MASS MOVEMENT:
THE DIGITAL YEARS VOL. ONE

Tim Cundle

Published by Earth Island Books
Pickforde Lodge
Pickforde Lane
Ticehurst
TN5 7BN

wwww.earthisland.co.uk
© Copyright Earth Island Publishing Ltd

This collection first published by Earth Island Publishing 2020

The moral rights of the author have been asserted.

ISBN 978-1-9997581-6-5

Printed, bound and distributed by Ingram Sparks

Earthisland
publishing

"For my family for my friends
for those that we've lost I sing
this is a message, this is for you..."

For My Family – Agnostic Front

Copyright Roger Miret & Agnostic Front

"You're just as important as we are
This much we know is true
So why don't you get up here
And tell us what matters to you..."

Get On the Stage – Spermbirds

Copyright Lee Hollis & Spermbirds

Contents

Foreword

Books like this are crucial for preserving the words of our subculture and I am so very glad that this collection will put Mass Movement in its correct place within the history of punk. There is little that I love more than the heartfelt work that goes into collecting and archiving important writing and interviews and Tim has done an amazing job here.

Just as with MM during its time as a printed zine, this collection is diverse, passionate, and interesting. It will help preserve this periods history on so many aspects of different sub-cultures – but all from a punk perspective.

I always loved that Tim interviews bands that he liked and people that he found interesting or inspiring, rather than the suggestions of publicists. I think that's what made MM retain its authenticity as it grew – that it wasn't a vehicle for promoting the next hyped band, but more one man's passions and preferences. This led to questions that had depth and purpose, and far better interviews than in the average zine.

The diversity of the bands and other individuals reflects Tim's loves, and this shines right through the pages. As both a writer, and someone working at record labels for years (Revelation Records for 20 years and now Pirates Press Records for almost two) I understand the difficulty in reaching this balance. I think it's crucial for a zine (or a website) to retain this integrity and it's something Tim's always managed to do.

Our history, our thoughts and emotions, and our collective punk scene must be archived in this way or it will be lost. Through this kind of dedication, hard work, and follow through, Tim is once more illustrating how the punk scene, especially in the UK, would have been far less rich and wonderful if Mass Movement had not been one of its cornerstones. And as it continues to be so, whilst Tim diversifies all the more with his writing, we take our hats off to him for putting together this collection for us all to either read for the first time, or take a lovely trip down memory lane.

Thank you Tim, from one zinester to another, for your hard work then, now and probably for always.

Vique "Simba" Martin.

Introduction

It was never supposed to last or be anything other than an underground punk rock fanzine. All Mass Movement was ever meant to be was a stop gap to fill the hours while, after losing my job as a Drugs Counsellor and gaining my journalism accreditation, I tried figured out what the next step on my journey was going to entail. However, these things, no matter how much we'd like them too, rarely work out the way that we think, hope or imagine they will. Which is why, twenty two years after I started mailing out the first illicitly photocopied issue of Mass Movement, it's still a thing. Granted, it's now entirely online and a denizen of the World Wide Web, but Mass Movement is still a thing.

Swept up by, and engulfed in, the nineties tsunami of zine culture and having written for a variety of publications, that included everything from the local newspaper to a veritable who's who of UK based DIY magazines that no-one except the handful of rabid devotees who gladly and fastidiously consumed them faster than they could be produced remembers, since the age of fifteen, I decided, with more than a little encouragement from my wife, to strike out on my own. And on, and following a phone interview with Tim Barry from Avail that was the first procured article for MM (which is how Mass Movement has commonly been referred to by the plethora of writers and readers who have sustained it for more than two decades), an unusually warm for that time of year April evening in 1998, Mass Movement was born.

Taking its name from an Underdog song after I'd been talked out of, having been made to see reason by both my long-suffering other half Emma and MM's co-founder Ian, calling it *Hail Satan*, Mass Movement took off faster than I ever thought it would. From an original, late night, illicitly copied on the office machine after hours run of a hundred copies, by the time it reached its tenth issue, Mass Movement was topping a thousand copies and being produced by a real life, honest to goodness professional print company.

Every copy that we had, we either sold or sent out to a record label that requested one; we didn't keep a single issue. It never failed to amaze me that people wanted to not only read Mass Movement, but were willing to spend their money to do so. Twenty years after Mass Movement started shifting copies, I'm still a little flattered and flabbergasted that every issue sold out. Maybe if I'd charged more for Mass Movement then, I wouldn't be broke now. But that's another story for another time and one that's probably best left to my accountant to tell. Or at least it would be if I actually had, or could afford, an accountant. Which I don't, and can't, because punk rock and comics don't pay and writing about them pays even less.

Where was I? Oh yes, Mass Movement... Slowly, but surely, Mass Movement started to expand its remit, as even the most holier than though and punkest of punks can't live on music alone, to include all of the things that I, and the rest of the miscreants responsible for creating its content, loved and were, and are, passionate about. Comics, wrestling, genre fiction and film and all manner of associated franchises, RPG's (that's Dungeons & Dragons and its ilk for those of you not familiar with these things) and everything in between began to appear in its pages and Mass Movement became something else. It became a zine, and later a magazine, that was devoted to all aspects of fringe culture, and the more facets of said culture that we featured, the more copies we sold. There was, and still is, far more to punks and punk than just punk rock. The underground popularity of Mass Movement proved that.

Then Beer City Records came knocking and offered to make Mass Movement a global entity by increasing its print run and giving it something that it had never had; a distribution network. It seemed almost too good to be true, so we leapt at the chance. Unfortunately, for one damnable reason after another, none of which I hasten to add were Beer City's fault as they were nothing but absolutely professional and we remain best buds to this day, it took nearly eighteen months for the first issue of Mass Movement produced by this joint venture to appear. And by the time it did, my personal circumstances had changed dramatically. My step father had discovered that he was terminally ill which meant that I wouldn't be able to put the time and effort that Beer City required into Mass Movement as I'd be spending whatever time I could looking after, and out for, Pops. Family always comes first, so Mass Movement and Beer City parted ways. We were on our own again.

All told, we (the "royal" Mass Movement we that is) made a bloody good fist of it too; being on our own that is. Having had a taste of the "big time", we decided that we liked it and went all posh and glossy. We looked good, we had great content – even if I do say so myself, and we were printing and selling the same amount of magazines as our super-market shelf distributed contemporaries. Mass Movement became the one of the biggest selling magazines that no-one in the mainstream, and a worryingly high percentage of folks involved in the underground and geek culture, had never heard of. Then the bottom fell out of the print market, production costs almost doubled over night and faced with the certainty of having to vastly increase our advert and cover prices, something that we were unwilling to do, Mass Movement ceased print publication and became a free, digital magazine distributed by an online platform.

For twenty issues, a number of one off specials and five years, Mass Movement existed solely as a digital magazine. We didn't have to worry about distribution or production costs and we weren't limited by a page count. We did what we wanted to, featured whoever we felt like featuring and reached a far wider audience than we ever had. It was fun, we were busier than ever and not only were we covering all of the bills, we actually making a little profit. A teeny, tiny, almost negligible amount, but it was profit nonetheless. The future was, all things considered, looking pretty good for Mass Movement. Right up until the moment that Microsoft and Adobe had a behind the scenes falling out which rendered all of our production and publishing software obsolete in the space of a single Bill Gates update. After seventeen years, Mass Movement Magazine lost the magazine part of its name, went completely online and our entire digital back catalogue became a thing of the past. Until now.

The book that you're holding in your hands is a compilation of the best interviews and features from the first half of Mass Movement's digital period. Some of you have probably seen a lot of it before, but I'm willing to bet that for the majority of you, this is the first time that you've seen most, if not all, of this content. And you know what? It's good. It's really, really good and while I'm happy, well as happy as a miserable old bugger like me can be, that this content is finally available again, what I'm genuinely thrilled about is that it shows how varied Mass Movement Magazine was and captures the spirit and essence of everything Mass Movement is and, probably, always will be.

Are you ready? Then let's begin. It's Mass Movement time...

Tim "Mass Movement" Cundle

South Wales, April 2020

MASS MOVEMENT:
THE DIGITAL YEARS VOL. ONE

Tim Cundle

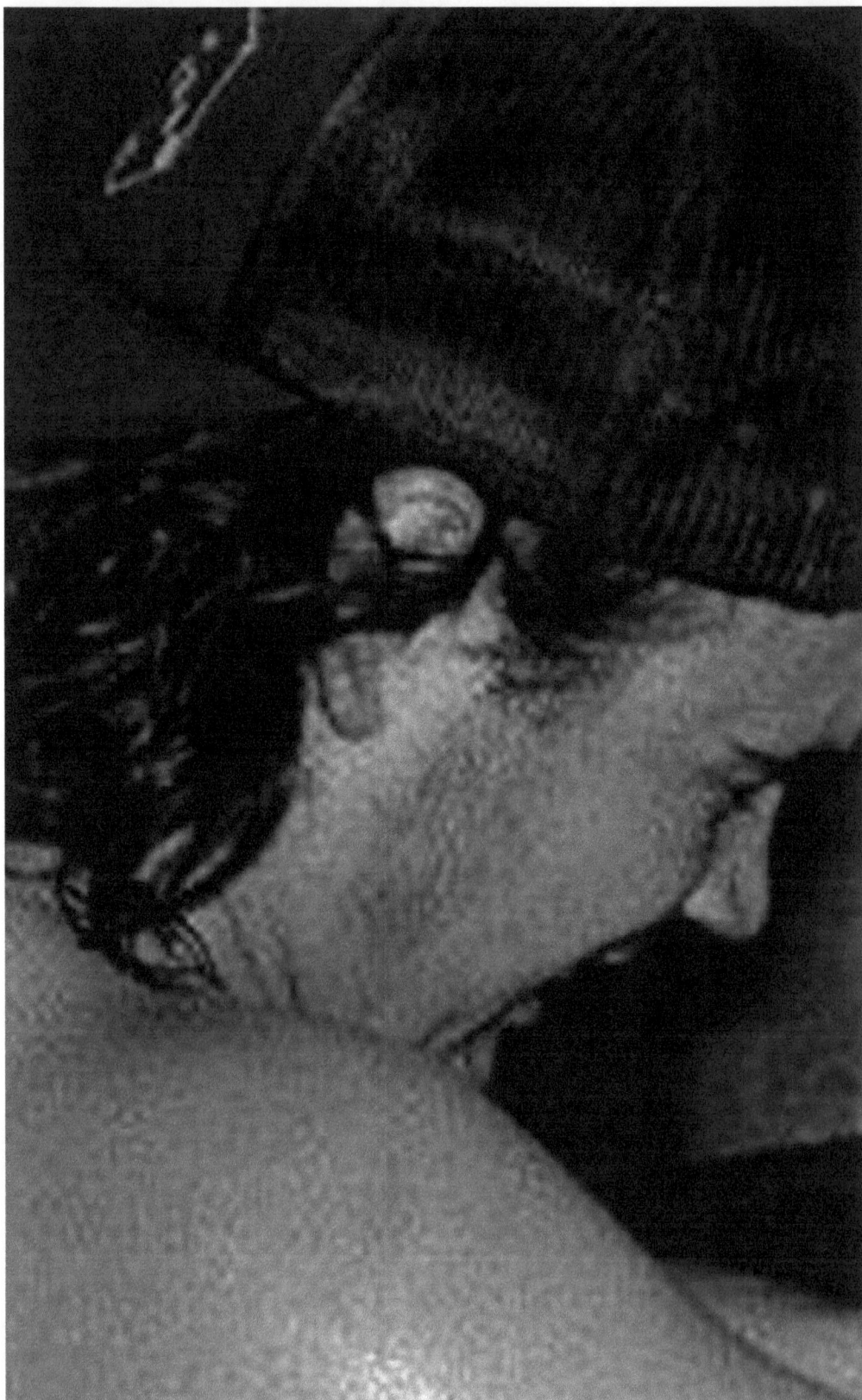

CHRIS KONTOS
(ATTITUDE ADJUSTMENT / MACHINE HEAD)

Being a thrash happy crossover fuelled thirty something who happily lived through (and wished that they'd never ended) the mosh crazed days of the mid to late eighties, I tend to go a little mental whenever certain bands are mentioned, and right up there, at the top of the list, are Attitude Adjustment, so when I found out that the band were back together and playing again, I knew I had to try and interview them, and after a bit of back and forth, I finally managed to get hold of Chris Kontos, and the rest as they say is history. And below...Ahem....

Interview by Tim Cundle

MM: When, where, how and why did the original Attitude Adjustment line-up get together? Did the bad form based on a specific sound – i.e. did you want to be a HC band, or a thrash (metal) band, or did you have some other sound in mind?

Chris: Eric and I started the band after we met Rick in Walnut Creek, CA. 1984. A friend that was skating too close to a bum one day was told that he was going to get an ATTITUDE ADJUSTMENT if he did not go the fuck away. Well we took that as our name that day. We all had the born gift to play music and this was what we were doing at the time, expressing ourselves with music, art and fun. The band was just a spark of light for us. It wasn't based on something like drugs or being straight edge, skin heads, Punks, anti-one thing or the next. It was just happening. We were 15 -16 years old at the time.

MM: What was it like being a part of the original Bay Area (thrash) scene? Was the scene really rooted at Ruthie's Inn – by that, I mean did the bands hang out when they weren't playing etc.? How close, tight knit or community minded was the scene? Did you have any idea at the time that it was going to be become a world famous scene, and what in your opinion, was it about the Bay Area that gave birth to so many famous thrash bands?

Chris: You're asking five questions at a time bro. I'll take this as a Ruthie's Inn question. When you are 15 - 18 years old you don't think to yourself "Wow...I'm part of something really incredible" I was just loving my friends and the bands I was seeing at the time. We did have trust in our scene. You could get killed at a show but at the same time your life could be saved. We did all hang-out at each other's shows back then. We all watched and slammed and did stage dives and the support was amazing back then. Being in a band that was getting love from that tough as nails, take no poser shit, crossover crowd was a the best feeling in the world. You could really never play that club again if you sucked. The Slay team told Slayer that they could come back, but ditch the make-up next time. Well the next time they just played in jeans and tee's Kerry just wore the nails! NO eye make-up No fake blood! It was just the proving ground. Live or DIE!

MM: Attitude Adjustment quickly became a part of the embryonic Crossover scene, and you played with HC, punk and thrash bands – which did you feel more at home and comfortable with, the thrash, punk or HC bands and scenes? Why? Did and do you think of the band as being a part of the HC or thrash scene, or do you think of AA as a true Crossover band? Again, why?

Chris: We did some of the first shows with metal bands like Exodus and Testament (then Legacy) and we played with the Circle Jerks too. DRI. The English Dogs. The Mentors.... We did all the shows and never thought twice about fitting in or if it was crossover or not. Eric and I have a vast musical back-ground. Some said it was strange that we played heavy music at all due to the wide taste we have in music. So anything that makes it better, faster, stronger, overall more musical within the lines we would try and pull off, be it Punk, Hard-Core, Rock n; Roll, Prog whatever We got to see some of the best metal bands in the world back then and it was easy to get hooked on that kind of picking and drumming when it is going off in your face. So yes, we are true cross over daddies!

MM: When you think about the term Crossover, what does it mean to you and why?

Chris: I think I just answered that one. I think about Attitude Adjustment!

MM: Why did Kevin leave the original line-up, and how did you find Andy Anderson? How did you feel about the line-up change at the time, and how do you feel about it now?

Chris: Well, Kevin got in some trouble and could not participate in the band for 8 months. Andy was a local jokester that was part of the Exodus Slay Team aka S.T.B. He was a friend of Rick's and myself and just fell into the spot really. Andy was in the band 7 months. He hit the hot spot in the band. At the time he came in the band it was cool because we had just got going and had a head of steam. But you could see he was just a ham ball and it was not his life long quest to be in bands. Much like the guys from that first LP, none of them play music any more, and some haven't for years and years now.

MM: What do you remember most about recording the *Dead Serious* demo, and how did the folks in the scene at the time initially react to it when you guys put it out there?

Chris: I remember it stunk in the jam room we recorded it in, big time. We would do a song and run out into the hall to get air; really it was bad. We were tight and ready to do it, so it was a hot day and one hot minute to say the least. It sounds like shit but has so much heart it comes off to this day. We sold so fucking many of them demo's. It was at the top of the pile for months. Other bands jumped in on the hype and did really well with demo selling right out of the trunk. Later on the Rappers started doing this too, guys like Too Short, and MC Hammer. People seemed to love that demo! It kinda blows away the LP if you ask me.

MM: Do you think, as seems to be the general consensus, that *American Paranoia* is the definitive Attitude Adjustment record? Why?

Chris: Well yes, because it sold so well. Like I said many times before, I don't like the vibe on that album. It is cool we got to do it. Eric is NOT on the record and that just made it sound empty to me. Chris C was a good player but Eric wrote the songs and had a killer picking style that is missing on the album. It was mistake to not have Eric on that fucking recrd.

MM: What caused the split, with Andy, Rick and Chris forming Attitude, and you hooking up with Eric and Kevin again to carry on with Attitude Adjustment? How do you think the band changed after the split?

Chris: Andy and Rick wanted too much change in the band out of the blue. They wanted to go all poser and do some lame ass butt rocking' They thought it was a joke but no one got it. Taking half the name was chicken shit and a gutless move. Stand on your shit and change your name if you want to bail out. I had AA back with Eric and Kevin in just a month or two and it was much better. The band was much more metal, way super hard-core with Kevin singing again. By '88 the *No More Mr.Nice Guy* album was out and you could hear we were not fucking around anymore with fun pop punk that Andy had been shooting for.

MM: I have to know – are you still in touch with Andy? Did and do you keep in touch with any of the ex-members of the band?

Chris: I see Andy around. I see some of the old members in town and online.

MM: What caused Attitude Adjustment to finally split up in the early nineties? Do you think it was inevitable, or do you think it could have prevented?

Chris: In the start of the nineties people were on hard drugs, drinking and had some fucked up girlfriends running them and then it was just over. I had been getting offers to play with other bands doing world tours and AA was just a drama boat at the time.

MM: Here it comes, the inevitable Machine Head question – what happened? The first album was great, you left, and then. Again, are you still in touch with the guys and how do you feel about Machine Head now?

Chris: Really dude? I mean it is like 15 years later, do you think anybody really cares about that old lame story man? I had a killer time in that band. I loved the music from that first CD and did some of the biggest shows ever - one being Dynamo with 156,000 people watching. The legacy of *Burn My Eyes* is really flattering to this day. I get mail from people that are moved by that CD and that makes me really happy. I see them at shows from time to time and we are cool for a drink and some hellos. But I will say I was so happy that I did not spend one more day in that band then I needed to. I have been involved in some really wonderful bands, played music around the world and I'm still doing my thing the best way I see fit. I think that is cooler than a bad trip replay from 15 years ago. But if not you can find all that lame shit online I guess.

MM: And now, you're back together again – Attitude Adjustment 2009. How does the AA of the twenty first century differ from that of the eighties and nineties, if it does at all?

Chris: This just might sound like a pitch to get people out to see the band, but I think we are stronger, faster, tighter and more focused than ever. This line up wants it and we bring top fuel crossover music played with 30 years of know how under our belts.

Originally published in Mass Movement #24, July 2009

BILLY BRAGG

Singer-songwriter, author, punk, political thinker, activist. All these words describe Billy Bragg. Breaking into the spotlight in 1983 with his first album *Life's A Riot* with Spy vs. Spy, Billy Bragg hasn't looked back. Writing songs with political messages, Billy has been out-spoken in his support for workers unions, and his ideas on racism, ideologies, patriotism and the world. I spoke to Billy at Blackwood Miner's Institute, following the final date of his June 2009 Welsh tour to commemorate 25 years since the miner's strike and his search to reconnect with ideas about collective provision by touring Welsh mining towns.

Interview by Leigh McAndrew

Photos by Vince Jones & Mei Lewis

MM: This is the last night of your Welsh tour – what were some of your reasons for doing this tour?

Billy: Well firstly, I have never done a tour of Wales. It hadn't really occurred to me until I at-tended an event at the Senedd in Cardiff last year which was a celebration of the 60th an-niversary of the welfare state and Paul Robeson's visit to Wales. The people at the Theatr Mwldan in Cardigan set up some little gigs like this, so that I could get into places that I wouldn't normally play, places like Caernarfon and places like that. Here we are, travelling around in a bus on the back roads of Wales.

MM: During the miner's strike in 1984-5, what sparked your interest in the plight of the worker's unions, and how did you get involved with the strikes at the time?

Billy: The miner's strike wasn't just about the miners; it was about the post-war consensus. The idea of free healthcare and free education, those kinds of ideas. It wasn't just about peo-ple losing their jobs, it was about whether or not we were going to stand around while the Tories closed down all those kind of things. We had to stand and fight. That was really what the strike was about. The miners were the point of confrontation. I was there to defend and to ensure that the sort of things that I grew up taking for granted which I outlined – educa-tion, healthcare –that those things would be around for my kids. That's why I was involved. I was writing political songs at the time so I had an opportunity to test whether the songs I was writing and the ideas that I had actually had any validity. I thought that that's where I should be. Right place, right time.

MM: With the current economic climate and with people fearing for their jobs, do you think that workers unions have as much power and influence that they used to?

Billy: The old industrial unions were counter-balanced to a free market government. Govern-ments have always lent towards the free market. The old Labour government of the 70s and 80s certainly did. The unions were a counter-balance to that. They were the people who said "With capitalism so far and no further." Get to the point where you're exploiting your labour for your own benefit and it's bringing you benefits – great, that's good. The unions ensured that if you were being exploited then it was on your terms. We've lost that, now people are just getting exploited. Britain has the longest working hours in Europe. We shouldn't really have that. That's what the unions were about.

MM: During this tour the BNP has unfortunately gained two European Parliament seats. Do you think this is an example of how tactical voting can be useful? For example, in Manchester where (Nick Griffin won his seat, nearly 12,000 voters spoiled their ballots – if they had voted for a moderate party this would have stopped the far right gaining a seat.

Billy: Yeah, if just a few more people had voted for any of the parties – it was a matter of a thousand or so votes in an area where there must be 5 or 6 million people. I think the real lesson from what happened is not really about proportional representation, it's about political parties giving people something that they really believe in. What happened last week was that people stopped believing that their votes could make a difference. They couldn't be bothered to vote. That's the real problem – cynicism, which I talk about on stage – that's our big enemy. People have got to be engaged, they've got to feel that the act of going out and voting can make a difference. The system of voting doesn't matter – those bastards [the BNP] will always be out there. It's apathy which is the deal-breaker for them, that's the most frustrating aspect of it. People's apathy, good people who have given up on voting because they are so appalled by the political mainstream. If asked now, after seeing the result of the vote, they would go out and vote, even if they cast it for one of the daft parties, they would still have gone and done it, I think

MM: How do you think the political mainstream will be able to regain the trust of working-class Britain?

Billy: For the white working-class in Barking & Dagenham they need to do what they did in the past. The BNP have no answers to the problems that are besetting the people of Barking & Dagenham which are unemployment and lack of resources. Barking & Dagenham has the cheapest housing in London, so people are coming from all over, so there is pressure on local services and houses, particularly. People are pissed off about that. If the government identified the places which had the larger influx of people to schools, hospitals and services, and put money in there to cope with that, then I think that people would be more conducive to voting for the party. What has happened in the last ten years is that New Labour has said "People who have always voted Labour, traditional Labour voters, have nowhere else to go". Shockingly, we find that they have and it's a racist, fascist party. That's how politicians need to reconnect, they need to put their faith in people and put their faith in communities and overcome the cynicism which is inherent in New Labour's politics and get on with what they did before. That's why it is important that we reconnect with those ideas of collective provision, because they are the ideas that worked.

MM: Do you feel, like me that for younger voters there are no mainstream parties which push forward the same ideas and values that we have?

Billy: You have to remember that during the miner's strike the Labour and Conservative parties were diametrically opposite. Completely opposite. At the end of the Soviet Union and the Berlin Wall coming down, we are kind of in a post-ideological society, and that's sort of the problem. It means now that the mainstream parties are trying to be all things to all people, rather than trying to represent a particular idea, and that is the politics which people want. They want politics of principle and not politics of pragmatism. So you want to know what to do? You've got to come up with a new ideology. That was the problem with the anti-globalisation movement. It was absolutely clear what it was against, but it was never able to manifest itself in a simple way that you could organise yourself around and what it stood for. So you need to declare those things that your generation wants to stand for. My generation stood against racism. That's why we're still here. That's why the people you find leafleting against the BNP are geezers my age who wear suits when they work, when they take those suits off you'll find they have a Clash tattoo. We keep the faith, you know, and your generation is not going to find that easy. There won't be another Clash. I just wish that you could feel the sense of revolutionary fervour and an opportunity to actually do something, which is what I felt when I was 19 and during punk, because it really felt like we had the opportunity to do something. The ripples of that carry on, which you feel generations later.

MM: Today's bands which are truly political and which reflect those ideals are now underground, and people have to search to find music which is reflecting the ideas that they believe in. There are no punk bands that are mainstream like the Clash were...

Billy: The Clash were reflecting the mainstream politics of the time. The National Front, who inspired Rock Against Racism, were actively saying that they would deport every black person in the country. They weren't just talking about illegal asylum seekers, they were talking about people you went to school with, and people were your mates, people who were in your favourite bands. They were actively going to take them and deport them. We have come a long way, and they wouldn't dare say that now. We have come a long way, but those old divisive ideas are still here. Maybe your generation needs something to push against, and maybe this [the BNP] is it. We had Thatcher, she was our monster. I'm not being ironic when I say that she was my greatest inspiration, she's what made me Billy Bragg. I'm sorry about that. The Clash had a big part in it, and so did a lot of other people, but Thatcher was what set me out there with my solo guitar playing for the unions.

MM: What does the future hold for Billy Bragg?

Billy: Well, I'm carrying on playing gigs and putting out records. Writing stuff – albums, books. My bottom line is communication, whether I'm on stage talking and singing to an audience, or making an album or speaking to your readers through the medium of this magazine. I want to communicate ideas. I know, through my own experience, through Rock Against Racism in 1978, that singer-songwriters cannot change the world, but they can change your perspective of the world – and that's what I'm trying to do, and thank you for your help with that.

Originally published in Mass Movement #24, July 2009

DEATH OF THE RAVEN
THE LAST DAYS OF EDGAR ALLAN POE

It has been said that true greatness and immortality share one thing in common – both are unattainable. The two also share something else in common – time (no pun intended). While greatness is often an overused term that is given out too freely in place of mediocrity, the measure of one's greatness depends more on the passage of time than anything else. Throughout history, there have been many "flashes in the pan," but true greatness is eternal.

Despite his errant lifestyle, Edgar Allen Poe was a writer of substantial talent. Considered by many critics to be, "the master of the eloquent narrative," his ability to convey the essence of absolute desperation through the written word is remarkably uncanny. Unlike many authors who struggled with nebulous accounts of human survival, Poe truly did live his deplorable condition, and he was able to fully express his most abject circumstances in a number of haunting poems and short stories. Few writers have had such a profound effect on both American literature and culture as he, and it is unlikely that there shall be anyone to match his mastery of macabre storytelling.

Each year, hundreds, if not thousands, of adoring fans visit Poe's gravesite with gifts of remembrance. And yet, it is sad to think that his last days on earth were marked by a series of tragic events more akin to one of his own stories than to reality. At the very least, his last, few earthly days were clouded in mystery.

The reports of Poe's death range from the tales of a dying man who spent the remaining hours of his life composing his magnum opus, to the woeful epilogue of a drunken derelict, dressed in ill-fitting clothes and spewing mindless gibberish. From all accounts, the truth of his demise was more closely linked to the latter, rather than the former.

It was October 3, 1849 in the city of Baltimore. A few congressional seats were up for the taking, but voter turnout had been scarce due to a combination of bitter winds and hard-driving rain. During this period in our nation's history, it was not uncommon to see the local tavern serve as a polling place. Equally as common was the practice of enlisting the aid of some unsuspecting drunkard to repeat his Fifteenth Amendment right in order to sway election results.

Just five days earlier, Poe had secured passage in Richmond, Virginia aboard a steamer bound for Baltimore. As verified by the ship's log, it was known that he travelled with a trunk that contained: clothes, books, and a manuscript. The mystery lies in what happened between the morning of September 27 and the afternoon of October 3, when he arrived in Baltimore.

According to various testimonies, the following information is the best-known account of Poe's final days. The first individual who supposedly set eyes on Poe was a printer by the name of Joseph Walker, in the afternoon of October 3. Walker spotted Poe at Gunner's Inn, a local tavern that conveniently doubled as a polling place.

From Joseph's perspective, it appeared that Edgar Allen was quite inebriated and very unkempt, as his attire was mismatched and dirty. Other than Poe's oblivious, intoxicated physicality, he seemed noticeably disoriented, with no recollection of his arrival in Baltimore or what had happened to his belongings.

Through the course of an incoherent conversation with Poe, Walker did manage to learn some rather sketchy details about Edgar's recent rendezvous in Virginia with his fiancé, Elmira Shelton. As confused as Poe appeared, he was able to relay a story about a mystery man aboard the steamer, who had threatened to kill him if he didn't write a poem while en route to Baltimore. Ridiculous as this sounded to Walker, he nevertheless listened to Edgar's nonsensical rant for almost an hour before the two men adjourned to a nearby parlour.

It was there that Poe relapsed into a stupefied state of consciousness, for which Walker immediately sent for Doctor John Moran. Very soon afterwards, Moran determined that Poe be relinquished to the nearest hospital for observation. The next seventy-two were crucial ones, for Poe's mental health continued to deteriorate, and it became increasing more difficult for Moran to gather any factual information about the situation.

In a condition of delirium, Poe repeatedly uttered the name of Maxwell McGovern, for whom Moran learned was aboard the same steamship as Poe. Upon further investigation, it was also learned that the two men had been seen together by several of the passengers.

At the height of his career, Poe was a very recognizable personality, and it is doubtful that the passengers would have mistaken him for someone else. To this day, however, it is unknown how Moran was able to determine that McGovern was in fact the same man that the passengers had seen aboard the steamer.

Research showed that McGovern's employer, Arnold D. Caulter, was a solicitor for The Louisiana Stamping Company, and he had sent McGovern to Baltimore on a business deal. Why McGovern chose to stop in Richmond, Virginia to board a steamer, instead of traveling directly from Louisiana to Baltimore via a train, is indeed a mystery. It is for certain that neither McGovern nor Caulter had any prior knowledge that Poe would be traveling aboard the steamer, which rules out any premeditated activity concerning the author's death.

Interestingly, Caulter was a known Southern sympathizer and there is some speculation that he may have sent Mc- Govern to buy some favours in the congressional election. But whether McGovern was the "mystery man" who had actually threatened Poe with his life in exchange for a handwritten poem is unsubstantiated, as well as the event itself, purely speculative on Edgar's behalf.

It is quite possible that Poe may have been lured with drink upon his arrival in Baltimore, and then beaten and robbed of his belongings. The fact that he was dressed in ill-fitting clothes and very inebriated suggests that perhaps he, like so many other unsuspecting drunks, was sent to different polling places to vote, each time with a different set of clothes. Another theory is that he may have been so intoxicated and, as a result, unprepared for the inclement weather, which may have been responsible in some way for his death.

Shortly after his admittance into the hospital, Poe received a surprise visit from his uncle by marriage, Henry Herring. Herring had wed Poe's aunt Virginia, more affectionately referred to as, "Muddy," and he had spent time with Poe during his early years in Baltimore.

Quoth The Raven, Nevermore.

ORIGINAL BURIAL PLACE OF
EDGAR ALLAN POE
FROM
OCTOBER 9, 1849.
UNTIL
NOVEMBER 17, 1875.

MRS. MARIA CLEMM HIS MOTHER IN LAW
LIES UPON HIS RIGHT AND VIRGINIA POE
HIS WIFE UPON HIS LEFT, UNDER THE
MONUMENT ERECTED TO HIM IN THIS
CEMETERY.

Fortunately, he was able to experience one of Edgar's more lucid moments, and the two men enjoyed some casual conversation. But Poe's lucidity was short lived, and he soon slipped back into a state of incognizant chatter. As the hours wore on, Poe continued his incoherent babbling, and at one point, began to speak of spectres and odd spirits that he would occasionally address as individual's names. According to Moran's notes, Edgar was absent of facial colour, and he was beading in a constant, clammy sweat. He was extremely anxious as if to signal an impending doom.

On the morning of the third day, another visitor made a quick sojourn in Baltimore while en route to New York City. It was Edgar's second cousin, Nelson Poe, a well-respected attorney at law and a journalist for the Whig political party. It seems that he had been in town to write a feature article on the political drama of the election, when someone informed him of Edgar's unstable condition.

Under different circumstances, Edgar would have refused to see his young cousin because of an earlier falling out between the two of them. For the moment, the younger Poe had mended any indifference that may have existed in the past, and he brought with him fresh linen and clothes for his ailing cousin.

On the final day of his life, Poe underwent several, anxious periods of consciousness in which he demonstrated a degree of residual sanity. His fever had withdrawn from its torrid pitch, and Moran seized this opportunity by gently questioning his patient about several unanswered events. When asked about his recent journey aboard the steamer, Poe had no recollection of it and began to utter names of past acquaintances. Curiously, in the final hours of his life, he was sane enough to cause the local nursing staff some hardship, by throwing his bedding unto the floor and demanding to be released from the hospital.

But in those final moments before death, Edgar became rather reserved. Turning his head gently on the pillow, he said, "Lord, help my poor soul," and expired. The exact cause of Edgar Allen Poe's death is still a mystery. The local newspapers attributed it to a condition known as "congestion of the brain." From a medical standpoint, it is safe to assume that alcohol may have played an important role in his untimely demise, most likely, "delirium tremens," or what is more commonly referred to as the "DT's." Whatever the cause, Poe left behind a timeless legacy of unforgettable literary works. Sadly, he was only forty years old when he died. As for his belongings, one can only surmise that he was too intoxicated to concern himself with their whereabouts.

As for Maxwell Mc Govern, he was never brought into question over Poe's death, even though, many years after the fact, he freely admitted to being with the famous author aboard the steamer, but he did not elaborate as to the extent of their encounter. Ironically, according to his death certificate, Mc-Govern died on August 4, 1863 of acute alcoholism.

Perhaps the mystery of Poe's death is a fitting epitaph to his bizarre life. He viewed his own existence as a series of disastrous events from which no escape was possible. Lonely and forlorn, Edgar Allen Poe did his best work under the duress of life's situations, and he was adept at cultivating a poetic mood of sheer misery as well as terror through the written word. Although he was plagued by ill health, much of his misfortune was brought about by a self-indulgent life style of drugs and booze. His reality and the natural world were on parallel paths, never crossing.

Poe said it best when he wrote:

"Take this kiss upon the brow!

And, in parting from you now,

Thus much let me avow

You are not wrong, who deem

That my days have been a dream;

Yet if hope has flown away

In a night, or in a day,

In a vision, or in none,

Is it therefore the less gone?

All that we see or seem

Is but a dream within a dream"

Doug Crill

Originally published in Mass Movement #24, July 2009

GARY SPENCER MILLIDGE

A while ago I was sent a book called *Conspiracies*, the third volume in a series called *Strangehaven*. It took precisely seven pages, or if you prefer to measure such things in units of time, five minutes, for *Strangehaven* to ensnare me, to draw me into the story. It was, and is, unlike anything else I'd read before, or have read since, and for my money is quite possibly the best British comic to have emerged in the last fifteen years. It's the cult that gives everything and only asks for a slice of your attention and a little of your time in return, and in order to find out more, I tracked down *Stangehaven* creator (and thus, 'Leader' – All Hail The Leader), Gary Spencer Millidge for a chat about *Strangehaven*, Life, and all the little things that fill the gaps in between...

Interview by Tim Cundle

MM: Right, let's start at the beginning, introduce yourself, tell us something about Gary Millidge and what's the strangest facet of your personality?

Gary: I've lived all but four years of my life in the south-east of Essex, about forty miles from London, a city I love. I grew up in the sixties and seventies and inadvertently my elder brother David greatly influenced me in regards to art and culture. His psychedelic band used to rehearse in our shared bedroom (a converted loft) and he went to Art College in London. He left all kinds of interesting books and magazines and records lying around the house. I think probably everything useful I ever learned about politics, religion and philosophy came from watching Monty Python. Probably what surprises most of my friends is that despite my cultural leanings, I am a huge football fan and have followed the famous Chelsea FC since I was about seven years old. That's probably not so strange for most people, but it's probably the most incongruous part of my personality.

MM: Let's talk comics – what initially drew you toward the medium? What was, and is it, about the medium that inspired, and continues to inspire you, and how do you think that inspiration manifests itself in your book(s)?

Gary: I grew up with comics of all kinds, from Rupert the Bear style nursery comics through to the glamorous American superhero imports. The Adam West Batman TV show was all the rage in 1967, and I drew my own Batman comics in crayon as soon as I could hold one. I have never understood the English speaking world's prejudice against comics, where they are viewed as juvenile. If prose stories and art and graphics and television and film can all be considered adult material, then why shouldn't the unique blending of words and pictures be considered as valid an art form or even respected as adult entertainment? I believe this is the way they are perceived on the continent, particularly in France – but not here or in the US. Comics are extremely labour intensive to create and often offer little reward, but there are very few means of self-expression that allow a single creator to tell a story verbally and visually without the inevitable corruption that collaboration brings.

The enormous diversity, invention and evolution of the medium continues to inspire me, and despite the huge amount of dross that inevitably accompanies the rare gems, the fields of comics, graphic novels and web comics continue to produce increasing numbers of exciting new talent.

MM: What made you want to create your own title? Why Self-Publish? Did you approach any publishers with a view to them adding *Strangehaven* to their roster, or did you always know that it was something that you wanted to do on your own?

Gary: That's an interesting question, because although I had produced and contributed to a number of fanzines, strip-zines and news-zines while at college and in my early twenties, my first thought was to find a publisher for *Strangehaven* It soon became apparent that in order to maintain full creative control of my work, I should self-publish. Self-publishing in the 1990s was the zeitgeist, with *Cerebus* creator Dave Sim leading the way, and Terry Moore and Jeff Smith following. In the UK, my attention was brought to Paul Grist's Kane and Nabiel Kana's *Exit*, both self-published and making inroads into the US market.
On seeing a preview of my first issue, a couple of 'mainstream' US publishers expressed an interest which they ultimately neglected to follow up; and my decision to self-publish was vindicated just a couple of years later when *Strangehaven* was nominated for two prestigious Eisner awards.

MM: What, in your opinion, are the positive and negative aspects of self-publishing, and with the advent of more and more creator owned titles, are the days of big publishers controlling the industry really a thing of the past?

Gary: The way the distribution of comic books was set up until recently made it very possible for a single creator with a minimal investment to grow a small publishing project into a viable career. Unfortunately recent contractions in the comic market combined with the global recession have moved the goalposts somewhat. The comics industry has been moving away from the serialised periodical pamphlet for some time, and moving towards a self-contained graphic novel as the default vehicle for new creator owned works. The Internet in terms of both delivery and sales has really become the new conduit for creative comics work, as it has done in so many other media. The industry giants of Marvel and DC still greatly control and dominate the traditional comics market, but the new bookstore and Internet markets are offering viable alternative outlets for creator works.

MM: Let's move on to *Strangehaven*…Where did the idea come from, and how would you describe the book to someone not familiar with it?

Gary: *Strangehaven* actually began as an idea for an ongoing periodical that could contain all kinds of self-contained stories, loosely linked by a common geographical location. It soon became a much more cohesive concept, but essentially it was a canvas upon which I could experiment with my storytelling, flipping between subjects, ideas, storylines and characters as I wanted, in order to keep it fresh for myself, and therefore hopefully the reader.
Dave Sim said once (and I paraphrase from memory) that the only way to find out if you have anything to say is to write. I had no idea at the time, but it seems to me that with *Strangehaven*, I am trying to say something about belief, spiritualism and our perception and interpretation of reality. And no one was more surprised about that than me. The actual series concept was inspired by my favourite TV shows from my childhood, like *The Prisoner*, *The Avengers*, *Ace of Wands*, combined with the desire to create a specifically British *Twin Peaks*.

From a comics perspective I was influenced by the slice-of-life works of the Hernandez Bros in their *Love & Rockets* and Alan Moore & Bill Sienkiewicz's aborted *Big Numbers* series. I was a big fan of Sienkiewicz and Dave McKean's arty, mixed media, photo-referenced illustrative style and I tried to interpret that in my own way, with my own limited abilities.

MM: Given that the town allows, and doesn't allow people to leave (and that it's a Hub, or magical nexus, which is more important, the town of the characters that populate it?

Gary: Well Tim, first I must point out that you should be careful not to take anything anyone in the village actually says as Gospel. Maybe the town does not want people to leave; or maybe they actually don't want to leave, consciously or unconsciously.
As I said earlier, the original concept was for an almost anthology-style book, different characters and stories, simply set in the same location. Indeed, I am currently working on incorporating a few guest creator strips which are set in different time periods. So I'd have to say the town itself is the star.

MM: Although the perception is that Alex is the main character, *Strangehaven* feels more like an ensemble tale to me, and I wondered how difficult it was to link each individual thread together to form the whole?

Gary: Alex was a late addition to the cast. I thought the plot needed a cipher, a character that the reader could identify with as he encountered the village and its inhabitants. As it's turned out, Alex is very much the central character of the *Strangehaven* books, but it's certainly not only all about him. The separate story threads were always meant to cross over, run together and split off in assorted directions, sometimes without explanation, in an effort to reflect the way real life tends to unfold. But as I have worked towards some sort of satisfying conclusion, the threads and have come together much more closely than I originally envisaged.

MM: I have to know, given the Hitchhikers and Roddenberry links, is Adam really what he seems, or is there much more to him than meets the eye?

Gary: Well, I dunno, you tell me Tim, what is it that he seems?

MM: With the Knights "controlling" Strangehaven, do you think that we're all at the mercy of the establishment and those who would abuse their power in order to manipulate it, and thus us for their own nefarious purposes?

Gary: Well, do the Knights control Strangehaven? Or do they just think they do, or perhaps hope that they might? Are they a dangerously powerful and corrupt organisation or just a bunch of guys looking to have a piss-up on a Friday night?
I mean, just because they may be delusional idiots, doesn't mean that they *can't* be dangerous, does it? Actually, I think if the 'establishment' had a modicum of intelligence or coordination, then we'd all be in big trouble.

MM: Given the direction that 'Conspiracies' takes, it feels like you're driving toward a climatic showdown between Megaron and John, and the groups that they lead and a part of – is that the case? Is the world really black and white in that it always comes down to good and evil and the inevitable confrontations between the two?

Gary: That's what people seem to boil it all down to, don't they? Trouble is perception of good and evil very much depends on what side you're standing. Ambiguity is everything. You know, good versus evil is always a good starting point for a story, but like life, there's just a patchy variation of grey. Oh, and if you are expecting a 'climatic showdown,' then you've come to the wrong place mate!

MM: It's been a while since the last issue of *Strangehaven* – what have you been up to, and are you planning on returning to the "town" soon? Apart from *Strangehaven*, are you working on any other projects?

Gary: *Strangehaven* has been on the back burner for a while. Self-publishing comics is such a labour-intensive process that it's hard to make any kind of survivable wage from it, despite *Strangehaven*'s apparent and perceived success. Therefore recently I have been taking on a number of freelance jobs in order to pay off the assortment of unhappy creditors which I have been collecting over the past twelve years or so. These have included a couple of how-to draw books from New Holland Publishing, book jacket and magazine illustration and even some website design. At the time of my response to this interview, my epic *Comic Book Design* has just been published in the UK by Ilex Press. It's a large format, beautifully produced, image heavy 160 page full colour analysis of the various design aspects of creating comics which is available from Amazon like all my other major works.

MM: How do you view Strangehaven? How do you see the town, and do you think your vision of it differs from your readers?

Gary: I think both Strangehaven the place and *Strangehaven* the story are wide open for interpretation. There's no definitive narrator of the series, so the reader really has to make up their own mind about everything. I could only answer your question if I solicited a few opinions from reader first and methodically compared them to my own. Which I'm not going to do. What I will say though, is that the letters from my readers are a constant source of amazement and amusement in the way they do interpret the story – often in way I would never have anticipated. So in a genuine sense, *Strangehaven* has taken on a life of its own.

MM: What's next for Gary Spencer Millidge?

Gary: There's possibly a follow-up to the *Comic Book Design* in the works, but more importantly, I am desperate to complete – or even start - the fourth and final volume in the *Strangehaven* series. It's something that weighs heavily on me and I need to complete it as soon as the time and financial situation allows it to become a reality.
Beyond that, there are a huge number of projects which I'd like to pursue, one or two slightly less ambitious (at least in terms of scale) comic projects, including a biography of my father, a novel and recording my solo album which I've been promising myself for the past twenty years.

Originally published in Mass Movement #24, July 2009

MUNICIPAL WASTE

I ain't gonna lie to you, if I had my way, we'd have these guys in each and every issue of Mass Movement. Been that way since *Waste 'Em All* and it'll probably always be that way – we've hung out shared more than a few beers along the way (Mass Movement and Municipal Waste that is), and I dare say that that we'll share more than a few more before either of us are done, but that's by the by. There's a Municipal Waste record, *Massive Aggressive* due out late August, and once again it's an orgy of thrashing goodness, so I thought we should catch up with Tony and Ryan, shoot the shit and find out what was going down with Municipal Waste...

Interview by Tim Cundle

MM: So what's been happening between the *Art of Partying* and *Massive Aggressive*?

Ryan: We've been touring a lot...A hell of a lot...

MM: Do you think that the new album is very different from your previous albums?

Ryan: I think we improvised with a lot of aspects of the band and influences that we really like. It has a lot of punk roots and a lot of metal roots

MM: And the name *Massive Aggressive*, where does that come from and how does it relate to the album as a whole?

Ryan: It's a play on words. In the States people talk about people being passive aggressive all the time. Basically I was describing an argument I had with my friend, someone I would always describe as passive aggressive and I wanted to be the opposite to that I wanted to be massive aggressive. It kind of reflects where we want to be right now as well, it's more aggressive than we've been in the past
Tony: Yeah it's a more pissed off record than the one before; that was a real fun record.

MM: Is this, your fourth album, the definitive Municipal Waste record?

Ryan: it is the best one to date I think. The best thing about thrash metal is that it comes from punk and it comes from metal and this record reflects that and I'm so proud of it.

MM: What lyrical themes do you guys explore on the record and what external factors, if any, have influenced *Massive Aggressive*?

Tony: We actually try to base things on real events. We'll take a true crime and try to create our own story with it. One of the songs is based on an axe murderer from London in the 1940s. We've got one based on Chernobyl
Ryan: We just basically didn't want to make another record about being fucked up all the time. We did that with the last record and that's all anyone expected of us and we didn't want to do that again. We wanted to take another approach

Tony: If you look at it there are like 12 different little stories and some of them are pretty gnarly but if you look at them they actually tackle real social issues.

MM: When you guys started playing did you have any idea that thrash would explode again the way it has?

Tony: No idea at all. You were writing about all this stuff before all these other journalists too so I think you're in the same boat as us. You were one of the first people to pick up on us and I think you worry about this too: that this explosion in popularity could turn into a long term trend and that generic is bad. I do this because I love it, and now we have been able to go from playing gigs in pubs in Bristol to playing Reading this year. We'd never have believed we'd be playing Reading and Leeds festival, but we're still the same guys, we still have a tour bus and we love it. We're having a good time.

MM: Do you feel like you are under more pressure playing the festivals than just playing a Municipal Waste show?

Tony: I liked Reading and Leeds because I got to fuck with Billy Corgan from Smashing Pumpkins... he pulled up in a minivan so I called him a soccer mom.
Ryan: Definitely the first year we started doing festivals that was the case, but we've started doing bigger shows in the States too and so now it's more natural for us.
Tony: The audience want you to talk to them and tell them what to do and it's great because you can get a larger circle pit going that way. It's incredible when you've got a couple of hundred people going round and round.
Ryan: In bigger rooms you have to yell at the people at the top of your voice just so they can hear you

MM: Have you been affected by the fame game: people recognizing you in the street etc.? And how do you deal with it?

Ryan: Yeah we do get recognized...
Tony: Any guy who's with us and has a beard and shades basically gets recognized as Ryan so I've got a load of my friends with beards to sign autographs as him
Ryan: We come from a punk background and its weird having people want your autograph. I think that's more of a metal thing, people coming up to you that way, but with hardcore fans will have a drink with you, but you can't be rude and act like you're better than them because you're not. They just want to get to know you and they are the fans so you want to give them what they want.

MM: Has the rising profile of the band had any effect on your personal lives?

Tony: Oh yeah...
Ryan: We're gone most of the time so we have less time with love ones etc..
Tony: We all have sacrifices that we need to make but we all love playing music.

MM: You've all got side bands as well No Friends, Cannabis Corpse...Why do you do it?

Ryan: Because we love playing music! We want to experiment with so many sounds, sounds that don't fit in with what we do with Municipal Waste that we need to find new bands to do this stuff under and with...

MM: Don't you ever think enough is enough and you'd rather spend some time at home?

Tony: You'd think that wouldn't you? But it doesn't ever happen like that, we never get fed up of playing

MM: What do you do away from music and what's this about Tony collecting art?

Tony: Yeah this is something that just went up on YouTube; I've got a whole bunch of paintings. I've been collecting art for about 8 years. I don't know a lot about art, about the detail of it and I've never studied, I just buy stuff that I like....
Ryan: I just hang out and do nothing. Rest. It's tough out there man!

MM: If someone were to do a Municipal Waste comic book, what would the story be about...

Ryan: It would be an easy job for a comic book artist because our songs are like a bunch of short stories which are all written out for them to work with.
Tony: It's funny but we've often thought about doing something like that.

MM: What's the craziest road story that you guys have, that you can share with us without fear of being arrested?

Ryan: We were in Vegas one time and I convinced the rest of the band to spend half of the merchandising money on black. There was maybe about $1000 and we bet on black and we won! But then someone tripped over and knocked all our chips over and people ran away with all our chips, so we lost half our money. We tried to go to security but they were having none of it but we managed not to get arrested which turned out to be the luckiest part of the evening.

MM: How do you think the band has changed since you started playing out as Municipal Waste?

Ryan: The band hasn't changed really. We have a broader audience but we're still the same guys trying to write music.

MM: What's next for you guys?

Ryan: Next year we're going to tour some places we haven't been be- fore like Brazil and Japan. But basically we're going to carry on sup- porting the record. This summer though we are going to be playing at a whole bunch of festivals in Britain and Europe.

Originally published in Mass Movement #24, July 2009

PAUL CORNELL

Some guys have all the luck. Take Paul Cornell for instance. Not only does he get to write for Doctor Who, but having helped shaped the rebirth of arguably the most important British Sci-Fi icon, he lands the Marvel gig of the year, the reinvention and rebirth of Captain Britain, arguably the greatest British Super-Hero. You know what's even worse? His vision of, and for, Captain Britain is nothing less than brilliant. On top of all that, he's just been head hunted to script, and drafted into writing, The Young Avengers. Like I said, some guys have all the luck, but in Paul Cornell's case, it's thoroughly deserved and has been well and truly earned...

Interview by Tim Cundle

MM: So which came first for you, Doctor Who or comics?

Paul: Comics actually. The first comic work I actually did was for the Doctor Who comic, which I got off the back of doing Doctor Who novels, so I guess it's chicken and egg really.

MM: How did you become involved in Doctor Who in the first place? I'm assuming you made the transition from being a fan to being involved in creating the mythology...?

Paul: I'd been writing fan fiction and made the transition to the books. The editor put out a request for pitches for Doctor Who novels and I just sent him my fan fiction –put it in the shape he asked for – and got commissioned on that basis. So I've literally gone from being a writer of fan fiction to being a writer for the show. It's like a dream come true.

MM: I was going to ask you about how you became involved with the show. Did they come to you or did you approach them?

Paul: Russell (T. Davies) gave me a call and said that he'd like me to go and write for him – this is a call you wait all your life for.

MM: Is there a sense of competition amongst the writers?

Paul: There's a sense of great comradeship amongst us all; after all most of us knew each other way before the show. Most of us were writing for books and audio books in the 15 years before the old show and the new show, which people call the wilderness years but actually you could call it the theme park years; because there was loads going on and it was all fun but most TV shows after a certain period of time should lie fallow for a period of time, like a field of crops, and Doctor Who did this during those 15 years. Then green shoots began to grow, fans started writing about the show in different ways and then there it is – back.

MM: Which Doctor is *your* Doctor? How true do you think it is that it's your first doctor, the one who you grew up with, who shapes you and that he's always your favourite, regardless of anything else?

Paul: It's your first regeneration that they always say isn't it? I grew up with Tom Baker and Peter Davison was surprising and wonderful for me. So of the old Doctors I'd say it was a toss-up between Peter Davison and Sylvester McCoy. I couldn't choose between all these wonderful actors that are the new doctors. They've all been absolutely tremendous. I've had the pleasure of both Chris and David doing one of my scripts. It would be wrong to choose between them.

MM: How did you feel when your first story was published?

Paul: Oh well it was a long time ago. I really recall the editor of the Doctor Who books writing me a letter and saying "If you're not careful, you'll be writing one of the four new adventure books" and I remember literally leaping up and down with joy in the hallway of my flat in Manchester. Then I remember thinking "What does he mean by 'If I'm not careful'? Just exactly how careful do I have to be?" They've all been fantastic since then you never get over the thrill. The wonderful thing about writing a show written by fans is that you never get a chance to be complacent because everyone is reminding you all the time of how fantastic it is that you're here.

MM: You made the transition to Marvel. From a comic book point of view, how different are the UK and US comic industries?

Paul: The industries are very different but that's mostly about scale; the British comic industry is much smaller. The art is the same in terms of everything that brings the story together, but at Marvel, they're looking for 22 pages per book and in Britain they're after 7 or 8 pages. So an advantage that British comic writers have is a tendency to tell the story very quickly, we're used to that. That may be why British comic writers have done so well in America. I have actually sometimes, struggled because from a British point of view you can do almost anything in 22 pages, even the brothers Karamazov...

MM: So how did you get the gig at Marvel?

Paul: Well I think this is something that young writers can certainly emulate: Mark Millar wrote to me and said that he really liked my Doctor Who episodes and would I like to write for Marvel? So that's all you have to do. Get a gig writing for a TV show that Mark Millar likes and then wait for him to call.

MM: How did you approach Wisdom? Do you think that this is the book that really paved the way for the return of Cap?

Paul: Very much so. It was my editor's idea. He was looking for someone to write an idea that he was calling MI13 at that time; we formed this fantastic partnership that has been going ever since. He sent me loads of pictures and photocopies and I recognised them instantly. I'd been reading them and loved them. You can imagine how fantastic it is when your first gig is writing a character which you already adored. Basically, I was just me: I assumed that I would never work for Marvel again and put in everything I ever wanted to put in to Marvel comics with the War of the Worlds Kill Ray and the Kung Fu Masters and any number of things. I'm very proud of those 6 issues; I think we go quite a long way with them. We do the very British thing of making the first 4 issues single issue stories and then bringing it all together at the end. I was a big fan of Captain Britain before I started writing for the series; it was another dream job for me really. I'm a huge fan of most eras of the strip actually. I think that right from the start they were doing tremendous things with it. The very best writers and artists have worked on it and there is an incredible history there – no pressure!

MM: How difficult is it to write about a British Superhero in a world of American capes and meta-humans?

Paul: Marvel have given me huge support, they couldn't have been more welcoming - when you get the top guys coming to you and asking if they can put Captain Britain into Mighty Avengers. That's always a nice feeling. It's a British book but it's not a whimsical book. Previously books like Excalibur have had this wonderful ethereal and whimsical view of Britain, and I have seen American fans on message boards complaining that this new book isn't British enough, by which they mean not whimsical enough. But whimsical books don't sell very well these days and it's about time we took Captain Britain away from that and found the roots of the character again. I'm very proud of doing that and I think by the end of this run we have put him back where he belongs at the centre of the British Marvel Universe.

MM: Do you think the book has been truly Captain Britain or more of a group effort with the MI13?

Paul: It's true that he is the central pivotal character, around which the other characters move.

MM: I kinda think that he's more like Xavier in the X-Men or Captain America in the Avengers...

Paul: Well yeah. But then it's also true that quite often the central pivotal character is not the most interesting character in the room; Buffy for example is not the most interesting character in Buffy the Vampire Slayer. This is something – perhaps if there's one thing I regret, it's that with one more arc I might have been able to give him some more drama. Actually as drama is conflict and the character had really been dragged apart too much by conflict I wanted to rebuild him. Some of the other characters get plenty of grief but we wanted to let him become something whole. Maybe with one more arc we'd have given him some grief. But I think he has a tamer voice now. He's very straightforward, quite tough. I was very, very influenced by the tremendous job Garth Ennis did on capturing Dan Dare's tone of voice. He did a marvellous job; it's just a shame that there were only seven issues. I wanted to capture a very British sense of grit which every now and then has this sort of wry quality to it that's laughing at itself

MM: How did you choose what characters would populate MI13? Were there any you particularly wanted to use but put to one side for some reason?

Paul: Spitfire was a fairly late addition. Maybe because people kept insisting that I'd really have fun with her but I kept saying "But I really don't like her costume". Then I saw her costume done really well and I got it and it worked really well in the end. We were "Uhmming" and "Ahhing" about Union Jack for the longest time, but I think it's because of Blade. Strange as it may seem you really need Jack and Blade occupying the same logical niche. Union Jack has a history of vampirism and is pitched towards mystical threats, so you have one or the other really, you can't have both. So what we've done is to set up Blade in a love triangle with Jack and we would of taken that further, but all of this is unformed because I've actually used up all the plots I thought of when I first started the title.

MM: One of the things you employ very well in the titles is the sense that Captain Britain needs that sense of magical history and mythology...

Paul: Well he's formed out of mysticism. He's one of the very few superheroes with a magical origin and I really think of him as a magical hero. I'm sure that was Allan Moore's idea when he brought the Captain Britain Corps into play, the idea that he was one of the deconstructions of a superhero. The trouble is he's been deconstructed out of existence so I wanted to reconstruct him a bit.

MM: Do you see Captain Britain as being a superhero in a traditional sense because of his magical powers and origins?

Paul: Yes. He is the British Captain America as far as where he is in the national psyche but he has a logical origin that fits Britain. I thought that was really important, but also I wanted to bring Merlin back and put him in the same costume as he wore in Marvel's Doctor Who strip...

MM: The books started with *Secret Invasion*, with *Vampire State* you seem to be moving towards a *Dark Reign* tie in. So I was curious as to whether the major arcs in the wider Marvel Universe, the big storylines effect books like Captain Britain and how much you...

Paul: Starting off with *Secret invasion* was a real bonus for us. It meant that we could have this really big thing happening that we didn't have to spend much time explaining and we had a really good reason for these people being together. People think that it must make me really angry to be part of a tie in to another story arc but it's fantastic for sales, especially when it's a Marvel tie in. As for *Dark Reign* at the end of *Vampire State*, I think it was just natural that we show it. It would have been quite odd not to...

MM: Moving on to the Young Avengers...

Paul: I'm really enjoying the Young Avengers. I've nearly finished writing it and I'm loving Mark Brookes' art. Cap will always be the thing I most love, but I think that the Young Avengers might be my best comic work.

MM: So you've tied up all the loose ends and the story arcs you wanted to with Cap?

Paul: Oh yes. The thing about Cap is we actually finish up having told, in a lot of ways, one big story from the start to the end. I always knew when we got started that there may be a possibility for a limited number of issues so I set out from the start to bring it to a close at this point. So it's not rushed and it has a proper ending...

MM: So Young Avengers: What can you tell us about it and how does it work with *Dark Reign*?

Paul: *Dark Reign* and Young Avengers is the story of a bunch of kids who find themselves with super powers and get together to form a team called the Young Avengers; and the, if you like, Old New Avengers.. Eli goes apoplectic that anybody else might be using the name, which is exactly the same problem as they had when they decided to call themselves the Avengers. So it's a question of what they decide to do about it. Do they recruit these kids? Do they test them to see if they come up to the standards set by the Avengers? What gives them the right to do that? There are so many Avengers teams, who owns the rights to the Avengers name anyway? It's one of the themes of the books – is there anything new? And we have various characters to explore various aspects of that and it's a very dark book. It goes to some very nasty places. But it's illuminated by the light of the characters themselves who still have the level of idealism which keeps them going. One of the questions we ask is with your superpower how do you actually decide to be a hero or a villain. One character has the power to melt everything with a gesture, and although he really wants to be good, it's very hard to be a hero with that superpower, and very easy to be a villain

MM: What's next for you?

Paul: We have a five book run of Young Avengers then I'm doing some work for the anthologies that will be Dark X-Men the Beginning. After that there are various things I can't tell you about. So stay tuned...

Originally published in Mass Movement #24, July 2009

The teachers at Lincoln High
have a very dangerous problem...
their students!

a MARK LESTER Film

CLASS OF 1984

CLASS OF 1984
Starring PERRY KING   MERRIE LYNN ROSS   TIMOTHY VAN PATTEN
STEFAN ARNGRIM   MICHAEL FOX and RODDY McDOWALL as Corrigan
Director of Photography ALBERT DUNK, A.S.C.   Music by LALO SCHIFRIN
Song "I AM THE FUTURE" performed by ALICE COOPER
Screenplay by MARK LESTER and JOHN SAXTON and TOM HOLLAND Story by TOM HOLLAND
Executive Producers MARK LESTER and MERRIE LYNN ROSS   Produced by ARTHUR KENT
Directed by MARK LESTER
Released by UNITED FILM DISTRIBUTION COMPANY

R RESTRICTED
UNDER 17 REQUIRES ACCOMPANYING
PARENT OR ADULT GUARDIAN

SCREEN DAMAGE

LIFE IS PAIN: THE NIGHTMARE PROPHECIES OF *CLASS OF 1984*

"Life is pain. Pain is everything. You will learn."

When Class of 1984 was first unleashed more than a quarter of a century ago, it was criticised for being unrealistic and too far-fetched. Few critics could buy into director Mark Lester's ultra-violent vision of kids taking weapons into American classrooms, drug deals in the playground or schools fitted out with metal detectors to prevent students hiding knives inside their homework. But fast forward almost three decades and history has proven Lester to be right. As he told Kamera magazine

"I way underestimated what could really happen. It is far worse than even depicted in this film. At the time, people thought it was outrageous. Back then, bringing a gun to school was unbelievable. Now, it is just everyday fact. Hostage situations and violence in schools, that's just normal now."

Lester struck on the idea for the film after paying a visit to his old school, Monroe High in Sepulveda, California, and finding it plagued by gang violence.

"I graduated in 1964," Lester said. *"We used to have a dress code. I saw kids in the hallways who weren't even wearing any shirts!"*

The secret for the film's success is not hard to pin down. Its young cast and school setting are hardly new - in fact, whole plot points are copied directly from the 1955 classic *The Blackboard Jungle* - but children had never before been portrayed as being so gleefully and realistically involved in crime, rape and ultra-violence. A *Clockwork Orange* visualised the antics of Alex and his Nadsat-speaking Droogs within a heavily stylised fantasy setting. By comparison, *Class of 1984* is all urban squalor and modern day familiarity.

"My idea was to update Blackboard Jungle, which I liked as a teenager," Lester said. *"I spent a year with the script and I did everything exactly right, and it became a huge success."*

Lester intended *Class of 1984* to be a wakeup call about the increasing levels of violence that he saw developing across the USA.

"I did some research, and found out there were 287,000 assaults in American high schools (in 1981). In Boston, they put the kids through metal weapon detectors. In Florida, they have closed-circuit television scanners."

Intrigued, Lester visited several other high schools and finished his tour convinced that the education system was about to implode.

"I used my original interest in politics and put it into a commercial context," he said. *"The film became controversial. I was on CBS Morning News. Time magazine reviewed it, Newsweek gave it two pages. The beginning of the film even predicts Columbine, years before, by saying that if we don't do something about high school violence now, it's going to get much worse in the future."*

Finding such social commentary in a mean little flick like *Class of 1984* is not so surprising when you consider that Lester has a degree from Cal State Northridge in political science. He also spent four years as a campaign manager for the Young Democrats of California and started his career by making political movies with American Documentary Films. Early credits include the prize-winning *Twilight of the Mayans* and a study of American involvement in Vietnam called *Cops of the World. Class of 1984* begins as naïve music teacher Andy Norris (an ideally cast Perry King, who probably wouldn't have done Lester's flick if his audition for Han Solo had been successful a few years earlier) leaves small town Nebraska for his first day at a tough inner city high school. Befriended by jaded biology teacher Terry Corrigan (Roddy McDowell in a superb supporting role), Norris is shocked at the heavy security measures in place at the school. CCTV cameras monitor the hallways, the teachers carry guns for protection, students have to file through metal detectors at the main entrance and a healthy portion of the school budget is spent employing a full time security team. The school itself is a foul place, its once beautiful walls covered in layers of obscene graffiti - something which landed the production in hot water once location filming had finished at Central Tech High in Toronto.

"We couldn't get it off in time for the kids to come back to school!" Lester admits. *"It caused a big uproar. When these nice Toronto kids went back to school, it had graffiti all over it. We had to sandblast the school to get the graffiti off the walls."*

The graffiti, much of it obscene, had been copied directly from the New York subway system for added realism.
Entering his classroom for the first time, Norris immediately clashes with Peter Stegman and his gang of punks. Rumoured to have scared Norris' predecessor into abandoning his post, Stegman (Timothy Van Patten) is a rich kid prodigy who has used his talents to carve out a profitable mini-empire of drugs, extortion, gang beatings, rape and prostitution - an all-round teenage Godfather. He is ably aided in his criminal exploits by Drugstore (Stefan Arngrim), the gang's chemist and resident drug addict, Patsy (Lisa Langlois), Stegman's sadistic girl-friend who is already sexually jaded despite her tender years, and the gang's two enforcers, Fallon (Neil Clifford), a vicious motorcycle-chain wielding thug, and Barnyard (Keith Knight), a hulking dimwit who carries a two-by-four into battle. The gang are avid followers of punk fashion and have an unhealthy interest in Nazi paraphernalia. They racially taunt their rivals in the high school drugs trade, and then demonstrate their ability to beat the living crap out of anyone who opposes them in hyper-violent, brutally vicious scenes of gang warfare.

The main gang fight scene was filmed over two days at a unique location - a piece of waste ground below two adjoining freeways. Lester wanted the action to be fast and realistic; all chains to the jaw and baseball bats to the face and kneecaps. It lasts less than a minute before the police arrive to break it up, but the heavy violence and racial slurs ("I'm gonna cut you, white meat!") meant that the scene was badly censored in many countries. Evading the police, the gang go cruising in Stegman's prized cherry red convertible. Donning masks, they ambush Norris outside his home, spraying him in the face with stage blood and taking note of his pregnant wife, Dianne (Merrie Lynn Ross, who also produced the film) - a grim warning of what will happen if the teacher insists on getting in their way. They celebrate their double victory by ripping up the mosh pit at a Teenage Head gig, then move into the grotty venue's back rooms for a little business. Lester is rightfully proud of the club scene where Teenage Head play *Ain't Got No Sense*. He recruited real life punk rockers to act as extras, and is quick to point out in the DVD's commentary that the haircuts and clothes are the real deal. (That doesn't explain why Stegman boasts a 'do that puts the 'wave' in 'new', but I guess you can't have everything). He also reveals that the slam dancing got out of hand, and some of the actors ended up getting hurt for real.

Among the first of the night's customers is Sally, a teenage girl who offers to hook for the gang in exchange for a steady supply of cocaine. Prompted by an aroused Patsy, Stegman orders Sally to take her clothes off for an audition, then invites Fallon to 'check this merchandise out'(Fallon, incidentally, is seen reading a pretty large book in this scene – a nicely understated hint that he is more than just muscle). As the girl strips before them, a clearly bored Drugstore dismisses her with a shake of his head. "Suburbanite," he mutters, before asking the half-naked teen what she does for a living. "What do you think?" she says. "I don't think," he responds, more interested in preparing a hit of heroin than in checking out her naked flesh.

The gang's contempt for all and sundry doesn't stop there. Strutting out of the music class, Stegman licks his middle finger and offers it up to Norris. "Sit on this, motherfucker," he tells the astonished teacher, who by now has worked out that he definitely isn't in Nebraska anymore. Norris sets about fine-tuning the talents of the fledgling school orchestra, but despite the pleas of Corrigan, he is unable to turn a blind eye to the criminal behaviour of Stegman and his gang or the challenge that it presents to his authority.

A series of minor confrontations and petty vandalism makes it clear that the teacher is set on a collision course with the gang. Interrupting a drugs deal, Norris reports the gang to the headmaster, only to be told that there is nothing he can do without witnesses. When Stegman demands to play piano in the forthcoming school concert, he surprises Norris, the orchestra and even his fellow gang members by performing an amazing piece of music that was composed on the set by actor Van Patten himself. The scene is a stand-out highlight – just check out the various tributes to it on You Tube - and establishes Stegman as something more than a two-dimensional villain. Cultured and brilliant he may be, but the boy is also hopelessly psychotic, and unable to curb his dark side. When the young thug screeches "Do I get the fucking gig?" at Norris, he gets turned down flat. That night, the teacher's car is fire-bombed, but as before, nothing can be proven without witnesses

The breaking point finally comes when a student falls from the top of the school flagpole (wrapped up in the stars 'n' stripes, naturally) while under the influence of angel dust supplied by the gang. Norris foolishly seals the fate of Arthur, a clean-cut kid who witnessed the drugs deal, when he tries to convince him to squeal on Stegman. After school, Corrigan is giving Norris a lift home when the teachers spy the gang threatening Arthur and his girlfriend in a grubby alleyway with a broken bottle. "School's out, teacher-teacher," Stegman tells Norris as Drugstore casually displays a straight razor. "You're not welcome here." Norris promises Stegman that he will see him jailed for pushing drugs. "Oh, I've got plans for you," the boy tells him. "Likewise," Norris replies before pushing Stegman out of his way. Within seconds, Fallon has floored Norris with a blow to the face and Drugstore has slashed Corrigan's hand wide open, but at least Arthur gets away. Corrigan insists that Norris does not report the incident, telling him that things will only get worse if he keeps on getting involved. He's right.

One cafeteria fight later and Arthur is in the hospital with a knife through his kidney. The fact that Arthur is played by superstar-in-the-making Michael J. Fox only adds to the delinquent fun and games.

Lester said of the actor: *"He came in for a reading and the minute I saw him, I said, this guy's a star."*

With no witnesses willing to reveal who orchestrated the stabbing, Norris confronts Stegman in the toilets and comes close to punching the teenager. This amuses Stegman no end. "When it comes to killing, teacher-teacher's just got too much to lose. Otherwise, you could have done me right - like this!" And the mad little bastard promptly smashes his own face into a mirror, cutting his forehead and smearing the blood over Norris' fists. "Hey, look what he did, man!" Stegman tells a security guard who rushes in. "He's crazy!"

With no witnesses to back him up, Norris is in the frame. Faced with an impending investigation and suspension, he takes matters into his own hands and visits Stegman's mother at her luxury apartment. The deluded woman can't see the monster that her spoiled child has become (he's sitting on the couch watching Lester's earlier hit *Bobby Jo and the Outlaw*), and vows to have Norris thrown out of his job. The teacher takes his frustration out on Stegman's beloved car, utterly trashing it. Later, he goads the enraged teenager, telling him that accusations are useless without witnesses

It might have been worth it to wipe the smirk off Stegman's face, but Norris has just moved the game up to a whole new level, as Corrigan discovers when he finds his beloved lab animals butchered, skinned and skewered. He reacts by going on a bender and teaching class at gunpoint - another standout scene that made it onto at least one version of the theatrical poster Asking Drugstore a question, Corrigan levels the gun at the teenager's head and tells him: "You simply can't afford to fail this class." Only Norris' intervention prevents the biology teacher from filling the gang with bullets.

Later, a drunken Corrigan ambushes the gang as they leave the punk club, gunning his car at them and forcing them to dive for cover - a stunt that actor McDowell did for real. Sadly, his revenge is short lived, and ends when the car overturns and explodes. As Corrigan perishes in the flames, the gang dance around the wreck, mocking the dying man by warming their hands on the blaze.

The death of his friend forces a change in Norris. "Are you ready now to give up that obsession you have with those kids in your class? " Dianne asks him, but Norris won't give in. When she tells him that she is going to stay with her mother, he persuades her not to leave until after the concert. She agrees.

The cracks are starting to show in Stegman's psyche, too. Confronting Norris in the school hallway, the boy shouts "I am the future! I am the future!" over and over. In his increasingly unhinged state of mind, the roles appear to have reversed, and the pupil promises to provide the teacher with the most important lesson of all: "You've got to learn – life is pain. Pain is everything. You will learn."

Such memorable dialogue was provided as part of a script polish by Barry Schneider, but when he saw the finished movie, he demanded that Lester remove his name from the credits. Other notable writers who worked on the script were *Child's Play* and *Fright Night* director Tom Holland and John Saxton who, having already written the shameful likes of *Ilsa: She Wolf of the SS*, was not so prissy.

That night, while Norris attends the school concert with a sell-out crowd, Stegman and the gang break into the teacher's house. Finding Dianne getting ready to go to the concert, the teenagers brutally gang-rape her. As if this wasn't enough, Patsy casually takes Polaroid's of the rape. "Smile for your photograph, honey," she tells the screaming woman. Pausing long enough to decorate themselves with lurid makeup stolen from Dianne's dresser, the gang set off to have some fun at the school. They present the souvenir snaps to Norris just as the concert is about to begin. Perry King puts in a great performance here as shock gives way to horror, and horror to fury. Shaking with rage and realising that his actions have put his wife in harm's way, Norris charges out of the concert hall into the darkened corridors of the school. But Stegman's gang are waiting for him. Ambushed in the gymnasium, Norris is beaten and left in a crumpled heap. But not too badly - this is a grim game of hide 'n' seek, after all, and Stegman, who is dragging a traumatised Dianne deeper into the school, wants the teacher to suffer for as long as possible. Norris goes after the gang and is again ambushed and beaten before he realises that he is playing into their hands. Instead, he hides in the school workshops and sets a trap of his own.

Fallon is the first to find him. "That bitch of yours is an easy lay, Norris," he taunts, provoking the teacher into a furious assault. The seasoned gang fighter easily evades the older man's lame attempts to brain him with a metal bar - but Norris gets lucky, and manages to drag Fallon's arm through the workshop's circular saw. Screeching with pain and sporting a bloody stump, Fallon pushes the teacher away and stands up -straight into a right hook from Norris that throws him back down onto the saw. As the blade digs deep into Fallon's thrashing body (oh, those noises!) and Norris is drenched in the boy's blood, the teacher realises that he has stepped beyond the pale - he has mutilated and killed a student.

There's no turning back now, and Norris becomes increasingly violent as the other gang members come for him. Ducking into the motor shop, he pours petrol over the floor, then emerges with a lit acetylene torch as Drugstore enters his trap. The teacher threatens to light it up if Drugstore doesn't reveal where Stegman has taken Dianne. Perhaps not willing to believe that a teacher would harm a pupil, Drugstore foolishly opts to taunt the man about how his wife has suffered. "Your little whore is ours now, Norris!" the addict jeers. "And it was sooo easy!"

Norris prevents the teenager from saying anything else by igniting the pool of petrol and burning the boy alive. Game to the last, Drugstore screams "I'll fuck you in hell!" as he dies. This scene is more shocking than Fallon's fate on the circular saw, mainly because you are left in no doubt that Norris has very willingly murdered the boy

"I wanted the teacher to make the transition and show the very ironic situation where they are there to educate, but all this violence is taking place," Lester said of these scenes. *"It was designed from the teacher's point of view. I was thinking, how can you have a teacher come to a school to teach kids, and by the end of the movie, they are cheering him for killing the kids? That was my concept – how could I get people to accept that and cheer for that to happen?"*

Drawn by the screams, Patsy and Barnyard burst into the auto workshop and discover Norris standing over Drugstore's cooked, twitching flesh. As Patsy gags at the stench, Barnyard charges, using his forearms to block the piece of pipe that Norris is wielding like a club and effortlessly tossing the older man around. But Norris gets the better of the young thug with a series of skull-cracking hits to the head. As Barnyard goes down, Patsy uses one of the auto shop cars to charge at Norris, but only succeeds in crushing Barnyard and trapping herself in the resultant wreck. Badly injured, she finally reveals that Stegman has taken Dianne up to the roof of the school, and Norris heads up there for a final confrontation. Stegman's grin falters only slightly when Norris appears on the roof top, his clothes red with the blood of the other gang members. But the boy is too far gone to care that he is now alone. Giggling and enjoying himself, Stegman gleefully nicks away at Dianne with a knife. "This is only the beginning," he tells the teacher. "We all go - together!" and he punctuates his point by dragging the blade deeply across Dianne's chest before turning to confront Norris. But the teacher has discovered a hidden talent for violence, and it's fair to say that he kicks the living crap out of the surprised teenager. The fight ends when Norris throws Stegman through a skylight set directly above the stage where the orchestra is playing. "Please don't let me fall!" Stegman begs as he becomes entangled in stage rigging. "I'm just a kid!"

He may have just sawn, burned and bludgeoned four teenagers to death, but enough of the old Norris remains to make him reach down and try to pull the boy up. Stegman uses the opportunity to slash at his would-be rescuer with a hidden knife. "Sucker!" he sneers, and that's the final straw for Norris. His face contorted with murderous rage, the teacher punches Stegman hard in the face, forcing him to let go. Screaming, Stegman plunges through the ceiling tiles above the stage just as the stage ropes pull tight to form a noose around his neck. The teenager meets his grisly end high above the heads of the horrified orchestra. As Stegman dies serenaded by screams from the audience, we see that his eyes have rolled up towards Norris and Dianne, framed in the skylight window overhead. Even in death, the young thug appears to be sneering at them

The film ends with a nihilistic shot of Norris and his pregnant wife clinging to each other on the roof top, utterly shattered by their experience. Nobody has won here - the teacher couldn't let his authority be challenged, and as a result he has been brought down to the level of the young punks. In a final touch of supreme irony, a title card reveals that Norris escaped prosecution for killing the gang due to 'a lack of witnesses'. And that, my friends, is how you end a first-rate exploitation movie.

If Lester's film is judged purely on its merits as an exploitation flick, then there is no doubt that *Class of 1984* is one of the greatest b-movies ever made, a first-rate cult action film that has withstood censorship cuts, an outright ban by governments in Britain, Sweden and Switzerland and a flood of carbon copy imitators, most of which have shamelessly recycled the film's lean, mean plot. Whether it was known as *Guerrilla High* in Canada, *Insan Degildiler* in Turkey or *I Taxi Tou 1984* in Greece, the film's $50m worldwide gross is proof enough of its enduring popularity - just $7m less than Lester's better known hit of a few years later, the Arnold Schwarzenegger classic, *Commando*.

"We got major coverage in Times and Newsweek," Lester recalls. *"It was a very big hit. In New York, it was the number one film for weeks."*

Perhaps this is because *Class of 1984* emerged during the mid-70s – late 80s golden age of the vigilante action flick. For every *Dirty Harry*, *Death Wish*, *The Exterminator* or, *Walking Tall*, there was a *Sloane*, *Savage Streets*, *The Ghetto Blaster*, *3:15: A Time For Dying*, *The Substitute 1-4*, *Detention*.... The genre has also seen something of an old-school comeback with the recent likes of *Death Sentence, Taken* and *The Punisher* and its sequel. But not one of these films has come close to bettering *Class of 1984*.

A major part of its appeal is the way Lester utilises punk music and fashion as a backdrop for the film. *The Blackboard Jungle* did the same thing, using the likes of Bill Haley's *Rock Around The Clock* as a weapon to worry the grown-ups. For *Class of 1984*, Lester brought in the likes of Fear, Teenage Head and Alice Cooper, later claiming that his movie had introduced middle class America to punk rock (he obviously hadn't heard the likes of The Stooges or The Ramones before making this comment!).

Lester kept a tight rein on his story, making sure that the characterisations were solid and the acting realistic. The punk look that he adopted for his young villains was a winner, and embraced something that had been scaring and baffling parents and authority figures for a number of years before the film came on the scene. And the violence with which the supposedly responsible adults punish the young villains was truly shocking - teachers aren't supposed to go around burning pupils alive or cutting their arms off with circular saws.

Respected critic Roger Ebert summed up the film's appeal after viewing it at the 1982 Cannes Film Festival. *"It tells a strong, simple story,"* he said. *"It is acted well. It is not afraid to be comic at times and, even better, it's not afraid at the end to pull out all the stops and give us the sort of Grand Guignol conclusion that the slasher movies always botch. You may or may not think its any good, but you'll have to admit that it works."*

Michael J Fox may have been the one who become a superstar (*Back To The Future* even features an in-joke where one of Marty McFly's siblings is seen wearing a baseball shirt that states 'Class Of 1984' across its front), but the rest of the cast didn't do so bad either. Timothy Van Patten did a few b-movies and worked with Lee Van Cleef on the TV ninja show *The Master* before becoming a sought-after television director, racking up episodes of *The Sopranos, Rome, Deadwood, Sex And The City* and *The Wire*. Stefan Arngrim starred in ace high school horror flick *Fear No Evil* (which also features a punk soundtrack) and formed a rock band called The Knights of The Living Dead. Neil Clifford became a successful sculptor, and Lisa Langlois married Robert Ulrich and continues to act. Sadly, Keith Knight died in 2007 from brain cancer, but not before appearing in movies such as *Meatballs, Siege* and *My Bloody Valentine*.

During his long career, Mark Lester has made a number of movies, including *Roller Boogie, Firestarter, Armed and Dangerous* and even *Class of 1999*, a loose sequel that expands the concept of high school violence and introduces cyborg teachers into the mix. Currently running a distribution company called American World Pictures, Lester continues to direct the odd feature. But he has a major soft spot for *Class of 1984*, which to this day remains his most controversial movie.

"I'm proud of that film," he says. *"Blackboard Jungle was sweet compared to this."*

Liam Ronan

Originally published in Mass Movement #24, July 2009

TIMOTHY TRUMAN

I've been interviewing musicians, writers, bands, film-makers etc. on and off for more than twenty years (since I was 16, doing freelance work for the local paper), and the following interview with Timothy Truman (which we did a couple of weeks ago) is one of my favourites. Easily in the top five. Why? Well, because it's with Timothy Truman, writer and artist extraordinaire (*Hawkworld*, *The Spider*, *Scout*), and because he's the man who breathed new life into 'Conan', and made Howard's 'Conan' live again. And because he's a genuinely good guy, an increasingly rare thing in this day and age. Ladies and gentlemen, I give you Timothy Truman...

Interview by Tim Cundle

MM: I guess, as always, the best place to start is at the beginning – would you like to both introduce, and tell us a little about yourself?

Timothy Truman: Well, I was a border pilot for several years, running guns and booze to folks in need of same. When things got too hot in that trade, I tried being a rodeo clown. Got busted up pretty bad and thought I'd give this comics thing a try. The work is a little less dangerous— usually— but the hours suck.

MM: You´re known as and for being an artist, a writer and a musician - which of the three do you primarily see yourself as, or are the three aspects an equal part of the whole?

TT: I'd rather be whichever one I'm not doing at the time. When I'm writing, I get the itch to draw. When I'm drawing, after a few weeks I want to be back at the keyboard. Truth be told, though, I'd rather play guitar at just about any time. I don't like dragging amps in at 3:00 in the morning, though. And, of course, I'm sure that if I was doing music for a living, I'm sure I'd want to be writing or drawing.

MM: Art, literature or music - which do you think has had the greatest impact, an influence on you as an individual? Why?

TT: Safe to say, all three— although I don't think most folks would call the stuff I read when I was young "literature". I think you're confusing me with my son Benjamin. Seriously, though, Jefferson Airplane, Pete Townshend and had as big an impact on the way that I write and draw as Jack Kirby, Joe Kubert, Spain Rodriguez, Robert E. Howard or George R. R. Martin. I fed on the attitude and imagery of their lyrics and music. The comedy albums by Firesign Theatre were a huge influence, too. Big time.

MM: As you worked as an illustrator for TSR, and in the RPG industry, I was wondering how you became involved with the industry, and what drew you toward to it? Have you always been drawn toward fantasy, and did a love of Howard´s `Conan´ play any part in your wanting to work in that industry?

TT: The latter. I never was a gamer. I tried it a few times when I worked at TSR, but never really got into it that much. However, I loved fantasy. It was always my favourite genre, and, except for history and mythology, it probably remains so. Howard's Conan and Gardner F. Fox's Kothar kicked the whole thing off for me. Right after I started making a living doing fantasy art for TSR, I got to meet Gar at Gencon, the big gaming convention, one year. He was taking a break, sitting with his wife on a bench in the hall. I went over and shook his hand, and the first words that I said to him were "I just wanted to thank you, man. You got me into swords and sorcery."

MM: Do you think the RPG medium and hobby is as strong today as it was in the late seventies and eighties, or do you think the emergence of the internet and PC gaming has irreparably damaged it?

TT: Sorry, but I really can't say. I've been away from the RPG market for about 5 or 6 years, and I imagine that things have really changed in that time. I had fun doing it while I was there, though, drawing all those beasties and critters and wizards.

MM: Sticking with the same theme for a while - what was, and still is, your favourite project that you worked on for TSR? Why?

TT: Easy one. The time that I got together with John Totleben, Rick Veitch, Steve Bissette, and a bunch of other ex-Kubert Schoolers to do designs for the TSR toy line was by far the high point. I flew out to New Jersey from Wisconsin; we holed up in a couple of hotel rooms for about five days or so and drew out freakin' brains out. Other than that, meeting guys like Keith Parkinson, Larry Elmore, and Jeff Easley was what made those days worthwhile. They were simply amazing. Keith and I became best friends. Sadly, he passed away a few years ago. I miss him a lot, especially when I'm trying to do a painting. Keith could always look at something and figure out exactly what I was doing wrong. And I would go over to his studio and tell him he was drawing legs too short. God was he a fun guy. My polar opposite politically— conservative, though not a right winger. Maybe that's one reason we got along so well.

MM: How did the RPG industry, from your point of view, differ from that of the comics industry?

TT: More editors, more art directors, more writers, all of them seeming to think that someone was expecting them to say something. Of course, I have a lot of editors on Conan, too— three to four people giving me input on any given script— and that can be pretty frustrating at times. However, I remind myself that it's nothing like TSR. Close, but not quite! Comics are usually a tighter ship, and they're by far more creative—at least the sort of comics that I've usually done.

MM: Did the `pulp' writers of the twenties and thirties help shape the way you write and indeed the way that you think about stories and characters? As well as Conan (and thus Robert E, Howard) you also adapted Norvell Page's `The Spider', and given that, I kind of assumed that you were kid of fond of the pulp's...If so, why? What is it about those stories and writers that makes them so influential and helped them to weather the storm of time?

TT: The pulps are a no-B.S medium. You know what you're in for, and the great ones give it to you good. Some of the greatest "literary" writers we have came from the pulps— Truman Capote, Raymond Chandler, Dash Hammett, on and on. Each of them carried something with them from the pulps. A way of colouring things, but a very direct way of communicating, and done with an economy of words. Working in the pulps sharpened their tongues and their eyes.

42

MM: With both Jonah Hex and Scout, although both are separated by time (and an apocalypse), there's a frontier /Wild West link and theme, and again, I wondered what inspired and inspires you about it (Wild West / Frontier), and do you think, given that some sort of ecological apocalypse is not only likely, but almost inevitable, that as a species we'll return to a simpler way of life (as in the nineteenth century), or do you think that we'll descend further?

TT: Who knows? It's kind of funny: Someone sent me a review of one of the Dynamic Forces Scout reprints a few days ago. If you'll remember, I did Scout in the mid-80's, and Scout's "universe" was set in 1999. The reviewer remarked that I had the world fall apart in, what, 12 years or so. I got a kick out of that. I told my wife, "Gee, I was pretty off the mark on that one. It only took 8 or 9."

MM: I have to ask you about *Hawkworld*. Did you feel any sense of pressure knowing that you were reinventing Hawkman? How do you feel about the series now, knowing how well its regarded. And did the Saturday Morning Chapter Plays (particularly *Flash Gordon* and *Buck Rogers*) have any influence on your reinterpretation, as I've always felt that Hawkman was DC´s answer, or their equivalent to those Larry Crabbe shows...

TT: You're pretty close. The series had its beginnings in a conversation I had with Gar Fox one time. he told me that if he ever did Hawkman again, he'd bring a John Carter of Mars feeling into it. I told him that if he ever wrote it, I'd draw it. Gardner died a few years later. So when I did Hawkworld, Gar's idea was in the back of my mind. As far as what's come after with Hawkman, I really didn't keep up with it like I should have. I use up so much energy on projects like that I usually want to get as far away from the character as I can for a while. They're like a girlfriend that stays around too long. (Not that I'd know much about that. I swear, it's just a metaphor, Beth. Honest...)

MM: Okay, a question about music -how much do you think a musician is shaped by the era, or decade in which he or she grows up, and by the musical genre's that he or she is primarily exposed to? How do you think your musical influences have both shaped your musical path, and manifested themselves in your musical output?

TT: Depends on the person. Lyrically, in most cases people gravitate towards things they can relate to. The lyricist's voice becomes their own. For music, I think that folks naturally gravitate to certain beats, instruments, or styles that trigger the release of endorphins and such in their bodies. Probably a biochemical thing as much as a psychological or cultural thing. I'm mainly a guitar player, so I gravitate towards guitar players. I have all sorts of music in my collection— San Francisco rock, British blues, some be-bop, Western Swing, Southern rock, old-timey, US electric and acoustic blues, country, country rock, prog, 70's hard rock, what have you. The thread that ties them all together is usually guitar .Not always, but 90% of it, anyway. The guitarists and singers that I like usually have a big blues influence in their work, though. In West Virginia, I grew up with gospel music and old-time music. All told, my favourite music is probably British blues of the 1960's and 70's. Peter Green, Danny Kirwan, Mick Taylor, Savoy Brown, Zeppelin, Rory Gallagher, Clapton, Climax Blues Band, John Mayall, Mick Clarke, and the like. My own music is a usually some unholy blend of blues, rock and country. "Bluebilly", I guess. Country and rootsy in the writing, but with a strong Brit Blues and Southern Rock emphasis on the lead guitar playing and sound. Whenever I do a lengthy session, I find there's a core group of people that I usually spend some time listening to: two Brit bands, Hookfoot (a bunch of guys who did a lot of work with Elton John during his early

"less pop" years) and Wishbone Ash. The production and engineering on their albums is absolutely flawless; The First Crosby Stills and Nash album and Deja Vu, especially if I'm going to be recording acoustic guitar sounds. I love their electric stuff, too; Anything by J.J. Cale. Totally free of ego, and stripped back to the essentials. he's the Dashiell Hammett of roots rock; and Led Zeppelin III, for the way the acoustic and electric instruments mesh. Jimmy Page is probably my favourite producer. If I'm doing to be laying down lead overdubs, there are certain guys who help me get my mind right, depending on the sound I want to go for: Peter Green and Freddie King for blues stuff; Leslie West, Peter Green, Dickie Detts, Andy Powell of Wishbone Ash for Gibson "humbucker" sounds; Jimmy Page, Nils Lofgren or Steve Stills for acoustic stuff; Roy Buchanan or Bill Kirchen if I'm playing the Telecaster; Nils Lofgren or Eric Clapton if I'm playing a Strat. There you have it— far more than you could ever want to know about my music tastes.

MM: I think it's time that we moved on to Conan. The first thing I wanted to ask you was, why do you think that Howard (and to a similar degree Lovecraft) have emerged as the lasting face of the pulp decade(s)? Why those writers in particular?

TT: I never was too fond of Lovecraft, so I can't really respond in regards to his stuff. As far as Howard goes, for one thing, he had a lot of good posthumous PR men who would pop up every generation or so to remind us of his virtues and keep his work in print.

MM: What, in your opinion, is it about Conan that has created such a lasting, timeless appeal, and rabid, fanatical fan-base?

TT: There's just something vital and visceral about his work. For those of us who respond to it, it just reaches inside and pulls our innards right up through our teeth. Howard finds that "alpha male" button and then keeps on hammering it.

MM: Given the nature of some Conan fans (i.e. the aforementioned fanatics), do you feel any sense of trepidation when you took over the book?

TT: Oh, yeah. You bet. You see, I was one of those guys who would never, ever read the Conan pastiche novels. It was really a daunting thing, and remains so. I would never, ever write attempt a Conan prose story. However, I approach the comics work like this: What if REH was still alive and had licensed the rights for a 32-hour long movie spectacular to, say, Howard Hawks or Cecil B. De-Mille? And for some bizarre reason they picked me to be the screenwriter? It's up to me to facilitate the transition of Howard's character from prose to a visual medium and, in doing so, to keep it exciting and dynamic. We approach all the Conan short stories, outlines , drafts, and the single Conan novelette as one very long epic story. As part of the job, I have to come up with linking stories here and there that pull all those elements together.

MM: How important is it to you to stay true to the world / universe that Howard created for his most famous `son´? Did he provide a wide enough canvas for you to work within? Does said canvas aid, or hinder, in adding to the canonicity of Conan´s world?

TT: It's a wide canvas, indeed, and it certainly helps me. I read through Howard's stories and try to pick up on little sentences here and there where he mentions places, people, gods, events, relationships, what have you... things that he might only refer to in passing, as a bit of background or colour. Those things are invaluable in creating the new arcs that link the adaptations together, and for giving more depth and continuity to the arcs that are adaptations of existing stories. It's very important for me to stay as true as possible to the things Howard created. That said, there are occasions where you have to juggle elements to help Howard's prose make the jump from print to visuals. I alter scenes as seldom as possible. However, there are occasions where it's had to be done— where the flow and action of the story would actually be lessened if we hadn't. On such occasions, I pretend that Howard is still around, and in my mind I knock on his door, sit with him at his desk, and say, "Okay, Bob, here's the problem." I just finished the adaptation of *Black Colossus*, and it presented a lot of challenges like that. When you read REH's original, it flows like wine. But when it came to visualizing it in picture form, there were some really problematic sections, mostly in regards to pacing. Plus— Lord, I'm sorry Bob!— as most Conan scholars tend to agree, while the bulk of the story rockin', the ending is a tad weak, especially when compared to some of his later tales. So the challenge was to pump it up some and give it a bit more depth while keeping it true to Howard

MM: Is it more difficult writing for an already established character such as Conan than for a character that you've created yourself, or does the amount of source material available make it easier? Why?

TT: It's much harder, because while I feel that Howard's background and my own are similar in many ways (rural boys, Scots- Irish upbringing, raised around a lot of hard working labour class folks, lovers of history, etc.) we grew up in different times had different influences. We both might dig Bob Wills and Harold Lamb, but would Howard appreciate Keith Richards and Phil Proctor & Peter Bergman? I just don't know.

MM: Which Conan story so far, have you most enjoyed writing and why?

TT: *Rogues in the House*, because it really encapsulates all I mentioned above. The prelude issues I did just before the adaptation established some cool setups for the adaptation proper. And I did an incredible amount of scene-juggling here and there that the hard-core Howard fans didn't even seem to notice. Most of them raved about what a "true" adaptation it was. In point of fact, Howard's original Rogues is a surprisingly "talky" story which, had it been adapted scene-by scene,
step-by-step-, point-by point, would have had sections that really lagged.

MM: How do you see Conan developing, and what can we look forward to in future issues? (I have to know!)

TT: It's going to get real interesting, I think. Between the first arc, *Cimmeria*, and the upcoming arc, *Iron Shadows In the Moon*, Conan completes his transition into manhood. In the current arc, *Black Colossus*, we see him become the commander of Princess Yasmela's army. This made me wonder what came afterwards. Would Conan really be comfortable in Yasmela's court— her paramour, a man of power, suddenly in the company of the petty princes and nobles? Despite the fact that he's pretty hedonistic, would a man who was born on a battlefield feel being a "kept man" in an environment where anything he wants is his for the asking? Or does his real enjoyment come from setting his sights on something and TAKING it?

MM: Do you have any other projects on the horizon, or are you going to focus on Conan for the foreseeable future?

TT: Actually, I'm pretty much focusing on COMICS, at least for a while. My life has gotten pretty crazy over the last couple of years—juggling rock music-related and book cover illustration plus the occasional comics art assignments while writing Conan. I just finished up a big Grateful Dead licensing project that I've been working on for two years— a board game, actually: Grateful Dead-opoly, which is WAY cooler than it might sound. Sort of an undergroundy, Mad-magazine take on board games. Really fun, and I was working with some great people As far as Conan goes, there's some exciting stuff coming up. Regular Conan artist, Tomas Giorello, had a baby a few months ago and Tomas wanted a break to spend time with his family. At this point, both Tomas and I have completed as many issues of Conan as Busiek and Nord did on their original run. So we're giving Tomas a breather. It gave us the chance to turn issues #14 and #15 into really special projects, especially #14. it's a "multi-generational" issue, creatively. My son Ben and I plotted the story, and to top it off Joe Kubert and I share the art duties. Joe's my spiritual godfather in comics, and my mentor as well— I'm a proud Kubert School Graduate, class of '81. So doing the story was a real treat. The story is a prelude to the next arc, *The Free Companions*. We're trying our best to keep away from "filler" stories that aren't related to the ongoing continuity.

That said, the following issue, #15, is a break in continuity. Scott Allie wanted Paul Lee and I to finish up the *King Conan* tales that Paul and I did in the original Conan title. Paul Lee is drawing that issue, and we decided to do the story of Akivasha, the Stygian vampire who appears in Howard's *Hour of the Dragon*. I always found the character really intriguing, and as it turns out Akivasha is one of Paul's favourite Howard characters. It's the *Hour of The Dragon* chapter as seen through HER eyes. We get into her head a bit— and extrapolate on how the whole thing turned out for her. Actually, going back to one of your earlier questions, of the "original" stories I've done, it might be my favourite so far. After that, we're determined to keep the continuity rolling strong. To help facilitate that goal, and to say "thanks" to the folks who've been asking my editors to let me draw Conan again, I'll be kicking off he first three issues of the *Free Companions* arc, drawing the bulk of those issues. Tomas Giorello fans need not fear: he will also be drawing some key sequences line that links the sequences together in a very cool way. After I finish pencilling those issues of Conan, I'm launching into my next major project: a graphic novel called INNER STATION, with my son Benjamin. Ben is writing the story and it's simply amazing .I can't tell you how excited I am about it. The story is a big, meaty, deep, science fiction retelling of *Heart of Darkness* by Joseph Conrad. Anyway, that's pretty much what I plan to concentrate on for a long while: Conan and Inner Station. I've been burning the midnight lamp to long, while Ben and our daughter Emily were in college. Time to ease up a bit. Of course, in the meantime, I'm desperately hoping to get to some outstanding commission work that I have to do!

MM: Do you still teach?

TT: No, I had to give it up four or five years ago. I just got too busy with comics work and illustration. Sometimes I miss it. They got a great man for the job, though: Bob McLeod teaches the classes now. I feel like taking the classes myself! I'm a huge McCleod fan. Folks can keep up with any new developments via my website.

Originaly published in Mass Movement #24, July 2009

ARVID NELSON

Ladies and gentlemen, boys and girls, meet Arvid Nelson. Arvid is one of the nicest guys in comics, and he's also the man responsible for *Rex Mundi*, *Zero Killer* and, in my humble opinion, one of the best books of the last twelve months, *Kull: The Shadow Kingdom*. Anyways, that's enough of my prattle, here's Arvid….

Interview by Tim Cundle

MM: Let's start, as so many things tend to, at the beginning. Introduce yourself to the boys and girls, and tell us something… "Different" about yourself, something, for want of a better word, "odd" about Arvid Nelson.

Arvid: The details of my life are inconsequential… No, I write comics semi-professionally. *Rex Mundi*, a story I created, finished up last August, after ten painstaking years. *Rex Mundi* is a quest for the Holy Grail told as a murder mystery. *Zero Killer* is another thing I created. It's an adventure set in a New York City where the United States never dropped atomic bombs on Japan in 1945. So things are ever so slightly different—there was a nuclear war in 1973. I've written a lot of other stuff, too, including Kull the Conqueror. We'll get to that in a bit, I'm sure! Some fun facts about me: I firmly believe pie to be inherently superior to cake, and my favorite Muppet is the Swedish Chef.

MM: When did you first become interested in the genre of literary fiction commonly referred to as 'comics'? What drew (I know, awful, awful, awful) you toward comics, what maintained your interest, and how has your taste in (i.e. the books that you read) developed or changed over time?

Arvid: My last year of college I got kicked out a band. It was kind of traumatic. I fell in with a disreputable group of people. Comic book types. We put together our own comic book and even conned our school into paying for it, by forming a "student organization". One night— we were all jacked up on caffeine and hydrogenated oils—someone suggested we start our own comic book publishing empire after graduating. The publishing empire has yet to materialize, but I'm still writing comics!

MM: Did you always want to be a writer, and if so, did you envision yourself working in the medium that you do? What and who influences your writing, and how do you think that these influences are immediately apparent in your work? Or do they lurk somewhere under the surface? Why?

Arvid: My first summer after school—this was in the midst of founding the comic book publishing empire—I worked on a few films, including a Woody Allen movie. I was just a lowly production assistant. The coolest part of it was that I got to wear a walkie-talkie with a hands-free headset. It made me feel very important. But really, it kind of sucked. It was a lot of "yessing" and "noing" and fetching coffee. The assistant director was a nice guy. One day, traveling between locations, he told me that if I didn't want to be an assistant director there was really no point in being a production assistant ever again. It's not like anyone was going to say "Hey! Arvid! You're so great at fetching coffee, why don't you direct this new movie we've got coming up." Then I learned Woody Allen dropped out of college to start writing. So

I thought I'd do the same thing—get out of the rat race and... Write.

MM: Moving away from comics for a while – you converted to Baha'i , and I was kind of curious about why, what you think the faith has both given you and taught you about yourself? Each faith has a basic doctrine, and I was curious about the approach that Baha'i utilizes and adopts, and wondered if you could briefly explain it?

Arvid: Sure! Basically, Bahá'ís believe in the unity of all the major world religions, from Hinduism to Islam. We believe a new world order is currently in the offing, one based on justice, tolerance, peace, and equality. That idea—no more racism, sexism or poverty—was and is very appealing to me. I became a Bahá'í about ten years ago. I was into straight-edge hardcore music at the time that was a big part of it. Bands like Shelter showed me there could be a "third way" through life. Bahá'í is that third way for me.

MM: I noticed that you were also a student of Opera - has this instilled a lifelong love of music, or did it have the opposite effect on you? What kind of impact has music had upon your life? Is it true that you dig the sacred riffs and love Metal, and if so, are you a traditionalist, thrash crazed, speed and power obsessed, or do you just get down with all the Devils tunes? So man, which bands make you raise the horns high and break out the air guitar?

Arvid: I'm absolutely berserk for this semi-new band, The Sword. I like Rush, too. And Amon Amarth, and Blind Guardian. Dungeons & Dragons Metal, I guess. I like Thrash, too. Exodus, Slayer, Death Angel, that sort of thing. And Death Metal! Nile is amazing. I also love electronic music. I don't know why, but all the best Electronica (you can't call it "Dance" in the States) seems to come out of France and particularly the UK. And Reggae, especially Rastafarian Reggae. It manages to be cheerful and devotional without being fake or annoying. Most Rap makes me want to jab ice picks into my cochlea. There's this new kind of music called "Reggaeton" which is all the rage here in New York. Somehow Reggaeton manages to be even more annoying than Rap. I didn't think it was possible. I feel really lucky to have been exposed to classical music. It's just really hard to "get it" if you don't sing it or play it. The Fauré Requiem has to be one of the most beautiful pieces of music ever written.

MM: Let's talk Rex Mundi – where did the idea come from, and what made you want to frame it in the way you did (the murder /mystery)? Did you find yourself (despite being there first) caught up in the inexplicable hysteria generated by the *Da Vinci Code* and its lucky stiff buffoon author?

Arvid: Heh, yeah—like you mentioned, *Rex Mundi* came out a good three years before *The Da Vinci Code*. I can't be angry at Dan Brown for all his success. Good for him. But it does irk me when people say I "ripped him off". *The Da Vinci Code* definitely made Rex *Mundi*'s journey through Hollywood a lot more difficult, but everything worked out for the best. One complaint I have against the *Da Vinci Code* is that it doesn't even touch Biblical themes in its subject matter. All the Jesus-had-kids' stuff is really just window dressing. *Rex Mundi* is Biblical on a much deeper level. The idea for Rex came to me later on in the Woody Allen/Comic Book Empire Founding summer, whilst I was working as a third arm on a documentary film in Paris. I was the Official Bag Holder. I got to stand outside of all these amazing monuments, guarding equipment bags, but I never got to go inside. Notre Dame, the Louvre, St. Sulpice—never went inside any of them. But it got my brain going. One day, I was sitting outside of a café and observing a church, St. Germaine des Prés. Someone sitting with me told me the church had been built in the 800s by the Normans. I was amazed something could be that old! All the stuff swimming around my head instantly dropped out of solution. *Rex Mundi* crystallized then and there.

MM: Did you manage to use all the ideas and finish the book (*Rex Mundi*) in the way that you wanted to, as it's run (number of issues) was smaller than it was initially supposed to be right? Did this have any impact on the story?

Arvid: It's actually longer than I wanted it to be! 38 issues instead of 36. I had to do a few fill-ins here and there so the artists could keep up. I feel good about how Rex Mundi ended. I mean, it's far from perfect, but I never cut any corners. Every single issue I put out was the absolute best we could do at the time.

MM: Come on brother, spill – is there going to be a *Rex Mundi* movie and is Johnny Depp gonna be in it? What's the deal with the movie rights, and when can we expect to see it in cinemas?

Arvid: As far as I know, the rumors are true! I mean, it's possible it's all a cruel hoax. I keep expecting a film crew to jump out of my closet and scream "You've been punked, mother-fucker!". But so far so good. The movie adaptation has come a lot farther than I had any rea-son to expect it would. We've got a home at Warner Bros., and we're working on the screenplay right now. But we've still got a long way to go. I'd say the chances of it getting made are better than even, but by no means assured. It's a nerve-wracking experience, and it's been like this for about eight years now. I've learned to live with it. As soon as I have some definite information, I'll be screaming it at the top of my lungs on street corners and subway platforms.

MM: Time to share the story about *Zero Killer* as well – why did it take an extended break and what was, and is the book about? What inspired you to write it, and how close, in your opinion, did we actually come to the 'big one' in the seventies and eighties?

Arvid: *Zero Killer* was inspired by 9-11. I was in New York when 9-11 happened (still am). There was this weird smell in the air for about a week. Something like gunpowder. I was walking back to my apartment the day after, and I heard jet engines overhead. But the noise was different. Sharper. I looked up, and I saw two F-15 fighter jets crawling across the sky. That's when Zero Killer came to me. The really scary thing about the Cold War is we were never more than 30 seconds away from a global nuclear holocaust. The people in the United States government responsible for such a holocaust, they'd have been fine, thank you very much. We learned that from 9-11. Bush, Cheney, and the entire United States Congress fled like rats into their secret, tax-payer funded bunkers. *Zero Killer* is a meditation on that kind of cowardice-from-on-high. Ah, yes, *Zero Killer* took a long break. A full two years. It really kills me, but it was out of my hands. I had the entire series written months before things ground to a halt. That's just comics for you. You're only as fast as the slowest member of your team. I know it hurt *Zero Killer*, probably mortally. But I did finish it, and I feel proud of what we ac-complished. I owe so much to my editor, Philip Simon, for sticking with it. It would not have come full circle if not for him.

MM: Moving swiftly, or not so swiftly on, Kull. How did you get the gig on Kull? Is the initial mini-series just going to be a one off, or can we expect more tales of the Atlantean Barbarian from you?

Arvid: Kull is a dream come true for me! He's my favorite Robert E. Howard character. I was talking to my editor for *Rex Mundi*, Scott Allie, and I think he appreciated my enthusiasm for Howard's writing. So he took a chance on me, for which I'm very grateful. I was really happy with how *The Shadow Kingdom*—the first and as of now only story we adapted—came out. Kull deserves a lot more exposure. Howard wrote Kull before Conan, in fact. I suppose Kull is to Conan what *Rex Mundi* is to *The Da Vinci Code*. There's a brutal honesty to the Kull stories that I find lacking in Conan. Kull isn't quite so self-assured. He's tortured. I think he's the closest Howard ever came to writing himself into one of his stories. Kull was just too far ahead of his time. But now I think the world is finally ready for him. I pray and hope we get to do more of his stories. We've got huge things planned for him. Epic things. That's another thing that makes Kull different from Conan—his life has a guiding purpose. Conan just kind of wanders. Kull's on a mission.

MM: How difficult did you find it adopting Howard's original source material, and how do you feel about the book now that it's been out there for a while, generating its own steam and fan-base?

Arvid: Not hard at all! I mean, I've read and re-read those stories so many times. It was great going them very carefully, figuring out how to tell the story visually. Getting paid to read Robert E. Howard—if there's a better job than that, I'd like to know what it is!

MM: Like me, you're a fan of Robert E. Howard – want do you think his lasting appeal is? What is it about his tales that separate him from so many of his contemporaries, and in doing so helps to create their own unique identity?

Arvid: I think that, first and foremost, it's because Howard wrote himself into his stories. I've always thought Conan is the person Howard wanted to be, and Kull is who he really was. There's something brutal and raw and brilliant in Howard's writing, something that that transcends literary genres. I think Frank Frazetta had a huge part to do with it, too. If you look at the original illustrations of Conan from the 1930s, he looks like a silent film star. Frazetta understood Conan in a purely visual way. He was able to show other people, too. Howard gave birth to Conan, and Frazetta was the midwife.

MM: Man, you gotta tell us about Thulsa Doom...?

Arvid: Interestingly enough, Thulsa Doom's "original appearance" consists solely of a few paragraphs at the end of a half-written Kull story never published in Howard's lifetime. That's it! The Doom most people are familiar with is from the Conan movie from 1982. James Earl Jones' character. It's not at all faithful to Howard, but I still think he's one of the greatest screen villains of all time. So the Thulsa Doom I'm writing is based more on James Earl Jones's character. The stories I'm writing for Thulsa Doom are set long after the time of Kull, and long before the time of Conan. Right after the fall of Atlantis and the ensuing chaos. To my knowledge, it's not a period of Howard's mythology that's ever been written about extensively, so I'm really excited for it!

MM: ...And you also have to tell us about *The Wolf Mage*...?

Arvid: Ah-hah! It's a fantasy novel I'm working on, the first of what I hope will be a longer series called *Therial's Song*. It's based on my love of Metal, and Celtic and Norse mythology. I want it to be on a more human scale than something like Lord of the Rings. No Evil Shadow Lords, no Quests to Save the World from Eternal Darkness. *Wolf Mage* is a term used to describe renegade sorcerers in Therial's world—Therial is the main character. Ah, there's so much more to say, but it's really too soon! I don't mean to be coy, but there's nothing worse than revealing too much of a story before it's ready.

MM: Do you have anything else on the horizon or planned that you can tell us about?

Arvid: Yeah! I'm writing something else for Dark Horse, *Deadlocke*. It's a one-shot, but I was really happy with how it came out. It's based on a film script of the same name. Dark Horse offered me the chance to work on it, and I jumped. The main character instantly appealed to me. There's a great tension in the story between fantasy and reality. I can't wait for it to come out! Not sure exactly when that will be, but it should be in the next few months.

MM: I guess that's about it, if there's anything else that you'd like to add, speak now or forever hold your peace...?

Arvid: I think I've dithered on long enough! All I can say is "thanks" for doing the interview, and whoever's reading this, thanks for making it this far!

Originally published in Mass Movement #25, December 2009

CANNABIS CORPSE

Most folks, who know me, know that I'm not exactly a fan of Death Metal, and can pretty much take or leave it, and there aren't really any bands that make me want to break out my dancing shoes. At least there weren't until I heard Cannabis Corpse, the thrashing monster that bridges the gap between Crossover, Thrash and Death Metal, a band that produces tunes so catchy you'll end up grunting them at your neighbours as you show them the claw...So, following a bit of good luck, good fortune and an email or two to Scotty Tankcrimes, and interview was duly set up, and Phil was cool enough to answer our questions about life, the universe and the bands weed obsession...

Interview by Tim Mass Movement

Live Photos by Beer Obsessed

MM: Okay, Phil, tell us all about Cannabis Corpse – when, why and how did the band get together, and where did the idea of the "tribute" to Cannibal Corpse come from? Was it something that you set out to do from the beginning of the band, or just something that popped in there on day....?

Phil: Well my twin brother and I have known each other for a long time (of course) and we have spent hours and hours smoking weed and cooking up ridiculous ideas. Cannabis Corpse was one of those ideas that was too good just to sweep under the rug, we couldn't stop laughing about all the possible song titles we could use. I think Josh and I were about 17 or so when we thought of it. It took us 10 years to finally get around to making it reality, I think our motivation basically was the fact that we thought Cannibal Corpse was the most brutal band in history and we wanted to be in a band that had that same sort of mega intense old school death metal vibe. We also enjoy our fair share of bong hits so combining our two favourite things together just seemed like a no-brainer. But I didn't want the music to come across half assed; I wanted it to be something totally legit that any death metal banger could get into. I put a lot of effort into writing and recording Cannabis Corpse songs and I hope it shows. It has been 3 years since we started and We have put out two full length albums and one four song EP and I couldn't be happier about how positive the feedback has been from everyone out there on the interweb.

MM: As a confirmed non-smoker of the herb, I was wondering if you could explain the allure of, and your obviously deep seeded affection for, the cannabis sativa plant? What's your favourite use of it, and what's the strangest thing that you've ever heard it being used for?

Phil: I would say that it is a love/hate relationship really... I love being able to relax and smoke a joint and let all my stress melt away with sweet chiba but I hate having to shell out sixty dollars a week (at least) on my habit, it can be a pain in the ass! I have also had my share of close calls with Johnny Law and that is no fun whatsoever, These days I feel like I need to smoke weed just to interact with human beings normally. Ha ha!

MM: The bong, the pipe or the straight forward smoke? Which is, in your opinion, the best route to take when following the highway to Highville?

Phil: One time I was in Oakland playing a gig with Municipal Waste, I saw a band called Cropduster, they actually made 3 or 4 entire Pizzas out of weed, I don't know how they did it but eating a slice of that was like eating a slice of heaven! I love it when people cook with weed, hands down that is my favourite way to get high.

MM: I'm assuming that, lyrically, you follow the path of the plant? Do you want to tell us what lyrical themes you explore within the band and how they both relate to and incorporate the bud?

Phil: Lyrically we are trying to create a vibe similar to the Scott Burns era Tampa Death Metal fathers like Deicide, Morbid Angel and of course Cannibal Corpse, We have songs about ancient societies that cultivate weed with blood from satanic sacrifices, Being driven insane by hash so potent it causes supernatural voices to command you to kill, shooting bud out of your cock, getting revenge on a dealer that has sold you fake weed and a museum dedicated to displaying horrific scenes of marijuana abuse gone wrong. We try to keep it as serious as we can because we think it makes the joke more "believable" in a way. I want Cannabis Corpse to give people the same "scary" feeling that I got when I heard death metal the first time as a kid ya know?

MM: I gotta know man, what does *Tube Of The Resinated* mean, and how does someone become *Mummified In Bongwater*?

Phil: Ha ha! Well *Mummified in Bongwater* is about a giant portal that opens over our home town of Richmond and dumps billions of tons of bong water onto the city, It is a spoof of the Cannibal Corpse song title *Mummified in Barbwire* as for *Tube of the Resinated* that is a spoof of the CC album called *Tomb of the Mutilated* that just sounded hilarious!

MM: Most people refer to CC as being the 'side-project' of Land Phil from Municipal Waste, so I was wondering how you see Cannabis Corpse, and how it makes you feel when people refer to the band as 'side-project'? Do you think the term 'side-project;' is seen or viewed as being less than a normal band by a lot of folks, and if so why, and if not, why not?

Phil: Cannabis Corpse has been playing shows and putting out albums pretty regularly, we just did a 30 day tour of the U.S that was really fun and we are doing a two week Euro run in Feb. next year. I love both MW and CC and treat both with the same amount of passion, I put 110% into everything I do and I really appreciate all the support I get from people out there that I meet on the road. I think now that people are starting to see us live we are starting to break through the "Side project" stigma and hopefully we are beginning to be seen us a more of a "real" thing.

MM: How do you feel about legalisation or decriminalisation of Cannabis? Given that as a drug it was legal up until the early twentieth century, why was it criminalised, and do you think the original reasons for changing its legal status still have any bearing in the twenty first century? Why or why not?

Phil: I have got to be honest and say that I really don't know what the original reasons were for changing marijuana's legal status, I know that I am sick of having to sneak around and deal with shitty weed dealers. I know the government could probably make billions of dollars off the weed industry. I also know that when it comes to dealing with people I would rather deal with someone who is super stoned than someone who is shit faced drunk you know?

MM: Do you know if Cannibal Corpse knows about the band, and if so, do you know what they make of you guys?

Phil: The funny thing about that is I actually asked Paul (the drummer in Cannibal Corpse) if we could use the name Cannabis Corpse for the band way before we recorded our first song. I have bumped into him since and he is stoked on the band, we have a pic of Alex (the bass player form CC) giving our first album *Blunted at Birth* the thumbs up on our Myspace page. I hook them up with merch every time I see 'em. I think they can see that I am doing this band in a very heartfelt honest way and in no way am I "making fun" of Cannibal Corpse. That band seriously impacted my life and I probably wouldn't be here doing this interview right now if it wasn't for them.

MM: You've got a new record out on Tankcrimes right? Do you want to tell us about it and how did you come to hook up with Scotty – Was it the MW connection?

Phil: OOOOOH YEA! Scotty is the man! I have known that guy for quite a while now and he is one of my best friends on earth, we have been all over the world and in all sorts of crazy situations together travelling with the Waste, He rolls the most killer joints and is the best dude to have around. I could go on and on about all the hilarious tour stories that involve Scotty ha ha! Working with Tank Crimes is something I have always wanted to do and there is no one else in the world I would rather have slinging the new album!

MM: How do you feel about term 'Stoner'? Is it derogatory or a badge to be worn with pride? Why?
Phil: I feel like the term "Stoner" makes people think that the band is going to be super slow and sludgy so using that word to describe us would not be accurate. CANNABIS CORPSE is way more aggressive than that, I haven't really heard anyone call us a stoner band though and I am happy about that I guess. I would rather just be called a DEATH METAL band than anything else. That is a badge that I would wear with pride for sure!

MM: To what do you attribute the longevity and lasting popularity of Death Metal? Why do you think Death Metal reaches the parts that other sub-genres just can't, and what do you think Death Metal's appeal really is? What's its secret?

Phil: I started listening to Death Metal as a kid because it was the most extreme form of metal I could get my hands on, I also liked the fact that it really pissed my parents off! I think there are many things that death metal has that other genres don't. Like attention to complicated musicianship, Badass album covers and passionate fans. There are always going to be people who want their music to be the most extreme thing they can find, so that means Death metal is never going to die. It was sent directly from Hell to devour your soul

MM: What do you do in the miniscule amount of free time that you have between the bands that you're in and their schedules? What do you do to chill?

Phil: This last year was insane. I played more shows and travelled more miles than ever before. I am actually in Chicago on tour with the waste right now as I do this interview, when I

get home I am going to spend some quality time with my girlfriend Luna and just relax hard as shit. Next year is starting to get booked up as we speak so there is no rest for the wicked, Evil never dies!

MM: Tell us something really, really odd about Cannabis Corpse and each of the members of the band- something weird that no-one would ever guess....

Phil: Well everyone in the band smokes tons of weed of course, I have seen people on the internet try and say that the weed smoking thing is just a gimmick, Fuck that! This is a lifestyle not a gimmick ha ha! I guess one thing that people might not know about us is that our drummer Josh "Hallhammer" is my twin brother, we grew up playing together and it is cool to be in a band with him that plays shows finally.

MM: What's next for Cannabis Corpse?

Phil: Cannabis Corpse has already written ten new songs! Hopefully we will get in the studio early next year and crank out a new full length album; we also have a Euro run in Feb to look forward to. We are just going to stay busy until everyone is slain in the upcoming marijuana wars of 4:2012

Originally published in Mass Movement #25, December 2009

CARNIVAL OF SOULS
AND PARALLEL UNIVERSES

The idea of mortals whose lives have been unnaturally prolonged because of supernatural events is brought forth in tales of vampires, zombies, and other creatures of the dark abyss. Stories of such immortal beings have been a source of entertainment for countless readers throughout the centuries.

But what happens when an individual's mortal existence is cut short due to an unforeseen occurrence, such as an accident? Could that individual dwell in two different plains of existence, simultaneously? And if so, could that individual also bounce back and forth between the two levels, spurred by specific events?

There is a compelling scientific argument that supports the theory of parallel universes and their relationship to the "real" world. Although more fiction than fact, the concept of another dimension does lend itself readily available to authors with vivid imaginations about hyperspace, time travel, black holes and specifically, the idea of parallel universes.

Such a topic is the premise for the occult film classic, *Carnival of Souls*. The protagonist, Mary Henry, seemingly escapes death, after the car in which she rides plunges from a bridge into a river in Kansas, killing her two girlfriends. Several hours after the fatal plunge, Mary, miraculously, appears before a search party with nothing more than wet clothes and a few, minor scraps.

From that point on, however, her life is turned upside down, as she teeters between the real world and a surreal existence of nightmarish encounters. She immediately leaves her familiar surroundings and accepts a job in a faraway city as a church organist.

Haunted by a zombie-like creature referred to only as "the man," Mary does her best to cope with his unrelenting presence throughout the film's stylish unfolding, but her connection to him becomes more and more obvious. She is obsessed by an abandoned amusement park on the city's outskirts, which just so happens to be the residence of "the man" and his zombie cohorts.

Her nosy and lecherous neighbor tries to reconnect her to reality with his unwanted sexual advances, and, for a brief time, she seems to respond. But the looming presence of the zombies is overpowering, and she slowly fades into an unsettling world of gloom.

In the process, Mary discovers that she is physically being blotted out of corporeal existence, alternating between the sights and sounds of the material world and the abject silence of her new surroundings.

To better understand her unusual circumstances, imagine that every thought, deed and event in your life has been replicated on some level of existence by an alternate version of you. That is to say, that you exist somewhere else in the vast cosmos. Now add one, small variant. Perhaps, instead of having blue eyes, you have brown. Or maybe today in this world, you turn left at a particular stop sign but in an alternate existence, you turn right. This scenario presents, as an outcome, a myriad of unique twists concerning any specific event.

If, for the sake of discussion, a certain pivotal occurrence, such as death, is disrupted by a cosmic crossover of one's self to or from another dimension, then the idea of a parallel universe and teleportation becomes a plausible explanation for Mary Henry's unique quandary.

Whatever the explanation, Mary eventually succumbs to her situation and returns full circle to the murky depths of her watery grave alongside her two companions. But how close to realty is this explanation? Or, for that matter, is such an example even possible in the world of science?

For nearly a century, cosmologists have grappled with the possibility that there are hidden worlds that lie beyond the human senses. Throughout time, mystics from every corner of the earth have claimed the existence of ghosts and spiritual entities that dwell in these dark places. Although the world of science could never openly align its beliefs to include such superstition, it, nevertheless, could not ignore the remote possibilities that such places do exist.

The single most intriguing factor that led science to such a conclusion came with the examination of subatomic particles. In their observations, cosmologists were puzzled to find that it was impossible to pinpoint the exact location of such particles. One probable explanation for this phenomenon was the idea that perhaps subatomic particles exist in more than one location at the same time.

Scientists now subscribe to the "M" theory, which suggests there are an infinite number of universes (also known as multiverses) that coexists next to our own, separated by the thinnest of imperceptible membranes or "branes." When these various membranes collide, as in the "Big Bang," they produce matter as a by-product. According to this theory, they are constantly colliding; therefore, an infinite number of universes are being created at all times.

Assuming that a man is wearing a shirt, the distance from one of these multiverses to the next is a trillion times closer than that of the shirt's material to the man's skin. Keeping in mind that each universe presents a unique outcome to any specific event, then someone such as Mary Henry, as a material byproduct of two multiverses colliding, could conceivably pass back and forth (teleport) through the various membranes to experience a different set of circumstances. In one universe, she dies. In another, she lives. In one universe, she is plagued by supernatural beings. In another dimension, they do not exist and so on. Multiply these scenarios a trillion or more fold and the results are mind-boggling.

Man's burning quest to know the origins of creation has brought him to the threshold of eternity. This insatiable desire to realize his ultimate, creative potential has ushered in a new age of reasoning about the process of life itself.

To me, *Carnival of Souls* is a thought-provoking excursion into what may lie beyond the five senses. Whether intentional or not, the film does offer a sense that life is eternal, albeit, complex. While science is still uncertain of how the whole creation process began, it does give credence to the idea of intelligent design. As for Mary Henry, she may have been the product of a parallel universe or just a glitch on the radar screen of eternity. No matter what conclusion you come up with, one thing is for certain...she has been immortalized on film.

Doug Crill

Originally published in Mass Movement #25, December 2009

GAMA BOMB

Gama Bomb have come a long way since MM first met up with this bunch of Irish Mosh Fuelled Lunatics two and half years ago at The Junction in Bristol, back when they were touring the UK via the National Express "travel" network. They've just released their second album, *Tales From The Grave In Space* on Earache (which is available for FREE download from the label), and without wanting to sound like I'm blowing smoke up their backsides, it's easily one of the best metal records of the year, crammed full of slam-happy, thrashtastic anthems, and in my humble opinion, they're poised on the cusp of thrash greatness. In all honesty, it couldn't have happened to a nicer bunch of guys. I figured that two and half years was long enough and decided it was time to play catch-up with vocalist Philly Byrne. Prepare for the gamma burst...

Interview by Tim Cundle

MM: So you're on tour at the moment, working your backsides off...

Philly: Yeah we're really good. Early this year we came up with the idea of giving the album away for free and we worked towards that for the rest of the year. We put ourselves under a lot of pressure to write the best music possible for the record. Then we released it a couple of days ago online and the response has been one hundred percent positive. People were just glad they could get it.

MM: I was going to ask you about that. Whose idea was it that you release the album for free and how did the record label take it?

Philly: We were just sitting round talking one night and the idea came up out of the way that we listen to music. We download all the time and don't pay for it – I don't think you should so we thought that giving it away for free download would be a cool thing to do and we all agreed. We played a gig in Shoreditch or Hackney – one of these tiny places in London and the guy from the label came round and we told him and he said "Yeah, great idea". We were really taken aback at that point. It's great though that we are going to be a little piece of history.

MM: You've started a revolution. It's time to gather up the brothers and sisters and carry on...

Philly: Yeah, yeah. I don't know if we've ever started anything before though. It's just a new way of releasing it. It could be one way of releasing in the future. While everybody else had their fingers in their ears we were seeing this. It's an instructional move, it's a career move – there are so many positive things to be gained from this. The response to it and the reaction – there is so much to be learned as well about how you can release music with a very small budget. We're breaking down the barriers a bit you know.

MM: *Tales From the Grave in Space* – Where did the album title come from?

Philly: We had a couple of names for the album from *Dracula, Dracula Frankenstein* to *Gama Bomb in 3D* – we were getting into that genre horror zone. Then Luke and I were talking and just throwing out random ideas and words from the genre with a bit of Hammer Horror and *Tales From the Crypt*...

MM: Yeah it's sort of like Agent Steel meets Amicus Productions...

Philly: Well that's exactly it. That's exactly what we wanted. You know for me the whole concept of the thing is almost separate from the music. It's just a question of thinking about what's moderately exotic and what's really going to jump out at you as an album title, and this really did. We had an idea, and then we thought we had a way to design the cover which in the end didn't work very well but in the end the album cover tells a story that really works together with the title and the music.

MM: Were you actually channelling John Cyriis on *Polterghost*?

Philly: I may have rigged up a Ouija board, set it up and found out where he is, yes. *Polterghost* was one of the first songs we wrote for the album. We all loved the film *Poltergeist* and thought it was really funny when the medium came to the door so we wanted to use the film as a basis for a song. It's a great song and it was a challenge to record as it's quite an operatic song, it's quite big.

MM: And is the *Mussolini Mosh* your answer to the *Milano Mosh*?

Philly: What's the *Milano Mosh*?

MM: Yeah okay I'll bite...An S.O.D. song...

Philly: No. Never heard of it. What this is though is just a song in the great tradition of short songs. Every time we recorded it, it just became more and more a real crossover song with a retro feel...

MM: It's a great song because it makes you want to slam round the room. And the same goes for the album; there's no filler on it at all – and that's really saying something these days. Do you want to tell us about your campaign to stamp out inferior metal?

Philly: I suppose it was just a fun tongue in cheek thing. People who got it reacted really well and people who didn't get it talked about it which works just as well.

MM: What do you think constitutes inferior metal?

Philly: I don't know... most other types?

MM: So what makes you want to thrash?

Philly: Hard to say really, screaming riffs? What makes you want to thrash really more than being in front of a room of people who really want to, you know? I'm such a lazy git, but it's amazing when you play in front of a room full of people and they're totally up for it. It makes it happen. But apart from that, our riffs make me want to thrash. A couple of tins, a couple of hot lights and a couple of hot girls...

MM: What do you think are the golden rules of Thrash Metal?

Philly: The good thing about it is that there aren't any rules... No there are rules, of course: number one –know what you're talking about. Don't start talking about a band or wearing their T-shirt unless you know a little bit about them and have an opinion about it; number two – don't start acting like a dick just because you think you're supposed to; and thirdly – don't get your hair cut.

MM: So conversely what are the big no-no's that no self-respecting thrasher should be caught doing?

Philly: One - Wearing an S-Club t-shirt, Two - Drinking shandy and Three- Peroxiding their hair

MM: What about perming?

Philly: Yeah perming's okay you know – I'm thinking of getting some of those crimping tongs and crimping my hair, see how extreme it looks

MM: We all know the Big Four – the supposed Thrash Titans but who do you think deserves a place in that elusive group?

Philly: I think Megadeth – they deserve to be in the big four, and from a personal point of view, my big four would be: Megadeth, early Anthrax, Nuclear Assault and Agent Steel. They were all great for different things; Nuclear Assault are really punky, Agent Steele for pure power metal, Anthrax for their personality and great big riffs and Megadeth just because they came up with the format, the style that created Thrash and underpinned all those bands

MM: I was going to say that about Agent Steel – on this album you sound scarily like John Cyriis in places. What's the best format for thrash – the album or live?

Philly: It has to be live. Because music has always been about the experience. People want to take something away from the experience and that's how it should be.

MM: So how do you feel about the album now that it is out there?

Philly: I think it's a real vindication. People get it really early. I haven't heard anything bad about it at all, we haven't had any criticism. Recording the album we didn't have the easiest time, we didn't have the best time, but listening back is great.

MM: What next on the agenda then Philly?

Philly: We're going to Greece for a couple of shows in January and February, then a European tour later in the year. That's the plan, we're not going to record anything else for a while.

Originally published in Mass Movement #25, December 2009

CHANGE

Jakob Anderson liked to whistle. It drove his parents crazy but he did it anyway. It satisfied him. He knew it was stupid. His friends teased him endlessly about it, for sure. Whistling may have been an annoying habit but it was his, and he wasn't about to change.

I hate tests, Jakob thought as he chewed on his pencil eraser. They make me feel so dumb.

Fortunately, it was last period and he could go home when he'd finished the math exam. With half the school year behind him and the other half still in the future, Jakob felt trapped in a quagmire of seemingly worthless education. He was going to play in a rock band and didn't need algebra to whip out hot licks. Groupies didn't care if he knew the value of 'x' or 'y'. They'd want his body simply because his last ten albums had sold platinum. His would be a good life, devoid of blank verse, logarithms and the capitols of all fifty states.

He barely finished on time. Finals took long enough without being distracted by daydreams. Jakob handed in his test just as the timer went off. Mrs. Baxter scowled at him alarmingly.

"When will you change those filthy jeans, young man?" she sneered.

"Change is for the homeless, Mrs. Baxter," he replied smartly.

"Which is exactly how you look, Mr. Anderson." she stated flatly.

He returned to his seat, smiling stupidly. The aging battle axe had hated him from the first day of school. After today they wouldn't have to put up with each other again. Trigonometry II was the last math credit he needed for graduation.

When the bell rang, Jakob leapt from his desk and bolted for freedom. Today was Friday and he had all weekend to work up the courage to ask Shelby Dearborn to the Senior Prom. She was the hottest girl in school and had once let Jakob carry her books to class when they were in the ninth grade. Her flaming red hair and brilliant blue eyes haunted his hormone-induced dreams. Her huge rack and rounded backside made his baggy pants embarrassingly tight whenever she walked by. As Jakob liked to tell his friends, she was stacked.

Since he lived so close to the school, Jakob had to get home without riding a bus. Riding his bike would be the end of his social life so he always walked. When it rained he caught a ride with one of his friends or their parents, though he greatly preferred the former. He liked to walk, though, because it gave him plenty of time to whistle. Sometimes he whistled his favorite songs from the radio, other times he made up melodies as he went along. Today it was songs he had learned in elementary school music class.

The day was cloudless and warm. A light breeze rippled through the trees and blew leaves along the sidewalk. It was a beautiful afternoon and just right for a slow stroll home. As he approached the last intersection between school and home, he heard the screech of car tires and a dull thud followed by a clipped yelp.

Somebody must have hit a dog. Jakob thought.

Curious, he looked around to see whose favorite pooch had just bitten the bullet. *Yankee Doodle* died on his lips as he saw the blue Geo Metro with the broken windshield. Instantly he knew that the accident victim must have been a person. A dog would have hit the bumper and rolled under the car, not over it. A still form lay beside the car, limp and bloody. Jakob ran over to see if he could help. Over the summer he had worked as a lifeguard at a local water park and basic first aid had been part of his training.

The woman driving the car got out and stood over the motionless person she had just hit. Hysterically, she rocked back and forth on her heels. Her eyes were wide and she pulled on her hair.

"Ohmygod, ohmygod, ohmygod, ohmygod," the distressed woman chanted painfully.

Sensing that the woman was temporarily worthless and obviously unhurt, Jakob fixed his attention on the fallen man. The victim was old, at least forty. He was bald, plump and poorly dressed in a stained t-shirt and ragged sweat pants. Jakob checked the man's pulse while secretly hoping he would not have to administer mouth-to-mouth resuscitation.

Oh no. No pulse. No breathing. This man was dead. Jakob was overcome with dread. His own heart raced and he felt dizzy. Sweat ran from his every pore. Bile rose in his throat. He felt sick, knowing he'd just touched a dead body. His skin tingled as he struggled not to lose consciousness. Time slowed to a crawl. His vision blurred as a single thought passed through his head. It's time to change.

For a single brief instant Jakob saw himself lying on the ground in the exact same place and position the crumpled man had been in only moments before. Now Jakob was lying on the asphalt, bleeding. He appeared to be unconscious. In fact, he looked convincingly dead. Disturbed, he stood up and brushed the dirt from the knees of his filthy pants. He moved to the sidewalk, away from the accident but close enough to tell the police what he had seen.

Flicking the last vestiges of teenage angst from his fingertips, Bobby Taylor waited to give his statement to the cops. It was an unfortunate situation the bald, plump man had witnessed. Someone's son was dead and no medical professional could change that. Life was so fragile, so precious and a single moment of carelessness could take it away. Bobby wanted to talk to the press. He knew the injured teenager was beyond help but hoped this tragic loss could change the course of someone else's life if the story were properly told. Bobby knew he could tell it; he knew there was a reason he had been there at that moment. From this point on, his life would be very different.

The cops arrived, sirens wailing. Bobby watched as the paramedics attempted CPR. He watched as the coroner from the black van pronounced the young man dead and covered his tattered body with a white sheet. After he talked to the police, he returned to his place on the sidewalk and watched as the emergency personnel completed cleaning up the site of the accident. For a while, Bobby sat on the curb, whistling softly and thought about the true nature of change.

Jim Dodge Jnr.

Originally published in Mass Movement #25, December 2009

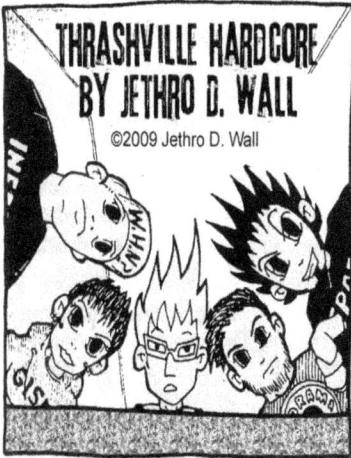

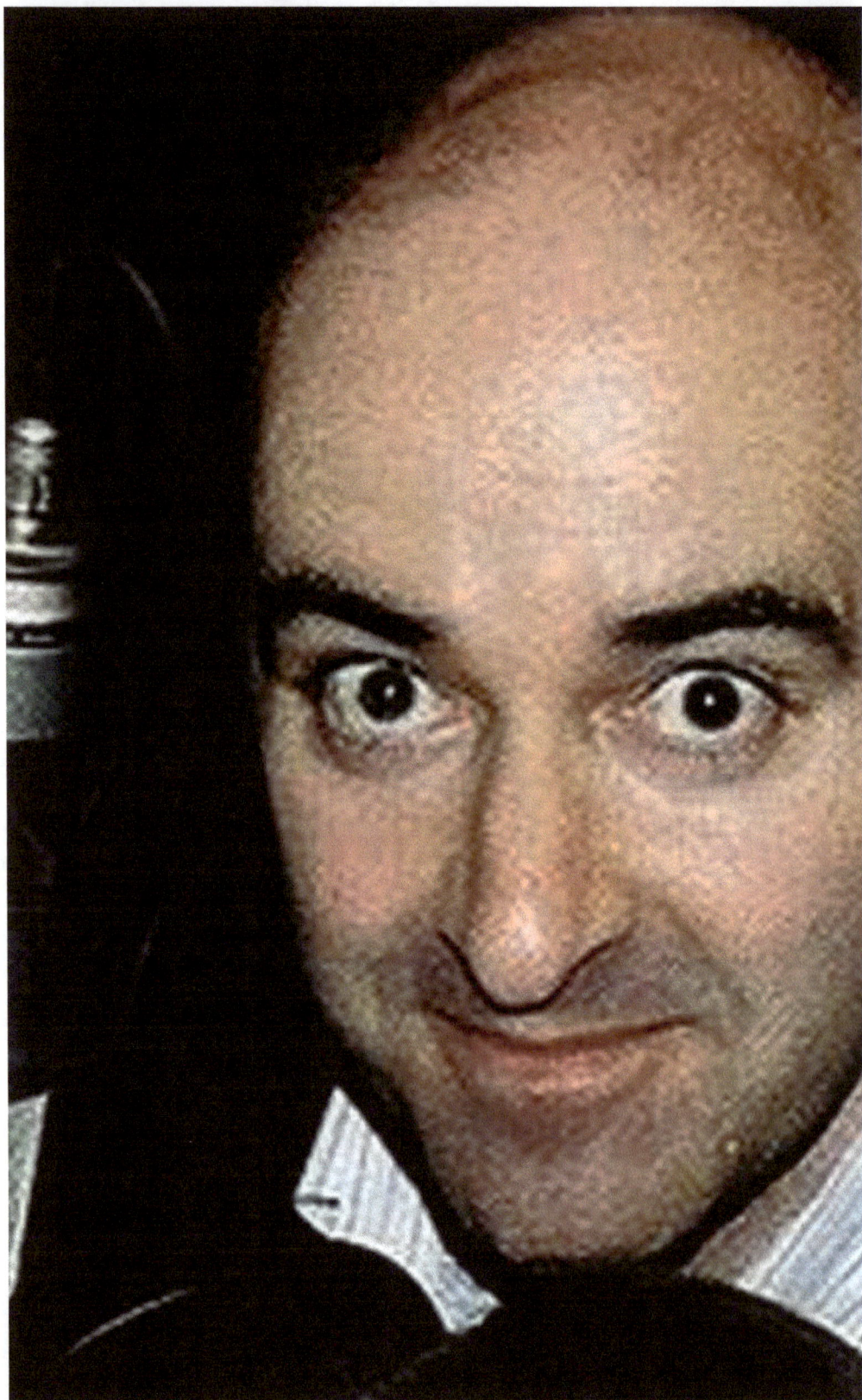

NICHOLAS BRIGGS

Nicholas Briggs. To a certain branch of fandom, his name is synonymous with Doctor Who. He's he executive producer for Big Finish, the company who have kept the Doctor alive with their series of audio drama's and he's the voice of both the Daleks and the Cybermen. Being a lifelong Doctor Who fan when I was offered the chance to talk to Nick about all things Doctor Who and Big Finish, I seized the opportunity with both hands. And this is what he had to say...

Interview by Tim Cundle

MM: As with all things, the best place to start is at the beginning...So, for those reading this who might not know who you are, would you like to introduce yourself and tell us something decidedly (in your opinion, of course) odd or strange about Nicholas Briggs...?

Nick: I'm the voice of the Daleks. Is that bizarre enough? I spent a large part of my childhood and teenage years sitting in my bedroom, fiddling with tape recorders and microphones, desperately trying to sound like a Dalek... and failing! So when I got the job, my mother said, 'At least all those strange noises we heard have amounted to something useful!' I can't think of anything particularly odd. But I'm sure there are a lot of odd things about me that I don't notice. My partner, Stephanie, tells me that I'm eccentric in so many ways, but I think I'm pretty normal. So what if I wear a deerstalker in bed! I'm joking. Or am I?

MM: How did you originally become involved with the Doctor Who universe? Were you a fan before you started working on productions associated with the series, and if so, what initially drew you toward, and thus made you a fan of, Doctor Who?

Nick: I was a huge fan of Doctor Who as a child. I don't remember why or how. I just remember that it was part of my life. I remember being upset when I heard that William Hartnell was going to leave! Ironically, though, Patrick Troughton, his replacement, ended up being my favourite Doctor. Then, years and years later, when I left drama school, I got involved with a group of people doing Doctor Who audio plays for fun. I played the Doctor and the Daleks... and any other monster going! Then, a few years after that, I was in at the beginning when Big Finish got a licence from the BBC to do Doctor Who audio drama. It's still going, and that's what occupies most of my life. From time to time, I travel to Cardiff to do Daleks for the TV series, which has been great.

MM: What are your earliest and fondest memories of the series? Did you ever hide behind the sofa when watching, and if so, what was it that caused you to do so?

Nick: I remember all sorts of bits from the middle of the William Hartnell era onwards. My earliest, detailed memories are of Patrick Troughton's first stories. I don't recall hiding behind the sofa... I never got the chance. As soon as something scary happened, my mother would put a newspaper in front of my face. So all my earliest memories of the scary bits have newsprint in them.

MM: Right, time to talk about Big Finish...Do you want to share a little of its history with us, and tell us how you came to be involved with Big Finish?

Nick: Big Finish asked the BBC for a licence to do Doctor Who audios in 1996, but they said no, because they thought the Paul McGann TV movie was going to be really successful and turn into a new TV series. It didn't, so three years later, we asked again and got the licence. In the meantime, we'd got the licence to do a Doctor Who spin-off range based on an inter-galactic archaeology professor called Bernice Summerfield. This demonstrated to the BBC that we knew what we were doing. I was in at the beginning of the Doctor Who's, writing, di-recting, acting, sound designing and composing. And over the years I worked on all sorts of productions. Then, when Gary Russell, the original producer, left, I became executive pro-ducer.

MM: Where did the original idea to create new stories and adventures for the Fifth, Sixth, Seventh and Eighth Doctors and their companion originate?

Nick: It was because Gary Russell and I had been involved in doing the amateur Doctor Who plays, and we'd both said that one day we'd like to 'do it for real' as it were. We decided to do the Fifth, Sixth and Seventh Doctors to start with, because we'd worked with them all in other contexts and kind of knew how to approach them. We didn't think we had a cat's chance in hell of getting Paul McGann. And we knew the proposition of Tom Baker would al-ways be, shall I say, complex. It is still proving to be so...

MM: How difficult was it to get the idea off the ground and keep its momentum rolling?

Nick: Once we'd decided to do it, Gary held a big meeting of writers to break the news and get people on board. Steve Moffat was there and famously left early, because he wasn't in-terested in rehashing old stuff. He felt we should pick one Doctor, create a new companion and then just go with that. But Gary knew Doctor Who fans through and through and knew they'd want something that 'fitted in' to established continuity. He was very wise. So that's what we did. He commissioned me to do the first one, and I more or less organized the whole thing. I cringe now at some of the mistakes I made. I sent Peter Davison the script for the Sixth Doctor! And I remember printing everything on tiny bits of paper in five-point text to save money. People were squinting at the scripts. Ah... those innocent days.

MM What, in your opinion, were the most difficult and the easiest things to work out and finalise about each series?

Nick: Each series presents a new set of challenges. The most difficult thing to get right is the script. It's an old, old story, but everything flows from that. And Doctor Who is fiendishly dif-ficult to write. Everyone kind of thinks they can just dash it off. But it's really, really difficult to get right. Then, of course, there's the casting. You have to be bold! That's why I get other people to make the difficult phone calls for me. And the post-production really needs to be followed in detail. You can make or break a scene with a misplaced sound effect or a piece of music that washes over the emotional content incorrectly.

MM: As the Executive Producer for the Doctor Who range, what do you think each Doctor (or rather the actors who play the various incarnations of the Doctor) bring to the role? Do you think that there are stories that are more suited to one Doctor than another (say the Sixth rather than the Eighth), and how, from the Big Finish (and of course your own) point of view, do you decide on what will or won't work with each Doctor?

Nick: Producer David Richardson, script editor Alan Barnes and I are dyed in the wool Doctor Who fans. We have an instinct for what works with each Doctor. By and large, the Sixth Doctor drives the plot along faster and commands the action. The Fifth Doctor is always right in the middle of it, apologizing and getting bogged down. The Seventh Doctor is mysterious, manipulative and aloof. Aside from that, they all largely behave the same way. The Eighth Doctor feels like a more modern Doctor, more like the bridge between the old and new series, possibly because he's got a touch of a regional accent. And certainly when we teamed Paul up with Sheridan Smith playing Lucie Miller, we felt we had more room to experiment with emotional content and story style.

MM: Which of the three jobs (actor, director and writer) which you fulfil on a regular basis for Big Finish do you prefer? Or isn't it that simple? How, in your opinion do all three differ, and are there any similarities between each of them? How do you manage to juggle the three roles?

Nick: I trained as an actor, so when push comes to shove, that's the job I'd do if a metaphorical gun was put to my head and I had to choose. But that would be a huge shame for me, because I really love doing them all. I particularly like the sound design and music. But I like variety in my life. I like to be able to flit between one discipline and the next. That keeps me fresh, and also helps me to do each job with a bit more insight each time. For example, directing for audio is much easier if you've done sound design before. You know exactly what you need to concentrate on. My sound design work has definitely helped me with the directing. Slowly it's dawned on me that more actors give their best performance in the rehearsal! They feel no pressure to get it right, so they relax! This has proved immensely useful to me as an actor as well. I try to pretend the first take is the rehearsal and it goes a lot better. Naturally, as a director, I do actually do retakes, but often you'll take most of the lines from that rehearsal. So it's not a question of juggling all of these jobs. Or rather the juggling is only about time management and that's a nightmare. When I direct something, it really stops me being the producer. So I have to find a way to keep in touch with everything else in BF when I'm directing. It's called email! I have my laptop open when I'm directing, so I'm always in touch. But at the root of it all, all these jobs have one vital similarity. They're all about communication and story. And that's what I love.

MM: Time to put you on the spot Mr. Briggs (sorry!) – which of the Big Finish dramas that you've been directly involved in (as a writer, director or actor) is your personal favourite? Why? Which was your favourite to work on, and what made it so pleasurable?

Nick: I don't do 'all time favourites', because I change my mind. And there are so many different reasons why things succeed and are good. I've just loved directing Paul McGann in two of the latest of his adventures. We had the most amazing guest casts and Paul was working his socks off. I don't think I've ever seen him throw so much of himself into it. So that was really thrilling and I can't wait to hear the sound edits. I suppose my favourite stories are the ones that feel more like they are from my heart. So, there's the *Dalek Empire* series and the first *Cyberman* series. These were written, directed and sound designed by me, and with

Cyberman we did loads of rehearsals and then performed it live. That was a real buzz. But I'm afraid you can't put me on that spot! I can't pick one. Oh, and of course, it was a massive privilege to direct Sir Derek Jacobi. He was amazing in Rob Shearman's *Deadline*.

MM: Following on from the last question (and putting you back on that awful spot again), which three Big Finish Doctor Who adventures / stories do you think best sum up everything about the character? Again, why?

Nick: I just don't do that listing thing. It's not in my nature. I know it's a favourite male pastime. 'What's your top ten… ?' etc. A lot of my friends do it. I can never make my mind up! But I will say that I love those moments of crisis in Doctor Who, usually when a companion leaves. I'm keen on that kind of emotional content, so as a result, I end up writing those things. I wrote the exit of our long-term companion Charley Pollard in *Blue Forgotten Planet*. And I wrote that emotional departure over three stories really. And throughout her story arc, I did rewrites on all the emotional content, to get it just right so that it would lead up to something very grounded in real emotions. I also stuck my writing oar in for the final scene of *Death in Blackpool*, when Lucie Miller parts company with the Doctor. And I totally rewrote the emotional fall-out of the departure of C'rizz. I always want those moments to be right and be what I feel is quintessential Doctor Who, those moments when we get an insight into the vast cavern of loneliness in his heart. I'm fascinated by how the Doctor deals with being so incredibly old and coping with all that loss. The only constant in his life is that people leave him and/or die. I think a real human being suffering that over a number of centuries would go insane. The Doctor doesn't. So I love exploring that in those particular 'leaving' moments. That's when I feel I get to the core of Doctor Who. I find that very exciting and rewarding.

MM: Are there any parts of the established Doctor Who universe that you haven't used yet (in a Big Finish production) that you'd like or love to use, and if so, what or who are they, why haven't you used them and in what kind of context would you like to use them?

Nick: Someone told me the other day at a signing that we should do a Yeti story. I'd love to do that, but there is, of course, a famous rights issue. I'll look into that at some point! I don't think there's any other particular part of the Doctor Who universe I have a burning ambition to do. I have a burning ambition to do great stories, and they can take many forms and be in all sorts of places in the Doctor Who universe.

MM: After hearing Frazer Hines' uncanny Patrick Troughton impression on 'The Glorious Revolution', I wondered whether you'd though about bringing the Second and Third (maybe using Sean Pertwee) Doctors back to life? Or given that Tom Baker has returned to the fold, and has been working on a new series for BBC Audio, whether you'd also thought about maybe opening the door for the Fourth?

Nick: The door is always open for Tom Baker. He just never chooses to walk through it. I've been in contact with Tom and discussed a few things, but he went very quiet suddenly. And then *Hornet's Nest* came out! But I will go back to him. I would love to do adventures with the other Doctors and recast, but I think it would offend most of our audience and the BBC might not be happy with the idea of us recasting. I don't know if that's true, because I haven't asked. I'd kind of like to do a sort of Unbound version of the previous Doctors. I'd love to do the David Whitaker *Doctor Who in an exciting adventure with the Daleks* book as a full cast dramatization. It's so different from the TV episodes that it would certainly feel a bit Unbound. And that, I think, would justify recasting. Just as an experiment.

MM: I have to know...When and how did you discover that you could do the Dalek and Cybermen voices? How do you approach playing multiple versions (for instance three different Daleks) of each, and how do you differentiate between which one you're playing at any given time?

Nick: I can't remember a particular moment when it happened. It just took a lot of childhood mimicking, I think! To do the different Daleks, I kind of give each of them a different motivation and squeeze my voice in a different direction.

MM: It was inevitable that the question would be asked – how did you feel when you first heard that the Doctor was coming back to TV? Did you approach the show, or did they approach you regarding your roles (Daleks, Cybermen, Nestene Consciousness etc.) in the show?

Nick: I was very excited. They approached me. Or rather, my agent.

MM: What are the differences between acting in an Audio Drama (or play as I'd prefer to call them) and acting on TV? Given that both are essentially Who, do you approach each differently, is one easier than the other and which medium do you think best suits you?

Nick: Doing Dalek voices for audio and TV is essentially the same job. Although, the good thing about the audios is that I'm in with the other actors. Even though on TV I rehearse with the other actors, when I do the voice I'm just sitting with the sound man and whoever else is sitting with the director and producer on location that day. When I stand up to do my voice, they can't hear the effect – the actors can on set, but not the people around me. So it's strangely humiliating sometimes! Like someone on a bus suddenly starting to spout Shakespeare.

MM: Do you ever worry that you've been and will always be typecast?

Nick: Shorthand understanding of everything is the enemy of creative thinking, and show business is full of it. No one wants to think more than three seconds about something. I'm the same, quite often. I have to stop myself and think, 'No, just because that actor played a policeman for me before, I don't have to keep casting him as a policeman'. But then I do! So I am totally typecast as a Dalek. I didn't realize how typecast I was until I did the part in *Torchwood*, and people were quite innocently saying to me, thinking they were being supportive, 'What's it like to be a proper actor now?' Newsflash! Doing Dalek voices is proper acting. It's more proper acting than, say, sitting next to the lovely Joanna Lumley, pretending to be a solicitor who hardly says a thing! I did an episode of *Lewis* a while ago. It was lovely. But spending a few weeks clashing with the Doctor in big dramatic scenes as a Dalek requires far more proper acting than that! I was shocked at how amazed people were that I could actually walk and talk.

MM: Being a HUGE Conan-Doyle fan, I wanted to talk about Sherlock Holmes. You played the world famous detective on stage. How did you approach playing him? Did you rely solely on the original source material, or did you think of other actors who had previously taken on the role, Basil Rathbone, Jeremy Brett, Peter Cushing etc, or did you rely on something else entirely? Did your involvement with Holmes play any part at all in Big Finish deciding to produce its own Holmes stories?

Nick: Of course my playing Holmes on stage (in three different jobs now) was the reason Big Finish is doing Holmes stories now. Holmes is sort of part of my psyche. I've seen most of the screen adaptations and I suppose a lot of that has subconsciously affected me. But when playing him, you use the script you are given as your main guide. The fierce intelligence and the fact that without a conundrum to solve he is almost nothing. So he is an immensely powerful personality, but strangely empty underneath, which is why when the game's afoot he's always firing on all cylinders... more cylinders than any other human being has. I love his arrogance too. When on a case, he has an unshakeable belief in his own conclusions and often believes that his views of justice are beyond the law. And I love his deep friendship with Watson. I think that's what brings him down to the level of mortal. He is just such a joy to play. An absolute joy. And not unlike a certain Doctor we know of!

MM: So Nick, are there any upcoming Doctor Who (Big Finish) spoilers that you can share with us? What can we look forward to?

Nick: There's loads of great stuff! I have such a fantastic team and we work together very hard to create new and exciting stuff. I don't know where to start... There is, of course, the return of Tegan in the Fifth Doctor adventures, and the answer to what happens after Lucie Miller leaves the Eighth Doctor – you'll never believe it! And Sylvester McCoy's adventures are about to take a very interesting turn. The Sixth Doctor, too, will be having a rather unexpected encounter. And there will be some other new projects that are just too secret to talk about... Well, we can't talk about them because the deals aren't signed.

MM: What's next for Nicholas Briggs?

Nick: More Big Finish. There's the possibility of writing and starring in another Sherlock Holmes stage play and there's an original sci-fi audio series to write and develop for Big Finish. And then, of course, there's the phone that might ring with my agent on the other end offering me something rather special. There's always that!

MM: If there's anything that you'd like to add...?

Nick: This feels like the longest interview I've ever done. But it's been fun!

Originally published in Mass Movement #25, December 2009

PAINT IT BLACK

Paint It Black have been snapping spines with their jaw-droppingly intense brand of melodic Hardcore for eight years now. Their two new EP's 'Amnesia' and 'Surrender' have, as did their previous LP 'New Lexicon, raised the bar for intense, thought provoking and, at the same time, effortlessly melodic Hardcore punk. After their set in LePub this September, frontman Dan Yemin allowed me another hour of his time after the tape from a previous interview I'd done with him had broken. We sat in a darkened stairwell to talk about the new records, religion and countless other things. We were joined later by Josh (Agran, Guitar) and Andy (Nelson, Bass), who also had plenty to say. I hope you enjoy...

Interview by Kai Woolen Lewis

MM: First of all, you recently released *Amnesia* and *Surrender*, how do you think they compare, both to each other and to your previous records?

Dan: I think that the thing we're trying to do with Paint It Black is evolve and stretch the boundaries of what permissible, if not permissible then certainly what's expected within the parameters of Hardcore punk, while still remaining firmly ground in the traditions of the style of music. You know, the speed, the aggression, the politics. We're not really interested in making music that people are gonna listen to and be like "Oh, this isn't really Hardcore." I'm not interested in pushing the boundaries that far, but I am interested in incorporating a lot of influences that most bands won't try. So I kind of feel as though we've been doing that from one album to the next and I feel as if we've continued to do that with these EP's. How these EP's compare to each other? Well that's not an entirely fair question as they were all recorded as one block of songs and we didn't know which songs would go on which EP when we recorded them. We decided that afterwards through a long, tedious process which we always go through when we're sequencing a new album, like what order do the songs go in? What song starts Side One and ends Side One and then what starts Side Two and ends Side Two. Y'know?

MM: I think it kind of made sense for *Bliss* to be at the end of the record?

Dan: Yeah. With that record, *Amnesia*, it just worked out that it starts with probably the most belligerent thing we've ever written and ends with the most...beautiful thing we've ever written and the least Hardcore, conventionally. That song sounds more like The Pixies and Jawbreaker than it sounds like anything else we've ever done before, except for my shitty voice. I'm glad we did that song. That song was written when we recorded *New Lexicon*, but I hadn't showed it to the band yet because I wasn't really sure what to do with it. I had no lyrics for it either. So I think that answers your question. I mean, I say this every time we have a new release: I think the angry stuff is more angry and brutal and I think the melodic stuff is more melodic and then we have a whole bunch of stuff with the lyrics that's basically just me.

MM: You recently said you're planning to keep releasing 7"s instead of full-length LP's, why? What does the 7" offer instead of an LP for a Hardcore punk band?

Dan: I've answered that question probably about a hundred times and I'm going to try not to repeat myself, but it's hard not to. I think I become really impatient in the time it takes to get a full-length album done.

MM: It seems to make more sense for fans as well, I mean I'd much rather have a new 7" every 6 months than an LP every two or three years...

Dan: Yeah, I mean you're looking at two, two and a half years between albums and with a 7" we can say "Hey, we wrote these four or five songs, we're gonna record and release them all in the next month or two months. It's much more spontaneous and it allows us I think a greater degree of freedom. I feel much more connected to the people that support our band and come to see us play when we have new stuff coming out on a regular basis. I start to feel frustrated and bored when we're not making music. Also, to be honest, there's no Hardcore band that's made more than three GREAT albums in my opinion. I mean Minor Threat released did a few EPs and then self-destructed. Maybe Fugazi's done more than three, but they're not strictly speaking a Hardcore band. The Bad Brains made three, but the first two were kind of the same...

MM: Bad Brains have always seemed to me to be a band that a lot of people who have a very anti-bigotry still very much seem to get off on in spite of their religious beliefs and the disgusting homophobia that came from it...

Dan: The Bad Brains are a unique band, and that homophobia is some crazy shit, but I'm just talking about Hardcore bands that have released three great albums. I'm not really interested in talking about Bad Brains right now because it's boring. Rastafarianism incorporates a lot of homophobic ideas and obviously I think that's bullshit, and ironic coming from a band of black Americans, because homophobia's just as tiresome and damaging as racism so I don't really understand that paradox. Back to the question; Cro-Mags put out one good record, Gorilla Biscuits put out one good record. Minor Threat put out 3 EP's and broke up. Name a Hardcore band who've put out three great records, cause I can't think of one and I'm not arrogant enough to think we're gonna be the band that can do that. I like that we put out New Lexicon last year and this year we put out two 7"s within the space of two months.

MM: When can we expect another 7" and who's it going to be released with?

Dan: I'm not at liberty to divulge that right now.

MM: Both your new records are on different labels, with *Amnesia* being on Bridge Nine and *Surrender* being on Fat Wreck. Why is it that you've avoided, staying with one label since Jade Tree?

Dan: We're just trying to change the way we do things. I personally have been with Jade Tree for fourteen years and three bands and just like we're doing 7"s instead LP's, we're just trying to radically change the way we do things and we're also doing a bunch of EP's because it's an opportunity to work with a bunch of new people. I also have to admit at the ego end of it, I was like "How cool would it be to release a record on the biggest Hardcore label and the biggest pop punk label all in the space of one summer?" I thought that would be cool. I'm also grateful and flattered that both those labels were interested in working with us.

MM: You seem to be getting more intense, angry and it's a lot more abrasive and at the same time, songs like *Bliss* show a far more experimental, for want of a better word, side to the band. Do you think having a steady line-up as you do now has allowed you to do this?

Dan: Yeah, I mean, we just have a really easy way of working together and we work together much more as a band and as a group of people than we did before. Prior to this line-up, I wrote the songs and told everybody what to do and that was it. Now I write all the parts, but Jared, Josh and Andy play an equally important role in arranging songs and filtering out the bullshit, stopping us from writing the same song over and over again. So yeah, I think having a stable line-up and in particular this line-up of people has helped us stretch beyond what I would call our "comfort zone". I mean, it's so easy to write like a fast, Kid Dynamite style song. I could write them in my sleep. I still like to write those songs and I write a lot of songs like that but I'm continually irritated by reading reviews and internet stuff where other people try to tell us what kind of band we're supposed to be. People are always complaining that we're not hard enough or that we're not melodic enough...

MM: Do you think that's to be expected, with the comparisons people are constantly going to draw with your previous bands?

Dan: Yeah, but those bands are different things. I'm so tired of hearing about Kid Dynamite, I mean, it was a lot of fun, but it wasn't particularly challenging. I'm interested in challenging ourselves and challenging the people who are into punk Hardcore. I don't want to be doing the same shit for nineteen years.

MM: That makes sense. The lyrics to *Salem* are pretty outwardly critical of religion, is there any chance you could elaborate a little on the massive sense of distrust for organised religion in your lyrics also where your massive dislike of organised religion stems from?

Dan: Well I don't like when power is abused to the disadvantage of the people who give you that power in the first place. That should be disturbing to anybody. As for organised religion, I feel myself to be a spiritual person. I think spirituality is an important part of being human. Having some sense of transcendence, whether it's God or music or art or love or sex, all of those things can be spiritual experiences. Some sort of connection with something larger than you, even if it's just a community. Some people prefer to have a specific structure for their spirituality and I think that's why organised religion serves a purpose. It helps people cut down on the ambiguity and the existential terror of living in this world and not really knowing anything about anything. Not even understanding the parameters of our ignorance about life and the universe and nature.

MM: I can imagine that such a view of the world would be far easier to comprehend than the vast nothingness of a world without religious meaning...

Dan: It's terrifying, you're right, but I think there are certain questions that are not meant to have answers and my distrust of organised religion starts with that, the notion that they have an answer to all those questions and a purpose for everything. Maybe there isn't a purpose for everything, maybe things happen randomly and we don't get to know why, because there might or might not be a reason why. And that can be terrifying. Basically, if people want to have a structure for their spirituality, then that's perfectly fine with me, but as soon as it infringes on the rights of other people, then we've got a problem. Once they start telling us who we can love and fuck and marry, then we've got a problem. I think those people need to spend more time living their own lives in accordance with their beliefs and less time telling others how to live theirs. I'm disgusted by that. The big inspiration for 'Salem' came from the notion of bringing a child into this world and being terrified that in the US, creationism is now competing with evolution as a scientific fact. It's like teaching witchcraft. It's crazy to me and I don't want my kid learning that shit in school, so that's the shit that really got me fired up to write that song. The fact that in 2009 we're having a dialogue about whether or not creationism belongs in science class and that any fucking drug addicted idiot can reproduce and at the same time there's actually serious dialogue about whether it's okay for gay couples to adopt a child? It's like "Really? What the fuck? How is that happening in 2009?" The notion of crazy people dragging us back, through history, has been a major theme in this band since the first album; turning back the clocks, rewriting the history books. I mean, it's some medieval shit, creationism.

(This is where Josh and Andy came out and joined us for the interview.)

MM: Are there any other major themes to your lyrics? Is there anything you're especially trying to express as a band or just yourself as a lyricist?

Dan: I think it'd be interesting if Andy had any notions on that.
Andy: Well, we always talk, as people, about hating the world but loving life.
Dan: Thank you, Propagandhi.
Andy: I don't know. I think what to me is really cool about Dan's lyrics and maybe sets them apart from some of our contemporaries is that he writes about real shit and he writes about it from a really authentic place. I think they're very much songs about him, about what he's thinking and feeling, stuff like that. Rather than trying to fit into any sort of mould, I mean, in punk it's so easy to just have 'Protest song X' or like 'Hardcore song Y', but even when he's tackling a similar sort of subject, it's like Dan Yemin's take on it. I mean, he's writing as a person of his age and his standing in the world, which is unique and interesting and I think that in music in general, you need an authentic, honest voice and all the great artists come from that place as well. I also like that there's also a feeling of like a rallying call to arms in a lot of the songs. It's not just like "Fuck you, here're a lot of things I don't like", I mean, there's plenty we don't like, more "This is a fight that we're in together and I dare you to join in" There's a lot of hope in that and it's very uplifting. It can be totally dark and scary, but it's like "Hey, we're fucked, why not fight? The worst that can happen is we're still fucked." I don't know about themes or anything in particular, this isn't some well thought out concept.
Dan: No, they're all kind of individual things. I mean, I get preoccupied with certain things at certain times. I mean, right now, it's sort of getting older and feeling kind of vulnerable in a different way and I think that's definitely crystallised in a lot of these new songs.
Andy: Yeah, that's what I mean. There aren't Hardcore songs that are like "I'm scared of getting hurt at the show because my body is fragile" and like "I'm not Derby Crash. I'm not going to stab myself with a broken beer bottle, because I might die and that would suck, I don't want to die." It's coming from a different place.
Dan: It's more like "I want to live" than "I don't want to die", but there's not necessarily a huge distinction.

MM: If you had to choose any one Paint It Black song to demonstrate what you do as a lyricist or as someone with something to say, do you think you could?

Dan: Fuck.

Andy: Probably *Four Easy Steps* (laughs)

Dan: I don't think I can answer that. Maybe you can pick one? You know, personally, I think one of my favourite sets of lyrics is New Brutality, even though I say *Fight Back* about a dozen times.

Andy: Really? Fight back times twenty? Are we really okay with this? An army of accountants counting matchsticks? That's like kind of the same word twice man.

Dan: I don't want to sound like a snob, but I'm not going to have my lyrics critiqued by someone who doesn't know what alliteration is.

Andy: I don't think there are many great lyricists where you could say "This is their one good song". Bob Dylan isn't a great lyricist because he wrote one good song, he wrote like a hundred.

Dan: Yeah, that's really hard to do, because we write lots of different types of songs. Some are very deliberately and belligerently political and some are a lot more oblique and personal. There's got to be songs where the personal and the political are balanced well and it would have to be one of those songs, but I can't think of any right now.

MM: You all do other things outside Paint It Black, how easy is it, then, to go about balancing it with things in your everyday lives, in particular, Dan, your profession as a psychologist?

Dan: I think it's hard for all of us for whatever reason. Everyone in this band does other things and is in other bands, but I think this band has been something that's a little bit difficult to organise.

Andy: I think in any band there's always a struggle of goals, schedules, aspirations and whatever else, especially when it's 'part-time'. It's hard to vibe your interests when you're playing like four shows a month. I think more than anything, it's geography that gets in the way, not necessarily like anything else. Sometimes someone will be in a different country so we can't record or whatever.

MM: How do you go about writing songs in that situation?

Dan: Generally, I'll bring the skeleton of the song to Josh, Andy and Jared and say "Have at it" and then they make it into something much more interesting than it was when I showed up with it. It used to be that I would demo everything on the computer with a drum machine, bass and guitar because I wanted to make sure they heard it the way I envisioned it and then did whatever they wanted with it after that. The new songs, though, were written far more face-to-face and I actually like that better. I think originally demoing stuff was a way of saving time, because we couldn't practise that often. It was much more satisfying to be able to say "I've got this bit, this bit and this bit" and have them bounce it around and refine it.

Josh: It took a few practises to get *Surrender* down. It took a few weeks. We'd practise all the other songs that we had and then we were like "*Surrender*, what the fuck are we going to do at the end of this song?"

Dan: Yeah, and the collaborative thing is fucking fantastic and magical. I think on *New Lexicon* and on these EP's we had songs that were like "This song's really cool, but I have no fucking idea how to end it." *White Kids Dying of Hunger* had this whole ending that was kind of mediocre and didn't really live up to the rest of the song and I asked "What do you guys think is going to make this work?" and Andy was like "Jesus Lizard!" He sat behind the drum set and played this beat and I decided to go home and rewrite the ending in that modality and it turned out to be this fucking huge crescendo of an ending that's probably one of my favourite things to come out of that record and the same thing happened with *Surrender*. It's was like "what the fuck are we meant to do here" and it was like "What about if we did a combination of what Dead And Gone did on this album and Dubstep?" At the time I didn't even know what Dubstep was so I went and researched it. Josh?

Josh: I remember, specifically, I was like "Jared, just pretend like you've taken a whole bunch of heroin and you're totally chilled out and just playing the drums, whatever the fuck you want."

Dan: It also ended up being largely improvised.

Andy: Yeah, that end bit was composed largely through recording it and cutting it up, a technique that a lot of bands utilise, but not really in Hardcore.

Dan: It was recorded in reverse too, you have this whole traditional song structure, y'know, fast, break, fast and then we kind of unravel into this more melodic Ink and Dagger type thing. We just recorded the bass playing 16th notes and then recorded drums and vocals afterwards, kid of chopping it up in the recording process. It was really cool. I had to leave, I had to fly home to work for a couple of days and they sent me rough mixes and I was like "Wow, shit. This is fucking cool." I was so excited.

MM: Do you prefer playing with Paint it Black to Lifetime? I've always thought it'd be more fulfilling to sing in a band than just play an instrument? Being the mouthpiece of the band?

Dan: The big mouth behind the band maybe. More in front of it; that's a terrifying responsibility. I'm still not sure, there's still sort of a 60% hit rate. I still only feel I get it right live about 60% of the time. The rest of the time I'm embarrassing all of us. It's scary and it's a lot harder than playing guitar was for me.

MM: When you were making the new Lifetime record, did you have any input on Ari's lyrics? Do you find it harder to be in that situation and watch someone else be the mouthpiece for the band since you've been doing that for PIB?

Dan: It was a nice relief, but I think that circumstance is part of what led to Paint It Black the band, all four of us, being responsible for our music, because that whole time we were making that new Lifetime record, we were writing New Lexicon and I was away a lot of the time, so during that period I'd say I only made it to practise about 40% of the time.

MM: Paint It Black, along with Lifetime and Kid Dynamite, are a huge influence in the UK punk scene – how does it feel to play with bands like The Steal who regard you as such a massive influence on them but also regard you their peers?

Dan: To me, I think The Steal was such an amazing thing to discover, because I think they did Kid Dynamite better than Kid Dynamite did Kid Dynamite. I'll say that for the record. It felt like there was this idea of what Kid Dynamite was supposed to be and sometimes we got it right and sometimes we didn't, but The Steal, they got the point and they got it right every single time. I mean, it's not like Kid Dynamite was original, it was all stolen from Gorilla Biscuits and Bad Brains and 7 Seconds. It's nice to be considered influential, but there's a dark side to that. I mean, a lot of the bands who cite Lifetime as an influence are fucking terrible. Is that a mean thing to say?

Andy: No. You're being kind.

Dan: You looked really sad when I said it, did you not like what I said or did thinking about those bands make you sad?

Andy: It's ridiculous, but I'm not going to go into it. It'll take up a lot more of your tape.

MM: What's next for Paint It Black?

Dan: More.

Andy: More everything, but for a little while, more resting.

Dan: I expect to get together with Andy at some point in the next month and fuck with some new stuff.

Andy: We're playing this a little close to our chest if that's okay? I'm not at liberty to divulge that.

Dan: I actually said that earlier. (laughs)

Andy: It just means it'll be really, really exciting when you find out about it.

'Amnesia' is out now on Bridge Nine Records and 'Surrender' is out on Fat Wreck Chords.

Originally published in Mass Movement #25, December 2009

STEWART LEE

2009 has been an exciting year for Stewart Lee. His TV show, *Comedy Vehicle* aired on BBC2 to critical acclaim. This enabled Stewart to break out of the arts centre circuit and play large theatres for his new show for the year, *If You Want A Milder Comedian Please Ask For One*. Having seen the fantastic Swansea date of this tour (reviewed in this issue), I spoke to Stewart the next day to discuss the tour, TV show and The Daily Mail, amongst other things.

Interview by Leigh McAndrew

MM: You are currently in the middle of your new tour, having already done the Edinburgh Festival. How has the tour been going so far?

Stewart: It's been going really great. In Edinburgh I did a hundred-seater room for a month, because I knew I'd be doing big rooms, and they are difficult to hear. You can't quite gauge the responses, so playing the little room which I normally do, The Stand, was really great, because I knew the show worked properly before I had to upgrade it to spaces that aren't always great for comedy.

The most difficult one yet was actually the Swansea one, because it was a big room which was only half full, so the bodies don't quite absorb the laughs. It's hard to get an atmosphere in the room and you have to trust your own internal timing as you can't quite hear the room, because all the sound disappears into the roof of the auditorium. So last night's show was a mixture of a real performance, but also I had to trust that it was going better than I could hear and sort of fake it a bit, which I think that all these comics who are properly famous and who are used to doing stadiums do, because you can't really get a proper flavour of what's actually happening in the bigger rooms sometimes, and Swansea was one of the biggest places that I've done so far. It was great, but it wasn't as sparky as some of the others have been, because I couldn't quite hear the room.

MM: One of the arcs of the show is based around Frankie Boyle's comment that after 40 you shouldn't really be doing stand-up. Do you think there's any truth in that comment at all?

Stewart: Ummmmm no. I think people in stand up get better with age, usually. A lot of musicians get worse. There's something about being in a rock band, it's kind of a naïve art form. It can be really great when you've got loads of energy and no technique. I think sometimes technique in rock music makes people kind of worse, actually. With comedy you tend to get better. The pitfalls are that sometimes you can get sucked towards blandness as your life becomes blander. You're not out there having adventures anymore. The other thing is that people tend to become more conservative politically as they get older, which doesn't always make for great comedy. We are living in strangely reactionary times where you could almost not be conservative enough to satisfy many audiences. It depends where you're coming from. When I was 21 and started doing stand-up I remember a quote from Victoria Wood, who is kind of a godmother of alternative comedy, and she said that no-one under 30 should do stand-up as you couldn't possibly know enough about anything. I don't agree with that, either. But I also think that it's part of Frankie's sense of humour. I don't think he would really think that. Or else he was talking about himself and what he's doing in his life. Stand up can be anything you want, particularly if you're Frankie Boyle, you know, he's really popular, so there's nothing to stop him doing anything he wants on stage. He could do a really thoughtful, nice show, or a story show, or he can do what he does now, loads of jokes.

The main thing about him saying that was that I had an idea that this show should be about what I'm supposed to be writing about. I thought, "What am I supposed to write about as a 40 year old comedian and a father of one?" I had this idea about something that happened to me in a coffee shop and I started writing about it and thought, "'That's so bland, so middle-aged". When I read that quote of Frankie's I thought that it was a great way to set up an argument in the show. There's someone who said you should give up doing stand up, so you have to prove why you should be doing stand-up. What have you got to offer, you know? So I suppose that's what the show is about. I'm talking about all the slippery ideas, things that make me feel that there's nothing left for me to relate to in culture as an older man who still has the political views he had as a teenager. I know Frankie; I wouldn't hesitate to tell him that I'd done that. It was just something he'd said in an interview and it seemed funny.

MM: There is a bit in your new show which talks about Richard Hammond [a TV presenter for any of our non-UK readers]. The Daily Mail took sections of this bit completely out of context for a story. What was your reaction to this 'journalism'?

Stewart: The guy came up to me in the street before the show in Edinburgh and said, "I write for the Daily Mail and the Mail on Sunday, I understand you are calling for Richard Hammond to be decapitated" and I said, "Have you seen the show?" and he said, "No", and I told him I wouldn't talk to him about it and he'd have to make something up. He said, "Well what's it about then?" and I said, "It's a joke, like they have on Top Gear". There's absolutely no point in talking to it about people, that's what I've learnt. There's no point in discussing it because there's no way that the nuance of what you're doing can translate to the Mail on Sunday.

The problem was that if I had tried to explain it then it would've spoiled the joke for people coming. And also no-one that reads the Mail on Sunday or likes Top Gear is going to come and see me anyway. So it doesn't make any difference. What I learned from *Jerry Springer The Opera*, which I co-wrote and got in trouble for, they sent me around the country trying to justify it when people tried to ban it, and there was absolutely no point having a discussion with any of the people because they'd already made their minds up. All that happened was that I was forced to explain what we meant by it, which I think spoilt it for people who were coming to see it, so I'd be happy to have a conversation about what I meant the show to be about with you, but there's no point doing it on the back-foot when you're being attacked by a tabloid newspaper.

Actually I thought the article in the Mail was really funny. The way it was written up was hilarious. They changed what I'd said, they had me saying, and 'I hoped his head had exploded into a million pieces', which is pretty funny. They had this picture of me smiling, looking quite nice, then next to it a picture of Richard Hammond's car exploding and then a picture of Richard Hammond's face looking unhappy. It looked like something they do in Viz, you know.

Anyone with half a brain reading between the lines would realise what the joke was, it's about...well you know what it's about. It's about if you are on Top Gear and you attack the weak and the defenceless and say, "It's only a joke", then what's to stop that being used against you? Nothing. You have no comeback on it because that's your defence when you pick on gypsies or whoever. The best you can come up with is 'it's just a joke'. It's just about that idea. No-one reading the Mail on Sunday would agree with that anyway, because they hate the poor (laughs). It's not as if I've lost any audience by it. At the end of the day, when you're 41 and have a family it's nice to get good reviews, but really all you're hoping is that bad reviews don't make it more difficult for me to pay my mortgage.

MM: This year you've gained more exposure with your BBC show. On your '41st Best Stand Up Ever' DVD you talk about the disappointment of having the show offered and then taken away. Were you surprised when the offer was then put back on the table?

Stewart: I was, yeah. It was offered to me in May 2005, withdrawn in April 2006, then back on the cards in spring/summer of 2007. So I was surprised and confused, because the offer was for exactly the same project that was already turned down by the man who had turned it down.

The thing about television is that there's no point trying to make any sense of it. It's like look-ing at the weather system. If you go out and it starts raining and you get wet, it doesn't mean that the weather was trying to harm you. It was just raining. Likewise if it's sunny and you're happy, it doesn't mean that weather likes you, it's just weather. So you have to view televi-sion and commissioning procedures as kind of a random system that there's no logic to. You can't start to believe that it means anything because there're lots of people much better than me who have never been on television and there're lots of people much worse than me that are on television all the time, so it doesn't mean they are good or bad, it just means that their face fitted at the time, and what strange decisions were being made behind closed doors about what kind of audience they were trying to attract.

That said, I still think that the BBC is out best bet globally for any kind of quality news cover-age or comedy or anything. There's a tiny chink of risk there, where they can afford to make things without having to worry too much. I know it's a deeply flawed system, but I've bene-fited hugely from it and I don't think there's any way that a commercial broadcaster would have made any of the things that I've done.

MM: In the series you did an episode criticising some aspects of television. Was there any-thing you wanted to add to that show but couldn't as it was on the BBC?

Stewart: No, there was nothing I was stopped doing in the whole series, apart from one sen-tence about David Cameron that I was made to slightly re-twig so that it was factually accu-rate. It was just something he'd said about religious schools, I just had to change it so it was right. One other bit was this idea I had about religious dog training schools, and I wanted to have an Islamic one for training dogs, and there was a concern that was never really resolved that because there's a cultural, but not a specifically religious, taboo about dogs in Islamic culture, although not necessarily in the Islamic faith, that it would look like I was being delib-erately provocative. I was asked not to do that, and to be honest no-one was really able to resolve whether this Islamic dog taboo was the case or not, so we just had to let it go. It actu-ally made the bit funnier. Those were the only things I was stopped on. But there's other stuff that I wouldn't have done on TV anyway, because there's things that I do in the live shows that are very long and they are contextualised and they have balance. You worry that on TV a sentence gets taken out of context and pinged around the world, and it's not worth the risk with YouTube and all this kind of thing.

MM: Some of your shows talk about religion and atheism. With books by Richard Dawkins and Christopher Hitchens hitting bestsellers lists in the last few years, do you think that atheism is being looked at more positively in mainstream society?

Stewart: Definitely. The worry about it then is that you have to remember to be polite. There probably isn't a God, but it's not worth getting too cross about. You have to be able to carry on your discussions with your mental enemies with a greater degree of politeness than they've historically shown to us (laughs). There's a worry now that in Europe, as the rationalist's cause starts to gain ground that you have to avoid triumphalism. Remember that there's still a lot of work to do and that's best achieved with a degree of cautious politeness, but you can understand people's frustration when their work gets banned and they get shouted down.

MM: The TV series recently came out on DVD and, as you mention in your new show, you've had trouble with people illegally downloading your DVDs, so will you continue releasing live DVDs?

Stewart: I will do, in fact the guy that put out the last one sold 57 last week, so he's just about to cover his costs, so he wants to do this show.

MM: Is that Go Faster Stripe?

Stewart: No, this is Colin Dench, who runs another company, but Go Faster Stripe are great as well, and I'll definitely do some more with them if they'll have me. Probably audio stuff or old archive, but the new show will be filmed with Colin Dench. He films it to broadcast quality which means you can flog it on to the Paramount channel or whatever.

Go Faster Stripe are really brilliant and what they've done is fantastic, because there a lots of really great comics who don't get on telly, and there's no documentation of them. Four or five of the DVDs that Go Faster Stripe have got are of the best people working today, people like Tony Law, Simon Munnery and John Hegley. Will Hodgson is amazing and it's really great that they are out there doing it. It's one guy in Cardiff, Chris Evans, and I think that the British Film Institute should give him a grant because he's documenting the best people, and they don't get documented as a rule.

MM: He's also bringing comedy out on different formats. He released your Pea Green Boat poem/story on 10", and comedy hasn't been pressed on vinyl for 20 years or so.

Stewart: (laughs) Just as everyone else is heading into downloads I'm going back to vinyl. Good idea.

MM: In your new show you tell a story about your youth and being friends with members of Napalm Death...

Stewart: Well there's no-one that I knew in Napalm Death who are still in Napalm Death. The only person from the line-up on the first album was Nick Bullen, who sang on one side. Nick Bullen wasn't at my school, but the other three were. The other three were, they were Daryl Fedeski, Simon Oppenheimer and Miles Ratledge. I didn't know them that well; they were in the year above me.

I was in a play with Daryl Fedeski, I was a butler and he was a sailor, I was in a walking club where we used to go walking in Wales with the other members of Napalm Death. I did see them when they had that line-up and around that time they were only 14 or 15. They got on these compilation albums that Crass used to put out called Bullshit Detector which were samplers of new anarcho-punk bands, but back then they sounded more like Crass or Poison Girls or something. They hadn't got that sound, even that's on the first album, where they sort of invented speed/metal/thrash/grind punk. They played sort of early 80's anarcho-punk.

MM: Speaking of music, in your new show you close the show with a song. Did you approach picking up a guitar live with some trepidation?

Stewart: I stopped doing stand-up in 2001 for three years, partly because I was never nervous and did the same sort of things again and again and I was sort of jaded with it, and I think that communicated to audiences. So every new show I do I try and do something I think is going to be difficult. In the last show it was trying to show a degree of sensitivity, I suppose, about having a kid and things like that. In the show before that it was about having one 40-minute routine which only had one joke at the end. This time around I thought I'd try and end on a song. It's sort of not something you'd expect from me, and also it'd make me nervous. It means I'll be nervous all the way through the show until the end, because I've got this thing coming up. It was a deliberate thing to do, and when I can afford to get him along I have a fiddler to play along as well. He helped me learn it. It was a deliberate decision to make it hard for myself.

MM: I think a few people may have missed the Sex Pistols reference in the song last night.

Stewart: Yeah... I do like the song *Galway Girl*, and I was sad when it was in an advert, that's what gave me the idea for the words, with Iggy Pop and John Lydon being in adverts. Also things you like generally, Nick Drake songs being in phone adverts and so on. I thought one of the only things you've got when you get older is culture that you love, books, films, music, comedy that means stuff to you. It's really depressing when it's taken away or the meaning is changed.

Although I hope that the song's funny, I am also serious in saying that we need to value these things more and let them retain their original meaning and not abuse them. You've only got one memory, you've only got one life and those special things are what keep people going, and certainly the Nick Drake albums that I loved, you just now think of that horrible fucking BT advert where his music is playing and they are talking about options for friends and family and stuff like that. It's insane, it's awful. I know that's an old-fashioned point of view, but that's what I think. Leave stuff alone (laughs).

MM: You also talk about the recent Magner's Cider adverts, and of course the comedian Mark Watson is the 'actor' in them...

Stewart: Yeah, I don't mention him in the show because I've got no personal animosity with him. I wish it hadn't been him and had been some anonymous actor. I know him a little bit. I've seen some of his work and I like it, but it would be hard to watch him again without thinking of advertising.

MM: I like Mark Watson, but wondered why he'd decided to do an advert...

Stewart: I expect he did it because he's got a family. He always does very well in Edinburgh, but for the rest of the year you don't really hear much of him. I would worry if I were Mark Watson. The brand of Mark Watson, as a quirky young fellow who thinks deeply about things and wears a Socrates T-shirt is compromised by being in an advert, on a purely practical level. I would imagine there are people who would stop going to see him because of it. But then he might pick up a lot of people who like cider (laughs).

MM: You're closing up the year with a month-long season at Leicester Square Theatre with *If You Want a Milder Comedian Please Ask For One*. **Have you done a season that long before in London?**

Stewart: I think it's six or seven weeks. I have done five weeks before at Soho Theatre, which is half the size. It may be that people won't come, but on the tour I've been getting 25-50% more people than usual, so maybe it will be all right. It's about a 350 seat theatre, and I could probably have done a shorter run at a bigger venue, but I chose this as it's sort of an optimum size for stand up, especially with what I do. It's not a big show. So I decided to do a longer run at Leicester Square and see what happens. I hope people come. It's been good around the country so far.

MM: Do you have any new projects for next year?

Stewart: I'm not sure yet. The BBC are supposed to tell me at the end of January whether we'll do a second series. If they will do a second series then I'll get on with that and I'll do some stuff in Edinburgh and film it before the summer of 2011. If they don't do another series then I'll write a new show for August next year and then I'll tour it and hopefully be back everywhere I've been before in about a year's time.

It'd be really nice to do a TV show again, because it's nice to earn that money, and it's nice to earn that money without being away from home when you've got a little kid. On the other hand, just having it on at all has been amazing and it's transformed my life. The money meant we could get a mortgage and stay in London and get a flat with a room for our son. And the exposure, it's not like being Michael McIntyre, but it does mean I get six hundred people rather than three hundred, and that makes the economics for touring so much easier. I can get someone to drive and come with us and help us with technical things, I can pay an opening act properly and I can pay a fiddler for some of the gigs and it just makes life easier.

I was just getting old and tired to be honest, and I don't know if I could've carried on doing what I did without a little bit of a leg up. I was getting burnt out. I was in a sort of funny quandary where I'd get really good reviews in broadsheet newspapers, but I'm not the kind of comic who does corporate gigs, I can't do them, I'm not very good at them, or do the commercial gigs like Jongleurs or the Comedy Store, so unless I'm on the small theatre/arts centre circuit it's hard to know what to do exactly, and the telly show has probably really helped get people along.

It will be interesting to see what difference this makes long term, but when I used to tour there was always 10-15% of the audience, maybe more, where I just wasn't what they wanted to see. They'd come to see some stand-up comedy and they end up seeing this boring bloke going on really quietly about things they aren't interested in. Because the TV show was an accurate reflection of that, those people aren't coming on this tour. There was a bloke in Worthing that hated it, but on the whole, most of the people who come know what they're coming to. You can have more fun with them and there are more of them. In fact, a lot of people who think they don't like stand up come and see me because it's not like other stand up. It's helped to whittle out trouble, the people who wouldn't get it in an audience, which is nice, but on the other hand all of us think that who we are now is the sum total of all our experience in the past and I wouldn't want to undo the twenty years I've had doing gigs to people who didn't really like me (laughs). I think it helped me become what I am now. It is nice now, at 41, when you have a kid and want to earn some money to be playing to large groups of people that actually want to see you (laughs).

Originally published in Mass Movement #25, December 2009

THRASHVILLE HARDCORE

©2009 Jethro D. Wall

97

THERAPY?

It's the big interview for issue 25, Therapy? are all set to go and … the Dictaphone won't work. Marvellous. Cue frantic calls to MM HQ before fate finally smiles on me and the bloody thing decides to start working. It's not the best start to an interview but being the thoroughly professional and nice guys that they are Therapy? put me completely at ease and proceed to talk about up the ups and downs of the music biz, their love hate relationship with punk and their critically acclaimed new album *Crooked Timber*.

Interview by Ian Pickens

MM: Welcome back to TJs and Newport!
Andy: Thank you, it's good to be back.

MM: It's been a while since you last played here; why did you decide to play small venues again on this tour?

Andy: I think we just really wanted make sure that we would have venues that would be sorta 'vibey' and that we wouldn't have to worry too much about ya know? When you play certain venues it's all corporate and it's all about selling the tickets, and all about making the money and getting the t-shirts out. With TJs it's like coming back and seeing old friends and that's the vibe ya know? We've booked a lot of venues like this simply for the fact that we enjoy it, cos next year is our 20th anniversary and ya know we're going to do all these things and we wanted a tour where we weren't putting ourselves under a lot of pressure. We're really pleased with the new album and it's a 44 date tour over two months and we've tried to get similar sorts of venues all over Europe that have the same vibe as TJs and the Thekla in Bristol. We were at Sin City in Swansea the other night and that was a lot of fun. Just so it's enjoyable and it's not really any pressure ya know what I mean? It's like you can get a couple of hundred people in TJs and it's a fantastic venue to play, somewhere else up the road might feel a little bit cold ya know. It's about keeping the energy levels up and keeping the optimism up.

MM: The last time I saw Therapy? was at Cardiff University with the Wildhearts which seemed a bit of an odd pairing; how was that tour for you?

Andy: I think to be honest it was an odd pairing; I mean we'd know Ginger and all for years and he's always been vocally a fan of Therapy? And we like the Wildhearts too and there's great respect there for one another, and he rang us up and said 'Shall we do the tour'? I think initially it was going to be a co-headlining tour and we were all going to play for an hour each but then ya know they an album out that had a radio hit, I think it was 'So Into You', and the promoter said 'we'll put the Wildhearts on as the headliner and you in the middle', so it kinda went to us be the opening act to the Wildhearts. So I think really we didn't know how it was going to go and also that was the first tour we'd done as a three piece again and we were in the middle of writing an album and finding our feet, so I don't think it was representative of how the dynamic works for the three of us now.

MM: The first time I saw Therapy? was here at TJs back in 1991 supporting Babes in Toyland; do you remember that show?

Andy: Yeah I do actually, I remember that very well because we toured in Ireland with them and got to share a house with them when we recording 'Pleasure Death'. The studio had this house that they put bands up in, and for about two weeks, on and off, we were living with the Babes in Toyland, so we were literally living under each other's feet, and then we did the shows which was fantastic ya know.

MM: You did the whole tour with them right? Was that the first major tour for Therapy?

Andy: Sort of, we came over first with Neil's first band, The Beyond, and then the second one was the Babes in Toyland tour.

MM: There was quite a short amount of time between the first two albums; *Pleasure Death* and *Baby Teeth* and it seemed to be a fairly meteoric rise for Therapy? from that point forward; were you surprised at how quickly success came to the band at the time?

Michael: No not really. We've often talked about this and we didn't really have a big Master Plan. It was all about do a good gig that night, next time in rehearsal write a better song than the last song we wrote ya know, quite organic and quite a natural progression. The most amazing thing was finding out that people actually liked the band; that wanted to buy the records and come out and see us. It wasn't like there were times where we were sitting in the back of the bus going 'Wahey that's great', smoking cigars. We'd always be thinking about the next gig, the next song, the next recording, stuff like that.

MM: The critical success of those early releases led to you inking a deal with A&M records; were you comfortable making the transition to a major record label or did you have reservations?

Andy: Oh we had big reservations, but the thing was that at the time we were touring a lot and I'd given up a job, Michael and Fyfe had given up college and it was like we want to do this and if we don't do this now we might not get another chance. This wasn't to do with signing to a major record label; this was to do with playing outside of Northern Ireland. John Peel had been playing us; we'd got this deal with Wiiija and we were selling shirts and making enough money for accommodation and petrol to get between gigs and that was all fine, and then it got to the point ya know where various record labels, whether it was Wiija or Touch and Go or Southern were saying "We want you to make this amount of money or play this number of dates, and we needed 'this' amount of money to do it", and I remember being told "Okay you're on Touch and Go and you need to do an American tour so you need to get yourselves flights" and we couldn't really afford the flights, so bless them they were like "Why don't you come down and work in the warehouse to raise the money'" and we were thinking to be honest, personally I don't want to do that.

It's not that I'm afraid of hard graft or anything. I mean I worked in a fucking factory for years; it's just 'is there any other way around it'? At the end of it we were just playing so many shows, the band was taking off and we had got to the point where there were six or seven record labels wanting to sign us and none of them were indies; they were all majors and eventually A&M seemed like the least bad of a bad bunch ya know? I mean I think it was literally overnight, we'd released *Pleasure Death* in January 92 and I was driving the van which had broken down on the Motorway in Belfast and been towed away for scrap, and all of a sudden we signed with A&M and were going to tour Europe. We signed to A&M and a month later we were in France.

Michael: A lot of people have this romantic view of the nature of record labels ya know but it wasn't about buying a Porsche; it's like Andy says it was about buying a van that was reliable enough for us to go out and play shows, buy equipment that didn't break down, drum skins, strings, those sort of little strings that ya know make the show work. And also if you needed to record a song you wouldn't have to do it all in three afternoons, you could spend a week recording it and then remix it later, things like that.

Andy: I think the thing that used to wind us up too was the people who accused the band of things when we went with a major label. In my experience all the people who do that, I mean we're from working class estates in Northern Ireland; all these people accusing us are these middle class punk kids who turn round and say 'you should do this and that', well ya know it's easy for you to say when your this big scenester in Northern Ireland and spreading this fucking hatred about the band and you live in Bangor, which is basically the equivalent to Beverly Hills in Northern Ireland. I mean this guy is a scenester photographer and his dad had built him a dark room in his house, and I was living off money I'd earned working nights shifts in the factory, Fyfe had a job in a bar, Michael was trying to save some money. To us it got the point where we just kinda said "Fuck it" ya know. It would have been brilliant if we could have done everything we did on Wiiija cos I loved that fucking label and I loved being on it and I loved Gary Walker; we're gonna see him on Monday which is brilliant.

It broke my heart not to be on Touch and Go because nearly every single record in that catalogue I had at home. The fall out with Corey (Rusk – owner of Touch and Go Records) because we signed with a major broke my fucking heart ya know? We'd go and play in Chicago and we knew he wouldn't be at the gig and there was all this kinda stuff. We did a tour with The Jesus Lizard, and they were really nice to us, but we did kinda get left out a bit after we signed to A&M; we were persona non gratis. I called up Steve Albini to do the *Short, Sharp Shock* EP and he was really, really nice but he said "Look, I'm friends with Corey from Touch and Go and you signed with a major so I can't do the EP". So there's a lot of that involved and it would have been nice if we could have done it any other way, but there wasn't. We weren't middle class kids living in the suburbs; we were fucking skint our parents were fucking skint too so there wasn't anybody to milk at home ya know?

MM: Did the onset of Grunge help bands like Therapy? who were bringing that whole vibrant, energetic rock music back into play after the excesses of the 80s hair metal bands?

Andy: Well we were already in existence when Nirvana's first album, *Bleach* came out and I was in Fyfe's house and we couldn't get a lot of the Sub Pop records, we had to get them through mail order and what we did was take turns and order them to the same address to save on postage, and this time it was Fyfe's turn and my copy of *Bleach* came and I really loved it, but Fyfe didn't cos he thought it was like Motorhead (laughs). At the time we were more into the noise-rock stuff like Oxbow, Sonic Youth and Big Black and we had already written things like *Meat Abstract* before we heard bands like Tad and Mudhoney. We were kinda more into bands like The Beyond, Die Kreuzen and Voi Vod ya know,? Slightly avant garde kinda rock. So I guess really all that stuff was running parallel, while we were discovering Black Flag and Big Black and all that stuff the Melvins were teaching Kurt Cobain about Black Flag, so it's just the two things were parallel. As regards circumstance, yes we were very lucky to be around that the same time and I do remember NME doing a grunge special in 1991 and we were featured in it. I think it helped I had hair down to my arse at the time.

Michael: I think Grunge had more of a traditional rock element to it, ya know Sabbath/Zeppelin, whereas we were more influenced by the Killing Joke/early techno/Acid House type thing. If you play *Baby Teeth* and maybe *Bleach* or *Superfuzz Bigmuff*, they're poles apart sonically but the energy of the early grunge bands was great and we could identify with that.

Neil: I think the connection is more in the attitude rather than sonically, we were both a reaction to all the hairspray, cock rock bollocks that was around at the time.

Andy: One of the places we were most popular, and recorded the *Shameless* album with Jack Endino, was Seattle; ironically because we were never really that popular in America but we were popular in Seattle, which is very much like Northern Ireland ya know? Not the average picture but ya know for years it was like an undiscovered part of the pacific North West and people are bored and they will gladly listen to Cheap Trick's Live at the Budokan next to Ted Nugent alongside Black Flag and Green River, they don't make any differentiation between them - 'The RAWK is the RAWK' (everyone laughs). I think that parallels very much Northern Ireland because no fucker ever came there to play and if anyone came, because of the troubles - people didn't want to go out. So when we were growing up we went to see anyone. I saw like the fucking Communards a week after I saw Metallica, six months after I saw the Smiths and I think you just take all these different influences in. In Seattle the FM radio scene is enormous, so you get up in the morning and you hear *Bad Motor Scooter* by Montrose and then in the night you can go out to a pub and hear the Murder City Devils blasting on the jukebox.

MM: Over the years you've recorded some eclectic covers; when you did the Reading warm up show here in 1994 I recall you asking the crowd if they wanted to hear a Misfits cover or a Smiths cover; you went on to record *Where Eagles Dare* for the Misfits *Violent World* tribute and also a fantastic version of Turbonegro's *Denim Demon* to the *Alpha Motherfuckers* tribute; it seems that punk has had both a formative and continuing influence on you?

Andy: It was until it got shit (laughs). This has happened all through my life ya know I was really, really into punk and I kinda went off punk when, I was also into bands like Magazine as well, and I kinda went off punk when it went (parodies UK82 style punk riff) Oi Oi Oi. Not that there's anything wrong with having a Mohican but when it got too much towards generic street punk, I mean some street punk can be exciting, but some of it was just ya know Lager Lads who'd got a band together, and that was when I drifted off and got into American Hardcore bands like Husker Du and I think later on the *Troublegum* album was really influenced by the punk we grew up on. And then post Green Day, don't get me wrong I really respect and admire Greenday a lot, but then you had every other Tom, Dick and fucking Dayglo Harry doing generic punk. The stuff I now consider to be punk are like your Converges or your Hot Water Music or bands like the Bronx who have got a really good spirit but I went round full circle and post Green Day went off Punk again. It was like I'd stick on a record from Fat Wreck Chords and every band would sound the same. It could be any band and I thought at that time that the last thirty years of my life have been a lie (everyone laughs)

MM: Musically Michael you lean more towards Metal like Voi Vod, Venom, Electric Wizard etc; do you feel you bring that side of things to the Therapy? sound?

Michael: No not really. It's not that our roles are really that defined in that 'he's the punk guy, I'm the metal guy'. There's just always something new in the metal scene that I haven't picked up on that Andy will have heard and vice versa.

MM: You have often been described a 'Metal' band which I've never really understood.

Andy: It happens more in the UK than it does anywhere else; I think it's because we played Download twice and Castle Donington twice and I think if you read the Guardian or you're a fan of Alpha Beat then we ARE Guns n Roses (laughs), they've got facial hear, they wear jeans and they have tattoos, I mean that's what it is, its just a bit lazy, but then what do you call us? I really don't know how to describe us, we listen to absolutely everything.

Michael: There's a lot of energy in this band and I think some people confuse energy with heaviness ya know? It's all about making that sound denser than anything else. You can be musically heavy and emotionally heavy without going *Roooaaaarrrr* ya know?

MM: Throughout your career I've found the albums have alternated between the more aggressive and vitriolic such as *Suicide Pact – You First* and the more polished and commercial such as *High Anxiety*; is this musical dichotomy intentional?

Michael: I know what you mean, we can be kinda schizophrenic. What I like about the band is it's not about going route one, it's about we can do this, but put a little twist on it ya know, that's sorta part of the challenge.

MM: Lyrically you have always made use of clever word play, puns and memorable phrases, much like Morrissey and the Smiths; do you write the lyrics specifically to make that impact or do they just come naturally in your song writing?

Andy: I just write bits and pieces ya know? I keep everything in little note books until the time comes to do a record and I just go through them until I find things that I like. I think an awful lot of the way I write is very, very dark and I think that just comes from reading. I've always liked books since I was a kid and I think I latched on to people like Spike Milligan, I really, really like Spike Milligan and he was like even before *League of Gentleman*, very dark but at the same time hilarious. And I like stuff like Flan O'Brian, a great Irish writer and some of James Joyce's work and I'm a big fan of Samuel Beckett and it seems like very much it comes from an absurdity that can kinda make it more... Sometimes my lyrics can be more direct and I enjoy singing them as much as the things that are a bit more obtuse, ya know? Things like *Potato Junkie* because it's kinda similar to the literature I would read. So far I've got two books full for the next record; its basically gibberish that I will write while we are on tour, or when I get back from doing the school run and normally it will be a line or a title and I'll run it past the rest of the guys and then we take it from there. It's always kinda been like that.

MM: Is it only Andy that writes the lyrics or do you all contribute?

Andy: Well actually our biggest hit worldwide, *Screamager*, the title came from Michael in a hotel room in Nottingham watching the Smash Hits awards and the song doesn't feature the lyric Screamager at all, but it got the ball rolling.

MM: What did you make of the mash up of *Screamager* with Electric Six' *Gay Bar*?

Andy: I don't think I've heard that one; I've heard the one with Destiny's Child.

MM: The Electric Six one is really good; you should be able to track it down on the Internet...

Michael: I love stuff like that

MM: Coming back to something you mentioned earlier; working with the legendary Jack Endino on *Shameless*; how did you find working with him? Some people have said he's quite demanding?

Andy: He's certainly very demanding (laughs). He doesn't party much but he's an interesting guy and we were there for two months and he's so intense, he would work from two in the afternoon until nine at night and then he's go and mix Zen Guerrilla and then go home and go on the internet until 2AM. He doesn't drink like so he can handle it. He was absolutely brilliant to work with but he doesn't like the band to go outside, he likes the band to be where he can see you. It's like if you're putting the drum sounds down, he doesn't want you to fuck off into town, he kinda likes the whole band to be there, it helped that we all like him; he's a brilliant lad ya know. I actually still keep in touch with him.

MM: He's not quite as intense As Phil Spector then? No handguns?

Michael: No, no there's no handguns. He's the master of the back handed complement, like you'd play a part and he'd go (in American accent) "Well THAT didn't suck" (laughs), so it's kinda like self-deprecating but he's also, like Andy said, quite a direct character.

MM: Things took a bit of a downturn in the mid to late nineties; problems with the record label, Fyfe leaving in 1996 and a few less than positive reviews; did you feel as if it all happened to fast and the move to the major was a mistake, or was it just a temporary lull in the bands fortunes?

Andy: I think it's like any band ya know – everybody loves you, then everybody REALLY loves you and then 'Don't mention their name again (laughs). You know the peaks and troughs. We've seen it in Northern Ireland, ya know everybody was going, Therapy? are shit, Ash, Ash, Ash and then two years later everybody was going Ash are assholes and we're like "No they're fucking not" Every band goes through that period.

MM: Download and Oxygene in the summer; the album is getting universally positive reviews...

Andy: Yeah it's been really, really good. We're really made up.

MM: Does this feel like a second wind for Therapy?

Andy: You know you hit it on the head really well; we tend to do one really experimental album and then one that's slightly more like *Troublegum* and it wasn't deliberate but I think with this record we took our time; it was a year ago we signed the record deal and I think we've really found our rhythm and our sound, but when it comes to the next album we're not gonna panic and try and do another *Screamager* or *Nowhere* like there's some kinda 90s revival just around the corner; we've kinda found THE sound for us and with the three people that we are it works perfectly, I think we're just going to develop that and not do a volte face and do another pop album. I think we'll just develop this sound into something more malleable than it already can be.

MM: It's quite a dark album but there's also a positive energy about it...

Andy: Well Ginger from the Wildhearts, our guitar tech – that's his two bands Therapy? and the Wildhearts, he played *Crooked Timber* to the Wildhearts when it first came out, and they had just done their album which is really melodic, and Ginger turned around to Steve (the guitar tech) and said how come three blokes that are so easy going and happy can make such a fucking dark and intense album and four blokes that are so bitter and twisted and gnarly can make such a happy one?

MM: Okay guys, I know you need to start getting yourselves ready to go on so I'd just like to thank you for taking the time out to speak to us.

Andy: Oh, you're very welcome.

MM: It says a lot about you as a band and as people that even though you could just do interviews with Metal Hammer and Kerrang you're still prepared to take the time out to talk to independent fanzines...

Andy: Well we're musicians and this is what it's all about.

Michael: It's not like we're trying to get our haircuts on the front of Vogue magazine or something; it's about going out there and communicating with people.

Originally published in Mass Movement #25, December 2009

THRASHVILLE HARDCORE

BY JETHRO D. WALL
© 2009

COME ON GUYS THAT WAS SO RAY OF TODAY!

END.

MIDGETT

My name is Blake Elmore, but the media calls me Lowdown. This is because my first few victims only had wounds on the bottom half of their bodies. When you're three foot four, you have to stab them where you can reach.

My life was one damn tragedy after another. I was ugly, unwanted and under-tall. That's a lot of u-words for a man like me to use, but there it is. Every time I stood up, life kicked me in the balls. After all the places I've been and all the people I've killed, I knew integration into normal society was going to be impossible. Yeah, you could say being a dwarf had its drawbacks.

I lived in a podunk town in Minnesota. I won't name it because you haven't heard of it. Think of any city in MN you do know and think of a place far, far away from it. That's my home. The people were nice (except to me), the homes were beautiful (except mine) and everybody knew everybody else. This was a bad thing. I was just beginning my career when the small-town blues struck. I left just in time to avoid the electric chair.

What good is an antisocial midget, you might ask. Well, I can't flip burgers because I can't see the top of the grill. I can't sell cars because I can't see the customers from the other side of the desk. Hell, I can't even join the circus because I can't juggle. It sure is tough being me.

Now I know you're tired of hearing me whine already but this is my story and I'm gonna tell it the way I want to. I'm the subject of this experiment and I get to choose which way I get through the maze. Cheese and w(h)ine go together after all.

So one day I was sweeping the parking lot at the Safeway when these kids start hassling me. I tried to ignore them, tried to pretend they weren't there when one of them said something about my momma. Now I've never met the dear old lady, but nobody but me gets to mention that. I freaked. I don't know how long the black-out lasted but when my head cleared again the boys were running away. They were crying and bleeding and it was hard to tell which one they were doing more. It felt really damn good.

After that experience I was more confident, even arrogant. I glared at passersby with evil intent and flashed invented curses at them with my tiny little hands. I loved to watch their eyes go wide as they hurried away from me. Being the town weirdo had its rewards.

I had never been an instigator; it didn't pay to start trouble when you live in a land filled with giants. You become so reticent that eventually the docs think you're dereistic and recommend pills and therapy to draw you back out. By the time you're as tall as the average third-grader, there's already enough hair on your scrotum to donate to 'Locks for Love'.

Imagine the teen-age years. Your hormones are raging and the prom is coming up. You want a date, somebody pretty who's willing to screw your brains out for a corsage and a mediocre dinner. Acne's not a problem, nobody's gonna look far enough down to see your face. The girls hear your voice and nearly trip over you while they try to figure out where that strange squeaking sound came from. It's like being a different species. I wasn't excessively hirsute. I didn't smell bad. My posture was good and I could maintain a quality conversation for hours. It's just that no teen queen wants to be seen with a circus freak. Stuck up bitches.

It's a terrible existence for anybody. It's so embarrassing even Oprah won't do a special on it. Don't get me wrong, I'm no timid virgin. But it would be nice to have sex without paying for it or having to dispose of a body afterwards. It's a damn nuisance and the clap is no fun at all.

After high school my voice was still an octave higher than any of my male peers. This fact created many fun hours for the jocks when they would come to the drive-thru where I worked part time. They would pretend they thought I was a girl until they pulled up to the window. When they got there, they feigned surprise and called each other 'fag' until they drove off. It made me bitter; determined to prove to them just what I was capable of. Flipping fries and making change was no way for an enterprising young man to spend his time, even if he was a pygmy.

I spent hours pondering. It was time for some serious contexture in my life. I needed to pull the pieces of my dawdling existence together. I needed a point, a purpose to drive me into the future. All I could think about was kicking the snot out of those boys in the parking lot. My blood ran hot and a red sheen covered my vision. I retreated into my own private nebula where stars and planets whirled around me in a froth. I became aware of my impending obsolescence and my ego puffed up like a blowfish. I was better than the average man, albeit of smaller stature. I was determined, no destined, for great things. I was as unique as the fabled dugong and at least twice as smart. I had a little money squirreled away under my mattress so I got it out and spread it out on the bed. There was almost enough there to buy an iced mocha from the Quik-E-Serv. My personal economy needed immediate defibrillation before it suffered permanent damage.

I formulated a plan. I had a knife and I was angry. I could have stolen a pair of panty hose from the convenience store but I figured that would be a waste of time since my diminutiveness would be a dead give-away. It was time to rob somebody.

Since the world seemed to consider me some sort of study on pathology, I intended to show them just how bad the disease was. I wouldn't be a cold sore. I was going to be cancer. I was skipping the small tumor and heading straight to the end-stage. This particular growth intended to be lethal.

I know you don't feel threatened. Nobody was scared of Kid Rock's midget before he died. He was just too cute to be frightening. Instead of worrying about this annoying factoid, I decided to turn it to my advantage. I knew I would be able to catch people off-guard.

My plan sounded great. Hide behind a bush, jump out when someone passes by and wave the knife at them. Simple right? The first time I tried this reasonably easy stunt, my pants got caught on the stupid hedge. I ended up standing on the sidewalk in my underwear and feeling low. The young couple laughed raucously at me and continued on their way. I had dropped my Bowie in the grass as I leapt so they didn't realize what the point of the whole situation was.

The second time I hid beside the bush. This worked much better. At the proper moment I stepped out of my concealment and brandished my pig-sticker at the old coot who was passing by. He muttered something about it being early for Halloween and kept walking. You'd think I would get indignant and sputter like Yosemite Sam, but it didn't work that way. Instead I grew calm. My thoughts were as clear and pristine as a wild mountain lake. I raised my knife as high as I could and slashed at his departing form. My blade bit deep into his derriere.

Old Man Farkus yelped and crashed to the ground in Mrs. Simlee's rose garden, thereby squishing her prized bushes. I could see the blood on my blade and was lost in the beauty of the streetlamp's refraction on its shiny surface. I demanded he give me his wallet. He called me a few names as he lay there with thorns in his hands and face. I'd been called most of them before and right now they meant less than nothing to me. He did hand over his money, though he had a clip, not a bill-fold.

Twelve lousy dollars. I had committed a felony for a dozen G.W.'s. I was pissed. Once again I blacked out.I heard sirens in the distance. I snapped out of my trance and looked down to see what angular thing I was sitting on. It was Old Man Farkus. What was left of him. It appeared that his intestinal tract would be fertilizer for the roses. I didn't know what else to do, so I ran.

As I lay face down in my own backyard, I reenacted the night's events. The smell of the dog shit from next door was a bit distracting but I managed. I felt shaky. I felt good. I felt powerful. I was a god. I was also a murderer. That could prove inconvenient. I did the only thing I could do. I left town.

The days were hot and without a breeze. Still I walked away. I walked until I couldn't stay awake. Sometimes I hitched a ride but I inevitably killed the kind-hearted strangers who were fooled into believing I was some runaway kid on his way to Grandma's house. This time the wolf was dressed as Little Red Riding Hood.

I experimented. I stabbed some of them once, aiming for vital organs. I stabbed some of them until they quit moving. One of them I carved up until she looked like red oatmeal. That one was messy. It took hours to get all the chunks of her spleen out of my hair.

I strangled some; I dropped heavy objects on their heads. I ran over one with his own car as he was changing a flat tire. I even managed to kill one bastinado, though that one took some time I assure you. Beating someone to death is challenging when you only hit their feet. It is, however, possible. I'll show you the pics if you want.

It became a game. I killed my subjects (never victims, too impersonal) in every way imaginable. I read books on serial killers and did some copycat stuff. It was fun trying to imitate another's style. It was like playing dress-up. Wearing Daddy's shoes or Mommy's dress. Using the Boston Strangler's choke hold or Gein's slicing technique. It didn't matter how they died. I loved the looks on their faces when they realized they were being killed by a citizen of Munchkinland. I certainly do not represent the Lollipop Guild and the coroner hasn't seen this many bodies in years. I was having the time of my life.

One day I was sitting on a park bench somewhere in Illinois trying to determine what had been the fulcrum, the point at which my rage had become deadly. I had only meant to mug Old Man Farkus...hadn't I?

Hey, who cares? I had a purpose. I had a dream. I had a career that excited me. The pay was usually okay but there was no insurance or retirement plan. I figured I'd be executed long before I was 60 anyway. Only Mudgett got away with more than a few dozen murders before he was taken down and I didn't consider myself on his level.

A couple years went by. I was still free. The cops were baffled. They were perplexed. They were looking for the wrong guy. The description they had was thus: 6'2", blond hair and blue eyes. Did I mention he was black? They had even considered the possibility I was a gang of homicidal Canadians or some other such nonsense. Life was dandy.

I was having so much fun that I decided to take a risk so monumental that not even the president would attempt something on such a scale. I bulldogged my way into a press conference in Seattle the mayor was holding in reference to my killing spree. She coughed and sputtered for a few minutes, the microphones like angry phalluses in her face. She hacked so badly that I wondered if she had taken a money-shot straight down her windpipe. She seemed to recover and left the podium. Apparently that was her speech.

The police chief was next and he opened up the floor for questions. One reporter asked him if he knew who the killer or killers were and what cult they belonged to. One claimed to have been attacked herself, which was patently false since I never left survivors. I even stepped up to the front of the crowd and pointed out that this could be the work of an angry drunken dwarf who was fed up with society's mishandling of his people. I was adamantly told that the ACLU could hold its damn own press conference if we wanted and not to interrupt with such nonsense again.

I walked away chuckling and shaking my head. I was the most successful maniac this country had ever seen and nobody knew it. Perfect.

I was galvanized and I knew it was time to take this to the next level. I needed to make this bigger, better and more efficient. It was time to be the Bill Gates of serial killers. It was time to make a Mt. Everest out of a mole hill. After years of practice, it was time to take the next big step, and I was ready. One thought stood out in my mind; repeated itself over and over in my sleep. I would need some collaboration if I was going to go global.

Jim Dodge Jnr.

Originally published in Mass Movement #25, December 2009

THRASHVILLE HARDCORE

©2009 Jethro D. Wall

LEE DORIAN
(CATHEDRAL / NAPALM DEATH)

That's right kids, Cathedral are back with brand new album, *The Guessing Game* and are raring to go, spreading their groove oriented metal vibe all around this, and any other, Cosmos the grand metal transmitters can reach. Lee Dorian shared the secrets of Cathedral, *The Guessing Game,* the intervening years and more with yours truly as Cathedral started to gear up for the album release and impending tours....

Interview by Tim Mass Movement

MM: Do you want to bring us up to speed with you guys in between *The Garden of Earthly Delights* and now?

Lee: We spent a couple of years doing pretty much nothing. It's our 20th year this year, so I guess that if you've been around that long you either stop doing what you're doing, carry on, or start questioning what you're doing. We fell into the latter as we always do; whenever we've done an album we've always had to stop and think about where we are personally and how we want to present ourselves musically and weigh up everything around us. So we spent a couple of years literally just wondering what our next move was going to be, or whether we were going to do it at all.

MM: It was that serious? You considered not going back to it?

Lee: It's not that we wanted to quit, it's just that we had to reassess why we wanted to continue. It wasn't until me and Gary got together again and started writing songs that we realised we wanted to get back together again. We did quite a bit of touring on *The Garden of Earthly Delights* but then we went about a year and a half without doing a show. The first gig we did in nearly two years was when we played Damnation festival about a year and a half ago, end of 2008. *Garden of Earthly Delights* came out in 2005 and we spent a year and a half ago touring that, going to Japan and everything, then there was a couple of years of silence.

MM: There's a new record in the offing now, I've heard some song titles bandied about like *Open Mind Surgery* and *Death of an Anarchist*. Does the new stuff differ lyrically from your previous output?

Lee: I think some of the lyrics are a lot more straight forward actually, but other people who read them might not think so. Open Mind Surgery didn't actually make it to the record... Musically it's got a sort of Amebix or Discharge feel....

MM: So it's kind of harking back to the old UK Hardcore scene...

Lee: Yeah, but it's still metal, but not pure Cathedral. *Death of an Anarchist* does have a punk message, well I don't know if you'd call it punk now, but when I was young I really believed, and I still do in the whole anarchy thing. The whole point of that song is just being trapped inside society itself, when you know that the things that go on around you, you can't really influence at all. Anarchy is a philosophy and it's just about coming to terms with that, without really thinking that you can actually change things. It's a song about frustration really, wanting to change the world around you but not being able to, and being so frustrated that you turn to drink or drugs to try to escape the environment you're in. When you wake up from being wasted you're still back to square one and there is nothing that you can do.

MM: You mentioned the two decades of Cathedral... How do you think that the band has changed over that time and how have you changed and are they interlinked?

Lee: That's a tough question to answer because with Cathedral we've always just followed our instincts, so there was never a plan as such. So if we've changed it's just a function of natural evolution for us as people. Obviously, musically we still have exactly the same influences we had when we started out, it's just that we've expanded on them I suppose. I mean there have been times when we've strayed too far from where we started... But you make mistakes, that's life. At least we're brave enough to do that and to own up to it. We make these – I don't want to call them errors – but we do these things and we learn from them and if we didn't we probably wouldn't be here today; we'd still be thinking about doing things that go against the grain for us, but you have to get these things out of your system.

MM: You mentioned straying away from your original influences, but how does it feel now that you are regarded by others in the same way that you once looked at your influences, that Cathedral are looked at in the same way that you looked up to your influences?

Lee: I don't know about that. Apart from the comment you just made, the only evidence we can see of that is that we're not extremely slow any more. That's certainly one element of being metal to me, playing really slowly. It's kind of hard to say. As far as Cathedral goes, we don't think of ourselves in that way. When we got started we didn't think Cathedral would be a long lasting band in terms of success or staying together. We had no grand ambitions for the band, even in terms of what we have managed to do. We've never sat down and developed some kind of master plan. We've just gone with the flow of our feelings and that. Ultimately, is what has brought us to here...

MM: You've been stuck with the Doom, Stoner labels - Do you think that does you a disservice?

Lee: I think it does, yes. It sounds a bit stupid but I don't think people are going to get us for quite some time, what we're really about. It's very easy just to say they're a stoner rock band, they're a metal band, a Sabbath rip off but there's more to Cathedral, but people don't see it. They just see what they want to see, not how vast our influences actually are. There aren't really any other bands that sound like us out there. Hopefully people dig what we're about now as much as they have over the years, but maybe we're one of those bands who in time people will sit back and reflect on and then understand a bit more. It's hard to say. We just do what we do and people think what they think.

MM: Do people still ask you about Napalm Death and how does it make you feel?

Lee: That's cool, but it's the last thing I want to talk about really as it left a bit of a sour taste in my mouth if I'm honest. That wasn't much to do with the music or the band, it was to do with all the stuff that went with it. I'm not ashamed or embarrassed about those days at all, in fact I'm very proud of them. I was involved in something that changed a lot of peoples' perceptions about music and about how people sing live as well. At the time I was in the band though I think people just saw it as some crazy novelty, the majority of people did. There were a lot of people though who did see the significance of what the band was doing lyrically and where we were coming from. It's a great thing that the band is still playing as the whole ideology and concept of Napalm Death is the most important thing and it's not really important who is in the band, it's the ideology and concept. If people ask me about it I'm happy to talk about it as long as it's not the same old questions...Which it usually is.

MM: It's amazing because you went on to Cathedral and Bill went on to Carcass and then Firebird... The legacy and impact of Napalm is incredible...

Lee: From the outside it probably feels really weird that the people involved in that band have gone on to do something so very different in some respects, but it's still very original and unique I would say. Like Justin, he was a real innovator in many respects and he's gone on to be in a rhythm and blues band which is very different in many respects and Mick went on and did a lot of electronic stuff and Shane's in a world of his own. I think the kind of people that were in that band were around at a time when things were still new, waiting to be discovered. We got into underground extreme music from around the globe because we had a curious nature. That curiosity was key I think because every time I heard a cool record I had to pick it up. So I think collectively the people in that band were just big fans of music, we were totally obsessed. When you have that curious mind set you explore more and more and expand it all the time. We were lucky as well because Napalm was a great launching pad for us to go on to other bands, it definitely made it easier for us.

MM: What do you think being a part of the Hardcore scene at that time taught you about music and the way the music world operates...

Lee: To be honest with you, you probably remember the good points of it, when it all started I thought it was the best thing in the world, I never wanted it to end, but that was when everyone was still friends. People were being good with each other, the music was getting better, everything was DIY, felt like you really belonged to something, you didn't know where it was going to go but you felt like it was going somewhere. I think there was a genuine belief, to a point at least, in the political ideas that went before. I think when metal became a major part of it and things did really start crossing over then those ideals really started to get dropped. Punks wanted to be more like guitar hero's than protestors. Then the age old thing of envy started creeping in, and really by about 1989 the scene had imploded on itself, but I think that there were a good four years that was a really killer time. What the scene is now, it's hard for me to tell, I don't know what it's like. ..

MM: With Rise Above, have you ever been tempted to release Cathedral yourself or do you prefer to keep the label and the band separate?

Lee: Well initially that was the idea. But to be honest with you, running a label is one thing, but I end up doing most of the stuff for the band anyway, so if I had to release the records as well it would just be too much, I'd lose any enthusiasm for actually being in the band. I enjoy the creative side of the band, and I also enjoy the creative side of running a label as well, but to bring the two together is not really my idea of fun, unless we were a bigger label and there were more people around to help.

MM: Do you have any regrets as far as Cathedral are concerned?

Lee: No. There were certain things we did, were if we had played the game a bit more when we signed to Columbia in America – it fell through in the end, but we were saying that the record label was shit and stuff in interviews, with this really expensive press tour and all we were doing was moaning. So I don't know what would have happened if we had played the game a bit more, and to be honest, don't care. We'd probably have broken up a lot sooner. We probably wouldn't be around now. The fact that it all fell through and half the band split off from each other just made us more determined to keep going and make something of the band. So regrets, no. Occasionally we have done things, musically, that occasionally, as an afterthought we shouldn't have done, but not many things. But I don't regret that because that's where we were when we did it.

MM: Given the power of the internet, what are the strangest rumours you have heard about yourself and Cathedral?

Lee: Rumours? Well I've heard that I'm a heroin addict and that I've died of an overdose and all sorts. The strangest things about ourselves... People have some kind of idea that we are aloof people, but people always want to write shit about you, it's just envy...

MM: Tell me about the new record? Tell me how you think it fits in with previous Cathedral records?

Lee: It's just a continuation really. When we did start writing, a lot of the songs were a lot slower and a lot more extreme in an early Cathedral way and we had literally a whole album's worth of stuff in that vein. The original idea was to do an album like that but then we thought why just do that when we can do things a bit more creatively and produce something that we have never really done before on record, at least never done it properly. For instance we've used a lot of melotron on this and we've actually found someone who can play it this time. I think musically it's a lot more interesting and a lot more diverse than last time. I don't know if you know this, but it's actually going to come out on an old fashioned double album with two discs. I hate it when bands do an album and fill up exactly 79 minutes because that's what they have to do. We have over 100 minutes' worth of stuff so I said to the record company that we either lose half the tracks and make it a 55-60 minute album or we release it as a double album and present it as a double album. Not additional songs up to 79 minutes and then a bonus disc, it's a proper double album, and the record company has agreed to that now, so we're pretty excited about that. We haven't released anything for pretty much 5 years, so to be away for that long and then to release something like this should keep people happy for a few years till the next one.

MM: So what's next for Cathedral?

Lee: Touring I guess. We don't have anything booked yet. Our agent's booking a few dates in the UK and I guess the release dates will be sometime in April. I'll be looking forward to it.

Originally published in Mass Movement #25, December 2009

BANG, BANG - YOU'RE DEAD
MESSING WITH AL CAPONE

With the passage of the Volstead Act in 1919, which prohibited the manufacture, sale and or distribution of alcoholic beverages in the United States, came a new breed of criminal. Prohibition, as it was called, paved the way for organized crime. Those enterprising but unscrupulous individuals who took up bootlegging the illegal libations profited greatly from their efforts. And no one profited more from Prohibition than Al Capone.

With half of the Chicago police force and city government in his hip pocket, Capone ruled his criminal empire with an iron fist. From his rise to power in 1925, to his eventual fall in 1931, Capone was the undisputed "King of Gangland."

During Capone's reign, only one other gangster served as competition – George "Bugs" Moran. Based out of Chicago's North Side, Moran repeatedly interrupted Capone's operations by hijacking his liquor shipments and by promoting "turf wars." Moran even tried to have Capone eliminated, but the assassination attempt failed.

Then on February 14th, 1929 – Capone had his revenge, as he orchestrated the famous St. Valentine's Day Massacre. Disguised as police officers, several of Capone's "hit men" raided a warehouse at 2122 North Clark Street, which was believed to be Moran's hideout. . The make believe officers, as well as two plainclothes assassins, lined Moran's men up against a brick wall and proceeded to slaughter them – seven in all – with machine gun fire.

Although Moran was not present at the massacre, the message was loud and clear. As a result, he faded into gangster obscurity and was sent to prison in 1946 for robbing a bank messenger of $10,000.00. He died of cancer in 1957 at Leavenworth Federal Prison.

As for Alphonse Capone, he died in 1947 of syphilis after having served eleven years in Alcatraz for income tax evasion.

The Aftermath and "Machine Gun" Jack

There was an immediate public outcry over the frightful events of the St. Valentine's Day Massacre, which resulted in an all-out investigation of the Chicago Police Department's possible involvement in the butchery. It seems that 235 department suspects were interrogated; yet no convictions were ever rendered.

In the passing years, there has been much speculation as to the identities of the mysterious gunmen involved in the famous slaughter. Some sources suggest that "Machinegun" Jack McGurn was among those trigger-happy participants. Certainly, he had sufficient enough reason for wanting Moran dead. Just a few years earlier, McGurn himself was the target of a Moran assassination attempt that left three other men dead. McGurn, whose original moniker was Vincenzo Gibaldi, was known for his lightning fast reflexes and violent temper, something that would serve him well as a member of the Capone gang. McGurn also had a proclivity for impersonating police officers, which might help to explain his involvement in the massacre.

Aside from his nefarious activities, "Machinegun" Jack McGurn was an avid golfer, and he had hoped to become a professional. On August 25, 1933, while participating in a golf tournament at Olympia Fields Country Club near Chicago, Jack was accosted by several police officers and served with a warrant for his arrest under the so-called "criminal reputation law."

Although Jack was charged with the St. Valentine's Day atrocities, he was never convicted, and, subsequently, he was released to resume his life in crime. Unfortunately, he had a very "loose" tongue when it came to matters of a guarded nature. On the night of February 15th, 1936, McGurn was gunned down in a bowling alley on the Chicago's North Side — a victim of the very mob to whom he swore his allegiance.

At the time of McGurn's assassination, Al Capone was safely tucked inside the secure confines of Alcatraz prison, and his right-hand man, Frank Nitti, was in charge of Chicago's crime syndicate. On a personal level, Nitti would not have had any compunction about doing away with "Machinegun" Jack; for fear that McGurn's free speech would incriminate the entire mob underworld. Although Nitti was never officially charged with McGurn's death, he still remains as the number one suspect.

Brotherly Connection

Al's oldest brother, James Vincenzo Capone, was an expert marksman, and he became, of all things, a Prohibition enforcement officer in Nebraska. Because of his younger brother's notorious reputation, James thought it would be a wise decision to change his name to Richard Hart. In doing so, he was able to enjoy a long and rewarding career as an agent of the federal government, without anyone knowing about his infamous sibling.

Al had five other brothers and one sister, but only James would end up on the "right-side" of the law.

The Famous Wall

So what ever happened to the bullet-riddled bricks of the famous wall on Clark Street? After the actual building of the massacre was torn down in 1967, Canadian businessman, George Patey, purchased the bricks for an undisclosed amount, and he used them to decorate the men's restroom at the Banjo Palace nightclub in Vancouver, British Columbia. Patey had placed a Plexiglas mural, which displayed a target-style motif, in front of the reassembled brick wall. Patrons, who visited the famous nightclub, could actually aim a stream of their own urine in hopes of scoring a bull's eye. If they were lucky enough to score a direct hit, the urinals would flush away the pee. According to Patey, this unusual gimmick was so popular that many famous celebrities tried their "hand" at hitting the mark. Just imagine how much fun it would have been to scrub Jimmie Stewart's piss off of a Plexiglas wall — something to tell the grandkids.

Doug Crill

Originally published in Mass Movement #26, March 2010

GOING TO THE GARDEN

Some years back, while writing for *New York Press,* I was asked by D*Generation, a local New York punk band that went on to be an international act, to do a story about them playing Madison Square Garden. They wanted a true story of what happened so they could show their grandkid's kids and stuff.

What follows is that story. Of course, *New York Press* couldn't handle it the way it was written and knocked it down to one page - which made it something it was never meant to be.

Anyway, read on, and know I love these guys, and getting to do this story for them was one of the biggest honors of my life!

Oy vey, such nice boys!

Punk Rock!

"I got you into the show tomorrow night", explains Uncle Garvey, DGeneration's publicist guy, to my answering machine.

I immediately pick up the phone. "The show?" I ask him.

"Oh, you're there," Uncle Garvey says to me, "why didn't you just answer the phone?"

I tell him because I hate the telephone, and am avoiding people like him.

"Oh," says Uncle Garvey. There is silence for a few seconds, and then Garvey speaks again. "So, the thing is, well, you kind of have to go in as a guitar tech."

"Roadie?" I ask him. He tells me yes.

"Oh, okay", I say, acting all annoyed, just to piss him off. Uncle Garvey is fun to annoy. I met him a couple of years ago at CBGB, and I was convinced he was the guy who played the reporter in Clint Eastwood's *Unforgiven*. That actor, Saul Rubineck. He looks like that. Wire frame glasses, curly Jewish hair, and all that. My first conversation with him was about how many "units" of a band he thought he could move. He talked like the guy in that movie. And why he calls himself "Uncle" is beyond me. Probably 'cause he likes to molest all the little girls DGeneration attracts. Like "Uncle Ernie" or something. Which is not a bad thing.

"So, you'll go?" asks Uncle Garvey.

"To the Garden, to see DGeneration and Kiss?" I say "Naw, tomorrow is Thursday night, it is Must-See-TV night. See if you can have them play like the next night or something".

Uncle Garvey says nothing.

"I'm kidding, Garvey. Of course I'll go. I'd love to see Kiss at the Garden, and well, I guess DGen too."

"Good," says Uncle Garvey, "I'll call you tomorrow and we'll set up a place to meet."

Tomorrow Uncle Garvey doesn't call and I wind up calling him. I get his "assistant", Jonna, on the phone. Eventually, she puts him on.

"You didn't call me, Garvey," I say to him.

He tells me he is sorry, but that things are crazy. He goes on to explain that they are having real trouble with Kiss's management and stuff, and this whole thing is turning into a night-mare. I feel bad for the guy, but don't let on. It wouldn't be punk rock.

"I don't care, Garvey," I say to him, "you didn't call me, and I have important things to do".

And I did. I just purchased this new game for my Super Nintendo System. It's called *Maxi-mum Carnage*. In it, you get to be Spider-Man, and get to kick lots of ass. I had already reached the second level, the one where you climb the buildings, and if I was going to have to leave the house and go to the show, I wanted to know now, because in this game, there is no way to save it, so you have to start from the beginning all over again.

"Sorry, George," says Garvey. He then explains that we are to meet the band at some place called the Paramount Hotel, in midtown. In some bar in there. Then we'll all go over to the Garden together.

"Cool," I tell him. "Bring your assistant, Jonna" I then say. I like her. She sounds cute over the phone.

"I'll try," he says, in that sort of voice which says, "Yeah, right."

So I get to midtown, and start looking for the Paramount Hotel. I know it's on 46th Street, between Broadway and 8th Avenue, but I can't seem to find the place. I walk up and down the block; see all the signs for all the plays and shit, but no Paramount. I start getting really pissed, and figure maybe I'll go to a peep-show instead. Finally, I ask some guy sitting out-side the stage door of some play where the fuck the Paramount is. He points across the street to a white building with lots of windows, but no sign. I say, "That's the Paramount?" He just nods his head.

I walk up to the door of the hotel, and these guys who look like male models in black t-shirts, and baggy black pants, open the door for me. I am dressed in my leather vest, stretch jeans, and sneakers.

"Ha!" I think to myself, "they think I'm somebody." As I enter the hotel, I wonder why they have no sign. Maybe it is because the hotel is so cool they don't want to advertise it. The fucking place is probably half empty 'because no one can find the fucking place. I guess it is the appearance that counts. Or the lack of appearance. Whatever.

I wander the hotel lobby for a bit, checking the place out. There are lots more guys with black clothes on, and they all have their hair slicked back, and some of them have pony tails. Now, if there is one thing I hate, it's a guy with a pony tail. Pony tails are sure-fire signs of assholeness. That and cowboy boots. And when worn together, well, you know the person is a dick.

I finally find the bar, and walk in. The first thing I notice is the air conditioning is on full blast. The second is Jesse Malin's, the lead singer of DGeneration's, hair. You can't miss it. It looks as if someone took an old mop that wiped up the Continental bathroom one too many times, and stuck it on a guy's head. His hair is all brown and dreaded and nappy and yucky and stuff. And long. It almost goes down to his shoulders. And the third thing I noticed was a girl who I assumed worked for the hotel with a tight t-shirt and erect nipples. I like air conditioning.

"How are ya?" says Jesse, in his Queens/Ramones accent. I tell him fine as I also notice Danny Sage and Howie Pyro, the guitarist and bass player from the band, seated by the bar. I have known these guys for years. Years.

I think I first met Jesse at A-7. Or Max's Kansas City. I'm not sure which one. Max's Kansas City was like my all-time favorite place in the world until it closed in 1982 or so. And A-7 was a blast. A-7 was on the corner of Avenue A and 7th street. It is now like a yuppie bar, but in the late, late seventies, and early eighties, it was a punk rock haven. Lots of bands played there, in a room the size of my bathroom. Well, my living room. The place was tiny. I remember trying to stage dive there, and hitting my head on the back wall of the club.

Anyway, I think it was there I first saw Heart Attack, Jesse's hardcore punk band. At the time, Jesse was around twelve, and he had a shaved head. All the Heart Attack songs would last like half a minute, and the band was very powerful. I remember once talking to him after a show at A-7, in Tompkins Square Park. I think it was a night a bunch of Boston bands played as well, because as we were talking, this little eight year old bald headed kid in huge boots walked up to us, and on his head, written in magic marker, were the words, 'Boston Sucks'. Jesse introduced me to the kid. He explained that the kid was named Harley. Harley later went on to be in a band called The Stimulators, and then, the Cro-Mags.

Jesse and I talked about lots of things that night in Tompkins Square. We talked about the difference between punk rock in Florida, and in New York. We talked about the political climate in a Reagan era America, and we talked about girls. I was impressed that this kid knew so much, and was so, umm, what is the word, umm, articulate. I was also impressed with his sex drive. I don't even think I knew what girls were all about at that age. I don't think I know now.

"Ya ready for the big show?" asks Jesse, as he sips his beer, at the bar in the Paramount. I tell him that I look forward to seeing him play at the Garden, and congratulations. He tells me that everyone is congratulating him, and he doesn't understand why. He says that he's been playing gigs forever, has lots of records out, and now everyone is congratulating him. I tell him that he is playing Madison Square Garden, for Christ's sake. He nods his head, and takes another sip of his beer.

The second band I remember seeing Jesse in was called Hope. Well, actually, at first it was called Jesse Malin and Hope. I remember seeing them on Avenue B, and 10th Street. In a rehearsal space. The same rehearsal space that the False Prophets rehearsed in. A band I was in at the time. We used to share the room with Jesse and his band, and lots of times I would sit in on their rehearsals. And they were a good fucking band. Not really punk rock, as much as just straight ahead rock. I think they even had keyboards in the band. I remember once seeing them at some club on 9th street near Avenue C. Jesse was running around like a wild man, and all these young girls were like going crazy over him. I was jealous.

"You gonna mention Hope, and how you thought we sounded like Springsteen?" asks Jesse, and then asks if I want a drink from the bar. I tell him sure I'll mention Springsteen, and no to the drink. It is too early in the day. I figured I had plenty of time to get drunk. Besides, I really didn't want a head-ache by the time Kiss went on. I'd let them do that for me.

"You been to Lakeside Lounge?" asks Jesse. I ask him what that is. He explains it is a bar, on Avenue B and 10th Street. I tell him that is where we used to rehearse. He says it is the same place, and the bathroom is exactly the same. I begin to wonder if my issue of Playboy with Sheena Easton is still in there. I wonder if all the roaches, cigarette butts, cum stains, and crack vials are there as well. The place was disgusting. And I think it was because of my band, not Jesse's.

Eventually I get a Diet Coke, and then walk over to say hello to Danny, and his big blonde hair. He is happy to see me, and we hug one another. I really like the guy. I remember seeing him in Heart Attack, with Jesse, and in Hope as well. It kinda seems that Danny has been Jesse's side man for years. I remember seeing them play together many times, and I tell Danny this. He tells me that he and Jesse love to play and create together. In his voice I hear a sincereness that first attracted me to Danny years ago.

Danny has always been into rock and roll. Ever since he was little. He was very young when he was in Heart Attack, like Jesse, and was always on the scene. Every show I'd go to, I'd see him there. He knew all the bands, and all the kids who hung out. He always wore a smile, and always seemed happy to see all his friends. And he seems no different now.

"You happy to be playing the Garden?" I ask him. He explains to me that it doesn't matter where he is playing. He goes on to tell me that playing music has been a dream come true, and that he is just happy to have gigs. He says that things haven't changed at all. That he always plays one hundred percent, whether it is The Continental or The Garden. And he means it. His eyes say it. His smile says it.

After Danny and I talk a bit more, I wander over and say hello to Howie Pyro, the bass player. Howie is another guy I've known for quite a while. He was in an early punk band called The Blessed, and later on played with one of my all-time favorite New York bands, The Action Swingers. Howie has an amazing stage presence, and in my opinion, is the punkest member of DGeneration. He has got spiky black hair, crystal blue eyes, and an "I don't give a shit about anything" attitude. When he plays, he bops his head up and down, and wears a mean smile that'll scare Satan.

"You excited about tonight?" I ask him, as I have asked the other guys in the band. Howie just looks at me with that Stiv Bator's "Fuck you" look. Punk Rock.

Eventually everyone finishes their drinks and some guy with the beginning of a bald spot tells the band it is time to get to the Garden. I ask one of the band guys who that is, and he explains it is their road manager. It figures. The guy looks like a road manager. Like a younger version of Monty, the Ramones road manager. Like that road manager guy I saw for AC/DC. Or that guy I remember with Lords of the New Church. All those guys had bald spots too, and all liked pushing the bands around. I think maybe they are guys who couldn't "succeed" in their own bands, so they took up baby-sitting bands instead. They still got to be in the "business". But I think they also got to lose their hair from all the stress.

As I pile into a cab with the guys in DGen, I notice the drummer, Michael Wildwood, for the first time that day, getting in the cab with us. I'm not sure if he was in the bar before, but he was in the cab now. Michael is a very quiet sort of guy, and doesn't say much. He wears tight leather pants all the time, and has a Johnny Thunders hair-cut. He looks like a poster boy for the St. Marks/East Village revivalist punk rock scene. And he has a nice smile. Like his brother in the band, Danny.

As we make our way to the Garden, Jesse keeps telling the driver to keep up with the cab in front of us. The cab carrying their balding road manager. He tells the driver that if he does, there is a good tip in it for him. The driver tells Jesse he knows where Madison Square Garden is, and not to worry. Jesse tells the driver to just follow that cab.

We arrive at the Garden, and as I get out of the car, I hear Jesse ask the other guys in the cab if they got any money to pay for the ride over. They all start taking out one dollar bills, and change, and stuff, and I get out before I have to give them anything.

We walk past hundreds of cops and guards, and in through a side door of the Garden. I remark to the band that this place is bigger than A-7. Danny says, "a little."

We are stopped by some guard guys at a huge desk, and the balding road manager explains to them that these guys are DGeneration, Kiss's opening band. The guard looks over at us, kinda sneers, and then tells us to go inside. We follow the balding guy as he keeps yelling "this way", and finally end up in an elevator with an old dude who is wearing a white suit and a matching cowboy hat. He is smoking a cigar thicker than my dick, and says, "How you boys doing?" We just look at him. He gets off at a floor before us, and I remark to the band that he probably owns the place. Someone on the elevator says that he thinks he does.

As we step out of the elevator, I get a good look at who is the DGeneration entourage. It is me, the band, the balding road manager, Rizzo, the big bouncer guy from Coney Island High who doesn't like to let me in for free, and this little guy with cut-off shorts, a very loud green paisley shirt, sandals, and curly red hair. I ask him his name and he tells me it is Marco. I ask him if he is in the band, even though I knew he wasn't. I was kinda kidding around. He laughs, and tells me no, that he is just the hair dresser. It figures.

"This way, this way!" the balding guy keeps saying as we walk down concrete hall after concrete hall. It was kinda like that scene in Spinal Tap, where the band can't find the stage. We all start to say "Hello Cleveland!", but finally we make it to the dressing room. Well, what appears to be the dressing room. Outside the door of the room was a small white piece of paper that said "Support Act". Danny and Jesse start bitching that in every other town, they have their name on the door.

We walk into what appears to be an oversized broom closet with no air-conditioning. It is very hot. There is a single table, about three chairs, and a tub of ice. Immediately the band starts whining about having no food, and nothing to drink. They tell the road manager that this is unacceptable, and to take care of it. He tells the band that he is really sorry, and that he'll get on it right away. He also tells the band to make up a set list for tomorrow night's show at "Irvine". Jesse explains that it is "Irving." The balding guy nods his head.

The band makes itself as comfortable as it can, with no A/C, nothing to drink, and only blank walls to stare at. We start to talk about how the tour with Kiss has been going so far, when a guy walks in the door with girl in a green cut-off shirt, and green matching dress pants. I ask Danny who the guy is, and he says it is their manager, John. I ask who the girl is, and am told that it is John's wife, Penny. She looks very Long Island. And kinda sounds that way too.

"How is everything?" asks their manager, oblivious to the fact that the band is in an over-heated broom closet with nothing to drink. Then I get a good look at the guy. First I start with his face. Well, his hair. He is wearing a pony tail. Uh-oh. Then I see he is wearing a black jacket, white shirt, and jeans. That's okay. Then I see what he has on his feet. Cowboy boots. This guy is an asshole. I begin to think DGeneration are in real trouble. So what if they are on a major label, have a nice following, and are playing the Garden. They are man-aged by a guy with a pony-tail and who wears cowboy boots. Yikes. They could end up at a dive like A-7 pretty quick.

Jesse tells his manager that there is no food and drink, and that he and the band are hungry. The manager with the pony tail and cowboy boots tells them to go upstairs to the commis-sary, get lunch, and when they come back down, he'll have taken care of everything. As we are about to leave, Uncle Garvey and his black rubber pants come walking in. He asks Jesse where everyone is going, and Jesse says, "To eat". Garvey says "Good", and starts to make his way out the door. He is stopped by the manager with the pony tail and cowboy boots, who tells him, and the band, that only the band can eat, because they have laminated passes. He says that me and Garvey and Marco can't eat, because our passes are only "Sup-port Act" stickers. We go with the band anyway.

We wander the concrete halls once again, saying "Hello Cleveland". At some point we enter the main part of the Garden, and I get a good look at the place. It is fucking huge. The stage stretches from the middle of the floor all the way to the back of the floor. I mean huge. Be-hind the stage is large light set that spells out "Kiss". On stage are a bunch of guys with walkie-talkies vacuuming and shit. I then remember the last time when I was at the Garden. It was a Slayer show. That night, the audience ripped out all the seats, and threw M-80's at each other. I hoped this night would be more of the same, but at $85 dollars a ticket, my guess was that they would behave themselves, and act their age. Oh well.

We finally make it to a small room where a bunch of tables are set up. We walk in and are told by a woman with large breasts and nice nipples, that we are early and the food is not ready yet. I remark in private how nice her nipples are to Howie, who tells me that I must be a journalist to have noticed such a thing. I ask him if he noticed. He just gave me that Stiv Bators look. Punk Rock.

We exit the food room, and wander around a bit. Somehow we end up at a counter where they are selling Kiss merchandise for amounts of money I cannot believe are possible. $25 dollars for t-shirts, $150 for Kiss books, and $650 for leather jackets and platinum records. The employees ask us if we are the band, and Danny tells them we are DGeneration, the opening band. I look at myself in the mirror behind the counter. I am wearing my leather vest and black jeans, but my hair is short, and bleached blonde. I wonder how they could mistake me for a member of the band. Either band. I don't have the hair for it.

Finally it is time, and we get into the commissary. The band gets food and starts to eat. So does Garvey. I don't. I'm afraid that someone will yell at me. They've done it before. Once, when False Prophets opened for the Ramones, me and our then roadie, Anthony, ate some of the Ramone's green beans. One of the guys caught us, and yelled to Monty, their road manager with a bald spot, "Monty, Monty, those guys are eating our green beans." Monty yelled at me so bad that I felt like I wanted to go up to my room and hide under the covers.

So, I'm watching the band eat and getting really hungry. I'm also listening to John, the manager with the pony tail and cowboy boots, tell the band that they owe him lots of money for the tickets they purchased, and that he'd like the money. Now. It turns out that each guy in the band only got five people on the guest list, so all of them had to pay for their relatives and friends. At $85 a pop. Shit, I wouldn't pay three bucks at Continental for my family and friends.

Finally I break down and ask Garvey if I too can get some food. He tells me to go for it. I get some salad, but try not to let the manager with the pony tail and cowboy boots see me. I kinda face away from him, and try to eat real quick.

As I take my third bite, Jesse announces that it is time to go back to the dressing room. As he leaves, the manager with the pony tail and cowboy boots announces that the band is supposed to vacate the dressing room fifteen minutes after their set. Garvey asks him why, and he explains that Kiss wants the whole place to themselves. They don't want anyone else even nearby. Nice guys, I think.

I walk into the broom closet with Danny and Michael, and there we find Jesse, sitting in a chair, with Marco fussing over his hair. I wish I had a camera. Jesse keeps running into the bathroom to see what Marco has done to his hair, and when the balding road manager walks into the room, Jesse asks if he can please get a mirror.

Eventually the band and Garvey go for a walk, and tell me and Marco to wait in the dressing room. Marco does, and I go out into the hall to check out all the activity. I hear Kiss on stage, tuning up and playing *Strutter* and stuff. I see a bunch of guys walking around with cameras. Big ones. I walk up to one of the guys with a huge video camera and check it out. It has the CNN logo on it. The guy sees me looking at his camera, and asks what I am doing back here. I tell him I am here with DGeneration. He says, "Well, shouldn't you be with them, then?" I say, "Shouldn't you be covering plane wrecks or something?" He just sneers. Jerk.

I return to the dressing room, and it is way too fucking hot, so I go back out into the hall. I run into a guy that looks really familiar. And he is with a really pretty girl. I ask him where I know him from. Maybe he was a TV star or a movie star, and just I thought I knew him. I sometimes do that. He tells me from San Loco on Second Avenue. "Oh," I say, "Good tacos".

We get to talking, and they both tell me they are here because she is doing the make-up for Ron Delsner. "The promoter guy?" I ask her. She explains that she is doing his make up like a guy in Kiss. As she is telling me this, some old looking guy in a black suit comes walking by. He looks like someone outta *Goodfellas*. He says to her, "You ready?" She nods her head and follows him. I say to the San Loco guy, "Ron Delsner?" He nods his head.

I go back into the dressing room and hang out with Marco. We start to talk about hair and stuff, and he tells me I need to cut my eyebrows. I go into the bathroom and look, and he is right. They are getting too long. Starting to curl up. I exit the bathroom and am about to ask Marco to cut them for me, when Ron Delsner quickly comes walking in. He walks to the center of the room. Looks around, and sees me, Marco, three chairs, and a tub of ice.

"How's the ice?", he asks, with all seriousness. I look at Marco. Marco looks at me. "It's fine," we say in unison. Delsner nods his head, gives us the thumbs up sign, and says, "good!". And with that, he walks out the door. Me and Marco just shrug our shoulders.

Eventually the band comes back, and a couple of them keep saying "Bow wow wow, yippie yo yippie yay!" I ask them what they're singing, and Danny tells me it is some rap song. I tell them Ron Delsner just came in. Danny says, "Bow wow wow, yippie yo yippie yay!"

The manager with the pony tail and cowboy boots comes back, and the band asks where the food and beverages are, and how come their stuff isn't on stage yet. The band was due to go on in less than two hours, and were kind of getting nervous. The manager with the pony tail and cowboy boots says he'll take care of it. Someone tells him to get the A/C fixed while he's at it.

A few minutes later some big guy in a green work outfit, and this little old lady , come walking in. He stands on a chair, feels the air-conditioning vent, and announces it is working. Just not very well. The lady agrees. The manager with the pony tail and cowboy boots asks them for a fan, and they says they'll get one. Jesse reminds them about the mirror, too.

While we all sit around waiting for the fan, Michael hits his drum sticks against an empty snare stand, and listens to his tiny little ghetto blaster he purchased for six dollars before the show. Michael seems very happy and content. His smile and nice attitude show it. Drummers.

The manager with the pony tail and cowboy boots starts to get kind of nervous and begins to pace around the broom closet. He opens the door to the bathroom, looks in, and points out, "This is the bathroom." Everyone just looks at him. Finally the fan and mirror arrive, and a few minutes later, the food, and beverages do, too.

The food is a box of Frosted Flakes, and a package of chewy chocolate chip cookies. The beverages are some Diet Cokes, and Bud Lights. The band immediately starts to bitch that they don't like Bud Light, and I tell them I'm with them. The manager with the pony tail and cowboy boots calls someone in, and orders some "rock". Wow, slang for Rolling Rock. Bow wow wow, yippie yo yippie yay.

Time passes slowly as the band discusses the set for the night, and how they have to tip the monitor and sound guys from Kiss so they can sound good. They also keep asking their road manager with the bald spot when their stuff will be set up on stage. Finally it is, and some of the band leaves the room. This gives me a good chance to talk with Jesse again.

"People have been calling me like crazy," Jesse explains as he sips a Bud Light. "People I haven't heard from in like 15 years. They tell me congratulations, and then ask if I can get them in to see Kiss. People who used to be bullies when I was a kid are calling me. People I hate." I nod my head.

"They keep saying congratulations about playing the Garden. I've been around playing for a long time. I'm getting sick of everyone saying congratulations. And also saying we are lucky. We want to have t-shirts printed up that say 'Congratulations' on the back, just so we don't have to hear it."

I ask Jesse what is in-store for the band and he tells me they plan to do more recording, a video, and a lot more touring. He says that a lot of people think he is lucky because DGeneration is doing well. We both agree that Jesse got where he is through years of hard work and dedication. I ask him now that he is playing the Garden, was it all worth it. "Of course it was worth it," he answers, "What else am I gonna do, anyway? Drive a van like I used to? Drive bands to play the Garden?"

As we are talking, Rick Bacchus, the other guitarist in the band, finally arrives. I was wondering earlier, at the bar, where he was, but forgot all about him. Rick sees everyone and says hello. Jesse asks Rick how the "internet interview" went. It turns out Rick was in some other room somewhere doing a live, on-line interview. Rick says that everything went well, but I can sense some kind of tension between him and Jesse. Bands. What else is new.

I start to talk to Rick, and he tells me he too, is glad to be here. He is wearing a green button up shirt, not much unlike the one Marcos is wearing. I ask him if he is gonna wear it on stage and he says yes. That's punk rock. But I guess Rick always was.

I first met Rick almost ten years ago. He was playing in a band called Sprocket, which was later called Viva La Wattage. He had long brown hair, and I thought he was the best metal/punk guitarist alive. Actually, Marc Rentzer, my old guitarist from Letch Patrol, and I, thought that. We'd go see every show Rick would play, and worship him from the side of the stage. We also liked his singer, Bridgette, who is now in New York Loose, but that is another story. Marc and I would give Rick the Devil sign with our fingers and bop our heads up and down while he played. I think Beavis and Butthead stole that from us.

Anyway, it turns out that Rick is from England, and he has this cute little accent. And it's not just me who thinks so. All the girls in the East Village do as well. He also has this cute little dog that he walks around, and everyone always goes, "Awwww!". It is hard to tell who is cuter, Rick or his Dog.

As Rick and I talk, I see a tall black costumed figure walk by, outside in the hall. I run out, and see Gene Simmons. In full devil make-up. Wow. He's tall. But skinnier than I remember. I yell to the band to come out into the hall and look at Gene Simmons. They do. Then I see the girl who did Ron Delsner's make-up walking behind Gene Simmons. I yell to her "Hello", hoping she'll introduce me to one of my childhood idols.

"Hi," she says back, "like my make-up job?" I suddenly realize that it is not Gene Simmons I am looking at, it is Ron Delsner. Doh. Delsner struts up ahead, kind of swaggering his hips, towards Kiss's dressing room, which we are not even allowed near. I tell the girl she did a great job.

I walk back into the dressing room, and Marcos is at it again doing Jesse's hair. This time, in front of a mirror. Also, Rick's girlfriend has shown up, and she is doing his make-up. She does a great job, and he looks very good. And everyone is drinking Rolling Rock, which means the good beer has arrived.

I open a "rock", and then Danny offers me a shot of some expensive liquor. I take the bottle happily, and then chug some down. I feel the warm rush of whisky go down the back of my throat, and it feels good. I take another shot. Danny tells me to slow down, and save him some. Oops.

The road manager with the bald spot announces to the band that they go on in less than half an hour. DGeneration seems to get visibly nervous, and don't say much. They all seem to be in their own little worlds. Suddenly I see a tall black-clad figure out in the hall, and know it is a member of Kiss. I run out there and look. It is only Ron Delsner, with a bunch of CNN people. He poses for the camera, and they take pictures of him, and interview him. Then I see someone else in black clothes and make-up. It's one of the guys in Kiss. He walks up to Delsner and shakes his hand. I ask one of the camera men who wasn't mean to me which guy in Kiss that is. I mean, it didn't look like Ace Freely. It wasn't Paul Stanley, and I don't remember Peter Criss looking like that. He says that it is Slater, the other promoter, and not a member of Kiss. Oh.

Eventually it nears eight o'clock, time for DGeneration to play Madison Square Garden. I think I am as nervous as them. I mean, I have seen these guys grow up through the punk scene, and I really want them to succeed. I want them to play well, and blow Kiss the fuck off stage. The road manager with the bald spot comes walking up to me and explains nicely that I should go up to the stage now, if I want to watch from there. I tell him I will, and thanks. Somehow I had begun to like the guy. I don't know why. Maybe it was just because he wants DGeneration to do well, too.

I made my way past all these really tall security guards to the stage. I couldn't believe the fucking size of it. It was like the fucking size of the entire CBGB's. Next to the stage was the monitor guy, and next to him, a stair case leading up. I walked up the stairs, and stood on the side of the stage. I could hardly see all the way across. I looked out into the audience and saw lots of people in Kiss make-up. But no one dressed like DGeneration. Not even a wig. Oh well.

As I stood on the stage, some Kiss roadie guy comes walking by and says, "Who the hell are you?" I tell him I am here with DGeneration. He says, "So?" I say "So" back to him. He then informs me that I can't stand where I am, because I am in the way, and how the hell did I get back here anyway. I tell him the band got me back here, and that I am writing a story about it. "I don't give a fuck," he says, "Get the hell out of here". I nod my head, and walk away mad. What a jerk. Now where was I gonna stand. How was I gonna see the band. I walk down the stairs and see someone in make-up backstage. A member of Kiss. I'll go ask him, I figure. I make my way toward the tall guy in black clothes, and then realize, that once again, it's Ron Delsner.

I start to make my way toward the dressing room, and see an older woman in the audience wearing a DGeneration t-shirt. I figure it is someone's mom. I say hello to her, and tell her I am here with the band. She says that she is here with Jesse's dad, and drags him over to meet me. I ask Mr. Malin if he is happy to be here, and he says, "I told Jesse I wouldn't see him play unless it was at the Garden. I've seen him play before, so, I guess I reneged. But, what do you know, here he is!" I looked at his smile, and it said "proud dad" all over it.

I decided not to go to the dressing room, but back to the stage. Fuck the roadie guys. I'd ignore them. Besides, the band was due to go on in less than five minutes.

As I got backstage again, I looked at all the guitars lined up on a wardrobe/case thing. It was the right side of the stage, so I guess they were Ace Frehley's guitars. Underneath each guitar was a label. The labels said things like "Brown", "Mirror", "Rhine", and "V". I think there were six guitars, and they all looked the same. Except for the Flying V.

"Wow, Kiss's guitars," I thought to myself. Just then the same Kiss roadie guy comes walking by, and sees me admiring the guitars. "What the fuck are you doing back here? I thought I told you to get lost," he says to me. I tell him I'll stay out of the way. "You better," he says to me, and gives me this really nasty look. Then he makes some comment to one of the sound guys about how he hates opening bands. Dick.

So a few minutes pass, and I keep looking at Kiss's guitars. No one is looking, so I touch one of them. Wow. I touched Kiss's guitar. It felt all hard and stuff. But smooth. Then I decided I'd be brave, and touch the strings that Kiss played on. I did. They felt like strings. Wow. Just like I played on. Still no one saw me. I kept admiring the guitars, gloating to myself that I touched them. Suddenly I am bumped into real hard, from behind. I turn around and it is the Kiss roadie dick. I think he did it on purpose. "I told you to watch the fuck out," he says to me, "and don't get too close to those guitars, I'm in charge around here." I nod my head, and think to myself how I'd like to take one of those guitars and shove it so far up his ass, that the tuning keys come out of his mouth.

The roadie guys leaves, and the lights start to dim. DGeneration is due to go on in about a minute, and no one is looking. So, to myself, I say, "take that", and then I twist some of the tuning keys on each guitar. Fucker. That'll show him. They'll yell at him like Johnny Ramone used to yell at me when I sent him on stage with an out of tune guitar.

Suddenly I hear the audience applauding, and the members of DGeneration rush past me, and up on stage. I follow them up the stairs, and watch them grab their guitars and stuff and start making noise.

"What's happening New York?" Jesse asks, and the crowd applauds wildly. DGeneration kick into their first song, *Scorch*, and they kick total ass. The band then continues the set, and everything goes very smoothly. The guys in the band jump around a lot, and Jesse sings his heart out. I am on Danny's side of the stage, so I see him run around all over, and go nuts. I can see on the other side of what seems like the ocean, Rick and Howie doing the same thing. Well, Rick, anyway. Howie just kinda stands there nodding his head up and down, being the punk rock God that he is.

The set finishes with *Degenerated*, and during that song, Jesse runs around and puts on a show that would have made Stiv Bators, or Darby Crash, proud. The guy can really perform, and I think he was born to play rock and roll. Either that, or be a life-support system for hair.

After the set, I follow the band back to the dressing room. As we make our way down the concrete halls, hearing the crowd cheering from the set they have just seen, we start with the "Hello Cleveland" bit again. As we get near the dressing room, I finally see Gene Simmons standing near the Kiss dressing room. I guess he was getting ready to go on. I say hello to him, and then realize, that once again, it is only Ron Delsner. Delsner says hello back to me, and then sticks out his tongue like Gene Simmons. Whatever.

We return to the broom closet, where the band falls back into chairs and catches their breath. Me and Marco and Rizzo tell them how good they were, and they just kind of wave us off, really overheated. The manager with the pony tail and cowboy boots walks in, and tells the guys he thought they were great. He then says that some woman from some label wants to come in and say hello. Jesse tells the manager with the pony tail and cowboy boots that he needs a few minutes to cool down and catch his breath. The manager with the pony tail and cowboy boots tries to talk Jesse into just letting her in for a few moments, and finally Jesse agrees. As soon as the door opens, the flood of people begins.

I start to feel uncomfortable around the band, and feel like I should give them some time alone, so I leave the room, and walk out into the circus, which used to be a hallway. There are tons of people out there, and they are all waiting to say "Hi" to the band. I see lots of familiar faces, and someone introduces me to Rick's sister, who flew in from England for the show. I ask her if she has seen Rick play before, and she says that this was the first time. Wow.

I see a commotion at the end of the hall, and walk toward it. As I do so, I am kinda not looking where I am going, and bump into the chest of a guy with nice shoes. I look up, and see Donald Trump. "Oops," I say, wondering if he remembers me from the time I did the same thing to him at the Bowery Bar. He just smiled at me, and kept walking. Again, his body guards gave me a nasty look.

I got to the end of the hall and saw Ron Delsner. Still dressed like Gene Simmons. He had his arms around like five girls, and everyone was taking pictures. I swear I saw him touch a couple of the girl's asses as he stuck out his tongue and did his Gene Simmons impression. After he got tired of posing, he signed autographs, and then he let all the girls kiss him, then walked away, toward me. I said "hello" to him again, since we were becoming such good friends. "I love show business," he said back, and then ran past me to some blonde girl who had a tattoo of each member of Kiss on her breast, which she wore out, proudly.

I made my way toward the DGeneration closet again, and ran into Howie, who introduced me to his parents. They looked like a couple of nice old Jews from Florida or something. Howie told them I was doing a story about them and Howie's father told me that this whole thing was "dreamsville".

"We're proud of our son," Howie's dad said. "Before this show, and after. It doesn't matter that he is playing Madison Square Garden. He could be playing anywhere and we'd be proud. We love our son". And I could see it on both their faces as we were interrupted by a zillion photographers who all wanted pictures of Howie with his parents.

I went back into the closet, which by now, was as much of a circus as the hall. I was introduced to Danny and Michael's mom, who told me, "I never thought I'd live to see the day my boys play Madison Square Garden. I cried almost the whole set.". Parents. Sheesh.

I took a beer, did a shot of the expensive whisky, and went back into the hall where I saw Ron Delsner with his arm around even more women, still sticking out his tongue, and copping feels left and right. I was jealous. I figured I should go look for that girl who did his face, and maybe she'll do mine. But I couldn't find her.

Suddenly I heard a voice from the stage say, "You wanted the best and you got it, the hottest band in the land, Kiss!", just like on the Kiss alive album. Then I heard a sour guitar note, and smiled to myself. Kiss kicked into their first song, Deuce, and I made my way out onto the floor to get a good look at them.

I was kinda shocked when I saw them. They all looked, well, old. Even with all that make up on. Gene Simmons looked like he had five chins, especially when they shot him on the big screen with a low angle. Hell, Ron Delsner looked better than him. And the rest of the guys? Well Paul Stanley looked as if he had been putting monoxidil on his chest to grow hair, Peter Criss played the drums about as hard as a flaccid penis, and Ace Freely took baby steps as he strutted across the stage. I bet they weren't letting us near Kiss's dressing room 'cause they didn't want us to see all the walkers and wheelchairs.

As I watch my childhood heroes play, I realized something. They were the Power Rangers of my time. The uniforms, the cheesy actions, and even the songs. What's the difference between the lyrics "I wanna rock and roll all night" and "Go, go Power Rangers!" Maybe I was just getting old. But then I realized it wasn't me. It was them. It's time for the Rock and Roll Nursing Home, if ya ask me.

I walked back to the DGeneration room to have one last beer, and then take off. As I did so, I thought about how good DGen was that night, and how Kiss sounded like a bad cover band of themselves. I ran into Danny and Michael's mom once more, who told me that she preferred the music of Frank Sinatra, Cab Calloway, or Vic Damone, to this Kiss nonsense. She said that with those guys, you could really sing along. But this, this was noise.

I also ran into Scot Ian, from Anthrax, and Sebastian Bach, from Skid Row. They were both making the scene, and scamming on Kiss's groupies. Like Ron Delsner. Only they weren't wearing any make-up, so they weren't getting half the action old Ron was.

I said good-bye and thanked the band, as well as the balding road manager, and even the manager with the pony tail and cowboy boots. They could have been bigger dicks, but weren't. Hey, they let me drink as much as I wanted.

I also said good-bye to Garvey and his rubber pants, and to Jonna, Garvey's assistant with the pink hair, who finally did get in to see the show, after all. I said good bye to Jesse's parents, Howie's parents, Rick's sister and girlfriend, and to my pal, Marcos the hair guy. He reminded me to trim my eyebrows. I said good-bye to everyone. I had had a good time.

As I made my way out to the street, some girl saw my "Support Act" patch. The non-laminated thing that really said, "no food for you." She asked me if I was with Kiss, and then said she really liked them. I looked at her, and in her eyes, I could see that she really did. Poor thing. I took off the patch, and stuck it on her chest. I explained to her it was a backstage pass. She screamed, just about fainted, then kissed me on the cheek and made her way backstage. If she was lucky, maybe she'd get felt up by Ron Delsner, and maybe even get his autograph.

I love show business. Bow wow wow, yippie yo yippie yay.

Jesse Malin is now doing his solo act thing and is amazing! Howie does *Intoxica Radio* on the net, and it's the best pod cast there ever was, will and shall be forever! And the rest of "the kids" are doing great!

George Tabb

Originally published in Mass Movement #28, March 2010

JFA

Just like Punk Rock itself, the original Skate Punk band, Arizona's JFA, has never gone away. The band has just released its first new album in ten years - the live *To All Our Friends* on DC-Jam Records - and is currently in the throes of recording a brand new studio album. I hooked up with vocalist Brian Brannon and guitarist Don Redondo to discuss the band, Punk Rock and, of course, skating.

Interview by Steve Scanner.

MM: JFA has just released the live *To All Our Friends* album – tell us a bit about that. I believe I'm correct in saying this is the band's first full-length release since 1999's *Only Live Once* album – why choose now to release it?

Brian: We've always been a live band and to really capture the essence of a live JFA show is pretty hard. When we heard these recordings we were stoked and wanted to get them out. As you mentioned, it's been about 10 years since our last release and most of our stuff is out of print so we figured this was a good way to get our music out to our old fans and also hopefully get some of the younger kids stoked on us as well.

MM: The album has been released on DC-Jam Records – how did you get involved with the label? Did you have any other labels interested, or consider releasing it with any other labels?

Brian: Darron from DC-Jam got in touch with me a while back and it just clicked from there. He's a totally cool guy and stands 100% behind his bands. Since we're really only interested in skating and playing music, we kind of need someone else to deal with the rest of it so it's been working out really well.

MM: Between the release of *Only Live Once* and *To All Our Friends*, there was the Alternative Tentacles compilation, *We Know You Suck*. Did AT approach you guys in releasing that? I do recall talk of a second volume – that likely to happen?

Brian: We've known Jello forever and at the time he was one of the few people we trusted to put out our old records and do a good job and treat us fairly. I'd say it worked out pretty well and we were stoked to have something out on AT, as they've had so many great releases over the years. As for the second volume, we're still talking about it but don't have anything in concrete just yet.

MM: What has the band done in the interim – have you continued to play during that time as JFA or in any other side project?

Brian: We're always playing. Mostly local shows because we all have families and jobs, but we do get around every now and then. Every once in a while someone calls us up to play a party at an empty pool, or jam at a skatepark, or do some totally killer old school punk gig with bitchin' bands out in the middle of nowhere and there's really no way we can say no.

So although we haven't toured in a long while, we've been playing continuously at select dive bars, sleazy holes-in-the-wall and skate bashes just like we've always done since 1981. But if you weren't there, you probably didn't know we did it.

MM: Going right back, you became the final piece of the JFA puzzle at the age of just 14. How did you get involved with the other three band members? Given the original premise of JFA was to be a band of full-on skaters, was it skating or Punk Rock that drew you all together?

Brian: It was both. At that point in time, being a punk was one strike against you and being a skater was another three or four. Being a skate punk basically meant you were due to get your head kicked in every day at school. So when you saw another skater or a punker on the street, you definitely felt a kinship. I met Michael Cornelius at a ramp in Scottsdale, and Don and Bam both skated High Roller, which was the big park in Phoenix. They had the idea to put together a band that played music that skaters would listen to and I couldn't have agreed more. It's been a wild ride ever since.

MM: How aware were you of the Punk and burgeoning US Hardcore scene at the time? I've read of a band you were 'in' called The Deceased. Did that band actually exist, or was it a mythical 'dream band'?

Brian: Nah, we never existed outside of our minds. I don't even know what I was supposed to play. Or if I was the singer. We didn't have instruments. All I had was one T-shirt. I wrote The Deceased on the front and spray-painted JOCKS SUCK on the back in big dripping black letters. The one time I wore it to school, the football team ripped it off my back. That was pretty much the end of the band.

MM: Tell us a bit about Phoenix, Arizona at that time. It's easy to forget in today's sanitized Punk Rock world that back in '81 you could get a serious kicking for being a Punk – but from what I have read, you actually went out to provoke such reactions from jocks etc yeah? I've also heard about a Phoenix Punk hangout called The Hate House – tell us a bit about that.

Brian: It's funny. Back then everybody hated punks: jocks, preppies, teachers, hippies, heavy metallers, moms, dads, little old ladies, cops, dentists, used car salesmen... They were all out to get you. All you had to do was have messed-up hair or some crazy shirt and they'd yell, "Hey DEVO!" because that's what they thought was punk rock at the time. A flock of hippies would be driving in a Camaro and throw beer bottles at your head for walking down the street. Jocks would mob your ass. If you ran across a cop somewhere, forget about it... Funny thing is that now all of those people are into punk. Or at least they think they are. Or at least they think what they're listening to is punk. Or even if they're listening to it, they don't necessarily understand it.

MM: I guess back then, the 'big' Phoenix bands would have been The Feederz and The Consumers (later 45 Grave). Did these bands prove to be an influence on the formative JFA? What about Meat Puppets – they would have been starting around the same time as JFA? You seemed to have strong connections with Huntington Beach band, The Crowd also – how did that come about?

Brian: We weren't influenced by The Feederz or The Consumers. They were the old guard. We were younger, played faster music and liked to slam and dive. The two didn't really go together. The Meat Puppets on the other hand, were and are simply amazing: super fast and intense musicianship from Mars with a great sense of humor. I will never get tired of seeing them live. Still one of the best bands ever. The thing I figured out recently is that to really appreciate them live, you've actually got to close your eyes so you're not distracted by everything that's going on around you and just focus in on the harmonic genius and complexity of their music. As for the Crowd, Don was originally from Huntington Beach and was a part of the early HB punk scene before moving out to Arizona to go to school. So he knew those guys really well. Nowadays, both he and I live in HB and we play with them from time to time. Our bass player, Corey, also plays bass with them.

MM: Your debut 7", the classic *Blatant Localism*, was released on local label Placebo something like a mere six months after the band formed! How did that deal come about? The band had a long relationship with the label – it must have been a good working relationship. Looking back at *Blatant Localism* now, what are your thoughts on the record?

Brian: Placebo was owned by Tony Victor and Greg "Mr. Wonderful" Hynes. They also put on shows in Phoenix. They liked our energy and our youthful spirit and backed us 100% until the label folded in about 1988. Without their support, it's doubtful we would have gone as far as we did. Tony was the brains and helped promote us and set up all our tours. He was really the mastermind and we owe a lot to him. Looking back on Blatant Localism, I think it captures where we were at the time, playing as fast as we possibly could and waving the skate punk flag high. It also shows what living in the baking Phoenix desert can do to you.

MM: The record featured *Beach Blanket Bong-Out* which suggested you drew a hypothetical line between the old Surf Punk ideal and the new Skate Punk idiom. Was there a great deal of rivalry between the two scenes at the time?

Don: Nah, the song was more of a Quadrophenia reference except instead of mods and rockers it was punks against (surf) hippies. That single surf punk line was more to distance ourselves from new wave. Everybody in AZ called you a surf punk if you weren't a Skynyrd hippie.

MM: While the debut album, *Valley Of The Yakes* continued the sound of the 7", 1984's *Untitled* album saw the band's sound developing with more instrumentals and the atmospheric *The Day Walt Disney Died*. Was this a conscious progression, or something that came naturally? Tell us the story behind the track, *ABA*, which has writing credits to both The Damned and Bowie.

Don: It was somewhat the luck of the draw, a lot of those songs were in our set when we recorded Yakes. ABA was in the first five songs we ever learned, it just did not get recorded until Untitled. ABA is a redone version of Andy Warhol by David Bowie; the intro is from the Damned (Teenage Dream). The title is a slap to Anita Bryant (Anita Bryant's Army) who was an early celebrity (sort of) anti-gay crusader.

MM: It was following this album that you wrote a letter to *Thrasher Magazine* requesting a Skate Rock Challenge to various USHC bands, who allegedly skated, to front up and take the JFA kids on. What was the outcome? Which bands took you on – and which ones failed dismally?

Brian: We never actually had a "skate off" with any other skate bands, much to my dismay. A few bands did take offense, but I won't mention any names. It would have actually been fun to have a skate band skate contest and maybe a gig afterwards, but alas, it wasn't in the cards.

MM: Original bassist Michael Cornelius left the band around this time – why did he leave? I recall it was because he kept some kinda secret about some skating pipes – that correct?? Was the bond of skating THAT strong to essentially cause a split in the ranks of JFA?

Don: He really did not want to tour in '84 (nine weeks on the road is a big commitment). The pipe thing also happened around then, but we found the pipes on our own anyway (hence the Untitled cover shot) so no hard feelings there.

MM: Your 1985 EP, *Mad Garden*, was named after a Phoenix venue that was an old wrestling hall yeah? What were shows there like – were there wrestling matches going on when bands played, or did the bands actually play in the wrestling ring?? Must have been a blast if Punks could slam off the ropes!!

Don: The wrestling was Friday night and the bands played on Saturday nights. One night, one wrestler threw the other one out of the ring and onto some old ladies in the crowd (on folding chairs). After that there was a floor to almost ceiling chain link fence all around the ring so you pretty much had to be in the ring to bounce off of the ropes. The ring had some bounce to it as well, so it was a fun "stage" to play on. Brian always got some good airs!

MM: I've heard rumours of an unreleased instrumental album also. Does this exist – will it ever see the light of day? Why did you never release it?

Don: That was between My Movie (with Alan Bishop on bass) and right around the time we got Mike back on bass so we shelved it to do Nowhere Blossoms thinking it would eventually get released, then Placebo folded. You can hear some of it on the Santa Cruz video Wheels of Fire.

MM: Obviously the split with Michael wasn't a major issue as he was back in the band for 1988's *Nowhere Blossoms* album. What brought him back to the band? And what brought about the album's ever-more keyboard-laced rock sound?

Don: With all of us working, we weren't into the 9-week tour thing anymore; plus Mike had some good songs so we just started working on those plus some new stuff Brian and I had. He only wanted back in if we were going to keep doing new stuff, which was good by me. More keyboards meant Brian was writing more.

MM: What happened to the band's morale after Placebo Records went bust? It must have had a double hit on JFA as Placebo's Tony Victor was also the band's manager. Did JFA ever consider splitting at this stage?

Don: Not really. After Nowhere Blossoms, Bam quit (again) because he was going to get signed with his other band (again). Then Bob (from ONS) had personal issues and then Mike quit, then Placebo folded and we just kept going. We were still having fun playing, we were still writing new stuff and still skating, so we found two new guys from other bands (bass/drums) and just kept going. If JFA was my whole life (to pay bills) I might have been more down, but it's hard to quit something you do as a hobby to have fun and have as an excuse to skate with your friends. Tony would still get us shows even after Placebo, but at that point we were not into long tours and then eventually Brian moved to California so the AZ shows were more rare.

MM: Brian, tell us how you got involved in not just writing for *Thrasher Magazine*, but becoming Music Editor and eventually Art Director. Did you not move to San Francisco to work there – how did you feel about leaving Phoenix at this stage? You still involved in writing for the magazine?

Brian: Don and I both freelanced for *Thrasher* for a long time off and on during the 80s, writing about the cement wonderland of pipes, pools and ditches in Arizona. Every time they sent me to write about a contest I'd get sidetracked and go skate a pool and end up writing about some killer pool session instead of the contest. Likewise, Don always had his own twisted way of looking at things that always caught people off guard, so they kept printing whatever we sent them. Then in August 1990, we were playing in Chino, California, and I got a call from Kevin Thatcher who was the editor of *Thrasher* at the time. He said Miles Orkin, the staff writer, was going back to school and did I want to come out to San Francisco and work full time at the magazine. Took me a little while to think about it because at the time, I had the AZ pool scene completely dialed with all my bros. We had our fingers on like 20 pools a week, but we'd only skate the top three or so because why mess around with quick transitions? That's when I decided that life's too short to skate crappy pools.

These days, whenever I go out to visit Salba he wants to take me to like 50 pools in a day and I'm all, "No bro, let's just go straight to the last one you were going to take me to because that's always the best and I don't need to crack my ankles trying to hit tile on anything cheap…" So anyway, I figured it was a once in a lifetime chance to work for Thrasher, so I moved out there and lived with KT for a while in the Hunter's Point 'hood. Learned to surf at Ocean Beach there, which is treacherous, cold, sharky, and gets huge and pummeling in the wintertime so that tends to keep the crowds down. They say if you can learn to surf there, you can surf anywhere.

Skatewise, I hung out with Noah Peacock and Coco Santiago and the rest of the boys and learned to skate downhill San Francisco style, throwing powerslides down the hill to control your speed. The early 90s were the dawn of street skating: tiny wheels, big pants and rap music, so I was the proverbial fish out of water as a punk rock pool skater, but you gotta do what you gotta do. So I learned to skate street a little, learned to ollie and noseslide. Skated the Safeway curb with Danny Sargeant, Stacey Gibo and Steve Rugey. Skated Bryce Kanights' Studio 43 vert ramp and Jake Phelps' and Max Schaaf's Oaktown vert ramp.

Mofo gave me the honor of taking over his Notes From the Underground column and I'd call up every band I could think of just to give them a couple sentences in the column to make it as bitchin' as it could be and after a while, Fausto and Ed Riggins offered me the title of Music Editor. So I said hell ya and kept on going, interviewing any band I wanted to, because when you called a record company and said you were from Thrasher, they were like, "Yeah, whatever you want to do."

Thrasher was also one of the first national magazines to use the Mac for production and I'd been working on old school photo typesetting machines so I picked up Quark, Illustrator and Photoshop pretty quickly. Next thing you know, they fired two art directors and I kind of fell into doing it, just because Fausto knew he could trust me not to ruin a good article and some killer skate shots by trying make an art project out of it. So I did that for a while. Got into making longboards out of used waterskis I'd pick up at garage sales for five bucks. Take the boots off them, turn them around so the nose is a perfect kicktail, put some soft wheels and real narrow Indy 88s on them. Then I'd make the trucks as loose as possible and go bomb hills in the Avenues, riding up driveways and popping off ledges at speed. The beautiful thing about the water skis was they had such a long wheelbase that even if you got speed wobbles the trucks were so separated that it was a real long swerve instead of a wobble, so you could keep the trucks super loose, which made the waterskis super maneuverable.

Well eventually, Jake Phelps and I had a falling out so I decided to move down to Huntington, to surf, skate and be by Don and the rest of the band, and I've been here ever since. Some call it Surf City and some call it the Asshole Capital of the World. Sometimes it's both, but I call it home...

MM: The band also released something on Nicky Garrett's (UK SUBS) New Red Archives label. How did that release come about? Could it not have been a long-term deal – especially considering JFA recorded the back-to-their-roots style *Only Live Once* album a few years later?

Brian: We were kind of going through (another) experimental period when we recorded with New Red Archives. We did a split single with Jack Killed Jill called "Secret Agent Man" and a song for a compilation called "Clown Party" with Jello Biafra singing backup. Neither was your traditional slam and dive punk rock, so it wasn't really what Nicky was looking for. Can't say as I blamed him as it was kind of different, but that's where we were out back then. If everyone else is doing punk rock, the punk thing to do is something different.. We were definitely showing our Damned influence (circa Strawberries album) round about then. We did "Only Live Once" with a buddy of ours from Chicago on Hurricane Records. You're right, it was kind of back to the roots. By then, we figured we could mess with people's heads more by playing straight ahead punk rock then by doing a bunch of weird stuff...

MM: Do you feel that, as JFA never officially split up as so many bands of the original USHC era did, the band never capitalized on its early influence? The line-up remained moderately stable (unlike, say, TSOL), the sound – while it progressed – never really mutated into something hideous (like, say, SSD), the band just never really went away in a blaze of 'Last Ever Tour' propaganda. Given the benefits of hindsight, do you think all of this possibly impeded the band's legacy?

Brian: I've heard that it's my singing that's impeded the band's legacy. That, and my keyboards. Oh well, I always give it all I have and if you don't like it, feel free to take a hike... Brent from Epitaph offered to sign us one time if we got rid of the keyboards and we were like, "Thanks but no thanks." It wasn't so much that we were married to the keyboards, it was just the thought of getting off on a bad foot by having someone tell us to change our sound before we even did anything with them.

MM: That brings us back to the live album – just tell us how you hooked up with current bassist, Corey Stretz and drummer Carter Blitch. Is Corey the same Corey who played with THE CROWD? You ever see original drummer Bam Bam or bassist Michael now?

Brian: Yeah, Corey's the same Corey from the Crowd. He was also in The Outsiders and China White and about a million other bands. He's been in so many bands that sometimes he has trouble remembering new songs because he's got so many stuck in his brain. But he's one helluva bass player and once he's got 'em memorized, he's got chops for days. Carter is the youngster in the band, but he's also the one hitting the most pools (I kinda stick to the ones I like). He's a super solid drummer and just wrote a couple killer songs for the new CD we'll be recording soon. Together, they're the perfect rhythm section for JFA. They've been playing with us for over seven years now and we're stoked to have them. As for Bam and Michael, we see them

about once a year when we go out to Arizona to play the Apache Skate Blast for our friend Doug Miles on the San Carlos Apache Indian Reservation. Doug is a great painter and runs Apache Skateboards. He's super good people and always takes care of us when we go out there. Looks like the next one is scheduled for the end of March, so it should be a good time.

MM: Looking at the flyers on the cover of the *We Know You Suck* comp, it appears you played with all the significant bands of the USHC era. For someone as young as you were then, that must have been quite an experience. Can you just tell us your thoughts on the following bands both as people and as a live band? Any stories about any of them you can tell also would be greatly appreciated!!

BLACK FLAG
Don: They were great until they got Henry. He just tries too hard and acts too heavy. The rest of the guys are just "back of the class screw ups" that had really loud amps. Really nice people... Really amazing shows!

DEAD KENNEDYS
Don: Just amazing. Jello is a one-of-a-kind front man and writes amazing songs. East Bay Ray is one of my favorite guitarists. All of those guys are really nice too (and really smart). Trouble is they are too smart; the folks they are burning don't ever get it (listen to Holiday in Cambodia sometime...its a slap against daddy's-money know-it-all college kids).

D.O.A.
Don: Their Hardcore 81 Tour was one of the reasons there is a JFA. I was bugging Mike for a long time to start a band... the night of that show he told me he was in.

AGNOSTIC FRONT
Don: Played with them at the L7 club in NY (really small, the size of a living room). Bam got really hammered and left some of his drum hardware. They grabbed it and made sure we got it all back the next day so we could make the next show.

BIG BOYS
Don: One of my favorite bands mostly because nobody sounds like them. Treated us like kings every time we went to Texas and good skaters too.

BEASTIE BOYS
Don: I think I missed them (or saw one song). Early punk band version opening for Reagan Youth (who were really good).

And lastly the UK's **DISCHARGE**
Don: I don't remember that one (must have been good?)

MM: Brian, your own skating has quite a reputation for being no-holds barred and you have associations with the likes of Tony Hawk and a long-standing relationship with Duane Peters. Have you ever seriously injured yourself by skating in such a full-on style?

Brian: I try not to dwell on the injuries but just avoid having them happen again. Broke my arm one time at Kelly Belmar's pool but don't remember the details too well on that. About the only serious injury I remember is dislocating my finger at Bryce Kanight's Studio 43 vert ramp. Every Friday night, he'd have a big session and this particular Friday night I had tickets to see the original Spinal Tap at the Waldorf and my favorite band at the time Swervedriver after that (note: don't confuse them with the idiot racist band that has a "k" in it). So I had my evening all planned out: a little skating at BK's, swing over to see Spinal Tap, and then finish off nicely with Swervedriver. Well, BK's ramp had a section that was about 40 feet long and 12 feet high with 20 feet of flat bottom. That connected to a section that was 16 feet long and 10 feed high with 16 feet of flat bottom. So I'd do this thing where I'd get hella speed on the long wide tall part backside and then do a front-side nose-grab on the lower part and just put the board up there at a full clip and see what happened: air-to-grind, tail-slide, lap-over, wheeler, whatever. This particular time I had so much speed that I missed the grind entirely and came down the wall still in the tail-slide/nose-grab position, with the tip of my tail sliding down the transition instead of my wheels rolling down it. Well, Bryce juiced every square inch he could out of that ware-house to make the ramp as big as possible so when I ran out of ramp there was nothing left but a solid wall coming at me. I flew right into it and put my left hand up to break my fall and my ring finger bent backwards and got dislocated. I was fine with it all dangling there until I thought, "Oh shit, I'll never play piano again..."

Then I went into shock and they took me to SF General. Being in SF General on a Friday night with a dislocated finger means you're not number one in the triage line. There were gunshot wounds, knife wounds, all kinds of stuff lined up before me. So I'm laying on the gurney, and this dude comes in with a hemorrhaging head wound, totally bleeding from the dome and they lay him down next to me. He gets into an argument with himself for a while and next thing you know, he's heading out the door. The attendants were less than on top of things and when they finally checked on us about ten minutes later, they said what happened to the other guy. I said, I don't know he just headed off into the night. Long story short, they finally pumped me up on lidocane, jammed my finger back the way it was supposed to go and sent me on my way. Well, I'd missed Spinal Tap by then but I didn't really care. So I had the taxi drop me off at my car at BK's and drove to see Swervedriver and they friggin' rocked. To this day, I still have a slight bump in the second knuckle on my ring finger, which my wife thinks is totally bitchin' be-cause it's almost impossible to get my wedding ring off. I have had to have it cut of two or three times since when I've hurt my arm and my hand started to swell up around it. That always makes her sad...

MM: In what ways do you think the relationship between skating and Punk Rock has changed today when compared with the early 80s?

Brian: In the most important ways, as far as stoking people out to get rad, I think it's stayed ex-actly the same. Sure you have a few more posers and the like running around because both punk and skating are more popular now than back then, but on the whole, when it really mat-ters, it's still there to provide fuel for the fire to get out there and rip it up.

MM: In 2001, you joined – I think – the US Marines (or was it the Navy?). Can you tell us a bit about that as an experience? You still involved? How did the anti-authoritarian, skateboard-ing Punk Rocker fit into such a strict regime as the armed forces?

Brian: I joined the Navy Reserve after 9/11 in 2001 because I wanted to do something more than drive around with a flag on my car. I'd always been interested in the Navy from way back to when I'd watch Victory at Sea on TV with my dad, so it was a natural choice. Since I've joined I've been all around the world, Nicaragua, Colombia, Panama, Hawaii, The Philippines, In-donesia, Malaysia, and Cuba, and I've never regretted it. Sometimes I bum out when it comes time to do the mile-and-a-half run because I've never been much of the jogging type. But that's kept me from getting fat in my old age so even that's good. One of the best things about the Armed Forces is that it's truly a meritocracy. You see people from all walks of life, and as long as they're good at what they do, they can go far.

MM: What are your thoughts on the situation in Iraq? Have you seen anything that has been so alarming that it has actually changed your perspective?

Brian: As for the places we're at right now, I can only say this. As a member of the Armed Forces I'm sworn to protect and defend the Constitution of the United States. And the Constitution is truly the document that makes us a great nation. The military chain of command goes up to the Commander in Chief, the President of the United States, and that's whoever our great democracy votes into office. I follow his orders through my chain of command because though I may or may not agree with him personally, I most assuredly believe in what this nation stands for and the right of the People to elect whoever they choose.

MM: How do you think that Obama has done during his first year as President of the States?

Brian: I think he came into a very challenging situation and he's done an admirable job so far.

MM: If you could change one thing about life in America, what would it be?

Brian: I'd like to see less poverty.

MM: A fun question – you and your skateboard could travel back to any time in history – when you would choose and why?

Brian: Honestly, I'm happy anytime I'm on my board. I've had some great adventures to be sure, but I'm still having great sessions all the time. Just the other day we have a session at Joker's Pool with Duane Peters, Dave Hackett, Jeff Grosso, Dave Reul, Jake Reuter, Arab and Nathan Groff and it was just as rad as any session I've seen in a long time. I'm still learning new tricks and still having a blast and skating with my friends. I wouldn't change a thing.

MM: So, what's in store for JFA now? In the wake of the live album, can we expect any new studio recordings also? Any tours lined up?

Brian: We're working on a studio album right now. Hopefully we're going to record in February or March. No tours planned as of yet, but if anywhere there's a punk rock dive bar or an empty pool session, we'll be glad to show up and play.

MM: Anything you want to add?

Brian: Thanks for the in depth interview. Tell all our brothers and sisters out in New Zealand and in the UK thanks for the support and ride on!

Originally published in Mass Movement #26, March 2010

R'LYEH ORCHID

March 15, 2003, The Journal of Alexander Berkeley, Ph.D.

On the island of R'lyeh, beneath which lies sleeping Cthulhu, grows a flower. Nowhere else on Earth does this noxious blossom grow. I came across this rancid bloom in my youth and I still remember it vividly, now on my dying day.

The year was 1963. Back then, when I was newly graduated from Miskatonic University, I was Professor Berkeley. I had earned my Ph.D. in botany and I was ready to make my way in the world. I knew the name, origin and catalogue number of every plant known to man. I would like to stress one point clearly. The phrase 'known to man' leaves room for a great many unknowns. I would like to stress another point clearly, too. Some things are better left unknown.

A dozen times I've put down my pen, determined not to write this horrific account. A dozen times I've picked it back up, certain the world deserves a warning. The thought that has caused me to waver so badly is this; will a warning make any difference?

June Marsh, one of my brightest students, approached me after class one day. She had been researching rare blooms in the university's library. While poring through the not-quite forbidden text of the Necronomicon she came across a hastily scrawled note in the margin. It said only:

R'lyeh Orchid? Only where Cth. holds sway

This cryptic remark had piqued her curiosity. The question mark indicated that the person who wrote the note wasn't certain if the bloom really existed. The second line seemed to show that they also didn't know what conditions it could be found in if it did exist. Cth. had no meaning to either of us so we assumed it was archaic shorthand for a weather anomaly or soil type. She dug further into the dread tome and found a map that showed the way to an island called R'lyeh. Knowing my intense desire to discover an unknown botanical specimen, she came to share her findings with me.

We immediately began to make travel plans for what would surely be an expedition of great discovery. The thrill of finding an unknown species of plant life was ecstatic and overwhelming. If we had been birds, we would surely have flown there on the spot. As it was, we created an itinerary for what became an increasingly complicated trip.

Our first order of business was to arrange for travel from Rhode Island to South America. The most direct across the Pacific Ocean to the fabled island of R'lyeh was to leave from the coast of Chile and to head nearly due west to latitude S 47°9 minutes, longitude W 123°43 minutes where the map showed the island to be. Getting to the South American coast proved to be the easiest part and the least filled with horror.

We flew out of T. F. Green Airport in Providence on a chartered jet paid for by the alumni of Miskatonic University. They had donated generously to our trip in the hopes that our discovery would bring prestige to their alma mater.

After a brief layover in Atlanta, we boarded a 747 headed to Mexico City. From there we took a bouncy ride in a miniscule propeller-driven plane to San Antonio, Chile. We felt that this thriving port town was the most likely place to obtain transport across the ocean to our destination.

When we reached San Antonio we were distressed to discover that this usually thriving port was mired by a workers' strike. Every captain, mate, dock hand, cook and porter had manufactured a picket sign and had refused to work until their outrageous conditions were met. June and I soon ran out of Spanish and patience. No boats were leaving to go anywhere from here in the foreseeable future. One worker, who spoke more English than we did Spanish, was able to give us the name and directions to a small coastal town where we should be able to arrange for transportation.

The lovely Miss Marsh purchased tickets for us on a rickety bus to the town of Talcahuano, a number of miles south of our current location. The ride was hot and uncomfortable. I tried not to complain too much due to the fact that my companion seemed to be enjoying herself. I swatted flies and tried to smile.

When we arrived in Talcahuano it was nearing dark so we decided to use a portion of our ample funds to find hotel accommodations for the night. All things being the same, we picked an establishment that had a decently wrought sign bearing an emblem of a creature half-man/half-fish. It seemed to bode well for our journey due to its aquatic nature.

We walked through the sagging doorway and went to the front desk. The clerk (who bore an alarming resemblance to the emblem on the sign outside) eyed us suspiciously and asked us, in Spanish, what we needed. When we asked for two rooms, he smiled obscenely and told us he only had one available. It was late and we were too tired to argue so we paid him. I took the key he handed us.

On the way upstairs I offered to sleep on the floor and to allow June to have the bed, though my feelings were becoming most inappropriate to a student/professor relationship.

She politely accepted my offer and I spent the night on a pallet, enveloped by nightmares of fish/men who wanted me as their sacrifice for some unspeakable ritual. I woke up drenched in sweat, certain my screams must have woken half the town. June was still sleeping peacefully on the bed so I determined that no sounds had truly issued forth. I lay back down and tried to return to sleep but I was unsuccessful. I finally gave up and took a shower instead.

The warm water washed away the sweat but not the lingering feeling of dread caused by the dream. As I headed down for breakfast, I found myself hoping fish was not on the menu.

After I filled my stomach with eggs and something resembling a tortilla pancake, I climbed back upstairs to our hotel room. I felt better after the meal and I had a spring in my step. Some of this was due in part to the prospect of being in the presence of June again, no doubt.

I entered quietly so as not to disturb her if she still slumbered. Since the bed was empty and the shower was running, I deduced that she was already up. I quickly packed up my things in preparation of leaving. Soon, June emerged from the shower, pink and glistening. I forced myself to avert my eyes even though she was fully clothed. My spirits were high and my willpower was low. June packed her things with quiet efficiency and we went downstairs so that she could partake of breakfast.

From that point on, the day declined. Of the few Latino sailors who spoke any English (or understood our rough Spanish) none seemed to want anything to do with our plans. Many just looked scared and scurried away. It was well past lunchtime before we found a captain staunch enough to be willing to carry us across the sea to what the locals obviously believed to be a cursed island.

Captain Gonzales' ship was a leaky-looking, rusty excuse for an ocean-going vessel. I wasn't certain if it could even hold its own weight, much less a crew and passengers. He assured that the Angelita Verde was more than able to take us to our destination. I hid my disbelief the best I could and paid him the advance we had agreed upon.

Relieved that we had finally found our transportation to R'lyeh, we went to the market district to eat a late lunch and to kill time. Since we wouldn't be sailing until dark, this left us nearly four hours to fill.

As the sun began to set we found ourselves increasingly bored with the stalls full of cheap junk for the tourists to buy. When the sun finally began to set in the western sky, we headed back to the berth where Angelita Verde waited to take us to the dreaded isle of R'lyeh.

Captain Gonzales met us at the dockside end of the gangplank and escorted us aboard. In the gathering twilight, I observed something extremely unsettling. Captain Gonzales bore an uncanny resemblance to the desk clerk from our hotel.

Our voyage started without any fanfare. The decks began to vibrate as the engines idled up, the deck hands untied the last lines from the dock and we were moving out of the harbour. Only the change in the sound of the waves lapping against the boat's hull gave any outward sign that we were no longer attached to the long, wooden pier.

A couple of hours later I was vomiting over the stern. It turns out that I am susceptible to seasickness. June, as radiant as ever, stood beside me enjoying the cruise. Her family hailed from sailor stock and she apparently had their strong stomach. She tried to help me feel better by sharing tips and tricks she had learned from her father as to how cure my current affliction. Unfortunately, nothing seemed to help. I dreaded the dry heaves that I knew were coming.

Around midnight, my stomach settled a little so I climbed wearily down the flights of steps that led to my diminutive cabin below-decks. I arranged myself gingerly into my narrow bunk and tried to think calming thoughts. My guts were still churning some, but I felt like I could keep it under control if I tried. Eventually I slept.

My dream started out wonderfully. June and I were in a small seaside cabin with the doors and windows opened wide to allow the evening breeze to blow through. We held each other close. We kissed deeply and started to remove our clothing. Things progressed and soon we were making love passionately (not that there's any other way, I guess) between the silken sheets. Then something changed. The sound of hundreds of voices chanting floated through the open windows.

"I'a, I'a, Cthulhu fhtagn," they croaked over and over.

I had no idea what this might mean but I tried to ignore it. That's when I noticed that June had gone. I was still in passionate embrace with something, but it wasn't her. When I looked down I was horrified to discover a hideous fish creature spread beneath me. Its skin was scaly and covered with foul-smelling slime. It reeked of death and evil untold. I tried to disengage myself from this monstrosity but it held me firm and continued to rock against me in vile ecstasy. I screamed and flailed in a futile attempt to escape its repellent grasp. The worst part was that this thing from the deepest abyss of the darkest ocean was staring at me with June's azure eyes.

I fell out of my cramped bed as I woke up. I managed to bang my head on the wall and my shin on the bedrail as I fell. I was so agitated I barely noticed. I sat up against the wall and tried to tell myself it was just a dream and that it was over but I could still hear that unearthly chant coming through the window.

"I'a, I'a, Cthulhu fhtagn."

I realized that it must be the crew of the Angelita Verde observing some obscure religious ceremony. Somehow my subconscious had incorporated it into my nightmare. This was little consolation to my bruised and bedraggled mind. I knew I would sleep no more that night so I decided to begin composing the speech that I would give to the students, faculty and alumni of Miskatonic University when I returned triumphant with the R'lyeh Orchid in hand.

The next morning I asked Captain Gonzales about the previous night's singing. He explained that the crew, himself included, worshipped gods that predated Christianity that lurked on the threshold of our reality. That particular chant welcomed them into the world of man. I nodded wisely and tried to disguise the chill that ran down my spine. I resolved not to ask any more questions about their religious leanings if I could help it.

I found June in the mess hall and joined her for breakfast. I felt guilty that I had had a dream in which she had played such an erotic part in but I knew that mentioning it, even to apologize, would create awkwardness between us. I focused, instead on trying to get a few bites of...well, whatever the greasy food-like substance was, to stay all the way down in my stomach. It was a hard fight and after a few bites I declared a draw and switched to drinking water. Only a few acidic burps came back up so I assumed victory was mine, at least this time.

We chatted pleasantly and I followed her above-decks to take a stroll in the morning air. No land mass was visible in any direction. Here, the sea was king. I found myself wondering if man had any right to ply the wide open ocean in the manner that we were. Surely the fact that the sea claimed many lives each year was a sign of saying 'Stay on land, foolish mortals. You don't belong here!"

All musing stopped, however, when the storm hit. The sky clouded up so quickly, it was like watching time-lapse photography. Whitecaps began to pound the hull of our vessel mercilessly. Angelita Verde rocked and moaned, as if in a lover's embrace. I would have headed directly to my cabin if my stomach hadn't violently erupted at that moment. I staggered to a rail and grasped it tightly. I vomited repeatedly and tried not to fall overboard. Sailors ran by, yelling at each other in Spanish. One of them tied a rope around my waist and deftly lashed it to the railing I was holding on to. I thanked him mentally and continued heaving. I barely spared a thought for June, but since I didn't see her from my vantage point, I assume she had fled for safety.

For three days and nights, the dilapidated little boat pitched and bounced across the storm-ravaged water. Wind blew rain in sheets and lightning crackled, striking the ship several times. Luckily, no real damage was caused and nobody was injured by the blasts. On the fourth day, the clouds parted and the sun regained its dominance over the sky.

I had managed to ooze my way back to my cabin shortly after the storm started, and now the whole tiny room reeked of stale vomit and sweat. I could barely stand but I wanted to breathe fresh air before the odours of my illness forced me into having a relapse. I grimly climbed the flights of steps leading to the open air.

The first thing I saw was June. She was standing at the rail, letting the wind blow her long, brown hair behind her in a cascade of beauty. Her eyes were closed and she seemed to be savouring the moment to its fullest. I watched her for a several minutes before I approached her.

She smiled at me without opening her eyes and I couldn't help but smile back. Aphrodite couldn't have possibly been as beautiful as June Marsh. No mortal man would have been able to cast their eyes on her if she had been.

I could hear gulls crying overhead. It took a while for this fact to register. When I finally realized that the cries of these seagulls meant we were close to land, I nearly wept in relief. My stomach spasmed briefly, as if to remind me who was ultimately in control of my continued comfort.

I nearly danced to the bridge to ask Captain Gonzales how soon we would make landfall on whatever piece of solid ground we were in close proximity to. His response was to point out the window straight ahead of him without saying a word. My hope crashed to the ground in a fiery blaze. Ahead of us lay the most forbidding piece of undesirable real estate I had ever seen. We had reached R'lyeh.

The entire crew seemed jubilant. They laughed and clapped each other on the back so much I feared they might break each other's ribs if this behaviour continued. June appeared to pick up on their excitement and was brimming with enthusiasm. She was rechecking our equipment and supplies in preparation for disembarking. I only felt trepidation now that we had reached our goal. The ancient rocks that lay ahead radiated malice and contempt. I wanted to go home.

As we steamed closer, I got a glimpse of some cyclopean architecture situated in the centre of the island. The shapes I glimpsed were distorted, misshapen chunks so weathered that even the crevices had crevices. The stone itself had a strange greenish hue that I assumed was caused by algae growing on its surface. By all that's good, I wish that had been the case. The truth is much less palatable.

We loaded our necessities into one of the shore boats that were aboard the ship specifically for the purpose of getting people and cargo ashore when there was no safe harbour in which to tie up. They lowered us into the waves and cast us loose.

We all helped to row the boat to shore, gruelling work that was made much more difficult by my weakened state. I was exhausted by the time we reached the rocky beach.

June and I arranged our equipment on our persons and we hiked up the beach. A hundred small crabs scurried out of our way. I observed that their eyes appeared to rest on elongated stalks and their rear-most legs appeared to be extremely flexible, not unlike a tentacle. I noticed many pieces of debris that would have been consistent with shipwrecks and once, a bone that looked eerily like a human fibula. I managed to convince myself that the marks I spied on its surface were from the grinding of the waves, and not from some creature gnawing the flesh off of it, perhaps one of the crabs' larger cousins.

Worse things lay ahead.

The land rose and it became more difficult to traverse the terrain. The rocky shore had given way to rocky cliffs with only one obvious pass between them. Boulders and loose scree made even a slow walk perilous. We eventually had to work our way parallel to the beach for about a mile before we could find a less hazardous path to the interior of the island. R'lyeh was just as forbidding up close as it had been from a distance.

After another hour's hard travel, June cried out in surprise at something that had caught her attention at the base of a stone outcropping. It was a carving of ancient design and inhuman craftsmanship. It depicted a creature that looked like a deranged octopus with the wings of a dragon. It had animalistic arms and legs that sported wicked talons. Its malevolent gaze was certainly a warning to trespassers. We forced ourselves to ignore it and continued on.

One thing we noted was that this island was much bigger than we originally thought. We had been struggling for hours in the general direction of the ruins I had seen from the ship and we seemed to be no closer to them.

No birds sang overhead and no insects scuttled beneath our feet. The island was quiet except for the low moan the wind made as it blew across the cliff faces. It was the song of the damned.

Around noon, the trail through the cliffs came to an end. In its place was a set of steps carved out of the stone itself. With only a moment's hesitation we began the arduous ascent. I was beginning to wonder if the crew members that had accompanied us could be convinced to carry me the rest of the way when we reached the summit. I dropped my dragging ass right onto the unyielding ground with a groan. I rummaged around in my pockets until I found my lunch. The others followed suit. June sat near me, a fact which lifted my spirits considerably. We spoke very little between bites but I knew every word was a gift to be treasured. In the midst of unspeakable ugliness, her beauty shone like a thousand suns.

We rested for half an hour before resuming our trek. Since we had no idea where we might find the R'lyeh Orchid, I led our party to the derelict building that was suddenly before us. Its walls cast an eldritch glow across the uneven ground that surrounded it. I inspected its stonework closer and discovered that the glow came from the rock itself, not any algae that might have clung to it. It was surprisingly clean and free from any detritus that might have adhered to it. Though I was a botanist, I had studied some geology during my quest for my doctorate and I was completely unfamiliar with this particular variety of stone. The vast quantity of it that this single immense block was carved from spoke of a monumental effort to transport it here and to work it into a usable shape. Even with the strange geometry presented here, several million tons of it must have been used to build this architectural nightmare.

Not only was the stone unknown to me, but the shapes and angles of the walls and spires were alien as well. Nothing humanity had come across previously had been formed in such a way. Fathomless gulfs of black space yawned before us and it scared me shitless.

I turned around to address the rest of the party. The hardened sailors were all lying prostrate on the ground before the steps that led up to a shadowed alcove. They began to chant, just as they had aboard the ship.

"I'a, I'a, Cthulhu fhtagn."

June stood in their midst, staring at the building with glassy eyes. Her face was motionless. I tapped her on the shoulder and she came back to the present. I talked with her briefly and we decided to leave the men to their veneration of the alien structure and continue our search for the mysterious flower.

We began by looking for any signs of moisture that would support life of that kind nearby. For twenty minutes we walked in what we hypothesized was an easterly direction. I was looking to my right when June restrained me gently by putting her delicate arm against my chest. I looked at her and she pointed at something up ahead. It was a small, blue flower.

I whooped with joy. June grabbed me and kissed me passionately, causing me to forget everything awful that had happened in an instant. We had found the R'lyeh Orchid at last! I could hear the applause of my peers ringing in my head. Success was at hand.

I got down on my knees to look more closely at our discovery. The petals of this rumoured bloom were midnight blue, almost black and most closely resembled a tulip. They had fine black hairs covering their surface. A piss-yellow stamen protruded proudly from their centre. Atop it was a cluster of small sickly brown orbs, probably its seeds. Below this, waving in the breeze, were its leaves. They moved sinuously, like a snake in the thrall of a charmer.

"By the gods, does everything on this island have tentacles and eyestalks," I cried.

June and I both laughed, though I wasn't really joking.

As my initial excitement began to wear off, I detected the scent of decay in the air. It was coming from the flower. This wonder of nature smelled like nothing as much as a corpse left to rot in the sun. Backing slowly away from this amazing plant, I found my enthusiasm had dimmed. The damned thing was ugly and it stunk. I hoped I wouldn't get fired for bringing this thing back to Providence.

June had hunkered down beside me and was still examining our find. I stood up, brushed off my hands and headed farther down the path. I saw several more Orchids displaying their attributes to this desolate world. About twenty yards ahead, the path opened up into a great meadow. Not much soil covered the stony ground, but apparently it was enough. Before me, stretching to the horizon was a vast field of fetid vegetation. The R'lyeh Orchid was thriving.

We collected a couple of specimens in bags designed to help their roots retain moisture during the long journey home. We celebrated with some crackers and warm water from our canteens. It was a wholly unsatisfying meal to mark a wholly unsatisfying find. The day had been full of trials and disappointment. It went downhill from there.

As we were moving back up the path towards the monumental monstrosity of a building, I heard the chanting begin to grow louder. I also realized it was coming from behind me as well as from in front of me. I turned to see June had begun to mutter those god-awful syllables under her breath. She looked pale and unhealthy.

"I'a, I'a, Cthulhu fhtagn."

She kept walking so I figured it was just an effect of the extreme heat. Her earlier excitement appeared to have passed, but the memory of her kiss lingered. I knew I'd never forget this day.

The closer we got, the louder the chanting got. I was surprised the sailors hadn't gone hoarse by now. June was also chanting louder now and it began to worry me greatly. She still looked pale and her gaze had gone slack. She looked like a plague victim in the early stages. Her eyes were wide open and staring and her arms hung limply by her sides. I tried to ask her if she wanted to stop and rest, but she didn't respond. When I tried to guide her to a rock she could sit on, she struggled against me and kept walking. Something was wrong with this island and we had to get off of it before it was too late.

As we came around the corner, my curiosity grew strong again. I began to feel compelled to enter this building of greenish alien stone, to discover what mysteries lay hidden within. I pushed past the frenzied bodies of the sailors and made my way up the gigantic steps. Thirteen stairs led up to a shadowy alcove, each nearly three feet high. What type of being must have trod these steps before the coming of man, I couldn't divine. I shuddered to think of it.

"I'a, I'a, Cthulhu fhtagn."

The darkness began to grow absolute. Even though the sun was shining brightly only yards away, it didn't penetrate this far to scatter the gloom. I felt that with a sharp knife, I could have cut a piece of it away and brought it back with us to the university. Fear began to gnaw at my guts.

I got out my flashlight. I had reached the doors that led to the inner recesses (lairs) of this darkly enigmatic place. They were carved all over, adorned with monsters that no human could have possible imagined in even the worst delirium. They were nightmares depicted as coming from the remotest gulfs of the universe. Here and there human figures were shown. They appeared to be in agony. Every person was either running from some beast or being consumed by it. My terror grew stronger by the moment. This was the most abhorrent thing I had ever seen. No longer curious, I fled the darkness.

The sailors were chanting at the tops of their lungs. They were nearly spasmodic in their religious fervour. They were reaching a fever pitch and June had apparently been caught up in their orgiastic display. She swayed and screamed right along with them. Her eyes stared blankly at nothing and her skin had an unhealthy green tinge to it. Upon closer inspection, it was somewhat scaly and oozed a sticky fluid. Obviously something on the island was making her very sick, very quickly. I grabbed her by the hand to take her back to the Angelita Verde. She shook off my grip and, instead followed the sailors as they now made their way to the steps of this domicile of evil. I caught a look at her profile and noticed that she was beginning to resemble our good Captain Gonzales and the desk clerk from the hotel in Talcahuano. She was walking stooped over and her shoulders hung off her body as if they had gained too much weight for her to bear any longer. I tried again to lead her away but she flung me furiously away. The maleficent mob continued on their way to the doors of the ancient temple, as I now thought of it.

I followed them up; though this was something I had to fight myself to do. The carvings that adorned those massive doors were better left unseen. I wanted to save June, and nothing would prevent me from doing so.

June looked worse, the farther up she went. By the time the crowd had reached the doors, she looked like nothing as much as the fish/man that appeared on the hotel's sign and had played so large a role in my recent dreams. I began to hope I was hallucinating, though I was certain this wasn't the case. Madness would have been easier to bear.

The sailors and my student began to bang on the doors as if seeking to enter. This seemed like the worst idea ever developed by humankind since we crawled from the ocean. I panicked and ran back down the steps. This cowardly flight saved my life.

As I reached the last step, I heard a groan as if a thousand tons of rock was being dragged across another thousand tons of rock. I knew the door to that colossal temple was opening. I screamed, though the sound of that portal being opened was so loud that I couldn't hear myself. The sound stopped as abruptly as it had begun. Screams followed in its wake. Whatever was contained in that building was slaughtering the rabid worshippers. June was among their numbers, but I wasn't going back up those steps ever again. I've never regretted that decision.

I saw a tentacle lash out from the shadows. In its grasp were several of the crew members who had so recently been prostrate on the ground where I now stood. They no longer looked as if they wanted to see what dwelt within that stone edifice. They looked as if they had seen it and it was madness incarnate. Their hair had gone white and their screams were silent. Only shattered souls remained.

One of those Herculean tentacles reached out for me where I was transfixed. I was paralyzed with fear and couldn't have moved under any urging. I was doomed. I was saved by the sun. When its lovely golden rays had touched the ichorous skin of the brobdingian monster its skin began to smoke and blister. It quickly pulled its serpentine appendage back into the darkness. I moved.

I ran back to the ship as if the Abyss itself had opened up and spewed forth all its foulest denizens to consume me. For all I knew, it had. I reached the shore with no recollection of the intervening distance. I was beyond exhausted but I managed to row the boat to the ship alone. The captain ordered me hauled up and questioned me as to the whereabouts of his crew members and my colleague. He looked scared.

My babbled responses were apparently enough to convince him that we needed to get out of there as soon as possible. Besides, a storm was coming and clouds had already begun to form overhead. We both agreed that we had no desire to be anywhere near R'lyeh when darkness fell.

I learned from him later that the palpable fear I had felt on the island was felt by all the sailors on the ship as well. Only the captain's furious discipline had kept them from mutiny. They pulled in the anchors and we left immediately.

Nobody talked about what I had witnessed and described to them so completely. It was more than a human mind could bear to discuss openly. The return trip was short and un-eventful. The storm that had been developing over the island hadn't followed the Angelita Verde on her trip home.

When we docked in Talcahuano, I took my leave of Captain Gonzales and went to procure a bus ticket back to San Antonio. From there I began the series of plane flights that eventually led me home.
I had much time to go over our notes and my experiences on my way back to Providence. The scrawled notes from the Necronomicon haunted my thoughts.

R'lyeh Orchid? Only where Cth. holds sway

I finally realized what the second line meant, while waiting in the Atlanta airport for another layover to end. It meant that the R'lyeh Orchid only grows where dread Cthulhu holds sway, i.e. only where he was in complete control. I was glad that this funereal blossom had never been seen anywhere else on earth. I meant to keep it that way. My only real quandary was this; what would I tell everyone at Miskatonic University that wouldn't get me committed to an insane asylum?

Upon reaching my home town, I went home to my small apartment before I reported to the university. I searched my luggage and clothing three times before I was convinced that I had lost my samples of the R'lyeh Orchid at some point during my return. I had hopes that I had dropped them on the island itself while running for my life. Any other possibility was too hor-rifying to consider.

I showered, shaved and changed clothes. I felt less harassed by this time so I reported to the college dean's office for a full, edited report of my distressing travels. I told him of the entire trip to the island, leaving out the dreams and imaginings I had. I told him that we reached the island but found only barren, rocky wastes devoid of any life or scientific interest. I told him of the storm that formed over the island upon our leaving its shores but I made it sound as if this storm engulfed our little ship. In this (untrue) version of the tale, several sailors, and the lovely June Marsh, were swept overboard. We were unable to rescue them and had to leave them to the sea. My story was met with sadness and disappointment, but no curiosity as to what the island might have held. My deception was taken at face value and no inquiry was ever held. I finished my career as a botany professor with no outstanding merit and no en-thusiasm. I retired in 2001, shortly after the terrorist attacks on the World Trade Centre. I had seen enough terror in my life, and I needed some solitude.

I bought a little cabin in the hills of North Carolina where my only neighbours were trees and wild animals. I wandered my property when the weather was sunny and barred myself in-doors whenever clouds threatened. I was content.

Two years passed between then and now. Two years of the most blissful quietude. Only infrequent trips to town to purchase supplies broke my desired monotony. I was finally able to get past those unbelievable events of so long ago. Until today.

I've been sick for about 6 months. The doctors say the tumour is too close to my brain to operate. It hurts, but not too much. Mostly it just makes me tired. I have a wonderful bed so this is just fine with me. I placed my bed directly across from the window in this tiny room so I could stare out at the sky when I was too tired to sit but not enough to sleep. I had a pristine view of a small meadow with snow-capped mountains in the background. It was the loveliest view I had seen since the death of June Marsh.

Many flowers and plants grew in the meadow. Bees buzzed and butterflies flitted from blossom in the spring and summer. It was a botanist's dream come true. Nature's beauty displayed itself proudly on a daily basis. One day I noticed something odd. There was one flower that none of the insects seemed to go near. With some trepidation I went to investigate.

There, to my deepest horror was a familiar bloom. It reeked of death and madness.

The petals of this abhorrent bloom were midnight blue, almost black and most closely resembled a tulip. They had fine black hairs covering their surface. A piss-yellow stamen protruded proudly from their centre. Atop it was a cluster of small sickly brown orbs, probably its seeds. Below this, waving in the breeze, were its leaves. They moved sinuously, like a snake in the thrall of a charmer.

There was only one fathomable reason why the R'lyeh Orchid was blooming outside my window. Cthulhu was coming.

Unfortunately, this isn't the end of this missive. While I was in town shopping for groceries today, I caught part of a news report on the radio. A strange new flower had been discovered all across the world. Sixty-three countries had already reported its presence, from the desert wastes of the Middle East to the snowy steppes of Russia. No scientist had ever seen it's like before. The petals of this exotic bloom were midnight blue, almost black and most closely resembled a tulip. They had fine black hairs covering their surface. A piss-yellow stamen protruded proudly from their centre. Atop it was a cluster of small sickly brown orbs, probably its seeds. Below this, waving in the breeze, were its leaves. They moved sinuously, like a snake in the thrall of a charmer.

The R'lyeh Orchid was growing all over the world. And it was thriving

Originally published in Mass Movement #26, March 2010

JUGHEAD'S REVENGE

During the early to mid-nineties, there was a whole slew of incredible bands playing out and releasing records, and thanks to Flipside, I managed to pick up records by as many of them as I possibly could. Amongst this onslaught of incredible punk rock goodness, was a band called Jughead's Revenge, and man, I couldn't get enough of the band. Each and every record was a blinder, and just as MM finally reached a position where I could reach and get an interview with them…They called it a day. Now, nearly a decade later, they're back and thanks to Joe D., I finally managed to get that interview…

Interview by Tim Cundle

MM: Alright Joe, let's go back to beginning – how, when and why did Jughead's Revenge first get together? What do you remember most about the formative period of the band? And, I gotta know, after all these years, where did the name come from and did Jughead ever really get his revenge?

Joe D: Joey and I met when he was in 80's speed metal band, Cholos on Acid, and we started Jughead's as a side project along with C.O.A. members George Snow and Kevin Heller. We did our first show in 1990. Why? To be the first band in Los Angeles that didn't sound like Jane's Addiction or Red Hot Chili Peppers in years. We did our first U.S. Tour in 1990 with nine people in a small van; looking back I don't know what I was thinking, but surviving that showed us what being in a band was all about. The name was strictly a metaphor, but I'd say in the end he did get his revenge.

MM: You guys were, and are, a part of the LA scene, which is sort of famous for being one of the epicentres of punk rock, which made me wonder…How did the LA scene take to you guys? Were Jughead's an instant scene favourite, overnight local heroes or did it take a while for them to warm up to you guys? Do you think that there was such a thing as a typical 'LA Punk Band' and how near or wide of the mark were and are, in your opinion, Jughead's Revenge? Why?

Joe D: Growing up in that scene throughout the 1980s we were friends with everybody anyway, so that worked out. However, back then we had three major LA gangs at every show, which made for "interesting times." I don't think that there is an actual L.A. sound because bands like The Germs, X, Black Flag and Bad Religion sound so different from one another. We weren't imitating, but of course were influenced by those L.A. bands as well as others like Poison Idea from Portland and BL'AST! From Northern California.

MM: Sticking with LA for a minute, and drifting off topic at the same time – being an LA scene veteran of long and good standing Joe, how do you think the LA scene and the people and bands who comprise it have changed during the last decades, and again, in your opinion Joe, have those changes had a positive or negative impact on the LA scene?

Joe D: Now that people aren't making money anymore it's gotten a lot smaller, but more genuine.

MM: Okay, back to Jughead's Revenge – why did you guys originally split? Was it entirely due to the lawsuit or were there other mitigating factors? With hindsight, do you think the split was the right decision and was unavoidable, or do you wish that you'd tried to find a way around it?

Joe D: The lawsuit was actually a bi-line to why we stopped. We had toured for eleven years and wanted to take a break; the lawsuit was an inconvenience in the middle of making that decision. I think it was the right thing to do because around 2000-2001, a lot of bands started seeing dollar signs and the climate was that either you sold out and sold your songs to commercials or that you weren't going to last in that world, and we didn't want any part of that.

MM: What, if anything, if you could bend the laws of physics and alter the progression of time, would you go back and change about the band and why? What, if anything would you change about Jughead's Revenge, and why would you change it?

Joe D: I think that we stuck to the principles we started off with, despite the band sounding different in the end than it did in the beginning, our philosophy stayed intact. So, I wouldn't change a whole lot.

MM: Let's talk about the lawsuit – what happened? What was it about? I've heard all kinds of different rumours that it happened because of the label, that it was just one of those things, so do you want to pick the flesh from the bones of the rumour mill and tell us what really happened? How it resolved and what was the end result of the suit?

Joe D: In 1998, Nitro received a cease and desist letter from Archie Comics complaining about a T-Shirt that Nitro's mail order was selling that had the Jughead face on it. This was something we told Nitro not to do; they ignored the letter and we were later served with papers telling us to be in court. Keeping in mind, we didn't know anything about the initial letter in the first place; so it was all news to us. In the end, Nitro paid out about $80,000.00 and we lost the name. Nitro then, not being able to sell our CD's, threw the remainder of our records and CD's away. In the end, Nitro's lawyers and Archie's lawyers, called me to say that the band's name was now "Jugg's Revenge;" a name we've never truly accepted. Nitro reissued Image Is Everything, Just Joined and The Pearly Gates last year on ITunes under the new name.

MM: And now, you guys are back – so, what made you want to reform the band? Whose idea, and how difficult was it? How have the initial rehearsals been going, and how are you guys sounding? How does it feel to be playing as, and a part of, Jughead's Revenge again?

Joe D: I always knew that we would play together again; we just needed to go back to our own lives and wait for the popularity contest between bands in the late 90s to blow over. Now, we can do what was always fun for us on our terms, without record companies making it feel like a job. Joey and I have talked about it over the last year and wanted to do a handful of 20th anniversary shows while he had time off from his band Black Fag. The rehearsals have been going great; we're playing a lot of songs from the first three records that we haven't played since the mid-90s. How do I feel about the upcoming shows? As long as Andy can keep his clothes on, I'll be alright.

MM: I know that you're only talking about shows at the moment, but what are the chances of a new record, and maybe a tour or two that would include an overseas jaunt…?

Joe D: I won't say that a new record is out of the question, but hopefully we do plan to return to Europe and the UK by the end of the year.

MM: What, for you, was the best period of Jughead's Revenge, and why? Likewise, what, in your opinion, was the worst time to be in the band and why?

Joe D: Playing with just about every band I grew up listening to was far more than I ever expected. At the same time, the disappointment of record companies was more than I ever expected.

MM: Which Jughead's Revenge album do you think is most indicative of what the band were and are, all about, and what makes it the definitive Jughead's Revenge album? Which of the bands records is your least favourite and why does it occupy that particular position?

Joe D: I'd say it's a tie between *It's Lonely At The Bottom* and *Just Joined* because those are two good examples of what our influences were. They were also the funnest to record. Thee Slayer Hippie produced *Lonely*. At the time he was a handful, but looking back it was really fun working with him. Trever Keith produced Just Joined. He's one of my favourite writers and an old friend of the band. Donell Cameron who worked with us on most of our stuff engineered it. The planets were aligned on that record. The Pearly Gates was my least favourite because I felt that the recording was rushed. I felt it made a good demo, but not a good record.

MM: During the time that Jughead's were originally playing out, you guys must have seen some crazy stuff – so come on Joe, do you want to share some of those strange, crazy and downright bizarre memories with us?

Joe D: On tour, I don't remember what other people are doing. I just don't understand how you can play a great show in Houston, TX and then wake up alone in a motel room in Cheyenne, WY with nothing on but a cowboy hat and a coke straw up your ass. Thank God for tour managers.

MM: On a personal level, what do you hope will happen with the Jughead's reformation? Do you have a plan, no matter how vague, or are you just going to take things as the come and happen?

Joe D: All we want to do right now is a handful of shows celebrating the 20th anniversary of the band; if more comes of it that would be great, but the most important thing is that we're having fun with what we're doing.

Originally published in Mass Movement #26, March 2010

KILLING TIME

A lot of things in life change, and whilst it's often necessary to embrace those changes, more often than not we all need a stabilising factor in our lives, something that we can depend on. For me, since the late eighties, there's always been NYHC, a loose collection of bands based in New York City whose music has been a constant factor in my life. So, when John from Dead City mentioned that he was putting out the new Killing Time record and asked if maybe I'd like to interview them, I jumped at the chance. I mean, c'mon one of the best bands to have ever emerged from the NYHC scene? Who wouldn't want to speak to these guys? Exactly...

Interview by Tim Cundle

MM: Even though it's kind of like preaching to the converted for MM, do you want to introduce yourself and tell us a little about Killing Time?

Drago: I'm Anthony Drago, the drummer for Killing Time and one of the founding members. Carl Porcaro, Rich McLoughlin, Anthony Comunale and I started the band in November of 1987after Carl, Rich and I split from Breakdown and Anthony left Token Entry. The original name of the band was Raw Deal but we were forced to change the name for legal reasons after we signed to the In Effect record label and released our debut album *Brightside*. We've been playing together for over twenty years. Our new album *Three Steps Back* is coming out February 9th on Dead City Records.

MM: Okay, so what have you guys been up between getting back together in 2005 and the release of the new record, *Three Steps Back*?

Drago: In 2005 we played a few shows on the east coast. In 2006, we did a European Tour and in 2007 we hit Japan for the first time. After the return from Japan, we decided to start writing some new material and that's what turned into the new album *Three Steps Back*.

MM: I was kinda curious about why the band went on hiatus after *The Method*? Were there any particular reasons why you called time on the band when you did? Do you think the extended hiatus was a positive or negative thing for the band, and how did you know, when you eventually got back together, that it was the right time for you guys to reunite? What did you miss most about the band whilst it was on hiatus?

Drago: I personally missed everything about the band during that time. Writing songs and playing out live is a tremendous release for me. There were a lot of reasons that brought on that long hiatus. One big reason was that we were seeing increased violence at the shows. The scene really didn't feel the same to us. Anthony and myself decided to take some time off to explore other opportunities. Carl and Rich went on to record and tour with other bands. I can only see the hiatus as a positive thing. I think we had to miss the band and each other enough to start talking about reuniting in 2005. The reunion shows in Brooklyn really woke us up to the fact that this band is a huge part of each of us.

MM: Given that you guys have, realistically, been around for over two decades, how, in your opinion, have both the band the individuals that make up Killing Time changed since its inception, since the formative days of Raw Deal? What originally influenced you as a band, and what influences you now?

Drago: I think that we have all changed a great deal since the time of Raw Deal but when it comes to the music and the band, nothing has changed. We play exactly how we want to play and when we want to play. We talk about things that are most important to us and to a fan base that understands us as we are. We would like to keep it that way.

Alright, let's talk about the new record, *Three Steps Back*… How do you think it compares to your previous records, *The Method* and *Brightside*? What does the title refer to? As it's your third album, I kinda get the feeling that the title is hinting toward a rebirth for Killing Time…?

Drago: Rich came up with the *Three Steps Back* concept, which is basically a way of saying a return to our roots. I think that the new album is definitely are best yet. I know there are people out there that think that we would never be able to top *Brightside*. I'm just hoping that those people will at least give it a chance. They might be surprised. Chris and Carl really opened up with the new music. Carl never ceases to amaze me with the riffs he comes up with. Chris has been such an awesome addition to this band. A lot of the flavour of this new record I can attribute to him. Rich laid down some incredible solos and Comunale just killed it from day one of the vocal recordings. Needless to say, I am very proud of this record.

MM: Why did you guys go back to where it all started for you, that is, your folk's garage, in order to write *Three Steps*…? Purely convenience, or was there another reason for retracing your roots, and if so, what was it?

Drago: My folk's garage is neither convenient nor comfortable. It's just a hell hole with a lot of spirit and memories. It seems to bring out the best in us musically. It was a good idea. It worked out very well.

MM: One of the things that always distinguished you guys was the way that lyrically you always avoided HC clichés and so I was curious about the lyrical subjects that you've utilised and explored on the new album, and wondered if you could kind of share the ideas behind some of the songs on it with us?

Drago: Killing Time lyrics have always been very personal. We've never touched upon politics or social causes. There may be a useful place for that in music but not in this band. I like sharing with people the things that affect me the most and those concerns have always been how I feel about myself or the people that mean most to me. I had to make up for a lot of lost time since the last record, so there is a great breadth of topics that are covered. Two of my favourites are *The Accident* which I wrote about my relationship with my father and *Lookout* which is about my relationship with my son.

MM: How does it feel when people refer to you, along with AF, Gorilla Biscuits, Sheer Terror, Youth Of Today, Cro Mags etc. as being 'Godfathers' of the New York Scene? Did you ever think that the band would last as long as it has when you first started playing out?

Drago: That's good company to be with. All those bands are great influences as well as friends. However, were probably more the "Fredo's" of the "Godfather" Hardcore scene. No other band has been more maladjusted than us. No, I didn't think that I would be in a Hardcore band at the age of 40 but I also didn't think I'd be a Police Sergeant either. That trips me out more to tell you the truth.

MM: So, how, in your opinion, has the New York Hardcore scene changed since you first became involved and first started playing in Breakdown? Do you think those changes have had a positive or negative impact on the scene? Why? From an inside perspective, did you ever think that NYHC would have the worldwide impact that it did and has had? How does that global acclaim make you feel?

Drago: I think that the only thing that's changed about the New York Hardcore scene is that I got older. The way I see it, I have no right to complain. It belongs to the young kids who are now just discovering it and making their contribution. I just want to have a place on the soundtrack. One of the new tracks *Rope-A-Dope* I wrote about that feeling exactly. I love the fact that the music has become some popular around the world. While we were in Japan I got to witness some of that first hand. I found it incredible to hear those fans screaming along to *Brightside*. You got to understand, when I wrote those lyrics in my basement at the age of 17, I didn't think that one person gave a damn about what I was feeling.

MM: Do you think that there's such a thing as first, second and third wave NYHC bands, and if so, what do you think separates and defines each wave, or do all the bands that have emerged from the city share a common heritage and are they all simply NYHC bands? Why?

Drago: I would probably tend to agree with the latter. No matter what musical influences are becoming more predominant, the lyrical content and the feeling is true NYHC. None of us are talking about mythic knights or demons. We're also not talking about fucking some girl in a car either. I hope that makes sense.

MM: As a serving member of the Police force, I wondered if anything that you discovered about yourself whilst in the HC scene, or took from the scene, encouraged your decision to serve as a police officer? Do you think there's any common ground between the HC scene and the Police Force – like belonging to something larger than yourself, wanting to make the world a little better etc.?

Drago: That's funny. I never thought to make that comparison before. You may be right on a couple of points there.

MM: I wondered if we could ask you a personal question for a moment – you were on the Police Force on 9/11, and if it's not too personal, I wondered what you remember most about the day that changed the world?

Drago: I was on the police force but I don't work for NYPD. I was part of a large group from my job that travelled down to assist in the recovery efforts. Probably the most I remember

about the tragedy was the feeling of helplessness that overtook me. I'm sure most of the country felt that way.

MM: What is it, I your opinion, about HC that inspires life-long devotion amongst those of us (yeah, I'm in my late thirties as well) involved in the scene?

Drago: Expression and Acceptance. That's all it boils down to.

MM: Given that the band has had two different names, do you ever find yourself referring to Killing Time as either Raw Deal, and when you think about the band, which name immediately springs to mind? Do you thin the change of name changed anything else?

Drago: I very rarely think of the name Raw Deal. The band has been Killing Time for so long, that's how it is etched in my head. The name change never affected the music or the direction of the band.

MM: So, are we gonna see you guys in Europe and the UK anytime soon?

Drago: That is being discussed now actually. I would love to make it to the UK. I have family there.

MM: What's next for Killing Time?

Drago: I had such a good time putting together this new album that I want to start working on a new one February 10th.

Originally published in Mass Movement #26, March 2010

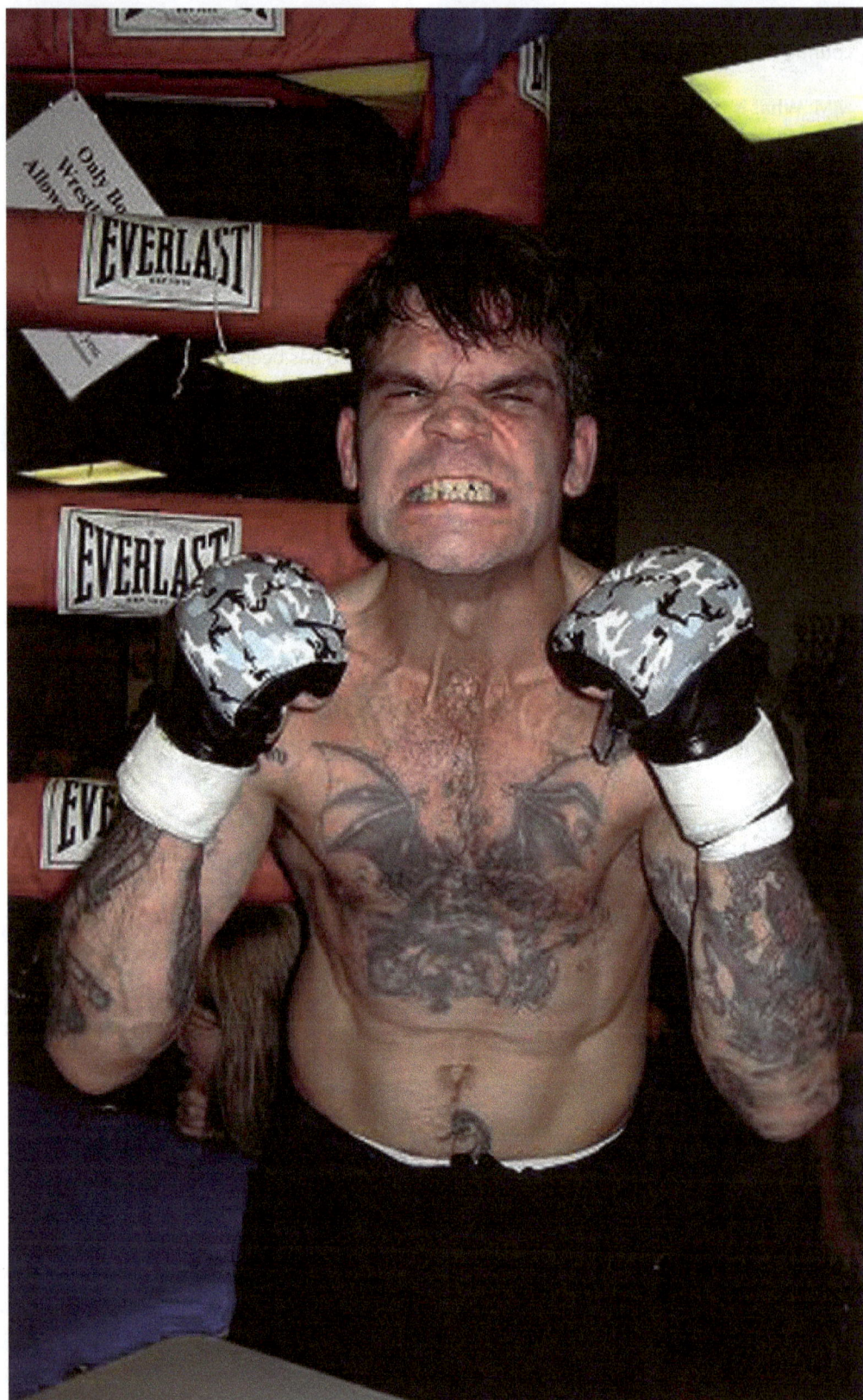

174

MARTIAL ARTS & HARDCORE

Hardcore Punk Thrash – loud, fast rules apply, 'there is no authority except yourself', chaos, anarchy – sounds familiar?

Now think Martial Arts – what are the most evident traits? An ability to kick ass obviously; but also grace, respect, spirituality, discipline and obedience.

The two seem almost irreconcilable, but......I happened to notice during conversations with other martial arts practitioners that many of them also had a background in, or love of, punk rock, hardcore and thrash metal. I wondered why there seemed to be so many sharing the same interests and how they reconciled the dichotomies. First of all let's take a crash course through the history of Asian martial arts and how they passed in Western popular culture.

One of the earliest references to a codified form of fighting was 'The Art of War', written by Sun Tzu in the 6th century BC during the Warring States period of Chinese history.

The origins of the modern martial art of Karate may be traced to 1400 – when the Chinese established trade links with Okinawa, exposing Chinese and Japanese martial artists to the indigenous Okinawan unarmed combat art of "Te" which over the next three centuries combined with traditional Chinese and Japanese martial arts.

In 1935 Karate became the official name of the Okinawan martial arts, based on the traditional art of "Te" (hand) and the term "Kara" (empty or unarmed) and in 1936 Gichin Funakoshi published the first edition of his work 'Karate-Do Kyohan' documenting much of the philosophy and traditional Katas (forms) of modern Karate.

In 1943 Judo, Karate, and Kung Fu were officially introduced in Korea and began to mix with the indigenous Korean arts. During the Second World War the first Korean dojang or martial arts schools opened in Seoul, and Korean military personnel received martial arts training. Following the end of WWII many British and American soldiers were exposed to Asian martial arts while based there.

In 1957 Korean martial arts were brought under the official name of Taekwando, although an alternative art called Tang Soo Do Moo Duk Kwan (often shortened to just Tang Soo Do meaning 'Hand Striking Way') was developed by Master Hwang Kee in 1945.

Although traditional forms of Karate such as Taekwondo and Tang Soo Do and more defensive arts such as Judo are probably the most well-known martial arts in the West, there are numerous other worthy arts that have been developed along the years such as Jujutsu, Brazilian Jiu-Jitsu, Aikido and most recently the concept of MMA (Mixed Martial Arts) which has been popularized in the Ultimate Fighting Championship (UFC).

The 1970s and '80s saw an increase in media and public interest in the martial arts, most notably due to the legendary Bruce Lee film *Enter the Dragon* (1973). The timing of course ties in with the rise of punk in the UK and the US and may partly explain why so many exponents and Masters are familiar with the genre.

The success of films such as *Crouching Tiger Hidden Dragon* and *The Matrix* in recent years, and the continued public desire to see Jackie Chan and Jet Li kick ass in films such as 'Rush Hour' and 'Fist of Legend' have been very much responsible for promoting martial arts in recent years, and one of the main reasons why the uptake of the arts is more popular now than ever.

The questions remains though why do so many people in the punk, hardcore and thrash metal scenes practice martial arts, and how do they reconcile the chaos and anti-authoritarian stance of their musical genre with the rigid discipline of their art? I asked two legends of UK and US HC scenes, and martial arts practitioners - Ian Glasper (Decadence Within, Stampin' Ground, Suicide Watch, Flux of Pink Indians and currently Betrayed by Many) and Harley Flanagan (The Stimulators, Cro Mags, and currently Harley's War) How they first become involved in martial arts?

Interview by Mass Movement

HF: I grew up in a very violent neighbourhood, on the lower east side of NYC in the late 70s early 80s, it was intense, lots of gangs lots of crime, drugs etc. That was the lower east side back then. And anybody that was young and grew up in NYC in the late '70s was into Bruce Lee and the whole martial arts craze that jumped off. I remember there were martial arts supply stores all over forty deuce even a couple on 14th and 23rd, that sold nunchuks, throwing stars, darts, swords - all kinds of knives and weapons, 007's and shit. They'd sell them to any-fuckin'-body - they didn't give a fuck. They'd sell them to little kids. There was a bunch of those stores up on the Deuce right there with the porn and horror movies, arcades, pimps, hookers, peep shows, drug dealers, pick pockets, thieves, etc. That was the Times Square I grew up with. But yeah, they had the Bruce Lee outfits - like the yellow and black one from 'Game of Death,' when he chokes out Kareem Abdul-Jabbar, posters of Bruce Lee everywhere, and all the Kung Fu movies playing. And it wasn't only up there and in Chinatown - on TV there was 'Drive-in Movie' or 'Drive-in Theatre' - whatever it was called and 'Black Belt Theatre,' that used to show Shaw Brothers films. Shit like *The Four Assassins*, *Dirty Ho*, *Master Killer* and *Return of the Master Killer*. All kinds of Bruce Lee movies, like at least two or three Kung Fu movies back-to-back, or some shit on Sundays on channel five or eleven. Kung Fu was the shit. You even had all the Blaxploitation Kung Fu movies. It was funny, I mean, just like the song, "Everybody was Kung Fu Fighting." That shit was no bullshit!

IG: Several of my mates were doing ninjitsu and telling me how much fun it was; I went along and found myself to be a bit of a natural at the break-falls and rolling and thoroughly enjoyed it... this was WAY back, probably in the mid-Eighties? I eventually fell out with the instructors there, and then did a bit of judo for a while, then tried out aikido, stuck at that for a few years, but again, the instructor eventually started to piss me off with his ridiculous demands for total commitment and subservience, so I ended up doing karate from about 2000 'til the current day. Last year I started Brazilian jiu-jitsu too, which is just awesome.

MM: Which art(s) do you practise and what rank are you?

IG: I have a first dan/black belt in wado-ryu karate, which would make me a senior grade, I guess? I don't put too much importance on titles and ranks, to be honest - the higher the pedestal, the greater the fall!

HF: When I was a kid I trained "Northern Eagle Claw" system with this Chinese Master up in midtown, but that didn't last. Through most of the '80s I trained with black belt friends of mine and just crazy street fighter friends of mine. I was a street fighter. I trained with some of my skinhead buddies who were black belts and kick boxers and we got into lots of street fights. That's where my most of my experience came from, real life - growing up. It wasn't till years later I got interested in BJJ after UFC 1 and 2. I'm sure everyone knows the history by now, how in 1993, Rorion Gracie and the Gracie family brought the concept of UFC to America. In Brazil, free-style fighting tournaments had been going on for years.

But amazingly enough, it wasn't here in America. I mean, it was in some places - they had similar type of shit. My roadie, I call him Red in my book since we did commit a lot of crimes and shit together, so I don't use his real name in the book, he had competed in underground K-1 type events with boxing gloves, and pretty much all kicks and strikes were allowed. But there was really nothing like UFC - with free-style rules. And back then, they had no weight classes, no gloves, and no time limits. When I caught that, that really re-sparked my interest in martial arts and fighting arts. I wished they would have had it when I was young and into fucking people up. That was really my introduction to BJJ - Brazilian Jiu-Jitsu. I saw the effectiveness of Jiu-Jitsu. So that was my introduction to BJJ - watching Royce Gracie fight. I got completely fascinated with Brazilian Jiu-Jitsu. I made up my mind that if I ever had the opportunity to meet any of the Gracies, I was going to get down with them. So anyway, I was dying to learn Gracie Jiu-Jitsu. I was looking in every martial arts magazine I could find, black belt Kung Fu - all that shit. I was waiting for a Gracie School to open up in New York City.

Like I said, it was still really the early days of the sport - they had only had the first few UFC's at this point. Well, one day I found a little ad in the back of a black belt magazine or some shit, that said something like "Gracie/Kukuk Brazilian Jiu-Jitsu: Renzo Gracie black belt and Craig Kukuk, etc. and an address and number. I went. This was in '95. First time I walked in there, it was this big loft space in the Twenties. The place was empty - maybe three people there. I looked around, and Renzo is standing over by the the mats. He walks up to me and smiles. I don't know what the deal is with this place - do I walk in and bow to this guy? What the fuck is the deal? I didn't even know if he was Renzo. I didn't know if it was some kind of rigid martial arts school, where you have to act like all traditional and shit, and bow to flags and all kinds of bullshit. I guess he could tell - he walks up, and says, "My friend," and puts his arm around me, smiles, and says, "Come in my friend, you come to train." I'm like, *"Oh shit"* - This motherfucker is cool as hell! None of this pretentious martial arts/bow-down-to-my-black-belt-bullshit. Just a real down to earth cat, with a big smile - who could totally fuck you up. It was so nice. I started training like two days later.

Back then, the shit was still underground. You couldn't get this shit on DVD's and stuff like that - you sought out VHS tapes. There was only like one store - on West 48th - that sold real MMA and some Jiu-Jitsu stuff on VHS, MMA from Brazil and the Netherlands. When I first got the "Jiu-Jitsu fever," I was so into the shit. If I didn't have a training partner, I'd find one - either a band member or a friend. Or I'd just sit and meditate on the moves or watch my VHS tapes of the shit. We'd share tapes, make copies, and circulate them amongst people who were down. UFC hadn't blown up yet - the way it has now. It was kind of the beginning of that whole shit. It wasn't as "on fire" as it is now, as everybody has incorporated Brazilian Jiu-Jitsu into their style. Back then, it was still all relatively new in America. It was still the old days of BJJ - before the worldwide Jiu-Jitsu explosion. But meeting Renzo was one of the best things that happened to me. He will always be a friend and an inspiration to me. Like I said I was fortunate to start training with him back in the day, when it was in its early stages - with just a handful of students, and I moved with him through several academies. The first one was at a Kung Fu school on 25th Street and 8th Avenue. Then we moved to 27th Street - between 7th and Avenue of the Americas. Then He moved back to the Kung Fu school on 25th Street. The shit was funny, there'd be all these people doing Kung Fu in one end of the place - with all their staffs and crazy spears and shit - and then on our side, people were getting mangled, choked, and arm-barred. It was great!

I think the Kung Fu school lost a lot of students to Jiu-Jitsu. Eventually, Renzo got a space on 37th and 8th Avenue by the music building. That academy was totally crazy - it was in this building that was partially under construction, so most of the floors were empty. There was a fucking methadone clinic on one of the floors, so there was always all kinds of scumbags in the building and hallways it was crazy, it was Hardcore yo, that academy was nuts. Renzo had some really crazy students, and the shit wasn't quite as organized as it is now. Then we finally moved to 30th Street - where he is now - and I have trained there for a long time. Now he has a legion of students and bad ass instructors - black belts like John Danaher, Daniel Gracie, Fabio Leopoldo, and so many others. But when I started training in the early days, it was just a handful of people. Now, my man has multiple academies and an army of black belts! Go Team Renzo! Like I said I received my purple belt from him a few years after I started training, but I was a part of his team in the early days - and in the early days of BJJ. At least here in America. It took me a while to get my purple belt cause of touring etc Now I teach my kids and a few friends. I have passed on what I know and I am still training. I have mats at home and me and my friends get together as well as training at Renzo's. I don't have "students" I show some moves to friends, I trained some of my band members even took them to compete at NAGA, they did real well but then I referred them to Renzo. He is the master. I have competed in Underground MMA events. Here in NYC we have the UCL Underground Combat League and other events that are closed door events. Some sell tickets, they are at boxing gyms and martial arts academies and stuff. I have competed in Grappling and submission tournaments like NAGA and others.

MM: How did you get involved in the Punk/HC/Thrash scenes?

HF: I've been in Punk and Hardcore since 77 playing music with The Stimulators, Cro Mags etc.

IG: I got involved in the very early Eighties, as a fan, and then as a musician, then writer, even promoter for a while, did my own CD label for several years... I've played in bands since 1982; have been writing for fanzines, magazines - and three books! - Since about '85...

MM: Do you see any similarities between martial arts and these music scenes?

IG: Well, they're both aggressive and physically/mentally demanding... you don't get an easy ride like you do if you're a pop fan!

HF: Yeah as far as aggressiveness and it gets me pumped up, but I'm sure other people who are into martial arts would rather listen to their style of music whatever it may be when they train. It's all relative, but yes I see a similarity in music and martial arts. I remember when I was young a friend of mine, one of our roadies in fact, his instructor was no fucking joke - he was very respected in the martial arts community, and in many other circles as well. He put it in a way that I really understood, he said, "Doing Kata and traditional martial arts is like playing classical music. Fighting is like playing jazz." With jazz, it's like whatever happens,

happens, and you just go with it. Whereas with classical music, it's very regimented and structured. He put it to me in a way that made complete sense.

Any early training like real training I had came from fucking around with dudes that trained under him. They were seasoned black belts, some bad motherfuckers. I remember he'd hold up a pen and say, "This is martial arts - a pen, anything can be a weapon. We would work out, stretch, practice our kicks, practice combinations, strikes and takedowns. Then when we got in fights, we actually used it, a lot. We were skinheads and I lived in a bad neighbour-hood, and this was the early 80's. We got more hands on training than most people do who fight MMA or train in academies and I'm not kidding. When I was young we were crazy, we'd get in fights with gangs and other groups of people, we were nuts. At clubs, on the street, with bouncers, gangs, jocks, the local Puerto Rican gangs in my hood, all the black gangs in my boys area and really anybody that fucked with us. We were just crazy when we were teenagers, it was some intense Clockwork Orange shit but we didn't beat up bums and shit, just lots of fighting.

MM: Do you see any contradictions? How do you reconcile the strict discipline of martial arts with the apparent opposition to leadership and hierarchy in the Punk and HC scenes?

HF: The Hardcore punk scene is all about leadership and hierarchy and conforming these days, so...

IG: I never have felt truly comfortable prostrating myself in a full bow, which is probably why I've finally gravitated towards BJJ, where there is very little of that master/student protocol. I appreciate the traditional etiquette of karate and aikido, and the eternal debt we all owe to those that paved the way for the arts in the past, but I also love the Amebix and they said, 'No gods, no masters!'

MM: Does the positive mental attitude promoted by martial arts cross-over into the PMA/Straight Edge attitudes in HC?

IG: Absolutely! Punk has always been about never rolling over and giving up, and you have to find some of that spirit when you train in the martial arts - especially when you're as rubbish as me, ha, ha!

HF: Hell if I know, I don't know much about these young kids today.

MM: Why do you think there are so many exponents of martial arts who are also fans or participants in the Punk/HC/Thrash scenes?

HF: I didn't know there was that many. I had a site for a while Hardcore-MMA trying to bring the two together and I did shoot a video in an underground fight MMA club in the Bronx with me competing. I lost the fight but it went 8 minutes which was longer then the dudes four other matches combined. He was tough besides the fact that I'm like 42 and he was 25 but it was a good fight. It's on YouTube and also on my new Harleys War CD/DVD. I had fun even though I lost, shit happens someone's gotta win, someone's gotta lose. I just had a good time testing myself and actually getting to hit someone without risking getting arrested. It was a good competitive environment, so it was cool. I have won more fights in competition and on the streets then I've lost but I've had my ass kicked a few times. When someone says they have never lost a fight you gotta wonder if their lying, or if they only pick weak opponents.

If you fight tough guys sooner or later you have to lose it's the nature of the game

IG: Fans of hardcore punk and thrash are usually some sort of closet adrenalin junkies, hence fans of the genre being attracted by dangerous sports like skateboarding, BMX... and martial arts!

MM: Have you ever used you martial art skills within the context of your music, either the spiritual or meditative aspects or any of the physical techniques?

HF: Well, I have sung a lot of songs about kicking peoples asses if that what you mean and I did shoot that video in a fight club. It don't get much more martial arts and music then that does it?

IG: There's very little room for meditation in the music I play and listen to, ha, ha! But I have tried to bring some of the positivity and never-say-die spirit to some of my lyrics... as for physical techniques; I've hit a few high kicks onstage in my time... and usually split my shorts!

MM: Have you ever had to use your art defensively in a real life confrontation?

HF: You're kidding right? You must not know me, ha, ha, ha, read my book.

IG: I've talked my way out of many a fight, and 99% of self-defence is all about awareness - just general avoidance of dangerous scenarios - if it gets physical, it usually means your 'self-defence' has failed! It's weird, but since I've done martial arts, I've not got in a serious fight... I get all my aggression out in a controlled manner at the dojo or through the band's music, and that leaves me to live my life as calmly as possible.

MM: How much does the spiritual part of martial arts play in your life? Does meditation play a big part in your art/life?

IG: Please see the answer above, Grasshopper, ha, ha. No, I don't have time to meditate. Which probably means I really ought to make time, but fuck it, I'll meditate when I'm dead!

HF: Yes it does play a part in my life, more so now than when I was young.

MM: Do you feel martial arts have lost some of their original intent and become too much of a business over the past few decades?

HF: That's life!

IG: Yes, indeed, which is again why I've gravitated towards BJJ - the Combat Academy where I train is non-profit and very much a club for its members rather than a business for its instructors; there are no extortionate membership and grading fees to pay, just a modest insurance and mat fee and talented people who have decided to share their knowledge and skills with others for very little financial reward - which, when you think about it, is quite punk rock really.

MM: Has the 'Hollywood' treatment of martial arts had a positive or a negative impact on the arts?

IG: Both. I took up aikido after seeing *Out for Justice* - and jacked it in after seeing *Out for a Kill*, ha ha! But seriously, I love a stupid MA movie as much as the next guy - *Ong Bak* fucking rules! There have even been a few serious entries recently that stand up to closer scrutiny - *Red Belt* is well-acted and pretty damn good, for starters...

HF: Well if it weren't for Bruce Lee where would we all be? So... I grew up with the films. By the way check out Renzo Gracie's movie *Legacy* and Rickson Gracies movie *Choke* they are great.

MM: Do you use 'breaks' in your art? Why do you think breaks are important? Can you give some examples of some outstanding breaks you have performed?

HF: I only break people's bones; that's about it. Not often though... as long as they tap.

IG: I broke my fingers once, does that count? (Laughs)

Originally published in Mass Movement #26, March 2010

BOBBY "BLITZ" ELLSWORTH (OVERKILL)

You know that old saying "You should never meet your heroes, because you'll only end up disappointed?" Well, its bullshit, and I have proof. See, I've been listening to Overkill since the mid-eighties, and as they're one of the only bands that have never, on a musical level, let me down, they have by definition, become musical heroes, to me at least, and with therelease of *Ironbound* (a career highlight from a career full of highs and zero lows), I finally got to chat to Bobby Ellsworth, Overkill's singer, about their new record and the band in general, and you know what? He's one of the nicest guys I've ever interviewed and living proof that good things do happen to good people...

Interview by Tim Cundle

MM: What have you guys been up to between *Immortalis* and now?

BE: Obviously a lot of touring. We did a lot of fresh touring with Immortalis. We hit the road as soon as it came out, toured with Motorhead, did the US run then over to Europe and back to the US so I guess that in the two years since the record we've done a solid year of touring.

MM: That must be three or four hundred shows...

BE: I wouldn't say three or four hundred. Obviously we have breaks and the reason we can do this for this amount of time is that we keep both ends of our lives in balance. So we go out for four weeks at a time then go home for four, five, six weeks then back out for four weeks. So probably 170 shows maybe. It's still a lot of shows, I'll tell you though that's still one of the major attractions for me, I love to tour, love the live theatre. You have to prove yourself second to second minute to minute. When you get that instant gratification, that instant success it's kind of like a drug. It's probably the main attraction to me

MM: *Iron Bound* is the heaviest album you've ever released. It's like you get heavier and faster with age. Like vintage wine, you get better with age... How do you do it?

BE: Thanks for the compliment! It's obviously a heavy record. It's hard for me to be objective about it because I had a part in creating it but I do get that thrash 'em, bash'em feel with it. There is a great immediacy to this record. We talked about the touring, and I think that's a big factor, you feel that energy touring for a couple of years and you bring that energy into the studio. That becomes the "X" factor that becomes that feeling of immediacy, because we were just on the road. It is, I guess a heavy record, I don't know if it's the heaviest. But sure I can go with that.

MM: What kind of lyrical subjects have you explored on *Iron Bound*? I was wondering, in particular, what Bring Me the Night and the SRC were all about...

BE: I think that there's a thing that goes on where you can't write about the same things over and over again and at the same time you evolve as a band and as individuals including my-self. Somewhere about the turn of the century, I was involved in some things that were per-sonally shitty or scary and it changed my outlook and I see this evolution going in much more or a positive direction. I truly notice and hold dear the value of what we do.. you obviously need an ego to do this, but I think there is a balance in understanding where the ego is and understanding that I'm only a very small part of this thing. If I start throwing myself parades, I'm the only one that's coming you know? I do believe what I say like in SRC when I say "If we want it we will get it" but what I mean be "we" is introspective but then also spreads out into this community of ours. I realise that over the years we've done this with a multitude of thousands so we've really become kind of an army, so when you look at the SRC, going back to your question, the we is collective. *Bring Me the Night* had that whole feeling of the wave of British heavy metal that influenced when we were just starting. It reminded me of where we came from. And I guess I felt that I and we excelled in the darkness, that's when we really come alive. It seems like it was the lunatic fringe, but it became through time a collective power, so that's really what that is all about

MM: It's nearly Thirty years of Overkill...Come on Bobby, spill...What's the secret of your longevity?

BE: I think the secret is...DD and I have kind of the same background. We both put huge value on family. I was just recently talking to his wife and she said that the only reason is works is because you're the same people, you have the same background and you put peo-ple in front of the band and that includes each other. It's true and it's really not about get-ting rid of the ego because you need the ego when you get up there on stage, but you need to be able to put it to one side and put people first. It makes a huge difference.

MM: How do you think your audiences and the band have changed since *Feel The Fire*?

BE: I don't know... Balder? I think one of the things is that probably until say 2004 or so we grew an audience who began to age and we went down that road with them. What's hap-pened since then is that there has been a revival and through that revival has come a new thrash kid with high tops and skinny jeans, it blows my mind... I've got all this stuff up in the attic and I could have sold it all to Warbringer. I do think that we have grown with our audi-ence, but there is a new audience now, and we inject that angst of youth. In some ways the younger bands are responsible for heavier releases than the old guard in 2010 and 2009; it seems to be the flavour of the month to have a good fucking record! The reason for this new interest and the new fans is just that the quality of the stuff around, and I think it becomes inspiring and everyone makes better records.

MM: I kind of feel weird asking about this, because it is an intensely personal thing...You suffered a stroke on stage in 2002...How did this affect you on a personal level?

BE: It hasn't. It was more of a seizure. It's called a TIA, it's a very minor stroke. I'm predis-posed on my mother's side of the family, I had no idea. When I finally found out I sat her down and said "You know mom, you've got to tell us these things, really". The rumours going round afterwards were awesome. I was pretty fine in an hour or so and back on my feet in no time. It was about two in the morning and I unplugged myself and I was wearing pyjama pants and what we call a wife beater – a white vest and a pair of white boots and I went up to the desk where the nurse was and she said "Mr Ellsworth you must go back to bed!" and I was like "I haven't had a Marlboro in like 15 hours, just point me in the right direction, I'm leaving the hospital whether you like it or not"; and if this was 8 hours after incident I was doing ok. I suppose mentally it did have an impact, it made me realise it is important to enjoy what's here you know?

MM: You guys have played anywhere and everywhere, is there any one place you feel particular affinity with?

BE: We haven't played Australia and I'd love to play there. It's always a big deal playing in our own back yard, I love playing New York. I also have a really good feeling about playing in Germany because my first show outside this country was Munich in 1986 when Chernobyl had blown up. I just remember saying "Who cares, I just won't eat the lettuce" so I remember that as being my first out of the county real tour – it was us and Anthrax and just a great feeling.

MM: Tell us something unusual about you and Overkill...

BE: I'm gonna be in a Simon and Schuster publication out next month called *Thrashed Potatoes*. There's a picture of me cooking tarragon salmon. My wife is like "I have really scored with you this is amazing" and I'm like "Out of my kitchen". She bought me pots and pans for Christmas. I've still got the other side to me but I like to eat good...

MM: Do you have any regrets?

BE: The one regret I have is telling you all that shit! I don't think so, I've had a nice ride and had a lot of fun doing it and I'm very satisfied as a man. There's always been growth in what we do, love us or hate us we've never stopped growing in our own way, never stopped doing our own thing. We're not a band to ever rest on our laurels and that carries over into our private lives. As long as you're really evolving you are really living. That's why I have no regrets.

MM: What's next?

BE: Tours. Like we were saying earlier we like to tour. We don't look way into the future either, 30 years doing this? We'd never have planned that. We just think let's tour this record then see what happens. I think that's part of the key to our success. If you don't have any laurels you can't rest on them. We never changed the world, we were just a part of that.

Originally published in Mass Movement #26, March 2010

PAT MILLS

Here's the thing...Pat Mills is responsible for me being a comics junkie. It's all his fault. If he hadn't run wild with 2000 AD during the late seventies, I would probably have never shown an interest in the medium and would have moved quietly through life never experiencing the joys of the weekly (showing my age here) and now monthly, coloured inks and words that when combined are the foundation of the literary medium that I adore more than any other. So, when I was offered the chance to 'chat' (via cyber-space) with Pat about *Requiem* (and other things), what do you think I did? Don't be so bloody stupid, I cancelled everything else and focussed solely on all things Mills. As you would...

Interview by Tim Cundle

MM: I guess we should start at the beginning Pat – where did the idea for *Requiem* come from, what caused the initial spark that the story sprang from?

Pat: A strange recurring dream about a German soldier dying on the Russian Front and being secretly involved with a Jewish girl in Berlin. He returns home on leave and sees her being taken away by the Gestapo, but is powerless to save her. Writing Requiem was a way of getting that dream out of my system.

MM: Unlike many writers and artists involved in comics, you chose (with *Requiem*) to focus on France rather than the US – why? I've read that it was a life-long ambition of yours to break into France - what is it about the French comic industry / market that appeals and appealed to you so much?

Pat: 2000AD was always heavily influenced by the French market - notably *Metal Hurlant* and never by American comics, except where they had a European flavour, with artists like Barry Windsor Smith, Mike Kaluta and Bernie Wrightson. When I left 2000AD the first project I put together was a graphic novel called *Mekomania* with a number of artists providing a chapter each of a robot history of the future. The artists concerned were Dave Gibbons, Brian Bolland, Mike McMahon, Kevin O'Neill and Ian Gibson. It was intended for Europe and was submitted to Dargaud (publishers of *Asterix*) in France and various other companies. It didn't work out but the interesting thing is that – at that stage – France was a first choice for those artists as well as me. So it was potentially a natural course for all of us. Progressively America has become the dominant force for UK creators but it wasn't always so and the best stuff always came from France. Look at Blade Runner where Ridley Scott acknowledges how the French artists inspired his work (and I suspect also the Italian *Liberatore* whose Rank Xerox predates *Blade Runner*) We have lost our European cultural roots in comics somewhat for a North American comic culture which relies heavily on superheroes .Our relationship with them sometimes reminds me of Blair's slavish admiration and obedience to Bush. Film also used to be heavily influenced by France – consider the cutting edge Fahrenheit 451. That happens less these days. Vidocq, for instance, a French steam punk fantasy I don't think made it over here. So against this background, you can see why working for, and in, France is a natural progression for me and also for other creators. Charlie Adlard (*Savage*) for instance. Requiem is one of a series of graphic novels I've written for France – others include Sha, Shadowslayer and Broz. Let's get away from this USA super hero point of view that hamstrings our creativity into the world of men in tights. French books are beautiful to look at, to write for and to own. Few North American products compare, except graphic novels like League of Extraordinary Gentlemen and similar – which, once again, have a European flavour to them...

MM: Following on from the above, how, in your opinion, does the French (comic) industry differs from that of the UK or the US? Is there a particular common sensibility or thematic undercurrent that defines and separates French comics from those of other countries, or areas, and if so, what do you think it is, or how would you describe it?

Pat: French books have to be high quality otherwise they won't cut it at the box office. The standard generally has to be higher than UK or US as I know to my own cost. It's like a Hollywood first weekend. If the book doesn't sell in the shops in the first week or so, it's dead in the water. This happened to me on a past book. Fortunately not to Requiem which is a bestseller. But it is a tough market which is why few of us venture into it. French books have a greater concentration on backgrounds and rightly so. I think it's valid for Hellboy to have that wonderful minimalism but I don't care for imitators who think it's an excuse for doing second rate work. I have even heard fans disapprove of strong backgrounds and see it against free-flowing sequential art. I actually like "heavy" illustrative comics' style, but in any event you can have free-flowing art and still have backgrounds. However, French stories aren't always that accessible to a Brit or US market. Bilal's work is genius but only has a cult following here. Westerns like Blueberry don't work here. Requiem is, however, written and drawn for a UK and US market as well as a French market.

MM: Staying with the industry questions – why do you think UK and US readers tend to focus on what they know (and I'm as guilty of this as anyone else), instead of trying to branch out and embrace comics and literature from France, Belgium, Germany etc? Do you think that there's more to it than the language gap?

Pat: Yes. It is hard because the stories are often rather art house or European, for want of another word. And the French are not into Hollywood endings. My French publisher and artist looked appalled when I initially suggested there should be a happy ending to *Requiem*. But look at what happens when the French do connect with the Anglo-American sensibility...

Perfume by Patrick Susskind. The French designs in *Fifth Element. Asterix.* And the wonderful *Persepolis* was originated in France. This country would never have had the balls to commission something like that. Reprint – sure, but commission. No way. We have been unlucky in that some French books once translated into English didn't sell. The brilliant and very beautiful *Magician's Wife* by Bucq. It wasn't hero based enough for us. You have to take these things one step at a time – if you go ahead of the market, you'll lose it. And there's all that super hero sensibility to deprogram from our brains. I did my best with *Marshal Law* - but there's a long way to go

MM: Back to *Requiem* – one of the major themes running through the book is that of rein-carnation, or rebirth, with the next life being shaped by the deeds or misdeeds of the pres-ent or previous one. I wondered if that idea was shaped by your own beliefs, and if so, how do you view, or see, the idea and / or concept of reincarnation. How would you define the human soul?

Pat: Yes it is shaped by my own beliefs and, in fact, by my own experiences which were ob-jective rather than subjective. I featured some aspects of them in an earlier series Sha. I think Roger Woolger's book *Other Lives Other Selves* probably expresses it better than I can. It is not New Age-ish and doesn't talk about people who believe they were Cleopatra or Napoleon. I think our knowledge of reincarnation is at a very early stage so to talk precisely about definitions of soul would be a difficult thing, especially in this space! Modern material-ist society discourages reincarnation from being researched further. If you talk about it too much – and you don't happen to be a writer who can turn it into a story – you could even be accused of having Multiple Personality Disorder. The brain is a reducing instrument which is meant to keep this stuff out. But there are some people who can let it in and work with it. Others let it in via trauma. Thus children in Lebanon had bizarre past life experiences. Scep-tics about reincarnation can rationalise it all away with psycho-babble, but with many experi-ences – including my own – they'd have to tie themselves in so many waffling knots, that their explanations would sound far more like mumbo jumbo than mine.

MM: The central character, Heinrich / Requiem, was a German soldier killed on the Eastern Front during World War II – why did you want to make the central character a Nazi, part of a movement that is widely vilified the world over?

Pat: He's a Vampire, he's evil, and he was the subject of a strange dream I had. Plus we are all fascinated by evil. We all like Darth Vader and comparable Men in Black far more than Luke Skywalker's. In fact, Requiem is a kind of dark Star Wars. That's why the little Cryptos takes the piss out of gurus in the opening book.

MM: I get the feeling that you see him as being part of the ultimate evil, and as such use it as vessel to propel the reader into your nightmare vision of hell, and by making Heinrich a German solider, you're challenging the traditional concept or role of the anti-hero / hero...?

Pat: True. But also people are fascinated by German soldiers. He's a German first, a Nazi sec-ond. The Eastern Front turned him – and would turn most of us – into an animal.

MM: How and where did the ideas for your vision of Hell, Resurrection, come from? The re-versal of everything that the characters previously knew in life, almost like reversing a pho-tographing negative? What shaped and helped you create this alien world of nightmares and terror?

Pat: When I was a kid I used to make huge three dimensional maps in plasticene - Battle of Waterloo, Ireland etc. I always intended to make a map of the world in the same way, re-versing out land and sea and see what it looked like. This stayed with me all my life. So that was a real motivation for Resurrection, although the seas are of blood there. And everything comes from this – time runs backwards, people admire decadence not progress. Olivier added to it greatly. For instance he came up with the archaeologists who bury the past.

MM: ...And, given Heinrich / Requiem's obsessive desire to find and once again be with Rebecca, do you think that Requiem could be seen as a love story, exploring the idea that regardless of behaviour, sanity, insanity, good, evil etc. that at the end of the day, we're all driven by the same needs, urges and desires, both biological and psychological?

Pat: I think when we're in love we can be very driven. Arguably, he's obsessed rather than truly in love, but when you're that close to the flame you don't know your own mind. I originally had it as more of a Romeo/Juliet love story and it still retains those elements but they are now, within a much wider canvas with lots more going on. Star Wars format, again, perhaps.

MM: I was also fascinated by the idea that on Resurrection, aging is reversed, its inhabitants gradually becoming younger until they become foetuses and gradually fade from memory. What prompted the idea of life in reverse?

Pat: It fitted the world of a negative and was a valid way of him coming back to life.

MM: Do you think that anyone can ever truly be forgotten, the passage of their life and accomplishments, no matter how minor, disappearing for good given that even the smallest parts of our history are now recorded, both personally and by those whose lives we touch?

Pat: Modern technology means the age of privacy is over and the subject of identity theft is explored in a science fiction story I'm doing with artist Clint Langley called American Reaper. It was commissioned by Xingu Films (they did *Moon* and *A Guide to Recognising Your Saints*) as a screenplay and also as a series of graphic novels. The screenplay is now complete and we're about to start on the graphic novels. Anyway, the identity thieves can recreate the lives of those whose ids they've stolen because there's so much info out there now.

MM: I was curious about the class system – why use the Undead and creatures of folklore and mythology, and how did you establish the hierarchy of said class system?

Pat: Once you start with Vampires and you have ghouls and werewolves, they all have to form part of a hierarchy. Ghouls – hypocrites – interest me in particular. Check the pirates in Book Two and see if you recognize a certain famous nun. What I've researched about her makes my blood boil. Without doubt a hypocrite. Not to mention my experience of being taught by nuns who were also total hypocrites. I wrote it quite passionately, and then remembered how often I've been discouraged from writing with polemics and anger by some UK readers. So I chickened out and toned it down. But Olivier liked my polemic, so he put it all back in.

MM: Following on from the above, and given that Requiem is a Vampire, why do you think people are and have always been fascinated by the idea of vampires?

Pat: Men in black – we love 'em. Batman, Lone Ranger, Judge Dredd. The dark other. And the sexuality of them in the case of Vampires, as well as the defeat of death.

MM: Requiem is much more graphic in its nature than a lot of the work that you're also well known for, and I was wondering if the freedom that it's given you to push those boundaries has helped inspire the story and the way it's evolving, or any other ideas?

Pat: It's darker, yes. Although other stories of mine like Defoe about a zombie hunter are also pretty graphic. At first I was going to put in some lighter elements, but Olivier insisted the tone should be unrelentingly Gothic and he is absolutely right.

MM: Did you ever think when you first started writing comics that you'd be able to create and publish a story like Requiem?

Pat: I always wanted to work for France after creating 2000AD. Just as many of my peers wanted to work for the USA. My first French book was *Shadowslayer* followed by a couple of other series, so Requiem was a natural progression.

MM: Panini have released the first two volumes (four issues) of the series, are there any more planned, and if so, when are they due?

Pat: If the UK edition sells, more will follow. I think it was great they brought out two books to kick off.

MM: Apart from its domestic market (France), which audiences, do you think, seem to have really embraced *Requiem* and drawn the book close to their dark hearts?

Pat: Lots of Goths (or should that be Emos now?) come to signings in Paris, especially signings in the Pigalle. Girls with pet rats on their shoulders etc. So I hope the same in the UK?! Actually we did a promotion in a Goth cellar club in Paris where we emerged from coffins to be interviewed by the most tattooed MC in France along with actors playing Requiem and Claudia. Each year we have a new Claudia model for promotions and one of them actually had a whole page of Claudia Vampire Knight (a spin off series) tattooed on her back. We also did a big tattoo convention in France and Requiem went down there well. So we should be looking at the equivalent in the UK. Maybe we should also do something at Whitby Festival. We had a big range of Requiem fashions launched at some metal concert in Paris. The Claudia fashions were amazing. And boots they'd die for in Camden. There were some problems with the production so that seems on hold just now – although some great t-shirts came out of it. So it would be nice to link into that dark fashion thing here. Requiem fashions were originally going to be launched at a counter-culture fashion exhibition in London connected with Skin 2., because Olivier is a great fashion designer, too, as you can see from the clothes in the story. I tried to get someone who makes videos with Cradle of Filth interested and he may have shown Requiem to the band by now. I think there's a large black t-shirt market in the UK that would like it. At some point I need to investigate and facilitate this further. And of course a lot of 2000AD readers and people who like dark sci-fi comedy will enjoy it...

MM; Can you share of any future plans for the book with us? Storylines, character development, plots etc.?

Pat: I'm currently writing *Requiem Volume 10*. It features a Vampire Samurai who does battle with Requiem. The current story could go up to Volume 16. (That would be Book 8 in UK editions as there are two volumes in each book). The overall storyline is about a vast conspiracy to destroy Dracula and Requiem holds the key to averting it because he has the Hammer of Thurim, his earlier incarnation in Hell. Events grow more apocalyptic each Volume. I particularly enjoy writing about the reptilian Dystopians. The Dystopian Empire is the Victorian British Empire in Hell. We are known in Europe as Perfidious Albion – something our history books back home play down. But they have good reason to remember this in France and so the Queen of Dystopia is Queen Perfidia, a reptile version of Queen Elizabeth 1st.

MM: Okay, I have to ask – *Requiem, ABC Warriors, Savage /Invasion* and *Charley's War*. A lot of your stories have been shaped by and through war, and I wondered why? What kind of impact, in your opinion, has War had upon your life, and why does it play such a major role in your characters' lives and stories?

Pat: War is a good template to generate ideas and one that readers respond positively to. I guess personally I've been pretty unaffected by war, but I was certainly affected by religion and I'd say that's even more prevalent in my stories. And corruption. I found most establishment figures inherently corrupt so that tends to drive my stories too…

MM: What's next for you and *Requiem* Pat?

Pat: A new spin-off, I hope, after Claudia. We want to do *Sabre Vampire Knight*. A Casanova Vampire, a lovable rogue, who is in Hell because he probably started the Bolshevik revolution. He was a Czarist officer in 1917 who was too busy screwing aristocratic women so couldn't be bothered to get out of bed and arrest Lenin

MM: If there's anything that you'd like to add, speak now or forever hold your peace…

Pat: I hope to get a website going sometime this year (about time!) and when I do I'm going to major on Requiem UK as it's a character very close to my heart and I'm delighted he's finally come home to his birthplace.

Originally published in Mass Movement #26, March 2010

WILL THE REAL WOLF MAN PLEASE STAND UP?

With the remake of *The Wolf Man* now on the big screen, I thought it might be interesting to briefly trace the derivation of such a beast down through the ages, including, his relationship to an actual wolf and to examine the etymology of certain terms that have become synonymous with both creatures.

Historically speaking, it is by and large the common, ordinary wolf that has surfaced in both literature and folk tales and not the monstrous creature of imagination. The confusion comes in trying to separate the two when reviewing ancient texts.

Unjustly reviled for their fearsome, outward presence, wolves are perhaps the single most misunderstood animals of all. From birth to death, from newborn cubs to fifth generation adults, these strikingly, beautiful creatures live together as one, cohesive unit, and seldom, if ever, do they stray from the pack. They are highly efficient hunters, and as a result, they have earned a nasty reputation for preying on cattle and livestock much to the hatred of shepherds and farmers alike. Yet, false horror stories of unprovoked attacks on humans have led to their needless slaughter.

Wolves are fiercely loyal companions to their mates and doting parents to their offspring, but the public's perception of them has been one of fear and loathing. Over the centuries, these false perceptions have expanded to include certain, socially maladjusted individuals, whose irrational behavior and inability to "fit in" with the social norm have branded them as cursed misfits, capable of beastly deeds. It is because of these distorted perceptions that some myths and legends have been created. Superstitious peasants and gypsies, who once inhabited the region now know as Romania, have helped to promulgate such myths, and even today, these beliefs still exist in parts of Eastern Europe.

The image of an actual two-legged wolf man, covered in fur, with gleaming fangs and razor sharp claws, is simply the product of one's over-stimulated imagination; a legend that has been handed down from generation to generation as fact rather than folklore. As a result, the words "werewolves" and "wolves" are somewhat interchangeable terms, and, in some instances, both lexes have been historically interpreted to represent the mythical wolf man.

Etymology

Perhaps the most common term associated with a wolf/wolf man is the Greek word "lycanthropy" (*lukos*, wolf and *anthropos*, man). According to Webster, one definition of the word is "a delusion in which one imagines oneself to be a wolf or other wild animal." The second definition states, "the supposed or fabled assumption by a human being of the appearance of a wolf." Notice that Webster makes no mention of a creature that is part human and part wolf in the definitions. Instead, both of the descriptions specifically refer to one's "delusion" or "assumption" of being the four-legged variety. Logically, one who suffers from this affliction would be a "lycanthrope."

The word "werewolf" (Old English *wer* or *were* for man and *wolf* taken from the original O.E. for wulf), according to Webster, is "a person who has assumed the form of a wolf." In the above example, the word "assumed" is defined by Webster as, "to take on or; become endowed with." Therefore, a lycanthrope and a werewolf are not necessarily the same creature. In fact, it is safe to say that the word "lycanthropy" or "lycanthrope" refers merely to a malady of the human mind, while the word "werewolf" is an individual who has magically transformed into a wolf.

It is important to note; however, that neither of the two definitions suggests that a wolf-like beast (wolf man) stands erect on two legs during a full moon. Again, the image of a fabled nocturnal killer is either the direct result of ignorant ethnic superstitions or age-old mythological tales that were intended to serve as a moral lesson.

Disease

The Latin translation for a wolf is the word "lupus," which is also the name of a life-threatening disease that attacks the autoimmune system. Victims of the disease breakout in a red facial rash that resembles the bite-mark of a wolf, thus the name lupus was given to this disorder by physicians of the mid-nineteenth century But as far back as 1575 B.C., superstitious Greek medicos referred to this affliction as "κόκκινο σήμα του κτήνους λύκος" or "red mark of the wolf beast."

Religion

Jesus, in the Master's consecration of the twelve disciples, tells his flock, "behold...I send you out as sheep amidst the wolves." Ultimately, it would be Christ himself as the sacrificial lamb. Several centuries after his crucifixion, some of the early Christian symbols crudely represented Christ's payment on the cross in the form of a wolf whose jaws were firmly secured around the body of a bloody, sacrificial lamb.

Starting in fourteenth century, there began a "push-pull" relationship between the various rival forces of religious thought that consisted of those individuals who were still loyal to the Christian code of ethics, those practitioners whose faith was imbedded in the dark and mysterious hues of demonology, and still, those individuals who sought to lift the human consciousness to a higher level of spirituality by acquiring knowledge from all sources.

During the Middle Ages, Western Christian doctrines introduced other doctrines of the Greek Church and far eastern philosophies. In some circles, this broadening spiritual awareness became all consuming, which resulted in a gradual amalgamation of traditional Christian teachings with those theretofore-alien practices. The most extreme examples of this new fellowship of thought showcased such superstitious beliefs as the incubus and succubus, the transmutation of men into beast, specifically wolves, and the power of flight, to name just a few. Procedurally, some of those same circles wished to distance themselves from anything that was remotely connected to Christianity. In doing so, they altered the sacrificial lamb image to one with demonic overtones, depicting a sinister wolf man beast who was devouring a beautiful, young maiden; the underlying objective of this image was to promote the spilling of virgin blood to a different savoir (see figure entitled "Wolf Beast"}.

The New World

As the centuries passed and civilization began to migrate beyond its once familiar boundaries, new vistas awaited those explorers brave enough to travel across the expansive Atlantic Ocean. European immigrants, who ventured to the New World in search of religious freedom, found incredible bounties of sprawling, virgin forests, lush, rolling hills, treacherous mountain ranges, and brutal winters. It was in this strange, new land that the settlers would encounter Native Americans, who practiced a different array of superstitious beliefs.

Native Americans held a special reverence for all creatures, and in particular, the gray wolf was exalted to an almost god-like plateau. Also known as the ghost wolf, it was thought to hold the power of life and death in its spirit, especially in the glint of its eye. One glance from the wolf could make a sick man well and a dead man alive.

The Navajo tribe believed that those individuals who were bitten by a wolf would gradually turn into a similar beast on two legs. Every cycle of the new moon would begin the victim's transformation, and his final state of a wolf beast would be achieved when the moon was full. They also believed that the only way to either save or destroy the afflicted individual was for a close relative to touch the victim with a nugget of solid silver. If the victim was pure at heart, he would be saved. However, if he had an impure heart, he would die. Of all of the myths, legends, and fables about a wolf man, the Navajo's conception of such a beast is by far the most faithful to the genre. The idea of a man being of pure heart is the basis for the famous poem from the 1941 film, *The Wolf Man*, which states, "Even a man who is pure in heart and says his prayers at night, may become a wolf when the wolf bane blooms and the autumn moon is bright." Of course, there was the problem of getting close enough to the victim in order to touch him with the silver...a minor point.

Some Indian tribes believed that a man could transform into a wolf merely by wearing its skin. And then there was the idea, according to some Native American tribes, that both the wolf and his cousin, the coyote, had god-like powers in which they could affect conditions in the universe. The Cherokees held one of the most profound Indian beliefs that there were two wolves inside every man, one good and one evil. The wolf that was victorious in a man's spirit would be fed; the other would go hungry.

During this same period in American history, the early Christian church struggled to gain an identity; something it had hoped to find in the New World. Moreover, church patrons were exposed to Native American customs, which, in some cases, brought about a change in their attitude towards life and death, heaven and hell. Instead of just one, universal god, Native Americans worshiped many deities or spirits, including animals. Some defectors of the Christian church embraced this ideology and hence, a heretical merger of "water downed" Christianity and Native American folklore gave birth to an offshoot of Old World witchcraft. The parishioners of such a faith (witches) were said to have all the powers of hell at their disposal, among those being: the resurrection of the dead, the conjuring of spirits, and the ability to change men into beast.

Literature and Folklore

One of the earliest accounts of a werewolf in literature is found in the story, "Gilgamesh." According to the legend, the Assyrian goddess Ishtar is forced to turn a shepherd into a wolf due to his neglect of the flock. Ironically, in nature, the wolf is probably the last creature one would choose in concert with a flock of sheep. Nevertheless, the story ends as the shepherd's very own dog devours him.

Another werewolf tale of antiquity is included in Ovid's narrative poem, *Metamorphosis*. A monumental piece of work, the poem is a collection of fifteen separate books that chronicles the creation and history of the world, as seen through the poet's eyes.
As a part of his grand poem, Ovid retells the tale of King Lycaon (lycanthrope), who murders his grandson and offers the flesh as a feast to god Zeus, telling him the meat is of a forest animal. When Zeus learns of Lycaon's deceit, he changes him into a wolf with some human characteristics. This is perhaps the earliest recorded introduction of a true wolf man, as opposed to an animal with four legs.

It has often been a source of question, among scholars, as to why Zeus chose to turn King Lycaon into a wolf, rather than, some other predatory animal. One possible explanation for Zeus' choice may have been the fact that a wolf is one of the few apex predators of the animal kingdom. As an apex predator, they are at the top of their particular food chain, and they have been known to devour their own kind, including newborns. According to Greek mythology, Lycaon was a cannibal, and he acted much the same as an apex predator in killing his own grandson and then attempting to feast on the flesh with Zeus. In his infinite wisdom, the supreme god perhaps felt that it was a fitting punishment for the king to share the fate of a wolf.

A poem of werewolf folklore is Marie de France's "Bisclavret" from Lais written in 1175. She tells of a medieval knight who falls victim to a werewolf curse, as he desperately searches to find his clothes before the next full moon. If he fails to recover them, his curse will extend beyond the cycle of the moon, and forever – he will remain a wolf. The knight's unfaithful wife and her lover are successful in keeping him from finding his clothes, and he is forced to wander in the cold for many years, until a kindly king helps him to once again become human.

Sexuality

The vilification of the wolf is a favorite theme in nursery rhymes and childhood tales, but one only needs to look beyond the literal interpretation of such stories to find a more symbolic and sinister meaning. In the familiar tale of "Little Red Riding Hood" (Charles Perrault), the wolf, after having eaten Red's dear, old grandmother, pretends to be the elder Hood in order to devour the innocent, young girl. On the surface it appears to be an innocuous, albeit, grisly tale about a wolf intending to satisfy his ravenous hunger.

Interestingly, Perrault, a French nobleman who has been credited with being "the father of the modern fairy tale," was also a devout student of Greek and Roman mythology. In being so, he often incorporated similar themes of an erotic nature into his "innocent" childhood fantasies.

In both Greek and Roman mythology, the wolf is sometimes dramatized as a devious and sexual predator of young, fair maidens. As mentioned earlier, this theme of a wolf beast was used by some of the more sordid religious sects in the Renaissance period. It is thought that perhaps Perrault intended his wolf to be a sexually lecherous creature with more on his mind than just dinner.

An even more overt example of the wolf's sexual role in fables can be found in the misty region of the Carpathian Mountains. Birth land to Vampiric legend as well as werewolf folklore, the gypsy inhabitants of this region (Romania) once viewed the wolf as a creature whose true identity would be revealed as the offspring of a sexual encounter with a virgin of tender heart. This unnatural union of beauty and beast, according to gypsy legend, would produce a wolf beast. It is not known for sure, the significance of such a creature other than his mere existence in werewolf folklore.

Summary

Mankind will always have a fascination for the dark mysteries that lie beyond the limits of mortal comprehension. It is this fascination that drives us to question our very own existence. Many myths and legends have, at their core, a basis in reality.

The legend of a wolf man, who prowls the fog-laden landscape of some remote and desolate countryside, is just that — a legend. Nevertheless, for those individuals whose lives are dominated by the fear of the unknown, reality and fantasy often coexist as ever-present figments of the mind. Allowing fear to control one's life is crippling. Accepting fear as a part of life is liberating. The discovery of truth will indeed, make us free, but the power of our imagination will keep us alive.

Wolf man or no wolf man...It really doesn't matter. The fascination with such a beast is in the legend

Doug Crill

Originally published in Mass Movement #26, March 2010

RICHARD HERRING

Richard Herring has been performing comedy for a quarter of a century. Gaining attention as part of the Lee and Herring double act with Stewart Lee, Richard has gained critical acclaim and a steadily growing live audience over the last few years with his solo shows such as *Talking Cock*, *Ménage a Un* and *The Headmaster's Son*. He returned to Edinburgh in 2009 with his latest show, *Hitler Moustache*, a hilarious, controversial and thought-provoking look at race, liberal hypocrisy and the Chaplin toothbrush moustache. I spoke to Richard shortly before his performance at Blackwood Miner's Institute in March.

Interview by Leigh McAndrew

MM: You performed your latest show, *Hitler Moustache* at the Edinburgh Fringe in 2009 and are still touring it; how has the tour been and how do you think this show has been received?

Richard: It's been really good on the whole. It's nice to have a bit more time, with Edinburgh you're always rushing to get it to fit into an hour, I never manage to do that even so, but it's nice to have the luxury to slow it down a bit and having two halves and adding extra stuff that had to be cut out at the previous stage. Every year I've been touring it's been slightly touring bit by bit, some of the smaller places, like tonight, there may be 80 or 90 in, but other places I've had 600 and 700 people in, so it's definitely building up. Over the years you can sort of see the numbers building up. On the whole audiences seem to like it, I've had a few nasty e-mails and some people taking offence at something, but everyone else seems to be very positive about it.

MM: Where did the idea for the show come from?

Richard: I think we started talking about it in the Collings and Herrin podcast when I was talking about growing a moustache and it sort of grow from there. I was going to surprise Andrew by having a moustache when he was meant to be coming to a cottage I had hired to write in. I was going to have a big gay biker moustache (laughs). We'd just been talking about moustaches (laughs). I'd thought about it in the past, why that moustache had the association with Hitler rather than anyone else and how it was sort of forbidden to have it and I just thought it would be an interesting starting point for a show, you know, just to grow one. I did it for the podcast for one week, just in the house and not going out and even that felt naughty and I thought well, what would happen to me if I actually went out with this moustache? So that was the starting point and I'd come up with this routine that was about the way that racists are more liberal than liberals in some ways and it'd been playing around in my mind so I sort of put those two things together at the point when I had to come up with an idea, as I had a title and poster and a vague idea of what might happen and you have to write it [for Edinburgh] which is around now, this time. I tend to write the shows in May, June and July so it was all sort of coming together. It accidentally became sort of zeitgeist-y, with the BNP winning the European election seats and stuff like that, but I wanted to do a show as a white guy doing a show about race and racism and sort of investigating those things, because you're not really meant to do that. It's all right if you are of the race to do jokes or to talk about it. I actually think that it's something that everyone should be talking about, and everyone's a bit confused about.

MM: Do you think that the majority of audience members 'get' the points that you are try-ing to make in the show?

Richard: Yeah, I kind of discuss that in the show a bit. I've had three complaints, there's a Madeleine McCann joke in it, even though I flag it up and tell the audience and get them to vote on whether they want to hear it, and someone said it was wrong, and made worse by the fact that I'd flagged it up. I think that when the audience have said that they do want to hear it then I've kind of lost the responsibility of it, and you can always not listen if you don't want to hear it. Someone else said that there's a lot about mental illness in there and some-one else thought that it was sexist. Apart from that... (laughs) I've thought about these things really carefully and I'm talking about these subjects because it is about my own hypocrisy and also about the way we make broad generalisations about things, so I think most people do really get it. I use the 'p' word in one of the routines and then later on discuss whether I was right to do that or not, but I actually think that everyone gets the context of that. It's about words, and that's what that routine is about. I discuss the fact that word itself isn't of-fensive, it's the intent, it's a word that I really don't like, but then it's quite interesting to throw it around and let the second part talk about it in a lot more detail, along with the Carol Thatcher 'golliwog' thing. But yeah, I think people get it and like it and the shows got kind of a nice message. There was a little bit of controversy before anyone had actually seen it, Brian Logan made out it was racist, but if you see the show you'd have to be really strained to think it's anything but slightly 'right on' if anything [the article and Richard's response to it is available on the Guardian online]. I've got an audience, and I don't think any BNP members are coming to the show, but it's also about making liberals aware of their own culpability and responsibility in the BNP's success, so it's not preaching to the choir, it's actually criticising the audience as much as anyone and looking at our own hypocrisies and culpabilities and even just discussing the way that we're meant to respect where everyone comes from, but isn't that against the ethos of treating everyone the same? We have to treat everyone differ-ently as well as we are all from different places. Human beings are actually all the same and we impose these things on each other, but maybe there's a good thing about imposing cul-tural differences (laughs). Constantly I've heard people say that they went to the bar and talked for hours about it which is all you can hope for from a comedy show, getting people thinking and discussing. It's not meant to have all the answers by any means, but it's meant to point people in the right direction and get people to think about stuff.

MM: Is there a fear with this type of comedy that, especially with the 'YouTube' genera-tion, routines can be taken out of context and videos put up onto the Internet. Stewart Lee had bits from his show taken out of context by the Daily Mail and certain lines from *Hitler Moustache* have also been taken out of context.

Richard: People do worry about that a lot, but I think that actually quite hard, unless you edit things out. It's worse in printed media, when someone can take a line out of context, but if you see something the said in the way that it's said it's more difficult to misinterpret it, un-less someone has literally taken one line out of context and then you can say, 'you haven't shown the rest of it.' A lot of comedians get worried about their jokes being seen online or their routines being misinterpreted online. There's a video of me dealing with a heckler on YouTube, but they asked me if they could put it up. I suppose that I could've said no, if it's one of those bad gigs that someone decided to put up, I'd be more worried about that, where things go wrong, you slightly lose control of yourself or of an audience, so I'm more worried about when I'm making something up or doing a gig where I fly off on one to see where it goes, to see that go up online would be awful, but I think you can be paranoid and too worried about it. For example, that YouTube video has been seen by a million people, which means that a million people are aware of me, so probably 80% of responses have been positive, so that's potential people to come and see you, and it's not as if I'm doing any bits from my show in that video. I think most of these things help, if you give stuff out for free on the Internet then stuff can happen and people will come and see you live. Stew's argument about people downloading his DVD, I can see why he's upset about that, but I think that people who download his DVD will probably then come and see him and so that's where he'll make his money. I give away a lot of free content online and I think people feel 'well I like this guy, I'll go see him live, he's given away 50 hours of free entertainment this year, so let's pay him back by seeing him live or buying his DVD'. If I start losing a lot of money I'd be worried, but I'm not feeling that anyone is stealing my intellectual property. I think you can worry about that more than you need to, but I can appreciate, like the guy from Seinfeld [Michael Richards] that there are certain things you wouldn't want to go up online (laughs). It could have some repercussions. I think, for me, that it's my online presence which is generating my live audience and building me up, quite gradually, but in a cool way.

MM: You have released over one hundred Collings and Herrin podcasts, how did you begin working with Andrew Collins?

Richard: We were contemporaries in the nineties, he was on Radio One the same time as Stew and me and we'd met in corridors. When 6Music started he did a show called Round Table and asked me to go on. He'd read my blog and saw an affinity with me. Just through that I started going on his 6Music show and doing half hour where we'd just discuss the newspapers and we did that for a year, either on a Saturday or Sunday and that finished. We felt it was a shame, it took about a year and we thought maybe we should do something. He'd done a podcast before and seen how easy it was to do, basically. I'm not very technically minded, but once we'd realised we could just do it on a computer and we'd found a nerd who'd put it online for us and very kindly provide massive support (laughs). I'm being very facetious by calling him a nerd. We realised how easy it was so we thought we'd give it a go, because we really enjoyed doing it. We figured we'd just do it for fun and in the back of my mind I thought that if it was successful it may bring some work. It's also a very good way of developing a relationship with someone, to talk to them for an hour every week (laughs). We've got a good relationship, we did anyway because I wouldn't have just done them with anyone, it was very organic. If you listen to the first ones they're almost polite, it starts to descend into madness. It was partly Andrew pushing on, saying it'd be a good idea, because if it was left to me I wouldn't have gone on and done it.

MM: Haven't you recently recorded some special podcasts for Go Faster Stripe?

Richard: We came to Cardiff and did four new ones, they are exclusively for CD. We just thought, given we'd done so many for free, it would be interesting to see if people would pay for them and I think they will, like with the DVDs online you may sell 3,000 over a course of time which wouldn't be enough for a big DVD company, but for Go Faster Stripe it's great, so we might try to experiment charging a pound now and again for one.

MM: You're recording *Hitler Moustache* in a few weeks with Go Faster Stripe, has the date been finalised for that show yet?

Richard: It's being recorded on 2nd April at Chapter Arts Centre, Cardiff. I've sold out the Glee Club for tomorrow night, so there's definitely an audience in Cardiff for the show. I'll probably record two performances of it that night, for a backup in case anything goes wrong. It's quite a hard show to get exactly right, so it's nice to have a couple of cracks at it.. It will actually be distributed by another company, so it will be in shops so it's slightly different to my other DVDs, but Go Fast Stripe will be recording it and selling it on their website. It will be owned by someone else, so we'll see if it sells in shops.

MM: Go Faster Stripe recently released your fifth DVD with them, *The Headmaster's Son*. What was the premise of that show?

Richard: My dad was my headmaster at school and I'd done a few shows about being 40 or being a debauched middle aged man, so I thought I'd like to do something a bit different, a bit sweeter and lyrical and also to look at why I'd become the person I was. I'd always assumed that my father being my headmaster had some huge psychological effect and I just wanted to look into it. That was the starting premise and it was a way of looking back at my teenage years and read my diaries out and have some fun with that, but also to investigate why I am the person I am and whether I'd be like this if my dad was the headmaster or not. It was a really, really nice show, kind of a theatrical show.

MM: How did you begin working with Chris at Go Faster Stripe?

Richard: He did Stew's DVD, and Stew pointed me in his direction. We sat down and had a chat and I'd seen a bit of Stew's DVD, I don't really like to watch him or myself (laughs), so I'd seen how it was put together. It seemed a shame to me that I was doing these shows and there was no record of them, it was nice that he was interested in filming it, and for me it meant that the DVD would exist and I could move onto the next show. I haven't done 'Christ on a Bike' or 'Talking Cock', obviously. I'm going to do 'Christ on a Bike' again at Edinburgh this year, so I've got those shows to pick up in a way and get on DVD, it's really nice, especially as things have picked up a bit again, people are going back to those shows which I think are good shows. They are still able to see them, when at the time people weren't sure, for example 'Someone Likes Yoghurt' really divided the critics and the audience weren't sure about it every night, but it was a really adventurous, experimental and funny show, so it's great that it still exists.

MM: The DVD of *Someone Likes Yoghurt* shows how it divided the audience, there are a number of shots of audience members who are really not enjoying it at all!

Richard: It's good to see that because that show is as much about what is funny and dividing an audience. The yoghurt routine itself developed in clubs. Trying to do that in a club was, and I didn't even realise it, a stupidly brave thing to do, because on a Friday night, a gang of pissed up lads aren't going to want to listen to that, so that's why it became longer and longer, it just became a case of 'the more you complain about it, the longer I'm going to do it. I'm doing this to annoy it'. It just developed organically from there. When the audience is behind you, when they are, generally (laughs) in that DVD is not as exciting as when there are people in the audience who genuinely hate you and want to kill you because of what you're doing. Again, I don't watch them so I haven't really seen it back (laughs).

MM: You've also got a book coming out this year. What's it about?

Richard: It's called *How Not To Grow Up*, and it's essentially about the year I turned 40. A lot of the stuff is from the blog, or things that I discuss on the blog. It's also filling in all the stuff that was happening behind the scenes as well. It's quite an honest look at me having sort of a breakdown and behaving a bit more badly than I usually word, sort of a borderline depression. I suppose it's about still feeling 18 when I'm 40. So it's about whether it's a good or bad thing that I haven't really grown up and have no responsibility. At the start of the year I'm getting into fights and halfway through I meet my girlfriend, so there's a good story arch to it, there're a few things that I moved around that some people who are massively observant of the blog will spot, I used things that are narratively good for the book, but most of it is accurate. It's a funny but true look at what I was up to.

MM: Being a veteran of the Edinburgh Fringe now, it seems that most comedians write for the Fringe, and then tour the show afterwards. Is this how you work?

Richard: The Fringe is a nice thing to do, for me it's an impetus and a deadline. It would be embarrassing if I didn't have a show, so that's how I work. I'm very bad at sitting down and just writing, but if I know I have a deadline and won't have a show, then that forces me to do it. I spend a month or two putting the show together, a month in Edinburgh performing it and then three months touring it, so it's about six months of my year is with the live show now. I earn enough money in those six months to get me through, and I do other things during those six months too, then I do other bits and bobs in the other six months. It's turned into a nice way to do things, it's nice to have a show every year and to tour every year, that's the way of building up an audience without massive TV exposure.

MM: What are your plans for this year's Fringe?

Richard: We're doing Collings and Herrin live, and I'm also doing 'Christ on a Bike', I was going to try and do a play, but I don't think I've got the time to do it, so I may do that next year, try and write the play in advance so that I can get good actors. I may do one 'As It Occurs To Me' too.

MM: What are your plans beyond that?

Richard: Up until September I'm fairly booked up, I'm doing another series of 'As It Occurs To Me' in May, 'Christ on a Bike' and the book is coming out. Up until the end of September I don't know, obviously I'm going to tour 'Christ on a Bike' about the same time next year and I'd like to start writing a play, I'd like to write a comedy drama, a sitcom maybe, we'll see what happens.

Originally published in Mass Movement #26, March 2010

WILLIAM PETER BLATTY'S
DER
EXORZIST III

Ein Film im Verleih der Twentieth Century Fox of Germany

DREAMING OF A ROSE
THE LEGION CHILLS OF EXORCIST III

Forget *Paranormal Activity, REC* or *Drag Me To Hell*: the last time a horror film managed to *really* scare me was way back in 1990.

It was a late screening of *The Exorcist III* at the UCI in Swansea. The Friday night crowd were rowdy and pissed. Smuggled beers were being passed around, the ushers had given up trying to keep us quiet and most of the lads, myself included, were having one last crack at impressing the available girls. But as the film began, everything slowly went quiet, and within minutes, we were given a new reason for not wanting to go home alone.

As the camera prowls down the darkened, quiet streets of Georgetown accompanied by a deeply unsettling soundtrack of guttural sub-Latin growls, a vaguely threatening voice utters one of the film's first lines of dialogue:

"I have dreams... of a rose, and then of falling down a long flight of steps."

The quiet sanctity of an empty church is violently shattered by some unseen force. Throwing the heavy wooden doors open, it charges in, a defiant windstorm of screams. As prayer books are scattered and candle flames snuffed out, any viewers who doubt the demonic nature of the intrusion are promptly put right when a statue of Christ unexpectedly snaps its eyes open. Then we are out on the streets of Georgetown again, gliding through the dark as the opening credits unfold.

At this point, the entire audience fell completely and utterly silent, and I knew then that we were in for one hell of a show.

The Exorcist III is a much-maligned flawed masterpiece that turns the rule of diminishing returns on its head. It ignores John Boorman's ridiculous *Exorcist II: The Heretic* to present itself as a direct sequel to the original film. Too bound up in provocative theology for the turbo-gore crowd, too tainted by the horror tag for serious movie fans, the film is stylistically similar to the original, but arrives as a far more entertaining package.

It was written and directed by William Peter Blatty, screenwriter for the classic *The Exorcist* which was itself based on his bestselling book. The movie began life as a project designed to re-team Blatty with *The Exorcist* director William Friedkin. Blatty initially resisted the idea, later revealing in the book *The Exorcist: Out of the Shadows* that "Everybody wanted Exorcist III... I hadn't written the script, but I had the story in my head."

Blatty's initial concept was to produce a movie about demonic possession without repeating the ritual of the exorcism that formed the final act of the original film. But Friedkin disagreed with the direction Blatty wanted to move in, and the project faded into development hell.

Unperturbed, Blatty developed his concept as a novel. Published in 1983 as *Legion*, the book was an instant bestseller, and by the end of the '80s he had fashioned it back into a screenplay. With studios such as Morgan Creek and Carolco now chasing the rights, Blatty chose to go with the former after executives at Carolco revealed they wanted him to change the storyline so that the daughter of the lead character becomes possessed. He refused, but Carolco still got their pound of flesh by producing the dire Leslie Nielson spoof, *Repossessed*, with Linda Blair in the central role.

With Morgan Creek putting up an $11m budget to realise Blatty's vision, the writer/director sought respected actors who would be able to carry the story's heavy themes of faith, friendship, belief and loss. The great George C. Scott agreed to star as Lieutenant Kinderman, the character played in the first film by the late Lee J. Cobb.

"It's a horror film and much more," he told *The Exorcist: Out of the Shadows. "It's a real drama, intricately crafted, with offbeat interesting characters, and that's what makes it genuinely frightening."*

Scott delivers a powerhouse performance as a man who has lost his faith in God after witnessing too much horror. When we first see him, he is standing on a riverside dock, examining the body of a young coloured boy who has been crucified on two rowing oars. The boy has been decapitated, his head swopped with one taken from a white plaster statue of Christ that has been done up in Al Johnson-style black face. As a final atrocity, ingots have been driven into the boy's eyes.

"Would a God who is 'good' invent something like death? I don't buy it, Father. It's not a winner."

Jason Miller returns from starring in the original movie to play Patient X, a hospital inmate who could well be Father Karras resurrected, while Brad Dourif handles Patient X's psychopathic alter ego, the Gemini Killer, and in doing so delivers the signature role of his long career.

The plot sees Georgetown plagued by murders identical to those carried out by James Venamun, AKA the Gemini Killer, a serial slayer who was electrocuted back in 1973. His execution took place around the same time that Father Karras was taking his final dive through Regan McNeil's bedroom window.

As the bodies mount up, Kinderman realises that the victims are all connected to the Regan case. He discovers a nameless patient in the local hospital's maximum security wing who looks exactly like the supposedly deceased Father Karras, but who claims to be the Gemini Killer.

It transpires that satanic intervention has caused the souls of both men to be entombed within the same body, as the Gemini Killer explains:

"A certain matter of an exorcism, I think, in which your friend Father Karras expelled certain parties from the body of a child. Certain parties were not pleased, to say the least. The very least. And so, my friend, the master, he devised this petty scheme as a way of getting back, of creating a stumbling block, a scandal, a horror to the eyes of all men seeking faith, using the body of this saintly priest as an instrument of - well, you know. My work. But the main thing is the torment of your friend Father Karras as he watches while I rip and mutilate the innocent, his friends, and again, and again, on and on! He's inside with us! He'll never get away! His pain won't end!... Gracious me, was I raving? Please forgive me; I'm mad."

Each death is prefigured by the presence of a blood-red rose displayed somewhere in the scene, a poetic visual touch that recalls the opening lines of dialogue. The murders themselves demonstrate a similar creative flair. A priest is attacked in his confessional box; injected with a drug that renders him passive but aware of all that is going on around him, he is messily decapitated. The killer carefully arranges the scene so that the dead priest remains sitting in the confessional, his severed head propped up in his lap for the next penitent parishioner to discover.

Father Dyer, Karras' friend from the first film and now a pal of Kinderman, is also targeted with the drug during a stay in the local hospital. Unable to resist, tubes are inserted into his heart and his entire blood supply is manually pumped out shortly after the two men watch 'It's A Wonderful Life' together at a cinema. The killer taunts Kinderman by leaving these very words written in blood above Father Dyer's headless corpse.

The police are baffled when they discover that the culprit leaves a different set of fingerprints at every crime scene. Are they dealing with more than one murderer?

The film strikes an unsettling, disturbing tone that is maintained and enhanced even further by each of the murders. But the real showstopper, the one that scared the hell out of us all those years ago in that packed cinema auditorium, that one occurs at the hospital, late at night and in near total silence.

Blatty's set up is masterly: the camera remains static in a side corridor looking onto the hospital reception desk. It's the graveyard shift, and a lone nurse chats with a bored policeman. All seems well.

Hearing noises from a side room, the nurse goes to check that the occupant is okay, first making sure that the policeman is still nearby. As she steps into the room, she doesn't notice the policeman being called away by a colleague. The nurse is now alone.

Nothing happens for several beats. It's a false scare; we start to relax as the nurse emerges from the room and heads back to her desk, and that's when Blatty strikes.

As the nurse strides back to reception, the camera suddenly catapults forward, shattering the late night silence with a terrifyingly loud synthesised shriek as we see that *right on the heels* of the nurse is a shroud-wrapped figure brandishing a pair of surgical bone-clippers at her neck. A split-second later, it is over, and the scene quickly cuts to the discovery of the nurse's body the next morning.

This simple set up is massively effective, and I still recall the wave of shock that washed over me when I experienced it for the first time back at the cinema. I remember the low burst of exhilarated chatter that broke out among the audience following this murder set piece, and when I looked around, I saw people digging themselves out of their seats and whispering 'did you see that?' to one another. The transition from static silence to synthetic scream really makes the scene work - had Blatty scored it more conventionally, the effect would have been far less impressive.

That's the thing with 'The Exorcist III'. It is one of the best examples I have ever found of how a director can combine fancy sound design with stark visuals to create unbearably tense horror.

A case in point is the episode where Kinderman visits the local Jesuit university late at night. As he and the university president discuss the murders, a door creaks in an outer office. Kinderman turns in time to see a pile of papers lift in the breeze, as if someone has just walked past. Half-whispered Latin reaches our ears as Kinderman steps out to investigate.

On the landing outside, the lights flutter on and off. Harsh, murmured growls emanate low on the soundtrack. Kinderman looks around; in the flickering strobe, a distant statue of a Jesuit saint suddenly appears demonic and evil. Kinderman steps forward for a closer look, unsure of what he is seeing. The growls swell; someone approaches.
As the noise reaches a crescendo, Kinderman collides with the university president's secretary. She screams, the lights return to normal, he apologises. She hurries on her way. Kinderman turns to look at the statue, which is utterly benign once more.

Sure, the payoff is a cheap shot equivalent of that cheesy cliché where a cat jumps out and spooks someone - but boy, does it work. Blatty pioneered the use of 'vocal violence' with this flick, and it's a shame that it hasn't been used as effectively in more genre offerings.

Kinderman realises that Patient X is possessing elderly residents of the catatonic ward and forcing them to commit the murders. When one victim-to-be, a priest called Father Kanavan, urges a charming little old lady to make a good confession, her response is chillingly delivered:

"Seventeen of them, Father. The first was that waitress in Candlestick Park. I cut her throat and watched her bleed. She bled a great deal. It's a problem I'm working on, Father. All this bleeding."

Blatty completed the film on time and only slightly over budget, but trouble occurred four months later when Morgan Creek suddenly realised that the director had delivered an Exorcist film without any exorcisms.

The original climax followed the ending of the book – with the Gemini Killer realising that the father he has sought to shame with his sickening acts of violence is finally dead, just as Kinderman shoots him in the head and brings the supernatural shenanigans to an end. Clips of this can still be seen in a trailer where Karras/the Gemini Killer/Patient X 'morphs' through a series of different faces.

Rather than let the studio bring somebody else in to make the required changes, Blatty opted to reshoot the ending himself. He introduced a new character at the eleventh hour - Father Morning, a priest who is briefly glimpsed in his room at the seminary as the evil entity that plagues Georgetown makes its presence felt. He then inexplicably turns up at the hospital to separate the two souls amid a fantastic battle of devilish special effects that cost an extra $4m to put on screen. It doesn't make a great deal of sense, but fails to totally ruin the film as well. Blatty himself said of the new ending in The Exorcist: Out of the Shadows that

"It is all right, but is utterly unnecessary and changes the character of the piece"

"The original story that I sold Morgan Creek, and that I shot, ended with Kinderman blowing away Patient X. There was no exorcism. But it was a Mexican stand-off between me and the studio. I was entitled to one preview, then they could go and do what they wanted with the picture. They gave me a preview, but it was the lowest end preview audience I have ever seen in my life. They dragged in zombies from Haiti to watch this film! It was unbelievable. But I decided, better I should do it than anyone else. I foolishly thought: I can do a good exorcism. I'll turn this pig's ear into a silk purse. So I did it."

The cast sympathised with Blatty's predicament.

"We all felt really bad about it," Brad Dourif told Blatty fan site theninthconfiguration.com. "But Blatty tried to do his best under very difficult circumstances. And I remember George C. Scott saying that the folks would only be satisfied if Madonna came out and sang a song at the end!"

Dourif elaborated on this to Fangoria magazine. "The original version was a hell of a lot purer," he said. "I liked it much more."

By the movie's end, Father Morning is dead at the hands of the demon and Kinderman has rediscovered his faith: you cannot believe in the devil, he tells Patient X, without also believing in God:

"I believe in death. I believe in disease. I believe in injustice and inhumanity, torture and anger and hate... I believe in murder. I believe in pain. I believe in cruelty and infidelity. I believe in slime and stink and every crawling, putrid thing... every possible ugliness and corruption, you son of a bitch! I believe... in you."

Blatty told Fangoria that when Patient X hisses "I must save my son, the Gemini," at Kinderman in tones that recall the possessed voice that the late Mercedes McCambridge provided for the original film, this was intended to suggest the demonic entity, Pazuzu, is back holding the reins. This time, the demon's voice was provided by an uncredited Colleen Dewhurst, an actress who was twice married to (and divorced from) George C. Scott in real life.

Prior to the film's opening across almost 1,300 screens in the USA, Blatty pleaded with the studio to call the film *Legion* – a title which 20 years later has been used by another movie to depict a war between angels and demons

"I begged them when they were considering titles not to name it Exorcist anything, because 'Exorcist II' was a disaster beyond imagination," he said. "You can't call it 'Exorcist III' because people will shun the box office. But they went and named it 'Exorcist III', then they called me after the third week when we were beginning to fade at the box office and they said 'We'll tell you the reason, it's gonna hurt, you're not gonna like this – the reason is 'Exorcist II'.'
"I couldn't believe it! They have total amnesia."

Nevertheless, the movie made a respectable profit at the US box office – more than $26m – and has proven to be especially popular with rock and metal bands around the world.

US group Beyond sample the movie on the song *Limbless* from their 1995 album *Reassemble*, and Canadian band Cryptopsy sample it for *Crown Of Horns* off their *None So Vile* album. Finnish metallers Children of Bodom top and tail the titular track from the *Fear The Reaper* album, and thrash stalwarts Slayer based their song *Gemini* on Brad Dourif's character - it appears on the punk compilation, *Undisputed Attitude*.

The film is also apparently popular with serial killers – Jeffery Dahmer was reportedly watching it on video when police raided his charnel house of an apartment, and later claimed that it was his favourite movie.

Despite the studio-imposed changes, Blatty remains proud of his achievements.

"It's still a superior film. And in my opinion, and excuse me if I utter heresy here, but for me, it's a more frightening film than 'The Exorcist'."

Interestingly, Blatty originally wanted to enlist John Carpenter as director, but as the man behind such classics as *Halloween* and *The Thing* later revealed in the book *John Carpenter: Prince of Darkness,* he shared the same problems with the plot that William Friedkin and the studio had expressed.

"Blatty is a fabulous writer, and much of 'The Exorcist III' is brilliant," Carpenter said. "But there was no exorcism in the third act. I was ambivalent about the script, primarily because it didn't have an exorcism... I kept suggesting a third-act exorcism and pushing the both of us to come up with some new, exciting and grotesque devil gags. Blatty was resistant, so I withdrew from 'The Exorcist III'."

Even with the studio meddling, the finished film demonstrates that bringing in Carpenter wasn't necessary. Blatty makes use of technology, directorial sleight-of-hand and solid old-fashioned acting to craft some truly scary chills, wrapping them in a satisfyingly intelligent and atmospheric horror movie that is crying out for a special edition DVD complete with excised (exorcised?) footage and more.

The director has tried for several years to locate the trimmed footage, which apparently includes an alternative opening where Kinderman views the dead body of Father Karras just after he has fallen from Regan MacNeil's bedroom window.

Morgan Creek claim to have lost the footage, but noted Exorcist expert Mark Kermode, who has described *The Exorcist III* as *"A restrained, haunting chiller which stimulates the adrenalin and intellect alike,"* has insisted on his BBC blog that the search for the lost footage remains ongoing.

So here we are, two decades later. I'm still waiting for a director to step up to the plate and scare me as badly as Blatty did all those years ago. It hasn't happened yet, and until it does, fans of *The Exorcist III* will have to content themselves with dreams of a rose... And then of falling down a long flight of steps.

Liam Ronan

Originally published in Mass Movement #26, March 2010

THE DUNGEON'S MASTER
A WORLD OF FIGHTING FANTASY

It was the 1980s and role playing fever was sweeping the nation, swept along in the ever-growing popularity of *Dungeons and Dragons*. I, for one, at the tender age of eleven, was completely unaware of *D&D*, or role playing for that matter. All that changed one fateful lunchtime at school, when a friend showed me a copy of *Deathtrap Dungeon*. With its lurid cover of a hideous, bloated monster, wallowing in a pit of pink slime, with its gaping maw of razor sharp teeth and a hundred eyes staring hungrily at the viewer (it was later, while daring that very dungeon for myself, that I learned that the creature was called a Blood Beast and just how dangerous it was!) that my fate was sealed and my life-long love affair with role playing in all it's myriad forms began.

Fighting Fantasy Game Books first crawled their way onto the world's bookshelves in 1982, but the real story started two years earlier. Steve Jackson and Ian Livingstone, the founders of Games Workshop (yes, THE Games Workshop! They had created the company as a means of importing and selling D&D and other role playing games to the UK market), proposed a series of single-player game books to Geraldine Cooke, an Editor at Penguin. Now, it must first be noted that the idea was not altogether new; the concept of an interactive game book had been around since 1959, when it was pioneered by the French writer Raymond Queneau and his publication *Story As You Like It*. The format inspired a number of imitators, the most famous of which was the Choose Your Own Adventure series by Bantam Books, which first appeared in 1979. In addition, the format had been used in a series of solitaire adventures as part of the *Tunnels And Trolls* role playing game. However, what set Jackson and Livingstone's interpretation apart was the introduction of true role playing elements - a character sheet with statistics, the random element of dice rolls and, here's the clincher, proper combat rules!

Interestingly, what would become the first Fighting Fantasy game book almost never made it to print. Jackson and Livingstone submitted the initial draft, called *The Magic Quest*, a short adventure designed to showcase the style of game that they wanted to create. However, Cooke didn't know what to make of it; was it a book or was it a game, was it aimed at children or adults. The manuscript bounced around Penguin, from editor's desk to editor's desk, for almost a year before the decision was finally made to publish it.

Then the next obstacle reared its ugly head, as the two authors had to turn their synopsis into a fully-fledged adventure. This was to prove to be not quite an easy task as one would think, as the creative pair had to run Games Workshop during the day. Consequently, they were forced to do all of their writing in the evening and at weekends.

To cope with their multitude of duties, Jackson and Livingstone decided to split the writing chores in half. Livingstone wrote the first half of the adventure, taking the reader up to the river crossing (I hope I haven't given anything away for any of you readers who want to read this particular book, as you now know that there's a river crossing!). Meanwhile, Jackson wrote the from the river onwards, including the final confrontation with the evil warlock Zagor (There! I've gone and done it again!), as well as the combat rules and the all-important key system that would prevent the reader cheating his way through the adventure. Finally, after six months hard work *The Magic Quest* had become *The Warlock Of Firetop Mountain*.

Soon after they had submitted the new manuscript, however, a very apologetic sub-editor explained that it still needed work. In fact, it needed a major re-write, as the writing styles changed from the moment the reader crossed the river. Without word processors or a trusty computer (Hey! It was 1981, remember! The best you could get was a ZX Spectrum!) Jackson and Livingstone were forced to go back and retype entire sections of the book.

The second draft was fine, but the next problem was who would publish it? Geraldine Cooke, who commissioned it, wanted it to be a Penguin title. Others within the publishing firm felt that it would be better off in their children's list as part of the Puffin Books range. Finally, it was agreed that Puffin would publish the title and thus in 1982 *The Warlock Of Firetop Mountain* appeared in bookstores across the nation. Sales were nothing exceptional, however, word began to spread around school playgrounds and colleges, and also, thanks to the Games Workshop connection, around the role playing gaming community (no internet viral campaign back then, kiddies!). Within the first three months *Warlock* was reprinted three times! Within the first year it was reprinted a total of twenty times! *Warlock* had become a runaway success and Penguin desperately needed a sequel. Jackson and Livingstone immediately began work on the next two books, but this time, to avoid any differences in writing styles, the authors were working on their own. Soon, *Citadel Of Chaos*, by Jackson, and *The Forest of Doom*, by Livingstone were released and by March 1983 the three books were topping The Sunday Times bestseller charts.

Of course, there was opposition to the books, as the anti-role playing witch-hunt began (strangely, in America before spreading to these shores. What a surprise!). Outspoken members of the Evangelical Alliance denounced the books as the work Satan and demanded that they be banned. Fortunately, Puffin's Editorial Director, Liz Attenborough, who tackled the thorniest of accusations, even when the sensationalist media asked whether stories of sorcery and demons were suitable for children, deftly defended Fighting Fantasy. But for every critic there were plenty of supporters, such as teachers, who cited that the books were brilliant at getting reluctant teenage boys to read.

As Puffin demanded more and more books to keep up with demand, Jackson and Livingstone became virtual hermits. They split their time between running Games Workshop and penning the next dangerous adventure, seeing very little of family or friends. Furthermore, Jackson had promised Cooke a more advanced version of the series to be published under the Penguin imprint.

So it was that in 1983 *Shamutanti Hills*, the first in the Sorcery series of books, was released on an unsuspecting fandom. The Sorcery series was far grander in scale than the previous Fighting Fantasy books, as it was aimed at an older audience. There were four books in the series, the aforementioned *Shamutanti Hills*, *Khare - City Port of Traps*, *The Seven Serpents* and *The Crown of Kings*, each released between '83 and '85, and were essentially one long campaign. As a campaign, the reader could keep their character from book to book, and although you could play the books individually and still complete them, if you had an ongoing character the adventure would be easier. Not only that, but you could decide to play either as a Fighter or as a Mage. If you were a Fighter then the books played in much the same way as a Fighting Fantasy book. However, if you played as a mage then you got to use the 48 spells that were detailed in a separate book that came in each slip-cased edition. Another nice touch was that dice were not necessary to play the game, as published at the bottom of each page was a pair of dice symbols with random numbers on them. The idea was that the reader could just flip the pages and randomly stop on a page and see what score they got.

This is something that Wizard has resurrected with their editions, but more on that later. Also in 1984, Jackson published *Fighting Fantasy*, a simple role playing game utilising the FF system.

Meanwhile, Livingstone decided that the emerging world of the Fighting Fantasy game books needed to be defined. As subsequent books, such as *Deathtrap Dungeon* and *City of Thieves*, were added so was the world of Titan, and more specifically the continent of Allansia detailed. Each book added to the characters, history and legends, providing more and more depth.

At the same time, other publishers were planning on releasing their own versions of the successful FF game books. To fend off these competitors, Puffin decided that they needed to release a book a month. Of course, this was an impossible task for the series creators and so additional writers were drafted in to pen these new epics. One of these writers was the extremely talented Marc Gascoigne, who not only wrote a number of adventures, but also wrote *Dungeoneer: The Advanced Fighting Fantasy Role Playing Game*, its supplements, *Blacksand* and *Allansia*, and the novels, but who also went on to become the series editor.

The Fighting Fantasy game books didn't just limit themselves to setting adventures in the fantasy setting of the Titan. The fourth book in the original series was a sci-fi quest, entitled *Starship Traveller*. Other genres followed, such as the horror thriller (and, I might add, darn near impossible to beat!) *House of Hell*, as well as the Mad Max-esque, post-apocalyptic *Freeway Fighter*, and the superhero adventure *Appointment With F.E.A.R.*

With a group of talented writers behind the series, *Fighting Fantasy* went from strength to strength. More products were released to an ever-eager audience. To meet the demand *Warlock* magazine was launched in 1984 and ran for thirteen issues - the first four of which were published by Penguin and then by Games Workshop. *Warlock* focused primarily on Fighting Fantasy and reprinted shortened versions of some of the game books, acting almost like a teaser. It also provided bestiary entries of the monsters that appeared in the books in a feature called *Out of the Pit*. In addition, it also covered other aspects of role playing, opening up a new world of gaming to the fans of Fighting Fantasy.

That same year, Proteus, another FF inspired magazine, also launched. Although its adventures were not set in the world of Titan there was an area of crossover, as it reprinted the final part of the *Flatlands Trilogy* by Ruth Pracy, after *Warlock* was cancelled. Proteus itself ran for nineteen issues before finally fading from the newsstands in '88.

Also in '84, a series of FF computer games were released for the Commodore 64, Amstrad, BBC and Sinclair ZX Spectrum, based on some of the game books, such as *The Warlock Of Firetop Mountain*, *The Citadel Of Chaos*, *The Forest of Doom*, *Temple Of Terror*, *Appointment With F.E.A.R.* and *Seas of Blood*.

In 1985 the ultimate FF bestiary was released. Taking its name from the regular feature in *Warlock*, *Out Of The Pit* detailed all of the monsters that had appeared thus far in the FF game books, along with two hundred and fifty illustrations depicting the creatures in all of their hideous glory.

The following year one of the most eagerly anticipated books of the Fighting Fantasy series was released (well, it was for me), *Titan: The Fighting Fantasy World*. This companion tome to *Out Of The Pit* revealed the history, the gods, the beasts, the legends and the lands of the world of Titan - codifying everything that readers had experienced thus far.

Also that year, Fighting Fantasy branched into the realm of board games, as Games Workshop released *The Warlock Of Firetop Mountain*. Now, players could enjoy the thrill of the game book on their table top. It came with a beautifully illustrated board, playing pieces, cards, dice, as well as a simple to understand rule book. As to be expected it was produced to Games Workshops exacting high standards.

While a steady stream of new game books was being released, Jackson, never one to rest and always eager to expand into new territory and technologies, launched F.I.S.T. - Fantasy **I**nteractive **S**cenarios by **T**elephone in '89. Players phoned up the specialist line and were able to use the telephone's touch keypad to make their decisions, as they listened to the adventure's narration, as well as sound effects to enhance the atmosphere. But there was more to F.I.S.T. than just FF by phone or paying an extortionate phone bill. Players could create their own character and advance as they proceeded through their quest, as well as saving as they went, keeping their character in limbo until returning at a later date.

Overtime, the Fighting Fantasy phenomenon encompassed practically every medium one could imagine, from jigsaws, posters, to the world's first collectable card game - Battle Cards. In total there were 150 cards in the series and the objective was to obtain the *Emperor of Vangoria* card by accumulating 8 treasure cards by fighting battles and completing quests. Unfortunately, Battle Cards didn't fair too well, as a few short months after its launch it was eclipsed by the arrival of Magic The Gathering.

Interestingly, the Fighting Fantasy series was due to end with the 50th book, *The Return to Firetop Mountain*. However, it proved to be a massive success and rekindled interest in the previous books. Consequently, it was decided to continue and finish on the 60th book, *Bloodbones*. However, this book was never released as the series was cancelled in 1999. After nearly two decades, Fighting Fantasy had dominated the children's fantasy market, with 59 game books in all, 4 Sorcery titles, role playing games, board games, novels and poster books, sold in 17 countries around the world, with sales exceeding 15 million copies. Fighting Fantasy had gone beyond being just a children's book. It had become a legend!

Now, Fighting Fantasy game books are back! Wizard Books have re-released some of the original books with stunning new cover art and some nice new additions to the original text. Whereas in the original books you always had to create your character, the new editions not only offer you the choice of 'rolling up' your character, but also choosing from three pre-generated characters. These characters all have a nice couple of paragraphs giving you some background and details about their personalities. Each one generally excels in one of the three statistics, Skill, Stamina and Luck. So you can decide whether you want your character to be exceptionally skilled, very strong or very lucky.

Another nice touch, which I have already mentioned earlier, is the addition of two dice symbols at the bottom of each page. This means that even if you do not happen to have a pair of ordinary six-sided dice to hand, you can begin playing immediately just by flicking the pages of the book and stopping at a random page and seeing what the dice symbols are.
For the diehard fans, you'll be pleased to hear that the original internal artwork is faithfully reprinted, as well as the original text.

City Of Thieves - Ian Livingstone

City Of Thieves was the first of the three books sent to me for review. So it was that on a Sunday afternoon I settled back in my armchair with a nice cup of tea, as I embarked upon my first Fighting Fantasy adventure in nearly 'cough' years.

As I opened the book and began reading the background I was confident. After all, I had played this game book several times as teenager. Venturing once more into Port Blacksand would be like walking down the streets of a town I knew really well. How wrong could I be! I should have remembered "Port Blacksand! Never will you find a more wretched hive of scum and villainy! We must be..." Sorry, slipped into another universe there. Still, the advice stands. Port Blacksand is dangerous. No, let me say that again Port Blacksand is very, very, very dangerous! And great fun too! My mission was simple enough, find the wizard Nicodemus, who resides in the city of Port Blacksand, and ask for his aid in defeating the evil Zanbar Bone (what a great name!). Of course, this being a FF book no mission is simple.

My first foray into the city limits I quickly met an unfortunate demise. My second attempt I lasted a lot longer, but found myself outside of the city walls with no way back in and all of the city guards wanting to kill me. My third attempt I succeeded, barely! There was some tense dice rolling involved and testing my luck, but I made it to the end and defeated the vile Night Prince.

All in all, *City Of Thieves* does exactly what it says on the cover. It is a city full of thieves, so don't trust anyone! It is a really great adventure, but not an ideal holiday destination. Iain McCaig's gorgeous illustrations are littered throughout, adding to the atmosphere and the sense of danger. If you're feeling brave enough, rush out and pick up a copy. You won't be disappointed.

The Citadel of Chaos - Steve Jackson

After having been beaten twice by the *City Of Thieves* I was determined not to be outdone by *The Citadel of Chaos*. Yes, I'd played this one too in my youth, but I wasn't going to trust my fading brain cells to guide me through this dark fortress. No, I was going to really pay attention and carefully weigh up my decisions before acting. After all, I wasn't just entering any old fortress. I was on a quest to kill one of the most dangerous sorcerers to ever threaten Allansia! None other than the infamous Balthus Dire!

Now, The Citadel of Chaos is a bit different to City of Thieves. Whereas in City of Thieves you play a fairly typical hero, in The Citadel of Chaos you get to play a warrior mage. One of the most crucial steps you make if you're creating your own character is choosing which spells to take of the twelve available, and how many of them. Having rolled my character and made my selection of spells, I braced myself for the coming dangers with another cup of tea (or was it my fifth, I can't remember) and set off into Balthus Dire's fortress. I penetrated my way deep into the citadel and it wasn't long before I was dead. Hmm, not off to a good start. Settling down with another cuppa, I attempted to defeat the denizens of the citadel once more and... died. With time running out I decided that I will return to The Citadel of Chaos another day and I WILL defeat Blathus Dire.

Overall, *The Citadel of Chaos* is a great read, but I think it's a lot tougher than *City of Thieves*. There are plenty of opportunities to get in a fight if you so choose to, but that's not what this book is all about. To succeed you must select your spells wisely (Creature Copy is a brilliant spell and saved my bacon on more than one occasion, I know, not enough to complete the quest though!), and make plenty of notes. The book is littered with incredibly detailed and sinister illustrations by Russ Nicolson. If you want a real challenge and also want the chance to fling some spells, then *The Citadel of Chaos* is for you.

Stormslayer - Jonathan Green
Firstly, I must state that *Stormslayer* is massive! Although it has the same amount of numbered paragraph entries as the previous two books, there is a lot going in this book. Also, unlike the first two books, the adventure is not set on the continent of Alansia, but in the Old World (check out your copy of *Titan* for details). In addition, it is an entirely new adventure! No mere reprint here.

In this book, as in the others, you get you choice of three pre-generated characters or creating your own. I decided to play Gorrin Silverblade, as his description reminded me of a fantasy Indiana Jones. You also get to choose two magical items as well as your mystical sword, Wyrmbiter. Of course, as I chose a pregenerated character, my items were already chosen for me. These items, by the way, have a bearing on the adventure as it unfolds.

In this adventure you find yourself on the trail of a renegade elementalist, who has created an elemental device capable of destroying the realm. Your quest leads all over the land (and under the ocean), as you seek out the items you require to defeat him and the elementals at his command. Not only that but it's also a race against time! The whole adventure has a truly epic feel to it and barrels along at a great pace, as you race across the land, gaining items and making allies.

Jonathan Green has penned a really great adventure worthy of Jackson and Livingstone. It really captures all the things I love about Fighting Fantasy, danger, excitement, great puzzles, vivid descriptions of incredible places and vile villains!
Furthermore, Green's words are ably accompanied by the incredible illustrations of Stephen Player.

Have I completed my quest? No, but I can't wait to give it another go!

If you're in the mood to treat yourself then you can't go wrong with any of these great Fighting Fantasy game books. Adventure awaits at the turn of a page!

Brady Webb

Originally published in Mass Movement #26, March 2010

STARBLAZER

FANTASY FICTION IN PICTURES No. 204

28p

THE ROBOT KID

CONFESSIONS OF A STARBLAZER JUNKIE

Mandroid. Starhawk. Hadron Halley. The Planet Tamer. The Suicide Squad. The Robot Kid.

If these names are familiar to you, then chances are that your childhood was similarly marked by an insatiable taste for comics that seemed only to exist so they could annoy parents and Daily Mail readers everywhere.

I still recall the adrenaline-driven years of 2000AD, Scream and Battle Action with a melancholic sigh, but the early eighties saw this habit punctuated by a sci-fi companion to those Commando pocketbooks you used to find everywhere: the Starblazer.

Baring the somewhat clumsy subheading "Space Fiction Adventure In Pictures", Starblazer charged out of the DC Thompson stable and rode the crest of the sci-fi tsunami that followed in the wake of Star Wars with two monthly issues to keep aficionados sated. But unlike Commando, Starblazers were fairly hard to find. Publication seemed to be sporadic, and you really had to scour local newsagents to hunt copies down. Despite this it still enjoyed a pretty good run, lasting for 281 issues between 1979 and 1991.

Throughout its twelve year lifespan, Starblazer featured some surprisingly well-known names. Grant Morrison, Walter Cyril, Henry Reed, John Smith, Mike Chinn, Mike McMahon, Colin Mac-Neil, Cam Kennedy and John Ridgway all worked on the title, although only the eagle-eyed or well informed would have been able to tell due to DC Thompson's reluctance to credit authors and artists. They relented somewhat in the dying days of the strip by including a 12-episode 'definitive history' column starting in issue 268 which provided the missing details.

Initially, only a single issue a month was published for the first three months, presumably to allow DC Thompson to test the market. But the sci-fi boom that had ushered in the likes of 2000AD secured Starblazer's future, and output was increased to two issues a month from issue four onwards.

The very first Starblazer story was *The Omega Experiment*. With hindsight, it is a little bland in depiction, but it succeeds in setting the tone, subjects and theories that would forever be explored in future issues. Testing an experimental transporter, Lute Fireball (!) finds himself on a world populated by robots who amuse themselves by creating weird cyborg creatures in vats of flesh, Terminator-style. Lute escapes after enduring many fiendish experiments and gladiatorial bouts with just enough time left to plant a bomb and arrange a rescue. Androids, laser guns, spaceships, monsters... all the main ingredients were there from the start as the Starblazer cannon unfolded, and variations on these themes would crop up again and again.

One aspect that Starblazer really excelled in was dodgy science. It was applied wherever possible to dead stars, star gates, worm holes - anything that allowed characters to go dimension-hopping, and always handy when escaping from enemy fighters or ambushing villains. Sneak alien invasions as seen in *Robots of Death* were also popular, especially if a long-forgotten hero returned to lead Earth to victory. Perhaps the best example of this was the King Arthur-ish *Space Warrior*. Escaped criminal geniuses planned the downfall of the universe in tales such as *The Tomb Of Tara* while futuristic fortress communities were attacked by hostile forces in *The Siege of Seabed City* and *The Battle For Beacon Bravo*. Amazing alien landscapes quickly became a selling point - who could resist the dreaded *Acid Seas of Koga*, or the ten-mile trees of *Terror Planet*?

STARBLAZER

SPACE FICTION ADVENTURE IN PICTURES No.1

12p
AUS 40c NZ

THE OMEGA EXPERIMENT

Wild aliens were also very much in evidence. Some of the best designs appeared in the energetic *Terror Tomb,* where a terra-forming team discover a cool Alien-type creature imprisoned in a weird craft. As with its cinematic inspiration, the alien UFO looks suitably disturbing, but this time stops short of resembling female genitalia.

Unfortunately, the majority of space ships were usually rather clunky-looking efforts emphasising huge phallic engines (my warp drive is bigger than yours?), and often differed in design from frame to frame. Exceptions included the titular Fortress Of Fear, fabulous mushroom-shaped domain of dreaded Mekon rip-offs, the Mind Lords.

With only so many galaxies, evil villains, noble heroes and basic storylines to be explored before the format become stale, the early issues of Starblazer were soon in danger of burning themselves out. After all, the plots and settings of the war-time Commando pocketbooks had merely been moved into space, with the human race replacing allied forces and alien scumbags taking the role of the dastardly Hun.

A solution of sorts was found with the introduction of overlapping storylines and recurring characters. Fi-Sci, the Fighting Scientists, became a regular 'Star Fleet' style organisation that served as a point of reference across a number of Starblazer tales. The concept allowed the characters to court danger and demonstrate big brains while exploring new worlds, developing deadly weapons or testing new spaceships - and then gave them the muscle to thrash any bad guy who got in their way. A case in point is *The Serpents of Sirius*, where a mining operation discovers huge Dune-like worms and an alien plot. Fi-Sci later turns to science to give both aliens and serpents a good bashing.

The Suicide Squad were a team of disgraced soldiers who specialised in dirty work and had a leader who was constantly sickened by the horrors of futuristic warfare. They graced the likes of *Rigel Express, Doomrock, Alien Invasion* and *The D Team*. Matt Tallis was a Galactic Security Service agent in *The Immortals, The Mask of Fear* and *The Megaloi Menace*. His main feature was unusual strength gifted to him by being born on a low-gravity colony world, and a telepathic link with his faithful android sidekick.

Fi-Sci boasted their own hero in Hadron Halley. He graced no fewer than nine Starblazers including *The Torturer of Triton II, Moonsplitter* and *Nightmare Ship*. Clipping him with appearances in 13 issues, though, was Frank Carter AKA the Mandroid. Not quite a cyborg, Frank was a normal police officer until he received a blast to the head and underwent experimental cybernetic surgery. He gained super strength and reactions, but lost his emotions, making him a particularly brutal cop. His tales boasted hardboiled titles that spoke for themselves - *Rough Justice, Desolation City, Rogue Mandroid* and *Carter's Fury*, for example.

Topping the league, however, was Mikal R Kayn (arcane - geddit?), another police officer injured in the line of duty. This time the main characters' eyes were burned out, forcing Kayne to wear special glasses to 'see' in infrared. Kayne featured in 16 issues of Starblazer, including *Citizen Kayn* (groan) and *Convict Kayn*. Kayne also teamed up with deadly female warrior Cinnibar, who herself appeared in three solo Starblazer outings, all based around her frontier home world of Babalon.

Starhawk was about a freelance adventurer named Sol Rynn who leaves distress cards dotted around the galaxy for those who need his help. Originally a flagship strip in DC Thompson's short-lived Crunch comic, *Starhawk* hit its stride in the pages of Starblazer. With a robot called

Droid and a space ship that could be summoned by remote control, Sol fought the evil alien Krells as they raided the crumbing Human Empire. Another lone wolf-style hero was Solo, a passenger on a universe-hopping spaceship whose peers died in a suspended-animation accident that left him the sole owner of an entire planet. The only snag was that advancing technology meant the planet was populated by the time Solo's ship got there.

In later issues, Starblazer dropped the sci-fi approach in favour of stories with a greater fantasy element (the subheading also changed to "Fantasy Fiction In Pictures"). This shift in focus gave rise to a quartet of stories about Skald, a young man living on a grim techno-feudal world ruled over by evil Warlocks. The Anglerre series was also set in a fantasy kingdom and followed a royal family across five issues as they dealt with war, magicians and demonic swords.

In the mid-eighties, Starblazer tried its hand as a 'fighting fantasy' role-playing strip. Again, it came with a new subheading, this time the even clumsier "Space Role Playing Game In Pictures". The strip required readers to flick back and forth between frames, and didn't prove to be very popular. It wasn't long before Starblazer quietly dropped the idea and returned to what it did best.

A more humorous angle was present in the later issues. Grok and Zero were police officers thrown together for a series of crazed adventures in the likes of *The Pirates of Penz-Anz* and *Beastworld*. The Robot Kid was a particularly inspired creation from Mike Chinn, and originated from DC Thompson's request for Chinn to come up with something that could rival the ABC Warriors *Meknificent Seven* storyline in 2000AD. Chinn imagined a lawless, Wild West-style planet where a group of colonists order a deadly Dethmek war droid to protect themselves from bandit attacks. What they get is a reprogrammed cinema usher robot with an encyclopaedic knowledge of cowboy movies. Second and third instalments parodied Kung Fu flicks and the Rambo series, and there were two further strips that sadly never saw print - *The Prisoner of Zante* (spoofing swashbucklers) and Robat (reputedly a parody of the first Tim Burton Batman movie).

The *Planet Tamer* series was a Starblazer gem that helped to hook me on the title. It featured a lone half-lawman-half-machine who travelled space on a flying motorbike, seeking out evil... what's not to like about that? His best was Galactic Lawman, a breakneck tale of escaped alien prisoners, ravaged planets and psychic villains able to summon forth towering monsters from the Id. *Planet Tamer* and *Return of the Planet Tamer* were good, but not quite as pacy.

So which were the best Starblazer stories?

It all comes down to personal taste, but *Operation Overkill* would definitely have my vote. This featured satanic villain Alta who escapes from prison and heads straight for Weapon World, the dumping ground for a peaceful universe's now-useless death machines. Using passing meteorite storm the Starhammer to stall his pursuers, Alta starts warming up the technological terrors found in this devil's playground.

Hot on his heels is a plucky ex-agent who circumnavigates the Starhammer and ends up facing a scary (and brilliantly rendered) Slaughtermek droid. The showdown sees Alta roasted by a handy atomiser some careless clerk has left lying around. After all, pick up what looks like a pebble on a planet of deadly weapons and you might find yourself wielding a bone-dismantling robot death-doorstop (outlawed on Charnok II, naturally).

My other all-time fave Starblazer has to be the classic future war epic *Killer Clones*. Humans locked in stalemate with warring Morgons on a strategically important planet come under threat from vast swarms of, erm, killer clones. Violent and savage, these mindless beasts resemble scaly gorillas and use cool weapons like acid gas, which allows for gratuitously gory images of flesh sliding from bones.

A reprogrammed enemy robot smuggles an attack squad into the Morgon base to reverse the orders of the clones. Key Morgon positions are successfully destroyed and the enemy space fleet gets a good kicking, allowing the humans to go home victorious. They leave the killer clones behind to live out their 48 hour life span. I know it doesn't sound like much, but the story moves at a fair old clip, the art is strong and there are some immortal lines, not least the one that follows the destruction of the reprogrammed droid: "You were a great guy, robot!"

There were a few Starblazers that I inevitably missed out on. Two that looked really interesting were *Space Ghost*, which boasted a spooky intergalactic Marie Celeste on the cover, and *Space Samurai*, which featured cool cover art of a laser-sword wielding Japanese warrior. I actually bought a copy of the latter, but lost it during a day trip to Barry Island Funfair. Moral of the story: never take a comic on the Waltzer.

I often thought about Starblazer as I grew older, but by the time I decided to try and seek them out again, they were long gone. The sci-fi boom had well and truly passed, reader tastes had moved on and the days of the Starblazer were finally over. Okay, so the artwork was sometimes dodgy, the dialogue stilted, the concepts silly and the outcomes predictable... but boy, were they fun to read.

It took me a long time to wean myself off the habit, but a big part of my childhood memories will always involve crouching beside my bike, waiting out the rain beneath a clump of trees with an issue or two in my hand. So rest in peace, Starblazer. You served us well.

Liam Ronan

Originally published in Mass Movement #26, March 2010

BRIAN POSEHN

It's a given that as a species, we all see ourselves as individuals, yet follow our basic biological urge to gather in tribal and social groups, identifying ourselves on wider scale with the title that the social grouping or tribe has been tagged with, and conforming to the behavioural patterns that have been established within the "tribe". As each tribe grows, occasionally a figurehead or spokesman appears, a leader figure without power, one with whom all the members of said tribe can identify. For those of us lucky enough to be members of the mid-thirties thrashers who are sort of settled down and still enjoy shows, comic books and other assorted "fringe" activities, Brian Posehn is the man. Hell, the guy is so damn funny, he's broken through the tribal boundaries and even "normal" folks dig him, and when the chance to speak to El Hefe was offered, I rose to the challenge. All hail the leader, we love the leader...

Interview by Tim Cundle

MM: How did you get your initial start in comedy?

Brian: I was 19 or 20 and I had a couple of friends who told me I should give it a shot. I'd never even been in a comedy club at that point. The one thing that I could do at that age was to write jokes, so I looked on it as doing research because I couldn't go in a comedy club until I was 21. So the week I turned 21, I went straight down to the comedy club and did the 5 minutes I had been working on and just had a blast. The second time I completely hated –but then still loved it.

MM: Which is tougher: doing standing up or doing TV and films?

Brian: I think stand up is harder, typically. Whenever I talk to actors about stand up they all are amazed that I do it as it's seen by everybody as one of the toughest things you can do, because you're putting yourself out there. When you're acting it's not as personal, there are lots of other people involved. But with stand up it's just you. If it sucks you suck.

MM: Which was cooler for you: Being in the *Devil's Rejects* or being in the video for *What Doesn't Die*?

Brian: That's a good question! They're both pretty cool. I've pretty much got to live the metal dream, I'm very lucky. I liked the rejects, it's always been my dream to be in a horror film – you get to kill or be killed.

MM: How did you hook up with Relapse? It's kind of unusual for a comedian to be on a metal label...

Brian: Yeah. I don't know if you're familiar with a comedian called David Cross, he's an old friend of mine, he and some other comedians I know went on a whole variety of labels including Sub Pop and that kind of stuff. So when I did my record, I self-produced it and decided to go to a label – right away I knew I wanted to go to a metal label straight away so I had a short list which I gave to my manager who also spoke to the indie rock labels who weren't really interested because they knew that I was going to be recording music with Scott Ian, so it was going to be metal in the way it sounded. Before he could even get to the list, Relapse got wind that I was going to be in Philadelphia and asked if we could have a meeting. This guy really impressed me, he started the label up basically from his garage. I really liked what they did and the kind of bands they put out.

MM: What's the most metal thing that has ever happened to you?

Brian: The most metal? Getting to be involved with the Revolver awards out here in the States, and doing the Golden Gods, getting to host one year. I think it was probably the first year I hosted because I got to meet Dio, and we actually did a bit for the TV show at my house with Dio and Scott Ian and loads of others. Even though Scott has been my friend for a while, it's still surreal because I used to be an Anthrax fan when I was a kid and then I get to have Dio come to my house!

MM: Why Short Round? Why did you name your number one boy after a small Oriental Sidekick?

Brian: Just because it's silly (laughing). That's the kind of thing that makes me laugh. When I thought of calling my penis Short Round it made me laugh out loud. That's how something makes it into the act. If it makes me laugh it's got to be worth doing.

MM: Does shouting Slayer really make it okay?

Brian: (laughing) It's the same thing really. It's so ridiculous that it just made me laugh when I came up with that concept and people seem to love it. It's a joke that really does well, and it's a joke that does well for people who don't even know Slayer because it's so surreal. What I love is that Slayer fans really don't get it – they think I'm taking the piss out of them and saying they're gay, but Slayer is so very far from gay that the idea that if you perform a gay act but scream Slayer when you're doing it somehow makes it not gay is so ridiculous.

MM: Why *Fart &Weiner Jokes* Brian? Why call the album that?

Brian: It's just something that was funny to me as a kid, and it's always gonna be funny to me. The record is more than that, but calling it Fart Weiner and releasing this material it's just a cool joke. *Fart & Weiner Jokes* just rolls off the tongue. The last record I named *Nerd Rage* after one of the jokes; so I was going through the record, looking at what the joke titles were and one of the things that I say at the start of the show is that I don't consider myself to be only low-brow, I do a mixture of smart and crucially dumb. I kind of tell myself to lower their expectations as all that's coming is a load of fart and wiener jokes – which isn't entirely true but it's a way of letting people know what to expect and I think the album title does the same thing: opening the show by saying "If you like fart and weiner jokes - this is for you"!

MM: Your show is really open, frank and at times brutal. Is there anything that you consider taboo?

Brian: Yeah, there are topics – I'm trying to think about topics that I just wouldn't touch. I guess for me, I don't really talk about politics and religion much because that's just not what I like to do. I like to shock people a little bit with the dirtiness, but I really don't want to alienate people. I used to talk about religion – I did a joke on my last album about it, but I prefaced it , I mean just bringing it up you're gonna lose half the audience. I'm not in comedy to offend people I just like to have fun. So I guess those two things are the things I tread lightly around purely because they're not my thing.

MM: You mention comic books on your record and seeing as you co-wrote the *Last Christmas* for Image, are you planning to go back to write more comic books?

Brian: For sure. I've been working on a concept for a while with the same guy that I wrote the other book with, my buddy Jerry – he wrote a really great book for image last year called *Horizon*. He and I are working on a super hero book. It's the kind of thing that would be ongoing not just a 4 or 5 book story arc. We'd love to get a book going for Image comics where we work on it for a couple of years, so we're working on the idea. But it's a tough thing because with Image you have to put up your own money, and there isn't really any money in comic books so we've got other things going on. I don't know how comic book riders take on more than one volume in one month, it's a hell of a lot of work.

MM: All comic book folks are always Marvel or DC. Which are you?

Brian: I'm a weird guy. Even as a kid I didn't make that choice. My first two heroes that I was really into were Batman and Spiderman. They were my two favourites. I have a ton of Marvel, I have a ton of DC I don't think it really matters. I've always loved them equally – I love their history and keep up with both of them currently. It's like – being a metal head and all that, that's not all I listen to too: sure I was wearing a Testament T-Shirt in the '80s but I was also listening to the Pixies. I've always been that guy. I've never just got into one thing and gone "this is it! This is all I am!"

MM: What bugs you about the phrase "Party like a rock star"? Why is it so annoying?

Brian: I just don't like when people repeat stuff – I'm a writer, I don't like anybody just repeating a cliché weather it's "Talk to the hand" or "Don't go there" or any of those phrases that become popular in language. They've just always annoyed me and that's what it all about. I mean, "Party like a rock star is so lame" people go to Vegas and use it as an excuse to be really gross and behave like animals and think it's okay. It's the same with "What happens in Vegas, stays in Vegas" kind of an excuse to be a scumbag, but you are using this "clever" phrase – except it's not clever because somebody else thought it up and it's been regurgitated a thousand times. Things like that really annoy me.

MM: Is night digging ever acceptable? And if so, under what circumstances?

Brian: (laughing) Yeah if you have a lot of property and nobody can see you. It's one of those things that when I was thinking about things that I just can't do because of my size and because of the way I look and it just really made me laugh. The idea of my neighbour looking over the fence and seeing me digging: he would alert a constable.

MM: How did you get the *Abracadabra Doo* voiceover gig?

Brian: That was really cool, it was just one of those things. I did an audition and they said "would you be interested in playing a villain in Scooby Doo?" I just said "Well.. YES" – it's just one of those iconic things. Growing up here with Scooby Doo that's one of the cartoons I was into when I was very little, and the villains always the best part with the "I'll get you" so I had to do it.

MM: As a self-confessed "nerd", what does the term mean to you?

Brian: Nerd, geek and dork are all kind of interchangeable. For me it's just about being obsessed with something, loving what I love and being into something in a way that other people don't get. Other people have hobbies, nerds have obsessions. By calling yourself a nerd you are accepting who you are.

MM: Does Wikipedia ever get it right or is it always wrong?

Brian: (laughs) All wrong. I left a thing up there that said I was a classical piano, I love putting it all up.. I do a lot of radio when I'm on tour, I go on the morning shows to promote my show when it comes into town and one said "So.. do you play a little classical piano" it was so funny. So don't believe everything you read.

MM: How do you feel about Hecklers and what's the best heckle you ever had?

Brian: I'm lucky in that I don't get heckled a lot. I had one recently, a guy in Chicago just laughing at the wrong stuff and it was just wrong so it really threw me off my rhythm. He threw me for a second because it was so weird. I'm very lucky, I get the kind of heckles that when you talk to them later I call them helpers because that's what they always think they are doing. They're having a blast they love you and they just want to get involved and participate. That Slayer sketch we were talking about earlier is a classic example. You'll find that long after that joke is over, people will continue to shout out Slayer for the next hour. They think they are being funny or helping.

MM: How's the album gone down so far?

Brian: It's getting a good response from people. I was the number one comedy record on Billboard which didn't happen last time. I had a good couple of first weeks and people will hopefully continue to check it out. The video will be out soon then I will be touring with the live show and hopefully people will check it out.

MM: So what's next for you Brian?

Brian: I think I'm doing Knebworth, which I think will be the greatest thing I've ever done. It will be wholly British comics except for me. It's certainly going to be an experience. Do you really want your first time over there to be a gig like that? I mean wouldn't it be better to be over there and do a couple of comedy clubs first to get to know the audience and make it more conducive to comedy instead of turning up cold in front of 10,000 metal heads. Although I feel like I have metal head love but that only gets you two minutes before people start shouting "You suck"...

Originally published in Mass Movement #27, July 2010

CRIME IN STEREO

The last time I interviewed Crime In Stereo they were in between albums, on a European tour with New Found Glory and very unsure of their future. Since then they have released another album that has stepped further away from their Hardcore punk roots, but closer to mainstream success. *I Was Trying to Describe You to Someone* was released by Bridge Nine Records this year to critical acclaim, and has garnered the band rave reviews in the mainstream rock press, festival appearances and tours with Glassjaw and Brand New. I spoke to guitarist Alex before their headline show at Le Pub in Newport.

Interview by Leigh McAndrew

Photo by Meghan McInnis

MM: Last time I interviewed you my final question was "what does the future hold for Crime In Stereo" and you said that you'd either "blow the fuck up or break the fuck up". Which one at this point do you feel that you're closer to?

Alex: That's actually a phenomenal question that I really don't have an answer for. I would say that it could go either way at any minute.

MM: You've just played some big tours in America, you supported Brand New and Glassjaw and now you're headlining a UK tour, so I'm guessing at the moment you feel that you're working more towards the former than the latter...

Alex: Yeah, we're doing all the big festivals over here like Download and Reading & Leeds and everything. Again, I don't know that I have an answer for that.

MM: The latest album (*I Was Trying To Describe You To Someone*) is even more experimental than the album which came before (*Is Dead*). Was it a conscious decision to be more experimental or was that something that naturally came from jamming?

Alex: Yeah, it comes more out of just messing around and the desire to not want to do the same thing twice. We don't set out to be the most experimental band or anything because obviously we are not going to be. We're not going to end up being like Rush or fucking Yes or The Mars Volta or some band like that. Here's the thing; people misconstrue personal experiment with the idea that as a band we're trying to be the fucking craziest band on the planet. That's not the case, we're not the best musicians on the planet, we're never going to be and again we're not going to be Rush or anything like that, we don't even want to be. We just want to push ourselves personally, we want to get better. We want to be better musicians; we want to be better at what we do than what we had been previously. What people are seeing as experimentation; it is, but it's us pushing our own personal boundaries, not trying to make some grand statement of 'we're going to change music' because we're not and we don't have any delusions that we are.

MM: I suppose it's a natural progression – starting off as a punk band, growing older and trying to break away from the boundaries of punk music and go in different ways.

Alex: Yeah, at this point we would have to make a seriously conscious effort to still play punk music, because we've just moved beyond that to a great extent and our skills as musicians, the various things we do whether it's drums or vocals or guitars, just where we're naturally at, we're doing other things than playing blast-beats and punk songs. So it would take a conscious effort for us to make a punk record. The truth is that us making a Hardcore record would be far more insincere than us doing what we do because it's not what comes naturally to us anymore.

MM: I spoke to you before about how it seems strange that your older punk records were on different labels and then you moved to Bridge Nine, a label known for Hardcore and you've experimented with your sound whilst on the Bridge Nine roster. Do you think that your band has helped Bridge Nine to open the door to what they can have on their label? Since Crime In Stereo they have signed bands like Polar Bear Club and Lemuria...

Alex: I'd like to think so, I'd hate to speak for them, but I do think they had a standard Hardcore roster before we arrived and I don't know that it's because of us, probably not. I think the fact that they signed us was indicative of the fact that's where they wanted to go. I think they had it in their heads that they wanted to branch out, so like 'Crime In Stereo fits the bill' and then 'Polar Bear Club fits the bill' and then Lemuria and all the other things they've done whether it's New Found Glory. Even Strike Anywhere and Paint It Black. I like to think that we've kind of helped them out, hopefully as much as they've helped us out, but I don't it's because of us but I think we were the first salvo in them wanting to branch out, which is awesome. You can't do the same thing forever.

MM: As far as being 'experimental', the artwork for the latest record is not what you'd expect from a punk band...

Alex: Do you hate it?

MM: I don't hate it, I'm just not sure I 'get' it, I can't work it out.

Alex: I don't really want to talk about the artwork, if that's all right? I know there's a lot of people out there who don't like it, that's cool, it's their opinion and they're welcome to it, I am very happy with it.

MM: You're in the touring cycle for the latest record now, have you started to think about writing new material?

Alex: I'm working on some songs only because I'm always working on songs. We don't say that we're going to write a record and then sit down and write it. I play my guitar every day and write pretty much every day, I'm always writing stuff, so we have some songs. We feel like we're at the very beginning with this record, *I Was Trying To Describe You To Someone*, so we're not even thinking about a new record. We love working in the studio, so we feel that if you put us in the studio any day then we'll give you our best effort and hopefully some really good material so we feel that we could go and make songs at any minute, but we don't have any plans to record or anything like that.

MM: Bridge Nine brought out their compilation last year and you gave them the song *War*. Didn't you write that song in the studio specifically for that comp?

Alex: We were going to do a cover, but the artist's lawyers said that we couldn't. We were working on the cover when we found out we couldn't do it and the pressing deadline for the compilation was the Monday morning, so our track had to be done by Sunday night, and we found out that we couldn't do the cover on the Friday. So we basically wrote the song on the Friday in the studio, tracked it on the Saturday, mixed it Sunday and sent it off Monday morning to be mastered. It's a strange song.

MM: I really, really like that song...

Alex: I like that song too. What's weird is that Scotty had plans or something that day, so wasn't planning on tracking and he came in, and there's basically only one drum beat in that song and he literally tracked that beat and left. It was all we had to work with so it was a crazy experience. Scotty basically gave us just one beat and we had no fills or changes, so we had one beat to work with and me and Kristian just sat down and started fucking around. The acoustic that you hear at the end of the song was me just playing that riff, Kristian just started singing that part and the mic happened to be running. We listened back and were like 'wow, that's great' and we built the song out of that. So that part that you hear at the end was off the top of our heads, just messing around and that was where the song came from.

MM: There are acoustic parts to songs on the new album that I'm guessing came about after the session writing *War*...

Alex: It feels good that we don't have to think 'well this isn't punk' or whatever. When we were doing Troubled Stateside we were trying to kind of push the boundaries of a Hardcore record, but we were still very much constrained and actually even on *Is Dead* there were still a lot of constraints where we would be like "Oh, how are people going to react to this" and by the new record we just didn't give a fuck. We were like "Let's do our own thing, who cares?"

MM: You were going to open Is Dead with a slower song, *Let Me Take You Out*, which ended up on *Selective Wreckage*. What were the reasons for leaving it off *Is Dead*?

Alex: I fucking love that song, I have such a soft spot in my heart for that song. Yeah, it was supposed to be on *Is Dead*, and so really was *Everywhere and All the Time*. *Let Me Take You Out* got finished, *Everywhere and All the Time* didn't. If they were both done then they both would've gone on Is Dead as they would've balanced each other out, but with *Is Dead* only being eleven songs, and we already had *Orbitor* and *Unfortunate Tourists*, we felt that *Let Me Take You Out* would've slowed the record down a little too much. That basically would've been a quarter of the record being slow, drawn out songs, so for that reason we decided to leave it off.

MM: When you're recording new songs, do you think about how it's going to go over in a live setting, like in a sweaty pub tonight?

Alex: We figured out with the new stuff how we were going to perform it live, but we didn't think "are kids going to be able to stage dive to this?" We feel that, with the new stuff, we were able to perform them live quickly, compared to the *Is Dead* songs which took us so long to be able to perform well live. We kind of recorded *Is Dead* beyond our means, so it took as a little while to nail it live every night, whereas with the new record we were very conscious about what our abilities and limitations were. We weren't think about whether kids could mosh to it. If you want to mosh or stage dive or whatever there are a million bands that do that better than we ever did anyway.

Originally published in Mass Movement #27, July 2010

JOE KEITHLEY
(D.O.A.)

DOA probably (as far as I'm concerned anyways) the best punk rock band in the world, have recently sent their thirteenth studio album, *Talk – Action = 0*, which gave me a perfect excuse (like I needed one anyways) to phone Joey Keithley to play catch up and chat about all things DOA

Interview by Tim Cundle

Photos by Bev Davies, Kevin Staitham & Michael Loccisano

MM: What have you guys been up to between *Northern Avenger* and *Talk Minus Action*? (I know there was a hockey album in the middle eh?)

Joe: We recorded two new tracks for that. It was just a thing for Canada; to reassert ourselves as kings of the ice hockey world... that DOA was the equivalent of it you know (laughing) Basically we've done a lot of tours. We went to China in January '09 and went to Europe although unfortunately not to the UK we're hoping to do that next year, but we did festivals in Germany. Then we recorded another album then there was another big tour, and we've just got back from that, then we're heading off to the States in about a week. I also wrote the book...You know the book and the movie *Hardcore Logo*? Well a friend of mine, he's theatrical and he's written a theatrical version of it so we had a lot of fun thinking about actors that could be punk rockers which took a while, then we had to try to train them how to play the part.

MM: *Hardcore Logo* is loosely based on you guys right...?

Joe: Yeah, the first quarter of the book really follows the DOA storyline, so the association makes sense.

MM: A lot of the reviews for *Talk Minus Action* have said that it's kind of your roots album; do you think that's a valid comment?

Joe: I think that's a fair assessment. This album has a bit less production – and I mean that in a good way. It's a lot looser; we wrote the songs and then we rehearsed it for a bit then went into the studio, and the good thing is that we would use an entire tape, we wouldn't cut it up with pro tools to create something on the tape that we couldn't play – we just played it so the whole thing was really loose.

MM; So the whole thing has a bit more of a live feeling...

Joe: Yeah... I think it's important with our kind of music, or with any great rock music. You can take it into the studio and give it some production, take in extra tracks, lay over guitar tracks and so on but in the end you've gotta have the sound coming from a place like you mean it. I think we've done that.

MM: What I've found funny about the album is that you've got an Ode to Star Trek. Are you Star Trek fans at all?

Joe: It was big when I was a kid and then I started watching it again recently. What I liked about that was when writing the lyrics – so opposed to modern day heroes and personalities where everything is about what you have, the bling and so on you can write about a fictional character who goes out and does the right thing just because it's the right thing. And that's very important. So for me it's like, okay, this is so much different to the heroes of today; they do it because it's the right thing, not for money.

MM: There's a song on the new album called *Don't Bank on a Bank*. Do you think the banking collapse and the financial ruin that followed were inevitable?

Joe: Sure. If you think about the banks in Europe and the United States and the government response, they were all about greed. It's a great idea that people can build on their house, but I don't think that in your or my lifetime because the disparity in wealth between those who have money and those who don't just gets wider and you can't put people in houses if they've got no money. Some of these people – it's not their fault they have no money. They are paying for kids or school or whatever. It's the same, endemic over here where the real poor people ending up staying in the same house for a long time, that's not bad, not like you should move a lot unless you have to do it for your job. It just is exasperating that the administration does nothing to help these people. As long as their buddies are getting rich, who gives a fuck right?

MM: *RCMP* is obviously a song about police brutality. Do you think that is ever going to end or is there an endless cycle of the police doing exactly what they want when they want?

Joe: There's been a case lately, which is what *RCMP* is written about, that said there was no discipline, no oversight and also they've gotten to be fully happy with their tazers. There was an incident recently where they arrested a guy who didn't speak any English and they locked him up without talking to him for 11 hours. So they left him there and he's waiting 10-11 hours to find out what's going on and within 30 seconds of them opening the cell door they had tazered him. The police were saying he had a weapon but when they checked afterwards he didn't have a weapon they were just too quick to act. If you're gonna be a cop, dealing with people is part of the job. You have to tackle people and talk to them and get to the bottom of what's going on. So this song is about police brutality but also about the report in Canada on the conduct of the RCMP.

MM: Do you think the album title is prophetic –that talk without action really is useless?

Joe: My whole thing is that change happens naturally. If you have a good idea and you tell your friends, your neighbours, your papers, your school or the people down the block and if it is a good idea and it can affect a change people it will create a groundswell in the local people. Once you have that locally you can build it from there.

MM: Do you think that one man or one woman can make a difference?

Joe: Yeah, incrementally. Obviously some people can change things more than others. Everybody can make a difference. It may not feel like much but it's worth trying. It's something I want to put out there – do not give up.

MM: It's nearly 33 years of DOA now isn't it Joe?

Joe: 32. It was Feb 10th the first show we ever did. I really thought that DOA was a really good platform for our ideas and we have fun doing it. We have fun travelling around, we have a good laugh. If we can go somewhere new as well - like when we went to China recently that was great and we went to Brazil and Argentina- so if that's your fun, we're men of action –then this is the life for you (laughing)

MM: DOA are widely credited with giving the Hardcore scene its name. How do you think the Hardcore scene has changed since the '80s and how do you think it compares to the '80s heyday...?

Joe: I think pretty much that the whole term has changed. Kids will say anything is Hardcore – you really have to make the distinction now by calling it Hardcore punk, where Hardcore is a lot nastier and trashier than mainstream punk. I think that Hardcore is alive and well but I think that it's changed a lot– which has to happen. First of all the change in punk fashion, but the sounds then were a lot different from the sounds 10 years later – things have to evolve – just remember that 20 years after punk was reviled you have Blink 180 having a number one single. I would have hoped that everyone involved in Hardcore would still have that revolutionary spirit which is the heart of the whole thing. It was part of what I liked about the early days of punk. I know you say that we popularised that phrase but really it just came out of our desire to be original.

MM: Do you think that punk rock is still a force for good in that it promotes a sense of political awareness, activism and self-awareness?

Joe: Absolutely. It requires empowerment as part of the movement. Political awareness empowerment, whatever you want to call it, these were all the kind of things that we wanted when we got started. We wanted to reflect a real free spirit. I think that now there are kids out there who hopefully have the same attitude, and they are there among the big bands. There are some good big bands. But you see it when you go out and about before the shows and talk to people. There are people involved in the anti-war movement, in the environmental movement and that's punk right?

MM: Tell us all about DOA day in Vancouver...

Joe: That was really funny. My friend just woke up and said he had an idea for the 25th anniversary. We would get a school –go to the city centre and get a school and asked if we could put on the show so we did and basically we picked up the mike afterwards and read out all this stuff like "On this day DOA did play " and "In the year... DOA won this" etc. It was a cool thing. The city helped us out to do that.

MM: How does it feel to be voted one of British Columbia's most influential people of all time?

Joe: That was really surprising. I know they had this poll, there were like 150 names on it and it was our 30th anniversary. There were a lot of writers on the list. Some dead, some almost dead and there I was with all of them I didn't really consider myself worthy to be on that list, but there I was and people where voting for me. So obviously, I think it's one of those things like with the DOA day that people realise that they really like DOA – they may not own any records, but they have really liked what they have heard.

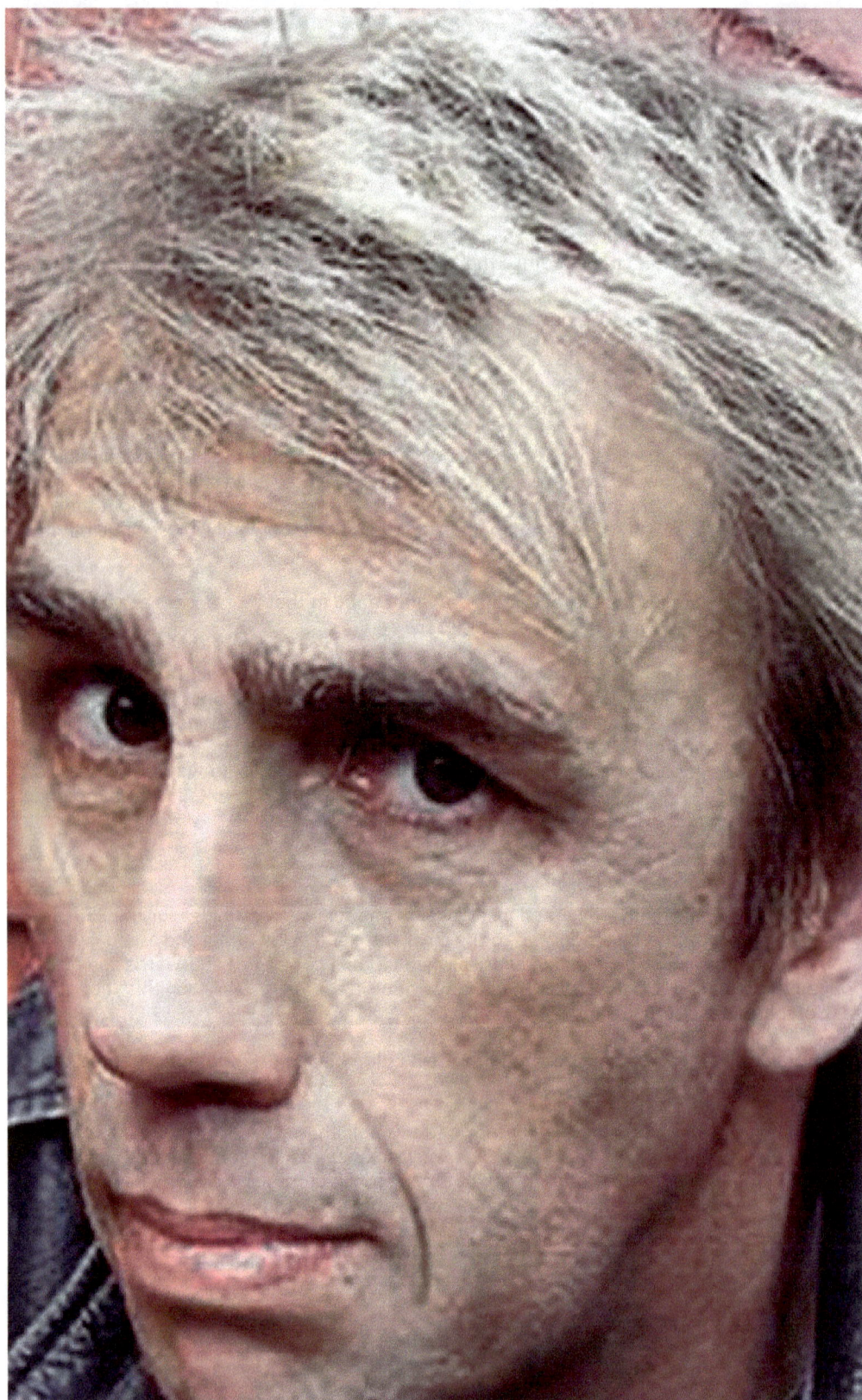

MM: it's been nearly six years since *I Shithead* was released. Are you going to write another book?

Joe: As a matter of fact in about two hours I will be in a meeting with the publisher of that book to talk about the next book. It won' be out by the Fall but hopefully January, February. What it's going to be is pictures. Posters stories – so you may get a picture and it will have a story to go with it or a poster – not very long winded but a quarter page, half page something like that. Together, the pictures and the stories will tell the story of the whole of DOA.

MM: I wanted to ask you about Sudden Death. It was kind of a part time thing for twenty odd years and now it's become a full time thing. With the rise of technology and the advance of the digital, how are things in the independent label market?

Joe: It's pretty tough. I put out and album recently that was catalogue number 888 so we've got albums, singles and all the other stuff and some of it sells pretty well and some of the stuff doesn't sell at all. So basically you've got to find ways to re-brand yourself and get stuff on the net. The vinyl stuff is pretty good but it's expensive to produce. But we're doing okay, it's a struggle to keep going but we're still there and still going.

MM: Now that it's actually out there, how do you, personally, feel about the new record?

Joe: On a personal level I'm really happy with it, we turned it around really fast

MM: So what's next on the horizon for DOA?

Joe: We're gonna start working on another record but one that's very different, but it will still have DOA's core sound.

MM: Anything to add?

Joe: The only thing would just be to effect some positive change...

Originally published in Mass Movement #27, July 2010

DOWN TO NOTHING

Sometimes, just sometimes, all you need is a regular dose of good old fashioned Hardcore, and that's exactly what Down To Nothing serve up, and then some. You want Hardcore? You got it...

Interview by Tim Cundle

Photographs by Todd Pollock

MM: Alright, time to introduce yourself to all the folks out there...You want to give us a brief history of DTN? When, where, how and why did the band get together?

DTN: The band currently is David Wood, Daniel Spector, Jared Carman, and most recently Alan and Hunter on guitars. Daniel and David have been playing in the band together since they were in high school. They have lived across the street from each other since they were born I think. The band used to be called Detonation and that got shortened to DTN and from there Down To Nothing came to be. The band really started doing stuff in 2003/04. That's when the first US tours and real stuff started happening and things got a little more real. Aside from a few splits and singles here and there we have released *Save It For The Birds*, *Splitting Headache*, *The Most*, and recently *All My Sons*. We're cool.

MM: Alright, you guys have a new record coming out on Reaper right? Want to tell us all about the new record...?

DTN: The record is called *All My Sons* and its six new songs recorded with our friend Jim Segal at The Outpost (Blood For Blood, Death Threat, Have Heart) in December of last year. I love the record and I think it's the best stuff we've ever done.

MM: Okay, kind of following on from the above question, how did you guys end up hooking up with Reaper, and why did you make the move from Revelation?

DTN: Being on Revelation was something that we all loved. They were always pretty cool to us and we were just happy to have the star on the back of a couple of records. They actually could have held us to another release if they wanted to but when we called them one day to see what the deal was Jordan at Revelation said he didn't mind if we wanted to do something else and that he would miss us. We just wanted to do something with Patrick because we respect his work ethic and he also puts out records for David and I's other bands, Terror and Trapped Under Ice. We deal with him on a regular basis and is a very close friend to both of us, not to mention the rest of the band now. He puts out great records and it was just a no brainer. It wasn't until we were half way through recording that I sent Kitzel a text and told him "Yo we're in the studio recording...Lets do Reaper..". There was nothing to even talk about.

MM: How do you think DTN has evolved, or changed as band and as people, between *Save It For The Birds* and *All My Sons*? Do you think that evolution, or change is necessary for a bands continued existence, or are change and evolution over-rated? Why?

DTN: That's a hard question to answer. We all pretty much grew up doing this band sort of. When I joined I was nineteen. I hadn't ever been anywhere and did it all with not a dollar in my pocket. This shit literally changed my entire life. The same goes for all of us. Ninety five percent of the travelling any of us did at the time, we did with the band and that shaped us in a lot of ways. We would tour eight or nine months out of the year and then go home and live together. There was honestly never a problem. That was five plus years ago now. I think the music and David's lyrics both show how we changed. Especially as of recently with the new seven inch. As far as any other bands it varies I suppose. I think there is a chemistry to all bands and everything works differently. Some bands get better by doing the same exact thing and others grow and are always evolving. That's what is cool about music.

MM: Members of DT' have also played, and / or still play, with Terror, Trapped Under Ice, Heathens amongst others, and have appeared with, or been in a HUGE number of other bands...So, I was wondering, what do you guys get on a personal level from playing with, and in, so many other bands? Even though you do play with other bands, you guys always come back to DTN, so what do you get from being in Down To Nothing that you can't get in any other band?

DTN: David plays in Terror, I play in Trapped Under Ice, Hunter has Bracewar and Heathens, and aside from almost being a doctor you might catch Daniel with Cold World from time to time. I think we all love playing music with our friends. If all of our bands ended tomorrow it is more than likely that new ones are going to come from it. We keep doing the band be- cause we like it and we don't want to quit yet. With this band we can do whatever we want. This isn't our last stand and we aren't running this into the ground. The band is the same there are just no standards to live up to now. More than half the shows were playing this year were playing for free. We don't need the money. We have all got other bands and jobs and school to worry about. We do this because we love it and we're chillin' with our boys and nothing more.

MM: As you guys are from Richmond, a scene which seems to play host to a large number of Hardcore (Municipal Waste, Avail etc.) and Metal (GWAR, Lamb Of God) bands, I wanted to know why you think so many bands come out of Richmond? What is about the town that helps promote and embody such a powerful scene?

DTN: People ask bands from here this all the time. I think it's because Richmond is so laid back. It's also one of the cheapest cities on the East Coast. I think it makes it easier for a "mu- sician" lifestyle. It's hard to put your finger on it though. There are seriously amazing bands from this area. Richmond got soul.

MM: I read a quote on your MySpace page from Dave that said "There are still a lot of things to do, places to go and people to meet. We got that PMA", and I wondered if that was some sort of mission, or focus, for the band, getting to play as many different places as possible? Why? It almost seems like you've got that Black Flag mentality toward playing live and touring, that 'Get in the van and just go' attitude...Do you think that spirit of DIY fun and adventure is still alive and well in the Hardcore scene, or has it died at the hands of cosseted bands and too-money men? Why?

DTN: At one point we were running at full speed. We we're going at it like nine or ten months out of the year and when we slowed down a lot of people were assuming that a last show was coming up. I guess that's fair but honestly you don't have to be a full time band to exist. You don't have to do world touring if you don't want to. So I think that's what he was talking about. We wanna see more of the people we don't get to see like we used to.

MM: What's the strangest thing that's happened to you guys while touring? You know, the most bizarre, way out there, odd experience....?

DTN: We were nearly arrested from trashing hotel rooms with Bane and when we tried to split we were surrounded by probably ten cop cars. The guy found out we were in a band and asked us if we know Agnostic Front. "That's my cousins!!". Another time our friend Chris was throwing unopened cans of soda at signs in the desert. He stands up out of the window while were going eighty miles an hour down the highway and the door comes up. I honestly thought he was dead. No one in the van said anything. He was hinged over the door where the window is at his waste and we had to pull him back in. I think we stopped fucking around for about a day after that.

MM: If music really is the food of love (although, you ask me, that sounds like hippie twaddle), what element of life and which emotion do you think you think Down To Nothing embody in their music? Which emotion do you guys supply the soundtrack for and to? Why?

DTN: This band is definitely about fun. We have cancelled shows in the middle of tours to go swimming. We called the promoter and told him David got jumped by hippies and that we didn't know where he was or if he was alive. We caught some serious shit for stuff like that but it was just too nice of a day! Almost every tour we have done we've taken days off to spend the entire day staring at the Grand Canyon or jump off some cliffs. We have literally kidnapped our friends and taken them on tour. We ghost ride, surf on, set off fireworks, and strap dead animals to the side of our van.

MM: Okay, what's next on the horizon for Down To Nothing? What are you guys going to be up to for the rest of 2010?

DTN: We play this shit by ear. We've got some festival appearances both East and West not to mention a weeks' worth of shows with Terror, Grave Maker, Foundation, and Naysayer. Then we are hitting Europe AND THE UK for a month on the Hell On Earth Tour with Terror, Every Time I Die, All Shall Perish, The Acacia Strain, and Thick As Blood. Come out!!

MM: If there's anything that you'd like to add, I guess you should speak now or forever hold your peace...

DTN: Shout outs to Reaper Records, Naysayer, Foundation, Mother Of Mercy, Dead End Path, Bracewar, Terror, and GUERILLA CREW! Keep making new friends. It's definitely a younger or newer band vibe and I see it in bands like Foundation, Naysayer, and Backtrack.

Originally published in Mass Movement #27, July 2010

KURT BRECHT
(D.R.I.)

Do these guys really need any introduction? If you're not familiar with their music, good old fashioned tooth chipping thrash, then chances are you'll have seen their skanking man logo somewhere, on a shirt or as graffiti in a club, so each and every one of you out there, subliminally or otherwise, knows this band. It's thrashing time, it's time for the Dirty Rotten Imbeciles. After listening to them for twenty three years, I finally got to talk to Kurt Brecht about all things DRI...

Interview by Tim Cundle

MM: What initially drew you to Hardcore and lead you to form DRI?

Kurt: I think what drew me to Hardcore was how close you could get to the bands. They were so much more accessible than a big rock and roll band; I liked the music a lot more and the whole do it yourself attitude and the fact that anybody can do it.

MM: Is it true that the name DRI came from your dad?

Kurt: Yes. We used to practice in my parent's house and the room didn't have any insulation and we were so angry – you know? He used to come home from work and he couldn't hear himself think or hear the TV or anything (laughing)

MM: So he used to call you Dirty Rotten Imbeciles?

Kurt: Yeah that and a lot of other stuff (laughs) But that stuck...

MM: So what was the initial reaction to the band like, because when you guys started, what you were doing was vastly different to anything else out there...

Kurt: We were, at that time, going out to a lot of Hardcore shows, we were into bands like Verbal Abuse and MDC and we didn't think we were that much different. We were very underground even for an underground band – we practised for about a year before we played our first gig, so people kind of heard about us. A few friends who came over to listen to us practise spread the word, so word started getting out there. So, they started pushing us to play live. We had a lot of songs but some of them were so short we weren't sure if we had enough to put a full set together to play. Finally we put it all together and started playing, then after a while we just moved to California.

MM: What made you move out to San Francisco? How tough was it on the band making that move?

Kurt: It was pretty tough. My brother, Eric, the drummer, and I were in art college and we had to quit that –just leave; Spike had a regular job and he had to quit that and leave, our bass player as well. We went out there, not really intending or knowing that we going to, to stay there for 15 years like we did in the end – we had just heard that we should go out there and that our kind of music would be more popular there. Our kind of music was beginning to be really popular in the San Francisco area.

MM: This was just before the Rock against Reagan tour right?

Kurt: Yeah, we went to California and we played the show and then our bass player quit so me and my brother went back to Houston and finished up the first semester of the college. Then we found a new bass player in San Francisco and started practicing with him, and then we got the call from MDC and found out we had got onto the Rock against Reagan tour.

MM: What do you remember most about that tour?

Kurt: Mainly just the shows – playing all sorts of big outdoor shows – lots of college kids and it was kind of like a musical protest road-show really and there were a load of bands on it we really liked so it wasn't like work at all. Of course we weren't paid anything; they used to give us some food and a bit of money towards gas, but for us it was really an opportunity for us to make some fans.

**MM: How do you think the band then progressed between the *Dirty Rotten Album* and *Dealing With It?*

Kurt: Well, a lot of them were the same songs but we knew that we could make them sound better because a lot of them had already changed since we'd been playing them live a lot. For us, because of the sound quality, the first album wasn't really anything more than a demo really. *Dealing With It* was really just a better recording of it. When we got Felix as a drummer – from my brother – he's got a really different kind of feel than my brother, kind of more like a Metallica kind of feel. He was able to add that extra metal edge into the band...y'know?

MM: Yeah, because after *Dealing With It* you get into *Crossover* which is a vastly different record from anything you'd ever done. How did your fan-base react to that ? You took a massive step forward with that record...

Kurt: There were some people who were pissed off about it – especially in Europe – but we also gained a lot more fans so... I don't know, it's... Any time you jump out there and put yourself out on the line like that you take a risk, but a whole different range of kids could get into us now. We headlined a punk festival a few weeks ago and to follow it up we're going to headline a metal festival in Baltimore. We're able to jump those two scenes comfortably now without anyone getting upset. It's a pretty good place to be actually.

MM: Did you have any idea how important *Crossover* was going to be as a record? That you would be helping to, in essence, create a whole new musical genre?

Kurt: Well we knew that people had already started labelling us as a crossover band even when Dealing With It was out. I don't really like labels but you're forced to use them so that people know what you're talking about... So, basically it was my idea to use that as the name for the album because that's what it was, and that's what people thought it was...

MM: After twenty eight years as a band, what do you attribute DRI's longevity to?

Kurt: The fans. Just rabid fans wanting us to play all the time. It seems like we don't get a moment's rest and it's "When you gonna go again? You gotta keep going for ever". We just love it. We're a touring band, we've always been a live band so that's the main thing. I get a normal job every now and then, working 40 hours a week but I really don't like it or prefer it. I'm happier when we can get to go back out on the road again and get to make our living with music

MM: I've heard lots of different reasons why there hasn't been a DRI album for fifteen years, so can you set the record straight?

Kurt: Well we brought out the last album – *Full Speed Ahead* and we toured off that for what must be three or four years. It just seemed to keep going. We'd finish off a 3-4 month US tour then we would be wanted in South America; we'd come back and it would be Dubai and Europe for 3 months and by the time you come back there's a whole other 3 month tour of the US. So we were having a great time with it, then it became the 20th anniversary in there somewhere so we toured that for 2-3 years. For us to stop touring and write a record we need to have some money built up and nobody's throwing money at us for that. Plenty of people want us to put out a record but nobody wants to help us with that too much.

MM: I guess by now most people know that Spike has been really ill and has thankfully now recovered. What kind of impact did Spike's illness have on a personal level and did it change the way that you view the band?

Kurt: When he got sick we were two weeks from doing a full US tour, so we just had to stop that, and like I said, we're just touring, touring, touring, so originally he just said we would postpone the tour for a short time; he'd have an operation and get back to it. We found out shortly after that, the Doctors said "You're insane you're not going anywhere for a while". It took me probably six months of sitting around thinking "What am I going to do?" before I actually got a job and all that, and started another band as a side project to keep me busy. I've always been very thankful to have the band, but now more than ever; during our hiatus – our time away thrash metal and crossover became quite popular again. We're riding the crest of the wave.

MM: You've just reissued *Crossover*, do you want to tell us about that?

Kurt: Actually it's been planned for a long time, it just wasn't the right time. It took a lot to get it together: we used to be on a different record label, we switched it over to Beer City, but basically the whole project was stopped during our whole period of time off – it just kind of waited until we were getting ready to get back out on the road again

MM: Any plans to re-release the follow-ups to *Crossover*?

Kurt: Some of our stuff we can't get near because it's on our old label – it's still out there anyway.

MM: Do you have a personal favourite DRI record: one which you feel really defines the band?

Kurt: I guess *Dealing With It*, or *Full Speed Ahead* – the last one. I don't really listen to them that often, but each album I like several songs on any given day then three weeks later I might listen to it again and like completely different songs. When you put out an album, cer-

tain songs which you think are going to be real good sometimes don't turn out so well, and others which you don't think are so good which turn out miraculous.

MM: Do you want to tell us a little bit about Pasadena Napalm Division?

Kurt: Some of the guys in the band asked me to come and sing with them. They are a local Texas band, they were called Dead Horse. They broke up a few years back but kind of made a pact to get back together, and they were from Pasadena which is right by Houston and they heard that I was just kicking around and asked me if I wanted to come over. I said told them I wasn't going to buy a microphone or invest even a quarter – I'd just come over and check them out and if it clicks –good and if it doesn't – forget it. They were really cool guys and we've got a seven song demo out and we've just come up with another 5-6 songs and I'm supposed to go in this week and finish the vocals on them then try to mix them down and we'll have a full album's worth of material –demo quality, but good demo quality.

MM: You ought to get Mike (Beer City) to release that...

Kurt: People can listen to it on Facebook and MySpace

MM: Away from the band, what else do you do? Do you still write? Any more books in the works?

Kurt: I've not written a book in a long time. I used to sell them as a book on CD where I would essentially read my own book then record it and put it onto CD. I sell them at shows and stuff. It's easier for me rather than print up 1000 copies and have them cluttering up my apartment...

MM: What does the rest of 2010 look like for DRI?

Kurt: We have a show in the Chezch republic next month which is kind of odd as we are flying in for one show and flying straight out again. Then we're touring Central America and in September it all starts all over again in the US.

MM: You guys should hook up with Municipal Waste and go out with them – that would be a dream tour at the moment...

Kurt: Yeah we think about all that stuff we've got a lot of dream tours at the moment, it's just the logistics that cause a problem. We've got a booking agent that looks after all that stuff. He does a pretty good job for us.

MM: Anything to add?

Kurt: If anybody wants to book us its First Row Talent – a US based company. You can talk to them about bringing us to your home town, we play just about anywhere from little café grills to pizza places to huge giant festivals. Also if there are any record companies out there willing to help us out – some kind of record deal would be sweet...

Originally published in Mass Movement #27, July 2010

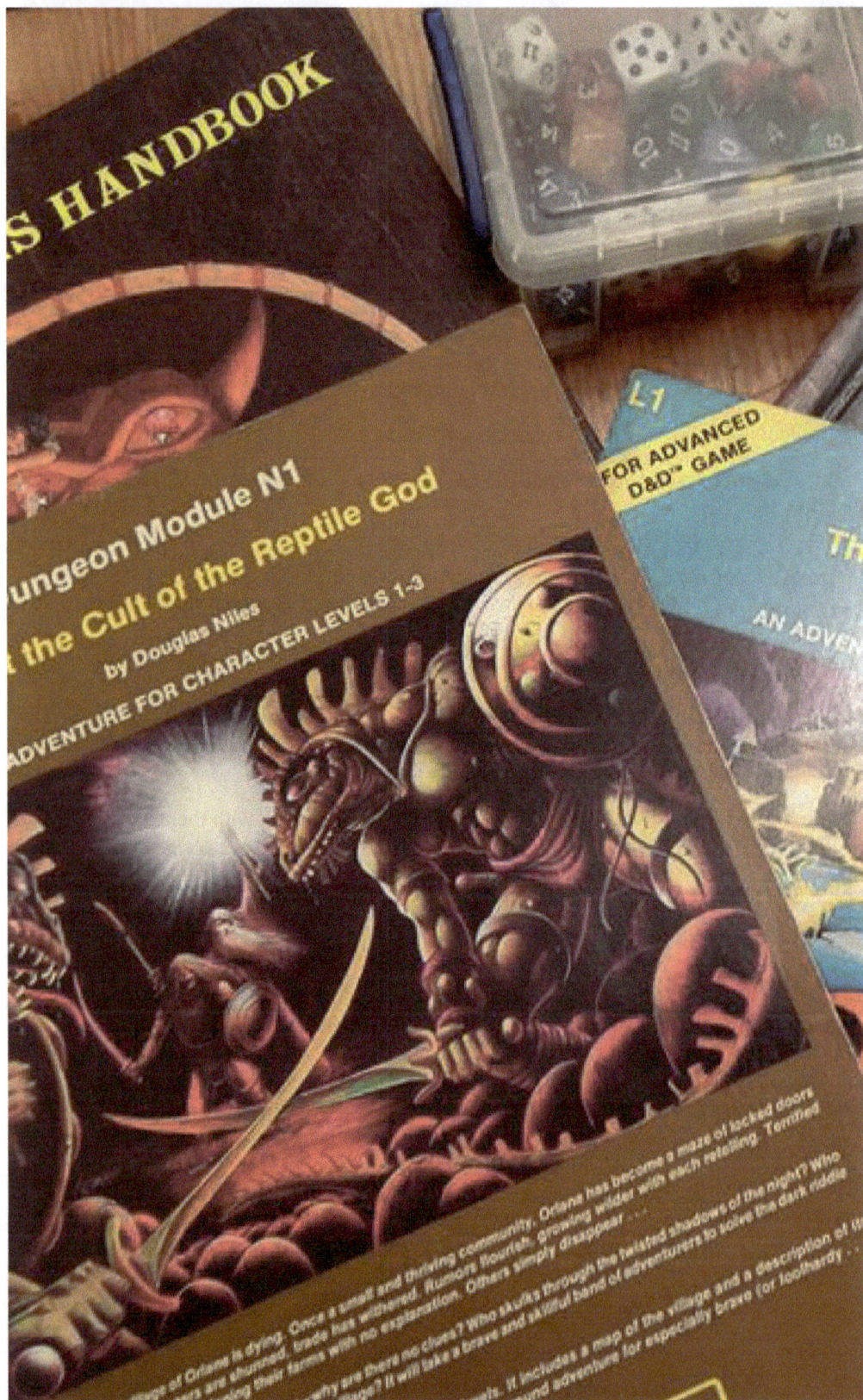

S HANDBOOK

Dungeon Module N1

the Cult of the Reptile God

by Douglas Niles

ADVENTURE FOR CHARACTER LEVELS 1-3

L1

FOR ADVANCED
D&D™ GAME

Th

AN ADVEN

The village of Orlane is dying. Once a small and thriving community, Orlane has become a maze of locked doors and suspicion. Outsiders are shunned, trade has withered, growing wilder with each retelling. Terrified inhabitants shy away, abandoning their farms with no explanation. Others simply disappear . . .

Why are they leaving? Why are there no clues? Who skulks through the twisted shadows of the night? Who can be trusted? It will take a brave and skillful band of adventurers to solve the dark riddle of Orlane. It includes a map of the village and a description of its inhabitants. A thrilling, fun-to-play, all-around adventure for especially brave (or foolhardy) . . .

MIKE MEARLS
DUNGEONS & DRAGONS R&D TEAM

It's no secret that D&D has been a part of my life for over a quarter of a century, so when, in email conversation, Charles (Ryan) at Esdevium mentioned that there was a possibility of getting an interview with one of the R&D Team (that's right folks, Dungeons & Dragons has a Research & Development Team – number three on my list of dream jobs), I leapt at the chance, and after a little too and fro in cyberspace, the following interview with Mike Mearls was set up and ready to go. Six weeks later and I'm still smiling...

Interview by Tim Cundle

MM: Let's start at the beginning...Do you want to introduce yourself and tell us how you originally became involved in the world of , and started playing, D&D?

Mike: My name is Mike Mearls and I am lead designer on D&D. I was first exposed to D&D in 1981, when my older brother and his friends discovered it. Perhaps by coincidence, or maybe it was simply a cultural shift, I also had my first taste of Tolkien, Conan, and fantasy literature. D&D was my chance to explore a world of fantasy and magic, and I dove into it head first. I wasn't allowed to play with D&D with my brother and his friends, but they didn't remain involved with the game for long. Soon after they gave it up, my brother sold me his Basic D&D rulebook. The rest is history.

MM: For the sake of those poor souls reading this who may not be familiar with D&D, would you like to briefly explain, from an industry insiders perspective, what Dungeons & Dragons is?

Mike: Dungeons & Dragons is a cooperative game where each player creates a character, a sort of in-game avatar, such as a wizard, an elf, or a warrior. The player's team up to defeat monsters in a fantasy setting that looks something like the Lord of the Rings. The big difference between D&D and other games is that in D&D one player takes on the role of the Dungeon Master (DM). The DM creates the fantasy world and builds scenarios for the players to tackle. The DM adjudicates the rules like a referee, allowing the players to try almost any action. While the rules cover a lot, the DM's judgment is the final arbiter. This makes games of D&D interesting because there are no limits aside from common sense and logic to what the characters can do. For instance, let's say that a ferocious ogre guards the entrance to a treasure chamber in the ruins of an imperial palace. The players could attack the ogre, but they could also try any number of other plans. They might offer it a keg of ale they found elsewhere in the palace ruins, hoping that it gets drunk and falls asleep. One character could challenge the ogre to a contest of riddles while another one sneaks past it. The characters could pretend to be allied with the ogre's master and bluster their way past it. The players are free to try anything they can think of. The DM is a big reason why after 36 years D&D is still around. Like a musical instrument, D&D shifts and changes in response to what a DM wants to do with it. Some DMs create vivid, detail fantasy worlds for their players to explore. Others build devious puzzles and traps for the characters to overcome.

MM: How did you make the transition from gamer to becoming part of the Dungeons & Dragons R&D team? Can you tell us a little about role of the R&D team, what it does and what you do within the team?

Mike: The R&D team is broken into three primary components. The designers are responsible for the creative spark that drives the game forward. They come up with new concepts for characters, new worlds to explore, and new ideas for the game. As lead designer, I set some of the big picture goals for the design team. The developers take the designers' work and ensure that it fits in with the game as it currently stands. They make sure that everything is balanced so that new options don't make old ones obsolete. At the same time, a new option has to be powerful and interesting enough that it's worth a player's time to look at them. The editors take the developed manuscript and work to make sure that the game is clear, easy to understand, and precise in its language. By keeping the phrasing of rules consistent from release to release, they cut down rules confusion.

MM: Do you have to separate and differentiate between being a gamer and a developer when working on new ideas? Does being a gamer help, or is it a hindrance to, working on D&D as a game? Why?

Mike: Obviously, you'd need to have some interest in games to work on D&D. Otherwise; you wouldn't have enough of the basics under your belt to do interesting work. You'd have to spend a lot of time catching up. The biggest benefit, though, lies in understanding the audience. D&D players like that they can bend and shift the game to fit what they want to do. For DMs, the game is a creative outlet. Having experience playing D&D makes it a lot easier to understand what players want and need. My rule of thumb is that I don't put anything in a book I'm working on unless I'd personally be interested in it. That's a good first test to see if an idea is worth pursuing.

MM: I'm assuming that you're directly responsible for all the minor and major changes within the D&D core system and rules, so I was kind of wondering, what changes, or additional rules were, and are, you directly responsible for? What impact, as an individual, have you had on D&D, and how do you think your changes have affected the game?

Mike: Most of my design work has come out from Player's Handbook 2 onward. I think my biggest contributions have been the class design in *PH 2* and the system of psionic magic we introduced in Player's Handbook 3. I like taking the core 4th edition system and twisting, turning, and bending it in new directions. Its fun showing how you can take what looks like a relatively static, predictable system and turn it on its head. I don't think people expected that.

MM: I guess the change that's still big news is the move to, and release of the 4th Edition Rules – how long did it take to develop, play test and refine the system before you, and the rest of the team, were happy for it to be released? What were the biggest problems that you guys faced during the development of 4thE, and how did you eventually overcome them? With hindsight, is there anything that you'd change about 4thE if you could?

Mike: The first work on 4e started in 2005, and I was intermittently involved in it from then until 2006. For the final year of the game's design I worked on it full-time. The biggest challenge was finding the right balance between making the game appealing to existing players while finding ways to make it more accessible to new players. It's easy to get lost in catering to your existing fans. They've seen all the basics and want to see more detail, more options, just more stuff in general. You have to fight that urge and remember that the game has to provide an easy route for new players. It's also easy to fall into the trap of creating a rule for every situation. That causes the game to become too complex to play easily. On the other hand, too few rules mean that DMs and players are stuck guessing or arguing over how something works. Finding that balance is an important part of developing a new version of D&D. There are a few things I'd change, but the one that springs to mind would be alignment. I understand why the alignment system was simplified, but I liked playing lawful evil characters!

MM: Okay, time to put you on the spot – are there any changes to D&D that you wish hadn't been made, and you think don't work so well within the overall system, and if so what are they and why, in your personal opinion, don't they work? On a similar note, what do you think the greatest changes to the game have been, and why do they work so well?

Mike: The biggest change to D&D in 4E was the shift in how characters advance. It used to be that each class had its own progression of advancement in level. A wizard might gain a new spell, a fighter gains better fighting ability, while a druid can shape-change into an animal. 4E changed all that, giving each class the same pace of advancement. Obviously, the classes all gain different types of abilities, but those abilities all look much more alike. The benefit is that it's easier for new players to learn how all the classes work. The drawback is that classes that used to offer more complexity are simpler, while simpler ones are more complex. There was some value to letting a player choose how complex he wants his character to be. On the other hand, it meant that anyone who wanted to play a wizard had to learn far more rules than the other players.

MM: Slowly winding things up....I don't suppose that you can tell us what you're working on at the moment can you? What can we look forward to, and what's new in the world of D&D...?

Mike: This fall we're rolling out the D&D Essentials, a set of books and boxed sets that are designed to serve as the ideal starting place for D&D. The Red Box introductory starter set is one of the first Essentials releases. It's the perfect way to start playing D&D. After that, we're rolling out player books with new options for the most popular classes in the game. Those books are a good place for new players to go after the Red Box. The content is also a new take on classic character classes, so even D&D veterans should find something interesting there.

Originally pubiushed in Mass Movement #27, July 2010

VAR THELIN
(NO IDEA RECORDS)

So, I guess there isn't anyone out there in punk rock land who hasn't heard of No Idea Records, the label that put Gainesville on the Mohawk map, but how many of us actually know anything about 'em, apart from the Stressface logo that adorns more and more of our ever expanding record collections? Bunky and me figured we'd find out as much as we could by talking to head honcho Var…

Interview by Tim "Bunky" Davies & Tim Cundle

MM; As ever, the best place to start is at the beginning - No Idea started as a zine didn't it? Why did you originally start putting the zine out and, how, in your case anyway, did a zine become a label? How many of the original No Idea zinesters are still involved with the label, and are you still in touch with all of the original crew? What do you remember most about the formative days of No Idea?

Var: The local high schools were rezoned in the mid-80's, so all of a sudden a lot of the punk, Goth, new wave, whatever-you-call-it kids ended up going to the same school. There was an energy to create that burned in our bellies. We were all kids looking for something to do. Hormones raging, questions abounding. Who were we? What were we doing? What does it all mean? Boredom is death. For some reason, a few of us decided to work on a zine. The main catalyst was Rats Magazine, which was a comic that Ken Coffelt and some friends of his had made a few issues of over a couple years. I was blown away by the idea that kids could actually do something like this. It was very empowering. I wanted in and I wanted to start creating something of our own. We picked up from there. It was simply the need for an out-let. Many of us were taking a Graphic Arts class as well. The teacher was very supportive too and allowed us to learn hands-on how to use the printing press, etc. This was 1985. For our sixth issue, we included a 7" by the local band DOLDRUMS.

This was the start of the label, circa 1988. We were very interested in hollering about the local scene and bands, so it was natural to ask to include our favourite local band at the time on the first record. (I just found out that Russ, the guitar player, died earlier this week at age 50.) I am the only one from the original loose group that remains. The last one to move was Ken and that was back in 1988, as I recall. He contributed a couple times after he moved and we remained friends. We infrequently talk, but for some reason I still feel a strong connec-tion with him. I'm just terrible at corresponding and consider it a fault of mine. I care so much it hurts, but get wrapped up in the panic of the day, leaving off the rest for the next day. With modern social networking websites, I do see that a lot of these old friends have created families and businesses… and I wonder what a grand reunion would look like! I re-member working bizarre long hours and fitting bits in between school classes, etc. I did poorly in school… but if I did not go through that process, I would likely not have met a lot of people or learned the cut-n-paste graphics of the pre-desktop-computer world.

MM: Having sprung from the ashes of a zine, have you ever been tempted to do another magazine, or is there some overwhelming reason stopping you? If so, what? What, if anything do you miss about putting together your own zine? How do you think zine culture has changed during the last decades?

Var: Creating a zine took so much time... it was overwhelming. As we started focusing more and more on records, that became a more motivating outlet. I just did not have what it took to start a new issue, knowing it would take a year or two to finish. Time was the reason I did not start issue #13. There were hundreds of free newsprint zines for a while there by the mid-90's. So many that came with free CDs. When we did the issues with CDs, it was still a pretty new idea. Within a few years, everyone was doing it. CD pressing prices fell, sales went up. Record labels had money to advertise a lot. Zines thrived. As that well dried up in the 90's, the zines fell away. Now it is mostly webzines. Ad money is scarce and spread thin. I have wanted to do a zine "in theory" over the years, but simply have no time. This is too bad in a way, but my focus is elsewhere. I do not write very often anymore either, which is a downside.

MM: Did you see it lasting this long? No Idea that is... What's been the most dramatic change in the label since you first put music on to a record?

Var: Absolutely not. I had no real long-range plan. In 1994, I had saved nearly $10,000 from working a job for four years and living cheap. I took that as a challenge to go full time with the zine and label. I expected that I would have to get a part time job within six months to help cover the bills... but I never did. Strange. I always had a "this could end at any moment" phantom in the back of my mind. I have never kicked that; it's still there. The most dramatic change? I suppose that would be the slow growth and mutation that has occurred. We started a "distribution" in 1995 that shifted and evolved. We operate now with ten people (plus a few interns running the various facets of what we do: label, mail-order, wholesale distribution, press wrangling / PR... I am the only one officially employed by "the label" but there is a lot of crossover. That is a big change! It feels great to work with people we care about and offer a job that allows them to do the things they are really here to do: play music, make art, start families and more

MM: Since you started the label, is there a band or record that you didn't get to put out but had the chance to and wish you had? Why, and why didn't you do the record?

Var: There have been a lot of bands that have asked when we were too busy to consider adding another. There were a few that I did not think to ask... and a few that were supposed to, but broke up instead, ha!

MM: Obviously you've released quite a few bands from Gainesville over the years, is there something in the water that makes them so good or is there an underground No Idea Boot Camp that you're not telling us about? Is No Idea a big part of the local community or do you try to keep yourselves to yourselves?

Var: That would be the mystery of Gainesville. There are a LOT of bands here, multiple labels and several great places to play. We sometimes electroshock bands and subject them to strobe lights and nature films. Does that count? I suppose you'd have to ask around. By extension, folks that help run this ship organize benefits, play shows, and otherwise participate in the local community.

MM: Do you think that Gainesville and Florida have had an impact on the label and bands from the area, and if so, what kind of impact do you think it has? How, do you think the scene in Gainesville differs from other well-known and long established scenes, such as LA. DC or NYC? Has, in your opinion, the Gainesville scene evolved purely though its own merits, or has any external influences or other scenes helped its development?

Var: Yes. Gainesville is far from being in a bubble. The individuals here are influenced by bands and scenes from all over the world. Perhaps vice versa? We live in a pretty small town.

MM: Like most labels you must get a lot of demos, how do you decide which ones to listen too? Or do you generally not have the time? Do you find that with the Internet and MP3's being around that fewer bands are sending demo's out through traditional methods?

Var: I rarely have time to listen to demos - every now and then, maybe? Right. Fewer bands are bothering to mail CDRs and whatnot.

MM: Following on from the above, what kind of impact and effect do you think the internet has had **on punk rock and music as a whole - in terms of label, bands etc.? From a personal perspective, has it been beneficial or detrimental to No Idea?**

Var: Computers are both great and horrible. I'm in a van with Young Livers right now, heading home after a couple days in Charlotte, NC, getting the van repaired. Yesterday they started organizing a tour that starts in a week. All but one show is now confirmed, two of which came together while I was typing my answers. That's the internet for you (and a few phone calls). Some people take all the music they can find, others do not. Some people will support bands, labels, and communities in various ways. Others do not. These are polar extremes and lots of people fall somewhere in between. If no one does their part, then it all collapses. If people pitch in, then things live on, evolve, and change.

MM: We're constantly being told that we live in the digital age, and as such I was wondering if you thought that the traditional role of the record label was changing, or evolving, and if so, how? How do you think this change will affect the way the music "business" operates? Does digital really mean the death of vinyl and CD? If so, why and if not, why not?

Var: We bob and weave. Sting like a butterfly, float like a bee. Nothing is static, everything changes. Some labels are shifting to managerial roles and act more as licensing and promotion companies and image builders... or so I hear. I've been hearing about the death of this and that for twenty plus years. Some people like records, some people like CDs, and some people like sword fish. Some people like burritos.

MM: As with any technical, forward thinking achievement, human nature always manages to twist and manipulate it so that it becomes part of the lowest common denominator, and in the net's case, that usually revolves around gossip and rumour. So, what are the strangest internet rumours that you've heard about both yourself and No Idea?

Var: You tell me. But really, you should read what that one bloke posted about you on "dubyadubyadubya dot bangers and mash dot co dot uk backslash wankers"

MM: Hot Water Music, Against Me! And Less than Jake went on to be pretty successful in their careers; did their success change your favourite record by each of them? Conversely, what's your least favourite record by each of the fore-mentioned bands, and why?

Var: When a record and band do better than break even, then they help to press another band's record. That's all there is to it, really. Of course it is gratifying to work hard alongside a band and champion them as they roll down the road. Sure, we're proud when they stick by their convictions and blaze a trail, undaunted. AGAINST ME! "Reinventing..." HOT WATER MUSIC "Fuel..." LESS THAN JAKE "Hello Rockview" No way in hell I'd say a bad word about any of those bands. Respect, support and inspiration.

MM: If you we're going to live on a deserted island somewhere and you could only take one No Idea Record with you which one would it be and why? Where did the Stressface logo come from?

Var: I love how you put two unrelated questions into a two-part question... ha! "Do you know how to change a flat tire? What's your favourite ice cream flavo(u)r?" I would take a compilation. Not sure which one. I drew the Stressface on break at my old job, circa... 1990? It originally had a bowtie and a topknot. It may have been an attempt to draw a character of mine from the 1980's called "Amazingly Boy." Ken's character was called "Pill Salad". They had adventures.

MM: Let's talk Fest - when, how and why did you come up with the original idea for Fest?

Var: I did not, Tony did. It's his jam. (I like toast.)

MM: How do you think it's changed and evolved since its inception?

Var: More bands, less sleep.

MM: Who do you think, have put in the best performances at Fest, and why?

Var: The people left standing at the end of the night always turn in the best performances.

MM: How do you think Fest differs from other music based festivals, what makes it different?

Var: Well, of late, there are a LOT more FESTS. I just went to RADFEST. It was fun and familiar. It was nice to be in someone else's town and fully off-the- clock. CHAOS IN TEJAS a couple years ago was great and with any luck I will be at the one in a week two. Those are the only other Fests I've been to since the mid-90's. Oh, but there was also one Michigan Fest in like 1999? I forget. That was the first REALLY GOOD, well run Fest I had been to. It set the level.

MM: I gotta know man...What's with the beards? Why do so many No Idea bands have beards, or start growing bands when they join the label? Is it some rites of passage thing, some kind of weird initiation type deal, a secret 'Order Of The Grand Beard' that exists within the confine of the label, or something else, and if so, what?

Var: I have no clue. I am not capable of growing anything beyond a teenage hoodlum scruff, so... I cannot comment from a personal perspective. They are either lazy or really into Grover Cleveland. They are smuggling acorns.

MM: How has parenthood changed you Var?

Var: Tim, it made me lactate more regularly. But that eventually dried up.

MM: Has it changed the way that you view and think about No Idea and punk rock, and if so how?

Var: Parenthood changes everything, but mostly diapers. We got a lot less sleep for a while. Matt just became a poppa too. They are busting out all over. No Idea nursery and day care and records. Ivo and Vivie know how to fold record covers and have hand-coloured a few. It makes me work harder and want to do right(er).

MM: Which No Idea five releases do you think best sum up everything that the label is? Why?

Var: Methane, Carbon Dioxide, Sweat, Urine, and Poop. Why? Because that's what we do.

MM: What's next on the No Idea horizon?

Var: Sinking other pirate ships and returning with galleys full of exotic spices and treasure.

MM: If there's anything that you'd like to add....

Var: I am so tired I am nearly delirious. All you can eat taco party plus an eight hour drive minus sleep equals who am we? I answered questions one to four a couple weeks ago. The rest in a van around midnight. I'm not driving. Do what you do because you are driven. And if that does not work out, try driving yourself.

Originally published in Mass Movement #27, July 2010

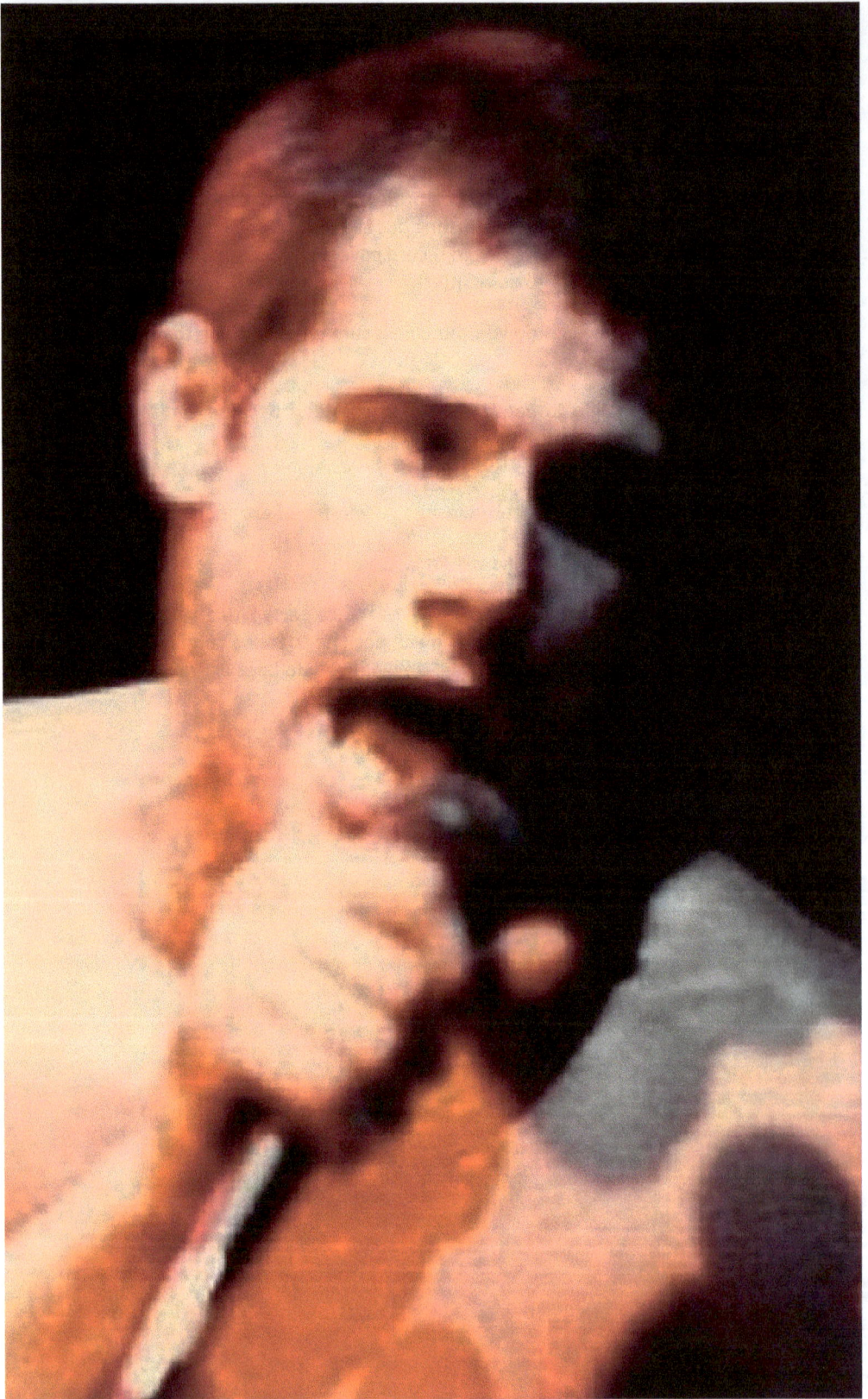

PETE STAHL
(SCREAM / WOOL/ GOATSNAKE)

Scream. Wool. Goatsnake. Apart from the fact that they're all incredible bands, what do they have in common? Come on, you know this one. You don't? Okay, I'll tell you. Pete Stahl. The guy was, and is responsible for being the voice behind some of the best records you'll ever hear, period. I spoke to Pete about his incredible musical odyssey at 2AM on a Friday morning and just for the record, he's one of the nicest guys I've ever interviewed. And that's the damn truth...

Interview by Tim Cundle

Photographs by Marcus Bastida and others (credits where available)

MM: What initially led to the formation of Scream?

Pete: My brother and I played in a band when we were kids and messed around, learned guitar in high school. We got into punk rock and new wave and we got together our own band, we were especially inspired by the Bad Brains.

MM: How do you feel now when people refer to Scream as one of the seminal DC hardcore bands?

Pete: Awesome. You know, being part of a community as a musician, in the early days people come to our shows and it became, I guess what people call hardcore and I kinda feel part of that. The people in the bands, the people who came to shows, the people who put on the shows, it's a real community.

MM: Do you think there is a definitive Scream record? One album that defines the band.

Pete: We really killed it with our last record, so I hope it was a culmination of everything we've done really. I feel that it had elements of everything we were about. If you were a fan of the band you generally pick the first record, so for the fans it's the first record. I don't know, I think all the records show growth in learning how to play the instruments and write songs. I like them all.

MM: How long after Scream split up did you and Franz start Wool?

Pete: Pretty much straight away. Scream was on tour when we broke up. Skeeter had bailed on us again and we were trying to find a bass player to get home – we still had 16 dates booked back to DC and we needed money. So we auditioned bass players, and in that time frame Chris and Kurt phoned us up and said they would come and help us play some shows and then ultimately joined the band. My brother and I, we thought, well we've done a lot with Scream, but let's see what we can do here, and put together a new band.

MM: Wool, I think, is a very different entity to Scream, and *Budspawn* was a very different entity to *Box Set*...

Pete: Just goes to show the part a drummer plays in the band when you play as a group as we always do. We jam stuff out and create that way, so the drummer has a real integral part in shaping the music. We've been lucky to play with great drummers to this day. So Pete Moffat had a certain style that fit with the heavier... makes *Budspawn* heavier in effect; but Chris Patton was a completely different drummer, completely different style and that's the main difference between those two records.

MM: I seem to remember you guys recording a cover of the Sonics' *The Witch*...

Pete: Yeah. We did, we played covers. Like with Scream there was a whole record which we never did which was a whole bunch of covers that we used to do.

MM: I was wondering why you never released *The Witch* as a seven inch, because that was one hell of a cover...

Pete: Thanks for saying that. It's funny, The Sonics were always one of my favourite bands and hearing them on commercials now? Weird. It's like I was saying with Scream, we had a whole bunch of stuff that was never release, pre Scream Me –it was how we really learned to play. Our first group of songs we used to play were by the Sonics, the Jam, Sham, Buzzcocks and other obscure stuff and that was pretty much in line with going from Scream to Wool, what we did. Wool was from Seattle and we did stuff like that.

MM: With the end of Wool it felt to me almost like you were moving towards a stoner vibe with *Short Term Memory Loss*...

Pete: Well it's funny, the whole stoner rock thing. I mean Scream used to play with the Obsessed, we always played together back in the day. Then when we ended up out here , I met this guy Hutch who does sound for Crooked Vultures, and does sound for Queens, and those bands. He introduced me to a couple of people out in the desert: David Hutchings who plays death metal and plays in Earthling which is another band I have we worked up that whole sound. We went on tour together and we laugh about that tour because we went all the way up the West Coast of America and no-one gave a fuck. There were about 20-30 people at each place, no-one knew who we were. I certainly wouldn't say though that Stoner rock was something we were aiming for at all.

There was this whole other record that Wool did that was never released that was definitely more garagey than stoner rock, and we were doing some really cool stuff when we called it a day. My brother was just over it at the time and wanted to concentrate on family life. But we might have an opportunity to release it someday. I'm hoping that we get to do that. Someone just approached me about releasing that stuff, and I'd like to do it. We did around 17/18 songs and got everything ready for the new record and then we were dropped by London...

MM: It was almost like, when you released *Box Set*, there was no promotion for it at all, and it was a good record. A good, solid, punk rock record but it got no promotional support at all...

Pete: Nah, they kind of had me gone by the time that was out, it's like what happens to a lot of bands with major labels...

MM: What happened with Goatsnake? Was it the Desert Sessions or Goatsnake that came next?

Pete: I met Greg Anderson when I was with Wool and he was in his band Engine Kid up in Seattle. We became friends and we kinda talked about him moving down to LA to make a band and of course Dean I'd known for years; he actually played bass in Scream too, he filled in on a tour. So when those guys were working on that and they asked me to sing for them I was like "Fuck Yeah" I love the blues and always have, for me it comes from that blues perspective.

MM: It's quite a musical journey from Scream to Goatsnake. Do you ever think about the path that you've taken musically?

Pete: It's one continuous journey for me. It feels natural. We have some opportunities that I want to take advantage of – we're doing some shows with Scream out on the East Coast, New York up until the summer and we may get together to do another Scream record. We have it written pretty much. Believe it or not we were going to do a split 7"– that was how it was presented to us and we jumped at the chance, so we came out here and recorded a new song for that split 7". I don't know what's happening with that label, there was no communication after we gave them the stuff. I've been talking to Ian and he's interested – I don't know if it's gonna work out, but we were seeing what we could put together, spoke to Grohl to get into a studio – he offered that. So I think that's gonna happen, it's difficult with people's families and living on different coasts but we are going to move it in that direction, work together on these new songs. We have enough material now to do a record.

MM: Is there any chance you may do a European tour with Scream, or just the US?

Pete: Certainly I would love to do that. I've been talking to a couple of people about doing some shows in Germany, but it's what we can afford to do in terms of getting away from work and all that.

MM: Is there going to be another Goatsnake record?

Pete: Greg Anderson is the lord, it's kind of up to him. I certainly would be into it, but if Greg wants to do it, we will. We haven't discussed it to be honest at all. I would hope so.

MM: I know you work as a tour manager, Pete, so which do you prefer... Touring with your own bands or working for touring bands?

Pete: No doubt about it touring in my own band. That's what I live to do – my music. That's the real passion in my life. I have a lot of experience and I can help other bands get around.

MM: Sounds like you've got a busy time ahead musically...

Pete: You know I've been focussing on working for other bands for the last couple of years and trying to do other things on the side. It's tough but things come back around and opportunities present themselves and you have to go for it. It hasn't been for a lack of wanting to, it's just that sometimes other things get in the way.

MM: Anything to add?

Pete: I'm glad that you were interested in some of the other bands I was in – I thought this was going to be specifically about Goatsnake for some reason. Great to speak with you.

Originally published in Mass Movement #27, July 2010

SCREEN DAMAGE
THE TALL TALES OF PHANTASM

The late 1970s proved themselves to be hallmark years for American horror movies. It was a pre-home video golden age, a time when independently made films could still be picked up for a long run around the country's cinemas, grindhouses and drive-in screens.

Nowhere was safe. Down at the mall, the zombies of George Romero's *Dawn of the Dead* were taking consumerism to extreme measures. America's desert wastelands were revealed to be the exclusive domain of inbred cannibals and cross-dressing psychopaths in movies such as Wes Craven's *The Hills Have Eyes* or Charles Band's bizarre *Tourist Trap*. Ridley Scott's *Alien* claimed the icy trucking lanes of deep space as the stalking ground for creatures with rapist tendencies and a knack for making an entrance. Back on Earth, the assault on small town America was led by the likes of John Carpenter's classic *Halloween* and Don Coscarelli's magnificent *Phantasm*. It seemed that horror had finally come home, and the fear flowed from the screen to mark the era as a truly unique period in the genre. But while *Halloween* took childhood bogeyman stories and made them real within a cosy suburban neighbour-hood setting, *Phantasm* followed the path of a fever-dream.

Phantasm was Don Coscarelli's third movie. A twenty year old UCLA graduate, his previous work included *Jim, The World's Greatest*, a grim drama about an alcoholic father and his sons, and an excellent childhood rites-of-passage piece called *Kenny and Company*. It was a Halloween night scare sequence in the latter film that convinced Coscarelli to try his hand at horror for his third outing. As he told the official *Phantasm* website

"When the monster jumped out of the darkness to scare the boys, the entire audience screamed. This was an exciting, new response... I determined that my next film would be loaded with shocks."

It was a logical step for the young director to take. According to an interview he gave to the Mopar Collectors Guide, as a child in the 1960s Coscarelli was often left with a babysitter whose lack of enthusiasm meant he had unlimited access to late night television horror shows. He called upon his memories of those happy nights when he set off to write the script for *Phantasm* in solitude, hiring a mountain cabin for three weeks and letting the isolation feed into his work.

"The longer I stayed alone in that cabin, the stranger my concepts became," he said. *"For instance, one night I finished a soda and accidentally punched my finger up through the bottom of the styro- foam cup. Watching this apparently severed finger wriggling in the bottom of my cup inspired me, and the result was a severed finger sequence in* **Phantasm***"*

In the 1979 advertising manual for 'Phantasm' that distributor Avco Embassy sent out to exhibitors, Coscarelli said

"I've been a horror movie buff all my life. But the more horror I witnessed on screen, the more difficult it was to scare me. That became the challenge of **Phantasm** *– to create a nightmare that would shock even the most jaded members of the audience."*

Of the film's title, Coscarelli struck on the word *Phantasm* mainly because it suited the hallucinatory tone of the picture – one dictionary definition defines it as being 'the delusion of a disordered mind' - and also because it was a phrase frequently used by one of his favourite authors.

"Edgar Allan Poe loved the word," the director revealed at the 1988 premiere of *Phantasm II*. *"He used it all of the time in his work, and that's where we stole it from."*

Adopting an experimental, deliberately non-linear approach for the film, Coscarelli took great care to anchor his story in sleepy China Grove, an all- American town that could have come directly out of a Norman Rockwell painting – albeit one boasting a surreal streak worthy of Buñuel or Dali.

*"Surrealism was always a component of **Phantasm**,"* Coscarelli confirmed in the Nucleus Films documentary, *Phantasmagoria*. *"I was heavily influenced by 'Un Chien Andalou'."*

This and its small-town setting were both traits that *Phantasm* shared with Willard Huyck's earlier, more self-conscious *Messiah of Evil*. Both films succeeded in capturing the otherworldly feel of life in an insular community where things aren't quite what they seem.

"Coscarelli has rediscovered the surrealist cinema of the 1920s - the destruction of the story line, the surge of symbols emptied of content, the systematic refusal to make sense," the Chicago Tribune would later report.

An obsession with mortuaries and the way in which society deals with the deceased determined Coscarelli's setting and tone.

*"The basic scenario of **Phantasm** came from my fascination and revulsion with death and how it manifests itself here in America,"* Coscarelli told Rue Morgue magazine. *"How the corpse is spirited away behind closed doors by the mysterious, black-clad mortician to a place that we are not allowed to go... I knew the subject would make for a great horror movie."*

Using threads of half-remembered nightmares, he began to weave a tale of ghastly goings-on at a small-town funeral parlour with thick strands of teenage angst, the fear of abandonment, musings on the inevitability of fate, the physical manifestations of bereavement fallout and the factory-like manner in which dead bodies are processed and interred. Using these themes as his parameters, Coscarelli applied the anything-goes anarchy of the dream state, and in doing so successfully captured the essence of a nightmare on film.

As *Phantasm* was made independently with his father, investment counsellor D.A. Coscarelli, acting as producer, and his friend and long term business associate, Paul Pepperman, serving as co-producer (and occasional stuntman), there were no studio constraints placed on the director's vision. Coscarelli had the luxury of shooting and re-shooting material over the course of three years, and he used the time to try out many different plot developments, including at least five different finales, most of which featured difficult action set pieces or elaborate special effect sequences.

In all, *Phantasm* had a budget of around $300,000 dollars to play with, but Coscarelli and Pepperman stretched it by spending most of the week planning ahead and then filming almost exclusively over long weekends. Doing this meant that not only could they ensure a smooth shoot, they could also save money on the actual number of days they needed to hire their cameras for.

For his cast, Coscarelli turned mainly to actors he was already familiar with. He had first noticed Angus Scrimm's ability at pulling facial expressions on the set of *Jim, The World's Greatest*. Scrimm (aka Laurence Rory Guy) had also played the title role in the 1951 short *Abraham Lincoln*, had written a stage-play for Sam Peckinpah, depicted Elias Disney in *Walt Disney: One Man's Dream* and had somehow found time to win a Grammy for his record liner notes, something which meant that he could later lay claim to having helped introduce America to The Beatles. Now Scrimm was to portray the Tall Man, dark emissary of a deadly force. Using just an undertaker's suit, boots with lifts in the heel, lank, straight hair and a permanent scowl, Scrimm was transformed into something suitably cadaverous and menacing.

"On my first film, he was the most accomplished and mature actor I had ever worked with," Coscarelli told . *"I was very intimidated by him, and felt that if given the proper role, he could make quite an imposing impression."*

When informed by Pepperman at a screening of *Kenny and Company* that the director had written a role for him as an alien, the cultured and gentlemanly Scrimm, who lists India's *Apu* trilogy as his favourite film experience, immediately wanted to know what country his character was from – France, perhaps, or maybe England?

"He's not from another country," Pepperman replied. *"He's from another world."*

"It came as a complete surprise to me," Scrimm remarked to Worlds of Horror magazine. *"(Coscarelli) pretty much tailored the role to what he thought I could do."*

For the film's trio of heroes, Coscarelli cast Michael Baldwin and Reggie Bannister from *Kenny And Company* as, um, Mike and Reggie. *Kenny and Company* had already turned Baldwin into a teen movie star in Japan, where his character's sassy attitude and open disrespect for adults had struck a chord with young filmgoers.

"We took a promotional trip to Japan when I was in the eighth grade, after the film came out, and when we stepped off the plane it was just like the Beatles," he said. *"It was awesome. We were chased down the street by 200 screaming Japanese girls and had to dive into a limousine to escape. And then, of course, they swarmed the car. It was great."*

Bannister had also acted in *Jim, The World's Greatest* alongside Gregory Harrison, Coscarelli's first choice for the role of Jody, Mike's older brother. When Harrison opted to play the lead in the short-lived television series *Logan's Run* instead, the role went to actor and musician Bill Thornbury.

With several other actors and actresses from his previous films playing supporting roles, the strange story of Morningside Mortuary was ready to unfold...

The film opens with the memorable sight of a couple having sex in an eerie cemetery. The boy is Tommy, a long-haired rocker in a denim jacket. The girl, a blonde beauty wearing a sleek lavender dress, is listed in the credits only as the Lady in Lavender.

"That was great, baby."

As Tommy lies back in satisfaction, the girl unexpectedly plunges a dagger through his chest. In a series of quick edits, the last thing Tommy sees before he dies is a close-up of the girl's face changing into that of a grim-faced older man.

The opening scenes are a statement of intent on the part of Coscarelli. He hooks the audience with a mix of sex, death and surrealism, and lets them know early on that this is the start of something new, something unlike anything else they have ever seen.

Tommy's funeral is held at Morningside Mausoleum, a local funeral parlour. Struggling to bear his coffin, his best friends Jody and Reggie can't believe that their buddy committed suicide.

"It's a hell of a way to end a trio."

Jody's thirteen year old brother Mike has been forbidden from attending the funeral, but he sneaks in anyway, riding a dirtbike across the graves with the supreme lack of respect that only a teenager can muster. Jody and Mike's parents are dead, and Mike is terrified that his older brother, who appears to work in the music industry, may also leave town. He follows him constantly, shadowing his every move. While secretly watching the funeral from a distance, Mike hears strange scurrying sounds in the shadows and glimpses small robed figures darting between the gravestones.

Meanwhile, inside Morningside, Jody is paying his respects to his parents when he also hears the scurrying sounds, this time seemingly coming from behind the vaults in the marble walls. He is about to investigate further when he is startled by a hand on his shoulder. Whirling, he stares up into the face of a towering, scowling undertaker, and the audience sees for the first time that it is the same grim-faced figure who killed Tommy.

"The funeral is about to begin.... sir!"

With its velour curtains, stone columns and bas relief sculptures, viewers could be forgiven for thinking that 'Phantasm' was filmed at a real funeral parlour. But the large number of action set pieces and violent stunts they had planned convinced Coscarelli and Pepperman that this would be impossible. Instead, they hired unit production manager Robert Del Valle Jr to come up with a cheap alternative.

It was decided to film on two main locations in California's San Fernando Valley. A small warehouse in Chatsworth was rented for set construction, and a house was leased at Pacific Palisades to serve as a set for the brothers' home and also as a production headquarters. Morningside itself was designed and built by Mark Scott Annerl and Marc Schwartz, two graduates who had just spent a summer working in construction. It was a masterpiece of movie manipulation – a single huge hallway incorporating two side corridors at a centre intersection and an eight-sided rotunda at one end. This allowed for a variety of different camera angles to make it seem that the mausoleum was a labyrinthine building. Its wooden walls were coated with marble-patterned wallpaper, and once the furnishings were added, the illusion was seamless. In their naivety, first-timers Annerl and Schwartz constructed the set as a semi-permanent structure. It was a happy accident – the set was so solid and heavy,

Coscarelli and his crew could sit on top of the mausoleum walls to get certain shots without fear of it all collapsing around them. A similar illusion was achieved for the surrounding graveyard, which appears to be surprisingly thick with landscaped pockets of trees and shrubs. Coscarelli simply hired out 20th Century Fox's entire stock of fake tombstones and placed them in the north section of Chatsworth Park, an area which, in the 30 years since the film was released, has been partially turned into a largely empty, very depressing parking lot.

"There were a couple of times when the headstones would just blow over," recalls Kathy Lester, the Lady in Lavender. *"They had to play around with those a bit to make them nice and sturdy."*

Doubling for the exterior of Morningside Mortuary was the Dunsmuir Mansion, a popular movie location in the Oakland Bay area that has also been seen in the James Bond film *A View To A Kill* and the Mel Gibson civil war thriller, *The Patriot*. Right before the *Phantasm* crew moved in, the mansion also played host to a porn film called *Little Girls Blue*. Finally, the arched gateway and tree-lined drive leading up to Morningside was more than 350 miles away at the Cobb Estate in Pasadena – the crew simply added fake metal lettering to the top of the arch and 'accidentally' backed a van into a road sign that was spoiling shots of the gates.

When all four elements were fused together, they brought Morningside to life as a vast, atmospheric and impressive location. They also gave *Phantasm* an air of class that defied its origins as a low budget film directed by a 20 year old kid.

Reggie: "Hey, it was a good idea not to let your little brother come to the funeral and see Tommy like this."

Jody: "Yeah. After mom and dad's funeral, he had nightmares for weeks."

After Tommy's funeral is over and the mourners have departed, Mike spies the undertaker, whom he has dubbed the Tall Man, stealing the coffin from its grave. Its apparent weight doesn't appear to be an obstacle, and the Tall Man picks it up and throws it into the back of a hearse with ease. (Scrimm was once asked by journalist Darren Gross how this effect was achieved. *"We removedthe body,"* he deadpanned).

Troubled by what he has witnessed, Mike calls at the home of an elderly psychic and her cute granddaughter for advice.

"I'm really scared about something that I did. I was messing around up at Morningside Cemetery, and I saw something - something really scary."

The granddaughter asks Mike to place his hand in a sinister wooden casket. In a sequence lifted from Frank Herbert's book 'Dune', Mike's hand starts to hurt, but he finds that he can't remove it until he has conquered his fear.

"Fear is the killer. That's what Grandmother wants you to learn. It was all in your mind."

The character of the fortune teller has long intrigued 'Phantasm' fans (or 'phans' as they have become known). Speaking only through her granddaughter with whom she appears to have a telepathic link, the elderly lady obviously knows more than she is letting on, and may even be a major part of the mystery. Coscarelli was quick to pick up on this, and would go on to drop further hints about her role in subsequent sequels.

Intrigued by what Mike claims he has witnessed, the granddaughter later visits Morningside. Wandering through its ornate corridors, she finds a door from behind which a high-pitched humming sound can be heard. Opening the door just a crack, she is bathed in bright light. We don't see whatever is in there as Coscarelli cuts to an exterior shot of the funeral parlour, but the girl's scream lingers long in the air.

A major element in the appeal of *Phantasm* is the film's unforgettable musical score. It was composed by Fred Myrow, a conductor and musician who had also produced music for the likes of *Soylent Green* and *Leo The Last*, and who had collaborated with Jim Morrison of The Doors. After scoring *Jim The World's Greatest* for Coscarelli, Myrow was happy to be asked to work on *Phantasm*.

"I very much enjoyed the working relationship," he told G.A.S.P. magazine. *"When Don called a few months later and said, 'I'm doing something that my family is putting together and have very minimal funds, but I have a hunch that this could become a cult classic of sorts, would you help us out?', I went down and met with him and I could see that it was really a labour of love on his part, so I agreed to do it."*

Using just a keyboard, a rock drum and a guitar, he produced a chilling, gothic theme that was as repetitive as it was simple. Because of the low budget, Myrow aimed for an atmospheric feel and styled the music so that it could be reused throughout the film.

"Don is much more sensitive to music than most film directors," he said. *"Some directors do a film that is basically completed and the music just adds a few elements, but Don is there the whole time. He really cares and has a great sensitivity to music. He's probably one of the most exacting directors to work for because every split-second of that thing has to make him happy. So, Don is very much involved, not in the writing of the music, but certainly in supervising the way it comes out, and that's one of the reasons I've tended to stay with him. He's really happy when you nail it."*

The *Phantasm* theme has certainly struck a chord with rock and metal bands. It inspired a thrash band of the same name, features in the likes of *Left Hand Path* by Entombed, was covered by Hungarian thrashers Tormentor and has been namechecked by the likes of The Ravenous and Toxodeath. Dialogue from the film has also featured in *Guilty For Being Tight* by Municipal Waste and *Hearse* by Marduk.

A short scene where Reggie joins Jody on the porch for a brief duet also deserves a special mention. Intended to show Reggie using a guitar tuning fork as a prelude to a later plot point, it offers Thornbury a showcase for one of his own memorable compositions, *Sittin' Here At Midnight*. It's a strange scene, not least because you can see that the two actors are really playing their instruments, and is one that has proven to be popular with viewers to the point that Thornbury recorded it as a special audio track for the laserdisc release of the film many years later

"We're hot as love."

The next time Mike sees the Tall Man, it takes place not at Morningside, but in broad daylight on the town's main shopping street, and is another stylish scene which offers a truly sublime chill. Wandering idly along and peering in through the shop windows, Mike turns to see the undertaker striding purposefully down the sidewalk outside Reggie's ice cream parlour. Reggie is at the kerb, loading fresh supplies into the back of his ice cream truck, and the cold vapours of the freezer compartment are billowing out into the open air. as the Tall Man passes through the icy cloud, he pauses. Turning slowly to face Mike, he raises his hands in a peculiar conductor-like fashion, his face a strange mix of ecstasy and revulsion. The hypnotic moment is over almost as quickly as it began, and as Reggie slams the freezer door shut and cuts off the cold vapours, the Tall Man recovers, turns and strides away once more. Mike's sense of growing unease causes him to start having bad dreams about the Tall Man. This allows Coscarelli to display his flair for staging a macabre set-piece with tableaus such as one where Mike climbs into his bed, only to 'awake' to find that the bed is now at the centre of the cemetery, and that the Tall Man is looming over him while ghouls burst out of the ground at either side.

"When you're in the vicinity of the Tall Man, reality can distort, time can distort, and things are not what they seem," Coscarelli later suggested.

The weirdness continues as Mike follows Jody to a local bar and watches while he picks up a beautiful young woman. Leaving together, she convinces Jody to take a stroll through the cemetery at Morningside. She is, of course, the Lady in Lavender. Luckily for Jody, Mike is still following. While hiding in the bushes, Mike hears those scurrying sounds again, and this time something small and cowled charges at him with a furious roar. Mike inadvertently saves his brother from suffering the same fate as Tommy when he bursts screaming out of the bushes, interrupting the lovers with hysterical claims that he is being pursued by hooded dwarves. Jody is not happy, especially when he returns to his date to find that she has vanished.

"It was probably just a... a gopher in heat!"

About those dwarves... there is no getting away from the fact that they look exactly like the Jawas of *Star Wars*. But Coscarelli swears that he had already conceived of the creatures and started putting them before the camera long before the George Lucas film took the world by storm.

"We first started shooting in April of 1977," he told Fangoria magazine. *"One of the first scenes filmed was of a dwarf jumping on Mike's back. A few weeks later, somebody comes in and says, 'Hey, I just saw that new science fiction picture and they've got a thing in there that looks just like one of your dwarves'."*

In subsequent sequels to *Phantasm*, Coscarelli would try to establish some distance by giving his dwarves hideously distorted faces and having them utter inhuman, guttural growls and shrieks.

Later, while working on their beloved Plymouth Barracuda car at home, Mike is beset by the dwarves once more. Seeing someone approach, he strikes out with a hammer – only to find that he has just injured his older brother, who scoffs at Mike's wild claims.

Mike: "They were jumping on the car, and making these...these weird sounds!"

Jody: "You sure it wasn't that retarded kid, Timmy, up the street?"

Once memorably described by drive in movie critic Joe Bob Briggs as "The most outrageous muscle car ever to legally prowl the highways," the 'cuda has long been associated with *Phantasm* and its three sequels. Together with Scrimm, Bannister and the silver spheres, it is one of the main constants that you can always expect to see in any of the entries in the ongoing saga. Coscarelli knew that he wanted to immortalise the car on film ever since seeing a high school buddy show off a Sassy Grass Green pistol-grip four-speed 'cuda with a white interior.

By the time he made *Phantasm*, such muscle cars were out of fashion, and the production was able to pick up a cheap 1971 four-speed model with a 340 engine. It was in bad shape, but one trip to the body shop later, the car was spray-painted mirror black (a job which was made easier by the fact that Thornbury's brother happened to be a custom car painter), featured slightly flared rear quarter panels and boasted Crager chrome rims. Unfortunately, the engine was shot, and despite its flawless big screen appearance, it caused the production a lot of trouble.

At the end of filming, the original 'cuda used for *Phantasm* was given to a crew member who later sold it for $1,000, and it has never been seen since. For the sequels, the producers were forced to find alternative models, including a convertible version, although Coscarelli would later hold onto a modified 318 model that was used for *Phantasm II* (he is also the proud owner of a red-on-red AAR 'cuda).

"You're crazy, man."

Jody refuses to believe Mike's tall tales, and tells a friend that he suspects his younger brother is inventing bizarre lies to try and stop him from leaving town.

"I'm thinking of sending him off to live with his aunt... He's a tough little kid. I love him. I'm going to miss him."

Unused footage from an early cut of *Phantasm* revealed that following the deaths of their parents, Mike and Jody now own the local bank, thus allowing the pair of them to put off the inevitability of having to grow up and face their responsibilities, and also explaining why a thirteen year old is able to openly drive motorbikes and muscle cars without being bothered by the local police – the tie-in novelisation features a line in which Jody jokes that he will 're-possess the sheriff's squad car' if the law dares interfere with them.

It is interesting to note that Coscarelli, a young man in his early twenties when he directed *Phantasm*, ensures that none of the film's main heroes have anything that could be regarded as being a 'serious' job. Jody works in the music business, Mike doesn't even appear to go to school and Reggie is an ice cream salesman – a dream job for many a child. For Mike and Jody, the flip side of losing their parents is the freedom that the brothers have gained. They have a maid, an entire house to themselves, the run of a whole town to enjoy and no rules or regulations that they have to live by – there is quite literally no one who can tell them what time to go to bed or what clothes to wear. It is a childhood fantasy that most of us have enjoyed, and a concept that director John Hughes would later create a whole franchise around in the *Home Alone* movies. But in *Phantasm*, Coscarelli is determined to show us the flip side of such a dark daydream.

Scared that Jody is going to accelerate his plans, Mike sticks a knife down his sock and heads off to Morningside in the dead of night to get some proof, thereby providing the film with its weirdest and most talked-about moment. After hiding inside an empty coffin to avoid being caught by a sinister henchman of the Tall Man, Mike sneaks through the funeral home's empty marble corridors. Hearing a strange, high-pitched whistling sound, he turns to see a bizarre chrome ball flying through the air. Throwing himself to the floor, Mike narrowly avoids being struck by the silver sphere. He flees as the ball turns for another pass, but runs straight into the arms of the henchman. Only Mike knows that the sphere is approaching, and a close-up reveals two vicious hooked blades sliding out of the ball and locking into place as it hurtles towards the struggling figures.

Mike finally escapes the henchman's clutches by sinking his teeth into the man's arm. He drops to one side and rolls out of the way, but the minion has no such chance of escape. The silver sphere thuds directly into the centre of the man's forehead, the hooked blades embedding themselves deep in the flesh. As the minion struggles to remove it, a drill-bit slides out of the ball and proceeds to pierce his skull. Mike looks on in horror as a great jet of blood and semi-solid matter erupts from the rear of the ball, until the henchman finally topples over, dead and drained.

It is a fantastic moment in a film packed with surprises, and leaves the audience wondering where Coscarelli will take them next. What is the silver sphere? Where did it come from, and why did it attack another of the Tall Man's minions? Perhaps not surprisingly, Coscarelli's inspiration for the murderous chrome ball came directly from a particularly vivid nightmare.

"I had a dream, just your basic nightmare, only I found myself being pursued down unending corridors by this silver sentinel which I could not escape," he told Rue Morgue magazine. *"While writing 'Phantasm', it seemed like a perfect device with which to arm the Tall Man - a digital vampire, if you will."*

To realise this standout set-piece, Coscarelli contracted a film effects craftsman called Willard Green. A specialist in mechanics, when Coscarelli and Pepperman first visited Green they found him hard at work constructing gigantic turntables for car commercials. For a grand total of $763, Green delivered a master sphere rig containing the blades, drill and blood pumping system as well as three interchangeable sphere faces which would allow it to be filmed from different angles.

He also produced several balls formed from moulded plastic which had been put through a vacuum-metalizing process to give them their chrome look – these could be thrown or tossed for shots of the ball travelling through the mausoleum corridors. For the effect of the ball's blood exhaust, the actor playing the Tall Man's minion, Ken Jones, had a tube running up his sleeve and into the unseen side of the sphere from where it could be pumped through. The fluid that would bubble up from Jones' head as the drillbit made contact was simply flushed through a syringe, but the stage blood had congealed slightly by the time that the scene was filmed. To unclog the syringe, art director David Brown desperately squeezed down harder, causing a fountain of gore to explode from the actor's head. It was a happy accident that Coscarelli was delighted with, and he decided to leave the finished effect in the film.

However, it also meant trouble with the ratings board, who wanted to give the movie an 'X' – commonly viewed as the commercial kiss of death because it is associated with pornographic films; to this day, American newspapers and broadcasters refuse to advertise such fare. Luckily, help was at hand from Charles Champlin, a respected film critic for the LA Times whose earlier championing of Coscarelli had also convinced Universal to pick up *Jim, The World's Greatest* for distribution.

"Charles Champlin came to our defence," Scrimm explained to Worlds of Horror. *"The ratings board was persuaded that the whole thing really wasn't gory because the audiences would invariably laugh at the end, because it was so outrageous to see all that blood pumping out. So they reversed themselves and gave us an 'R'."*

They may have opted to stick with their original rating if they had noticed the flow of urine which runs down the dead henchman's leg and pools around the feet of a clearly horrified Mike, something which Coscarelli believes has been obscured by years of dodgy prints and washed-out video conversions, and has only really come to light in the age of laserdiscs and DVDs...

"The filming of the sphere was actually pretty funny because for the first few days, we didn't realise that they were mirrors," Coscarelli said. *"We kept trying to light them... It wasn't until about day three when somebody on the set realised and actually yelled it out - 'You don't light the sphere, you light what's reflected in the sphere!' Once we realised that, it was a whole new ball game."*

To achieve the shots of the sphere in flight, the production went for another low-fi approach.

"We had someone on the crew who was a high school baseball pitcher, so we had a plastic ball that we fabricated, filled it with sand and then he would skim behind the camera," revealed Pepperman. *"We would run the camera in reverse, and he would just throw it right over the camera towards the opposite end of the hallway. Playing it back, it looks like the sphere is coming right toward the camera. It worked out great."*

D. Kerry Prior, who would provide spheres for other films in the *Phantasm* saga, told France's Cinefantastique magazine that the sphere was the 'perfect monster', its simple design allowing it to adopt a gimmick first seen on screen in the 1960 movie *Peeping Tom*.

"It reflects the general surroundings, but also the fear, the terror that is written on the face of its prey," Prior said. *"This effect of capturing the victim's own death image is more terrifying, more horrible, than any mask of a monster who grimaces, froths at the mouth and drools blood... I am convinced that the spheres have touched the unconscious of the public as few monsters have."*

This single scene ensured that *Phantasm* stood out in a season crowded with genre flicks that were all vying for attention, as author and artist Stephen Romano recalled in his afterword for the release of the *Phantasm* movie tie-in novel.

"Though I was too young to understand such things at the time, the image of the flying silver sphere with the drill that sucked out your brain was impossible to escape that summer," he said. *"Everyone was talking about it. The media was buzzing. My older, braver friends, who had snuck in with their parents to see it at the drive-in, gasped that it was the freakiest thing they had ever seen."*

More was to follow. Immediately after witnessing the work of the silver sphere, Mike encounters the Tall Man. It's a supremely chilling moment; unable to take his eyes off the body of the dead henchman, Mike doesn't see the Tall Man stepping out of the shadows at the far end of the corridor. For several seconds, the undertaker simply stands there unseen, silently observing the boy. When Mike finally realises that he is being watched, he whirls around and slowly edges his way forward toward the corridor intersection.

The Tall Man mirrors him step for step. After a brief silent standoff, Mike makes a run for it, and the Tall Man explodes into motion, frantically chasing him through the backrooms of the mausoleum until the boy finally manages to slam a steel basement door shut, preventing the Tall Man from following. Mike pauses to catch his breath, but Coscarelli isn't done with us yet. A frantic tapping sound alerts the boy to the fact that the Tall Man's twitching fingers are caught in the jam of the door. Without a pause, Mike hacks at the hand with the knife, severing several of the undertaker's fingers. This causes a welter of blood to splash messily across

the wall and floor, and delivers yet another tremendous sucker punch – the colour of the Tall Man's blood is abright, inhuman yellow.

As if to accentuate the implications of this revelation, the undertaker lets out an unearthly wail of pain from the other side of the door while Mikes watches the severed digits wriggle and writhe in a puddle of the yellow blood. Realising that he finally has the proof he needs, Mike picks up one of the fingers and narrowly escapes the clutches of several hooded dwarves before climbing out of a broken window and running back home through the menacing dark.

Given his concerns over the similarities between the hooded dwarves and the Jawas of *Star Wars*, Coscarelli was equally as alarmed when he heard reports that the android character in the just-released *Alien* was also revealed to have yellow-coloured blood. When he caught up with the Ridley Scott film, he was relieved to find that it was actually white fluid.

The next morning, Jody finds Mike asleep on the stairs, a shotgun and a small wooden box containing the Tall Man's finger cradled in his lap. Telling his big brother the whole story, Mike opens up the box to reveal the finger, still twitching and oozing in a puddle of yellow gore. Faced with the evidence, Jody immediately supports his little brother.

"Okay, I believe you... What's going on up there?"

It's a deft move on Coscarelli's part, one which allows him to sidestep the usual genre cliché of nobody believing the hero's warnings, and moves the plot quickly and efficiently forward while also strengthening the audience's affection for the bond that exists between the two brothers.

As journalist David Flint has noted, *"Coscarelli's script foregrounds loyalty, courage, friendship and perseverance... instead of simply setting up 'empowerment' clichés, he gives each of the three leads the capacity not only to face the horrors, but also to appreciate each other's worth in the process."*

This is apparent in the scene where Reggie arrives just as the brothers decide to take their evidence to the sheriff. Checking the box, Mike discovers that the Tall Man's severed finger has transformed into some kind of red-eyed bug from hell. Reggie watches in amazement as the brothers struggle with the creature, which is eventually destroyed when they force it down a kitchen garbage grinder.

"What the hell is going on?"

The hell-bug was created by Kate Coscarelli, who performed sterling production design, makeup and costume work for *Phantasm* under the aliases of S. Tyler and Shirley Mae. Unable to afford to have the monster created from scratch, she simply bought a model from a store and adapted it. Sadly, the effect as executed on screen doesn't really match the level of creativity with which it was conceived, and whenever it is seen in close-up, the hell-bug is a rare low point in the film's stable of special effects. A scene was shot near the climax of the film which involved Mike seeing the creature again, this time sitting at the centre of a vast web. However, Coscarelli chose to discard it from the final cut.

"It didn't work out so good," was all he said by way of explanation.

But there is no faulting the energy and effort which Baldwin and Thornbury throw into their struggle with the beast, and they make the finished film's hell-bug scene work through a very convincing display of physical acting.

"You'll be safe here. Just lock all the doors and windows. And don't follow me."

With their proof gone, Jody sneaks into Morningside to have a look around and see if he can score something else that he can take to the authorities. But the law was something that Coscarelli wanted to avoid featuring in his movie (they didn't feature in any of the sequels until the fourth instalment, and even then turned out to be agents of the Tall Man).

"A horror story isn't a police story," the director explained in the *Phantasm* advertising manual. *"The cops would have injected a note of logic into the movie that would have stopped the action dead in its tracks. There are enough police on television – why let them spoil the fun?"*

At Morningside, Jody doesn't make it further than the basement before he is gang-tackled by hooded dwarves. Fleeing down the driveway, he is followed by a speeding hearse, and manages to fire off a shotgun blast before diving out of its path. As the headlights swing back towards him, he prepares for another shot – but the vehicle is revealed to be the 'cuda driven by Mike, who has ignored his big brother's orders to stay put. The pair race away as the hearse gives chase, and they are forced into a high-speed duel that ends when Jody fires the shotgun into the hearse's engine and causes it to crash.

"There's nobody driving that mother!"

Examining the wreck, the brothers are shocked to discover that one of the hooded dwarves is behind the wheel of the hearse. Even worse, the dwarf resembles Tommy, their friend whose death opened the movie. Using a strangely isolated phone box, Jody calls Reg and asks him to come and collect the dwarf's body in his ice cream truck.

"What's all this yellow shit coming out of his head?"

Back at their house, Reggie and the brothers try to figure out what the Tall Man is up to, and what they can do about it. While Mike worries that the bodies of his parents may have been stolen from their caskets and transformed in the same manner as Tommy, Reggie comes up with a plan.

"What we've got to do is snag that tall dude, and stomp the shit out of him, and we'll find out what the hell is going on up there!"

Jody is more concerned about keeping Mike safe, so he asks Reggie to take Mike to an antique store run by two sisters, Sally and Susie. Mike protests, but his brother appears to be finally facing up to some of the parental responsibilities that he has inherited, and will brook no argument. Reluctantly agreeing to his elder brother's demands, Mike allows Reggie to drive him over.

In the original cut of *Phantasm*, Sally and Susie were the girlfriends of Reggie and Jody, but the majority of their scenes were left on the cutting room floor as Coscarelli chopped and changed the course of the movie. Most of the trimmed footage can be found on recent special edition DVD releases – they include a scene set at the China Grove Bank where Jody enters his office and canoodles with Susie, a teller, and a light-hearted scene set at Reggie's ice cream parlour where Sally helps a drunken Jody turn Mike into a human sundae.

As it stands, there is no real reason why the two girls should be running an antique shop, but the movie tie-in novelisation reveals that Jody has used his position as owner of the bank to install Sally as manager and keep the business going mainly because he knows Mike loves rooting around in all the old junk that can be found there. At the store, a worried Mike takes his mind off his concern for Jody and Reggie by half-heartedly wandering among the antiques. But the mystery of the Tall Man has permeated even the history of China Grove, something which Mike realises when he finds an old photograph featuring Morningside Mausoleum.

In front of the funeral home stands a black horse-drawn funeral carriage, and sitting on it wearing the sombre uniform of an old-fashioned undertaker is none other than the Tall Man. As Mike's mind reels with the realisation that the Tall Man is not a new phenomenon, the photograph comes to life in his hands; we see the Tall Man slowly turn his head to look out of the image at the audience, and hear the horse whinny softly before the photograph returns to normal. A startled Mike realises that he has to tell Jody and rushes back to the girls.

"No questions! You must take me home!"

The sequence that follows was filmed inside the darkened Chatsworth warehouse and makes for another eerie scene – so much so that it graces the back cover of the film's Japanese souvenir cinema programme. As Sally drives and talks to Susie, a worried Mike spots Reggie's overturned ice cream truck lying at the side of a mist-shrouded road. Urging the girls to stay inside their car, Mike investigates. There's no sign of Reggie, but the truck's freezer compartment door has been forced open, and the dwarf-corpse of Tommy is missing. Realising that they are not alone, Mike hurries back into the car, but the girls have had enough, and demand some answers before they leave the scene. It's too late – the car is attacked by a pack of hooded dwarves, and as the girls are mauled, Mike is thrown through the rear windscreen.

He recovers in time to see the car's tail lights fading into the darkness as the creatures whisk their captives back to Morningside.

Meanwhile, Jody has fallen asleep while waiting for Reggie to return, and suffers a nightmare in which the Tall Man bears down on him in a Morningside hallway while clawed hands emerge from the marble vaults to drag him down to hell. He wakes to find a bruised, dishevelled Mike standing before him. Mike tells Jody what has happened, but if he was expecting his brother to tell him to go fire up the 'cuda, he is dismayed when Jody locks him into his bedroom to keep him from further harm. Distraught, Mike watches as Jody leaves for Morningside without him.

"You're never coming back, you goddamned bastard! Don't leave me alone!"

It's a strange scene, one where Coscarelli plays on Mike's fears of being abandoned and Jody's (terrible) attempts at being a responsible adult. As scary as the Tall Man, the dwarves and the silver sphere are, Mike is more frightened of losing his big brother, so he focuses his attention on using whatever is to hand to get him out of the bedroom. One inventive (and dangerous!) trick involving a hammer and a shotgun shell later, Mike is racing down the stairs and heading for the front door, intending to take the motorbike to catch up with Jody. Pausing only to slip a Colt pistol into the waistband of his jeans, he yanks the door open – and finds the Tall Man standing unexpectedlyon the other side.

"I've been waiting for you."

The Tall Man pauses only to show Mike his newly-regenerated fingers before grabbing him by the neck and hauling him outside. Mike puts up a game fight, but the Tall Man defeats him by casually lifting the boy a foot off the floor and carrying him to a waiting hearse. It's a seamless shot, smoothly executed in a single take, and in common with some of 'Phantasm's' best moments, one that was achieved simply and cheaply by having Mike step off the porch of the house and onto a wheeled camera cart which the crew then rolled down the driveway towards the hearse.

*"'**Phantasm** was entirely from the attitude of 'let's put on a show',"* Coscarelli later said in the documentary *Phantasmagoria*. *"The crew was entirely friends and students. The production designer was my mother, and the special effects were done by my college roommate. We were figuring out things as we'd go. The basic challenge was to put together some pretty sophisticated effects with paper clips and some tape."*

Locked in the back of the hearse as the Tall Man whisks him off to Morningside, Mike tries to kick out the rear windscreen before remembering the Colt. His first shot shatters the glass window; before the Tall Man can react, he aims a second shot down into the wheel of the hearse. As the Tall Man loses control of the speeding vehicle, Mike dives out of the broken window, rolling as he hits the ground in time to see the hearse strike a telegraph pole and explode (the explosion is somewhat illogical, but is perfectly in keeping with the anarchic tone that Coscarelli has taken pains to establish, and besides, it's a bit late to start worrying about logic at this point).With the Tall Man seemingly vanquished, Mike continues on his way up to Morningside to find Jody. Jody, meanwhile, has broken into the vault containing the remains of his parents and has dragged his father's coffin out into a mausoleum corridor to check if the Tall Man has interfered with the remains. Steeling himself, he prepares to open the lid – but loses his nerve and slams it shut at the last moment.

"He HAS to be in there."

By the time Mike arrives, Jody has moved on, but the coffin is still where he left it. Offering up a silent prayer, Mike opens the coffin and peers in. Whatever he finds (or doesn't find) sends him screaming in terror through the marble corridors, but his flight is brought to an abrupt halt when a familiar sound is heard. The silver sphere is returning, and as its hooked blades lock into place, this time there is nowhere for Mike to hide.

"Oh my God!"

Mike is saved from a horrible death when Jody appears at his shoulder and shatters the silver sphere in mid-air with a blast from the shot gun. The brothers embrace as Mike awkwardly tries to describe what he saw when he opened the coffin, finally giving up. It is interesting to note here that Jody declines to reveal to his younger brother that it was he who opened the vault, or that he tried and failed to do what Mike has done. When Mike suggests that they forget about it and try and find out what lies behind the door where the humming sound is emanating from, Jody readily agrees. But before they can do so, Reggie surprises them.

Mike: "Hey Reg, you ain't dead!"

Reggie: "No, and I ain't three foot two yet, either."

Reggie reveals that after he was brought to Morningside, he hid inside a casket before rescuing the kidnapped girls and sneaking them out through a window. A superb deleted scene which would have elaborated on this shows Mike trying to free his friend from a locked coffin, oblivious to the fact that Reggie has just entered the room through a doorway behind him. If Reggie is the one who has opened the door, who the hell is inside the casket? As the two friends ponder this, the casket lid begins to rise, forcing them to lock it tight before fleeing.

Jody: "Well, after you, my friend."

Reggie: "You be my guest!"

Whatever we were expecting to see inside the room, Coscarelli manages to side-step us once again. At the centre of the grand old mausoleum is a startlingly bright futuristic chamber. Almost surgically white, the room is empty save for stacked rows of barrels that face a pair of chrome waist-high metal poles. The poles are reverberating, and are the source of the intense humming sound that fills the air. Mike approaches the poles while Reggie and Jody check out the barrels. As Mike discovers that the space between the poles forms some kind of invisible void where his outstretched hand disappears from view, Jody is revolted to find that the barrels are filled with freshly transformed dwarves. Suddenly, Mike is sucked in through the void. Tumbling through the air against a blood-red sky that churns over on itself with furious motion, Mike is saved by Jody, who has managed to catch hold of his belt. In the few seconds before he is pulled back into the white room, Mike looks down upon a fantastic sight: a rocky, desolate landscape, identical in all directions for as far as the eye can see, broken only by a long line of hooded dwarves who are carrying barrels off into the distance.

Jody and Reggie haul Mike back into the white room, patting down his smoking clothes as Mike realises what is going on at Morningside Mausoleum.

Mike: "They're using them for slaves - the dwarves! And they've got to crush them, because of the gravity... and the heat. And this is the door to their planet."

Reggie: "Yeah... and these guys are all ready to go."

At this point in the film, savvy genre fans may notice a distinct similarity between *Phantasm* and what is generally regarded as the worst film in movie history (but not by me – as far as I'm concerned, that particular honour goes to *Jaws: The Revenge* every single time). David Flint nailed it in his review of the movie.

*"'**Phantasm** mixes genres with such smart but unselfconscious verve that it is only later you realise you have been watching a sci-fi horror film about grave robbers from another world,"* he said. *"That's right - the same plot as 'Plan 9 From Outer Space'!"*

The startling effect of what has become known as the red planet was achieved by filming on location at the Santa Fe Dam. Coscarelli created an optical illusion by placing the camera at the foot of the dam's sloping walls and filming up over its rocky surface. He and Pepperman then gathered twenty neighbourhood kids, packed them inside the Tall Man's hearse, drove them out to the dam, dressed them in dwarf robes created by his mother and placed them with the barrels at strategic points along the wall of the dam. With a series of cardboard cutouts set up at the furthest end, Coscarelli was able to film what looked like a long line of dwarves stretching over the horizon.

The red, churning sky was added as a matte later – Coscarelli painted a wall of the Chatsworth warehouse red, installed red studio lights and filled the warehouse with smoke to provide an eerie, rolling, red-on-red effect. Mike's tumble through the gateway was achieved by filming him on a trampoline, then editing his high-speed acrobatics to make it look like he was in freefall. Together with the silver sphere, the red planet is among the three major scenes that people refer to whenever *Phantasm* is discussed – but Coscarelli saves his biggest surprise for the very last scene.

The three friends are separated when the humming stops, the brightness dies and the mausoleum is plunged into darkness. Using a lighter for illumination, Mike is confronted by a hooded dwarf and flees the room, followed closely by Jody. When all returns to normal and the humming resumes, Reggie finds that he is now alone in the white room, and the only one who can shut the Tall Man's operation down. Inspiration strikes as Reggie studies the reverberating chrome poles and is reminded of the tuning fork that he used while performing his porch duet with Jody earlier. In that scene, Reggie stopped the instrument from humming by pressing his hand against its twin forks.

As he summons up the courage to do the same with the gateway, Jody and Mike are searching for each other in the cemetery outside the funeral home. The Lady in Lavender creeps up on Mike and is about to stab him in the back when, inside the white room, Reggie clamps his hands over the chrome poles and stops them from reverberating. The effect is instantaneous; as the Lady in Lavender gasps and falls to the ground, a mighty storm rises up, and Morningside is lashed by howling winds. In the white room, the humming noise has returned, except this time it is growing steadily louder as everything starts to get sucked through the space gate. Reggie battles his way out of the room as barrel after barrel is dragged into the whirlpool-like void between the poles. Making his way outside, he shields his face against the flying debris of the wind storm, and struggles across the front lawn to help a lone female figure who has apparently already succumbed to the rigours of the storm. But Reggie is in mortal danger, for as the audience can see, the unconscious woman is really the Lady in Lavender...

The actors also found themselves in danger during this scene thanks to the film's mischievous thirteen year old star.

"I wanted to get this scene first time because I am cold, and I am dirty, and I am pissed off, because sweet Michael is throwing stones and debris in front of this HUGE wind machine," Lester recalled in the documentary *Phantasmagoria* – something which Bannister also remembers with a wry grin.

"I got hit more than a few times," he said.

"Oh, that's because that's the only story they can remember," Baldwin retorted. *"They're all so old, they can't remember any other interesting stories, so they always come back to 'he put rocks in the wind machine'!"*

Out in the storm, Jody finds Mike just in time for the brothers to witness Reggie being stabbed through the heart by the Lady in Lavender. Like Tommy before him, the last thing that Reggie sees before he dies is the woman turning into the Tall Man, who looks none the worse following his fiery death in the hearse crash.

Mike: "Come on, we've got to help him!"

Jody: "You can't help him. He's dead."

As the brothers speed away in the 'cuda, the humming noise reaches a crescendo, and Morningside dissolves in a fuzzy bright explosion of light as the entire building is sucked through the space gate – an effect which eagle-eyed viewers will recognise as the exact same one used for the 'beam me up' scenes in the television show *Star Trek*.

Mike: "What are we going to do without Reggie?"

Jody: "Reggie's the last he'll ever get, 'cause we're going to run that bastard straight down to hell."

The brothers decide to try and lure the Tall Man out to an old mine shaft 'by the end of Singer's Creek - a thousand feet straight down'. Jody heads off to remove the shaft's warning barriers and get the trap ready while Mike gathers more ammunition and weapons at home. As he moves nervously around the house checking that the doors and windows are secure, Mike appears subdued and exhausted. It doesn't last long; opening the curtains to check the lock on his bedroom window, Mike finds himself face to face with the Tall Man. As he throws himself backwards, the undertaker smashes his way through the glass and into the room (a scene that required several takes to get right as it was among the first that Baldwin and Scrimm filmed together, and Baldwin couldn't stop grinning whenever he saw the villain leering in at him through the window).

Mike tears through the house and looks for a way out, but Coscarelli catches us by surprise again when the front door suddenly blows inward and hurtles past Mike to reveal the Tall Man waiting on the other side – another ingenious scene that was achieved in a simple, lo-fi manner.

"Paul Pepperman put some straps onto the door, and stood behind the door holding the straps," Coscarelli revealed in Fangoria. "The door was unhinged so that, on cue, Paul could just run as fast as he could across the set, finally landing on his back with the door over him. He was wearing a helmet and was thoroughly padded to avoid injury."

"You play a good game, boy. But the game is finished. Now, you die!"

Mike runs out of the back of the house and heads for Singer's Creek, pursued all the way by the Tall Man, who appears to have established a telepathic link with the boy. Mike is plagued by nightmarish visions as he flees – tombstones burst out of the earth, and hands erupt from the ground to seize at his ankles. Finally, Mike makes it to the creek, and with the Tall Man hot on his heels manages to leap across the mouth of the mine shaft. The Tall Man is not so lucky – he plunges straight into the pit, and with one final lunge at Mike, down the hillside to seal the top of the shaft. The brothers have done it; Mike looks up lovingly at the elder brother he adores as Jody punches the air in triumph... just as Mike wakes up in his own bed, and Coscarelli throws us another curveball, this time one inspired by *Invaders From Mars*.

Throwing back the covers, Mike heads downstairs to where Reggie sits playing guitar before an open fire, and reveals that everything we have just seen has been a dream. It is Jody, not Reggie, who died, not long after Mike's parents had their own accident. Reggie has been looking after him ever since, but Mike is still convinced that the Tall Man is real.

Mike: "I know those rocks aren't going to hold him. First he took mom and dad, then he took Jody, and now he's after me."

Reggie: "Mike, that tall man of yours did not take Jody away. Jody died in a car wreck."

So is Mike just a troubled kid, one whose fear of abandonment has caused him to imagine and dream about everything we have just witnessed? This was certainly the case in the first draft of the screenplay, and if Coscarelli had gone with his original vision, the film would have ended with Mike turning away from a visit to Jody's grave to see Angus Scrimm as a preacher overseeing a nearby funeral – an imposing figure that the grief-stricken boy has woven into his fantasy. But the director wanted something with a bit more punch, and tried a number of different endings before finally settling on one which has ensured that anyone who watches *Phantasm* will never forget it.

Reggie: "You know, partner, what we need is a change of scenery. Why don't you and me hit the road for a couple of weeks?"

Mike: "Where would we go?"

Reggie: "Well, I don't know. I guess we can figure that one out when we get there."

As Mike agrees and heads upstairs to pack a bag, Reggie starts playing his guitar again - *Sittin' Here At Midnight*, the same song that we saw him play with Jody earlier in the film. It's another odd moment, one which jars with Reggie's assertion that Mike has been dreaming this whole time.

Upstairs, Mike enters his bedroom and starts selecting items that he wants to take on the road trip. Picking up a Polaroid photograph of Jody, he considers it sadly for a moment before moving on to get some clothes.

Noticing that his mirrored cupboard door is open, Mike swings it closed – and reveals the reflection of the Tall Man on the other side of the room. Seeing him, Mike whirls around, his back to the mirror. Coscarelli zooms in to the Tall Man's face as the undertaker booms out a single word, one that resonates with malice and sinister intent:

"Boyyyyyy!"

The mirror shatters as clawed hands erupt through the glass to seize Mike and drag him back into the shadows, and the credits roll on *Phantasm*.

It's a fantastic way to end a film in which you are never sure what is real and what is fantasy, and plays on some of our deepest childhood fears – the monster in the closet, the beast under the bed waiting to clutch at your exposed ankle and so on. The Tall Man is the ultimate bogeyman: he lurks in the shadows, hides in your bedroom, kills parents and siblings and tears you away from your family and friends.

In his much recommended book *Nightmare USA*, David Flint describes the Tall Man as *"...a negative Peter Pan, trying to draw Mike (like Wendy) into a never-never land beyond adulthood, out of time."*

The impact of the final scene is so shocking that most viewers miss the fact that when the Tall Man is revealed in the mirror, he boasts short, neat hair. This was because Scrimm had assumed that filming on *Phantasm* was long over, and by the time Coscarelli called him back, he had got rid of his long locks. A fast zoom and some clever lighting helped to disguise the change in his appearance.

Trimmed down from three hours to a more respectable ninety minutes, *Phantasm* was picked up for distribution by Avco Embassy, a name familiar to horror and sci-fi fans as the outfit that distributed several important genre flicks like *Escape From New York*, *Scanners*, *The Howling* and *The Fog*.

Avco Embassy struck on a clever marketing campaign for the film. Instead of trying to explain its premise, they cut a series of trailers that played upon its weirder aspects and invited viewers to guess what it was actually about - 'Phantasm: is it a nightmare... an illusion... an evil... a fantasy... is it alive?'.

With a programme of midnight premieres and a whirlwind promotional tour for Coscarelli and Scrimm, the publicity worked, and the distributors soon struck on fresh ideas to advise the paying public that the movie was now 'open everywhere like a freshly dug grave'. Describing the film as 'The ultimate in terror' and 'A fiendish undertaking', they also coined the now-classic tag lines 'If this one doesn't scare you, you're already dead!' and 'If your skin doesn't crawl, it's on too tight!'

The advertising manual is a fascinating glance into a bygone age of movie hucksterism that has all but vanished. It advised exhibitors on a number of different ways in which they could promote the film. These included competitions to find the loudest screamer, employing a local basketball player to dress up as the Tall Man and hand out certificates congratulating patrons on 'surviving' the movie, hiring a hearse for a 'spot-the-hearse' radio phone-in promotion or staging a hearse-stuffing contest as "the kind of publicity stunt that will launch a sensational word-of-mouth campaign... and the 'reel' winner will be your box office." It also suggested using local radio to invite people to describe their worst nightmares and reward the most vivid ones with 'a nightmare on the town' – a complimentary funeral bouquet and a chauffeured hearse to enjoy a meal at a local restaurant before heading back for the opening night of *Phantasm*.

The publicity campaign tried to establish an air of doomed mystery about *Phantasm*, not least of which was the sad fact that silver sphere creator Willard Green died before the film's release and never got to see the ball in action.

"Mysteriously, all of his notes and drawings for the lethal looking gadget vanished," the manual stated. *"And thus far, no one's been found who knows how the complex mechanism within the sphere works. There were too damned many accidents involving professional experienced people who knew their jobs,"* it went on to quote Coscarelli as saying. *"First, a wind machine went beserk and started spinning in reverse. It caught a crew member's scarf and would have sucked his head in with it if Mike Baldwin, who co-stars in the picture, hadn't caught him around the waist and held on for dear life. Then there was the scene in which an avalanche of rocks rolled downhill into a pit. The rocks had been carefully 'tracked' so we knew their trajectory to the last inch. But somehow, one giant boulder flew over the pit – as if it had been hurled by a giant hand – and smashed headlong into a $100,000 camera."*

Another Coscarelli story in the advertising manual could almost have been a scene lifted from his screenplay.

"We had just finished the sequence in which ghoulish hands reach out of the grave, trying to drag Michael in with them. Mike returned to his home which is on a hillside in Tujunga Canyon, about twenty miles from Los Angeles. That was the night that torrential rain hit California and made headlines across the country. Suddenly, in the wee hours of the morning, a gigantic mudslide began moving towards Mike's house. A small cemetery on the hill above had literally shaken loose, depositing caskets, cadavers and tons of mud in Mike's front yard... it had to be a nightmare for the youngster. Somehow, he shook it off. When the canyon was cleared a few days later and he was able to return to the set, he simply asked me, 'Is someone trying to tell us something?'."

Phantasm was released to positive reviews.

Writing in the Hollywood Reporter, Robert Osbourne said "The Avco-Embassy release is a genuine spooker that's been constructed with a vivid imagination - and a great many funeral tours at night time - and more than once causes the hair to go skyward...(Coscarelli) deserves credit for producing a genuine chiller. It won't win Oscars, but it'll win him a mass of friends among those who enjoy having their blood run cold."

 Dave Kehr described the film in the Chicago Tribune as "One of those happy surprises that sometimes bubble forth from the depths of low-budget filmmaking."

And Joe Bob Briggs nailed the saga's appeal for many viewers when he said "Basically it's about this real ugly lookin' old skinny guy who goes around collecting dead bodies, and the way you know he's coming is that a flying Christmas tree ornament with daggers stickin' out of it tries to imbed itself in your skull. There's always a lot of talk about who the Tall Man is, where he is, where he comes from, whether he's dead or alive, why he wants the dead bodies, what the flying Christmas tree ornaments are for - and I never understand a WORD of it. But it's neato-mosquito."

Audiences responded positively and Phantasm managed to score a $12 million dollar return on its $300,000 budget – not bad for a film about grave robbers from another planet.

It was a huge hit overseas, especially in Japan where the Tall Man become an unlikely movie star pin-up, and Avco Embassy sent Coscarelli and Scrimm on a world-wide trip to promote the film – if you can find the out-of-print MGM special edition DVD, watch the hilarious short promo that Scrimm shot in character for Australian television (where the film was released as 'the Never Dead' to avoid similarities with Fantasm, a soft-core sex comedy). In the same way that Coscarelli borrowed the idea of dreams becoming reality from Invaders From Mars, Phantasm has influenced a number of films that followed in its wake.

 Just a few years later, Wes Craven would lift the concept wholesale for A Nightmare On Elm Street, now a classic in its own right – the near-identical climax of Craven's film even features a character being yanked backwards through the glass panel of a door.

A paler imitation of the Tall Man turned up in Poltergeist II: The Other Side and Poltergeist III under the guise of Preacher Kane, and the scene where Morningside Mausoleum is sucked through the space gate was referenced at the climax of the original Poltergeist. Even Stephen King isn't above lifting an idea for his book It from the scene in Phantasm where the photograph comes alive in Mike's hands.

Following the success of *Phantasm*, Coscarelli resisted demands for a follow- up. He had proven that he could deliver high quality on a low budget, but this quickly became both a boon and a curse – he was inundated with new scripts, but they were all for low-budget hor- ror and sci-fi pictures. Wisely declining to helm the likes of *Piranha II: Flying Killers*, Coscarelli seized upon the sword and sorcery boom of the early 1980s to write and direct *The Beast- master*, a film which has earned itself huge audiences thanks to repeated cable broadcasts. Coscarelli's mark was all over the finished film, but the experience of making the movie was not a happy one, and he has since described it as a film over which he ultimately lost control. The producers edited the movie beyond the director's original vision, and Coscarelli felt that it suffered greatly as a result. The experience was so painful for Pepperman that he left the film business altogether and parted company with Coscarelli on a professional level, although the two remain good friends.

Coscarelli experienced further heartbreak when he wasted several years working on an adap- tation of Stephen King's *Silver Bullet*, finally leaving the project altogether.

His next film, *Survival Quest,* was a violent backwoods survivalist thriller in the *Deliverance* and *First Blood* mould, but his concept was again compromised, and the finished movie lost a lot of the bloodshed that he had originally envisioned. Finally, Coscarelli yielded to studio pressure and agreed to helm a big-budget sequel to *Phantasm* for Universal.

Unfortunately for Michael Baldwin, Universal forced Coscarelli to use James Le Gros to play a more mature version of Mike.

*"**Phantasm** was a long time ago,"* Baldwin said. *"I continued being an actor until I was prob- ably 22 or something like that. I did lots of commercials and television and the whole routine. Studied acting, became a musician, and then when all my friends went off to college, I went off and found an Indian guru and lived on an ashram and had a grand time there."*

Baldwin returned to the series when Coscarelli helmed *Phantasm III: Lord of the Dead* and *Phantasm IV: Oblivion*. Currently a resident of Austin where he has his own acting studio, Baldwin continues to work in film and television, writing and co-producing the movie *Vice Girls* starring the deceased Lana Clarkson, who was famously shot dead by Phil Spector. He is also alleged to have introduced his friend Brad Pitt to Jennifer Aniston.

Reggie Bannister has maintained a healthy presence in low budget movies in the years since *Phantasm*. He has appeared in most of Coscarelli's films to date, even in minor roles such as that of an aeroplane pilot in *Survival Quest*, and has become a true cult figure, regularly par- ticipating in fan conventions.

He has also recorded and released a number of albums with his band, one of which featured a version of the 'Phantasm' theme tune. *Phantasm* transformed Angus Scrimm into a screen villain of the highest calibre, and permanently associated the actor with the role. He has en- joyed a lot of subsequent film roles as a result of his stint as an alien grave-robber, and is an enthusiastic, gracious and entertaining regular at horror and sci-fi conventions around the world. But he has admitted to feeling honoured to have become so deeply identified with such an iconic screen villain.

"What I think of him ethically and morally, I don't know!" he said. *"But I love the role, it's marvellous to have so indelible a character to be associated with... I have a warm affection for the old son of a gun."*

Bill Thornbury made a few more films after his stint on *Phantasm*, including Jim Wynorski's *The Lost Empire* where he appeared alongside Scrimm, but he later dropped out of acting to concentrate on teaching music. Like Baldwin, Thornbury made a return to the fold for the next two entries in the *Phantasm* saga, but seems genuinely puzzled by its impact and the obsession that it inspires in some viewers – an encounter with one unhinged individual who entered his home and announced that he was going to become the next Tall Man probably didn't help (Thornbury convinced the guy to leave by giving him armfuls of *Phantasm* memorabilia).

Phantasm has transcended its low budget horror/sci-fi roots to become a bonafide global phenomenon. Since it first saw the light of a projector in 1979, the film has spawned fanzines, comic books and action figures. Collectors compete to pick up ever-rarer memorabilia from around the world – the most sought-after items are probably a promotional yellow finger in a plastic box embossed with the *Phantasm* logo, a 12" 'blood yellow' vinyl single featuring a disco remix of the *Phantasm* theme tune, the original 'X' rated British cinema quad poster, a limited edition die-cast model of the Plymouth Barracuda car and the hard-to-find first vinyl release of the soundtrack on the GEM label (if your copy has colour stills on the back of the sleeve instead ofblack-and-white, then it's the original release).

Opportunistic fans regularly design their own unofficial artefacts dedicated to the Phantasm saga – a cursory glance at eBay will reveal Phantasm cigarette lighters, clocks that bear the grim leer of the Tall Man and spheres fashioned from materials varying from Christmas baubles to custom-made chrome orbs.

"To think that some decades later, people would still be watching, talking or thinking about 'Phantasm' was totally unimaginable at the time," Coscarelli told Rue Morgue. *"However, as I shot the film, I was the first to see that certain things were working really well. Angus was terrifying as the Tall Man. Michael Baldwin was giving the best performance by a child actor I'd ever seen. Bill Thornbury was great, and Reggie Bannister was creating this super-cool persona with the potential to be a major ass-kicker of the undead. The sphere prop was actually working as an onscreen driller-killer and the black Plymouth muscle car simply rocked. So I had a notion that it might turn out okay. But if anything, it was the fans who elevated our little tale into myth. They're the ones that created the word of mouth, the superheated speculation about what the intentions of the film were. They enthusiastically supported each and every sequel and swarmed the conventions barraging us with questions about it **Phantasm**, by design, is an open-ended storyline that allows audiences to fill in the gaps. I think this is the charm and the allure of it."*

So with episodes of the *Masters of Horror* show, the acclaimed Joe Lansdale adaptation of *Bubba Ho Tep* under his belt and a proposed movie of the novel *John Dies At The End* in the works, does Coscarelli think that we have seen the last of the Tall Man?

*"One thing I've learned about **Phantasm**,"* the director said, *"Is that it is never over."*

The *Phantasm* saga's sheer sense of fun is best summed up by the copyright caution that follows the end credits of each sequel warning that infringements 'may result in the wrath of the Tall Man'. What better guardian could a film have?

Liam Ronan

Originally published in Mass Movement #27, July 2010

THE DUNGEON'S MASTER
MEETS STEVE JACKSON & IAN LIVINGSTONE

In the history of role playing games there are two men who stand held and shoulders with the greats. Steve Jackson and Ian Livingstone not only founded Games Workshop, but brought RPGs to these shores; as well as creating one of the most enduring and unique fantasy book series ever… Fighting Fantasy! So it was that I, the Dungeon's Master, found myself in the privileged position to interview two legends of the industry (and I didn't use torture once! Well, maybe a little)!

Interview by Brady Webb

MM: You are friends from your school days; please describe how you met and what your first impressions of each other were?

Ian: I can't actually remember how we met. But we soon found out that we shared a big interest in wargaming and Subbuteo.

Steve: Maybe Ian doesn't want to admit it – we used to go to the same pub! We had some mutual friends who played together in a jamming blues band. We joined in. Ian played harmonica (still does) and I play guitar.

MM: At what age were you when you first discovered the world of roleplaying games and how did you first stumble upon them?

Ian: I was 25 and Steve was 23. It was 1975 and the early days of Games Workshop. We'd heard about this amazing new role-playing game that had just come out in the USA called Dungeons & Dragons. At around that time a copy of *Owl & Weasel* found its way into the hands of Gary Gygax whose company TSR published Dungeons & Dragons. He sent us a copy of D&D and we were soon hooked. We ordered six copies and ended up with a three year exclusive distribution agreement for Europe!

MM: What was your first experience of role-playing like? Are there any moments that are especially memorable?

Steve: We'd heard about Dungeons & Dragons - the term 'role-playing games' hadn't come into existence yet – but when we got our hands on a copy, we were dismayed. It was impossible to follow what was going on. No winner. No end to the game. One player didn't even 'play' in the traditional sense! Was it even a game at all? And no rules on combat – you were referred to a set of medieval battle rules for tabletop wargaming called 'Chainmail'. We couldn't make any sense of it. But then we discovered a D&D gaming group at City University in London lead by Andrew Holt and Steve Biggs. They showed us how it worked and that was an moment of epiphany. Our lives would never be the same again…

Ian: I remember spending days designing my first dungeon on graph paper. It was called *Temple of the Golden Skeleton*. I still have it today I'm pleased to say. I also remember 'rolling' my first character. He was a barbarian called Anvar. Sadly he is no longer with us…

MM: You both founded Games Workshop together, along with fellow friend John Peake. Is it true that you all shared a flat together in Shepherd's Bush? What made you decide to found the company, how did you come up with the name and what was the original vision for the company?

Steve: All three of us were bored with our jobs - and indeed our existence in a poky rented flat. So, one drunken night we decided we were going to change our lives. We'd start up our own business. But what in? We all had an interest in games. But what would we do? So we decided to publish a monthly fanzine, sell obscure games, do game-related services. John was a talented woodworker. He came back from a holiday in Greece with a backgammon set and made a perfect copy. He also liked the Japanese game of Go and made a Go board. These were professional quality and Ian, the salesman of the three, manages to sell John's games into Just Games and Harrods. Hence the name 'Games WORKSHOP'. But when D&D came along and it was obvious what direction GW was taking, John lost interest and left. He didn't enjoy playing D&D at all.

MM: You published a magazine called *Owl & Weasel;* was this your first foray into publishing? Where did the title *Owl & Weasel* come from?

Ian: We had started Games Workshop but nobody knew we existed. So we decided to tell the world about Workshop by publishing Owl & Weasel. In February 1975 we mailed out the first issue free to everybody we knew in games hoping that they would subscribe. Luckily quite a few did subscribe but the circulation always remained in the low hundreds. The name was supposed to represent the characteristics of a good games player; the owl is wise and the weasel is cunning. But after 25 issues it was time for a change. And that was *White Dwarf*.

MM: In 1976 you went to GenCon, the role-playing convention in Lake Geneva, USA, to get exclusive deals to European distribution deals. That convention also happened to be the event first funded by TSR to support the growing popularity of their game D&D. What do you remember of that convention, whom did you meet and what was it like trying persuade companies like TSR to give a deal?

Steve: It was a very amateurish affair, with trestle tables and sheets for covers. Games packaged in zip-locked bags selling for $10 a time (very expensive, but the publishers could only afford short print runs) For us it was a turning point. We got to meet Gary Gygax, Dave Arneson and Brian Blume, along with many of the other future big names in the hobby like Mark Miller (Traveller). But at this stage they were all garage companies, who were delighted to think that their obscure games were going to be sold in Europe. We were the only Europeans at the show and so we signed up the entire industry!.

Ian: I remember it took a long time to get there! We decided to see a lot of the USA on the way! We landed in New York; we being myself, Steve, Steve's sister Vicky and her friend Jane. We drove to Los Angeles along Route 66, to deliver a Buick Skylark. We dropped that off and picked up another car to San Francisco. We then delivered another to Chicago and eventually reached Lake Geneva, Wisconsin in time for GenCon. It was a memorable journey and made our arrival at GenCon all the more amazing. We met Gary Gygax and Dave Arneson and loads of other designers and writers. We already had the TSR distributorship and had been doing well with D&D. All the new role-playing companies were keen to get us to distribute their games too.

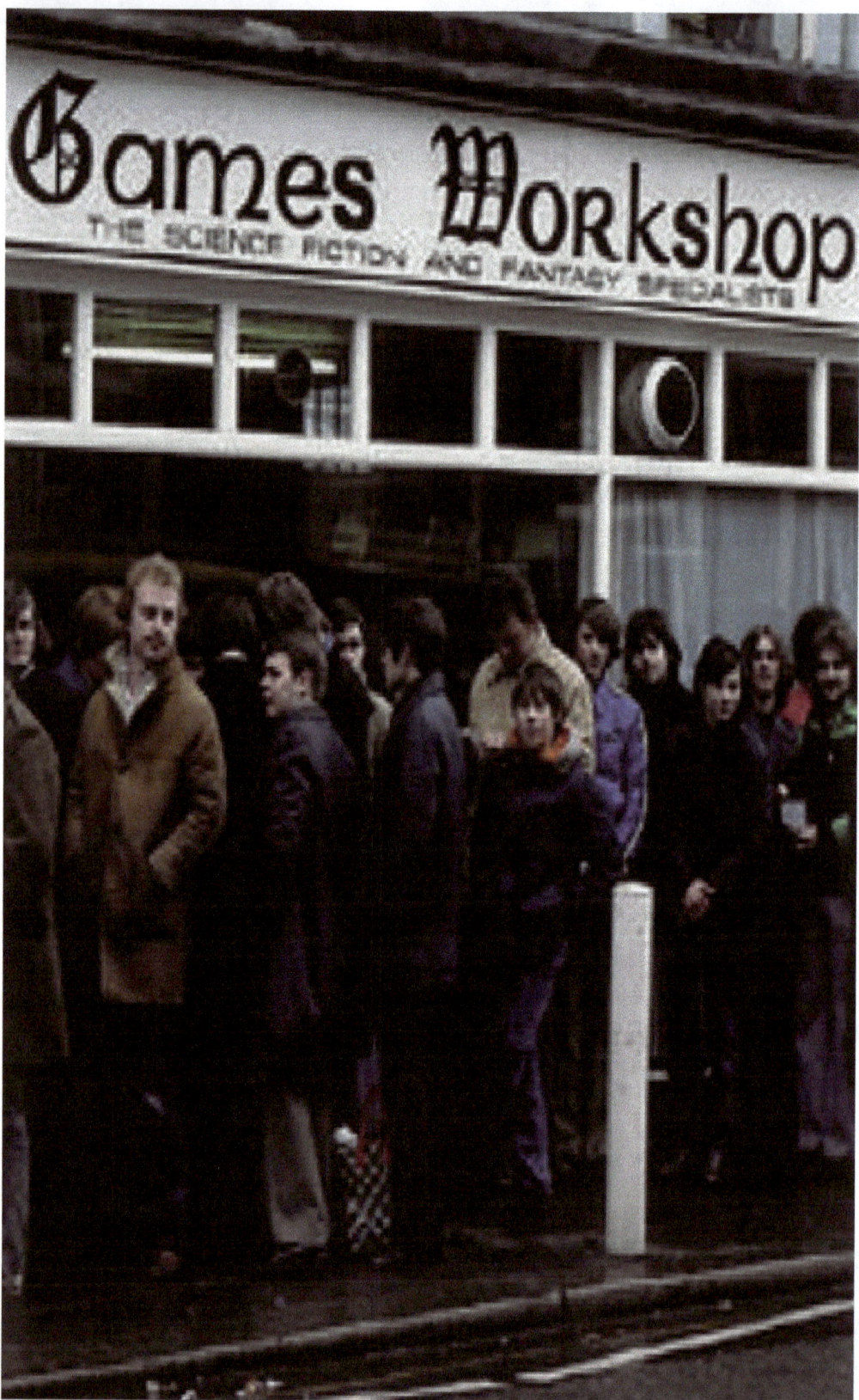

MM: In 1978 you opened your first Games Workshop store in Hammersmith; what were the early days of the company and running a shop like?

Ian: The main reason we decided to open our own store was because we were having trouble getting other retailers to stock role-playing games. They just didn't get it. All the rule books, supplements, figures, dice, etc was a nightmare for non-specialist retailers. But for us it just seemed like a natural extension of our mail order and distribution business to have a flagship store. Tucked away in a side street in Hammersmith, the first store became a gaming Mecca for role-players, some of whom travelled hundreds of miles to visit us. Steve and I had our office above the store and usually worked behind the counter on Saturdays. There was always a great feeling of excitement in the store and we felt very lucky to have turned our hobby into a business. We were far from being the best retailers in the world but our knowledge and enthusiasm for D&D rubbed off and the games began to sell themselves! They were great times.

MM: 1980 you came up with the idea for the first Fighting Fantasy novel, the legendary *Warlock of Firetop Mountain*. How did you come up with the concept and what was it like writing the first books, especially as you were both running GW at the time? Is there anything you would have done differently?

Steve: Those were balmy days. How our girlfriends stuck with us through 1982- 86, I'll never know. Up at 7, off to Games Workshop for a day at the office. Home at 7- 8pm. Then typing away until midnight, working on the next FF book. Anything different? Perhaps we should have published the FF books ourselves (through Games Workshop). That would have given the company the mass market game we were always looking for. But we couldn't actually foresee how successful they were going to be. And by that time, we were well and truly in bed with Penguin.

MM: Steve, you're responsible for the first of the FF books that weren't fantasy based, moving into the realms of horror (*House of Hell*, which I still haven't beaten!), Sci-Fi (*Starship Traveller*) and superheroes (*Appointment With F.E.A.R.*), as well as creating the Sorcery series. What made you want to step outside the safe boundaries of the fantasy genre and what was the readers' response like?

Steve: I was keen to take the idea to different genres. After I'd written a few fantasy adventures I wanted to see where else we could go. In retrospect I think fantasy was the best genre; it suited the game system best. But I was having fun trying it out with a multi-part adventure (Sorcery), horror (*House of Hell*) and superheroes (*Appointment with FEAR*)

MM: Ian, with Steve forging into new genres for the FF books, you continued to explore the world of Titan. How did you create the world and what influenced you? Did you discuss with each other any new additions or directions that you wanted to take?

Ian: I wanted to keep all my adventures in a one world, Titan, and particularly within Allansia. The plan was to build a fantasy world and introduce people, places, legends, characters, races, monsters and history that would be consistent and recognisable in many of my books to try to build up some familiarity. Hence recurring characters like Yaztromo became popular. I did stray away from Titan once with *Freeway Fighter*!

MM: What character, race and continent are your favourites?

Steve: I liked the little Jib-Jib that you encounter in Sorcery. When you enter its lair you hear this ferocious roar and fear for your life. But turns out it's a small furry creature which is not dangerous at all. Its bark is worse than its bite.

Ian: My favourite character has to be the grand old wizard of Darkwood Forest, Yaztromo. Favourite race are Lizard Men and favourite continent is Allansia.

MM: Which of the FF books are your favourite and why?

Ian: *Warlock of Firetop Mountain* because it was the first and gave us a great sense of pride. *Deathtrap Dungeon* because it was a great dungeon bash and gave readers a bit of a moral dilemma when they were obliged to fight to the death a friendly NPC called Throm. *City of Thieves* because of the story and the atmosphere of Port Blacksand.

Steve: Has to be the Sorcery series since I put so much time and effort into those books. But *Warlock* will always have a special place for me since it was the first.

MM: The FF world is populated with numerous races of a near unending variety, as chronicled in the excellent *Out of the Pit*. However, are there any creatures that you look back and say to yourselves, "What was I thinking?"

Ian: Actually I quite liked most of my monsters! They were mostly created to fit a specific purpose or scenario. But there was one in *Armies of Death*…. It was a chubby dog-headed human with a blowpipe. I called it a Blog. Not quite like the blogs of today's internet generation.

Steve: The Wheelies in *Citadel of Chaos*. Ouch!

MM: The Fighting Fantasy novels were brilliant fun. What inspired you to take the world of Titan into the realm of the prose novel? The principal character of Chadda Darkmane first appeared in *The Trolltooth Wars*; what influences, if any, were there on this characters conception? Are there any other tales that you wanted to tell and if so, do you think that you will ever be lured back to the world of Titan for either a novel or a new gamebook?

Steve: *Trolltooth Wars* was the book that took me longest to complete. Very different from writing a gamebook, that's for sure. Originally I'd intended that *Trolltooth Wars* would provide the solution to *Warlock of Firetop Mountain*. The solution had not been published anywhere, and there was no Internet for people to post up their own solutions. I thought it would be neat to have Darkmane follow the 'one true way' through Firetop Mountain. So anyone who was inclined to could work out how to solve the original book. But when I submitted it to Penguin, the Editor said the book seemed completely unbalanced. The beginning and end were relatively short, with this whole great long Firetop Mountain episode in the middle. It didn't work. So back to the typewriter. I finished the book off whilst I was living in Spain, and it was all written on a new-fangled – and very expensive – gadget that I was in love with. A word processor. How I wished these things had been around in 1980…!

MM: After stepping back from the FF books and eventually leaving GW, you both have forged very successful careers in other areas. Steve, in the '90s you devised a number of very successful interactive telephone games, such as *F.I.S.T.* as well as *Battlecards*, a collectible card game, and moved into journalism and game design.

 In addition, you are a Honorary Professor at Brunel University teaching a course in Digital Game Design. Ian, you have gone on to have one of the most influential careers in computer gaming, being involved on such incredible franchises as *Tomb Raider* and *Hitman*, to name but two, and have earned an OBE. Considering that you are both now so heavily involved in the worlds of computer gaming, how do you see computer games developing in the years to come and Fighting Fantasy's place in the market? Also, considering that computer games have eclipsed tabletop role-playing in popularity?

Steve: No question the future is in digital games. The size of the market is enormous, and board games have unfortunately become very much a niche market. The future will see constant expansion of games into all walks of life. We've seen console gaming become a multi-billion dollar industry, yet iApp games sell for 59p. And free-to-play Facebook-type games are making millions. Huh?? Gaming has become a creative area of the entertainment industry like music and movies. Who'd have thought that in 1976 when we were wandering around GenCon with 100 other bearded hippies equally as hooked on games as we were. It's been a fantastic journey

Ian: The games world is growing rapidly. Advances in technology allow new ways of delivering and playing games. Computer and video games is now the largest entertainment industry in the world. It is estimated that global revenues from games will exceed £50 billion, yes BILLION, by 2015. Diverse content available on diverse platforms, both online and offline means that 70% of the UK population now plays games of some type. The important thing is that games have become much more socially acceptable and there is something for everybody to play. Fighting Fantasy might not have the audience it used to have in book format but *Warlock of Firetop Mountain* and *Deathtrap Dungeon* are available as Apps on iPhone. That's pretty cool.

MM: I understand that you still meet up for regularly and play board games, which you call the 'Games Night Pro' and compete for an annual trophy, the 'Pagoda Cup'. How long have you been holding this night, and what is your favourite board game and why? Also, who has won the cup the most and has anyone been caught cheating? Do you, or are you ever tempted, to play any role-playing games? If so, what is your favourite genre and what games do you play?

Ian: The Games Night Club has been running since 1986. There are six members and we meet usually every two weeks at 'The Club'. The members are myself, Steve, Peter Molyneux, Clive Robert, Mark Spangenthal and Skye Quin. It is very much a spoof of a Gentleman's Club. As Secretary, I arrange the meetings, keep score on the night and publish the Games Night Newsletter in which I berate the members and report on the games played. I am currently publishing issue 343. Points are given for every game played, double if it qualifies as a 'game of substance' which is one that lasts over two hours and causes headaches. At the end of the year, the person at the top of the league table wins the Pagoda Cup and gets their name engraved on it. I am pleased to say that I have won it the most times. Let's say there have been a couple of incidents over the years that could be termed mild cheating but the perpetrators shall remain nameless. They know who they are. But as a result a new phrase entered our language called 'the practice roll.' We only play board games or card games. Our current favourite is Caylus although it is only 5-player which means we need one of us to be away. As for RPGs, well at our age we feel far too self-conscious to play them.

MM: Lastly, what projects do you have coming up that you think we should really be looking out for?

Ian: At Eidos I continue to put my finger in everybody else's pie. By that I mean that I work with our studios adding creative input. Just Cause 2 recently came out and reached No.1 in the charts. Kane & Lynch 2 will be our next release. I've also recently invested in a couple of start-up companies that are making social games although I can't really talk about them right now. I'm also involved with Socialgo.com, a solution that allows people to build their own private social networks and monetize them should they wish.

Steve: You may be aware that a movie producer, Superteam Productions have just bought an Option to turn House of Hell into a movie. But more than a movie it will be playable on-line and via Blu-Ray. This is an exciting project. There's a long way to go yet. But if it is successful, where could it go? Remember there are 70+ other books in the FF series...!

Originally published in Mass Movement #27, July 2010

RUSS IGLAY (UNDERDOG)

Underdog. Just thinking about the band sends shivers down my spine and makes me smile. They were, and are, the definitive New York Hardcore band. Hell, this magazine is named after one of their songs, so that should tell you about the kind of esteem that these guys are held in around these parts, and so when I was offered to talk to bass player Russ about the band and their new discography, *Matchless*, I jumped at the chance....

Interview by Tim Cundle

MM: I guess we should start at the beginning. When where and why did Underdog first get together?

Russ: We first got together when I was in Murphy's Law and Richie was in Numbskulls and they opened up for us a few times and I thought they were a pretty good band. When I got kicked out of Murphy's Law I immediately phoned Richie and asked if they still needed a new bass player – I had seen them a couple of times and they had had some girl on bass who they said was just filling in – so I called Richie and told him that I wanted to do it, and he was all excited and told me to come over to his house to get a tape. I was living in Manhattan at the time with my girlfriend and I didn't know it but he lived just a couple of blocks away! So I went right over there and he made me a cassette, booked a couple of practise sessions, learned the songs that week and that was that. Once that happened, his band the Numb-skulls were like a fun comedy band kind of like Murphy's Law and we both wanted to move in a more serious direction with the lyrics. Numbskulls was kind of like a joke name so once I'd joined the band, we changed the name and we changed the direction. We went from being a fun party band to being a more serious band. We wanted to move away from that fun party feel to do something more like what the Cro-Mags were doing.

MM: Right from Underdog's inception you weren't like the other bands in the New York Hardcore scene, you weren't following the set course. Did you always want to shake things up a little bit?

Russ: Yeah. Before I was in Murphy's Law even, and before Underdog – if you look back there was a band called Child Abuse, that was me and Dean's first band. I quit Child Abuse before they put that 7" out, but I was in Child Abuse for the same reason: I wanted to move up a lit-tle bit; I wanted to progress. When Underdog got together a lot of the bans were doing a standard fast then slow then fast format for their songs. We were listening to a lot of reggae back then, a lot of reggae, and some old stuff –some Sabbath and the Who and Stiff little Fin-gers and stuff like that. There were enough bands doing that fast slow fast stuff that -do you know what we wanted? Music that we would listen to. So I guess we weren't looking to shake things up as much as we were looking to be ourselves really. Underdog has really al-ways gone its own way and not really wondered what the crowd was doing.

MM: What do you think makes Underdog unique? What makes you different?

Russ: We didn't follow the crowd. We didn't do what was cool. We weren't afraid to be dif-ferent. It was cool to fit in but we weren't afraid to not fit in. A lot of people would wear a uniform, but I was a skateboarder and would go down to CBGBs with my skater shorts on and a backwards baseball cap and my board, and skinheads would shout things like "What are you doing here skater boy?" and they didn't know who I was and before they knew it they had a skateboard round their heads and they didn't say it again. And with Underdog we just always went our own way.

MM: Were you surprised how well that first 7" did?

Russ: Well back then we didn't know how well it did. When I got really surprised about the 7" was when the internet came in and I saw the 7" on sale on EBay for $250. It did well, but I wasn't really aware of how well it did.

MM: When the album *The Vanishing Point* came out it really stood out, and has stood the test of time better than a lot of the other albums that were around at the time. I was wondering how you felt about the album now and if your feelings about it have changed over time?

Russ: The songs on *The Vanishing Point* is a lot of the reason why the band is still playing now. Those songs, I love them and I'm so proud of them, and if they were more like our really old stuff that's kind of more like regular Hardcore then we would have been a dime a dozen. We were always a little bit different but it was what we managed to achieve on *The Vanishing Point* kind of sums up why I wanted to play. If you listen to any one part on that album: the drums, the bass, anything it's all just good music. It's so much different to a Youth of Today record or something like that. I don't think you can even compare. The only thing I don't like about *The Vanishing Point* is the production on it. The production could have been so much better especially the guitar sound. It's all out of our hands now, and back then we didn't know anything about it until the record was out but it's very disappointing.

MM: What was it with you guys and guitarists? You seemed to go through them like most bands go through drummers...

Russ: I don't know. We just seemed to go through them and be unable to keep a guitar player. Like in 1989 when we got rid of Chuck and we had been through so many – almost one a year and it seemed like so much work to keep teaching the guitar players the songs, I think that if we had managed to keep our guitar players we would have kept going.

MM: How did the short break after that first US tour turn into sixteen years?

Russ: Well, we went to take a short break, but then the whole idea of having to teach someone the whole set, to be able to find a guitar player who could play all that reggae and play all those leads.. we would find somebody who could play the chords for the songs but couldn't play the leads or the reggae, or they could play the reggae but couldn't do something else. It was so hard to find somebody but we just didn't keep in touch.. I didn't keep in touch with Richie, and after a while he moved on and started Into Another, so I guess Into Another was the real end to Underdog.

MM: Did you miss the band during all that time and did you ever feel there was unfinished business with Underdog?

Russ: I always felt that there was definitely unfinished business with Underdog. It would have been a different story if we hadn't taken that long, if we'd kept on playing. I think Richie's heart wasn't in it, as Underdog could have kept going when he set up Into Another, and Underdog could have changed and evolved to sound like a cross between Underdog and Into Another. If we didn't take that break it might of gone that way and that would have been something really special. When Underdog did break up I kind of got bummed out about what kind of music was going on, what kind of music the American market was listening to and buying and wanted to hear and didn't even think about music for a while. After a few years, me and Dean started up a new band called Huge … we've just recorded 5 songs and it sounds pretty cool. It's basically the three guys from Underdog except without Richie, I do lead vocals and we have another bass player; but basically, because we are working on Huge, that's why it was so easy to get Underdog back together, because we were all still working together. It was all because of that unfinished business like you say, but then Richie got back in touch with us in New York and we were all ready and willing to start doing Underdog again

MM: Do you want to tell us a bit about *Matchless*?

Russ: The Bridge 9 thing – they are brilliant, awesome. I had talked to a lot of record labels about doing this and nothing was sticking out, or showing much enthusiasm, then Revelation really wanted to do it. After a show in Chicago I was introduced by a roadie to Chris Wren the boss of Bridge 9, and he was saying how he'd love to do an Underdog discography, but I had to tell him that we were doing it with Revelation. After that we weren't really keeping in touch with Revelation, things were moving really slowly and I kept checking out the Bridge 9 website: they really looked after their bands and were really working hard at promoting bands. They put a lot of effort into the packaging and the branding and their bands were touring. So after a few months I emailed Chris Wren and said that I'd like to talk to him about bringing the Underdog discography to Bridge 9 and he called me within 2 hours to follow it up. He was really excited as Underdog had been his favourite band since forever. They re-released our first single last year and that went really well, they did a fantastic job on that. They've been setting up all kinds of promotional support, we're really happy with Bridge 9 and we're very excited, the packaging and everything is looking great.

MM: Any chance of a new Underdog album?

Russ: I don't think there is much chance of a whole Underdog album. There definitely is a chance of a 4 track EP or something like that though. We were thinking it might be cool to do some obscure cover songs, maybe two covers and two new songs.

MM: What do you guys have planned?

Russ: We are trying to play in the States every Saturday in the summer. We are trying to do one off shows where we can drive home every night. The reason being that between the four of us there are now 9 children in Underdog's family and it's important to us to get back from the show and get up with the family on Sunday. We are hoping to get over to Europe to play for you guys, maybe do 5 shows in a row and then come back so we would be away from the family for maybe 7 days. That's what we are trying to set up right now. I'd like to do the same thing for Japan and Australia.

MM: If there's anything that you'd like to add…

Russ: I would just like to thank the younger kids for listening. To encourage them to go out and buy the record so that they can hear where the younger bands got started and hopefully these younger kids will accept us and see that we're a bit different: with a little bit of reggae, a little bit of rock, a bit more singing instead of screaming. Tell the skateboarders to come out and see us too.

Originally published in Mass Movement #27, July 2010

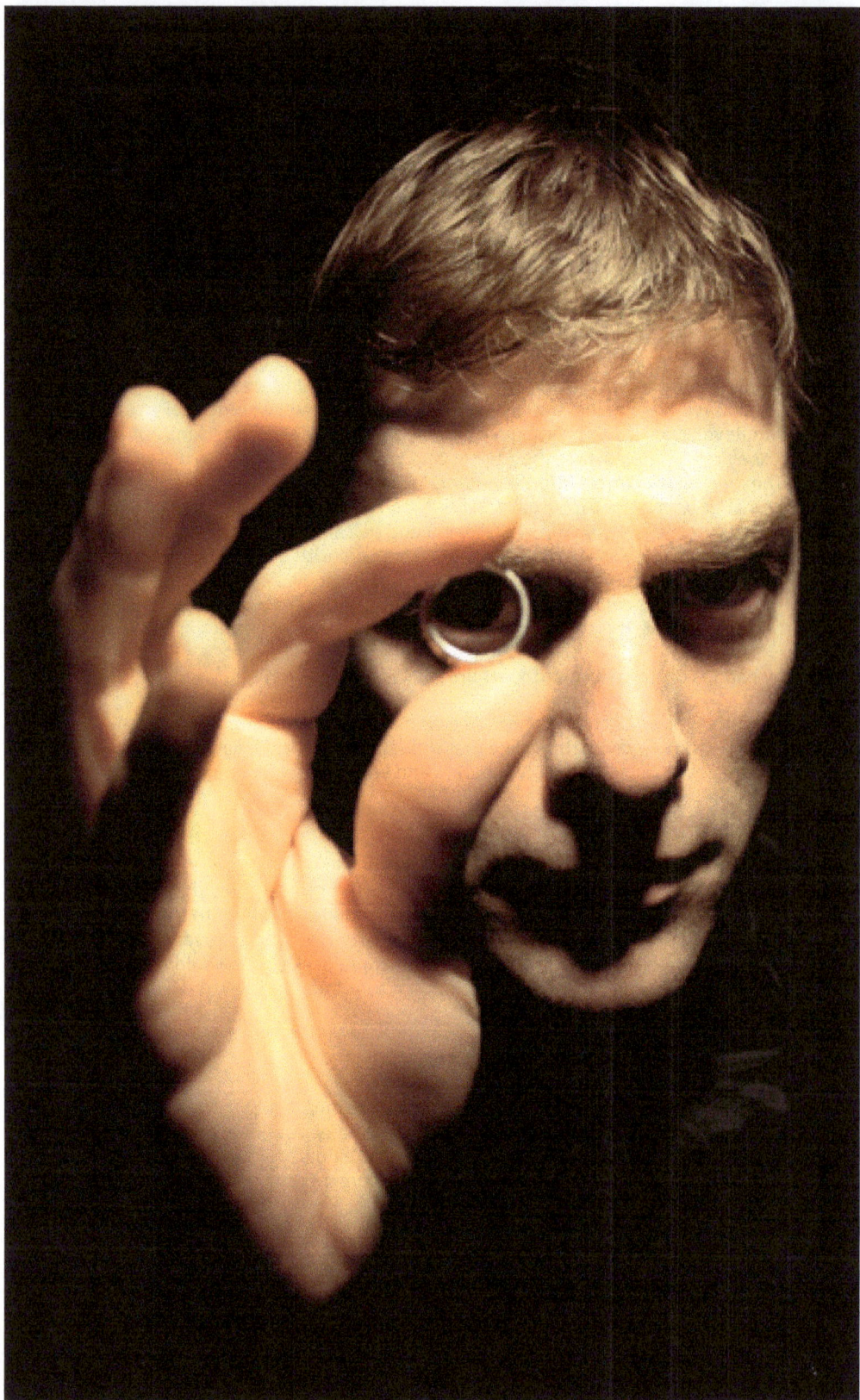

CHARLES ROSS

Following the success of his One Man Star Wars Trilogy show (that's the original trilogy), Charles Ross is back with a One Man adaptation of The Lord Of The Rings, and following his stint at The Edinburgh Festival, I managed to catch up with him for chat about all things LOTR and Star Wars in an effort to find out how one man really can make it different...

Interview by Tim Cundle

Photographs by Nancy Hebden & Lisa Santos

MM: What makes you a professional geek Charley?

CR: A professional geek? Because it's what I do for a living. I get to judge my own geeky level and get to be myself and not really have to hide it. I wanted to be just an actor growing up and try to do my thing, but I've found that this way I get to be a geeky actor and lean more towards the geeky side of things. I still get to do the jobs I want to do but I get to be more exuberant and have lots of fun.

MM: So what do you think constitutes being a geek?

CR: I think you can be a geek about sport, about motor cars, whatever. The thing about being a geek is the passion, so you basically wear your heart on your sleeve so that people can basically mock you because you love something. Whether you dress up like a Klingon or you decide to call your kid Andy Rooney, whatever it doesn't matter. You've opened yourself up to ridicule and sometimes people take the bait, take the obvious and they will ridicule you but you don't care because you feel so strongly about it.

MM: Before Lord of the Rings you adapted the Star Wars trilogy. So where did the idea for the one man show originally come from and why did you choose Star Wars?

CR: I did a fringe tour in North America; I was with a theatre company at the time. We did alright but we didn't really make any money. I noticed that the people making the most money were actually the one man shows and I had a friend who was doing a one person show and he was playing Kirk from Star Trek. He did this incredible William Shatner impression and I thought that if he can do that and people will just come out because they know who William Shatner is and they know who Kirk is then there has got to be a way to do something but not to copy him directly – this was 1994 by the way – I thought maybe if I could do a show which kind of referenced movies then it would be cool. Star Wars was one of the films that came to mind, then I thought – can you imagine doing Star Wars in five minutes and kind of encapsulate it? And I did it! Now flash forward to 2001 and that idea had metamorphosed into being a one man Star Wars show – just the first film – so I'd turned that into a 25 minute comedy sketch and it went down so well at the comedy clubs that it became something that we worked to extend into a one hour show. It's weird, it wasn't like an overnight realisation but more like a long formed good idea, weird idea that if you asked at the very beginning you would have thought it wouldn't have worked.

MM: You then chose Lord of the Rings... What is it with you and trilogies? You're not making life easy for yourself are you?

CR: I guess not, no. But a trilogy is great. If you're going to chop a film down to 20 minutes or so – Lord of the Rings comes down to about 23 minutes –they all have kind of the same story structure which means that you can squeeze it down with Lord of the Rings the same way that you can with Star Wars. They are both the same in that they are the stories of a hero's journey. This made it easy to follow the same pattern in doing Lord of the Rings as we did with Star Wars. If you follow the whole story arc there is the main story which is always there which then kind of has these side-lines shooting off but the meat of the story is really Frodo and with Star Wars the meat of the story is Luke Skywalker so if you just follow their stories, really, it's very easy, even though they are such epic stories.

MM: Was Lord of the Rings easier or more difficult to adapt than you thought it would be?

CR: it was easier because it was my second time around. I wouldn't say it was ever easy, but having had the experience of doing Star Wars, when I approached Lord of the Rings I knew sort of how to begin, whereas when I started doing Star Wars I was pathetic and I didn't know where to begin, what an audience would find funny and how much humour to use but once you've done it once you find your confidence.

MM: Did you work from the books or the films or combine both for Lord of the Rings?

CR: I worked from the books mostly as a guide, and the film makers worked in the same way too, in a different fashion, but when they wrote the script they used the books as a guide, but when the re-writers come in they were more interested in more Liv Tyler or less something else in terms of the film which fundamentally changes things and the end product is different. So by using the books, I can set about reducing it, using them as a guide so I know what to cut out for example Liv Tyler's character plays basically no role, so it's a big tour from the original text. It's a bit different with Star Wars because when you've got something written down sometimes the way it's expressed lends itself pretty well to being reduced and abbreviated.

MM: As you play all of the characters in Lord of the Rings, are there any characters you found particularly difficult or easy to become or any that stand out for you?

CR: No, actually I found all the characters pretty easy to become which is kind of terrifying. I don't know why it is I can become all of the characters in Lord of the Rings; with Star Wars it's more difficult. In the world of doing impressions, I'm much more of a Kermit the Frog rather than a Miss Piggy, and because Yoda is played by Frank Oz who does both Miss Piggy and Yoda I got a block. I tried my best but I kind of ended up sounding like a dying goat. So I try to concentrate on the information in the lines rather than the sound of my voice and people are usually pretty kind about it. Sometimes people would come up to me and do their version of Yoda at me and be really good; but I don't feel bad about it because of everyone who could do a good impression went out and did it, there would be millions of people out there all over the world doing their own thing, but I'm the only one with the legal permission to do it, so that's cool, because I don't get sued.

MM: Both Lord of the Rings and Star Wars are notorious for their rabid, faithful and fanatical fan bases, so before you started, were you at all worried about how these fans would react?

CR: No. Not really, because I think I'm part of it. Any time you do anything: put yourself up on YouTube, put yourself out there at all – as soon as you rear your head you're opening yourself up to critique, to ridicule. It seems rather strange that people would be so rabid about something. It's okay loving something but there are some people who don't want anything to be touched. They want things to be sacred and pristine. I can't spend my time trying to please them because they are unpleasable by their very nature. This is for people like myself who have a love for Star Wars or Lord of the Rings; and if that includes people like George Lucas who don't mind having a bit of a sense of community about what they have created. Part of loving anything and even being a geek is a bit like when you poke fun at your mum – you might seem like you're doing it in a way that's mean but you're not at all because there's that one little idiosyncrasy that half drives you crazy. In this case it's like a giant family where that mum is Star Wars or Lord of the Rings, and it's not an excuse at all, it's done out of love. And for those people who don't like to see anything touched or played with at all it's like having a sister in whom you don't see a single fault and no-one is allowed to comment on because it's disrespectful.

MM: Thinking about Lord of the Rings, is it steadfastly written or do you find it's a constantly changing and evolving beast depending on audience reaction?

CR: Well, the script is fine as it is, that's what I follow but the jokes, asides and whatever are constantly revealing themselves to me based on the reaction of the audience. If I get a fun audience you never know what's going to come up and what's going to stay.

MM: What has the audience reaction to Lord of the Rings been so far?

CR: Oh it's been great. It's funny going to the US and coming over here, for people who are actually fans of Lord of the Rings and who don't know what's going to happen in the show, it's very well received. I don't know why that is, it's not like it's a hot topic or anything but it's a story that lends itself to being told. It took me five years to put together the Lord of the rings show and get my legal permission. At one point, when I first started doing the show it was popular everywhere and people really loved it because the films were popular, but now that the general populous has moved on to absolute shite like Twilight and stuff like that, there's nothing that I can do about it. I'm not going to do a one man of Twilight. For those who are true fans of the books, they know exactly which way it's going to go.

MM: Have you noticed any difference in audience reaction in different cities or locations, or is there one place where the audience really stands out?

CR: You know I was pretty surprised about the reaction both in Edinburgh but also in Washington DC! I was there for a month and I couldn't figure it out, it's like they're Lord of the Rings mad or something. Maybe that is the source of the Ring of Power, maybe it's all a bit close to home. It was amazing that after a month, instead of the audience reaction starting to mellow, it actually built and became more enthusiastic. In some ways I could have been there for another month, I was very surprised. In Edinburgh I was very lucky to sell out the venue every show which is quite a claim to be made in Edinburgh, and it means so much to me because there is so much to be lost by going up there and so much to be gained so it's a

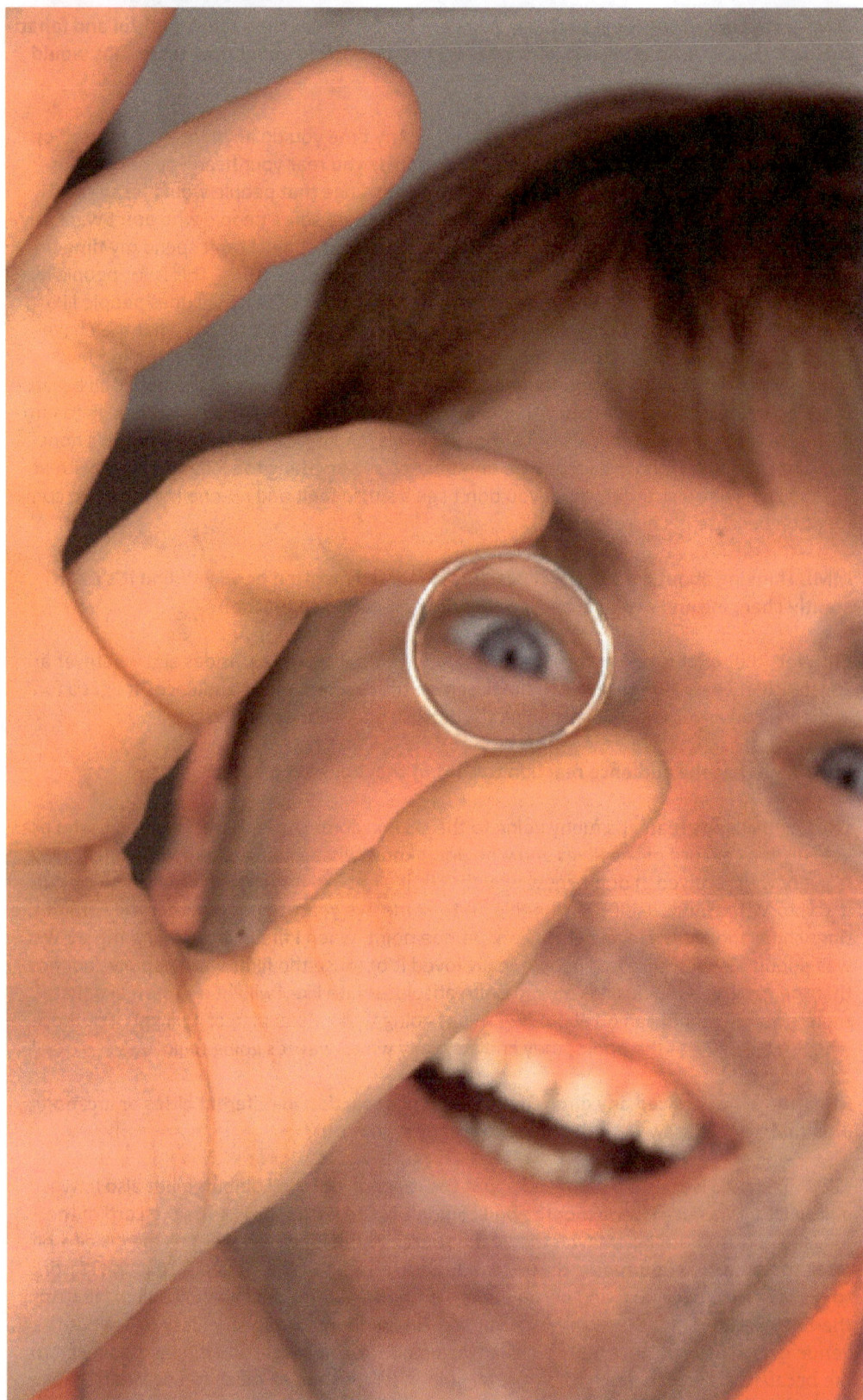

huge gamble. I don't think I'd be going up there with an autobiographical story, I would much rather risk the big things like Lord of the Rings and Star Wars to play fair against 2200 other shows.

MM: What's the strangest place you've performed either Lord of the Rings or Star Wars?

CR: Lord of the Rings has been pretty good so far, not many weird ones, but I did actually perform the Star Wars one to German backpackers. I was in British Colombia in Canada and my friend who is an art dealer really liked these girls and he convinced me that it would be a really good idea and that I should do this show for these two girls. So he ended up finding a large sort of lounge at a hotel where we could do the show and I did the whole thing and it was rather surreal because doing a show for two people, you end up giving out a lot of energy and I think that they – plus they knew Star Wars, but they didn't know it that well, and they were German and although their English was alright they weren't necessarily savvy enough to understand what I was saying – so if they hadn't enjoyed so many libations with us beforehand it wouldn't of worked. As it was it worked out fine for my friend.

MM: if you had to describe your Lord of the Rings show to someone who was unfamiliar with the source material, how would you go about doing it?

CR: I would say that it's the story of a person who is disenfranchised and how he manages to effect real change against oppressive powers that be. And in the meantime there are ancient tales of fighting working round that. It's just me telling a classic story with no real costumes, props or sets, and trying to be everything from 10,000 Orks to Firey Mountains, great battles and lead characters. We go from the Shire to Mordor and back in an hour and ten minutes; and whether you named your kid Frodo or whether you don't know anything about Lord of the Rings I guarantee you'll be entertained because I flop around like a frying fish.

MM: So thinking way ahead, have you started raiding the annals of Science Fiction and Fantasy in preparation for your next show?

CR: you know it's hard to do that. You kind of have to fall in love with something. The way you fall in love with something is by paying attention without really knowing. I'm trying to be open rather than actively search. The thing with both the Star Wars and the Lord of the Rings shows is that they were completely natural. I've thought of so many different things, from the Matrix to Indiana Jones, it goes on and on, but nothing in my mind is bigger or more significant to me than Star Wars or Lord of the Rings. So anything new needs to either reveal itself or just never come and I'm ok with that, to just let it be.

MM: What's next for you?

CR: I'm still touring the shows. I have thought of trying to do something else, maybe write the second version of Star Wars, the second trilogy, but I don't know about that. I mean, they are good, but they aren't the original Star Wars. But maybe I thought if I could make half an hour out of that, take an intermission and then come back and do the original trilogy.

Originally published in Mass Movement #28, November 2010

CHRIS JERICHO

Write a book, release a DVD, film a gameshow, star in a film, win the World Heavyweight Championship...This year, WWE Superstar Chris Jericho has done it all, but right now he's taking time off from wrestling to tour Europe with his critically acclaimed heavy metal band Fozzy, who released their fourth album 'Chasing the Grail' earlier this year. We caught up with Chris on the second night of Fozzy's European tour in Cardiff to discuss Fozzy, their new album, his wrestling career and more. Here's what the self proclaimed 'best in the world at what he does' had to say...

Interview by Leigh MM and Michael Skehens

MM: You've had a busy year so far – you've brought out a new album, on an extensive European tour, written your second book and had a stint as WWE World Heavyweight Champion – how have you managed to fit it all in?

Chris: Did *Downfall*, did *MacGruber*. Yeah, it's been a busy year and in this day and age if you're lucky enough to be busy you should take advantage of it. Especially with Fozzy, we've been doing this for eleven years now and the band has got to a point now where we're really growing, a lot of good stuff is going on so I want to take as much time as I can because I've been a musician a lot longer than I've been a wrestler. I started playing in bands when I was twelve years old. So this is something I've always wanted to do and I probably would have done it first, but there wasn't a big music scene where I grew up in Winnipeg, Canada so wrestling was a more viable way to get into show business because of the Hart brothers camp in Calgary, but I still always continued to play music and write demos and songs, stuff like that. I'm busy but it's worthwhile.

MM: You're European tour started last night, how do you find touring Europe compared to touring North America?

Chris: It's like our second home here in the UK; we've been touring here since about 2005. It really is a second home for us.

MM: You're always well received here.

Chris: Yeah, exactly. We play here more than we play in the States and people always ask me why. It's because we have a really great fan base here. We're going to continue coming here as much as we can. The UK is our number one territory.

MM: In terms of lifestyle, how does touring with Fozzy compare with touring with WWE?

Chris: Its two separate levels of success. Touring with WWE is more of a five star environment for hotels, playing in the big arenas and stuff. With Fozzy... (looks around tour bus) this isn't too shabby either (laughs), it's a great bus.

MM: I'd happily live here.

Chris: Exactly, this is nicer than my first apartment...my first three apartments, actually. There's a little bit of a difference with the level of what you're doing. The thing about Fozzy for me which is really cool is that on our first tour here we had this little van with little bunks that were built in and we've kind of built our way up the ladder and it reminds me of the same thing when I started to get to the next level with wrestling. I've done that once with Chris Jericho in the world of wrestling and to see that happening again with Fozzy is very rewarding and gratifying.

MM: It's good to see yourself climbing the ladder in whatever you're doing...

Chris: Yeah, exactly. You can always see the difference in the record sales, the places that we play, and the people that show up. The buzz about the band, more than anything. Some gigs are sold out, some are not as well sold, but you judge it more on the big picture of all the opportunities that you're getting and the buzz that the band is getting.

MM: Do you think that your wrestling career has given you the confidence to be the front man of a band?

Chris: They're always intertwined. One didn't come before the other. I think I played a junior high school Battle of the Bands when I was fourteen, so I think my experience with music and in bands really helped me when I started wrestling. I've created this persona and got this confidence which I had a little bit of when I first got into the business. Take that to music, then to wrestling, then to music again. It' all intertwined. They've both helped each other because it's show business. When I first started in wrestling I wasn't the biggest guy. I was small, actually. It was 1990. I had to think how I could have the biggest presence, the best personality, the best charisma. With music it's the same thing. David Lee Roth, James Hetfield, all these great front men are larger than life. You influence the vibe of the crowd; make sure they're having fun and a good time. That's what we do with Fozzy.

MM: Heavy metal does have that theatrical crossover. Bands like Iron Maiden and Metallica know how to use these elements to work a crowd.

Chris: Exactly, it's all a creative, show business element. They definitely do intertwine.

MM: In your latest album *Chasing the Grail* I've noticed a heavier sound to a lot of the songs than on *All That Remains*. Was that a conscious decision or a natural progression for the band?

Chris: The thing that made *Chasing the Grail* take off and be our most successful and critically acclaimed is because it's very diverse. It's got some of the most heavy songs we've had, but it's also got a ballad in *Broken Soul*, we've never had a song like that, or *New Day's Dawn* which has a weird European vibe to it and a song like *Wormwood* which is fourteen minutes long and pretty creepy. There are a lot of different styles of music, but it's all Fozzy. That's why the record works. We didn't sit down and discuss doing a fast song or a slow song. I just give my lyrics and ideas to Rich and he came up with all these great riffs. *Broken Soul* originally was a much heavier, darker lyric, but because of the music that Rich was inspired to write around it, I changed some of the lyrics to not be as deathly and downtrodden. It's more a relationship song rather than being a dark song. None of this was ever calculated, it's just how it came out. It's real and that's why I think it works.

MM: I think it's the riffs that a lot of people have gotten into…

Chris: Yeah, Rich Ward is one of the best songwriters in the world. The guy just has riffs upon riffs upon riffs. It's great working with him because the lyrics that I have are very diverse as well. I don't just write about cars or girls. I can write a song about the Revelations, or about 16th Century Vikings killing their enemies and eating their hearts and I can give all this stuff to Rich and he can make interesting songs out of them.

MM: When did you realise that Fozzy had progressed enough as a band to stop playing exclusively covers and start bringing our records of your own material?

Chris: Our first record, we were signed by Megaforce Records by a guy called Johnny Z who signed Metallica and Anthrax in '83. He was really into the whole cover thing, he loved the back story that we came up with and he thought that this was going to be the next big thing. He even said, "Are you ready to be the next Metallica?" and we were like "Dude, we're playing covers and wearing leather and spandex!" It started off as a fun diversion, basically, and I think the chemistry between Rich and myself and Frank who's been with us since the beginning too is great. We thought 'we're having a good time doing this, there's some good chemistry'. We all come from the same place, we're all world travellers, we're all experienced show business vets and we all love heavy metal and all that sort of stuff. When we started recording the second record *Happenstance*, that's when we thought 'we can take this to the next level'. As soon as that record was recorded we did the Howard Stern Show and that's when we decided to drop the whole persona and just be ourselves. We thought 'do we change the name of the band?' Fozzy is kind of a strange name, but then there's Red Hot Chilli Peppers, Limp Bizkit, Kiss, Helloween and the worst of all Def Leppard. That is the worst name for a band, but because you hear it so much it's cool.

MM: You don't think about it…

Chris: That's the thing, and that's how it is with Fozzy. It's just the name of our band.

MM: It was shortened from Fozzy Osbourne wasn't it?

Chris: Fozzy Osbourne was the name of a covers thing that Rich had in Atlanta. Anybody who was in town would show up and play. The first two gigs we had were as Fozzy Osbourne and after that we dropped the Osbourne and continued on. So we kept the name of the band and, like you said, it's just irrelevant; it's just about good music and bad music at this point.

MM: When you bring younger bands on tour with you, is it the same sort of attitude that you have when putting younger wrestlers over?

Chris: We had two bands that we toured with. I think this is our eight tour of the UK and probably five or six of them were with a band called Forever Never and another band called Nineteenth Century who changed their name to The Jokers. We loved playing with them so much that we just always had them coming back with us on tour. This last tour and this tour we started using other bands. We've started using different bands to shake it up a bit. It's exciting because these are bands coming up the ladder and doing everything they can. It's a hard business. For us to get to this level is cool for me because it's hard to break through.

MM: Do you think that you're helping other people through as well?

Chris: Yeah, that's kind of the time honoured tradition of rock and roll. You get a good support band and give them a shot to move themselves to the next level too.

MM: Wrestling wise you are known as a guy who will put the younger wrestlers over. This year you've put over the likes of Evan Bourne and Heath Slater. Do you think it's important for the established stars to give the rub to the younger guys?

Chris: Of course, it's the same with music, we'd love to go on tour with Iron Maiden, Metallica or someone like that, but at this point we're kind of a little selfish and like to do things our own way. We had an offer to do the Black Label Society tour, it was a cool concept and it would have been great, but we would have been second on the bill, playing for probably half an hour a night, but we like to play longer than that. I'd rather play to five hundred people of my own for ninety minutes than play to two thousand people for thirty minutes. Hopefully in the summer we'll do some bigger tours and some festival tours and stuff like that. The circle of life continues, especially in the WWE, and you have to build new guys. I'm not going to be around forever, I may never wrestle again; it doesn't matter at this point. Somebody has to come up. Same in music, when Paul McCartney and U2 retire, who'll be playing stadiums? Somebody had better step up soon.

MM: Who on the current WWE roster do you think will be the guy to take the company forward?

Chris: I think The Miz has got a lot of potential, I think Wade Barrett has got a lot of potential, John Morrison, I love Jack Swagger, he's very untapped right now.

MM: We've been really high on Jack Swagger for a while now...

Chris: There are a lot of guys that are coming up, but you just can't teach experience. A lot of those guys don't have it; they just have to keep working to get more experience.

MM: Conversely to the new guys coming up, this year we saw Bret Hart's return to the WWE. Did you think you'd ever see Bret in a WWE ring again and what did you think of his return?

Chris: I thought it was great, it was much deserved and necessary, you don't want the legacy of Bret Hart to end on a bad note. As far as standing in a ring with him, it was cool. It's not like we could have had a full blown match, but being in the ring with him was cool, but I enjoyed it from a professional standpoint and not a fanboy standpoint. It was good for business and it was cool to be aligned with him. As a character I think he can come in and out of the show.

MM: From a fan's point of view, it was great to see him back. His run with Vince McMahon was a nice sense of closure to the Screwjob story after thirteen years...

Chris: Yeah, he's an asset to the show and he's an asset to the guys in the back, so they should use him as much as they can.

MM: You've finished writing your second book, *Undisputed: How to Become World Champion in 1,372 Easy Steps*. Where did that title come from?

Chris: You have to read the book to find out. It has a meaning though.

MM: Does it pick up where *A Lion's Tale* ended, with the Raw Is Jericho promo?

Chris: Yeah, it picks up right after it. Two seconds after the first book ended, and I wrote the first one that way. I knew that I had so much material that I couldn't put it all in one book. Whether I wrote a second book or not, I structured it so that I could always leave the next book wide open.

MM: Does the book end with the breaking the code vignettes that aired back in 2007?

Chris: It ends when I walk to the ring with Randy Orton in 2007. Exact same ending as the first one, just with a different guy.

MM: Do you think there'll be a third book in the making?

Chris: I've definitely got enough material for it. I think there will be a third book at some point. Books are very hard to write, though. They take a long time. It took me a while to get motivated enough to do this one. It takes a long time to get into it and then when you start writing it, it took me about ten months of working on this on a daily basis to get it done, so it would have to be a few years before I do a third.

MM: Your DVD *Breaking the Code* is out in November in the UK. What can fans expect from it? A lot of people have been clamouring for a DVD from you for a while now.

Chris: Yeah, it's a great documentary. It's kind of like a movie version of my first book *A Lion's Tale* and a trailer for *Undisputed* as it's a combination of both. I handpicked all of the matches on it to make sure that they're all good or meaningful matches.

MM: I'm particularly looking forward to your first match with Lance Storm.
Chris: Yeah, that's cool, that's a good one. There's some great stuff on there, some stuff that's never been seen before. They definitely had a lot of stuff to pull from, twenty years of being in the job, there was a lot of stuff that they could use. It definitely is well worth it for sure.

MM: With the Fozzy tour ending at the end of this year, what does the future hold for you? Can wrestling fans expect to see you back in a WWE ring anytime soon?

Chris: I can't say at this point. I'm happy doing what I'm doing right now. I really want to focus on the band and continue to see the band grow. I want to do another record, we're going to start working on that in the new year. Like I said, we've got a lot of opportunities. Tours in Australia and Canada, and maybe Japan in February or March, so there's a lot of stuff coming up.

Originally published in Mass Movement #28, November 2010

DANI FILTH
(CRADLE OF FILTH)

Whilst genre's come and genre's go, music remains a constant, and while the bands whose music is dictated by genre disappear almost as fast as the emerge, bands who exist only to play music, bands that are driven to create something original and unique, like music, remain, and this has been true of Cradle Of Filth for more than a decade. Born from black metal, forged by the world at large, the band have transcended the confines of the scene from which they emerged, and in the process of doing so, have become of the most exciting, inventive metal bands of the last two decades. On the eve of the release of the band's new album *Darkly Darkly Venus Aversa*, MM caught up with Dani Filth...

Interview by Tim Cundle

Photographs by James Sharrock

MM: First a question which I guess you'll get asked a lot. Why has the new record been released on your own imprint?

DF: It's mainly because – well we've done it since *Bitter Suites To Succubi* which was on Flapper and we did it through Sony and Roadrunner. It just gives us a feeling of self-control, and if we should want it, it gives us the option to release bands ourselves. Obviously we haven't done that as yet, but it's something –like a trademark or something. But if you're asking me about the move to Peaceville from Roadrunner – towards the back end of our relationship with Roadrunner, they let go of a lot of cool people at the label, like the head of European markets and a close friend of ours, the A&R guy who signed us. They seemed to lose touch with the kind of markets that most of their big bands came from and started signing anyone they thought would make a chart hit record. They had such high expectations of the bands that they got someone in to rearrange one of Killswitch's songs, which then prompted them with the next album to be heavier and less patchy I guess. Also we feel like a bigger fish in a smaller, more creative pond. Their independent and that's cool.

MM: The new album, I understand is a concept album based around the story of Lilith, the mistress of Samael?

DF: And his first wife, yes. She's the main protagonist in the story. We've woven this home grown gothic horror story partly based on fact, mythical spiritual fact and laced it with our own unique kind of shit. It involves nuns and has Middle Eastern and Greek mythology woven round it and goes all the way through to the fourteenth century.

MM: So you haven't made it easy for yourself with a story this involved...

DF: Yes but it was even more difficult making sure that each track was a standalone track on its own, that can be enjoyed and appreciated separately, but beneath the surface there is a whole labyrinth of complexity underneath. The artwork which is done by Natalie Shau, is like religious iconography that walks you through the story of the album. It's representative; and when you get it all together it's so much more..

MM: So why Lilith? Why, as important as she is, choose this particular figure from the religious history of humanity?

DF: Lilith is big in many cultures and also she has been standing in the shadows behind Cradle of Filth for a while - ever since *The Principle of Evil Made Flesh* which it about sort of vampiric dark femme fatal, dark figures like Lilith or Persephone, passionate and original archetypes. So it was kind of inevitable really and a kind of escape route for me. I had four or five tracks, and I knew I had to write some songs and I was a bit stumped because I didn't want to write throw away songs on just any old subject matter – you know like sports cars or footballers or something like that I wanted something more in-depth. The music at that point kind of suggested it to me. It seemed to be staring us in the face for a long time like with the previous record where I investigated all that about 10 years earlier. It was a matter of circumstance as much as anything else.

MM: Your previous album was a bit of a concept based project too, so I wondered if you thought Cradle might become synonymous with the idea of a concept record?

DF: That was a concurrent story as well but no-where near as involved as there wasn't the historical criteria of this record. We've had two loose concepts and three very tight concepts throughout our career. I think there is a danger there, especially as last time I swore blind that I wasn't ever going to do it again. Obviously what we do with records is to try to make it as standalone as we can. That may come out of a number of things; the people in the band, whether we have been on tour or not and it's all reflected in the way it comes out. Immortal for example were never going to be recorded in Barbados!

MM: From a creative view point is the notion of telling a story through the tracks of a record more satisfying than writing a series of disparate songs?

DF: Maybe for us, but I didn't want to do it in such a way that it didn't interfere with the tracks themselves. On the special edition we actually wrote 16 original tracks and they're not short, they're not 2 minute punk bursts, so all thirty one songs are all stand alone and don't interfere with the story at all.

MM: The new album is released on November 1st, the day following All Hallows Eve… so is that just a happy coincidence?

DF: No it would have been a happier coincidence if it had been the day before really.

MM: So what do you think of the 21st Century's version of Halloween?

DF: Obviously it's really great that we live in the 21st Century. People can be – well I'm into 19th Century literature and I'm fascinated with that era of ghost writers and Empire, but I wouldn't want to live in that time it's far more comfortable now, but it's fun to reminisce. I think that's what a lot of people do with music as well. The older they get the more attached they get to the music they grew up on. We all say "I won't be like my dad all into sixties music and stuff" but when we get there, we'll be listening to 80s and 90s stuff.

MM: So do you think Halloween is still a time to break out the Misfits discography and the Hammer Studios back catalogue?

DF: Oh yes. Every year on Halloween I always get out the Misfits and Samhain, it has to be done. Halloween is about reminiscing so it's good to have all the pagan stuff and the dark stuff with it but if you can marry that with 21st century – good music, good company, good food – or rather horrible food and the modern trappings of horror films, dressing up and all that kind of shit which is essentially what it's all about. Which is what our album's about basically, it's a marriage of opposites.

MM: I've always seen Cradle as a fusion of music and art and I wondered if you'd ever thought about making full length films or animation to go with the albums?

DF: Things like that do cross our minds. Like our friend for example he's on the board of a new film company with the grandson of Douglas Fairbanks Jnr, the guy who basically invented Hollywood with Charlie Chaplin et al. And he's talking about... Just to do a standalone movie with just a few people in it, not a huge crew or anything of maybe $3-4million. So yes you can think about that stuff, you can be as ambitious as you want, but the great thing about our medium for fusing music and art is that basically you are not hemmed in by cost. You've got free range over your imagination. Films are also made for the majority and you have to visualise them and see them as such. We approached someone about doing a graphic novel for this album and I know some people who do graphic novels as well but again it's cost. It costs a fortune to produce that stuff...

MM: Do you still think of Cradle as a metal band or do you think that's too limited a genre...

DF: I think it is too limited a genre, so I don't really think of us as a metal band any more. Like I said there are just so many fusions and the hybrid children that have come out now; to say anything else is debilitating and restricting. I would like to be remembered as a metal band, although the ultimate accolade would be to just be remembered as Cradle of Filth, you know like Iron Maiden are – you know exactly what they are but no-one says Iron Maiden – part of that new wave of British heavy metal do they?

MM: How would you describe Cradle's current sound to someone who is completely unfamiliar with you?

DF: We are very fast and ornate, heavy, angry – lots of emotion. It's very cinematic, it's angry it's dark, vampiric, gothic. Iron Maiden on crack in a graveyard of angels.

MM: Sticking with the same theme, why do you think there are so few successful British metal bands?

DF: I don't know. I had this conversation with an Italian journalist earlier on. I don't know why. Europe is big and so is America but then both places have a marriage with that in their charts. Our charts are dominated by shit off the X factor...

MM: Going back to the new album, it feels almost like a new start for the band. How do you think it's going to be received by the existing fan base?

DF: I think very well. People have had access to the material. We put a track up online and we've been streaming bits of different songs online all the way up to the release. All I can say that the cross section of journalists that I've spoken to so far have all been thumbs up so I think it's cool. We're a really strong, passionate band, and I never thought about it in the beginning, because it's always just been one step up every time we do a record.

MM: With the band's image, there has always been this neo-fascist undercurrent in the mainstream press who want to make links with Satanism. Why do you think the mainstream press is so willing to label something as satanic?

DF: I look at it a totally different way; the British press loved us at one point, as they do with all bands and then just went the other way. It's something that's particularly unique with the British music press where they have to iron out any kind of individuality on the band's behalf and then destroy them. You'll see it so many times. They'll build a band up and then destroy them. It's just the way they are. The whole Satanic thing is the same. They don't warn people because they are worried about the readership or anything, they do it because they can.

MM: Following on from that, what do you make of the notion of divinity?

DF: Divinity? Yes I do believe in something. I don't like the idea of this being a complete non-event. My mother used to have a house in India and we used to travel out there a lot and I've seen all kinds of cultures as I've travelled round the world and whether it's Voodoo, Hindu, Egyptian or Sumerian culture there is always a God. God is everywhere. Humans see symbolism in everything and that's where we find our gods – it doesn't mean it's a bearded white man handing down judgment.

MM: I've always wanted to ask you about *Cradle of Fear*. How did you get involved with the film?

DF: Alex Chandon, the director and a couple of his friends, they worked on a Cradle promo. We all became friends and to cut a long story short we wanted to make a film so we used everybody on a work now pay later kind of thing. We raised about £80,000 and everyone got a percentage later. Actually it's a good way of making a film but you couldn't do that anymore...

MM: Is it something you've looked at returning to?

DF: Yes of course, but we are a prolifically active band and are developing all kind of endeavours such as an orchestral record we've got coming out next year called *Midnight In the Labyrinth*. So there are things we have on the back burner, but yes it is something I'd like to go back to one day.

MM: I'm assuming you're going to tour this record? I've seen your stage show a couple of times and it's always well done, well thought out and executed, making it better and bigger than almost any other bands stage show. What have you got planned this time...?

DF: We've only just started thinking about it but one of the things we wanted to do was to bring the stage show in line with the story. Obviously we can't bring the whole story to the stage but we want to bring the key elements. Plus up the ante with the pyrotechnics as well to make it a bit more of an event.

MM: You mentioned your love of Victoriana. What else inspires you?

DF: Horror movies, the environment, well my environment – my family is so fundamental to me...

MM: So what's next?

DF: We're doing some live shows for MTV then some touring. After Christmas we'll be finishing up that orchestral record I told you about. Then we're touring in the States and the UK and playing a smattering of summer festivals. Then we're working on the special edition or rather the ultimate edition with tons of extra stuff like a sixty four page booklet, a documentary and loads and loads more.

Originally published in Mass Movement #28, November 2010

JOHN ARCUDI

As has been well documented, I'm a sucker for both Hellboy and the BPRD, and when John Arcudi started writing BPRD with Mike Mignola, it was almost like the book kicked up a gear, arcs started to tie together, and it just felt, well, even more rounded, so when I recently got a chance to talk to John, I jumped at it. Ladies and gentlemen, boys and girls, I give you John Arcudi...

Interview by Tim Cundle & Brady Webb

MM: I guess we should start at the beginning John, do you want to both introduce and tell us a little about yourself? Did you always want to write, or was it something that you stumbled across and into during school, college or later on?

JA: Well, I always wanted to write, but not comics. That didn't come until years later when I found out (under Larry Hama's tutelage) that I had a knack for it. Or Larry had a knack for teaching, which may be closer to the truth.

What initially drew you to comics, and does it still draw you to the medium to this day? Do the same things that initially excited you about, and drew you toward, the medium still hold true, or has the way you feel about, and view the medium, changed? If so, how have they changed, and why?

JA: I was a fan, but again, I didn't give a whole lotta thought to writing comics until just about six months — or a year, tops — before I became professional. Nothing drew me to the work initially other than a chance to make better money than I was earning writing prose, but I learned to love it. The collaborative process, the versatility of the medium, the visual vocabulary you have to develop, all of those things are really amazing and wonderful and unique to comics. And the potential is limitless, so what's not to love?

MM: How did you make the transition from fan to working within, and for the medium of comics? What was your first gig and how did you feel when you were handed your initial story, finished and fresh from the presses?

JA: I can't say I recall all that clearly, but what I do remember is that Larry indoctrinated me into the philosophy that what we do is a job and you have to be professional or you'll lose that job. So generally the way I felt early in my career is still the way I feel; very much like any other guy who digs ditches or paints houses or fixes cars. I feel the pride of a job well done. No shit.

MM: As a writer, what and who (in terms of other writers) influences you and your work, and how, if at all, do you think your influences manifest themselves in your work? Do you think it's possible for a writer or an artist to escape the boundaries of their influences, or do you think that all literature, no matter the format and those who create it are the sum of their influences channeled through their own imaginations? Why?

JA: One of the major influences on my writing was Charles Willeford. There's a guy who could write like a motherfucker. And what I try to do with my scripts that he did with his novels was say as much as I can by writing as little as I can.

This frustrates a lot of readers, but I've been lucky that some have found the less-is-more approach enjoyable. Can you escape the boundaries of your influences? Experience is influence, right? What you had for breakfast, what TV shows you watch, what books you like, what books you hate, and what you see out your window are all influences, so no, you can't escape experience itself. It shapes you and if that isn't you writing, well then who cares?

MM: I guess one of the characters that most people know you for, or are familiar with is The Mask… How did you go about creating the character? Given that most people will be familiar with the character via the film, as the initial writer, how do you think the book differs from the film? What do you think about, and of, the film, the cartoon series and the belated movie sequel?

JA: All part of the collaborative effort. The Mask character existed before I ever wrote a word. Doug Mahnke and I changed it very much, and more or less into the character you saw in the movie. Still, we didn't start with a blank slate. The movie sorta skips the whole social commentary about violence that we were playing with in the book, but you aren't gonna sell a lotta tickets with your "hero" killing everybody.

MM: Which Mask story arc / story-line is your favourite and why, and which arc/ story-line do you think best sums up the character? Again, why?

JA: Huh. Well, I got to work with Doug on all of them, which was great, but Lobo/Mask was the most insane story, AND I got to work with the legendary Alan Grant, who was a lot of fun. Never got a chance to work with Alan again. Shame. He was hilarious!

MM: You've also worked for both DC and Marvel, and I wondered, if there was a different set of "rules" or "guidelines" for writers at each? I mean, both are famous for publishing books that revolve around Superhero's, yet the books published by Marvel and DC have very distinct, separate identities, and having worked for both, I wondered if you could maybe shed any light on why they're so vastly, and at the same time, subtly different?

JA: A million years ago, when Larry was still there, Marvel was a lot of fun. You knew there were restrictions, parameters within which you had to work, but as long as you did a good story within them, you were good to go. DC is still like that, and actually, DC also offers some genuine creative freedom. Look at what Brian Wood does there, or Bill Willingham, or Mike Carey or, for that matter, what I did with A God Somewhere which was a book published through Wildstorm that I did with Peter Snejbjerg and Bjarne Hansen. Sure, DC is part of a large corporate entity, but the people there seem to recognize that the medium can't survive without new, original works out there.

MM: Having written for two of the "Big Guns", Superman and Batman (which is like being given the keys to the executive suite) amongst a cast of hundreds of other Supers, I was kind of curious about which of them was your favourite to write for, and why? Which character did you most identify with whilst writing, and why?

JA: Really, Superheroes have never been my thing. I'm just not very good at writing them – probably because most of them just don't make much sense to me. Superman is probably the only one who does, so I was really happy to get a chance to write him.

MM: Sort of sticking with the same theme – how did you become involved with Wednesday Comics, and how did you feel when you were asked to write the Superman (arguably DC's flagship character) for the title? How do you approach writing Superman, and how do you think your Superman differs from other versions of the character? How did, and do, you feel about the format, and is it something that you'd like return to?

JA: Editor Mark Chairello asked me to be a part of Wednesday Comics and I said "Hell yes!" The way I saw this particular project was as an art showcase. I didn't want to get in the way of the beautiful work by the amazing Lee Bermejo, so I tried to make the story organic to the art. All I really wanted to do was to visually explore each world Superman lives in. Metropolis, his relationship with other "heroes' (in this case, Batman), his relationship with Lois, Smallville, and Krypton. In essence, a travelogue of Superman's world. Not as easy as it might sound, but I figured why do this if we can't look at the whole of Superman? It was a challenging format.

MM: From a writers perspective (in terms of Superheroes), which do you prefer writing for, individual characters or teams / collectives? Why?

JA: I prefer not writing for superheroes at all. All I ever care about is writing characters that make sense to me in stories that are fun and interesting to read (and write, if I'm lucky). That's all I've ever cared about. I've done some work solely for the bucks, but have regretted each and every job like that.

MM: Talking of teams...It's time to talk B.P.R.D.. How did you initially become involved with writing the BPRD? Where you at all wary about writing for a book that, at the time, was so heavily identified with Mike Mignola?

JA: Mike and I had kicked around the idea of working together for years before we finally agreed that this was the book to do it on. It was a little intimidating and I can't say I got off to the absolutely best start, but Mike did everything he could to make me feel as if these were my characters. That helped a lot.

MM: How does the writing partnership for the BPRD work? Do you bounce stories and ideas off each other until they start to take shape? Do you build on separate ideas, linking them together as the story progresses, or something entirely different?

JA: It was different with every series. Sometime Mike was heavily involved, sometimes barely at all. Lately Mike's let me take a lot more control of the storylines. He's got an endgame and some pieces he wants on the board at certain dates, but for the most part I'm free to go in many different directions. That sort of sounds like I'm a loose cannon, which is not quite true. Mike and BPRD editor Scott Allie are there to make sure I stay on track, but I do have a lot of freedom.

MM: Did you have a definitive vision of where you wanted to take the team when you initially took up the reigns, or have your ideas and stories changed as you've written the title and become more and more familiar with, and used to, the characters?

JA: Not when I started, no. I've got some firm ideas now, but mostly it's Mike's larger vision that provides the ultimate direction. Still, what the characters do individually is a byproduct of my comfort level with them.

MM: Have we seen the last of Ben Daimo? Is he doomed to walk the Earth as the Jaguar creature / spirit/ demon forever more or does he have a further role to play in the team?

JA: Readers already know the answer to this question... more or less.

MM: With each arc getting progressively darker, I get the feeling that it isn't going to end well for the Agents...Anything that you can tell us about their collective or individual futures? Any future plans for the book that you can share with us John?

JA: I can tell you that we're going to see more and more of the world outside of the BPRD HQ's walls. We'll become acquainted with some vitally important characters that will not have their origins within the established BPRD mythos, and some that people will recognize from earlier books. The BPRD is going to need all the help that it can get. Saying anything beyond that is giving too much away.

MM: Let's talk about *A God Somewhere*....What's the book about, and where did the idea for it come from? How do you think (if at all) if differs from your other work?

JA: *AGS* is about a lot of things. The main characters are two brothers, the wife of one, and the brothers' best friend. One of the brothers somehow gets god-like powers and the story takes off from there. The POV for this story, however, is not that of the superhuman but that of his friend. This is how we get a clearer picture of those people who are still normal, and what happens to their lives, which has always been the story I wanted to see in comics. It's more personal to me than the BPRD stuff, or really anything else I've done. Honestly, I've been struggling to find a way to tell a story of this nature for a while. The medium is overwhelmingly concerned with super-humans and I just couldn't make much of them – until I finally figured it out with this book. It's as close as I can come to telling a superhero story well — I flatter myself to think.

MM: Okay, nearly time to finish up – I wondered, both a fan and an insider, how do you think the comics industry has changed during the last three or four decades and how do you think these changes have affected the medium as a whole?

JA: Who knows? You get to a point where you realize your perspective is hopelessly skewed by your experience. It does seem to me that the current crop of independent comics are so numerous, and so creative that it's possible they will save the art form at the very least, which is what we should care most about.

MM: How do you feel, and what do you think of, the way in which Hollywood seems to be plundering the comic medium for new ideas and movies? Is it a positive or negative development, and what impact and effect do you think it will eventually have on comic books?
JA: If independents will save the art form, it's entirely possible that Hollywood will save the industry. Somebody'd better.

MM: What's next for you, John?
JA: More BPRD and a personal project or two — if I'm lucky.

REVIEW

A God Somewhere – John Arcudi, Peter Snerjberg, Bjarne Hansen (Titan Books)

Like so many other comic fans, I'm a fan of the capes, the super-hero's, the meta's, call them what you will, they're the lifeblood of the four colour universe, the big guns that keep the battle going, the fuel that keeps the comic wheels turning. We know the origin stories, we read the universe changing events that they fight and sometimes die in, and we know everything about them. Except what it's really like to be them. How untold power and ability effects and changes them. Because at the end of the day, when you break each and every hero down, they're just men and women. They're haunted by the same neuroses and psychoses, driven by the same desires and needs, laugh at the same jokes as the rest of the us, they feel the same heartbreak and heartache as the rest of us, but they never show it, because they're hero's and that's not what hero's do in comics. But what if they did? What if a normal, average everyday working guy suddenly became as powerful as God? What if a normal everyday guy suddenly became the equal of the Deity that he'd spent his life faithfully worshipping. How would it affect him? What would happen to him and those around him? John Arcudi asks, and answer those questions in *A God Somewhere*.

It's the story of Eric, Sam, Hugh and Alma, and how, when Eric survives a mysterious explosion at his Apartment Building and suddenly becomes Super-Human, their lives are changed forever. It's a story that doesn't end well, mirroring the real world as it does, how could it? In exploring the human condition, Arcudi reaches the same inevitable conclusion that so many of us, that underneath everything, we're just flesh and blood, and given that kind of power and freedom and the ability to do anything, each and every one of us would be driven insane and we'd drag our loved ones and friends, down into Hell with us. Peter Snejbjerg's art is a powerful testament to Arcudi's story, often horrific and soaked in violence, but with touches of delicate beauty and tenderness, again, perfectly mirroring the real world. Thought provoking, honest and touching, This is the art of the graphic novel at its finest, the written word and art fused together to create something more than the sum of its parts, coming together to create a truly incredible, endearing story...**Tim Cundle**

Originally published in Mass Movement #28, November 2010

STEVE IGNORANT

Love them or hate them Crass are/were one of the most significant bands to grace the music genre, and as the pioneers of Anarcho punk they played a vital part in the development of punk as a real social threat rather than a simply another form of rock n roll. When the band called it quits (fittingly in 1984) the majority of its members disappeared from the limelight, but not vocalist Steve Ignorant. With his distinctive Dagenham twang Steve went on to sing with Schwarzenegger and the Stratford Mercenaries with occasional forays into theatre and more bizarrely the world of Punch and Judy. In 2007 Steve made the controversial decision to perform Crass songs with a handpicked bunch of musicians. Despite the inevitable backlash from some quarters the shows went down well and prompted Steve to take the show on the road. I caught up with Steve after the first few British dates of the tour.

Interview by Ian Pickens

MM: First of all congratulations on the way the tour is going; you must be pretty pleased with the reception?

SI: Oh the receptions just been amazing I didn't expect that at all. Every night has been sold out and the response has just been fantastic.

MM: Were you expecting a lot of negative feedback performing a whole set of Crass songs without the rest of the band?

SI: Yeah I was expecting a bit but so far I haven't seen any or heard any, so we seem to be doing something right.

MM: *The Last Supper* – the last time you intend to play songs from your time in Crass or the last time you intend to tour?

SI: It's the last time I intend to do Crass songs live. Um, when this tour is over, which is going to be some point next year, I'm going to take a year and a half off and really knuckle down to some new material and then I'll go out on tour again; but that will be like a spoken word thing, but I want to produce it almost like a play. So there will be a stage set, a three piece band – just a bass, drums and keyboards and just um… talk really; and if it goes alright I'll open it up to the audience as a question and answer set, sort of like ' An Audience With.." 'cos you know I'm sure there's people out there who have a lot of questions. I dunno I'll give it a go.

MM: So it will be a combination of all the artistic threads of your life, the music, the theatrical (Steve had the lead part in the play *Tooth of Crime* by Sam Shepard and also ran his open Punch & Judy show) and the spoken word you've done?

SI: Yeah. What I plan to do is perform at little art galleries and smaller clubs, you know small venues where it can be quite intimate.

MM: You're playing fairly large venues on this tour , and with the exception of the *Feeding of the 5000* show at Shepherd's Bush Empire, this must seem quite a long way from that last Crass show in Aberdare back in 1984 in support of the Miners. How does it feel playing these bigger venues? Is it more difficult to connect with people?

SI: Um, no I feel fine with it. I have no problem with it at all. Um I think maybe we lost some of that intimacy playing the Empire to several thousand people but when you're playing to like 600/700 people then the intimacy is still there you know what I mean?

MM: I guess it's about striking a balance between the bigger shows like *Feeding of the 5000* where I get the impression from your book that things were a little out of control at times and the badly organised DIY shows you've done in squats?

SI: I think the problem there, with the *Feeding...* show was that I was incredibly nervous be-cause of all the build up to it and that was when, I mean I hadn't even played the gig and I was getting negative comments, so that really undermined my confidence, so I um... I don't know it was uh... out of control, how do you mean it was out of control?

MM: There were elements to the organisation of the show that maybe weren't quite as professional as they should have been - problems with the vegetarian catering, sound engi-neers, bouncers etc?

SI: Oh right. Yeah well I think a lot of that was because we were dealing with so many bands. When you've got like 12 bands playing some things are bound to go wrong.

MM: *The Last Supper* tour seems to be a lot more professionally organised?

SI: It had to be. My first stipulation was that it had to be done properly as it's the last time I'm going to do it so you know if we had cocked up in Bristol there's no way I can repeat it, so we've gotta do it right first time and part of what comes with that is that things have to be made easier for us as musicians so that's why I wanted to work with bands like Goldblade, because there's no problem with them getting on stage at the right time and getting off at the right time, especially when these places we're playing have such early curfews and its very rigid, so if you're late going on by 5 minutes then you're not going to get that back. The main thing for me is that everyone, the bands, everyone has put so much hard work into this that I want it to be fun you know, an enjoyable experience.

MM: Yeah one thing I noticed at the Bristol show was that everyone seemed to be having a good time, having fun, almost the antithesis of a Crass show in a way where everything was a lot more serious, maybe even a little po-faced; was it enjoyable to play those songs again minus the baggage that went with Crass?

SI: Yeah absolutely, I enjoyed doing 'em and what I think I'm really enjoying is that Beki, when she does the 'female' songs from *Penis Envy*, she gets the same amount of applause as what I do, there's no separation, no preference and the response she's been getting has been absolutely fantastic.

MM: It's a big set of shoes to step into with Eve Libertine vocals being such a distinctive element of the Crass sound...

SI: Yeah exactly, but it's nice doing those songs and just being able to you know enjoy them, without as you say the baggage.

MM: The band as a whole (featuring ex English Dogs and Prodigy guitarist Gizz Butt, former Morrisey drummer Spike T Smith, Steve's ex Schwarzenegger band mate Bob Butler on bass and the afore mentioned Beki Straughan from Loaded 44 on vocals) have gelled together really well...

SI: Well Bob even though he probably wouldn't admit to being a 'professional' bass player is just amazing and Gizz is just you know a great guitar player and Spike on drums, they're all just great musicians. We've rehearsed and rehearsed and they all take it really seriously, I mean in the sense of getting it right and when we played Edinburgh on uh Saturday, um we really wanted it to come together and it did.

MM: Coinciding with the tour you've just had your autobiography, *The Rest is Propaganda* published. Would it be fair to say you had a fairly dysfunctional childhood?

SI: Absolutely. What I tried to put across in the book it's that it didn't really bother me that much um, but you know I think really my stepdad and my mother just weren't very good at being parents, and that's all there is to it.

MM: Do you think that contributed to you being an 'outsider' and pushed you towards the scenes you later gravitated towards, the skinhead scene in the late sixties and then later the whole Punk/Dial House/Crass/Anarcho scenes?

SI: Uh yeah. I mean there was no particular feeling of love and I don't remember getting many cuddles or fitting in, so I found it elsewhere, and where I found it was you know dressing up as a skinhead and at football matches.

MM: Do you think that if you hadn't ended up in Dial House and its Bohemian atmosphere you may have gravitated more to the aggro end of punk, and ended up in an Oi band like the Rejects or Sham?

SI: I dunno really, um.. I think I would have got into punk anyway regardless and I think I would have (coughs violently), sorry I've got a bit of a cold going on...

MM: No worries I know the feeling...

SI: I think I would have met other people in that scene and I think I would have learnt off of them, so I think it would have taken longer but I think I would have felt the same as I do.

MM: Do you think Crass was of its time? The band ran pretty much concurrently with the Thatcher Government during their most significant years?

SI: I don't know that if Crass as a band started tomorrow, I don't know if it would work now, um because what we did as Crass at that time, remember there was no Internet, no email,

no mobile phones, there wasn't any of this amazing technology we have now, and what we did was kind of like nailed together likes bits of wood, very basic and what we did back then was introduce young people to things they hadn't heard of, for example Anarchy. They'd heard Johnny Rotten say it but they didn't actually know what it was, and things like CND (Campaign for Nuclear Disarmament). Now kids can just Google it so it's like "this is a song about.", yeah I know Steve I googled it last night...So I don't know that a band like Crass would mean the same thing now.

MM: Do you think kids are more cynical today? That there was a more idealistic element to youth back in the eighties?

SI: Well I mean you can just get anything you want these days really, it's just at your finger-tips, um... so it must be really hard to be a young person today because what the hell do you rebel against apart from the obvious like your parents and your school and obviously wars and all that, but I mean actually what can you rebel against these days as a teenager?

MM: In light of that what's the motivation behind Southern Records re-releasing the Crass albums? *Feeding of the 5000*, *Stations of the Crass* **and** *Penis Envy* **have been released so far right?**

SI: Yeah. Well firstly Pen (Penny Rimbaud – Crass drummer and founding member with Steve) went into Southern and all the albums were on 4" or 2 " tape and were starting to de-teriorate, so it's all been put on digital and while he was sorting all that out he re-mastered them all and I think he realised that back when we recorded them we actually used to try and put so much on that that's why they all sound so tinny, there's wasn't any more room for more bass. So he just re-mastered it and it sounded great and then it was realised that you know when the records went into CD format you actually lost half the artwork so Gee de-cided to redo the artwork and just kind of bring it up to date, enhance it, and I think it has

MM: Uh huh, the graphics were as much a part of the Crass message as the music...

SI: Exactly.

MM: Do you plan on re-mastering and re-releasing the albums you recorded with Schwarzenegger and the Stratford Mercenaries?

SI: Uh... no I don't know about re-releasing the Mercenaries, but I'd like to redo some of the Schwarzenegger stuff, because I know the ways things are with those records, sometimes Ben's guitar was so loud you can hardly hear the vocals, that was Ben when he was going through his Steve Jones and the Sex Pistols phase... But no I'd like to. I'll get all this stuff out of the way and then I'll look at that.

MM: Following the breakup of Crass it was noticeable that you were the only member who really pursued musical projects; Penny concentrated on his poetry and writing, Gee contin-ued working in the visual arts; did this expose the class differences at the heart of the band or was it simply a question of where personal interests lie?

SI: I think it was more personal interests. For the rest of them it was a case of 'Oh well that's that phase done' but for me it was 'I like doing this' and what could I go back to? Working in a supermarket? So you know I think that's why I kept on with it. And I like meeting people, I like being at gigs and things, but for Pen.. I asked him 'Pen don't you wish we had carried on or done another band or something?' But for Pen, he always says that he's had his 'John Lennon' moment <both laugh> and you know I've had my David Bowie moment but I still want it (laughs).

MM: I understand that the rest of the band are happy with you going out and playing the songs live and the re-release of the albums now, but initially there was a little bit of antagonism?

SI: Well it's all gone very quiet on that front, um... me, Eve, Gee and Pen are all happy about it and Phil, Joy and Pete are not and Pete Wright (Crass bass player) said that if things went ahead and we re-released the albums then he would take us to court, now it's all gone very quiet, so I don't know what the hell's going to happen. I've got a sneaky feeling that something very nasty is going to happen, so uh... yeah.

MM: Coming back to the autobiography; how much of it was actually written by you and how much was done by ghost-writer Steve Pottinger? The way it's written it actually 'sounds' like the way you speak which is quite effective...

SI: Well what Spot (Steve Pottinger) did was he would come down and basically interview me, ask me things about the family and memories and stuff, and then I'd answer them, he'd transcribe it and then he's come over here or I'd go over to his place and we'd go through it and I'd say 'No that's not how I would have said it, the way I would have said it is 'this'', so we very carefully so that when you read it, it does actually sound like me, if you know what I mean.

MM: Do you think it will surprise people to discover sides to Steve Ignorant that they haven't seen before?

SI: I don't know. Maybe. We'll have to wait and see mate. (laughs)

MM: How has the book been received so far?

SI: Really good. It's gone on mail order today, but I've had a couple of people email me about how much they enjoyed it. So yeah it's looking good.

MM: Totally unconnected with your artistic projects but nevertheless an important part of your life is your involvement with the Sea Palling volunteer Life Boat crew; how did that come about?

SI: Um.. well when I did the Shepherd's Bush Empire gig back in 2007, I always like to give some of the money to cause and I thought I don't just want to give away a load of money to something where I can't see where it goes, you know where it goes to putting petrol in the organisers car, that sort of thing and I thought no, I wanna see where it goes and I'd seen the crew in my local pub and I just said to them, you know I'm doing this gig and I'd like to donate some money to you, and they explained that they weren't part of the RNLI (Royal National Lifeboat Institution) and totally independent and existing on donations, and so anyway I gave them the money and they bought new life jackets with it. So they took me out on the boat and showed me what they do.

This year we've had about 19 call outs and saved 8 lives using those life jackets, so anybody who contributed to those Shepherd's Bush shows actually contributed to saving lives. Anyway after I'd given them the money and they'd got the jackets they asked me to join, but I said I couldn't commit myself to giving that much time, they explained that if you can only give 10 minutes of your time to sweep the floor then that's it. Anyway they took me out on the boat, I had six months training and now I'm a full member of the Sea Palling Volunteer Life Boat crew.

MM: So you've taken those egalitarian lessons from your punk days and applied them in your middle age...

SI: Well if you'd told me ten years ago that I'd be on a boat in the middle of the North Sea I wouldn't have believed you but it's just something I've got to do. When the bleeper goes off I'm out of the door and running without even thinking about it. I'm incredibly proud to be a part of it and the crew do such a good job, it's not just me.

MM: So... singer in one of the most significant bands in history, actor, Punch & Judy Professor, author, life boat crew member.... What's next?

SI: Well the spoken word will be the main focus when this tour comes to an end. I've already done spoken word a couple of times in the Vortex Jazz club in London and it's gone down really well, and you know I like to talk and I like meeting people, and what I like about these spoken word things is that a lot of people can come up and say 'You know I can really relate to that'.

MM: I think that's probably why so many people are still coming out to hear you belt out *Do They Owe Us A Living*? Okay well thanks for taking the time out to do this Steve, much appreciated. All the best with the rest of the tour...

SI: It's a pleasure mate.

Originally published in Mass Movement #28, November 2010

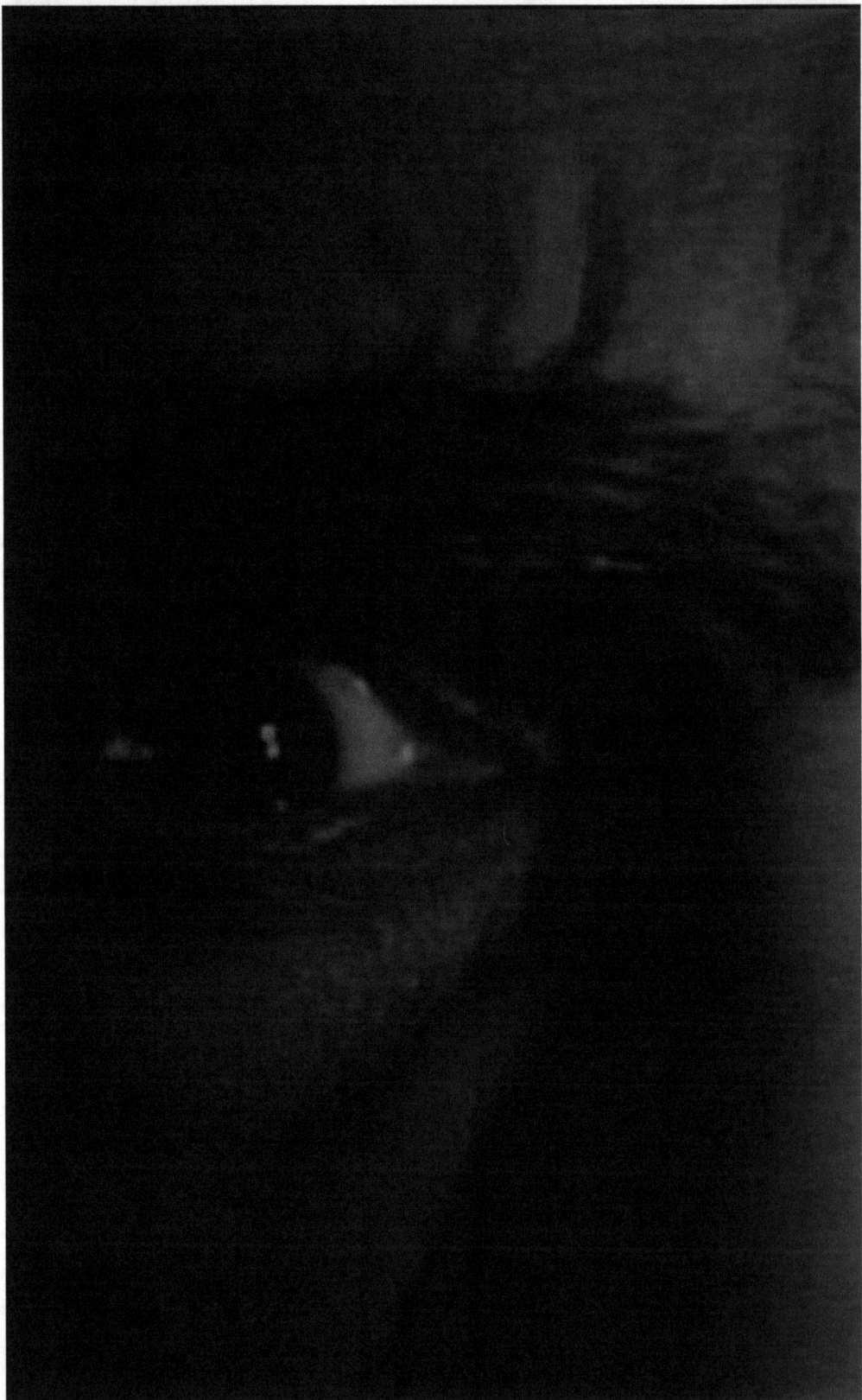

THE POWER OF THE POWDER

The examination of the Dutura plant and Voodoo

The West Indies has always been associated with beautiful and exotic surroundings, but beyond the obvious aesthetic value of these picturesque atolls is a more sinister backdrop. The ritualistic practice of Voodoo originated in West Africa and later migrated to the West Indies, specifically, to the country of Haiti. A brief history lesson suggests that Voodoo was a primitive belief held by the ignorant African slaves, who were being transported to the West Indies to work in the sugarcane fields. Roughly translated, the word "Voodoo" means "spirit of god."

Over the centuries, the various nomenclatures associated with the cult have been grossly misaligned to represent an even more distorted perception of the religion itself. The idea of mindless zombies who are at the "beck and call" of some unscrupulous taskmaster is the image that Hollywood has embellished to sell an audience on the horrors of this geographic region. The truth is far less ghastly.

Interestingly, this particular "tinsel town" devise used to generate ticket sales has, as do so many other cultural myths, a base in reality. Not unlike werewolf and Vampiric folklore with their various nuances, the notion of mind control as a means of enslavement is certainly a well-established tool linked to Voodoo. The question is –- by what means?

Ironically, the religion of Voodoo itself makes little or no reference to mind control for manipulative purposes but does, however, suggest that the basis for such a belief is more spiritual in nature. In an effort to mentally obliterate the horrors of captivity, the newly transported slaves used a form of self-hypnosis to soften the harsh realities of their existence. Aided by a mind-altering, herbal concoction (distilled from the Datura plant), they would render themselves oblivious to worldly distractions and enter into a reduced state of consciousness, a condition compared to the "black-out" stage of acute alcoholism.

Due to the potent combination of anticholinergic substances it contains, *Datura* intoxication typically produces effects similar to that of an anticholinergic delirium (as contrasted to hallucination): a complete inability to differentiate reality from fantasy; hyperthermia; tachycardia; bizarre, and possibly violent behavior; and severe mydriasis with resultant painful photophobia that can last several days. Pronounced amnesia is another commonly reported effect.

No other psychoactive substance has received as many "train wreck" (i.e., severely negative experience) reports as has *Datura*. The overwhelming majority of those who describe their use of *Datura* find their experiences extremely mentally and physically unpleasant and often physically dangerous. The intoxicated subjects appear as glassy-eyed robots with abnormal strength, capable of performing spectacular feats of endurance.

The Datura plant is ground into a fine powder and can be taken internally by a number of different methods. A zombie producing agent unknowingly ingested by some unsuspecting soul has been used as the premise in several movies, most notably — *White Zombie*.

In the 1932 classic, Bela Lugosi, who plays the evil Murder Legendre, instructs a man to use just a pinch of the powder in order to win the love of another man's wife. After the wife unknowingly smells a flower laced with the powder, she becomes the stereotypical zombie with

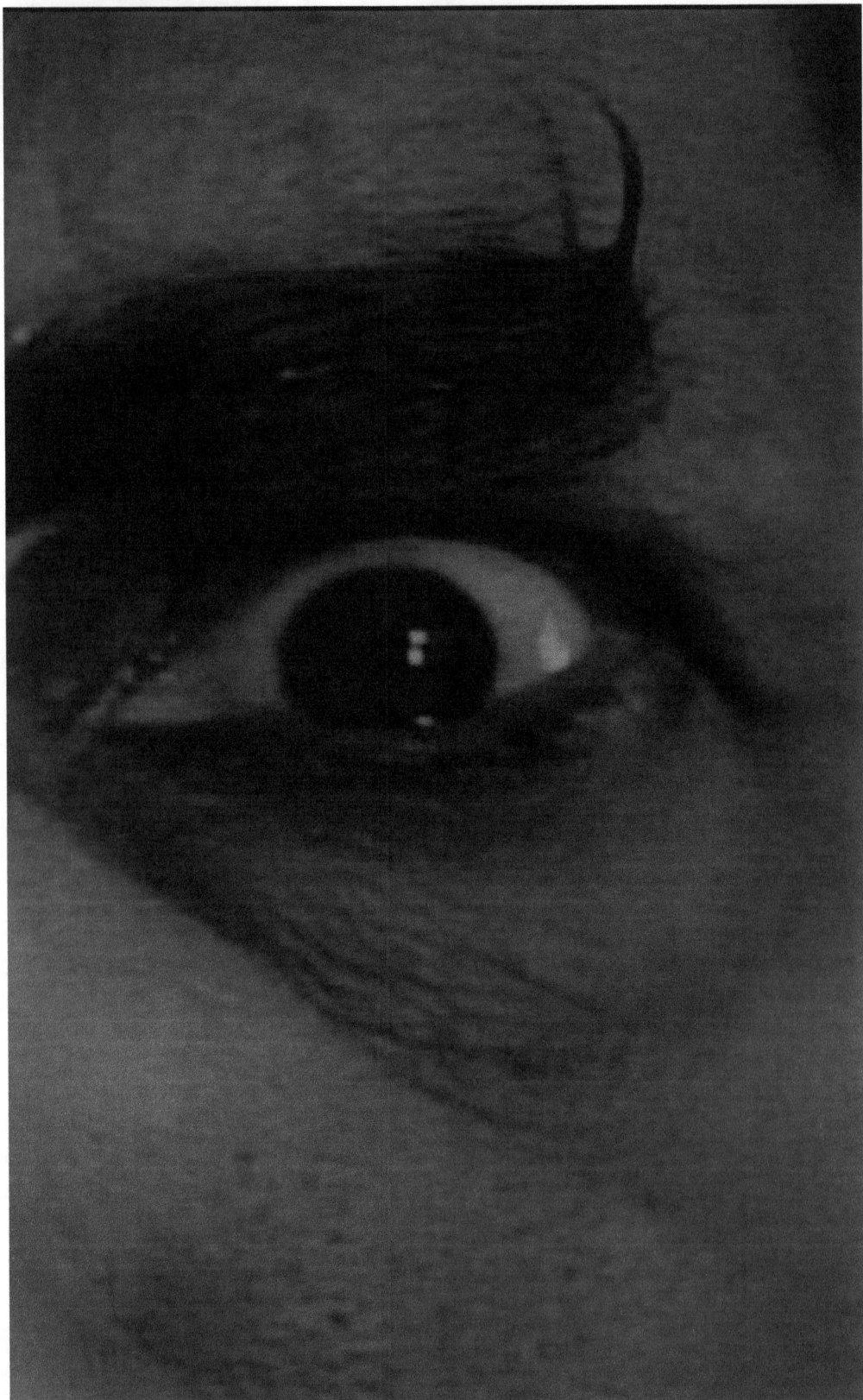

absolutely no desire for any type of romance. As a matter of fact, she has absolutely no desires whatsoever, except, to stand on the balcony of a lonely mansion and stare into space. (On a side note, the woman's actions are a closer representation to the zombie myth than the flesh eating variety that we see so often in films.)

Lugosi, on the other hand, has many nefarious desires, which includes lording over a troupe of zombie slaves to work in his sugarcane mill. His affections for the woman, whom he helped to enslave, run very deep. And, as one might predict, he has "other plans" for her. With the situation well in hand, the menacing Lugosi paralyzes the original adulterer, so that he may have the beautiful, young woman for himself.

However, in typical Hollywood fashion, true love prevails; the woman's husband finds a way to break her zombie spell; the adulterer destroys Lugosi and his followers, and everything is as it should be...good triumphs over evil and love conquers all. Yeah, right!!! In reality, the use of the Datura plant to control the will of an individual is highly improbable, but it does make for a very interesting premise. As for the religion of Voodoo, only the dregs of Haitian society practice it, while the vast majority of the population is Catholic.

If anyone is interested, my friends and I are going to enjoy a bit of the plant in the near future. We will report back to Mass Movement should all go well...?

Doug Crill

Originally published in Mass Movement #28, November 2010

ALAN DAVIS

I remember when I first discovered Alan Davis. Or rather, I discovered his work. It was around the time when I started to notice writers and artists names, and he was sharing a credit with Alan Moore in a 2000 AD strip called D.R. & Quinch, and following my initial exposure (the first part of *D.R. & Quinch Go Straight*) to the strip, I was hooked. It was unlike anything I'd read before, the characters were crazy and chaotic, but what really struck a chord with me, was the artwork. The way the characters leapt off the page and submerged themselves in the reader's imagination.

More than a quarter of a century later, I'm still a fan, and the chances are, that it you read comics, you are as well, as Alan Davis has pencilled, illustrated and written some of the biggest names in the comics universe. Don't believe me? You sure? Want some names? How about Batman, The Fantastic Four, The Avengers, X-Men, Captain Britain, 2000 AD and that's just the tip of the iceberg. That's right folks, Alan Davis has worked on them all, and in doing so, has become a legend both in the comics industry and to fans, and when the possibility if interviewing him came up, how could I say no? Admittedly, the fan-boy in me was screaming with a mixture of excitement and panic, but with great will, I overcame my fan-boy nerves and knuckled down. So, without further ado, I give you Alan Davis...

Interview by Tim Cundle

MM: A lot of British artists and writers initially gravitate toward 2000 AD, but your first break, or rather more mainstream work, came via Marvel UK. Do you want to tell us about it? How tough, as an artist, was it to break into the comic industry at that time?

Alan: I never had any ambition to work in comics but was lucky enough to be in the right place at the right time. A short time after I contributed a few sketches to Fanzines published by Les Chester and Mike Conroy they told me Paul Neary was planning to relaunch Captain Britain but couldn't afford to pay the industry rates so was looking for new blood.

MM: As we've already mentioned 2000 AD, I wanted to ask you about your time there – what was it like working on and for 2000 AD during what, has arguably become the comics "golden period", when it was on a creative high, pushing all sorts of boundaries?

Alan: Comics were selling pretty well then and the target was to sell comics (not as an ancillary to a franchise) so there were opportunities to experiment and take risks.

MM: As you're one of the co-creators of D.R. & Quinch, there's something I've always wanted to know – where did the initial ideas for the characters come from?

Alan: Alan Moore had based the script on the movie, OC and Stiggs—with a giant bug and lizard as the stars. I wasn't aware of that and assumed it was 'homage' to the movie Animal House so thought it was meant to be big foot cartoon. Steve MacManus didn't want it to be a cartoon because there were already three 'humour' strips in 2000AD so it was a bit of a confused hybrid of influences.

MM: Did you ever think that they (D.R. & Quinch that is), would have anything like the kind of impact on readers that the characters had, and still have? What do you consider to be their (again, D.R. & Quinch) finest moment? Why?

Alan: When I'm working on a comic I'm just trying to do the best I can. I don't think too much about how successful it might be. I always enjoyed drawing D.R. and Quinch and still do.

MM: As one of the famous British contingent who made the move to the US market during the early to mid-eighties, why do you think the US started to look to the UK more during that decade? Why then?

Alan: I think the industry was expanding, lots of new titles with the start of *'direct only'* titles which sold a year ahead, and parallel to, newsstand sales. I was grateful because the exodus created a vacuum I was allowed to fill at 2000AD.

MM: What made you want to work for DC, and how did it feel to be handed Batman, the company's flagship character, as your first job?

Alan: DC paid more and offered a consistent volume of work not available in the UK. My first work was actually an Aquaman miniseries but, after pencilling the first issue I was asked to take over on Batman and the Outsiders for a year while Jim Aparo moved onto the direct only issues.

MM: What do you think you brought to the title at that time that no-one else had up until then?

Alan: Nothing. I was still very new to the business, on a very steep learning curve and doing my best to fit in.

MM: Having worked for both DC and Marvel, was it easier to switch between companies, going back and forth during the eighties and nineties than it is now?

Alan: I think the level of difficulty was, and is, one of individual security and reputation. It's difficult to walk away from a good job to risk and uncertainty. And most editors will try to keep you happy while things are going well—even if it's just for convenience.

MM: Why do you think so many writers and artists seem to stay exclusively with either DC or Marvel these days?

Alan: Because of the incentives from exclusive contracts.

MM: From a creator's point of view, do you think long run's on titles are beneficial or detrimental to a writers or artists career?

Alan: That would depend on how successful the title is and how fast and versatile the creators are. But I think it's academic nowadays because it isn't really possible to have a 'pure' run with regular big event crossovers.

MM: Again, drawing on the fact that you've worked for both DC and Marvel, the rivalry between the two publishing houses blown up and exaggerated for the benefit of readers and fans, or is there a real tension between both companies?

Alan: I'm sure there is serious competition but it's not something I worry about or involve myself in.

MM: Do both operate completely differently, or are they more similar than anyone might suspect...?

Alan: In my experience, now over ten years past, DC was more corporate. Every decision needed a committee. Marvel is usually more straightforward. But ultimately it depends on the editor you are dealing with.

MM: You're part of an increasingly rare breed in comics, that is, you're both a writer and an artist. How difficult was it to make the transition from being an artist to being a writer as well? What made you want to make that move?

Alan: It was relatively easy for me because Terry Kavanagh, then editor on Excalibur, knew I had aspirations to write and he wanted me to pencil the book so asked if I'd take the reins.

MM: Do you view yourself as both a writer and artist, or do you think of yourself as an artist's first and writer second or vice versa? Why?

Alan: I'm a storyteller first and last. I try to subordinate the writing and illustration to the needs of the story— Which isn't always easy if it means scrapping a nice drawing or line of dialogue.

MM: Creatively, what does writing give you that drawing and illustration doesn't, and what does illustration and drawing give you that writing doesn't?

Alan: Drawing, though still fraught with problems, is easier for me. Writing is always a struggle and while I'm confident of my storytelling abilities I'm not a writer.

MM: Which of the titles and books that you've worked on so far, are your personal favourites and why? Conversely, which of the books that you've worked on haven't exactly made your top ten? Why?

Alan: I've always said that Killraven was the most satisfying because the realisation matched the conception. Having said that, *The Nail(s)* and *FF: The End* were great fanboy outings and creating the ClanDestine was very fulfilling.

MM: Having been a part of the comics industry for the last three decades, how do you think it's changed? In your opinion, have those changes been beneficial or detrimental to the industry as a whole? Why?

Alan: The industry is struggling to survive in a world that is losing interest in reading (books or comics) and also appears an obsolete medium alongside technological developments.

MM: I wanted to go back a bit if that's okay, and ask you about Captain Britain – how does

it feel when readers refer to your work with Alan Moore on the character as being the definitive era of Captain Britain? Why do you think that particular era of the character is so popular?

Alan: I think that depends on who you're talking with. Alan Moore's current high profile is useful to promote anything he has worked on but, my experience from meeting fans at conventions, is that preference depends on age. I still hear from people who favoured the original Chris Claremont/ Herb Trimpe CB, slightly younger readers only know him as a member of Excalibur while others only know the more recent incarnations.

MM: Have you read Paul Cornell's recent run on the title? What do you think?

Alan: I'm afraid I haven't seen it. I haven't read many comics for some years now.

MM: And, finally (I know, these multi-part questions are a killer, sorry...), why do you think Captain Britain has never had the same kind of impact on the mainstream market as Captain America has had and continues to have?

Alan: I have no idea.

MM: Is there a book or character that you'd love to be both artist and writer on that you; haven't had the chance to yet, and if so, who or what is it and why?

Alan: I've been lucky enough to draw all of my favourite characters at both Marvel and DC. Of course there are many I'd like to revisit but it would depend on if I could devise a worthwhile story.

MM: What's next for you Alan? What are you working on at the moment that you can tell us about?

Alan: I recently finished a one off *Young Avengers: Children's Crusade*. I'm currently working on a Wolverine annual which is the third in a trilogy. The other two, already completed are, Fantastic Four and Daredevil.

Originally published in Mass Movement #29, February 2011

BRENDON BURNS

Australian comedian Brendon Burns has a reputation for being loud, obnoxious and outrageously funny. Garnering rave reviews for his trilogy of Edinburgh shows, spread across three years at the festival and outlining his breakdown after a relationship break-up, Brendon went on to win the If.comedy award in 2007 for his *So I Suppose This is Offensive Now*. A prolific performer, Brendon has recently hosted a TV show, released his debut book and released a CD of his *Thinking Man's Idiot* tour, I caught up with Brendon before the Bristol leg of his *Y'Know, Love 'n God 'n Metaphysics 'n Shit* tour.

Interview by Leigh McAndrew

MM: Stewart Lee recently wrote an article saying that comedians should be thanking Michael McIntyre because he's encouraged people to go out and see live comedy. Do you agree with that?

Brendon: Oh yeah. It's very comparable to the wrestling industry. Remember when The Rock was around? Everyone knew who The Rock was, so every wrestler was making tons of money because there were more people tuning in to that genre than previously. They had ten million viewers because they had a major star at the time. Nobody had a bad word to say about the guy because they were all making money hand over fist. He brought interest into the industry. They haven't had a star like that since. Not only that, McIntyre is the closest that Britain has ever had to Jonny Carson, in terms of making stars. He's got a Midas touch to him and for what it is it seems to work quite well.

There are now sixty-eight shows on tour, more than there's ever been. I've been doing this for twenty years now and ever since 1990 when I started there's always people saying 'the boom is over, the boom has subsided', but then it keeps getting bigger and bigger. Not only that, I actually think he's funny. And pretty much every foreign guy thinks he's funny as well, because he's a posh bloke tearing himself to shreds. I've discussed it in this show – classism is everything in Britain. That's why he appeals to the working classes and why he's got such broad appeal. It's like Frasier – upper class bumbling idiots. He's just this posh, middle class English bloke and what he says really tickles me and yet every middle class white English guy I know can't fucking stand him.

MM: It seems that a lot of people dislike McIntyre because they perceive the people that do like him to be less intelligent than them.

Brendon: Yeah. Nothing bores me more than hearing a fucking open spot talk about how shit Michael McIntyre is. You know what? Try going on after him in somewhere like Cardiff before he was famous and then tell me he was fucking shit. He didn't get famous from bombing. He tore the roof off from start to finish. He went out there to make them laugh as often as possible.

MM: Since his TV show has been on, more TV networks are open to broadcasting stand-up comedy. You recently hosted an ITV4 show, *FHM's Stand Up Hero* which showcased new and upcoming comedians.

Brendon: I'm in the middle of pitching a show now, as sort of an antithesis to Michael McIntyre's *Roadshow*, but not sneering at it. Whenever this happens people say, "What happened to alternative comedy?" and I'm like, "It's alive and well. It's bigger than ever, it's thriving". It's a very English attitude. The moment that Britain has anything good, they always fuck it up. Peoplewho don't know what they're talking about... You see a lot of people shooting themselves in the foot, people who are on the outskirts of the industry, who make their living off the back of it and who complain and I just think, "Shut the fuck up. Without it there is no you".

It's self-sabotaging, it doesn't make sense. But yeah, having done the stand-up show they seem happy with it and seem interested in me hosting something else. So I'm currently working on a pitch, because they've tried to do *Saturday Live* again so many times, but they've always got the wrong people. So I'm going to try and assemble a comedy dream team of people that wouldn't ordinarily be on telly and also people that are so respected and well-connected in the industry that we could probably get a pretty major headline guest each week, so we'll see.

MM: You've also brought out a book this year (*Fear of Hat Loss in Las Vegas*). Is that another avenue for you to go down?

Brendon: I've got a lot of irons in a lot of fires, but none really very big profile. I'm still comedy's secret handshake (laughs). You really have to know your stuff to even find out who I am, because I've been such a techno-tard for so many years. I've finally got off my arse and got a website. There are guys who are brilliant at the Internet side of it and were really tapped in from the get-go.

MM: I know that Richard Herring is great at building an online fanbase...

Brendon: Ross Noble, too. When he was eighteen or nineteen after his first Edinburgh his website was immense. He just toured and toured and toured and built a bigger audience and did it all himself. I probably should have taken note of that, but I've always been more about the writing process than the marketing process, which I probably should. I'm not getting any younger; I should get better at that. I churn out about three hours a year, I try and get at least two albums or there's another DVD coming out. Now there're a few production companies interested. Also, it takes about five years of sobriety for the industry to go, "Right, he's not going to fuck up any time soon". It takes the right people introducing you places and saying, "He's all right, he's back, he's stable".

MM: With the DVD which you mentioned, is it this tour or the *Thinking Man's Idiot* tour?

Brendon: The DVD is this show. Talking about maybe collaborating with Phil Nichol to set it to music, but that depends on his availability, but I'm also working again with the two guys who directed *So I Suppose This is Offensive Now*, the live show. When we got picked up by Universal they brought in their own producers and directors. There was a lot wrong with that DVD. One of the key things was that when we had the reveal of Sajeela and Steve coming out to do the dance number, the whole audience was aghast. You can hear them, but you can't see jaws dropping at that whole process. At the beginning we say that "I like the jokes with the hang time, when the people realise that the butt of the joke was actually their dilemma". Seeing that lit up in hi-def in everyone's eyes and IT'S NOT THERE!

MM: Were both your *Sober Not Clean* and *So I Suppose…* DVDs recorded on the same night?

Brendon: Yeah. It was supposed to be a double DVD and then, I dunno, something went on. They thought, "Let's try and churn it out and sell two". The only way you're gonna shift my stuff is to give people value for money. I think if things pick up in the next year and my profile gets bigger, then there will probably be a two disc set on Universal. I would have liked to have done more extras for it. Hopefully we'll get to do loads for this.

MM: *The Thinking Man's Idiot* had the theme of class and race issues running through its core. What would you say was the overriding theme of this show?

Brendon: I think with all of them the overriding theme is being human. Whilst I think that the British comedy circuit is the biggest and the brightest and the best in the world, I also think that there is a bit of party line. There's party line edgy, as well. There're certain places that people won't go, but they'll happily say "The Bible ain't real". I'm like, "Uhhh, I don't need you to clear that up for me". Nothing bores me more than seeing someone being smug about that. Not only that, but it's not even fucking relevant in England. Does religion really mess with any of our lives in England?

That's why I dig guys like Jim Jefferies. I mean, Ed Byrne went there only because they went after him. Stewart Lee went there because they went after him. Glenn Wool and Jim Jefferies go and do it in the States, where it's relevant and it's everywhere. Here, I don't think I've heard a politician mention God ever. I dig the fact that their career would be over if they did. The reason that it's set to five verses was a) because I wanted it to be kind of lyrical and b) so that everyone forgot what was at the beginning but hammer it home in the fourth and fifth verse to show that everything was there for a reason. I always try to structure things so that everything is there for a reason. My favourite shows get written when I just have to write them. When I see a lack of balance in my society or in my industry I think, "Hang on, there's some bullshit going on here".

There's a saying – 'whenever there's a status quo in comedy – break it'. I tried to make a logical case for belief, but then realised slowly but surely that you can't. It's emotional. The more I tried to be understood the less funny I was being. I got very frightened of being misunderstood and misrepresented. The fact of the matter is, if you just cut to the funny and let go of people's perceptions and interpretations then that's down to them. I'm pretty happy with where I've ended up with it. I like performing it, I feel good doing it. It's taken about five years to write, a lot of the stuff has been on the backburner for a long, long time. Between that and the book, they both took about five years. There's been a lot of quiet whispers on the circuit, of other comics coming up and saying, "I'm sick of all this bullshit too".

MM: You mentioned being misunderstood – do you ever worry about parts of your shows being taken out of context?

Brendon: It's going to happen. If that happens and I can then turn around and go after, it's all just fodder. The thing that's really grown now is talking about a paedophile fucking a kid is worse than the Daily Mail saying that a paedophile fucked a kid. Originally I just did that joke and then my fiancée said to me, "Yeah, the Daily Mail is full of shit, that's not what people are taking umbrage with, it's not clear enough". So then I added the internal argument of "Does that mean you like the Daily Mail?" on stage. Back and forth, back and forth, because it happens, you can see it in the audience, because there's such a party line with comedy here, such a party line. I see a lot of guys get away with saying shit and pretending that the Daily Mail said it. It's like, "You wanted to say that, man".

There's a real element in this country that thinks it's liberal, but it's really fucking bigoted. I reiterate, I've become a British patriot again about British comedy, but when that whole Brian Logan thing came out, guys that I thought I knew and we were considered equals, were saying, "Yeah, you and Jim I can understand him going after, but Richard Herring and Jimmy Carr?" and I was like, "Really? The English guys understand what they're doing better than I do? The guys that haven't been going as long as I have understand detached irony better than me, do they?" Detached irony, by the way, is one of the simplest of comic vehicles. It's a shortcut, it's not complex. To keep on harping on about this great British sense of irony, that's one of the dumbest jokes you can make. It's not highbrow, it's really lowbrow and a guy that has adhered to that idea of classism and everyone hails him as such a great wit is Clive James. He's just adopted Radio 4 rhythms. He's not really actually saying anything.

Some of the guys need the extremist opinion for theirs to hold water. So when the whole Brian Logan 'offensiveness in comedy' came along, pretty much across the board people said, "I can understand you and Jim, but not Richard and Jimmy". It's like, "Wow, so I don't have the right accent? Okay, I thought we were equals. I thought I was smart, but apparently not.". (laughs) It sounds like a lot of sour grapes.

That was the issue that was burning inside of me. Then the art came from that, I had a real chip on my shoulder about it and I was fucking mad, I was very, very angry. So you start off angry, trying really hard to be understood and then slowly but surely you start to come around and realise that you can get more done with a tickle than a slap. No one is beyond parody on this matter. You can talk about butt raping Jesus with a pig until the cows come home, but I then went after a couple of atheist comics making fun of them and everyone was like, "Woah, here comes the rivalry" and I was like, "What?". I even sent Stewart Lee an e-mail saying, "Are you aware that you're a sacred cow now?"

I even told Robin Ince, who I think is hilarious, that I made a joke about him. It was, "I wear a cross, not because I'm a Christian, but because my house has an infestation of Robin Inces. They run around, being mad at you because you haven't read the same fucking book as they had read that day. The only way to get rid of them is to wear a cross, put up some shelves and satisfy a woman". Good joke, I like it, and I told him it and he said, "You had to drop it because I'm not famous enough, didn't you? You had to say Stewart Lee instead".

I think another difference between here and the States is that people get bogged down with whether they agree with what the comic has to say. In the States it's "He's funny" or 'She's funny". Here it's, "I'm not sure if he's clever enough." Who gives a fuck? It's a comic. It's the classism thing again.

MM: You performed this show at Edinburgh and have toured it since. How has the tour been?

Brendon: Up and down. I've been going to some new towns that I've never been to before, I'm with a new promoter now, so I think sometimes without the regular TV presence it's tough. But then you go to towns that have comics visiting regularly and it's pretty packed houses. I definitely will be pleased to get down to Australia and get some sun. Touring through the British winter is fucking hard. It's pretty brutal.

MM: Have you ever toured Australia?

Brendon: No, I've played Sydney and Perth and done the Melbourne Festival twice.

MM: I suppose as it's such a vast country that it would be a tough place to tour.

Brendon: I would love to do it one time though, I would love to get a big comedy bus and drive around Oz. Everyone wants to drive across America, but it's not as challenging or dangerous as driving across Oz I think.

MM: Jim Jefferies is successful out in America. Do you think he could open doors for you to go out there to perform?

Brendon: Oh yeah, he's offered for me to open for him. He's been doing this for ten years, so when he came here everyone asked him if he'd heard of Brendon Burns. We grew up in the same place and are of similar mind-sets. He even said, "You can perform to my audience, do you want to open for us?" and I was like, "Yeah, in a heartbeat". But, there's an element to his audience of, "Say cunt!" and I would much rather play to fewer people. I'm getting too old, I don't really have the time or patience to slow down for a moron. The funny thing is, I think Jim's stuff is really smart and he's hysterical, but by his own admission, there's an element of cunt. There's some cunts in his crowd.

MM: The last few years have seen you being prolific in your output. What does the future hold for you?

Brendon: Hopefully I'll get the TV show off the ground. I go back to the States to perform this show for the buyers in America for a possible TV broadcast and then we come back and tape it here.

Originally published in Mass Movement #29, February 2011

FUNERAL FOR A FRIEND

In the last twelve months Funeral for a Friend have recorded a new album, released an EP and said goodbye to guitarist Darran Smith. Bassist Gavin Burrough moved onto guitar duties and the band brought in Rich Boucher to play bass. With the album recorded and hugely positive reaction from fans upon release of videos for *Front Row Seats to the End of the World* and *Sixteen* it looks as if the future of the band is brighter than ever. I spoke to vocalist Matthew Davies-Kreye about this new chapter in the band's existence.

Interview by Leigh McAndrew

MM: Did you feel more pressure going into record the new record (Welcome Home, Armageddon) with the new line-up?

Matt: Umm...no. If anything it was a kind of chilled out, relaxed thing. It was making a record for the sake of making a record. There were no pre-conceived ideas or any desires to do something pre-planned. We wrote the songs and, obviously, made sure we liked the songs before we went in to record them (laughs). That was it. First and foremost we wanted to write songs that were really...I guess that made us feel what it was like to be in the band back when we first started. It was fortunate having Gav and Rich in the band that they really fed into that and what we created really allowed us to settle and to enjoy the process more.

MM: The new album has some heavier songs and a more aggressive feel to it that your previous couple of albums. Was that a conscious decision or more of a natural thing, with having the new line-up?

Matt: A mixture of both of those elements, probably. Some of the guys in the band really wanted to push that aspect of what we do further, which is fair enough. I'm not a particularly huge fan of overly heavy stuff. There's got to be something there that really draws me to it, some kind of catchiness to it, whether it's the riffs or the melodies and I think we wanted to finally do a record that was heavy. Everyone says that *Casually Dressed* was the heaviest album we ever wrote. I think people have mothballs in their fucking head when they say that (laughs). That's nowhere near being a heavy album. People will probably listen to this and still think it's not as heavy as *Casually Dressed* (laughs). Daft. But it was just about the fun of it. We've always loved bands like Vision of Disorder, Glassjaw and their heavier elements. A lot of the more heavy hardcore bands like Indecision and Most Precious Blood. We're big fans of In Flames and At the Gates as well, so we had a big mix of sounds. We really wanted to make sure that everything was presented in the songs, whether it was heavy, whether it was more hardcore, whether it was more pop punk or whatever you want to call it. It's all of our influences and what we like as members of the band. That's what we were aiming for.

MM: Are there any big lyrical changes to what you've done on this album compared to previous records?

Matt: Not great leaps. The biggest change I ever made writing-wise was when we did *Tales Don't Tell Themselves*, which was deliberately an attempt to do something completely different. Even from my point of view, being a concept album, it's about something that people have to look at as the definitive way that the album is supposed to be. The lyrics on the album are very open to interpretation as I write a lot of things in metaphors.

There's obviously a reason and an idea behind the song, but what I write about people can look at and interpret in different ways. People may think that *Welcome Home, Armageddon* is a concept album. It's not, it's about themes that I have progressed with from *Hours*, from *Memory and Humanity* and onto this through just being more aware of things as a person, growing up as a person, informing myself both politically and socially.

When you start writing your first bunch of material in your teens you write about teenage things. You write about relationships, you write about situations, "Woe is me, fucking hell my life is crap, I can't work it out of here blah blah blah". When suddenly you do this for a living and you get to meet other people, see other cultures, experience different things and absorb all these things, it comes out in whatever art you create. Lyrically or musically it flows out. So it's not a concept album, it's not a wholly positive album, it's very much a pissed off album lyrically, with a message there. I think it's very hard to deliberately interpret something else. I think the bare essence of it is that there is a little hope there so I think people can latch onto it and get the idea of it, but make it their own and apply it to them personally, which is something I've always tried to do.

MM: You released *The Young and Defenceless* EP having taken pre-orders from fans through Pledge Music. Do you think with the state of the music industry that websites such as Pledge are the way forward for bands to be able to record and release music?

Matt: I don't know that the Pledge format is necessarily the only options that are going to be viable, but I think what it does is that it shows the audience that they can get music directly from bands and all these things the band can offer. It cuts out the whole bullshit of the middle man and the need for the big corporate rock monopoly. I think that with the Internet and social networking sites such as MySpace and Facebook, it allows people to be more in contact with the band. It makes the bands more reachable, really, which, for better or for worse, is definitely the way things are going. I think that things like Pledge are a unique way of offering things and giving the fans something.

As a music fan you are investing in your favourite band and into music that you want to hear. That's a good thing. It's no different, really, to what a record label does. Giving the band money to record a record and when that record goes on sale it goes back into the people that pay for that record. It's quite similar, it's a cyclical thing. For some reason people see it as the band getting lots of money from a record label and the money they pay goes somewhere else. It's almost like paying off a loan. If you do it directly with the fans then they are investing in your music and getting something unique in return. More and more bands are realising that you can do that and bands are able to do it outside of the mainstream, corporate way of doing things and I think it's definitely a positive way, because you're able to take more artistic risks in that format. Major labels are really limiting themselves to what they are signing, because of financial restraints or what's popular. The way that the industry is going, they are signing less and less bands and more and more throwaway artists that they can make a quick buck on. Actual bands are having to do things on their own terms which gives more power to them and allows them to gain the rewards and benefits of creating their own art.

MM: You mentioned earlier about meeting new people and seeing new cultures. You went to Brazil at the end of last year – how did that tour go?

Matt: Brazil was awesome. We've been trying to go there for a good while but we never managed to get it to work, but when we got there it was just chaos.

It was beautiful, beautiful chaos. We played in little clubs, but it was nice to play in intimate venues in a country that we've never been to before. It allowed the fans who came to the shows to really connect with us and us to them and it was a lot of fun. It was hot. Being over there in December and seeing all the Christmas decorations in 35°celsius heat was weird. It was nice to finally actually get to go over there and meet some kids we'd been communicating with on the Internet. Playing songs and having a load of Brazilian kids singing your words back to you. It was one of the most passionate audiences I've played to in a while.

MM: You used live shots from the Brazil tour for the video for *Front Row Seats to the End of the World*. What have you made of the reception to the song and video?

Matt: I think it's been really positive. That video in particular really resonates with our audience because it's us in a situation where there're no frills. It's a live video and I see us in that video and think 'that's how we are'. We've very rarely done a video like that before and it allows everybody an insight into and experience what happens, to a degree, within Funeral for a Friend in those circumstances. I think it's probably one of the best videos we've done. It captures the spirit of the band and the essence and the working class element which the band is about. The video puts us in a place where it's real. This is what the band is about. There's no bullshit.

MM: You've also got a live DVD coming out soon. What are the details on that?

Matt: It's the *Casually Dressed and Deep in Conversation* show we did in Shepherd's Bush last summer as a farewell to Darran. We had a film crew there and it was rad because we wanted to capture that moment, not just for ourselves but for those who were there and those who couldn't make it. It's Darran's last Funeral show and he was a big part of the band for so many years. There's no weirdness between us or anything like that. We're all on good terms. It's kind of like a tribute, really. I haven't seen it yet, so I'm excited.

MM: What do the next few months hold for Funeral for a Friend?

Matt: It's all pretty much kicking off. The album is out in March, we're going to South Africa for the first time, playing a festival called Ram Fest. We're playing three shows there. Then it's a UK tour, we're going back to mainland Europe in April, playing a bunch of festivals in the summer. Then we'll be heading to the States, back to Australia and Japan and hopefully other countries that we've not been to. A smaller UK tour before Christmas too, probably. So that's our year in a nutshell.

Originally published in Mass Movement #29, February 2011

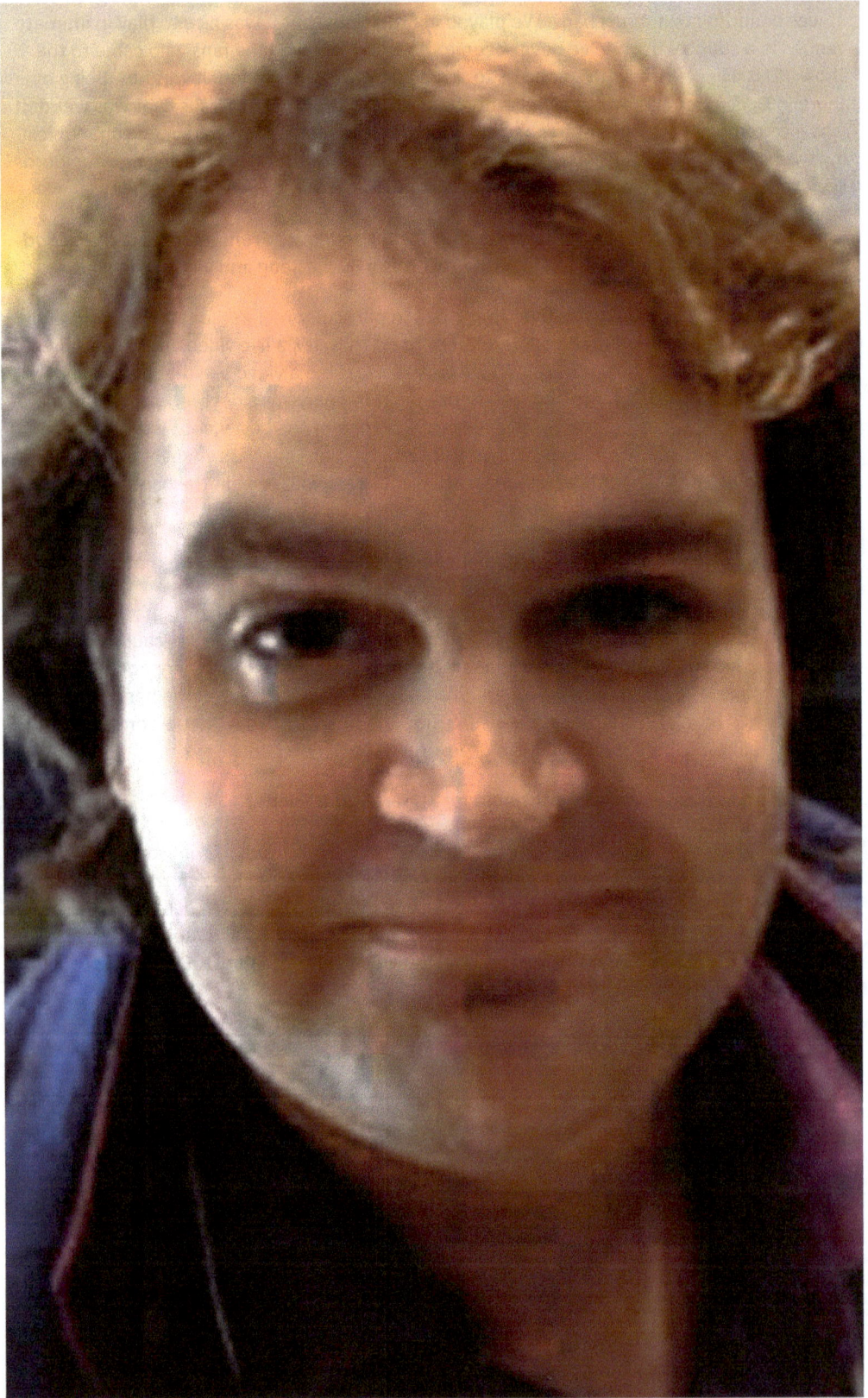

NEV FOUNTAIN

Whether you know it or not, the chances are, that in some way, shape or form, you'll have stumbled across Nev Fountain. Not literally of course, that would be silly, falling over him. Unless both of you were drunk, and Nev had already fallen over and then you proceeded to trip and stumble over him while he was lying on the floor, a direct result of his having fallen over before you. Which could happen I suppose, but it's not very likely. No, by stumbled I mean, you'll be aware of, or will have encountered the man via his writing. Whether it was through *Have I Got News For You, 2DTV, Dead Ringers* or 'Doctor Who' (*Omega, The Kingmaker* and *Peri And The Piscon Paradox*), there's a more than fair chance that Nev Fountain has had some sort of impact on your life. Having recently finished the incredibly funny and thoroughly enjoyable Mervyn Stone Mysteries, I thought it was about time that Mass Movement caught up with Nev to talk about the trilogy and explore the world of Mervyn Stone a little further...

Interview by Tim Cundle

MM: All good stories need a beginning, so would you like to introduce yourself, and tell us a little bit about Nev Fountain...? What do you think is the strangest facet of your personality, and how does this "strangeness" affect your daily life?

Nev: I'm Nev Fountain, formerly Steven John Fountain. I was born in Stamford, in Lincolnshire. I've been a professional writer for radio and television and magazines for a while now, mainly satirical things like *Dead Ringers, Have I Got News For You, The News Quiz, Private Eye*, stuff like that.
I am a 'comic' writer, but I've also been a teacher, a bin man, a toilet attendant and the Man Who Scooped Dead Animals Off A Conveyor Belt Full Of Broccoli Before It Got Frozen And Put In Bags. You need a steady hand and a keen eye for that one. Unfortunately, I have neither. If you're the person who found a mangled mouse in their veg in 1990 – I'm sorry. I'm so, so sorry.

I'm the grandson of a gamekeeper, the son of a lumberjack, the brother of an ex-professional pool player, the boyfriend of a Doctor Who companion, and the father of two wonderful boys who are both funnier and better at making up stories than I.

I used to be quite eccentric, dress up in waistcoats and colourful clothes and the like – but I don't that anymore. I realised there were two types of people who do that; those who do it to compensate for their lack of personality, and those who have genuine mental problems who want to assure the public their madness is cuddly. I used to think I was the former, but now I'm not so sure.

The strangest thing about me is my brain. It works like the film *Inception* – on three different levels playing at three different speeds all at the same time. This is great for plotting stories, but not much use for driving, cooking, eating, listening to what people say... and, well pretty much everything else you need your brain for to function in society. I act a lot like David Bowie in *The Man Who Fell to Earth*. Not the gratuitous sex and the lack of a penis – I never worked out how that worked – but the multi-skilling stuff, like watching eight tellies at once. I have to watch TV programmes while I'm writing, because only by concentrating on one thing I'm able to concentrate on the other. Is that freaky enough for you?

MM: Let's talk Mervyn Stone. Share your creation with us, tell us about him – where did the idea for the character, and the novels, come from? As Mervyn seems to have popped into existence fully formed with an incredible back story (that we discover more of as the novels progress) how much (if anything) of the character is based on "fact", that is, how much of Mervyn is based on yourself, people you know and your own experiences?

Nev: 'Write about what you know' – that's what they say, isn't it? That's what I decided to do about six years ago. I was worn out writing sketches and jokes for shows, and wanted to write something that I felt enthusiastic about, something just for me. I took a cold hard look at myself and asked myself what was really 'me'. I looked at my shelves and realised what I loved above all else – more than sci-fi, horror, comedy – was a good, well-told murder-mystery.

I'd always enjoyed Simon Brett's Charles Paris books, humorous detective novels with an actor-cum-sleuth as the star. Each book took him to a different arena of his career, and inevitably a murder or two – there'd be murders on the set of a sitcom, at a Fringe show, during the making of a corporate video, etc, and I liked that idea. I thought it would be great to take something of that concept and make it even more incestuous, keep it to one world, and have the same characters turning up from book to book, sometimes as suspects, sometimes as victims, sometimes as murderers.

In my capacity as script editor of *Death Comes To Time* – one of Doctor Who's many false dawns before the TV show returned – I'd been to a lot of conventions. I had shared hot-tubs with Frazer Hines, shared a drink with Terrance Dicks, went shopping for women's things with Katy Manning and danced badly with Michael Sheard. The more you attend those things, you more you realise what an hermetically sealed world it is – it is a fascinating existence, where entire lives are shaped by one old show, travelling gypsy-like across the country from convention to convention, signings, documentaries and whatnot, and your life is spent reliving the past with others who you've worked with for about five minutes twenty years ago, and would have otherwise been barely on nodding terms were it not for this artificially created 'family' of fandom. It's a world where no secrets stay buried, and rivalries are allowed to mature and fester – and when you're writing a murder-mystery, who could ask for anything more?

Mervyn Stone is not me, sorry to disappoint! Unlike Mervyn, I love going to conventions, and I love talking about old TV shows. There are hints of other script editors I've met and chatted to in Mervyn, but mainly he's based on an old friend of mine, who has a fatalistic, world-weary outlook on life. And yes, he does know Mervyn is partially based on him. I suppose the fact I used him shamelessly in my work is another sign for him that life stinks...

So Mervyn isn't me, but on the other hand we are both writers – so I really empathise with that desperate scrabbling for money, work and status, the fear of being shaken out of the tiny media club that pays your wages and not being let back in. I understand Mervyn's habit of clawing away at the fringe benefits of being Mr *Vixens from the Void*, whether it be hotel rooms, free coffee, or the warm beds of impressionable young fans. He knows this is as good as it's going to get, and if that's all he's going to get, he might as well partake of it. I think that's why some famous writers are such notorious shaggers – what other perks do writers get, other than the attentions of moist, adoring young graduates fresh from studying you as part of their English degree?

I also understand Mervyn's frustration with legacy; his dormant novel in his laptop that's going to solve all of his problems. Every writer has aspirations of leaving a body of work they can be proud of, so to end up as a TV writer is a cruel irony. It's such an ephemeral world and when it does preserve something it's all the stuff you'd rather forget about. Imagine William Shakespeare if he were working now – he'll have written thirty-odd plays, all incredibly well-received, but in interviews all they'll want to know is if Steven Moffat's asked him to write for Doctor Who.

It's been a bare four years since *Dead Ringers* finished, and I'm bored of talking about it, even though it was a happy and artistically rewarding time for me. God knows what it might be like for Mervyn. I can only imagine and shudder.

MM: *Vixens From The Void (*the show that Mervyn was the script editor for), again, I have **to know, where did the idea for that show come from? Mervyn pitched it as** *Dallas* **or** *Dy- nasty* **in space, but it seems to be more,** *Blake's 7* **meets** *Howard's Way* **featuring lots of women in Lycra….Could** *Vixens* **have been the product of any other decade apart from the nineteen eighties, or is it a product of its time? Why?**

Nev: *Vixens from the Void* came out a little bit at a time, truth to tell. I thought about this funny little show a great deal. I knew I had to get it right because I was going to be stuck with it for the whole range of books.

To give you some idea about how much I thought about it… Well, it was originally called *Space Vixens* and I eventually decided that that was too obvious a name; I thought that was exactly the kind of title a sci-fi fan might give to a fake space series. I wanted something much clumsier because, truth to tell, the really popular sci-fi shows all have really embarrass- ing clunky names that no sci-fi fan would dream of coming up with! Just say a few cold to yourself and you'll see what I mean. Hello Doctor Who! Hello Star Trek! Hello Buck Rogers in the 25th Century and Battlestar Galactica! So I thought *Vixens from the Void* seemed nicely crap.

It took a while before I settled on the 'Dynasty in Space' angle. It went through several incar- nations – it was the *Tomorrow Corridors* for a long while – the premise being a war between alternative Earths from different dimensions; 'Dinosaurs didn't get wiped out' Earth versus 'Nazis won the Second World War' Earth, that kind of thing, with the *Vixens* being some kind of multi-dimensional police force.'

The trick in the end was to fit the series around the range of books, and the main reason I settled on 'Dynasty in Space', a huge empire-spanning soap-epic stuffed with a cast of dozens, was that I could throw in more characters once I'd bumped off the first lot! If it was something like Blake's 7, you wouldn't have many more books to write once you'd killed three actors, because that would be half the crew gone, not counting Orac.

But you are right – there is Blake's 7 in there, as well as The Tomorrow People, Star Maidens, Doctor Who, Star Trek and Battlestar Galactica (both original and new spicy flavours), Buck Rogers, Babylon 5… But if there are elements of post-Eighties shows, I do try not to make it too sophisticated or too 'slick'. Whenever anyone says that *Vixens from the Void* was ahead of its time, it should really prompt a hollow laugh from the reader…!

Vixens is a quintessentially Eighties idea for a show. The premise of an intergalactic empire run by a woman hinges on the novelty that it still WAS a novelty, even with Mrs Thatcher in number ten. At that time TV was still deeply sexist, because it was reflecting the vast bits of the country that hadn't been troubled by women's liberation in the Sixties and Seventies. Lesbians were still freakish creatures not even fit to be seen drinking the coffee in Kath's Café in Eastenders, and Benny Hill was still running around slapping bottoms. The best way that women could be noticed is to wear next-to-nothing in a pop video, or date a member of the royal family.

The Eighties was the time when we were right on that cusp; women's liberation was still a novelty; women could be in charge but they had to be seen to be 'womanly'. That paradigm shift had happened by the next decade, so *Vixens* could not have worked in the Nineties.

There's also that idea of the grab for power or money. Dynasty, Dallas, Big Deal, Falcon Crest, feuding factions in opulent surroundings with no poor people in sight – it's a uniquely Eighties thing.

MM: When we first meet Mervyn in *Geek Tragedy*, he's returning to the convention circuit after an self-enforced absence and is instantly plunged into this world within a world with a different set of rules and values, and I know that you've had personal experience of conventions and fan-gatherings, so again how much of the convention world in which Mervyn finds himself is based on personal experience? How do you feel about conventions? Do you have a personal convention horror story (you can change the names and locations) that you'd like to share, and at the opposite end of the spectrum, what, so far, has been your personal convention highlight, or favourite moment?

Nev: As I said, I enjoy conventions immensely. I enjoy talking to fans, hanging out in the bar, doing panels. My favourite bits of conventions are very personal to me and, thus far, I prefer people to ask me what I'm sniggering at, and for me to shake my head and say, 'You had to be there...'

I can't place my hand on my heart and say there's a single incident that I've transcribed word-for-word into the books. There are many things that have happened to me since which have prompted me to go, 'D'oh! I want to write another book RIGHT NOW and put that bit in!'

So how much of it is fact? Okay, let's throw metaphors at the wall here and see which ones stick. All a writer needs is a grain of truth for his fiction to flourish or, if you like, it takes one drop of food colouring to turn a glass of water completely red. You take an amusing bit of truth, and you stretch it in all directions until it almost snaps.

But to break it down: a lot of the *observations* are true. I don't think there's any point in making up stuff about conventions when there's so much mad stuff out there. The *characters* are inventions, because they have to fit the story. They may start out as recognisable 'types' because again, there would be no point populating a book about a convention with characters you wouldn't find at a convention.

But once you've picked your 'type' of character, that's where the 'reality' of it stops, because that's the point when you start saying to yourself, 'So what would make a good story here? What would happen if that Nev Fountain-type character was an insane gun-toting maniac with a pathological hatred of the colour blue?'

Obviously the character starts moving in a direction that's not Nev Fountain in the slightest, and becomes a tool of the story.

MM: Fandom really isn't all that bad is it, Nev? Really…? Have you witnessed or been party to the extremes of fandom, and if so, if the experience isn't too painful, and isn't too raw, would you like to tell us about it? You're among friends….

Nev: Fandom is a fabulous cross-section of the adorable and the insane, just like life. So many lovely moments… The armed police running through the hotel in LA, frisking 20-stone fans in their nightshirts for concealed weapons… The hilarious and informative slide presentations of Doctor Who expert Eric Hoffman… I think my favourite is my first moment in my first convention. I saw a guy dressed up as William Hartnell walking from room to room in the hotel, clutching his lapels and looking around, muttering to himself asking what planet he was on. I had this burning desire to run up to him and shout, "EARTH! IT'S EARTH! IT'S OBVIOUS TO ME YOU HAVEN'T VISITED THIS PLANET A LOT, BUT YOU SHOULD AT LEAST RECOGNISE EARTH WHEN YOU SEE IT!"

MM: Mervyn seems to take the role of anti-hero, the reluctant centre piece in the unwitting drama that his life has become, but he seems to be surrounded by a multitude of utterly abhorrent characters…Actors, producers, directors. Television isn't really that bad is it, Nev? Is it? Surely not…? If not, then where did the inspiration for the supporting cast come from?

Nev: Television is great, a really fun place to be, but sometimes it can be like a nursery for adults. It's a cosy, pampered place where lovely people are allowed to be really lovely, but unpleasant people are also allowed to have free rein, throwing building blocks, having tantrums and soiling their nappies. The culture shock from certain individuals finding themselves not in that cosy world any more is just as profound as it is for shell shock; for a lot of those bad-behaving types it's like Post Dramatic Stress Disorder – literally. It's the mental problems that ensure when you can't get to be a drama queen anymore, and the effects can last decades…

The inspiration for some of the more horrid characters comes from morphing together what you know with what you imagine and then put in what you've heard from other professionals, writers, directors, actors… Everyone in 'the biz' knows who the monsters and idiots are – and there's not a great deal of exaggeration needed when talking about them. I recently heard tell of an actual producer of an actual television show walk into a studio and complain that the set was far too green… And, of course, it was a green-screen set! Not an urban legend! True story!

MM: Back in Mervyn's world, in *DVD Extras*, the novel centres on a seemingly impossible crime committed while our hero is recording a DVD commentary for the show he used to script edit. Why do you think we have such a keen interest in nostalgia, especially as far as TV, film and literature are concerned? We seem to dedicate huge chunks of our lives to it – TV stations broadcasting shows from yesteryear, DVD releases, fan-clubs, conventions and more. Is it a longing for the less complicated world and things of childhood, or something entirely different?

Nev: There's a lovely quote I put in one of the books from Bill Vaughan: *"Progress is a continuing effort to make things as good as they used to be"*. There's an understandable need for

humans to crawl back into nostalgia, to relive times when things were better than what they are now, or at least how we perceived them to be. I'm sure the first cavemen were grunting round the fire, complaining and talking about how much bigger the mammoths were last year...

Half of life is living moments and the other half is recapturing them. Actually, now I say that, I think it's about 30/70 now, so many people are intent on reliving moments as they actually live them, on camera phones, on Twitter and the like. Memories prove to us we're alive, and nostalgia proves to us we've experienced. Even memories of a crap TV show help proves we've experienced *something*...

MM: Why base *Cursed Among Sequels* in Cornwall? It's a beautiful part of the world, and hardly the quarry heavy setting for Sci-Fi location shots...Now, the Welsh Valleys I could understand. Especially South Wales, but Cornwall...? Come on, spill the beans...
Nev: I know and love Cornwall. I've spent a lot of time down there. But that's not really the reason why I chose it; I chose it because it amused me!

The infrastructure of television production is negligible down there, but I just know that a television company would be prepared go out of their way to move their base of operations to the middle of nowhere, spend shedloads of money that they couldn't afford, just on the basis of some bit of mad logic dreamt up in a boardroom in London or on the other side of the world.

It was just a funny, bonkers idea to me. Like moving Question Time – the show that depends on the availability of politicians from Westminster to make it work – to Glasgow. Sheer bloody madness.

MM: With all three of the Mervyn Stone novels being published by Big Finish, I wondered if there's been any behind closed doors, not too hush-hush discussion about possible audio adaptations of the Mervyn Stone novels? Come on Nev, you can tell us, we can keep a secret.... If, and only if, mind you (wouldn't want to ruin any possible delicate contractual shenanigans), there were to be audio adaptations of the Mervyn Stone Mysteries, who would you like to be cast as Mervyn? Why? Any other ideas for casting? Vanity Mycroft? Ken Roche? Graham Goldingay?

Nev: Well, we have already done some free podcasts with John Banks as Mervyn and Nicola Bryant as Vanity. I think it's only fair they reprise their excellent interpretations if a 'big' audio gets commissioned.

John Banks is an actor friend of mine, and he's the 'face' of Mervyn on the books.
He did a play with Nicola and watching him perform, he struck me as a perfect actor to do Mervyn – he has that quality, both physically and in his voice. He comes across as polite, intelligent and well-spoken, but you can imagine he has great reserves of exasperation ready when things go wrong. You could pose John in a photo with Eric Saward and Terrance Dicks, tell everyone he script edited Doctor Who in the late Eighties, and it would look completely plausible.

There's talk of audios – and those are ongoing. I would imagine that audio versions of the books will be available, but not for a while yet. The great thing about books as opposed to CDs is they can't just get ripped off and passed around the Internet. Making an audio version this year would be a bit of a gift to the pirates!

MM: How did Steve O'Brien and Nick Briggs feel about becoming characters in another of Mervyn's exploits? Was it difficult to persuade them to become involved and lend themselves and their beings to the tale...?

Nev: They were delighted! Both agreed happily. I don't think Nick's even read his bit, he's that confident I wouldn't do anything naughty to him. The poor fool.

MM: Are there going to be any more Mervyn Stone Mysteries? Surely the initial trilogy isn't it for our script editing sleuth?

Nev: I would love to write more, but of course, that is in the gift of Big Finish. Sales will determine whether Meryvn soldiers on, but the signs are very positive. Reviews are great, and Mervyn as a brand is certainly making a mark. So I'm planning ahead. I've got a lot of ideas for book four, or *Ten Little Figures*, as I've already decided to call it.

I have two piles of ideas in my head. The first, huge pile is 'Things that would be quite funny to do for a Mervyn Stone book', and the second, much smaller pile is 'Things that would actually work as a story for a Mervyn Stone book'.

MM: Moving away from the Mervyn Stone Mysteries, you're also a huge Doctor Who fan, aren't you? What is about Who that initially appealed to you, and what has maintained your interest in the show? Would you call yourself a devotee? Do you think of yourself as being part of Who fandom? How, in your opinion, does someone know that they've become part of that exclusive breed, how does someone know that they've entered the uncharted waters of 'Fandom'?

Nev: Doctor Who appealed to me in a way that Star Trek and Buck Rogers didn't, because it was a show that rewrote all the rules. It looked past the heroes in the foreground and gave the keys to the show to the odd-looking boffin with the weird hair standing at the back; the one who was only meant to be there to explain the plot to Doug McClure. I loved Doctor Who because it was the space adventures of a terribly interesting man. A witty, grouchy, eccentric pacifist who never used guns except when he did. I think with Who you come for the madness and stay for the history; the sheer fun of unearthing volume after volume of interesting silly stories sprinkled with love. I feel part of fandom even though I don't watch all the new episodes exhaustively, or read the books, or do stuff, but I like to be sociable to like-minded idiots. I think you might be considered part of fandom if you find yourself arguing about roundels in a hotel foyer, and then end up singing Roger Limb's *Arc of Infinity* incidental music in the bar after everyone else has gone home, and when you do finally go to your room you end up sitting in an Internet chatroom at one in the morning waiting for 'Davros342' to turn up.

MM: You've also recently written a Companion Chronicle *Peri And The Piscon Paradox* for Big Finish – how do you think it compares to your previous Big Finish work? Was it difficult or challenging to feature both the Fifth and Sixth Doctors in a story that revolved around their shared companion?

Nev: I think *Peri and the Piscon Paradox* is my best BF audio to date. I think it has a great premise, it's well structured (and I'm a structure fetishist) and most of all it has heart. I love both *Omega* and *The Kingmaker*, but I think *PatPP* has the perfect fusion of humour and drama – a satisfying script where everything pays off both logically and emotionally.

It comes across as being insanely complicated, but it was actually quite simple to write, like dominoes. I knocked one plot element over, and that helped knock the rest into place. The only struggle was with act two, and how to bring both Doctors and Peris together – I originally had them all being taken to the Piscon ship, but I scrapped that and came up with something much more fun...!

MM: Go on, you know you want to, which of the stories / audio dramas that you've written for Big Finish is your personal favourite? Why?

Nev: See previous question! *Peri and the Piscon Paradox* is my favourite audio, but If I'm being asked 'What is the best story I've written for Big Finish?', I would say Mervyn Stone book three, *Cursed Among Sequels,* which is my utterly favourite thing I have written ever ever ever.

MM: Having written for Television, Radio and Audio Drama, and being a published writer, which is your favourite medium as a writer? Television, radio, audio or literature? Why?

Nev: At the moment I love books, because I love the precision of storytelling, the ability to describe everything. It's like working in oils rather than chalks; slower, but much more satisfying. Having said that, I do love radio/audio. It also provides a great deal of freedom, and it's great fun handing it over to a producer and a cast to see what they can do with it.

MM: What's next for Nev Fountain?

Nev: Definitely something Mervyn Stone-related! And I have ambitions to go back to where I started and write a stage play; perhaps a thriller.

MM: If there's anything that you'd like to add, speak now or forever hold your peace...

Nev: *Buy my books!!!*

The Mervyn Stone mysteries are available to buy from Big Finish Production.

Orignally published in Mass Movement #29, February 2011

RETURN OF THE GEEK

In February last year I did something that I hadn't done for 16 years: played a game of Warhammer. Pushing little men around a table for the first time since 1994, drinking a bottle of wine and chatting to some regular game-playing friends, I was hooked, back in the fold of something I had discarded as just too geeky, even for the geek I am.

I'd spent from 1991 to 1994 playing Games Workshop (GW) games like Warhammer Fantasy Battle (WFB), Warhammer 40,000 (40K) and Epic regularly and religiously, painting the miniatures and reading the background. No doubt, even if you've never played a table-top wargame, you'll be aware of GW stores, their windows filled with miniature toy soldiers, and with a floor full of hygienically-suspect young men playing games. In the 1990s the company expanded hugely, opening stores nationwide, catering for a rapidly-growing customer base made up mainly of teenagers, even in a world of burgeoning video game consoles and general hand-wringing over the demise of kids' social interactions.

Over the years since, the company has had its up and downs, but its expansion has continued and its stores are still filled with small soldiers and small boys. It finds itself in 2011 still the pre-eminent tabletop wargame manufacturer in the world, and anecdotally there are more and more people like myself getting back into something we probably thought we'd shelved for good. This phenomenon got me thinking about why this should be: why is it that people in their 30s and into their 40s (mostly men, yes, but some women too) spend some of their time rolling dice and pretending to cast spells?

GW stalwart Andy Chambers worked for the company, most recently as lead designer, from 1989 to 2003. He is currently the creative director of American computer games company Blizzard Entertainment. What does he think it is that brings adults back? I explain that for me it's a mixture of nostalgia, a social element and raw enjoyment of the game.

"Your experiences seem to be common. I've also noticed a lot of dads coming back to the hobby with their sons. For the younger fans there's so much exploration and discovery involved that they have a very different outlook; older gamers take pleasure in following the development and seeing how things change (and complaining about it), mixed with a sense of continuity."

Now that WFB and 40K – both invented in the 1980s – are old enough for two generations to have been exposed to them, it's that sense of development-versus-continuity that gives adult gamers one element of their interest, but it's not enough to keep us hooked. I ask Andy whether, when he was involved in the development of WFB, GW ensured it catered for a wide age range. "It was a constant debate," he says. "No-one wanted to make real kids' games but at the same time demographics showed that most money was being spent by pre-teens. It was hard to keep more complex games in the stores that might appeal to older gamers when they consistently made less money."

Thank goodness for the hard-headedness of the games designers in holding out against the temptation to dumb down their systems. Coming back to WFB this year, the rules are still challenging and complex (although not as labyrinthine as they were in 1991), providing something for people of all ages to get their teeth into. Indeed, the recent issue of the eighth edition of the game has seen a surge in interest – and it's largely agreed to be the best edition the company has yet released.

Alessio Cavatore, senior games developer at GW from 1996 until 2009, and now co-founder and managing director at River Horse Games, has a slightly different take from Andy. "[The age range] policy has changed through the years. Warhammer has gone from a very 'adult', heavy metal phase to a colourful, almost caricature-like period, and to the present, more balanced approach. In general though, the underlying philosophy is that it should be aimed to older gamers, as the young ones would find that inspiring anyway, feeling grateful for being treated as adults and wanting to grow into 'veterans'."

Alessio thinks that it's the background (gamers call it 'fluff') that brings adults back to the hobby. "It's the thing that keeps it all together, because now one can still interact with that background even though one is not actively playing Warhammer. You could be reading a Black Library novel [GW's own publishing arm], playing a computer game or a board game set in the Warhammer world. And that background will at times trigger again one of the factors you mention, whether it's the nostalgia for the camaraderie of the gamers, the love for the toy soldiers or the passion for the gaming itself... it will be different for each person, but it's the background... that allows this all."

The background is a huge element of GW's success. In WFB they've developed a world based loosely on the Earth, with a mix of medieval atmosphere (the Holy Roman Empire of continental Europe in the middle ages), Celtic mythology, classical Tolkien fantasy, plus Norse and even steampunk aesthetics. Since GW invented the twin universes of WFB and 40K in the 1980s, they've had 25-plus years to develop and hone them, to the extent that many novels based in the worlds have been released, and each rulebook and army book is stuffed with illustrated vignettes, timelines and glossaries adding the fluff. It adds not a jot to the ability to play, but it's what's marked GW out for years. When I got back into playing WFB last year, it was this background that once more elevated from a game of luck and strategy to one that had a sense of narrative, and added a nostalgic pleasure.

But is it possible to say which element is more important? Andy Chambers: "Each is important: without a good setting people never take an interest in the game; without a good game they don't stay interested. Personally I value a good visual style more than game rules – if you don't like the rules, they are easier to change." Alessio Cavatore agrees: "Both are important, but... in a wargame I believe the atmosphere is more important than the rules. On the other hand, if the rules are broken, there's no setting that can make the game playable... so there must be a mix of them all. WFB has a great background, fantastic models, excellent rules, all working together in a very exciting mix."

For many returning gamers, and I include myself in this, the fluff was hard-wired into us as teenagers. So it comes as no surprise that talking to adult gamers now, I've found that it's the gameplay that is the more important element. Stuart Mack recently came back to WFB after 12 years. "When I was younger... the background and imagery were of major importance to my enjoyment of the game," he explains. "Now I spend just as much time, if not more, reading rules and writing lists. I do still enjoy the fluff, but I enjoy the game and the social side far more now that I'm older. With that in mind, I could not play the game without the in-depth background."

Suffice to say, if the background wasn't so strong, so atmospheric and rich, I doubt players would be coming back to the game and the hobby. The fluff explains why certain troops and characters do certain things, and help the player remember why they do those things – to condense it, the number of dice you roll and the scores you need to get are directly consequential from a narrative. For example, imagine there's man defending his village who's fighting a multi-limbed evil gribbly that's trying to eat his brains. He needs to get fours or greater, on three dice, to survive. No matter how little importance a gamer puts into the fluff, were it just 'roll fours on these three dice' it would lack that certain je ne sais quoi. The more you play, the more the fluff becomes subconscious, but it's still there.

I'm also interested in what it is that adults get out of WFB that they may not have done as teenagers. My own teenage gaming wasn't especially intense, being chilled, drawn-out affairs sound tracked by Bon Jovi and Guns N' Roses. I did, however, know some kids for whom tantrums were par for the course. These days, my gaming is occasional, still relaxed, still sound tracked by cheese rock but also accompanied by a large glass of red. I asked Andy and Alessio what they thought. Andy: "Winning every game definitely becomes less important as you get older, and I think players start to value having fun with their opponent more." Alessio, meanwhile, says: "If I try to put myself in a pure gamer's shoes... I can say that I personally have changed from being very competitive to being now a lot more 'fluffy' and friendly... I just cannot take it that seriously any more."

Alex Gisborne, the man who got me into GW in 1991, never gave up gaming, but he has thoughts on what adults get out of it. "The more complex elements of the game systems and the detail available is something that is more appreciated by advanced gamers, partly for the mental aspect but also years of experience of immersing yourself in another world is something I think you appreciate more as you get older. As far as returning veterans go, the hook comes partly from nostalgia but it's a hobby that uses their brain, allowing them to be creative in some way too. Because it is a social thing for me, that is what has kept me hooked. As an adult, meeting friends and the socialising that now accompanies it definitely improved the gaming experience."

Phil Bridge, another of my gaming friends, who also never shelved the hobby, chips in: "We treat the game as a source of entertainment, whereas many people take it very seriously and put a lot of emotion into playing. It is definitely a social event for us, and I personally wouldn't feel particularly motivated to join in with any tournaments, as this defeats the purpose of the game for me."

Each to their own, of course, and the WFB tournament scene is very healthy, as the likes of the BadDice, Heelanhammer and Podhammer podcasts attest. There are some very competitive adult gamers out there, old and young. Alessio says: "I don't think it's a matter of age, I believe it's a matter of personality. I've seen very serious power-playing youngsters and very relaxed old bearded chaps, and the complete opposite!"

Dan Heelan, the man behind Heelanhammer, and one of the top WFB players in the UK, tells me: "Most gamers I know tend to have a break, I did myself for a few years as life alters course or the game/hobby become 'stale'. I think its a vital part of continuing the hobby that you have a break every now and then. I tend to find a lot of the time is the social aspect that draws people back. Regular listeners of the show will know of Warhammer legend Alan Thompson. He got me into the tournament game when I was 16 (just read that... makes him sound like my pimp!), one of the best players of his time, then has a serious gap for a few years and is now right back into. He never really lost the love of the hobby or game, just people around stopped playing and life moved on. People/friends returned to the hobby and now he is back. So to answer your question I think it's a combination of love of the hobby/whatever drew you to it in the first place and more importantly the social aspect."

So, the fluff is fun, the gameplay is complex enough to be interesting (Alex says: "Having tried other tabletop games, the GW ones tend to be easy to get into and play, but also can be as complicated as you are willing to make them. The variety of races in WFB requires thought rather than just being able to slug it out toe to toe; that definitely appealed more as I advanced in years.") and there's a massive sense of reliving lost youth that appeals. But there are two elephants in the room. Firstly, I'm aware that I've been very positive about GW and WFB so far, but it's expensive. Very expensive. Representing armies on the tabletop can cost hundreds of pounds. Some adult gamers almost have a house deposit or a car sitting in various cupboards. Secondly, there's the reason we gave it up in the first place. Nerdishness.

I knew that my interest in girls, going out, drinking and 'cool' was directly opposite to my interest in WFB. Once I got to university, there was no way I was going to seek out gamers; those 'out' gamers were more often than not people I'd choose to avoid. Shallow, yes, but most of us are at that age. Phil says: "By 13 or 14 it is no longer 'cool' and those who have an innate love of all things sci-fi or fantasy tend to hide it from others, as what other people think (especially girls!) tends to be important at that age." Stuart agrees; "I played... until I was eighteen and arrived at university, at that point I decided that the social stigma that follows a wargamer was best left in my youth."

But now, with a house, a girlfriend, two dogs and a car, behaving in a horribly middle-aged fashion, I have no pressure to be cool, no reason to present a façade of style and élan to potential girlfriends. My friends and I play WFB but can all hold a conversation and maintain eye contact. While 'Dungeons and Dragons' and 'roleplaying' – synonymous with wargaming to the average punter – are still shorthand for a nerdishness that's deeply unappealing to wider society, I suspect more people than you'd expect have an interest in it that stems from their childhood.

Phil goes on, with a thought about GW players' wider characteristics: "I think that virtually everybody who plays does so because they are of a certain 'ilk'... if you were to survey 1000 WFB players about their likes and dislikes, you would find a strong trend: it is likely that most of them like Star Wars, and aren't that bothered by sport. By its very nature it is more of an 'academic' based interest. As such, those who get back into it at a later age will commonly have shared these traits throughout their lives."

A generalisation of course but an apposite one. Getting back into the game over the past year has exposed me once more to the benign, intelligent geekiness of its core player base. Is that such a bad thing? Of course not. Adults all need some escapist, inconsequential hobby that can have invested in it a degree of enthusiasm that's up to the individual. Whether it's gardening, doing up cars, hardcore punk or Warhammer, it's good for sanity. That's my excuse and I'm sticking to it. Pass the dice. Right, I need three fours...

James McLaren

All pictures taken in Firestorm Games, Cardiff.

Originally published in Mass Movement #29, February 2011

BLAG DAHLIA
(DWARVES)

The Dwarves Are Still The Best Band Ever my not only be the first track off the new Dwarves album, *The Dwarves Are Born Again*, it quite possibly be true.

Actually, I'd say *The Dwarves Are The Best Band Still Around*. That's more like it. We have to remember The Ramones, Black Flag, Dead Kennedys, etc. But since they are all dead, some of them actually six feet under, The Dwarves win. They play loud, fast, and snotty. And some how, also very very melodic. I guess we can blame that on Blag's (the singer) brain. The guy thinks in ways that are always creative, always "outside the box" (which he has not problems getting into, wink wink, nudge nudge) and always funny. And I mean FUNNY.

Like the song *Working Class Asshole* on *The Dwarves Are Born Again*. If you just listened to the music, you'd think it was your better than average Oi band. You know, with all the silly tough guy shouts in the background, and lyrics about blue collar working and stuff. But when you listen, you hear it's actually about how those baldheaded walking penises are just suckers, following a system that actually fucks them over.

Then there's the tune *Masturbate Me*, which starts out very Meatmen-ish, what with the low Tesco voice, and words about one's Johnson. But as the song progresses, as a jerk-off session would, it goes faster and gets funnier, finally spurting clever gobs of lyrics all over the listener's face. And the cool thing is you enjoy it. Even if you're not gay. Or a girl.

Also, it should be known that the Dwarves are hated. Not by everyone, but by lots of folks. And what good Punk Rock band isn't? These clowns will poop in your living room, and you'll like it. But unlike the late G.G. Allin (a good friend of the band's), it smells like roses, not dope, whiskey, shit and piss. These guys rule.

I guess I really started to really like them with the release of *The Dwarves Are Young And Good Looking* first out on Recess Records in the mid-nineties. Never had I heard a band with such mean, evil and funny lyrics so, well, poppy! In a Punk Rock/Hardcore sort of way. Lyrics about crushing skulls under you limo, and boffing thirteen year old girls. This band spoke to my soul! From there I went a bit backwards with their history and found albums like *Thank Heaven For Little Girls* and *Sugarfix* fun, and their first big hit album on Sub-Pop, *Blood, Guts & Pussy* almost as short and cool as the first Circle Jerks album, *Group Sex*, but it just wasn't as good as what they had become. And the stuff before that, to me, is just raw rockabilly.

Oh, it needs to be mentioned here that The Dwarves are the kings of media manipulation. Which is probably why they are so hated. Probably by rock reviewers. They've faked their own guitarist's (HeWhoCanNotBeNamed) death, fucked over major label douchbags, done five minute to five second live sets and the like. God, am I jealous!

Next up for Blag (real name Paul Cafaro) and company was a brilliant follow-up with *The Dwarves Come Clean*. More Punk Rock Pop that showed the youngsters how it was done. The right way. When this album came out, a whole new generation of kids were just discovering the Punk Rock, and this album was a brilliant introduction. Songs about NOT getting laid from lesbians, fucking, killing, and getting high (typical themes for The Dwarves), and of course, rape, made this a "naughty" album that would piss off any parents who actually listened to the lyrics. But at that time, the whole "Punk Pop" thing was in full swing and every band sounded the same, The Dwarves used that cover wonderfully to slip in ideas to make kids really think, while listening to music that was actually enjoyable.

The Dwarves Must Die was the last album before this one, and just hearing Gary Owens of "The Gong Show" fame announce the players in the band thrilled some of us old-timers to no end! Our peers had become the Gods Of Rock who ruled stadiums. At least in our minds and in our hearts. And fuck if these guys don't deserve that. Their music is light years ahead of anything else you've ever heard, mixing all kinds of genres together, creating what can only be called "Dwarvecore". And it's so unique no other band will ever come close to sounding this good, and anything like these guys. They are as unique as The Beatles.

Which brings me to my next point. The Dwarves Are The Beatles of today. They started out in a very raw rockabilly punk rock arena, sounding like everyone else. Just like The Beatles doing covers. But then something changed, and the band started to experiment with sounds and genres, and something totally new and wonderful was born. Then that sound was mixed up again and something else beautiful and fun was born. Kind of like *Sergeant Pepper's*. And now comes the wonderful violence on the new album with songs like *FUTYD (Fuck You Till You Die)* and *Your Girl's Mom* that have you wanting to fuck, kill and laugh, all at the same time. Awesome. It's The Beatles *Helter Skelter*.

To really understand The Dwarves, you really have to listen to the new album, *The Dwarves Are Born Again*. You'll hear all the musical stuff I'm talking about, and then some. Also check out Blag's side project, *Candy Now,* which is also the name of a song on the new album. It's a sort of retro-lounge act sort of thing that is funny, melodic, and catchy as hell. It WILL make you smirk.

To say the new Dwarves album is the best one yet is probably an accurate statement. The Dwarves continue to grow and grow, and Blag continues to learn how to push and pull knobs in all sorts of directions, like Dr. Who on the Tardis, and beautiful things and tones happen. It's pure magic. Blag puts something there that no one could even think of. Except for Blag. Being outside the box.

Anyway, after I heard *The Dwarves Are Born Again* I knew I had to interview The Dwarves' lead singer. It was time. We've both run in the same circles for quite some time now, and I've always admired the guy, but wondered about him and his origins as well. Like Spiderman or something. Blag's a cartoonish super-hero to me, so finally getting to ask him some questions for Mass Movement is quite an honor.

What follows is a few words with a man who is a true artist, pervert, egomaniac, man-boy, stud and creep. And I really sincerely mean that from the bottom of my dark and jealous heart. Oh, did I also mention he's one of the kindest human beings on the planet?

But you knew that, didn't you?

Interview by George Tabb

MM: According to the internet, you were once a band called "Suburban Nightmare" from Chicago. Who in the Dwarves was in that band as well, and what years did that band exist? Any recordings?

BD: According to the internet girls like anal sex, so you can't always trust the internet. In this case though, the interweb was correct. Suburban Nightmare made the *Hard Day's Nightmare* EP way back in 1985 on Midnight Records. By 1986 we had morphed into the Dwarves with drummer Slambeau replaced by Sigh Moan who wrote the classic *Fuck You Up and Get High*. See how it all fits together?

MM: What was Paul Cafaro like in Elementary, Junior and Senior High School? Did you have good grades?

BD: I alternated between wiseass and dumbass, working little and getting average grades. Then I discovered drugs and, ultimately, vaginas. That was the beginning of my undoing.

MM: How old were you when you first got laid? How old was she and where did you do it?

BD: I was 16 years old and so was she. I don't remember where we did it, but it didn't take very long. I still prefer dry humping to intercourse sometimes.

MM: How did the name "Blag Dahlia" come about?

BD: It started as Blag Jesus, then Blag the Ripper, Blag Tuesday, Paint It, Blag and Blag History Month.

MM: Ha! Does being in The Dwarves get you laid more than not being in The Dwarves?

BD: It's impossible for me to know that. I do get far more pussy than most guys in bands, but that's because my band is so good and so many of the rest are retarded.

MM: There's a recording on the new album about *No Cunnilingus*. Do you yourself follow that idea? I'm not a huge pussy-licker myself, so I sneak my finger in instead of my tongue a lot. Do you know any good tricks?

BD: I would advise buying the brand new record the *Dwarves Are Born Again* to find out exactly what we're talking about. If you hate music just watch the free DVD!

MM: Can your body still handle lots of Cocaine?

BD: It's not so much my body as my brain.

MM: Do'h! The *Candy Now* album is very awesome. Everyone I play it for loves it. Even old people and five year olds! How was it working with Angelina Moysov, and are you guys dating? If not, would you consider it? Can you put in a good word for me...

BD: *Candy Now* was a cool record that kind of went under the radar. I would consider dating Angelina if she would stop putting on that fake Russian accent and admit she actually comes from Duluth, Minnesota. But we are going to make more records together with Tom Ayres,

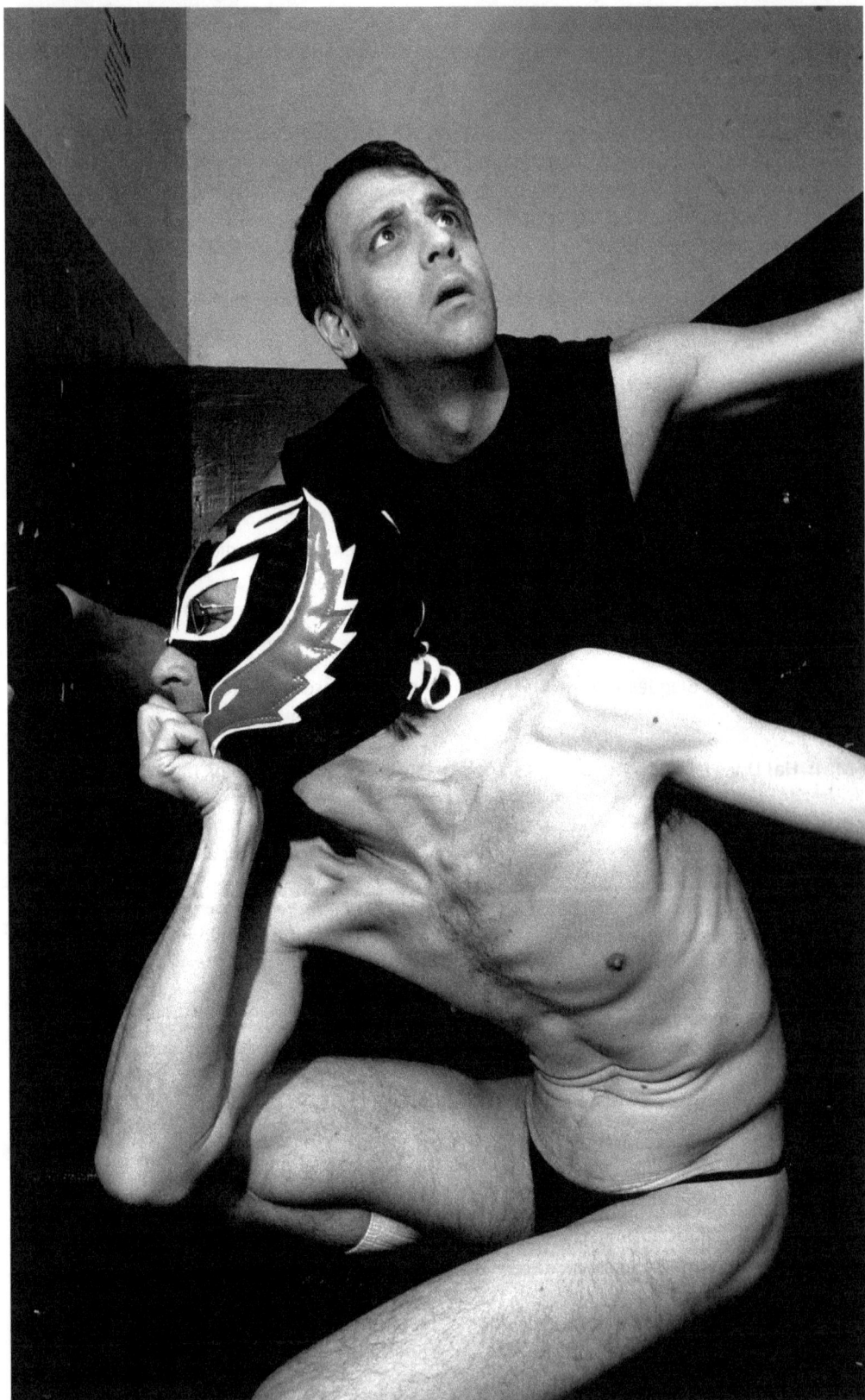

the guy who played every instrument on that record.

MM: Speaking of Candy Now, which came first, the band name or the Dwarves song?

BD: In was driving this girl home late one night, it was about 10 minutes to closing time and she wanted a piece of candy. I said I'd stop, but I kept forgetting and the minutes were winding down. Every time we would pass a store she would get all excited and scream out, "Candy, candy" and I kept putting her off until she really got pissed and screamed, "Candy Now!", and that's how another legend was born.

MM: Are you and HeWho friends outside of the band? Do you hang out together?

BD: HeWhoCanNotBeNamed is a Rock Icon, he is all things to all people. You serve in the Dwarves at his pleasure!

MM: I had a great experience working with Todd and Recess Records. How do you feel about him and his label?

BD: Todd is a lyrical genius. That's why I suggested he try his hand at pantomime and he's doing really well with it.

MM: Double Do'h! What do I do if I find out AFTER I sleep with a girl that she is way underage?

BD: Thank God for the low self-esteem of underage girls.

MM: When you played here in NYC at Coney Island High, you went on and on about "rockstar pants" they had across the street at Trash & Vaudeville. Do you now own a pair or two?

BD: I am a proud wearer of the Dogpile variety, but T and V will do in a pinch as will any comically tight pants. You feel like Spiderman.

MM: Cool! How did it feel seeing Jim Carry sing *Motherfucker* in *Me, Myself & Irene*? Did you get laid from it?

BD: It felt great seeing Jim sing our song. If I didn't get laid, I at least got a hand job.

MM: What the best advice you'd give any youngster getting started with pussy? WWBDD? (What Would Blag Dahlia Do?)

BD: Leave some for me!

Originally published in Mass Movement #29, February 2011

DAVE "ODERUS URUNGUS" BROCKIE (GWAR)

How do you go about interviewing an Intergalactic Warlord hell-bent on dominating the Universe through the medium of devastating metal? Well, you start by saying 'Hell-O'….Just kidding! In between collecting skulls for an interdimensional game of brain ball, skinning the only living virgin in the South Wales Valleys and consuming vast quantities of drugs, Oderus Urungus consented to a discussion about the limited future of the human filth and all things GWAR with Ian and me. I suspect that his Herculean consumption of crack was the only reason that we both escaped with our lives…

Interview by Tim Cundle & Ian Pickens

Oderus: Yeah my name is Oderus Urungus Aaaaaaaaaaaaarrrrrrrrrrrrrrgh! I've just got all this fucking shit right in the eye! It's the most since Liz Taylor died. I was with her when she died and she fucking shit herself screaming my name, it was beautiful…

MM: With you behind her?

Oderus: Oh yeah I was there with her family and it was beautiful. She's such a fat whore, I love that. They don't make sluts…They don't make prostitutes like Liz Taylor any more. Do you know how many popes she had blown? She was the biggest fucking Papal fucker since Salvador Dali…

MM: What's GWAR has been up to since Beyond Hell?

Oderus: Wow. Okay… After we found out the devil was Jewish – which really made the producer of the album mad, because he's Jewish too – it was just horrible. I was like "Look Devon, the devil's a Jew, he's called Jewcifer, it's no big deal get over it". Then somehow, when the final mix came out all the lyrics had disappeared! It went something like "They run banks, they run the courts, but don't worry they're not good at sports, the Jews" I don't know why he didn't dig that, I don't know why. It's like at the Olympic Games when the PLO slaughtered all those athletes. It wasn't because of any political system, it was just because they weren't good enough to compete and it was just their way of saying "We don't want you with your sports its stupid." What about with the flags, the flag dancing, that's not a fucking sport! They can't have skateboarding in the Olympics but they can have untalented Israeli flag dancers over 50 years ago getting blown up by German anti-terrorist police…

MM: What evil lurks behind, and in, the chapters of the latest GWAR epic?

Oderus: After we kicked Jewcifer's ass we came back to our Antarctic fortress and just when we got there we were attacked and all the humans of the entire world had built us a brand new GWAR temple, and as soon as I walked up to it and put a key in the door and opened it, it fell over because it was shit. Right as this happened we were attacked by Sawborg Destructo and his identical – well part identical name – twin Bozo Destructo and a lot of bullshit ensued, we got in a Scumdog warship went back to outer space, found out there was no crack in outer space and had to come back to Earth. Beyond just being a bloody bit of horror, it's just more GWAR being back on the planet; the latest hare-brained idea is to slaughter the human race, zombiefy them, pile them into the Scumdog warship, go into outer space with the human race as our own personal zombie army and reclaim the stars. But once again my titanic alcoholism and drug addiction kept us here.

MM: So now that you've added zombies to GWAR's awesome arsenal of weaponry, would undead humans make an effective weapon of planetary destruction?

Oderus: No they turned out to be pretty rubbish actually. The simplest of orders, reloading a weapon, forget it. All these guys seem to want to do is to bump into each other. The only thing that really gets them going is a GWAR show. You know I'm trying to lead an army into battle; I don't have time to be rocking out old school. So, as a fighting force? Demon zombie army get a D minus....

MM: How were the festivals (Download etc.)? How were the folks and zombies there?

Oderus: They were fucking idiots. It was perfect GWAR weather, they were covered in blood and mud and all sorts before the GWAR show even started. Because of this the crowd seemed to be all the more keen to get covered in shit. Wash the mud off with Oderus's blood and sperm!

MM: *Litany of the Slain* – it's all about all the celebrities you've dispatched during your career, so which members of the rich and shameless have been your favourites to toy with and destroy?

Oderus: I think the Popes were the best; they are certainly the most deserving of the torture that we heap upon them. These men are supposed to be the harbingers of all that is good and kind in the world and about the human race, but here are these men, raping four year old boys and people like the Pope make sure that when they get caught they are moved just a state or two over and it's not just in the United States. A large part of the Catholic religion is based around molesting people in churches. Churches are not churches so much as collection points for gay anal sexual galleries. I've always seen the Pope as an excellent target, even when he was that mumbling prick that dude from Poland.

That was the greatest thing, when I saw Gor-Gor come out on stage and bite the fucking Pope's head off, but even better, force that eight foot long Gor-Gor penis into the pope's spurting neck it was a pre-Cambrian, Mesozoic, Jurassic stump fuck of fucking epic proportions. And to think that I'd had something to do with it – because you know Gor-Gor and the Pope's headless corpse kind of hit it off after that. They went on to create the next Pope, Pope Dinner Dick ex member of the Luftwaffe who apparently didn't shoot his gun. Okay, when you've got an ex-Nazi for a Pope and he protects legions of dudes who, the whole reason they get involved is so they can have sex with children, that's the coolest thing you guys have on the planet and that's why I love killing religious dudes so much.

MM Which celebrity would you most like to painfully introduce to a GWAR show?

Oderus: The Queen had a birthday recently, so we asked her "Would you like to take this opportunity to come out and meet the GWAR fans and celebrate your birthday as they are some people you wouldn't usually get involved with." She said fuck no – don't call me again. But by that point I was in the room, so I grabbed her and she's here with us tonight. We got her all wasted, so she's actually having a great time so the Queen will be here tonight. She's ready to rock and she'll be opening the show, introducing us and encouraging people to come and meet her after the show behind the trash cans where she will service all the GWAR fans, right here tonight, anyone who comes to the show will be blown, sucked off by the queen. And she'll not just suck your fucking cock, she'll lick the shit out of your ass, she will clean peanuts out of turds and she will comb your pubes until your dick looks like Englebert Humperdink's hair. It's just one of the extra things we give the fans, not many of us do that kind of thing any more...

MM: You're going that extra mile...

Oderus: Yeah, and it's not just that. We've brought Osama back from the dead. He was the most wanted man in the world for many years and it's not fair just to blow off half of his head...

MM: I wanted to talk to you about that... What if GWAR had been put in control of tracking down and dealing with Osama Bin Laden and Al Qaeda, how differently would things have panned out?

Oderus: Osama's been hanging out with us for years. Everyone knows he's an excellent falconer and he went to Iran every year for that big convention, and the only reason he survived as long as he did was the same reason Slobodan Milosevic took fucking ten years to get to The Hague; it's like there's deals being made. Osama's dad is a very, very big construction magnate, very good connections in America. It was like after 9/11 every plane was grounded except for the one that took all the Saudis and Bin Laden's back to Saudi Arabia. So basically they were like "You can't kill him for another 10 years", so when they did, we got in there, got his body and resurrected him from the dead. He's back now and called Ozombie Bin Laden and he appears with us in the show. There's a bunch of other guys too, Sawborg Destructo is here, and he wants to be in the band, or just kick my ass or both, he's really after my job. But as for celebrities, Lady Gaga will be here tonight as well just to show people that we understand that David Bowie doesn't really do it anymore, but you don't have to replace him with some terrible, travesty cartoonesque plagiarism. Please Lady Gaga or anyone out there have a fucking original idea, is that so fucking hard?

MM: It's like Madonna for the next generation...

Oderus: You know I have a lot of respect for her, because if you look at Madonna through the ages she had very distinct moves that she made. When she dyed her hair I was all pissed at first and then admitted she did look pretty good like that. Then you have these other artists. You've gotta wonder, as you start getting older, at what stage do your criticisms of people who are younger than you and trying to do things differently, not valid simply because you're too fucking old? I was like that with house music for a long time. I was getting older and sitting in the house. I thought it was shit, so I pretty much came to the conclusion that it is shit is just that the people who listen to it are too high to care. There's really not a lot of fucking alternative now is there? Punk rock is just; it's gonna be just a lame ass... The biggest thing about punk rock now are the come backs, the reformed bands making a comeback. It's like nothing is going to fill those shoes. You're not going to do what the Sex Pistols the Clash and the Dammed did, or what Black Flag or the Bad Brains did. You're never going to have that again, so stop pretending. Don't merge metal and punk and do this metal-core, screamo or whatever. Fuck all the preconceptions just get out there and try to make something original. Those are the bands I respect. A lot of times – you know you've got to support bands; even if they suck I still support them. Being out there and doing this is the hardest job in the world...

MM: How did GWAR become involved in the world of video gaming with *Tap Tap Revenge 3*?

Oderus: They phoned us up and said "Do you want to do it?" and we said Hell yeah! We'd been trying to find somebody with the balls to do a GWAR video game for years...

MM: What would a GWAR video game look like?

Oderus: We've talked about it a lot, and I would very much like it to be a first person shooter. You would start the game as a lowly human doing something really dull, living a retarded existence when you're picked up by GWAR and thrown onto the ice plain in front of the GWR fortress. If you try to go through the main gate you're killed immediately, but if you find the secret way in you get to the GWAR dungeon. You can start your adventures in there, get a new power, build up your weapons, and slowly build up your character until you can get into the levels of the temple where GWAR lives. All of the GWAR characters have their

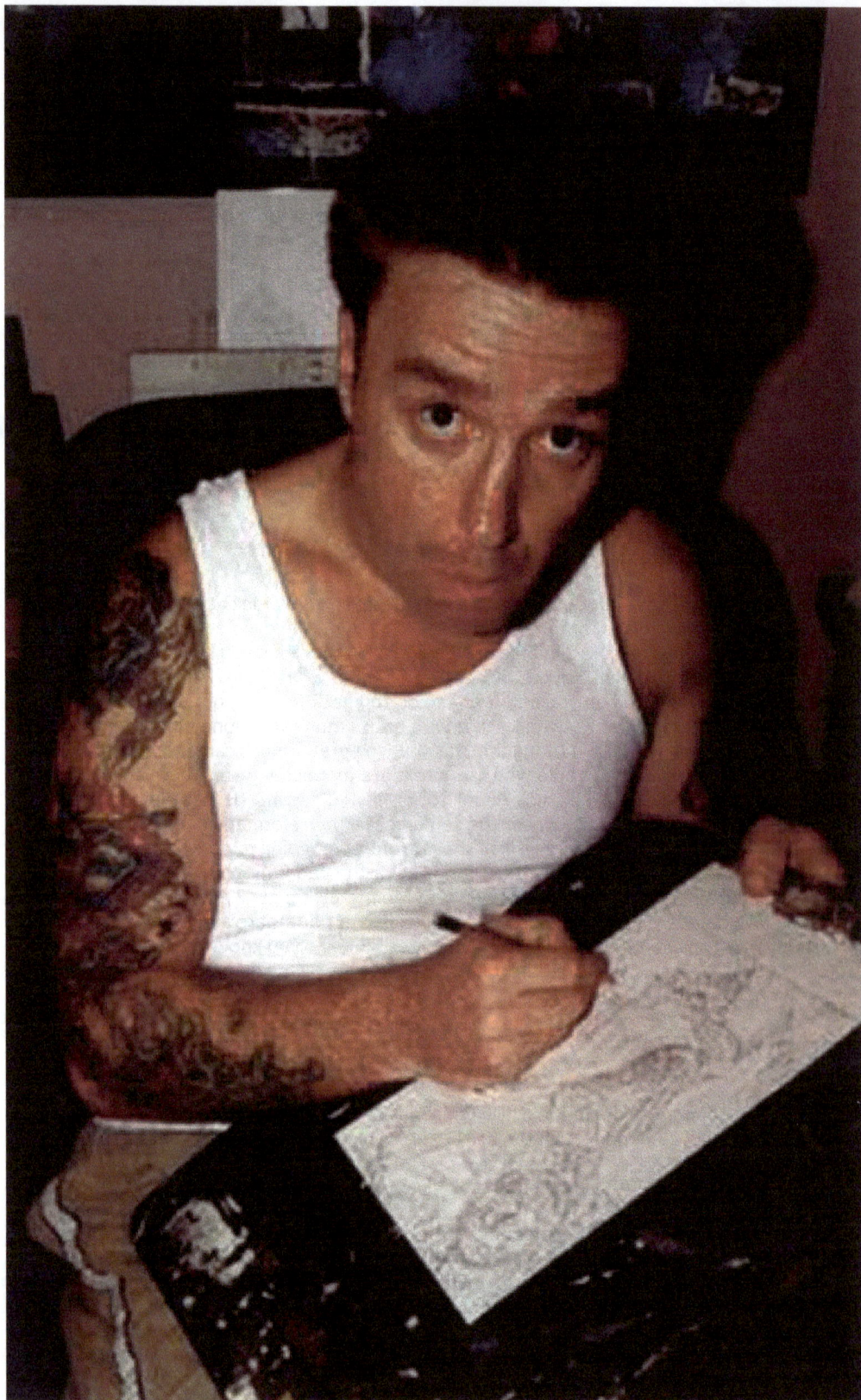

own distinct areas like the Keep of Balsac and you creep up on it and actually come to the room where Balsac has his sleeping chamber, where he has his repose and he takes off those gigantic steel jaws of his and puts them on the ring. You have to sneak across the floor like fucking phantom of the opera and you have to touch the jaws before Balsac notices you. If he sees you, you get to see his face in the game, but if you touch the jaws then you become the character of Balsac so you can actually at that point interact with the other GWAR members and eventually end up defending the GWAR fortress from its invading enemies, maybe going on tour or even maybe going on the Scumship and blasting off to space to fucking fight Cardinal Sin. It could be a total war open ended, multiplayer online game. It would be nothing less than the sickest bloodiest, most fucked up game ever.

And considering what GWAR is and everything we've done, its past high time that someone had the balls to do this. These video games cost so much money to produce they might have fucking factories filled with monkeys in Korea or somewhere writing code, but shit, their boss is going to have to get paid and these people don't make so much money once they find out they can't sell it at Wal-Mart or Costco. So they are always looking for new people. Probably what will happen is that we'll end up getting some kind of shareware engine that we can use for free and some dedicated GWAR fans and we'll sit there over a couple of years and just do it ourselves. I'd rather get a bunch of Korean monkeys to do it, but all things come to GWAR in time. We'd never thought about selling GWAR out to anything unless the time was right and this *Tap Tap* thing just came out of the blue so we went for it. We gave it the thumbs up and it actually turned out really good...

MM: It's a first because some of the things you tried to do previously, like the GWAR toy models never really happened...

Oderus: Yeah this company said they were going to do this and that and just crapped out entirely. A lot of people were like "Why don't you do action figures" and we tried to do action figures for years until one time a company (McFarlane Toys) actually sent out a photographer to take photos that would be turned into models, they were going to do these dolls for a toy company. He did full body shots and all angles and took them away but we never heard a word from them ever again. We attempted communication, then about a year later a new line of KISS dolls came out and that was the line of Kiss dolls where if you remember, about 12 years ago, where they looked a lot more bad ass? One of them even had, like, Balsac jaws on the shoulder pads. Those dudes just looked at the GWAR photographs, took some elements – I'm not saying they're exactly based on us – this is KISS for God's sake –but they looked at how they can incorporate some of that cool stuff into that shit you know? There are lots of companies out there, people like Rob Zombie who have all the money in the world, who could help GWAR with these things but they are not going to. It's not about anything else for them; it's about making money...

MM: What about a GWAR comic book*?

Oderus: Again we messed around with this. For years we did a GWAR comic but we ended up lugging box after box of these comics and selling them semi regularly but couldn't really formulate enough profit off them to make it worthwhile. And this is important because these are little vanity projects. When you expend a lot of time, energy, resource and money doing things to convince yourself that you're an artist that you're not, that's kind of what it is and we don't want to be like that. If someone would step up and say "We could have fun with a GWAR comic" we'd do another one, but we're past the point where we want to put a load of money into something simply because we want to do it. We used to do it all the time: *Phallus in Wonderland*, we were like "Yeah we're gonna make a 35mm film, we love it" we thought it was gonna be awesome but we had no idea really what that meant. By the time that we'd worked out what it meant and that it would cost all the money in the world it was too late, it was already in production. In order to survive into the new millennium GWAR had to cut back on a few things like in the GWAR shows. People would go and see a GWAR show in the 80s and 90s there would be like 15 people up there and we had to do this. We worked our

asses off and toured the world with this amazing fucking show but we got to the point where we just couldn't do it anymore so we cut back on some of the theatrics and concentrate on more of the traditional aspects of the show, great music, good production, but first and foremost we're going to do great fucking songs. GWAR took about two years off around the turn of the century and came back with a leaner GWAR and had to see if people would like it. We just played Download, and I'm not saying that GWAR is back to the level we were over here in the early 90s but we're getting it back. We went from dropping off the radar entirely to kind of clawing it back over here. We've always been solid in America but we really lost you over here for a while. There were about 5 or 6 years where we didn't really come here at all. It's so sad, we'd read the emails and letters asking when we were coming back and we did, playing festivals, starting with the last few records and gradually we're building it back. Then last year we played all these festivals and that's what we're doing this year, except this year we're going to be adding a club tour as well. Then we are coming back in January to do a full club tour of England and Ireland and the rest of Europe so that should be good...

MM: I've got to ask you about Lordi, because they totally copied what you do, and when they won Eurovision, you should have been paid for that, it was such a rip off....

Oderus: There are no laws that cover this. Those guys were really good at covering their tracks. It didn't bother me until I read an interview with the guy and they asked him about GWAR and he was like (adopts faux, comedy Finnish accent) "I've never heard of GWAR, we've never heard of GWAR, who is this GWAR?" and he was a liar, he was completely full of shit. Come on, throw some props to GWAR that's what you need to do. Unfortunately, his costume was basically a lamer version of Oderus, he had little horns, a little pig nose and all the studs. Then there's the drummer... It's obvious they studied GWAR intensely and said "Let's do a PG rated version, a version of GWAR without the sex and the violence and see if we can make it work" and they did.

But then they basically pretended that they had never fucking heard of GWAR before. At one point the dude said something like "We are from Finland we don't have access to the internet" so he was obviously aware of where GWAR were from and that you could see them on the internet. But it really fucking helped us because every time Lordi's name came up so did GWAR and then it's a chance to talk about the new album or a tour. Then we'd go back out and we had Lordi's head on a stick for a couple of years. But it was really funny, I was bashing him in the press and he would never respond – I'd say horrible things about him and he didn't respond because try to get into it with Oderus in print and you're in a whole different world.

MM: You were justified in the end though because they disappeared entirely...

Oderus: Well, totally and when that happened people were phoning us up and saying what would it take to get Lordi on an American tour with GWAR? And we said give us a European tour with Lordi. Let us open up for Lordi in Europe and we'll do the same thing in America and we'll do this thing when Lordi and Oderus fight and in America I can win and drive you back to the void, and in Europe you can win and drive me back to the void. It would have been great but they were like "No we don't do that". They are very talented but they are completely uninspired. They are the kind of guys who do special effects for films, super amazingly talented but they couldn't make a movie if their fucking life depended on it. So they're done. It was worth it for me to hear reports of when they were playing in the US and people were phoning me up and telling me that the crowds were like "GWAR, GWAR, GWAR" and to be that dude and to hear that, must have been so crushing, and he deserved it because all he needed to do was to give us our props. I don't know if that would have had much of an effect on them or anything, but I think they would have had more success. I mean with Oderus' blessing they would have done 10 times better in America. We could have had them open up for us and we would be like "They can't touch us they're just a bunch of stupid humans but check them out anyway. It would have been cool, it would have been polite and it would have worked for GWAR.

MM: What's happened to the other members of GWAR? Have you recycled them, converted them into meat paste and stored them in the flesh vats...?

Oderus: They come and go. Slymenstra is in Hollywood, she's doing a lot of art direction and design for music and shit, and she does her own solo thing. She's in California which is like another world entirely. We see her every now and then and she'll do a few shows with us. The rest of the gang are all splendid. I'm glad to say that nobody's died and the core of the band is very much intact. People come and go but the real core of GWAR people has been the same, the same musicians. The same drummer, the bass player and my lead guitar guy has been here for 10 years. It really is the most consistent line-up. I've been making music with these guys since fucking 1984!

MM: It's been 27 years, did you ever think you would last this long?

Oderus: Oh fuck no, even when we started getting successful we couldn't believe it and to this day we still can't...

MM Did you originally see yourselves as more of a side project to Death Piggy?

Oderus: Absolutely. We used to open for Death Piggy. We didn't even have any real songs we just used to get up there and groan, tell some really bad jokes, split and then Death Piggy would come out and play. But after we'd done three or four shows, every time we'd do GWAR, we'd come back on as Death Piggy and everyone had gone. There would be like five chicks and it became very obvious; Death Piggy were played out and GWAR was what people really wanted to see. So we said we'd do Death Piggy later and work on GWAR a bit. Sean the drummer from Death Piggy, we tried to bring him into GWAR but he didn't want to know, which was probably a mistake because he was one of the few members who did die. He died in police custody in Boston – it was fucked up. It never should have happened to him. He was never someone who took authority well. He was actually arrested once for breaking in to a prison. But he really wasn't right for GWAR and Bradley is. Once we found him for *Scumdogs...* we never looked back. He's like my favourite drummer in rock and roll. He has this amazing train wreck of style. He's got this big R&B influence and he's a great

metal player but he doesn't really like metal. He didn't even want to play double kick! On the first few records you barely hear it but it just builds and builds. He's like the premier combination of Dave Lombardo and Keith Moon.

MM: You mentioned *Scumdogs*, and that's the only album that's not on Spotify?

Oderus: I don't know. I know we just got the rights back for *Scumdogs* though. We are trying to move it into all the licensing areas it's supposed to be but we're not quite there yet – that might be why. We've managed to get some smart decisions and some very canny business decisions plus some positive court decisions and we managed to get half of our back catalogue back.

MM: *Scumdogs* was originally released by Master wasn't didn't it?

Oderus: And Master totally tanked so we managed to get that back. We've always just licensed them out to Metal Blade. Then we were working with DRT and that went bankrupt so we got all that back. Then we realised it was smart that every time we did a record with Metal Blade we just licensed it to them and the same with AFM. That way we retain the masters, they have to pay us a licensing fee every five years. Now with crowd funding you can get a Kickstarter and say "Hey we need $50k to produce the next record. If you contribute we'll send you a free autographed copy" then you turn around and get that money, make the record then get your fee from Metal Blade. That's the sole thing with Kickstarter and all this other funding is that it really makes it possible. People think we have all this money, but the thing about GWAR fans is that a lot of them are in their 30s and 40s, they have professional careers, have jobs and families and there is nothing that they would like better than to send money to GWAR or to buy every last bit of merchandising that we have. They will follow us around for 10 days and go to every show. If they get a chance to actually fund a GWAR project and be an executive producer? Well we did that thing for the Blood Vomits which is just a little side project we are working on which is a puppet show with a kind of medieval thing going on, a kind of comedy puppet show, and we put it up on Kickstarter to make a demo. The next thing I knew we had $1700 that was just given to us by our fans. All we had to do was to make the pilot and show it on GWAR TV and there we are, boom! Kickstarter is rewriting the way the music industry is put together. It's re-establishing he DIY ethic and I really encourage all artists to look into that. Labels that aren't with it are making their last stand right now. They lock their bands into shady contracts. It's like, we're dying. Why would you sign your life away to some record company who don't give a fuck about you? Especially if you're only going to sell 800 copies anyway. Every day you've got to have your fucking head on in this business, because you've got to be on lookout for opportunities coming down the pipe. If you blink you'll miss it.

MM: What's next for GWAR?

Oderus: A few festivals, more shows, then back home, finish up the blood vomits which is in editing right now, get ready for the Crackathon on the 15th September in New York. The GWAR-B-Q is a big outdoor party that we hold in Richmond in September. Then we go on tour again in the States in October and that's about as far as I can see right now...

MM: Anything you'd like to add?

Oderus: Well it's been 27 years of GWAR's domination of the planet and we still haven't done it yet and we're not giving up any time soon. Most bands last for 30-40 years tops. GWAR being immortal will just keep coming back and coming back until you guys just say "You know what GWAR – fuck it, we give up" ...Tonight will be another step in that direction...

*In the intervening years since this interview, the GWAR comic book has come to fruition. It's actually a graphic novel called *GWAR: The Enormogigantic Fail* . It was written by Matt Miner and Matt Maguire, illustrated by a whole bunch of incredibly talented folks and published by Renegade Arts. You should check it out. It's all kinds of awesome. And Dave would have loved it.

Originally published in Mass Movement #30, June 2011

MARK WATSON

Mark Watson is a stand-up comedian and novelist from Bristol. Having followed his career over the last few years, I have had the pleasure of seeing a number of his shows and read his novels. In the last year and a half Mark has released his third novel *Eleven*, performed stand up across the UK and Australia and fronted BBC Four show *We Need Answers*. Mark is currently on a tour entitled *Request Stops* and, having seen the Cardiff leg of the show at the Glee Club, I spoke to Mark the week after over the phone following a show.

Interview by Leigh McAndrew

Photography by Giles Wakely.

MM: You're on your 'Request Stops' tour at the moment. How has the tour been going?

Mark: Pretty well, really. It's fun to go to places, a lot of them I haven't been. Cardiff is a familiar and favourite venue, but some of the places are new venues for me. It's been nice to keep it fresh. It's special to go to places for the first time.

MM: Something that I have noticed about your shows is the way that you open them; on this tour you start typing on a laptop with the words appearing on the screen and I saw you a few years ago open a show at the Glee by standing at the back of the room shouting. Is that something that you look to do - do something different at the very beginning of the show?

Mark: Yeah, I do. I haven't done the 'shouting at the back of the room' thing for a while, because it was ruining my throat. I was getting home and I was absolutely knackered (laughs). I have always tried to make it different from the start, mostly just because it is always kind of awkward, the audience are always a bit nervous at the start. There's just a sense of awkwardness at the start of a show, I find. Some people try to get through it by really building it up and coming on with a big fanfare and stuff, but I'm always searching for a different way to start the show just to set the tone. It's a bit different from your average show, I suppose. It also helps to get the audience relaxed as soon as possible.

MM; The Glee Club like to have the big musical number...

Mark: They have the countdown, don't they?

Mm: Yeah, it's pretty ridiculous, so it's refreshing to see something different.

Mark: Yeah, it just keeps the audience on their toes and you create a different atmosphere at the start, otherwise it's a bit awkward for the first ten minutes because you're not quite sure what the atmosphere is going to be like.

MM: The other thing that sets your show apart for me is the sense of audience participation. In Cardiff last week you had audience members attempting to get into the empty seat at the front without you noticing. It adds a sense of fun to a show. I go to see comedians which are funny, but your shows have the added sense of fun.

Mark: That's something that I've only just started doing. I've only ever done that a few times, it's kind of a new idea, like a lot of this tour. I think it's true what you said, there are a lot of comedians that are very proficient and do very good jokes, but there's not that sense of fun. People forget that with comedy, because people can get so aggressive on stage or the atmosphere can be...you sort of stop and think 'We're all meant to be on the same side here'. I like an element of chaos in the show and I also like that feeling that you're playing games and having fun. However good your jokes are, there comes a point when the audience kind of want to be more relaxed and something like that helps.

MM: It gives the audience a sense of camaraderie, it brings the audience together more.

Mark: It does, everyone is on the same boat. Whereas sometimes you can feel certain people being isolated and they are feeling that everyone else is going to laugh at them. I just don't like that sort of atmosphere. I don't think it's useful to the show. With games like that, it's so stupid that it brings people out of themselves.

Do you think that idea is something that has stemmed from your twenty-four and thirty-six hour Edinburgh shows?

Mark: I think that those shows made me more confident about just messing about with the audience. I used to never interact that much with the audience when I started, because it does take a bit of nerve to do that. After doing those long shows, you'll never be nervous about audience interaction and participation again, once you've kept them busy for thirty six hours. That was pretty good training. I almost feel that if I hadn't done those long shows then I would be able to keep the audience happy in some way.

MM: I interview a lot of punk and Hardcore bands for this magazine and I've been involved in those scenes for over ten years. The main thing people involved with punk and Hardcore say is that there is a real sense of community between bands and other people involved. My thought on the longer Edinburgh shows that you did was that they showcased this sense of community in the comedy scene. Quite often at Edinburgh, comedians are competing with each other for audiences, whereas your shows were more about inclusion...

Mark: Yeah, that's very true. It is true that there is a sense of camaraderie between comedians, but Edinburgh often does challenge that a bit, because, although it's meant to be fun and it's meant to be a comedy festival that everyone can enjoy, it can end up being very tough. It's very competitive. With the long shows one of my favourite things was how everyone would get involved and people would come in unexpectedly and you do get the sense of community which you would hope it is all about, really.

MM: Yeah, you had people like Tim Key, Brendon Burns and Adam Hills joining in...

Mark: All those people were real regulars, actually and Hills in particular was sort of a hero with those long shows, he got me through it a lot of the time. It's very exciting doing that sort of thing where you're collaborating with people. It becomes less like a show and more like the acts and the audience united in this bizarre experience.

MM: Yeah and that's what I was saying earlier – you're starting to incorporate that into your newer shows...

Mark: Yeah, I'd like to think so. Definitely with the game with the seat and stuff like that, I don't really do very long shows, I haven't done one for a couple of years, I just try to achieve that atmosphere of people being in it together and if I can do that with my regular shows then I'm happy.

MM: Would you say that there is an overriding theme to your new show?

Mark: At the moment there's not, really. The show, like in Cardiff, is a mixture of the previous show and the new show and I'm gradually letting it take shape. At the moment there's not really one theme, it is unconnected material. There are certain themes; I'm a dad now as is mentioned in the show and I'm into my thirties, so the material is about that, trying to come to terms with increasing age and trying to make sense of life. These themes appear a lot in my shows, anyway. Hopefully it will become more focused. Some comedians set out to write a show about a particular thing, but I try to pick jokes and they will naturally settle into a theme.

MM: I noticed that you are recording a DVD at Bristol Hippodrome in two weeks...

Mark: Yeah, Sunday week. [Sunday 3rd June]

MM: A DVD of yours was supposed to come out a year ago, I had it on a pre-order, but it didn't come out. What happened with that?

Mark: That's right; it was a strange thing, really. The company that were doing it were releasing a lot of DVDs at the same time and they decided that it was too much at the last minute. It was up on Amazon and a few sites like that, so it was a little bit awkward for me because I told loads of people that it was out and then had to say, "Actually, it will be another year". When it does come out it will be one of the longest awaited DVDs possible. People have been waiting a year and a half for it (laughs).

MM: So is that one going to come out sometime this year?

Mark: The one that I'm recording on the 3rd is out in November and the one that was meant to come out is quite old now, so I'm not sure that it will come out in that format, but we'll probably use quite a bit of it as extras and stuff like that.

MM: Last year you released your third novel, *Eleven*. How do you manage to fit in doing stand up and writing novels?

Mark: A lot of the time they go quite well together. I do a lot of writing when I'm on tour in hotels and places like that. Obviously I perform at night, so I sort of come alive at night and still have a buzz going after the show so I find it quite easy to write. It is a bit tricky to do that and have a normally family life as well; I am sort of cramming quite a lot of things into my life. I just about fit it in; when I am working on something I tend to be quite obsessive about it so I write in quite short bursts, but do loads while I'm doing it. I juggle a lot of things, but I

write whenever I can. I do a lot of work travelling between the shows; I'll take advantage of time spent on a train.

MM: I haven't had the chance to read *Eleven* yet, but I have read *Bullet Points* and *A Light-Hearted Look at Murder*. I thought *Bullet Points* in particular was brilliant...

Mark: Thank you. I'm probably proudest of *Eleven* so far. I'm older now, more experienced, so I'd like to think I'm getting better as I'm going along.

MM: Is novel writing something that you want to continue to pursue alongside stand up?

Mark: Definitely. It's quite a big part of what I do and it gives me the chance to explore subjects that I wouldn't necessarily be able to do with stand up. It's definitely a big part of my career.

MM: I spoke to you about collaborating with other comedians. Your BBC show *We Need Answers* was a collaborative effort with Tim Key and Alex Horne. Is there any chance of a new series?

Mark: We hope so. We couldn't get any more commissioned by BBC Four because they had their budget cut and they weren't allowed to take on any cult comedy shows anymore. It was watched by quite a select audience. We're hoping that it might find a home on another channel. If possible, we might go back and do some more of the live shows. It was a live show originally. That's also a possibility, I would think.

MM: The tour that you're on is quite extensive this year. Are you doing Edinburgh?

Mark: I'm doing a handful of shows in Edinburgh, mostly to try out this new material and get a feel for what I'm doing with the next show. So I'm doing work-in-progress shows in Edinburgh, but as you say the tour goes on for ages (laughs), until Christmas, basically.

MM: You've performed in Australia a lot over the last few years, are you looking to go back there as part of this tour?

Mark: I tend to go out once a year, normally in spring when there are festivals out there. It's a lovely place and a really good place to do comedy. I'll probably be back out there next year. I tend to tour a show here and then tour it in Australia, or vice versa.

MM: Australia doesn't seem to have the same comedy circuit that Britain has. It's more festivals and things like that, isn't it?

Mark: They have festivals and touring shows. The big cities have plenty of theatres, but it's not as big a circuit as Britain. There are club gigs out there, but there're nowhere near as many. Here, there are an incredible number of venues and you can make a living as a comic just by doing club gigs. In Australia you could never really do that. Away from the festivals, there is just not enough of a circuit and all the best Australian comics end up over here, because there is so much more work. It's such a big country that you can't really tour it, it could take three or four days to travel between shows, whereas here the places are crammed together so much that you can work every night.

MM: At the moment stand-up comedy is in its biggest boom period since the nineties. Can you think of any reasons why this is?

Mark: Well, there's so much more on TV now. When I was at school there was very little stand up on TV, I'd only really seen three or four stand ups, like Eddie Izzard, Jasper Carrot, Lenny Henry, these sorts of people. You never had shows like *Mock the Week* or *8 out of 10 Cats*. There was very little showcase of stand up. There's just more awareness of how many comedians there are out there. Before, there were only a few comedians on TV and no-one knew about the rest. Also, I think that the Internet helps. YouTube makes it really easy for people to search for comedians. The main thing is the TV coverage has given a huge boost to the live scene and now the live comedy scene, as you say, has never had such a boom time.

MM: With that increase in interest, though, comes the scrutiny from mainstream press. You had a public falling out with Frankie Boyle earlier this year over certain jokes of his. You have blogged about this on your site but (and this is a question I have already asked Richard Herring) do you think that his brand of offensive comedy for the sake of offensive-ness is detrimental to other forms of stand up?

Mark: Yeah, I think if it looks as if you're just kind of bullying particular groups who don't have much of a chance to defend themselves, I think that's probably bad for comedy in general. Obviously, it's a controversial area and it's everyone's own right to do comedy about whatever they want, if they think that they can justify it morally then it's not really my business, although I made it my business for a bit (laughs). I do think that it's important to not alienate or bully people for the sake of it; I think that does give comedy a bad name in general. If you're going to make jokes about minority groups or illness…There are a lot of bad people in the world and someone will make jokes about them. If you're going to do that then I don't think you should be unnecessarily…people say that some jokes will hurt everyone and that is true, but there are certain groups that you should go a bit easy on.

MM: I think that some comedians think they can say whatever they want because they are on stage with a microphone, no matter what the outcome of what they say is…

Mark: That's right, that was what the original blog that I wrote was about which caused the trouble. As you say, the fact that you are up there doesn't mean that you can say what you want and not suffer any consequences. At the end of the day it is you that is saying that stuff and it will hit home with some people, so you have to take responsibility for what you say on stage, even if you do claim that it's part of a performance. Other comedians don't necessarily agree with that, but the more successful a stand up becomes then the more they need to think about the responsibility and the areas they cover.

MM: I think that in Frankie Boyle's case, he has always been a part of a TV show where he had to check himself, as he was on the BBC with other comedians, whereas he was given free rein on the Channel Four show…

Mark: That's true, that's why he went to Channel Four, I think.

MM: Richard Herring said very much the same as what you have said on the subject, that if you are going to make a joke about something then you should have an argument to back it up if anyone pulls you up on it...

Mark: Well I would agree with that and someone like Herring always will have an argument, he thinks very carefully about what he talks about on stage, but not everyone does. For some people, if there's a gag in it then they'll just do it, which is fair enough, because it is up to you in the end, but as a general rule comedians would do well to try and think about what they're saying. If you are going into controversial areas then you should think about specific reasons for why you are doing that, rather than just because it's a cheap laugh. I think most people would agree with that.

MM: You started the environmental project 'Crap at the Environment' in 2007. Is that something that you are still actively pursuing?

Mark: Yeah, although I'm not doing as much now. I'm still trying to live a generally more eco-friendly life, but what I haven't done for a while are the PowerPoint presentations. For a while I was doing climate change lectures, which I got trained to do by Al Gore and that was all quite good. I had to put it on the backburner a bit, because it just took up too much time. I might go back to it, I'm still a trainee of that course, so I do have the right to use that material, so it's something I could go back to. I'm still interested in the subject.

MM: This tour is going on until the end of the year, you are recording a DVD in July; is there anything else people should know that you are getting up to?

Mark: I'm writing another book which will come out next year, so I'm working on that at the moment. I've also got a pilot for Dave channel which is an improvisation show and that's on in a couple of weeks' time, sometime in July. Apart from that I'm doing lots of bits and pieces, as usual. The tour, to be fair, is going to occupy most of my time.

Originally published in Mass Movement #30, June 2011

SITTING SHIVA WITH MICKEY AND CHARLOTTE

It's been exactly ten years since my friend, Joey Ramone, passed away. This is a sort of Obit I wrote for him in *The New York Press* at the time. I miss my friend. I think we all do.

"My mom would rather call it RECEIVING GUESTS than sitting Shiva," explains Mickey Leigh, brother of Joey Ramone, and son of Charlotte Lesher, as he and I and Wendy, my now Ex-Wife, and Evan stand on his mom's terrace in Queens, watching the sun set over the Manhattan skyline.

"Uh huh," I say as Mickey passes me the joint he and Wendy are busy toking away on. I sniff the thing, then give it to Wendy. Pot makes me crazy. And crazy wasn't what I needed. I was already INSANE since I'd heard the news on Sunday that Joey, aka Jeff Hyman, had passed away from cancer.

About an hour earlier, Wendy and I piled into Evan's father's car to make our second journey out to visit Mickey and his mom at her apartment. The first time we went, Evan, my ex-bass player of Furious George, reminds me was in 1995. We were doing a segment for my cable television show, Destroy TV, which still airs every Friday night/Saturday morning at 3:30 a.m.

"It was the day of Mickey Mantle's funeral" he tells Wendy and I, as we make our way over the Williamsburg bridge in his father's car.

"Another great New Yorker," I tell him and we all sigh.

"So where's your grandfather's car?" I ask Evan, wondering what happened to his last car. The one that took Furious George on so many tours.

"Oh, I rear ended some French bastard last week," Evan explains, "and there was no damage to The Frog's car, but I fucked up mine $3500 worth."

We laugh, and talk a bit about Evan's new career as a SAG extra. He tells us that lately he's been getting cast as a crackhead, homeless father, and dead junkie.

"When I did the junkie role," he says, "they told me I didn't even need make-up."

We talk some more about how I agreed to let the United States Army use Furious George songs for free in their training films. We talk about everything except Joey. None of us want to think of what's really going on. That we're going to pay our respects to his mom and brother. That we'd never see him again.

We arrive at Charlotte's place and find a great parking spot. As we make our way into the building, Evan comments that he's looking forward to the food. I know Wendy was as well, as she hadn't eaten in hours.

As we all rode the elevator up to the their floor, Evan was the first to say it.

"All of a sudden I feel really creepy".

He had said what we all were feeling. That this was it. We were about to go into the home of a grieving family. Of a mother who had just lost her son. A brother who had just lost a brother. Fucking Joey Ramone.

We got to the correct floor, found the apartment, knocked on the door, and heard Mickey yell "Come in."

As we entered, the first thing we saw was this great spread of food. I mean, fucking beautiful. Roast beef. Turkey. Bagels. Meatballs. Pasta. Coleslaw. Potato salad. The works.

The next thing we saw was Mickey, filling up his plate with all the food. After a few quick hellos and hugs, Mickey begged us to dig in.

I asked him who all the people in his mom's apartment were, as I didn't recognize any of them except for his mom, his wife, him, and some pussy rock critic.

"These," said Mickey, as he pointed to the crowd, "are people who are hungry."

We all laughed and Evan and Wendy dug in.

I made my way around the apartment checking everything out. There was a nice mix of children and grown-ups. All who looked like close family or friends. It was really nice, and the room had a very peaceful vibe.

Set upon a table in the middle of the living room, were lots of pictures of Joey and Mickey and their mom. When they were kids, and when they were adults. It was very sweet, and I felt my throat lock up as I clutched the Furious George album in my hands that I had brought for Joey's mom. It had Joey singing on it, and since I knew that she collected EVERYTHING her sons ever did, I wanted her to have our album as well.

A few minutes later I found myself in Mickey's mom's bedroom, alone with him, Wendy, and Evan. Wendy and Evan were eating. And I was jealous.

"Didja ever see this?" asked Mickey, as he showed me a picture of him and Joey from an old issue of New Musical Express.

I told him I had, and that I actually still have that newspaper. It is amazing to see how he and his brother looked so much alike.

We talked some more about Joey, or Jeff, as his family calls him, and about his last moments on Earth. Mickey tells us the story of how he played a U2 song for Jeff as he drifted away forever.

"He was such a professional," said Arlene, Mickey's wife, as she walked into the room, "he even died on cue."

We all laugh. Laugh away the tears that we all feel welling up in our eyes.

"George," says Mickey, as he watches Wendy and Evan finish their bagel sandwiches, "go get something to eat. What's wrong with you?"

I tell him I will, as soon as I give my album to his mom.

Mickey pushes me out the door, and toward her. As I get closer to her, my heart beats faster and faster. What do you say to your idols mom? The idols being both Jeff and Mitchell (Mickey's real name).

But, as it turns out, I didn't have to say anything.

"George," said Charlotte, "It's so nice to see you again! Both my sons speak so highly of you. Have you had anything to eat yet?"

I give her the album, hardly able to cough out any words, and she tells me that her and Mickey are thinking of writing a book together called "I Remember You" about Jeff. Joey. Whatever. I get goose bumps.

We talk a bit more, and I was amazed at how GREAT she looked. I mean, even Wendy commented on how strong and beautiful she looked.

"George," Charlotte says, snapping me out of my thoughts, "Eat!"

So I do.

Roast beef. Turkey. Meatballs. Lots of coleslaw. Pasta. And even a piece of a bagel. And it was fucking delicious.

Sometime later, Mickey and Arlene took Evan, Wendy and I out on to the terrace to smoke some pot. As the joint was passed around, we watched the sun set over the city as we heard Ramones music playing. We turned around to look inside and saw that VH1 was airing a Ramones special. We all looked at each other and smiled.

We talked a bit more about Joey, remembering the good times of his life.

As the sun disappeared somewhere behind The World Trade Center and The Empire State Building, Mickey spoke.

"Ya know," he said, "My brother, Jeff Hyman has left us, but Joey Ramone will be with us forever."

Punk Rock. And Shalom.

George Tabb

Orginally published in Mass Movement #30, February 2011

SCOTT IAN
(ANTHRAX)

A stunning return to form. That's the only way I can effectively describe Anthrax's new masterpiece Worship Music and the bands glorious performances at the most recent 'Big Four' festivals. The album also marks the return of Joey Belladona, who left the band in 1992. After nearly thirty years, it's gratifying to know that this legendary New York band still know how to thrash with the best of them. Guitar player Scott Ian knows what his band needs to do in order to make 2011 an excellent year for the 'Thrax'...

Interview by Martijn Welzen

MM: Becoming a dad, going on tour with the Big Four, and releasing such a highly antici-pated new album. Would you say 2011 is THE year for you and Anthrax?

Scott: Oh yes, 2011 is shaping up to become a great year. And we still have the Big Four in Yankee Stadium coming up, which will probably be the biggest thing we've ever done. I'm pretty sure about that actually...

MM: Can you feel that anticipation within the band, about the upcoming release, or do you feel any pressure about it's release?

Scott: No pressure at all, I'm just really excited. Things have taken their course so there's no need to feel pressured by, or about, anything.

MM: In the years leading up to the release of *Worship Music* things were all over the place with Anthrax. Was there ever a time you wanted to call it quits?

Scott: Calling it quits would have been suicide, almost literally. I'm not the sort of person to back away from a challenge, so even when the band hit a few bumps in the road, I wanted to push forward. I didn't want to show any weakness by giving up.

MM: What I wondered when listening to the new record, is whether it was only Joey's vo-cals which had to be re-recorded in the end, or if you had to change some melodies or lyrics to make things work?

Scott: That's the thing. We never write songs for a vocalist, just pure Anthrax songs. Doesn't really matter if it's Joey Belladonna, or John Bush, or anyone else stepping in. They'll defi-nitely put their own signature on a song, but each song is written as an Anthrax song.

MM: I just feel his voice fits perfectly, so I can imagine work needed to be done on the music and lyrics as well...

Scott: Yeah, things did work out, and we had high hopes it would work out as good as it did. Producer Jay Ruston and Joey hit a home run, to use a cliche...

MM: Looking back at thirty years of Anthrax, with it's ups and downs... Do you have any regrets musically speaking?

Scott: Yeah, I regret not having written *Back In Black* (laughter) But no, no regrets. I think you should never have any regrets, well maybe if you're in jail or something, and as I'm not in jail, regrets don't really make any sense. You know there're things in the past I could have done differently, but if it was the case that I had a time machine and could go back and chance these events, I wouldn't be talking to you and the whole present would have changed. I love the present and my mistakes in the past made me and Anthrax what we are.

MM: I remember you saying 'what doesn't kill me, only makes me stronger', does that still ring true?

Scott: Sure is, I'm still living by the same rule.

MM: Songs like *Revolution Scream*, *I'm Alive* and *Fight Them Till You Can't* all seem to have this message of never giving up, and fighting for what you love or feel is right?

Scott: When looking at my past as a lyricist, and I started writing lyrics for the first time in 1985, when we were recording 'Spreading The Disease', there are always three or four songs about not quitting a struggle. It's just who I am. Back in the 80s, when we first started out, no-one gave a shit about our music. We weren't a new wave band, and didn't play Van Halen covers. It really was an uphill battle in the beginning. So this is what has shaped me, and it might not always be that obvious in my lyrics. Off the new album I would say *Fight Them Till You Can't* sums up my current mindset pretty accurately

MM: I love that title *Worship Music*, but I'm curious about how you're still able to worship something you're this close to?

Scott: Does the Pope, the guy the centre of the Catholic Church, feel less impressed by faith? There's always something to look up to. The Beatles or Led Zeppelin still have the same amazing appeal, and their magic will never be broken.

MM: Anthrax could be, and most likely are, the subject of worship to some metal heads...

Scott: Following my own train of thought, of course it can. We might not be as big as some bands, but some people consider our band to be very important. And I'm very grateful for that support and will never take that for granted.

MM: The cover also suggests, to me at least, that you can also lose yourself in worship. Is there maybe some (cont.) underlying message about not losing yourself in faith?

Scott: In all honesty, I don't really know what the cover is about, other than I think it looks cool. (laughter) You know if I could really sit down and think about it, I could probably come up with a nice story, but that wouldn't be totally fair....

MM: I read somewhere you called the new album the "Most Emotional Album", was that in reference to the rollercoaster you've been on while getting it recorded and released, or does it also relate to the lyrics and music?

Scott: I only have to mention the lyrics to *In The End* which is about us losing our friends Dimebag Darrell and Ronnie James Dio. You can easily connect to the whole vibe set by that song, which I hope will touch the listener both lyrically and musically.

MM: *Earth on Hell* also is a pretty strong song title, what can you tell about it?

Scott: Eh, you caught me of guard there. I don't really know…. Let me listen to the first few seconds of the song, and I can tell you from there. (Ian blasts *Earth On Hell*, and continues after a brief pause.) Right, there's a few ideas going through that song, but the main idea would have to be about public uprising and humanity taking control. You know this song was written before the uprising in Egypt, but that would be a good example of what it's about. Trying to force a country to change. I don't think there's one place on this earth which isn't fucked up, well maybe New Zealand or some far corner of the planet. I can see it clearly in the United States. Back in the sixties people made things happen. This country really changed back then, but in the twenty first century the US is deeply divided and I don't think that's going to change soon. I could go out protesting with a sign all day long, but it would take tens of millions of people doing the same thing to see change happen.

MM: Isn't it difficult combining serious topics like death, revolution or feeling alienated on one hand, and songs about zombies and comics on the other? Or is that just like life, the good and the bad wrapped up together?

Scott: I know there are bad things in this world, but you can't be too stressed out about it ALL the time. So yes, I'd say our albums have always been a mixture, that touches on serious subjects and having fun. It's important to have fun. Otherwise you might just as well go out with a gun shooting people, just like that madman in Norway. It's about balance. I really enjoy what I'm doing, and playing shows, it's hard work, but it's also a lot of fun. I love being around friends and family too. And playing with this band is something I can hopefully continue to do for a long time. Life's just too short to get stuck on the negative stuff.

MM: Metal is also a very physical style of music...

Scott: It sure is, and we always want to give one hundred percent. I can give you two great examples though, on why we can continue for a long time. First one: AC/DC. I've seen them a few times on the *Black Ice* tour and I can honestly say I think they're better now than they were on their *For Those About To Rock Tour*. The second one: Motörhead. We played with them on a festival in Montreal, and when Lemmy walked out on stage, he said; "We're Motörhead and we play rock n roll" and then *Iron Fist* kicked in. Goose bumps that's all I can tell you. And these guys are at least ten years older than I am. Even so, if you take Tom Araya of Slayer who as had severe back and neck problems. He can't head bang on stage anymore, but the intensity of his performance didn't suffer from that. There's always a way of adapting to every new situation...

Originally published in Mass Movement #31, October 2011

EVAN DORKIN

So, a while back I chatting to Aub at Dark Horse about upcoming books and he mentioned that they were going to be releasing a *Milk & Cheese* Omnibus collection, the definitive collector's edition, to which I replied something like "Seriously? Milk & Cheese?', although my actual reply might have contained a few more swear words and may have been written by my inner fanboy. Aub, who deals with this kind of thing on a daily basis, said that yes, he was very much on the level, and would he like me to hook up an interview with Evan Dorkin to talk about it? "Does a bear defecate in the woods?", replied I, knowing full well that it's the species' potty place of choice, "Heck Yes"! Aub, good as his word, set it up, and after some hyperventilation on my part, it was interview-a-go- go time with Mr. Evan Dorkin...

Interview by Tim Cundle

MM: As with any story, the best place to start is at the beginning...Do you want to introduce, and tell everyone a little about, yourself?

Evan: My name is Evan Dorkin, I'm a cartoonist and I write and draw for comic books, magazines and occasionally for television. My first comics job was in 1986, and I've been making comics full-time since 1991. Some of the comics I've created are *Milk and Cheese, Dork and Hectic Planet.* Currently I'm writing a comic called *Beasts of Burden*, which is illustrated by Jill Thompson and published by Dark Horse Comics. I've done work for Marvel, DC, SLG, Bongo, Oni, Mad Magazine, Spin and other publishers and magazines, many of whom are now out of business. I've done a few book illustrations, some CD and record covers and I've worked on several television series along with my wife and partner, Sarah Dyer, including *Yo Gabba Gabba!, Space Ghost Coast to Coast, Superman* and *Batman Beyond.* I once created a pilot for the Adult Swim called *Welcome to Eltingville* which was a complete failure. Some people like my work, some people don't, most people have never heard of me.

MM: What first attracted you to comics? What drew you to the medium? Which book first hooked you in, and why? What was its appeal? Has your love for, and thus what draws you to the medium, changed over time, or have the things that you love about comics remained constant? What's changed and why, or why do you think it's stayed unchanged?

Evan: Man, that's a lot of questions. Let's just say I've always been attracted to cartooning, whether it's for comics, newspaper strips or animation. I grew up on newspaper comics, read Tintin early on in a kid's magazine I had a subscription to, and eventually got into Mad Magazine and Marvel Comics. I read almost all of the Marvel titles, but my favourites were Spider-Man and the Fantastic Four. With Spider-Man I liked the humour, the character – like a lot of readers I could identify with his problems – and the rogues gallery was really strong, I've always been a fan of the villains and Ditko designed a lot of great-looking characters. The same goes for Jack Kirby's designs for The Fantastic Four, that book was just full of adventure, fun, it had a real sense of wonder and humour and invention. And I really liked The Thing, I thought he was a great character. I don't know why I love the comics medium as much as I do, it's not a simple thing I can just boil down briefly. I love books, movies, and music, but comics is where my heart is. As I've gotten older my tastes have broadened, I like all kinds of comics, new and old, foreign and domestic, all genres. I'm just drawn to the medium, no pun intended. I think the cheap old newsprint comic paper caused the ink to rub off on your hands and poison you with it. Comics got under my skin, I have ink in my veins.

The things I dislike about comics mostly have to do with the business end of things. Becoming a professional means now I know a lot of what goes on behind the scenes, and so much of that can be depressing and disheartening. Like any business, obviously, but comics was presented to the readers as a kind of endearing, genial clubhouse. And it's not. I love the medium, but I kind of hate the industry. There's been a lot of progress but it's still such an ass-backwards and immature industry, we hate being regarded as second rate but we do a lot of things that make us look second rate. That being said, there's never been so much good work being done in comics, the so-called "Golden Age" is revered for nostalgic reasons, but most of it was throwaway dreck. Comics sales may be relatively lousy these days, but we've never seen so many quality books coming out across all genres, not to mention all the terrific reprints and translations being done. And the production and art design end of things has never been better. I'm not a fan of the modern versions of the superhero comics I grew up on, but that's fine, they don't make things just for me, Marvel and DC are free to do what they want, obviously, even if I think a lot of its dreary. Sometimes I think it would be cool to have a fun, comprehensible, enjoyable superhero comic to read featuring the characters I enjoyed as a kid. Then again, there's stuff like Hellboy and B.P.R.D. to fill the superhero/ pulp void, and old comics reprints. So it's not something I get upset about. As I've gotten older some comics lose their appeal, some don't, and there are comics I used to dislike that I now enjoy. It's a process, you're always looking for new stuff and reconsidering what you've already read. The constant is the medium, not any one type of comic.

MM: Sticking with the same sort of theme, when and why, did you know that you wanted to work in comics? How did you get your first break in the industry, and how, if it all, does the life and world of a professional comic artist and writer differ from what you thought it would be like before you entered the world of the four colour book? Which writers and artists, if any, influenced you and your work, and how and why did they influence you?

Evan: Cripes, where to start? I wanted to draw comics since I was a kid. I wanted to draw Spider-Man. My early influences were Peanuts, Mad (the magazine and the reprints of the Kurtzman/Elder/Wood's fifties comics), Jack Kirby, Stan Lee and most of the classic Marvel Bullpen, as well as Warner Brothers, Disney and Fleischer animated cartoons. Steve Gerber was an influence although I didn't realize that until later. Kurtzman, Elder, Kirby, Lee, Schulz, those are the main guys, I think. Obviously you're influenced by what you like, a sort of osmosis sets in after repeated exposures to the material. It shapes your eventual style. You pick up additional influences as you age but the kid-hood interests are always lurking in the heart of things you do. I think. Especially if you're at all immature, which I am.

How I got into comics: when I was older, a comic shop opened near me that carried all sorts of comics, including the new small press stuff that was bubbling up like *Love and Rockets* and *Neat Stuff*. I ended up working there, then the co-owner left to open his own shop, and I ended up working there, at Jim Hanley's Universe. There I met a writer named Alan Rowlands who was breaking in to comics, he was getting some fill-in work at DC and Marvel, and he had a series idea for a comic and asked me to do design work for it. This was around the time of the Teenage Mutant Ninja Turtles craze, when speculation on black and white small press comics spawned a ton of new publishers out to make a buck, hiring any monkey who could hold a pencil to fill up pages. Alan set up some meetings with several publishers, which was good for me because I was too nervous to show my work to editors, I still hate pitching stuff to people and have never had professional portfolio.

Anyway, to try and make a long, boring story shorter and less boring, eventually the comic, *Phigments*, got picked up by a publisher, Amazing Comics, and we put out two issues. It ended up being a lousy experience, but it was a start. Work often leads to work, and I ended up doing my own series called *Pirate Corp$!* for Eternity Comics, which led to me attending my first San Diego Comic Con in 1987, where I ended up meeting other professionals and editors which led to my getting more work. I went full-time in 1991 after getting a pencilling gig on a *Predator* series from Dark Horse and a job writing and pencilling the doomed-from-the-start *Bill and Ted* comic series for Marvel. That same year I put out the first issue of *Milk and Cheese* with SLG. I wasn't a very good artist or writer at the time, but you learn while doing, and I was lucky to get my foot in the door and keep it open in the wake of the black and white bust.

Comics turned out to not be anything like I thought it would be, as far as the business went. I grew up reading about "Smilin'" Stan Lee, "Jolly" Jack Kirby, "Jazzy" Johnny Romita – Marvel made it sound like it was one big happy   family that had a ball making comics. It sounded like everyone was friends, they wanted to be your friend, too, and writing and drawing comics was nothing but fun. Of course most of that was bullshit. Most everything is bullshit. You grow up, and for good or bad, you learn about the entertainment industry being a business, first and foremost, and you learn about all the unfair and petty crap that happens in comics and animation and what have you. It's a rude awakening, especially if you were as naïve as I was about the grown-up world of making funnybooks. Nowadays almost everyone in comics is there because they want to be, but the business is still the business, still weighed down with a ton of bullshit. That's life. You try to avoid as much bullshit as possible and make good comics.

MM: I guess most folks know you as the creative force behind *Milk and Cheese*, so let's talk *Milk and Cheese* - where did the original idea come from? What, if anything, influenced its creation, and over time, influenced the way the book developed? How, if at all, do you think these influences manifest themselves in *Milk and Cheese*?

Evan: I first drew *Milk and Cheese* on a napkin while I was waiting for food in a restaurant. I had been to a ska show at CBGB's and was drunk. So, the influence there was beer and boredom, I guess. And hunger, maybe. I continued drawing them as a lark – I'd draw them for people at conventions and doodle them on envelopes to friends – but I never considered making comics with the characters. That was suggested to me by a guy named Kurt Sayenga, who I met at the San Diego Con in 1988. He was doing a music/comics zine called *Greed* and he said if I did a *Milk and Cheese* comic he'd run it. Which is how they first saw print. One thing led to another, and *Milk and Cheese* became whatever it is they've become. Obscure cult comic book stars. Glorified napkin drawings.

MM: Alright, assuming that there are some folks out there who are unfamiliar with *Milk and Cheese*, so straight from the horses (a turn of phrase, not that I'm making any equine comparisons or anything you understand Evan...) or rather creators mouth, how would you describe *Milk and Cheese* to a virgin reader? How would you explain the book in order to convince someone to pick it up?

Evan: The tagline for *Milk and Cheese* is "Dairy Products Gone Bad" and that's pretty much the gist of it. They're a carton of hate and a wedge of spite, two misanthropic alcoholics who take out their frustrations on everything they hate —which is just about everything – by resorting to mindless violence. It is what it is. People either like it or hate it. I like it.

MM: I hate to put you on the spot Evan, but I'm going to do it anyways…. Do you have a favourite *Milk and Cheese* strip and, or, book, and if so, which is it? Likewise, is there anything *Milk and Cheese* related that you wish you hadn't done, or given the gift of hindsight, would change in any way? If (again…) so, what would you change and (yeah, I like to ask why, I blame my parents) why?

Evan: I like some more than others, and there are a batch I'm not happy with at all, but I don't have a single favourite strip. I tend to like the more recent strips and the material from issues #6 and 7, for the most part. The earlier Milk and Cheese strips are baboon ass-ugly and hard for me to look at now. My art was very rough at the time, and while we were putting the *Milk and Cheese* collection together I had to resists the urge to redraw almost everything.

One regret I have regarding *Milk and Cheese* is that I wasn't able to do that many strips in the past ten or so years. I also wish I had been able to keep more of the original art from the series, I had to sell a number of pages over the years to supplement our income. What I really wish is that I had made better copies of some of the art because when it came time to do the collection we had a hell of a time finding the best source material for some of the comics. There are other things I regret having done or not done, but I'll leave it at that. You make decisions and hope for the best, in life and on the page.

MM: Okay, I guess we should mention the new hardback collection, *Milk and Cheese: Dairy Products Gone Bad* - how did the whole thing came about? With things having been kind of quiet on the *Milk and Cheese* front for a while, did you ever think there'd be a definitive collection, and how do you feel about the book as a representation of your work and *Milk and Cheese* as a whole? Guess I'm putting you on the spot again huh? I'm not a bad guy, honestly…

Evan: I always assumed there would be a collection at some point, but I also assumed I'd finish up an eighth issue before a new collection, and after ten or so years I only had enough material for half a comic. Without getting into it too much, I'd been doing more work with Dark Horse over the years, and my relationship with them had been growing to the point where I thought they would be the best place for me to do a *Milk and Cheese* book. I was with SLG for over twenty years and that's a long time to be associated with a publisher. I'm grateful for what we accomplished together but the industry's changed a lot in the past decade and putting my work out through SLG became more and more difficult based on my situation and their business model. It was nothing personal, and it wasn't a decision made lightly, because I had a close relationship with SLG. But I've also had a twenty-year relationship with Dark Horse, which is why I felt comfortable doing the *Milk and Cheese* book with them. A chunk of strips in the book were originally published in Dark Horse anthologies. As far as how the book represents my work or *Milk and Cheese* – I don't know what that means, exactly – it's a collection of my *Milk and Cheese* work. Unless it comes out with a bunch of Batman comics in it I think it'll represent *Milk and Cheese* pretty decently.

MM: I heard a rumour a while back that there was going to be a movie version of *Milk and Cheese*, or at least that it was going to be adapted for the movies, and then it didn't happen because you weren't sure about it…What happened? Most creators seem to be chomping at the bit to get their books on the big screen, but then you went in the opposite direction…?

Evan: There was never any deal to make a *Milk and Cheese* movie or T.V. show. I had a decent amount of offers in the 90's but I wasn't interested in selling off the characters. Also, most of the offers didn't involve my participation, and I can't really see someone else writing and drawing *Milk and Cheese*. I'm not against dealing with Hollywood or licensors, we did a pilot for *The Eltingville Club* and *Beasts of Burden* has been optioned for a film. But I'm very protective of *Milk and Cheese*. They're not the greatest characters on Earth, they're not genius, but they're mine.

MM: And the *Milk and Cheese* figures, what's happening with them? Have they seen the light of day yet, if not, when can we expect them? How do they look?

Evan: They came out several years ago from SLG/Monkey Fun Toys. They sold terribly, and the fact that you weren't aware they were produced speaks volumes about how well that particular project went. I think they came out really well, we were very happy with them, as far as the actual toys went.

MM: Cartoon time…. You've also worked in animation haven't you? How did, and does that differ from working on comic books? Which do you prefer? Animation or comics? Do you want to tell us a little about *Space Ghost* and what it was like to work on? Do you plan on returning to animation?

Evan: Animation provides a lot of opportunities you don't often find in comics in that if can pay well and there's a mass audience for it, both of which are desirable and rarely the case in comics. On the other hand, animation is often intensely collaborative, and sometimes it involves people who take your work and mis-interpret it, or just tear it apart. That hasn't happened to us too often, as we've had the opportunity to work on shows like *Space Ghost Coast to Coast* and *Yo Gabba Gabba* where the producers and creators were respectful of the writers and artists they hired and trusted them to do their job. We also had a ton of leeway when we worked on the *Eltingville* pilot for the Adult Swim. We've actually had only one really negative experience in animation, and that was on the *Shin Chan* show, doing dialog punch-ups, so we've been pretty lucky.

Regarding *Space Ghost*, basically, it was a fake talk show where Space Ghost would interview with celebrities while dealing with his rebellious, evil sidekicks. The writers took videotaped interviews done with mostly B-level celebrities and chopped them up to use as they saw fit in their scripts, which would have Space Ghost and the other cartoon characters interacting with the celebrities (who would be on a view screen) and one another. It was a fun show and a great experience, I'm really happy we were a part of it.

As far as new stuff goes, we've just wrapped up some animation development work and I was just offered a writing gig for a short cartoon project, we keep our hand in animation when the opportunity arises. We don't have an agent or a manager and we don't pursue T.V. work, basically, we like to work on things we like, and every once in a while an offer arrives and we end up doing some animation work. The work can be fulfilling and fun, but I prefer

comics, even if they're more time-consuming and the industry is so frustrating. In comics, you're in complete control; I write and draw what I want. Even on a work-for-hire project, what the audience reads and sees are my words and art. No one's come in and rewritten my dialog or reworked my art. I prefer to work that way whenever possible.

MM: Apart from *Milk and Cheese*, you've also worked on a load of other comic series, *Dork*, *Beasts Of Burden* etc. - Which of your comic creations is your personal favourite, and which do you think best represents you as a writer and artist? Wait for it, here it comes….Why?

Evan: Different projects mean different things to me, it's like being asked to pick a favourite child. *Beasts of Burden* is my main passion at the moment, it's the project I think about the most during the day. It's equally as important to me as my other books even though it's not a solo effort. I can re-read an issue of *Beasts of Burden* and marvel at Jill's artwork and what she brings to the project and I can't marvel at much of anything when I look at my own comics. Most of it makes me cringe. It's like looking at high school yearbook photos. The work's very personal and I'm very critical of it. That being said, I'm very fond of *Milk and Cheese* and *Dork*, on the whole. Along with *Beasts of Burden* those are my favourite series I've worked on. I don't know what best represents me as a writer or an artist. That's up to the reader to decide, it's not something I really think about By the way, every time you tack on the question of "why" it makes me feel like I'm taking an essay exam. Which is a really shitty feeling. Tonight I'm going to have nightmares of being back in school.

MM: Having talked to a number of comic writers and artists, one of things that constantly seems to come up is how fast the comics industry is changing, and the speed with which the changes are becoming standard practice, so I kind of wanted to get your take on it…. How has the industry changed since you first became involved as a writer and artist? Do you think the changes are beneficial for, or detrimental to, the business as a whole and the creators who ensure its continuing longevity? You guessed it, my favourite add on….Why?

Evan: The industry has changed a lot since I first started working in it, I couldn't even begin to go into all of the sea changes over the past two decades. I don't even feel like I'm part of the industry anymore at times, to be honest. Comics has become some sort of miniature Hollywood, only without the money and prestige. And it's not like sales are going through the roof to justify all the swaggering, it's just the internet and the film options and adaptations working a lot of people up. You can fool yourself into thinking comics are more viable and popular than they are by the number of movies coming out based on them, or the success of individual creators or projects, or by the growing amount of coverage of comics on non-comics websites – but sales are still falling, overall. The DC 52 launch is a shot in the arm for the Direct Market, but it's not likely to have a long-term impact. I mean, I hope it does bring new readers into the medium, and I hope some of them look into books beyond the superheroes so there's some growth across the board, but I don't think it will do much more than sell a lot of extra copies of DC comics for the next few months. The massive superhero events have become a sort of heroin for their hardcore fans, but they always need another fix, bigger than the last to get any kind of kick out of it, and they erode the overall customer base by burning them out or becoming too expensive a habit for them to keep. Book stores were shoring things up for publishers who are often ignored in the Direct Market, but now bookstores are faltering.

Obviously the biggest change is digital, and who knows where that will take things. It's all up in the air. All I know is the days of knocking out a goofy comic and getting it in shops are pretty much dead and gone. Things were looser and more seat of the pants when I started out. You could go to lunch with some Marvel editors, crack some jokes, and end up with a one-shot project that came out a few months later. Now everything is an event or a big deal, which means almost nothing is really a big deal, just like Hollywood. Tons of hype, a lot of noise, and a week later everyone's on to the next big thing. Now if you knock out a goofy comic you put it up on the web, which is cool and all, but kind of unromantic to me because I'm a print guy. I'm not at all anti-digital or anti-web comic, it's more democratic than the Direct Market and allows for more diversity and makes getting your work out there easier, but it's bewildering to me as a reader. So many comics, so little organization.

I have no way to know what the hell's out there and no time to slog through it all. Anyway, digital is the future, and I'm not a fortune teller, so who the hell knows what's going to happen. I'm sure there will be a lot of shake-up as print continues to cough up blood and publishing continues down the rocky digital road.

MM: What's your take on fandom? Do you dig Comic Con and Expo's and shows? What do you dig about them, and what (in your opinion), if anything, sucks about them and what, if you could, would you change about big comics shows?

Evan: Despite what people might think because of how I've portrayed fans in *Milk and Cheese* and the *Eltingville Club* strips, I'm fine with fandom in general. I mean, I'm a fan. That's what some people fail to realize when they criticize my comics. My problem isn't with all of fandom, it's with the fans who cross a certain line into stupidity or know-it-all obnoxiousness or have an outsized sense of entitlement, all the professional complainers, haters and whiners who inundate the internet. The defensive posturing and nastiness that often crops up in comments threads only serves to prove my points about idiotic fans, the Eltingville Club-types out there who give fandom a bad name. There's a lot of great fans and readers out there, there's a lot of socially awkward fans out there, and there's also a contingent of pushy, needy creeps and imbeciles. Which is par for the course for society at large. But that latter group is the one I target in my comics, I don't go after the lonely, messed-up fans, I go after the alpha jerk offs who make their hobby their life and their life a 24/7 nerd arena of combat. Nerds are almost always portrayed as meek in pop culture, but I've been a fan, a retailer and a creator and I've seen plenty of shitty behaviour from people in fandom. And I've acted indefensibly in the past, especially when I was younger. That's what Eltingville is about, that and the fact that creepy fan behaviour has pervaded modern comics, gaming and the media to an unfortunate degree.

As far as conventions go, I enjoy them on the whole, but I enjoy them a lot less than I used to. When I started out the shows were more intimate and more about comics. The big shows are too big and crazy now, everyone's on the move, hustling, pushing, drawing, taking meetings. It's less fun. I prefer smaller, friendlier shows like Heroes Con, as well as the smaller, independent and art comics-oriented shows like TCAF. San Diego isn't about comics like it used to be, and that's a bit of a shame, but the reality is, comics will always lose to movies, T.V. and video games. We're still kicking poetry and radio drama's asses, though. I'm not interested in going to a con for movies or celebrities, but when I was a kid I would have enjoyed those things, I went to Star Trek and Science Fiction conventions back in the seventies. Things change, conventions change, fandom changes, nowadays more people enjoy the pop culture shows than ever so who am I to say they're wrong?

If I had a say in how the bigger events are run, I'd mainly change things like crowd and floor traffic control and how loud the booths get. They really need to do something to better prevent people being packed in together too tightly and blocking the aisles, especially the complete pains in the asses who stop in the middle of an aisle to take pictures of female cosplayers. Maybe they should designate an area off to the side where the cosplayers can pose for the sweaty upper-lip crowd. It doesn't take long to get tired of being bopped with backpacks or poked with prop swords; sometimes you just wish you had a force field because walking the aisles can be incredibly frustrating. Anyway I wouldn't do anything else to change the big shows, people obviously like them as they are. I'd rather start my own show

MM: Okay, finally, I was reading your blog this morning and noticed that you mentioned that you'd recently got round to reading *Doc Savage* and that you were sort of disappointed as the novels weren't as good as *The Spider* (who, admittedly, is a king amongst the pulp hero's) novels and stories, and so I was kind of wondering why you thought *The Spider* was, and is, so much better than *Doc Savage*? I sort of have a soft spot for Doc Savage...

Evan: *The Spider* pulps are batshit crazy and relentless, much like the character himself. Everything is over the top, the plots, the violence, the action set pieces, everything is cranked up to eleven. The pacing is just as amped, the stories often take place within the confines of a day or two and the characters rarely ever sleep or eat, everybody pushes themselves to insane limits to the point where sometimes the stories are almost exhausting to read. Another plus for *The Spider* is that his girlfriend is equally as fanatically driven as he is, she's always involved in the action and the intense, bizarre romance between her and *The Spider* is as engaging as it is nuts. I just find *Doc Savage* dull and uninspired next to *The Spider*.

MM: What's next for you Evan? What are you working on, and what, if anything, can you tell us about your future projects?

Evan: I'm working on a number of comics projects, none of which have been announced yet. Sarah and I are still doing stuff for Bongo, and we just finished up a spot illustration for Mad, we usually work with them a few times a year. We might have some more animation work, but I never believe that until the contract's signed. Otherwise I'm drawing some comics for the next few months and hopefully I'll be able to write some more *Beasts of Burden* stories soon.

MM: If there's anything that you'd like to add, now's the time...

Evan: Why?

Originally published in Mass Movement #31. October 2011

MARK KERMODE

There are very few critics, regardless of the medium they review and critique, whose word I regard as being gold, and whose opinion I regard as being law. Mark Kermode is one of the few. A man who has devoted his professional (and a good chunk of his personal) life to film in all it's facets, Kermode has an uncanny knack of saying the things that every film buff over the age of 35 is thinking, but says it far more eloquently than we, the fans, ever could.

His latest book, *The Good, The Bad And The Multiplex* documents everything that is wrong, and everything that is right (the former outweighs the latter) with the modern film industry and the way it treats those, it's worldwide audiences, who ultimately ensure that it remains rich beyond the dreams of mortal men. On a September afternoon, I caught up with Mark Kermode to talk about his new book, film and cinema...

Interview by Tim Cundle

MM: With the new book, what made you finally want to put pen to paper and talk about what's wrong with the film industry?

MK: What happened was that things happened just at the right time. I'd written a book before – *It's Only a Film* - all about how I loved films and how I grew up with cinema; the fact that everything I knew about the world I had learned from cinema. And we were coming up to the 10th anniversary of doing the Radio 5 show with Simon Mayo; and essentially what happened was that things came together. We started getting an increasing number of emails from people who had been to multiplexes and had a poor experience; whether that be the film being poorly projected, the audience being badly behaved, the staff not looking after the audience properly.

That started to increase quite noticeably, and then we started getting emails from projectionists who were losing their jobs or retiring because everyone felt that with the changeover to digital, we would be able to do away with the projectionists art which I think was a major mistake. At the same time we had a couple of summers where the level of blockbusters was particularly poisonous – I'm thinking of Michael Bay's *Transformers* franchise and the *Sex and the City* movies – films which really, almost seem to flaunt their awfulness. All these things kind of came together including the rise of 3D which very much came in with digital projection. If you know anything about the history of cinema, you'll know that 3D always was and always will be a con. It's something that's used by a studio to essentially combat whatever they consider the current threat to cinema to be; whether that's TV in the '50s, video in the '80s or piracy more recently, 3D has never been led by popular demand, always be studios.

All these things came together and I just found myself getting more and more agitated by the fact that they were just presenting this as the normal state of affairs. If you're a critic people tell you all the time that you are elitist and out of touch and that your views don't reflect those of the "ordinary man on the street", and yet we've all been sold this big massive lie: that cinema is like this – big, stupid, loud and badly projected. Now 3D is the future and there's nothing you can do about it. So it just kind of grew out of that. The first chapter of the book that I wrote was *Why Blockbusters Should be Better*, because if you know anything about blockbuster financing you realise that the whole idea that studios are risking money in the pursuit of art is just not true. And from there it was ".. and another thing.. and another thing.. and another thing.."

MM: Do you think the multiplex really is the death of cinema though?

MK: I don't think that multiplexes are the death of cinema any more than supermarkets are the death of retail grocery. It's just that on their own they are not enough. I think the supermarket analogy works quite well; if you live in a village of a little local shop and a supermarket comes along, well maybe you'll have a great choice because you'll be able to have organically produced, home grown food, support local industry, or maybe if what you want is a six pack and a ready-made meal you'll go up the road to the supermarket. In fact I live in a village where that pretty much is the situation. The trouble is that when the supermarket puts the other place out of business, all you are left with is the supermarket, and all it sells is a six pack and a ready-made microwave meal for one.

It seems to me with multiplex cinemas, is that there's nothing wrong with them per se, it's just that some people only have access to multiplexes, and as long as multiplexes are only showing homogenous pre-packaged fayre, that's going to really have an effect on how cinema looks to you. The other thing is that multiplexes, if they are the only show in town need to get their act together and start behaving like cinemas. And the first way to behave like a cinema is to have a proper projectionist; then to treat the cinema like a cinema and not like somebody's front room, in which talking and texting and bad projection are just the way things are. The amount of time I've spent sitting in the cinema – and I talk a bit about this in the book – I was watching a Zac Ephron film and it's being projected wrongly and the cinema just refusing to do anything about it. Someone asked me if I'd made that story up and I told them that if I'd made it up it wouldn't have been a Zac Ephron movie for a start, would it? It would have been *Citizen Kane*.

MM: I was going to ask you about cinema etiquette because I'm fast approaching 40 and I remember going to the cinema when you would go to see a film. It was a social and communal thing, but you went to see the film. Why do you think cinema etiquette has died?

MK: I think it's died as the direct result of cinemas treating themselves and their customers as if it is nothing more than a front room. I do think these things are interconnected. Once the cinema chains realised you could have 15 screens operated by one guy pressing "on" and then not looking up at the projection of the film; once it became the case that if there was something wrong in the projection or in the auditorium there was no-one there to do anything about it; once there was no-one there to put people in their right seats; no usher to tell you to turn off your mobile phones, no projectionist to make sure that the film is played in the right order, in the right ratio; then people started to think: "Well this is like being in my front room."

It's the same as watching something on a DVD, you press go and watch it". I think cinema etiquette declined as a result of the multiplexes allowing it to happen. Let's not forget that cinema shares it's roots with theatre, and yet, because theatre involves live performance, the idea that you would talk or misbehave in a theatre is just anathema. In fact, as I mention in the blog, if you do it when Richard Griffiths is on stage he'll come of the stage and remonstrate you. But I think unfortunately multiplexes thought that because it didn't involve performance, it's just watching a film, just pressing "on", that it wasn't a theatre any more, it's just a way of showing a film.

And I think that audiences responded to that. If you go to cinemas that look feel and smell like cinemas people don't behave like that, the same way that people act differently when they go into a church because they know it's a different kind of area. Multiplexes kind of brought it on themselves; basically treating the audience as if they were sitting in its own front room.

MM: Now that the rot's set in is there any way to combat it?

MK: Yes there is. The best way to combat it is to support your local art house cinema, visit regularly and give them your business, because when it's gone, you'll miss it. If you have a local multiplex cinema that's doing a good job and projecting the stuff properly then great, but if they aren't then complain.

The whole thing with the Zac Ephron screening thing is that so many people have said to me "Yeah the same thing happened to me, but I never complained because nobody else was". It's like we accept this universal corporate awfulness and that complaining about it is some-how wrong, it's not, it's right. If you're in a cinema – well what I actually say to people is this: when you phone up to book a ticket, ask them how many projectionists and ushers will be looking after that performance, and if the answer to that question is none, ask them where the money is going.

MM: Yeah, because you're paying as much for a cinema ticket as you are for the DVD when the DVD is released. Then you're being asked to pay more for 3D and wear those awful glasses...

MK: You're right, it's a con. It's not the future of cinema, it never was and never will be. That is just the way it is. Unfortunately when the latest 3D revolution happened, anyone with a sense of history knew we'd been here before at least 4 times, it's a four year cycle and we're now in the end throws of it. They've really, really tried hard to ram it down people's throats and even now it's failed again. In the end it was never led by popular demand it was always led by studios pushing it every single time. It's always been the same, audiences don't want it.

MM: I wanted to ask you because you mention *Pirates of the Caribbean* in the book, will it ever be possible to make a successful film franchise out of a theme park ride?

MK: Well, never say never! Who knows what can be done? The history of film is littered with films surprising you, films turning out to be interesting... I'll give you an example: the *Night-mare on Elm Street* franchise. The first film was directed by Wes Craven, the second he wanted nothing to do with, the 3rd he's back, then there's 4, 5, 6 and the character of Freddy becomes more and more depressing and less and less scary. By the time the franchise is fin-ished, even Wes Craven is embarrassed by it. Then, he goes back and makes *Wes Craven's The New Nightmare* you'd think that they had kicked that corpse to death, that there was nothing you could do with it. But he makes *Wes Craven's New Nightmare* which was by far the most interesting film of the year that year and leads directly on to that sort of post-modern *Scream* thing that happens. If you'd asked me before then; if you'd said Wes Craven is going back to the *Nightmare on Elm Street*, I would have said No, surely not. So what I'm saying is that in the end you can't say it'll never happen. What you can say is that the odds are against it.

MM: On the subject of blockbusters, do you think big budgets kill creativity?

MK: I think the idea that once you have a large amount of money you have to be stupid in order to appeal to the largest number of people possible, is fundamentally bogus. What *Inception* proves is that's not true. Being intelligent will not make a blockbuster lose money, just as being stupid won't make a blockbuster lose money. We see plenty of stupid flops and plenty of intelligent successes.

Before *Inception* opened everybody said that it would fail, no-one would understand it, it could never succeed. Then when it opened and it did succeed everyone said "Well of course it's successful, it's because of blah, blah, blah...." *Inception* did well because it's a good film. The point is though that it didn't fail to succeed because it's intelligent. The whole idea that when these movies cost this much money that you have to dumb them down otherwise you run a real financial risk, is just not true. What Nolan demonstrated was that you just make a good film. People say " Ooh you critics are so high brow, you don't know what the average multiplex goer wants." Well on the evidence of *Inception*, what the average multiplex goer wants is something that stops treating them like a fool.

MM: I thought there were strong elements of *Dreamscape* in *Inception*...

MK: *Dreamscape* is basically the blueprint for *Inception* and I do say very clearly in the book that *Inception* is not a new idea. In fact one of the things I like about it, is that it owes a debt to *Dream Warriors* – the third Nightmare on Elm Street film – and *Dreamscape* and seems to be made by someone who's seen quite a lot of trash. I like trash. There's nothing wrong with good honest trash.

MM: Yeah, there's nothing wrong with genre cinema when it's done well...

MK: Exactly. It basically comes down to whether you treat your audience with contempt or respect. If you look at a movie like *Pirates of the Caribbean 3*, the people who made that had nothing but complete contempt for the audience.

MM: You talk in the book about international cinema and how multiplexes don't often show films with subtitles or films from other territories. Do you think that if international films were more widely shown they would naturally find an audience or do you think that an English speaking audience just won't embrace subtitles?

MK: It's an interesting question and my feeling about it is that if people watched more subtitled movies they'd be happier. Not that there's anything inherently brilliant about subtitles, it's just that if you're not watching films with subtitles, you are effectively walking round with such blinkers on, you're missing out on a massive part of what is good about cinema. When people say they love cinema but they don't watch subtitled movies, what they are essentially saying is that they love American cinema – which is fine, loving American cinema is fine.

But every year the things that surprise me – yes there are Hollywood blockbusters, there are great foreign language films, there will be bad foreign language films, but the funny thing about the UK is that there seems to be a reticence about reading subtitles. I think it's because English is so ubiquitous as a language around the world, it's been possible to imagine that other languages are somehow less important. I never understood the problem with subtitles. Every day around the world people watch films with subtitles and it doesn't bother them, so I think the answer to it is that we simply have to get over it. I would say to anybody that if you think you don't like subtitled movies, do me a favour, give it a go. Make a decision to see four subtitled movies this year and at the end of the year see if it has changed your view of international cinema.

MM: The way I came to subtitled and international film was through Cantonese cinema, and martial arts films...

MK: Yes, absolutely. I grew up as a horror journalist, I'm a horror fan. I've written for *Fangoria* and lots of specialist horror publications over the years. One of the things about horror cinema is that it's genuinely international, just like martial arts movies. The fans of these movies want to see them in their original uncut version the way they were intended right? If you ask a horror fan if they've seen such and such Italian film, they would want to see it in the original version right? It's funny that people often sneer at genre cinema, yet the people who watch those movies are far more open to international cinema. I've never heard a horror fan say they've heard a film is really good but they are not going to see it because it has subtitles. In fact quite the opposite is true.

MM: One of the best horror films for me last year was the Korean film "*I Saw the Devil...*"

MK: It's that interesting thing that in that area of cinema which is considered to be so trashy that you get this open-mindedness, that nobody seems to mind the subtitles and it's often the case with genre cinema. They wouldn't dream of saying "I wouldn't watch that it has subtitles" what they might say is "I'm not seeing that it's dubbed"

MM: On the subject of horror, is there one sub-genre of horror that you are particularly drawn to?

MK: I grew up on horror when I was a kid and I used to sneak downstairs and watch old Hammer horrors on TV, then when I was pretty young *The Exorcist* came out. I didn't see it until I was 17, but I remember all the hoo ha when it came out. I think people have a temptation to say things were good when I was a kid but they're not so good now, but that's just not true. *Pan's Labyrinth* was a good example in the horror tradition, people said it was a fantasy film but it was a horror by any other name. Guillermo's work in this area is as good as any in this area I think. I think he's brilliant, he's the new Orson Wells.

In general, any horror fan will tell you there are good films and bad films and the only thing that gets boring is when you see the same thing over and over again. Like recently there has been a real glut of really boring what is known as torture porn movies. If you look back to the seventies and eighties it's the kind of stuff that used to play the drive in circuit; it's always been around, but not only has there been an awful lot of it lately, it has also been a lot more corporate. I did an onstage thing with Kim Newman, and Kim said a very interesting thing. He said "If you watch the old grindhouse movies of the late 1970s, they look like they've been made by rebels – students who actually cared about these things. Those new movies look like they've been made by corporate suits. There is underlying all of those movies the question of whether you think it's been made by someone who really cares about it or whether it's just production line shlock

MM: It's widely known that you consider Friedkin's *Exorcist* to be the best film ever made, but if you had to recommend five horror films what would they be?

MK: It's difficult because it all comes down to personal taste really. The films that meant the most to me – *Don't Look Now* is a personal favourite, and I would include *Pan's Labyrinth* as well; *Eyes without a Face* which is quite beautiful and terrifying, really, really scary, *Audition*, that's a great film... These are all films that work partly because they're so surprising. I think the film I really love is *Dark Water*. I talk about it and the remake of it in the book, where in the end it's really sad rather than scary, it has that underlying tragedy of a lot of horror films.

MM: Going back to the topic of the book – do you think cinema can be saved?

MK: Yes absolutely. It's like a lot of people have said – *Empire* said it was a funny, angry book and I wanted to write back and say "Not angry, just disappointed". I must confess that I'm very nostalgic for things that have gone. I write in the book about the passing of celluloid and of projectionists. But we're in the second century of cinema now and everything is digital. The thing is that we need to demand more. We know 3D is a con, my only worry with the book was that by the time it came out 3D had died. I think people who frequent multiplexes should get used to complaining more. If the film is poorly projected or the auditorium not manned, complain. And if you live near an independent cinema patronise it. See a foreign language film once every few months even if it's not something you think you'll be interested in, because in the end it will pay off. All these things would improve the cinema experience for everyone. They are doing what they are doing now because they think we all want them to be stupid. But we don't.

Originally published in Mass Movement #31, October 2011

Gadgie 32
Star Wars Fanzine

GADGIE 33

NOW THEN GADGIE...
ADVENTURES IN RECORD COLLECTING

We all know that "Record Collectors are pretentious assholes" but be honest, we all like collecting records (or CD's, or stockpiling mp3s on an ipod – the format may change but you are still a music nerd!) don't we? I am as guilty as the next crate digger for getting excited at the prospect of rifling through a box of records in a charity shop, second hand record emporium, car boot sale or record fair and have whiled away many an hour doing so, stretching the patience of my wife and daughter beyond human endurance. An expensive trip to a fashionable boutique dealing in impossibly high heeled shoes and a Pokemon card outlet beforehand usually buys me an extra twenty minutes, but I digress. Unlike when entering say, HMV where you may bag a good zombie movie on DVD or a couple of cheap CD's in the sale, you really never know what you are gonna find when plunging in to the realm of second hand records.

You may find that you are simply wasting your time as piles and piles of marching bands, classical collections, Mario fucking Lanza and dreadful 80's pop and soul make you want to gouge out your eyes. You may find a long lost treasure. You may find a few bargains. You may take a chance and drop a couple of quid on something that looks like a long lost punk classic. It might be. It probably won't, but once the bug has bitten, there's no going back. I was bitten at an earlier age ... the screen, as it always does, goes wobbly ...

We travel back to deep in the eighties ... Dad, as Dads like to do, was ripping out a "built in" stereo cabinet in the living room. What was it about "built in" things in them days? Why did nobody buy furniture? Built in wardrobes, beds, kitchens, cabinets. Everyone then spent the next decade ripping the buggers out, but again ... I digress. Behind this built in cabinet on which sat an aging record player, also being "traded up" for a mini hi-fi, was a small gap in to which many things had fallen over the years. A sort of time capsule cum Room 101, this gap of doom was the place where things that fell would not come back. Until now!

The backing card from my Emperor's Royal Guard *Star Wars* figure was in there, as were a couple of swords and goblets from the Playmobil knights in armour set. Intriguingly though, two dust encrusted cassettes also emerged. Handwriting that looked like our Dad's scrawled across them the words "Dead Kennedys – this tape is kaput" and "Blondie – Parallel Lines". If I had to pinpoint a moment in time when I can honestly say my life changed it was now. Life changing moments are meant to be like a light bulb going ping or a chorus of "Hallalujah!" ringing out. My moment was a little more downbeat. Mam, suggested we might as well "sling'em". "Slinging" something was Mam speak for disposing of anything that would cause clutter or was "out of date". I decided that before any slingage would occur I should investigate and I am so glad I did.

Giving the Dead Kennedys a whirl first, I was appalled. The tape certainly was kaput. Whining vocals, squealing tuneless guitar ... little did I know at the time that the tape was in perfect working order and I had at the age of about 13 being exposed to *Fresh Fruit For Rotting Vegetables* an LP which in later years would become an all-time favourite. The other tape must be better then and Oh. My. Fucking. Word.

A telephone rang, and before I could wonder what on earth was going on the most incredible, delectable and down-right punk fucking rock (before I even knew what punk fucking rock was) woman I had ever heard roared "I'm in the phone booth, it's the one across the hall...." I was besotted. All I had heard was a voice.

I didn't know who it was. I didn't have any idea who Blondie was and indeed what she looked like. Or what they looked like. Where they a band? Was Blondie this woman with the voice of an off the rails angel? I didn't care. This cassette had been rescued from the void and I spent weeks listening to it over and over again. My parents, who I assume at some point, made the tapes, were taped them, or at least listened to them, seemed quite ambivalent to my new love of Blondie and offered very little in the way of further information.

On my a future bus trip to 'Boro to stand and suffer the usual indignities that come with being a Middlesbrough season ticket holder, I had a flash of inspiration and ducked in to HMV to see if they had any more records by this enigmatic new woman in my life. It appeared Blondie were sadly no more and the vinyl and CD racks were bereft of bleached new wave nuggets. Resigning myself to the fact that an ancient tape which someone tape to taped Dad yonks ago was still all I had, I headed for the exit . Then it happened.

The clouds parted. A huge hand reached down. A shaft of light broke through and there on the sale rack by the door for a grand total of 49p was a peculiar looking cassette that caught my eye. It was if the cassette was jumping up out of the rack like a bairn at school who is desperately trying to get teacher's attention as he knows the answer. "Mmmm! Ohhhh! Urghhh! Pick ME!!" The words *Blondie Parallel Lines* shone like a beacon of light in a sea of darkness. The Holy Fucking Grail was calling me! Grabbing the tape I was finally introduced to the woman whose voice had followed me round and burned itself on to my brain. I had done paper rounds with this woman. I had done my homework with her. I had turned the stereo up to eleven and got done off Dad because of her. And now here she was "in the flesh". Sort of.

Despite the diminutive nature of cassette front covers, I had never seen a woman like this before. Exquisitely beautiful. That white dress and high heels combo. Anabsolute goddess but with a snarling don't fuck with me attitude and motley assortment of gadgies behind her. It was all about her though. That cover was the beginning of something that to this day has endured, that has out lived the torture of teen hormones and has lead me to all corners of the record collecting world in search of more and more records with pictures of Debbie Harry on. Of course, pocket money and paper round dosh would only stretch so far and the HMV sale rack had to suffice for a bit. When I started College at Redcar and had half an hour to kill at the bus stop on a Friday night after footy training my love of Blondie morphed in to a love of records. Finding a dingy little, damp smelling record shop behind the bus station where a bloke in a big cowboy hat and long hair sat smoking cigars doesn't sound like someplace the typical teenager would hang out but with the pocket money friendly prices it became my Friday ritual to pick up a bargain.

I had the full set of Blondie LPs, each one added to my record shelf over a six week period as weekly paper round wages were handed over. I had also, as a more typical teenager discovered the joys of U2. Looking back I was embarrassingly earnest and the white flag waving, Amnesty International supporting, heart on sleeve, chest out rockers ticked all the boxes for me. The Friday Record Shop had a huge collection of early U2 singles that now go on eBay for astronomical prices, and as with my newly found punk pin up, on a weekly basis I acquired a burgeoning collection of, now extremely rare and daftly dear, early U2 7"s for peanuts. In my record collecting naiveté however, two of the rarest U2 records in the racks were much sought after promos, and one, a 12" with an otherwise (to this day I think) unavailable 12 minute epic version of one of the Irish troubadours tracks, was a whopping, not-going-to-the-footy-tomorrow-if-I-buy-it nine quid! For one song! The only one I didn't buy now goes for anything up to seventy ruddy quid. Lordy . I remember standing outside Woolworths on the day of release to buy *Achtung Baby* later that year .

Record fairs at Middlesbrough Town Hall Crypt were the next logical progression and as I knew a bloke who worked the door, could be snuck in for free. One time I went with a gang of mates and I also got in to *Alien 3* at the Odeon down the road as I knew a lass who was an usher there . Me and my cousin Richard, who was also a big fan of U2, would spend hours poring over every single record and CD at these fairs and as he had a job our Rich could splash out on expensive bootleg CDs. I, as a pezzy student, had to make do with stretching my limited funds over a carefully selected vinyl haul – usually Blondie and U2. About to leave one day, I spied a bargain box – "All LP's £2". That's gotta be worth a geg hasn't it? Pulling out a Sham 69 LP it looked intriguing and I gave it a go. I'd dallied with punk rock and, along with another mate who had acquired a couple of punk records, had investigated the likes of UK Subs and The Exploited but this was to be my first punk rock record that I had bought. At two quid you can't fall off I thought and it was mine. The next day *Borstal Breakout* was blaring out of my bedroom and me Mam wanders up the stairs.

"What are you listening to?" asked mother with a worried look. "Put U2 on, I like them!"

"This is punk rock Mam, don't you like it?"

"No I bloody don't!"

Of course, this was great and life as I knew it was never the same again...

Marv Gadgie

Originally published in Mass Movement #31, October 2011

KEITH MORRIS
(OFF! / CIRCLE JERKS / BLACK FLAG)

We're sitting in a van (we being myself and Smiler bass player Gave Gates) outside the Thekla in Bristol interviewing Keith Morris. Yes THAT Keith Morris. Original singer with Black Flag and the Circle Jerks and now fronting OFF! One of the most unmistakable voices in music (irrespective of genre) the diminutive Morris speaks with a surprising authority; discussing his career in some of the genres' greatest acts, love of a good steak and dislike of British weather...

Interview by Ian Pickens

Photographs by Dan Monick

MM: First of all Keith welcome back to the UK again, and thanks for taking the time out to speak to us tonight.

KM: Well, when you say 'Welcome back to the UK again', the last time I was here was 1985 and it was just 3 shows. We were with Gang Green, they were our label mates, and it was like a co-headlining bill. Our label over in the States, Roadrunner put us together; it was fun. We did three dates in the UK. We did the Hammersmith Clarendon, which was next to the Hammersmith Odeon. I've heard that it's no longer there...

MM: No, it's gone...

KM: And we played Nottingham and Birmingham.

MM: Was that around the time of V...

KM: Yeah I think so. I don't remember it so well. I do remember not really enjoying myself, the weather was really horrible and we were over here, and on the continent for about two weeks; and in that two weeks we had about 3 hours of sunlight.

MM: That's about right for the UK. I've read that OFF! Was formed almost by accident as a result of an aborted Circle Jerks album which Dimitri (Coats -Guitar) was going to produce?

KM: I've known Dimitri for quite a while because I worked at a record label called V2 and his other band, the Burning Brides, were on the label and they were one of my favourite bands on the roster. It's like on any label, there are going to be bands you don't really like, and there's always a handful of cool bands; and they were one of them. Dimitri and I developed a friendship, because the guy that I worked for was his A & R person who signed them to the label, handled all their business deals, all the tour plans, all the recording plans, this is who you should talk to as a booking agent; you know just giving them advice and then them taking that advice and running with it. I guess I've known Dimitri maybe 8-9 years and he was always one of my favourite characters amongst all the other characters that were in the bands on the roster. We dealt with the White Stripes...

My boss and I were responsible for signing bands like Neon, the Icarus Line – they came over here a couple of times, Burning Brides came over once and that was all on the record company tip. A lot of the times these bands can't make it over on the guarantees – they won't survive; sometimes they won't make enough money to cover their flights. They need someone to give them that bump; give them that kick.

MM: Do you find that the costs for travelling to, and around, Europe are now prohibitive to most independent bands touring?

KM: Its extremely expensive because first off – the flights; if you know you're going over far enough in advance, you can maybe save yourself some money. We waited until the last minute and I think it was fairly expensive. Then if your tour isn't set up properly and you're bouncing around all over the place, that can be extremely expensive.

MM: I'm guessing that's something you have experienced quite a bit over the years touring with Black Flag and Circle Jerks?

KM: Over in the US; yes. Where the booking agent or whoever is putting the tour together throws darts at a map. With Black Flag they would be calling towns for maybe a week before; but Flag was THE band that basically mapped out the touring route that's now standard in the United States and Canada, and there were a batch of bands right at that time that were going along with that, trying to figure out where you could play that was All Ages, because at that time we were playing nightclubs, and you pull up and the only way you can play to the kids is if you play an early show; which meant you were playing two shows per night.

MM: Stephen Blush, mentions that a lot in the book and film *American Hardcore*; are you surprised when you look back at the impact that you, and the bands you have been a part of, have had on people?

KM: Um; Yes; because we're just fans of music, and a lot of time you just play music and you go out and do what you do, without really knowing what you're doing. I've been asked this question before. When we set out we didn't have...there were no guidelines, no list of things that you needed to do to get to where you wanted to be. It was kinda like the blind leading the blind; you just feel your way through and hope for the best. Drink a lot of beer and smoke a lot of pot, do a lot of drugs, try to get laid and have a great time; see where it takes you.

MM: I was going to raise this a little later on but as you've mentioned some of those things; I was wondering if you felt that the lifestyle you were living was a contributing factor in the development of your adult onset diabetes? If you could go back and live your life differently, would you?

KM: I have Type 2 Adult Onset Diabetes, insulin dependent. I've actually just read some reports that claim they are able to reverse diabetes through diet, just eating raw fruit, vegetables; but I don't get to do that, because first off I love meat; gotta have a steak now and then, or a couple of slabs of fish, some poultry, and ...(at this point we are interrupted by a couple of guys who recognise Keith and poke their head in the van)

"Hey man, what time you on..."

KM: I have no idea.

"Fancy coming to see the Dickies later?" (*the Dickies are also played Bristol on the same – which we also managed to catch – what a night - Ian*)

KM: Uh, probably not.

"We're putting them on late so maybe you could come and see them?" (*at this point it becomes clear these guys are promoting the Dickies show - Ian*)

KM: How far are they playing from here?

"About 5 minutes away..."

KM: Okay, but I've only seen the Dickies a few hundred times and played with them a few dozen times...

"Uh yeah, I guess you must know them pretty well... OK maybe see you later. We can take you over if you like? Bye"

KM: Love the Dickies. He's the promoter?

GG: Yeah his names Johnny, he's a good bloke. He's one of the few you'll come across who really looks after the bands.

KM: Getting back to the diabetes, that had absolutely nothing to do with my lifestyle, because at a point my lifestyle changed; the drinking and the partying – I stopped doing that about 23 years ago. I don't miss any of it. I watched a couple of women smoke over here earlier today and I was like thinking to myself 'You know what, I'd really like to smoke a cigarette', and then I started
salivating, started to taste the cigarette in my mouth, the tobacco and then realised I don't wanna smoke that stuff, that's nasty, that's just hideous shit. They can have it. But the lifestyle didn't run into the diabetes; the diabetes came along much later.

MM: Do you find that the diabetes affects you more when you're on tour? Where a good diet is difficult to maintain...

KM: One of the things I try to do is just eat when I'm hungry; plus I do the insulin in the morning and I do enough so that I can do two meals on it, and have a 4-5 hour window, so if I don't have something healthy to eat. I'll eat a candy bar or have some fruit juice...

MM: From OFF!'s videos it's still apparent you have an immense amount of energy and a passion for playing this style of music. When you were putting this band together did you just naturally gravitate to this style?

KM: This would be getting back to when we were writing the music, writing the songs. We were working on another project. The guys in the other project, the guys that were involved with the other project became un-involved in the project, and at one point Dimitri and I were in my living room and I said "Dimitri we'd better be prepared; these songs that we're writing, we're not gonna let them go to waste. There's not going to be any sort of coup, any sort of

skulduggery, we're gonna come up with a Plan B and if, and when, the time presents itself we move with it; and the time reared its ugly head. At the time it was, I wanna say spiteful and hurtful things towards the other people involved, but I'm here doing this, and having a great time, and I can blame it on them; at the same time I ought to thank them for allowing me to have this opportunity. I'm having a blast. I'm playing with really great musicians. We're having the time of our lives and we're older guys; maybe it should be easier; maybe this should be a bus instead of a van but hey it is what it is, and we're presented with this opportunity, it would be ridiculous not to take advantage of it.

MM: You still enjoy touring...

KM: Yes. Getting back to the vibe of what we were doing on the original project; you were dealing with a bunch of guys, of a certain age, who have a set mentality, and it's gonna be like 'this', and there'll be power trips and power plays, the struggle as to who says 'this is how it will be'... the prevailing mentality was we could just get away with doing whatever we feel like doing because of who we are... and established, we have our fan base, and all I could say to that was 'Your heads couldn't be further up your assholes". That's a really complacent attitude. We needed to get back to a time and a place where it was fun, where it was almost like a train coming off the rails and (sirens wail in the background)... that's a nice sound. Sounds like getting your teeth drilled when you go to the dentist. Just that vibe... that energy... that mentality. Not this "the bass has to be placed here" and "in this process we need to add this to it" and "when we do the next process we need to take this away". It just became very...

MM: Contrived?

KM: Yes, very contrived. Very 'we're in the studio and we can do whatever we like'. We weren't gonna bash it out. We were just gonna go in and play the songs in the studio and overdub the guitars and "The bass isn't right so we're gonna redo the bass", "We'll add some cymbals", "We'll add some compression and reverb here'. One 'process' after another and it just loses what it's supposed to be in the first place.

MM: Do you feel that retrospectively that feeling had started with albums like _Wonderful_ and _V_ which had a more hard rock vibe to them?

KM: We were doing the metal/crossover thing which I though was kinda lazy, I just felt like I was kinda going along with the program. It was just kinda (imitates a droning one chord riff) which there's nothing wrong with, but for bands like us it just didn't work. It was a hoot and we found some hilarity in it, found some sarcasm in it. But it was just really lazy. A couple of us had grown really lazy and I will raise my hand and I be the first to step to the front of the line and admit I was messed up, doing so much cocaine and drugs that I didn't care; that's the wrong attitude and the other guy who's supposed to be stepping up and saying "Hey, what are we doing? Why are we doing this?" was just showing up to collect a pay check.

MM: You sound pretty bitter with how it had become. So does this mean that the Circle Jerks are no more, or just still on hiatus?

KM: It's a very, very, very long hiatus. It all depends on the weather; which way the wind is blowing on that particular day. I'm not closing the door on the Circle Jerks but there's no reason for me to even think about the Circle Jerks, or consider the Circle Jerks with what I'm doing right now. We just played at the Rebellion Fest. Rebellion had been asking the Circle Jerks to play for about the last 6 or 7 years and we couldn't even get it together to say yeah. We couldn't get it together enough to say to our booking agent 'who do you work with over in Europe; that could get us on a tour over to Europe; who could make this happen?' We didn't even have it together enough to ask that question.

MM: How did you find Rebellion? It's come in for a lot of criticism for just being a punk nostalgia event...

KM: Well you have to take into consideration that I've never really toured England, I mean, back in '85 – 3 dates, that's not really... how can you call that a tour of England? You can't; that's just - fly your ass in, play and then get on a ferry to Holland. So I'm whole heartedly enjoying all of this. Yeah it looked like a very nostalgic type of scenario but at the same time there were new bands that were playing. They gotta keep it fresh so they gotta pull in some of these newer bands; maybe pull in some bands that are not part of the punk rock genre, maybe that have that same kind of energy as the hardcore bands... I could rattle off a whole load of bands. I know Fucked Up played there, that's a step in the right direction. I mean how many times can GBH play there? The Exploited? Discharge? Cockney Rejects? Cocksparrer? UK Subs? I love all of those bands; they're part of our upbringing; some of the bands we rubbed elbows with so it's not a diss on any of those bands; but they need to infuse something new in there.

MM: Some new blood...

KM: Some new blood and let them mix it up on the major stage.

MM: On the subject of nostalgia and reunions; a Black Flag reunion has been touted now for many years; do you think it will ever happen?

KM: It's not gonna happen. It won't happen. They did two shows in LA, at the Hollywood Palladium and it was nothing like it was supposed to be.

MM: Raymond Pettibon who did a lot of the artwork for Black Flag and other SST bands has created a piece of work especially for OFF! How did that come about? I understand he was pretty disenchanted about working with bands after his experiences with SST?

KM: Raymond is one of my very close friends and we lost track of each other because what happened was, over the years, like we talked about this earlier when Flag was out mapping the tour circuit for bands in the US; we'd get in the van and we'd be gone for 3 or 4 months at a time. We would come back, we'd be back two weeks, we could be back two months, then we would go back out and do it all over again, hitting every little town that had a place that would allow our band to play, and in that process, I guess like the Process of Weeding Out, we'd be gone and everyone else was just left at home waiting for the band to come back and strike it all up all over again; and over the years this gap emerged and eventually I felt like, I need to go back and see my friend Raymond. So we struck up our friendship and we talked about a couple of things... He said something that completely blew me away because we're at his place and there's these pieces of art all over the place, on the walls, on the tables. He said "Keith, I know how my brother treated you. I know what he did. I know what he's done to a lot of the people he should have been straight forward and upstanding with. If you ever get into any kind of trouble, you can just come in here and take anything you wanna take out of here", and that's like beyond... beyond friendship. With the SST bands, and Flag, Raymond would do this artwork and then the bands would take it and change it.

MM: He felt they compromised his artwork?

KM: Yes definitely. You don't take a piece of art and then without asking the artist start gluing things or adding things to it.

MM: I know this is an old 'classic' but do you feel that punk and hardcore are still relevant or is it just a stale social club?

KM: It's just a form of music and just like your parents before you and their parents before them and their parents before them and all the way back, we've always railed against some authority figure. If it's not the government and it's not the police and it's not the mayor or the city council, then it's your aunts or your uncles, your grandparents and your parents, and that's always going to happen; so to me punk and hardcore, softcore, inbetweencore, metalcore, foxcore, grindcore, treecore, indiecore, whatever – it's all a form of "I don't wanna be like you" and that's the bottom line. It will always be relevant to the people that make it. That's kind of a very simplistic statement but it's the truth. (At this point the tour manager pops his head in and gives us the times up sign)

MM: Just one last question; what's next?

KM: We're gonna write a new album. We're gonna tour Australia. Play a few Festivals. We've been offered a mini tour with Dinosaur Jr. I believe some dates with the Melvins...

Originally published in Mass Movement #31, October 2011

FROM THE PRODUCERS OF
DAWN OF THE DEAD

THE THING

MANKIND'S GREATEST DISCOVERY COULD BE ITS LAST.

BINNENKORT IN DE BIOSCOOP

436

SCREEN DAMAGE

WEIRD AND PISSED OFF: THE RETURN OF THE THING

In late 2011, man is the warmest place to hide once more as the prequel to John Carpenter's *The Thing* is unleashed upon the world.

Given that the much-loved 1982 original is highly regarded as being a classic of the genre, the knives have been sharpening for some time in readiness for this one. Some fans have openly cursed newbie director Matthijs van Heijningen Jr for daring to encroach on such hallowed ground, dismissing him as somebody who got the gig because of his producer daddy.

I don't really understand this kind of thinking. True, the recent onslaught of remakes, sequels and re-imaginings of some of our favourite cult horror films has had more misses (*Black Christmas, When A Stranger Calls, Friday the 13th, The Fog*) than hits (*Fright Night, The Hills Have Eyes, My Bloody Valentine 3D, Dawn of the Dead*), but it's not like the originals suddenly cease to exist.

Maybe it's because such fans are sick of seeing remakes, but if that's the case, they are forgetting that Carpenter's film was itself a remake of the 1951 Christian Nyby/ Howard Hawks production of *The Thing From Another World*, and that back in the early '80s, the announcement that he was to stage a new version of this old favourite also drew howls of protest in some quarters - not that it should have come as a particular surprise. Carpenter is a proud admirer of Hawks, and even had clips from the 1951 version playing in the background of *Halloween*. As the director himself told the Chicago Sun Times in 1981: "I saw (*The Thing From Another World*) when I was six years old in Bowling Green, Kentucky. I saw it again when I was studying film at USC, several times, in fact. There's a lot of Howard Hawks in it, and Hawks is my favourite director".

It's easy to forget just how vilified Carpenter was for delivering *The Thing* - critics hated it, and audiences stayed away in droves. The film was released in an age of upwardly-mobile greed and opportunity, just a few short weeks after the worldwide success of *ET: The Extra Terrestrial*. In such a climate, people couldn't get enough of sweet, friendly aliens, and a shape-shifting menace which violated your body and stole your mind, especially one that arrived packaged within such a cynical, suspicious and subversive thriller, was quickly given the cold shoulder.

Carpenter's films are infamous for being ahead of their time, and titles that were considered a disappointment on release – such as *They Live* or *Prince of Darkness* - are often re-evaluated and praised some years down the line. But looking at *The Thing* now, its most amazing aspect is that it was ever made in the first place.

Think about it: there are no female parts in the film whatsoever (aside from an uncredited Adrienne Barbeau, who supplied the voice of the Chessmaster computer in the early scenes). The only onscreen sex we see is a twisted, alien version of the act (perhaps making it the beast with many, many backs?). The film is stocked with character actors, the majority of whom would never figure on anyone's list of Hollywood hunks. The heavy Arctic clothing makes it difficult to keep track of who is who.

Kurt Russell as the film's nominal hero, MacReady, does not play him in a particularly heroic fashion – in fact the aggressive, churlish character is barely likeable. The ending is downbeat and open to audience interpretation, and the first big special effects set piece commits what is possibly the most unforgivable crime in American movie-making: it shows us dogs being killed, and splits man's best friend wide open to reveal that he is really an evil, malevolent, slimy monster. Compare this with how the dog in the alien invasion flick *Independence Day* would fare just 14 years later – not only did the mutt survive an apocalyptic fire cloud, it even got its own heroic slow-motion leap to safety against the backdrop of the inferno.

Set against the upbeat, everything's-gonna-be-all-right optimism of most of Hollywood's nineteen eighties output, *The Thing* was a relic more in tune with the downbeat cinema of the seventies.

"More disgusting than frightening... most of it is just boring," said New York magazine. "Instant junk," moaned the New York Times. "A mindlessly macho monster mash," stated The Time Out Film Guide (you just know the author was proud of that one). But The Scotsman went one better and came up with my favourite line of criticism concerning *The Thing*: "The only avenue left to explore would seem to be either concentration camp documentaries or the snuff movie."

Carpenter himself had sensed that the timing was wrong just before the film was premiered in LA (complete with a 'best dressed Thing' competition hosted by Elvira, Mistress of the Dark). He suggested to the studio that the film should be held back until (heh!) Halloween, and also retitled *Who Goes There?* in line with the original 1938 novella by John W. Campbell. Carpenter went further in that he begged the studio heads not to advertise it as 'The ultimate in alien terror', fearing that this obvious cash-in on the Ridley Scott film from just a few years before was going to backfire with the critics (it did – more than one lazy reviewer complained that the film was basically an empty re-tread of *Alien*). But the studio ignored him on all counts – the $15m movie took in just over $3m in its opening weekend across 840 screens, and finished off the year by grossing just under $20m. It wasn't a total financial washout as many have since claimed, but it killed Carpenter's studio career stone dead.

In a move that has since been re-appraised, most critics complained that his film lacked characterisation or suspense, and tried to patch its many plot holes by distracting viewers with stomach churning scenes of increasingly gory special effects. But this was a time when film criticism was not a young person's profession, and sci-fi or horror films were seen as something of an embarrassment, guilty pleasures which could not be praised without also being denigrated for belonging to the genre.

It seems obvious with hindsight, but what these critics couldn't see at the time was that Carpenter had delivered a modern masterpiece that refused to play by the rules and which fully embraced the new age of special effects wizardry that had been ushered in by the likes of *2001: A Space Odyssey* and *Star Wars*. As for not establishing suspense, I've long maintained that you could remove all of the shocking gore scenes in *The Thing*, and still have a first-rate thriller about paranoia, trust, isolation, sacrifice and the loss of identity.

More than that, the film is a master class in cinematic tension, character deconstruction and screenwriting. For example, it defies cinematic logic by opening half-way through a chase scene, and disregards dialogue in place of showcasing a sprawling, epic, sterile vista that tells you everything you need to know about the isolated setting, and man's place in this frozen wilderness. Conventional wisdom would demand that we see the flying saucer crash land in the prehistoric ice, followed by the Norwegian's discovery of the alien occupant and its subsequent destruction of their camp. But no – Bill Lancaster's incredibly fat-free script carves its own rules for how the action should unfold. Even when he asks you to swallow some hokey leaps in logic ("Thousands of years ago this spaceship crashes, and this thing, whatever it is, gets thrown out, or crawls out, and it ends up freezing in the ice."), he hides it in plain sight by following through with the unflinching scepticism of the other characters ("I just cannot believe any of this voodoo bullshit!").

It's true to say that *The Thing* really found its audience on video. The medium was still in its infancy at the time, and the number of available titles from the big-budget Hollywood studios was relatively limited. Such a high-quality sci-fi gorefest found willing viewers among the teenagers to whom home rental was a heaven-sent gift. Like me, many had been too young to see it play at the cinema during its original theatrical run, and although I have since managed to catch it on the big screen twice, I can still vividly recall how badly I longed to see it after my elder brother came back with a scene-by-scene breakdown. I had to wait until it played on ITV in the mid-eighties before I could get my chance, but even the woeful limitations of the panned-and-scanned format couldn't spoil its many charms.

Of course, principal among these dubious delights is the alien itself. Writing in the New York Times, Vincent Canby complained that "One of the film's major problems is that the creature has no identifiable shape of its own." But this very fact is why so many young viewers fell in love with Rob Bottin's amazing monster SFX. Carpenter himself told critic Anne Billson in 1996 that "In terms of just pure imagination, I don't think I've ever seen anything equal to The Thing." Bottin himself has described how he devoted so much of his life to the film – even going as far as sleeping rough in the studio-owned Hartland Effects workshop in north Hollywood – that he ended up entering hospital suffering from exhaustion. And yet it could have all been so different. Bottin was not Carpenter's first choice of effects man for the film, and in fact he replaced Dale Kuipers, who had been forced to bow out due to ill health. Kuipers' own take on the look of the Thing was that it would have a single, lizard-like form, but would possess the ability to change its shape by inducing hallucinations in the minds of the humans it encountered. When Bottin came on board, he praised the design but described it as looking like 'a big bug', and lobbied Carpenter to let him go with something different. He eventually ended up leading a team of 40 illustrators, designers, sculptors, painters and mechanical effects technicians, and his effects budget stretched from $750,000 to $1.5m. As a comic book fan, he also had the pleasure of working alongside Marvel legend Mike Ploog.

The first big special effects scene, though, belongs to the late, great Stan Winston – he and his team were called in to handle the dog transformation in order to allow Bottin more time to concentrate on the film's other set pieces, like the never-been-topped moment where medic Copper tries to revive Norris with a defibrillator, and plunges his hands and forearms into the man's gaping chest, now transformed into the razor-toothed maw of the Thing.

Layering shock upon shock, Bottin then goes one better by having Norris' head detach itself and grow a set of spider legs and eye stalks. It's a moment of pure cinema – one which was partly achieved by having a genuine double amputee don a 'Copper' mask with prosthetics attached to the ends of his severed limbs, a calculated move on the part of Carpenter who rightly reasoned that the audience would be too shocked to notice the switch.

Considering how gruesome it is, the scene avoids splashy red blood in favour of vivid yellows and greens – a deliberate effort to make the images more fantastic than horrific. As Bottin said to Cinefantastique magazine, "That's not gross – it's fun!."

But to my mind, the classic scene in this classic film has to be the one where MacReady ties up the rest of the cast and forces them to undergo a blood test. Carpenter's set-up is masterful and assured, and the tension is superb. We just know that at least one of the men is not what they seem to be, but Carpenter and Lancaster have taken pains to misdirect our suspicions in different directions, so when MacReady plunges the hot needle down into the petri dish of infected blood and the alien fluid reacts by leaping into the air, the inhuman shriek that accompanies the move is quite possibly intermingled with our own surprise.

If the film has a disappointing moment, it arrives with the final confrontation between MacReady and the Thing deep in the bowels of the research station. Originally, the Blair-Thing was going to grab the explosive plunger with a thick tentacle, then burst out of the frozen floor and rear up high into the air. Deleted footage shows the creature contemplating MacReady as its chest erupts and a huge snake-like appendage bursts out with a snarling, dog-like visage at its head. The tentacle would then go after MacReady, who throws his last stick of dynamite at the beast and signs off with '"Fuck you too!" Unfortunately, Carpenter was not happy with the stop-animation executed by Randall Cook for the scene, and he trimmed it back to the bare minimum. I've always thought that the tense confrontation ended rather suddenly as a result, but it leads directly into one of the ballsiest, most epic endings in any film of the last three decades.

The climax – in which we are left to ponder if the two survivors, both dying from exposure, are entirely human – was certainly a scene of contention when the film was screened to test audiences. Speaking to The Prince of Darkness author Gilles Boulenger, Carpenter described how he attended one such showing and interjected when a girl complained that the film didn't deliver a straight answer at the end. "That's the whole point," he told her. "You have to use your imagination." To which the girl replied: "Oh God, I hate that." At that point, Carpenter claims that he realised that the film was "doomed"

*"Nobody wanted to hire me for a job after that because of the reputation of **The Thing**. Not only was it a box office failure in their eyes, but it was also an artistic failure. I was treated like slime. I was just good to lie down with the dogs. I was the guy who was doing this kind of pornographic violence... I can't think of a way it didn't change my career."*

Ironically, in 1981 Carpenter had already told the New York Times that *"The basic reality of working in a big studio is that the work is extremely expensive and extremely complex and you must produce a movie that makes money... But every big star, every director, has failed at doing that, and I'm going to fail miserably sometime."*

And yet the power of the film was enough to affect a handful of critics, even if they couldn't quite put their finger on the reasons why. For example, while simultaneously dismissing the film as being ' forever a footnote in history', Ted Mahar also wrote in The Sunday Oregonian in 1983 that "Somehow, The Thing stays on my mind... Carpenter didn't so much remake The Thing From Another World as he did film the original story for the first time."

Time has, of course, proven Carpenter to be right. His version of The Thing regularly appears in the top ten lists of modern film critics, and a brand new digital pint of the film was struck in 2009 for a limited big screen re-release. Sequels have been produced through the medium of both comics and a bestselling computer game. The director has also stated that he has his own idea for a sequel, but that he largely abandoned all hopes of ever seeing it come to fruition after an abortive meeting with studio executives in which he was asked if he could think of ways of getting teenagers over to the Antarctic.

Now the prequel has arrived, and in a strange case of history repeating itself, the film appears to be dividing fans straight down the middle. The trailer looks promising, although many have bemoaned the film's reliance on the use of CGI and the complete absence of Rob Bottin from the project. In a sign of the times, the script appears to have shoehorned not only a female character into the action, but also people from different ethnic backgrounds, too. Whether this works or comes across as a move required by the studio remains to be seen, but I'll be keeping an open mind when I finally get to see it - I'm just hoping that the auditorium won't be filled with cries of "How much more of this bullshit is there?", "I know how this one ends" and – of course – "You gotta be fuckin' kidding!"

In the meantime, why don't we just sit here a while, and... see what happens?

Liam Ronan

Originally published in Mass Movment #31, October 2011

SEAWEED

Seaweed. The band's name still send shivers of pleasure up and down my spine. Their music was, and is, incredible. Energetic, tuneful, insightful with melodies and choruses that stay stuck in the front of your brain long after the records have finished, and live...? Well, these guys were something else, and from the night I was lucky enough to catch them until this very day, I've always maintained that they were, and are, one of the five best live bands I've seen in more than a quarter century of going to shows. At the tail end of the nineties, the band seemed to disappear, but fear not kids, as now they're back with a brand new seven inch on No Idea, and hopefully, sometime in the not too distant future, there'll be a brand new album as well. The incredibly cool and patient Wade Neal was kind enough to provide the following answers...

Interview by Tim Cundle

MM: I guess we should start with the bands return... I know that you guys have been back for a while (since 2007), so to bring us up to speed - What originally caused the band to break up, and what precipitated your return? What, if any, factors influenced your decision to reform, and why did you decide that the time was right to put the band back together?

Wade: Well, we always said that we did not really "break up" because we didn't have any bad feelings between the band members around 1999, when we sort of stopped playing and recording together. In 1999, a lot of us were doing some different things like moving to other parts of the country, starting school, jobs, etc. Got to pay the bills! After a few years, enough people expressed interest in a kick-start of the band, so we decided, "Why not?"

MM: Okay, I want to go back to the early days of the band....When, where, how and why did Seaweed originally get together? Did you know from the very first practice how you wanted the band to sound, or did the bands identity and sound develop over time?

Wade: I was just talking about this with an old friend of mine the other night. As you may or may not know, Tacoma had a very vibrant punk scene, which really came to a crescendo in 1988-89. We had a lot of touring bands coming through, largely because Seattle's main punk/alternative venue Gorilla Gardens had been shut down and there had been a couple of small "riots" with the cops - so it was hard to get shows up there. We had amazing bands like Dag Nasty, Fugazi, Firehose, Circle Jerks, Butthole Surfers, No Means No, Dr. Know, Flipper, Scream, 7 Seconds, Bad Brains, Redd Kross, The Doughboys, all come through a town might normally have been skipped on the way to or from Portland! As 16-17-18 year olds, we were all drawn to music, so ended up going to these shows, most of them at the Community World Theatre - now a dive tavern I believe.

 Not only did national bands come through, but the local music was insanely good. I mean, it's legend now, but we could not believe that a bands as good as the Melvins, Green River, Nirvana, etc., were actually from around here. Plus, we had a bunch of awesome Hardcore bands that were pretty different from the punkish/ /metallish/Stoogesish/Sabbathish resurgence that was associated with Sub Pop, C/Z and other labels: SubVert, Silent Treatment, False Liberty, Coffin Break, AMQA, The Dehumanizers. There were also great and very interesting bands from Olympia – Beat Happening, Danger Mouse, Nisqually Delta Podunk Nightmare. Defying all classification were our heroes, Girl Trouble. We liked 'em all!

Tacoma was the birthplace of the Wailers, Sonics, Ventures, etc., so there was some major music history going on way before we were coming up, so we always thought that if you were from Tacoma, you should probably be in a band. Seattle and Tacoma were still pretty out of the way cities at that time - it felt a lot more like lumber and fish ruled the area rather than coffee and software - that came later. I was in a band when I was 17 called Cat's Cradle with Simon Smith - he sang for Silent Treatment, who were awesome.

In my mind, Simon was a very cool, charismatic lead singer - I thought this was going to be a good band. A few weeks later he abruptly dissolved the band, but told us we would now be in a straightedge band called Inner Strength, whose singer and guitar player were looking for other musicians. The singer was Greg Anderson, now of Southern Lord, Sunn and Goatsnake. We played one show opening for No Means No, but the band didn't really work out because the band was only 2/5 straightedge, but the music was great though. Simon then introduced me to Aaron Stauffer and Clint Werner - we had common band interests, hit it off right away, and started playing together.

Aaron had been in a cool band called Cactus Love - Clint was his old friend who was really, really into playing guitar and recording, and also loved classic rock as well as range punk and metal - he had a very broad range of musical tastes. I did too – I recall owning a Devo and Iron Maiden homemade tape when I was about 13 not really knowing or caring that some might think of them as opposed to one another. The three of us auditioned a few drummers and bass players, who were all good musicians, nice and lovely people - just not right for what we were trying to do; whatever that was. I think our goal was to be like a DC band like Dag Nasty and then mix in some heavier elements a la the Melvins - I don't think we got there, and woe to me to compare us to those bands, but that's what we were going for, consciously or no. We knew Bob (drums) and John (bass) from another band called Alphabet Swill, who were sort of a country punk band with really funny lyrics. They had opened for the Circle Jerks, so to us they were a "real" band. They had broken up so we asked if they wanted to play music - they said okay. That's how the band was formed between 1989- 1990

MM: With a lot of bands, when you listen to their music, you can often identify influences as they tend to manifest themselves, musically and lyrically, in the overall sound, but with you guys it's a near impossible task, as your music, and thus sound is so unique - So, I was wondering, what influences you and how you thing, if at all, your influences appear in your music? Have your influences changed over time, or have they remained constant? How have they changed, and / or why do you think they've stayed the same?

Wade: Hmmm, that can be good and bad, right? I think we definitely took the DC, Dischord stuff like Minor Threat, Dag Nasty, Rites of Spring, and mixed a bit of Black Flag/ Agent Orange LA punk in. We drew from a local history of great garage bands like the Sonics, Wailers, etc., so we maybe were a bit looser sounding than some "Hardcore" bands. We also loved the stuff coming out on SST - Dinosaur, Sonic Youth...Maybe that shows up here and there, I know we lifted an ending from Dinosaur for sure. We also really were influenced by the bands a few years older than us - Nirvana, Screaming Trees, Mudhoney, Soundgarden - they were good.

MM: When the band first started appearing in the music press (at least in the UK), you'd just signed to Sub Pop, and as such were widely, and rightly or wrongly, regarded as being part of the whole Seattle 'Grunge' movement, and I was wondering how you originally felt about being tagged and pigeonholed as part of that scene, and how you feel about it now? Do you think being regarded as part of that scene helped or hindered the band? Why?

Wade: Well, at the time, we were really trying to carve out our own niche so we may have bristled a bit at being called grunge, maybe because we grew up in the scene and saw that there was actually a lot of variety between the bands. Tagging it with "grunge" seemed simplistic at the time. We also didn't want to get lost in the "grunge" tide, and thought we should differentiate ourselves. Looking back on it, who cares what you get called? Plus, we were on Sub Pop, so I wonder why we were associated with Grunge with a capital G. Another aspect of it was the press made clear it was very trendy to be Grunge. We thought of ourselves as anti-mainstream and independent so having the jocks and local newscasters start talking about your music like they liked it the whole time annoyed us. It definitely helped us - thanks to Nirvana, etc., every label was hanging around the Pacific Northwest and spending money!

MM: Being part of the whole Sub Pop scene, different people always regarded you guys differently – one person would label you a grunge band, one a punk band (the genre I always thought you were closest to,), other thought of you as a power pop band and others as an indie band with a new wave sensibility – so, I was wondering how you guys always saw yourself as a band and why you thought or identified Seaweed as being part of that particular genre, and whether the way you've always envisioned the band has changed over time? If so, how has it changed and why?

Wade: I mostly just think of us as a hard rock band with elements of punk and metal. I guess I don't think we are that much different from other bands...we just try to do something that sounds cool to us.

MM: I saw you guys when you played TJ's back in the mid-nineties (Newport, South Wales, UK) with a band called Bivouac (I think), and you were down as main support, and you absolutely destroyed them, and like many others, I've always regarded Seaweed as being one of the best live bands I've seen in nearly twenty five years...So, my question is, how did you originally develop your fearsome live reputation, and do you, personally, regard Seaweed as more of live band or a studio band? Why?

Wade: First, my brothers in Bivouac will always be close to my heart, and I love them. Second - glad you liked the show, wow, that is a nice compliment, thank you. I don't know about being that good, but thanks. We just felt really energized by being on stage and just got into it. I blame the Doughboys for teaching us how to jump around so much.

MM: You also toured relentlessly, and I wondered what touring so much taught (if anything) you about being in a band, what it taught (if anything) you about the music industry as a whole and also what it taught you or what you learnt, about yourselves as individuals and the world as a whole? What, and why, were, and are your favourite, and worst, touring experiences in Seaweed?

Wade: Touring is the heart and soul of music - if you don't tour, or play a lot of shows, you can never get the band to really come together. So, here is what touring taught me and probably us, stream of consciousness:

1. A/C is very important.

2. You can only listen to Steve Miller so many times.

3. Avebury is actually a lot cooler than Stonehenge.

4. Electronic tuners are the most important band accessory.

5. If you ask for a vegetarian rider, you usually get spaghetti or something like broccoli and French Fries.

6. Cliff jumping can be scary for some people.

7. Getting up at 7:30 in a Motel 6 after getting back from the show at 3am to drive to the next show that is 400 miles away - Not good!

8. Floor punks rule.

9. People who allow bands to stay over should never leave plates of food on the floor where they are sleeping, is that too much to ask?

10. Europeans like music more than Americans, in general.

11. The Alps really are amazing.

12. If your fuse goes out, use a cigarette wrapper as a temporary fix.

Favourite tour: this is a hard question to answer - I really look back on all the good and bad times touring fondly. My favourite tour may have been the Bivouac tour of the states - it's hard to explain why, but we had some good old times on that one. Or the first one in 1990 with Superchunk and Geek. We were in a pickup truck! It was just pure adventure.

MM: Which Seaweed album, in your opinion, best represents the band as a whole, or as a musical entity? Why?

Wade: Probably *Spanaway* - we worked hardest on that one. *Four* was more straight ahead, and I love it, but *Spanaway* has some great overdubs and crazy sounds from small amps that I really like.

MM: Talking about records, how did the new seven inch come about? How did you come to hook up with No Idea for the seven inch? Is there a new album on the way, and if so, anything you can tell us about it? There was a rumour a while back about an album called *Small Engine Repair*...?

Wade: We have been SLOWLY working on new material for an album, and that's what came out. Var at No Idea booked our first Florida show way back when at the Covered Dish in Gainesville - we had great shows there and became buds. They flew us out to the Fest in 2007 and thought, let's give them a single if it comes to that. Var asked, and we said okay. Simple as that. *Small Engine Repair* is a working title I came up with while driving down a street in Tacoma. Not sure if we will get an album under that name or if we will keep it...

MM: Given that the music industry as a whole nearly completely changed with the advent of the internet and the digital revolution, during the seven year period whilst Seaweed were dormant, do you think that the way it's changed is positive or negative, and should be embraced or rejected? Why?

Wade: Old man speech coming up! Well, there are a lot of great things about easy access to music. With some of these services, you can pretty much listen to anything for free, albeit at a lower quality stream. When I was a kid, I had a sci-fi fantasy "what if someday there was like, a music cube, that could hold like 50 albums!!! Whoa, that would be amazing..." Now we got that x 1000, it's crazy, and you can't help but think that that kind of access is really cool. However, I have seen the money for smaller indie bands dwindle to basically nothing, where when we were coming up if you sold 10,000- 20,000 records, which was actually possible for a lot of bands, you could almost make a minimum wage living and even more if you toured a lot.

I am also a vintage / hi-fi audio enthusiast and am disappointed that people seem to be satisfied with lower quality reproduction. Computer speakers and earbuds satisfy most people, and they generally sound bad. It's like watching movies on a phone, which is also problematic for artists. Also, most streams or files sound awful to me - the bass and mids are all mushed up and the vocals are all garbled sometimes! Kids are growing up not hearing the difference between a good CD or LP and an overly compressed file . It's too bad.

The old man part of me wants to cancel the Internet and only buy vinyl and move to a city with no billboards. The other part of me wants to embrace the new technology - I would really, really like it if artists got a fair cut, but it seems like the income is going to the streaming services through advertising and to the labels, where it is mangled in accounting trickery. The deals are confidential in a lot of cases, so we have no idea how the money is being split up at that level. To be fair to the record labels, they now have way less revenue, so are less willing to take chances on new or different artists. I believe the decrease in revenue probably should be solved by some kind of tax on Internet services that would create a large royalty pool to be split up among artists It does seem to me that the digital "revolution" has weakened some artists' dedication to keep going. I think money really is a motivator for artists and musicians, and it has become harder for them to get paid, even minimally. In addition, there are so many artists out there now, thanks to cheap recording, that it's easy to be overwhelmed by the sheer number of choices in music, which is also good and bad, for obvious reasons. It is amazing to look up an artist and have their discography in front of you in seconds, but I always feel guilty - "They are not getting very much in royalties for this stream!"

MM: How, if at all, do you think that the Seaweed of the twenty first century differs from the Seaweed of the nineties? If the band is different, how do you feel about the differences and what kind of impact do you think they have on the band?

Wade: I don't think we are really that different. We are the same people, maybe a bit mellower, and the music tends to stay pretty much on track. We're like AC/DC - no acoustic sets!

MM: What's next for Seaweed?

Wade: Hopefully an album and visits to a few other countries!

MM: If there's anything that you'd like to add...

Wade: Thank you very much for asking us to be included in your magazine!

Originally published in Mass Movement #31, October 2011

CRONOS
(VENOM)

After listening to, and being a, Venom fan for twenty five years, I finally managed to fulfil a long held ambition. I got to speak to Cronos, and finally Venom are in Mass Movement. With an incredible new album (seriously, it's a classic return to form for the band), *Fallen Angels* about to be released to the slavering hordes, Cronos called on the Hotline from Hades to chat about everything Venom...

Interview by Tim Cundle

Photograph by Doralba Picerno

MM: The title of the new record *Fallen Angel* does it refer to the original inhabitants of hell or does it have a different meaning entirely?

Cronos: No it's basically saying Lucifer and the angels they were not kicked out of heaven, they decided to leave because God was a petulant child and the real fucking evil. We are the children of the fallen angels, we are the people who stand up for ourselves, do what we want, believe in what we want and are strong willed, powerful. It's part of what Venom have been talking about over the years with the witchcraft, Satanism, against the church. It's just another angle on that.

MM: 13 songs on your 13th album: a conscious decision or a happy coincidence?

Cronos: Nah, just a happy coincidence. It could have been 20. We've written so many cool songs and this line-up has been together now for over 2 years and we're getting on really well, the gigs are going from strength to strength and people are telling us that they would prefer to see Venom this way with strong powerful members who can put on a fantastic show rather than going to see the original guys who can't be bothered with this music any more. A lot of the fans that we have at the shows are young guys and the newer albums are much more important to these guys. It's only a minority, who are the older guys, who were around in the days of *Welcome to Hell* and *Black Metal*. So we're finding that the fans are telling us that this is what they prefer and the gigs have been going from strength to strength. We've been getting tighter and tighter and if you go to the Venom YouTube site, we've got some of the shows that we've played over the last few years and you'll see the audiences are going absolutely wild. In some of the new territories we've been going to like Poland and Russia, even though they are smaller concerts and we can't put on the whole stage show like we'd like to do, there's no pyrotechnics but there's still the energy, the power, the crowds going crazy. So yeah, fantastic...

MM: Musically, the album seems to incorporate some of the raw visceral power and fury of the earlier records, coupled with confident, technical song-writing ability. Did you have a specific musical goal in mind when you sat down to write this new record?

Cronos: Well, the thing is, when we put this line-up together we worked on the live set, that is thirty years of Venom, playing songs of every Venom record so it's ingrained in this band. But this is the Venom of the 21st Century, so there is a 30 year history to the band, so we need everyone to understand this because we can say to the audience "choose a song for

Venom to play and we can play those songs". Because this is Venom and everybody in this band is a 1000% committed to the band. Writing for the new album, songs came so easily but we stayed in the black metal theme and the songs were very Venomous and harked back to the old way of doing things, before everybody was using all the pro-tools and the technology which we have used in the past, I'll admit to that – samples, triggers etc. But for this album it was all microphones, real drums marshal stacks guitars, you know, just like we did back in the day. It sounds raw, it sounds aggressive, it sounds more like the band would sound live.

MM: Has the way you write with the new line-up changed in comparison with the way you wrote with the original line-up?

Cronos: Yes absolutely. Look at what made the band special back in the day, and we just want to continue without all the computers, without the tricks, the producers we wanted the essence of Venom. When we came to writing the songs, all the members of the band brought ideas in; Dante would say "Hey I've got this great new drumming idea what do you think of this?", Rage would come in and say "Hey I've been playing with some new riffs". Dante would start playing along to the riffs and I would come in and say "Fucking hell, great, let's put some bass on this" and "What words would fit to that?" and boom, boom, boom the songs just grew track after track after track it came together really quickly. Do you like the new album?

MM: I love the new album. I grew up listening to you chaps. I'm from the eighties, one of the original legion and the new record is an absolute return to form…

Cronos: You see the thing is, when we got back together we weren't thinking about album deals or record companies. We were just … In the beginning, we didn't know about publishing deals or any of this. We were just some young guys who wanted to write some cool songs and be in a band. I just wanted to bring that back. The honesty, just three guys who are friends and who want to make good music. That's how this album came about. It's a very honest album but it's also quite an arrogant album in that it knows it's a good album. Every song is a killer song

MM: it's not afraid to be what it is…It just flows naturally. I wanted to ask you about your lyrical approach; do you still get grief from people who falsely label you as Satanists and practitioners of the black arts?

Cronos: Not so much nowadays. I think people understand that it's only entertainment. Fucking hell, even Lady Ga Ga is bringing out stuff with fangs and horns and all that stuff now. I think people understand that now. Whereas people in the old days used to be worried about Satan and Witchcraft, I think people nowadays are more worried about UFOs (laughing)…

MM: Sticking with that idea, what was the worst thing that happened to you at the hands of the crazy fundamentalists?

Cronos: It was more the bullshit… Like in the States where they would picket the concerts. I think that they made more trouble than they prevented and they ended up looking like a joke. There was a thing where I had to go on television because either Judas Priest or Ozzy Osbourne (*it was Judas Priest – Tim*) had supposedly put satanic messages on their records and I made a cassette tape before I went to do the interview. This was on a big news channel and they said "What about these messages that make people go and kill themselves?" and I said "Backwards messages have got to be down to a studio technician so how can they be Satanic, it doesn't make sense" and they said it was the devil and Satanism. Then they played the tape and it made weird backwards, long slow sounds and they looked really frightened.

At which point I said "Do you not feel hungry?" and they said "What?" to which I replied "Do you not feel hungry? Do you not want to go and get some food?" and they said "No. why?" so I played the tape forwards and the tape was "Gravy and chips, beans and sausages" which when it was turned backwards it's supposed to be a subliminal message so it should have made them want to go to the shop and buy some food. It just shows how dangerously stupid these people were. If I was going to put a backwards message on there it would be "Go and buy ten copies of this record. Buy everything we ever do." (laughs) Where did the Satanists of 1000 years ago get the tape machines to play their backward messages?

MM: I've read that there are going to be lots more records and tours from the band now. Does this mean that with this new line-up it's like a rebirth for the band?

Cronos: Absolutely. It feels like we finally found the right people. I put the band back together in 2005/2006 for "metal Black" and it was easy to put a band together for an established band. It was always going to be a temporary lineup so we were always on the lookout for new members for the band. I now feel like this is the Venom that could last the next 10-20 years

MM: With the album about to be released it feels like your future is finally, where it should always have been, in your hands. That said, what's next for Venom?

Cronos: Great gigs and more killer albums. We still like to put on a great stage show, see what's new out there, new special effects, new things we can do with the stage show to make it more exciting. Keep this music going, be creative and try out new things.

MM: Anything you'd like to add?

Cronos: Really hope you guys like the album, we're so proud of it

Originally published in Mass Movement #31, October 2011

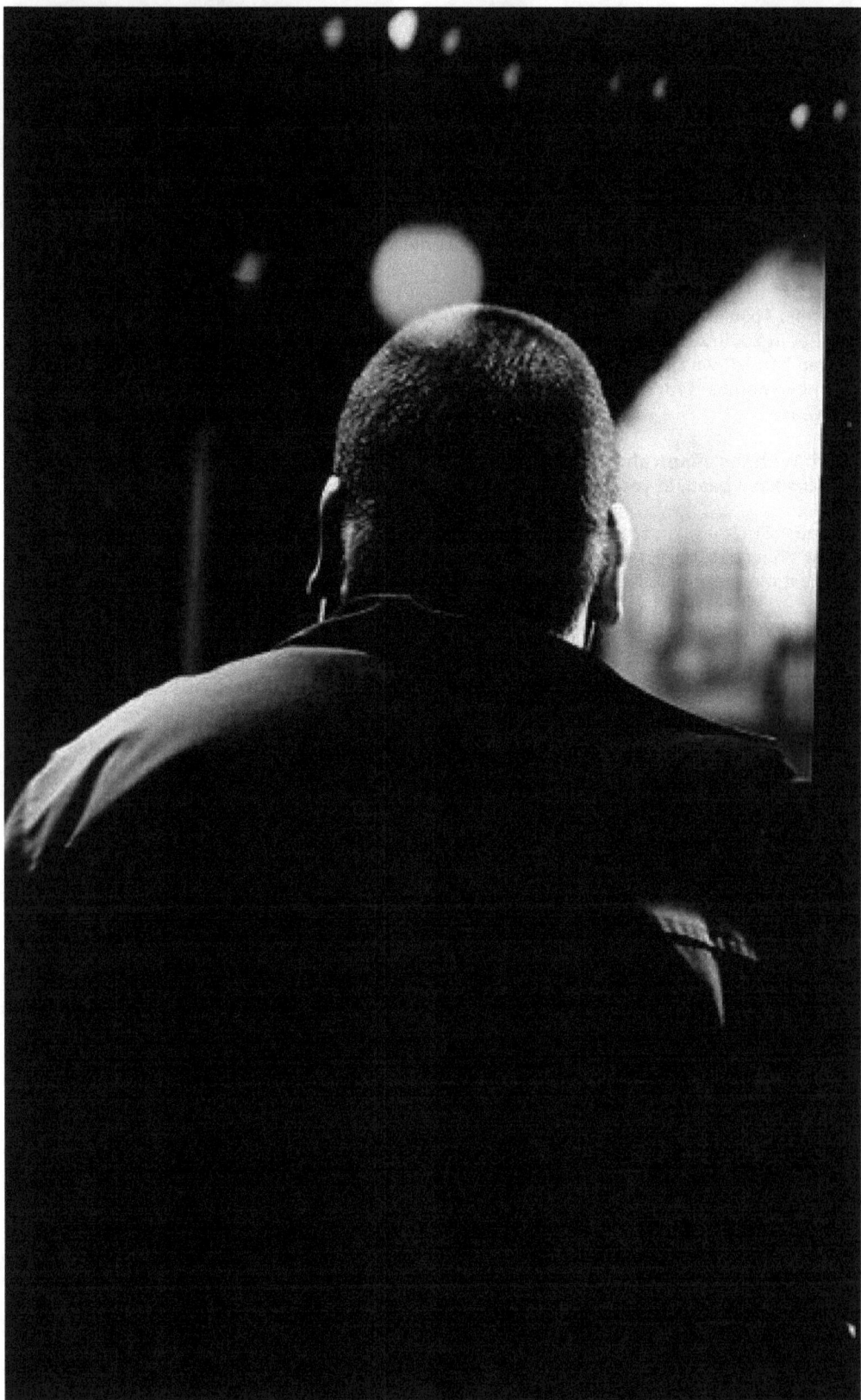

PAUL BEARER
(SHEER TERROR)

I can still remember it as if it were yesterday. It was the tail end of 1989, and there, hidden in the racks in Spillers, was *Where the Wild Things Are*, a NYHC compilation from a new label called Blackout! Back in the eighties, music was fundamental to how I viewed the world, and there were lots of bands who challenged my thinking and made me see the world in a new way, but I can count on one hand the ones that REALLY changed my life; and *Where The Wild Things Are* was one of them.

Truth be told, most of the bands on the record are just sort of 'Meh, y'know, heard it all before', and while I was a big Gorilla Biscuits fan and they had a track on the record (a cover of the Buzzcocks *Sitting Round At Home*) there were two bands on that record who changed NYHC, or at least my idea of NYHC completely: Norman Bates And The Showerheads and Sheer Terror. The latter, man, they've been with me ever since. I wore out the grooves on both *Cup Of Joe* and *Not Giving* Up, playing them over and over again; and from the grainy photo of the band in the accompanying booklet, I tried to imagine what they were like live. What inspired them? What their shows be like? I swore then and there, that one day I'd get to see them. Two decades, a lot of heartache, good times, false starts, broken promises and all that other crap that life throws at you and some spare change later; and after finally finding my feet and happiness; after having obsessed over their albums and nearly giving up hope because they'd broken up, I finally got to see Paul Bearer and Sheer Terror. They were worth waiting for, and at that point, everything felt right. At that moment, I wouldn't have cared if I'd never seen another band again because nothing and no-one could have topped that night, and I figured that was that. All was finally right with the world.

Roll on a couple of years, and rumours that a new Sheer Terror album was going to surface were beginning to circulate; I happened to mention this to George Tabb, probably in a state of near frantic excitement, and he casually says, "Oh I know Paul, he's a good guy do you want to speak to him about the band?" At that moment, at that second, a million different thoughts went through my head: I reformulated Einstein's theories to incorporate a realistic model of time travel; considered the minutia of universal replication from the microscopic to the infinite and what it means to the human condition and the God equation; realised the truth that inspired the Bacon Shakespeare conspiracy; thought of the perfect way to incorporate Flash Gordon into Captain America's timeline and re-evaluted a hundred different personal relationships which in turn led to a new acceptance of eventuality and fate and a calmer, more controlled perspective on life. And then I answered George's question with something like "You're damn skippy I do buddy!".

So, after some back and fore - and working out schedules between recording albums, jobs, families and all the cool, crazy stuff that makes life so much fun; on a Sunday evening not so long ago, I finally got to speak to Paul Bearer. And this is what he had to say...

Questions by Ian Pickens and Tim Cundle

Interview by Tim Cundle

All photographs appear courtesy of Sheer Terror and Paul Bearer.

MM: So Where did it all begin for you Paul, where did all this hardcore stuff start for you?

PB: I got into punk rock in 1979/80, because when we really started hearing it was the 1970s in New York; you started hearing about it and the Sex Pistols and the guy who killed his girl-friend – that was always in the papers anyway and I thought it was crazy. Then in about 1979/80 I went to the public library and stole a copy of the Sex Pistols album – I didn't have any money to buy it and I wanted to hear it so I stole it from the library. By then the whole Hardcore thing was just kicking off and it all started then for me. And it's still with me, still killing me, all these years later...

MM: So what was it like for a band coming up in the early 80s in the hardcore scene in New York? We always got the impression that it was really tough for you guys.

PB: Well yeah, certainly it was tough because of things like where you'd go to see bands, they weren't exactly the best of neighbourhoods, but if you minded your P's and Q's you were okay. We were all kids too, there were some of the old guard there from the early punk rock days who watched out for the younger ones, but if you didn't act like a jerk you were okay. You went into the venue and hung out there, and maybe hung out outside the venue or not too far away; I guess what I'm saying is that you don't go looking for shit. Sometimes in these neighbourhoods the gangs would come up to us and want to cause trou-ble, but mostly they just looked at us and thought 'These white kids are just fucked up, com-ing to see a bunch of crappy bands' – God knows what they thought of the music – they just thought we were crazy and they'd better leave us alone...

MM: So when did Sheer Terror start and what were the early days of the band like?

PB: Sheer Terror formed on December 30th 1984. There were some guys from a band called No Control and they broke up and they were looking to do something else so I tried out for them and we started playing together. December 1984 is when we came up with the name Sheer Terror, but I can tell you we stunk back then. A lot of people like to go on about the good old days and how everything used to be great, but we were rubbish when we first started out. We thought we were great – but everyone does – but the truth is it took a while for us to find our sea legs or what not. I don't know, we were young and dumb and trying to do something different. I don't remember when we did the first demo – the first demo that we sold anyway – I didn't want to be at a disadvantage or anything like that so I was to incor-porate in some of the slow parts some singing and crooning type thing – half assed mind you, but I was trying to do something different, you know, (may he rest in peace) – that fucking nut – who were doing that shit. There was HR doing his whole thing but I don't think that re-ally counts because there was more like a reggae thing and whatever so it was different. So I give credit to me and Pete for starting that shit. So many bands have been writing it and doing it over the years but fuck them, I started it.

MM: Did *Where the Wild Things Are* really help you out at that time?

PB: I guess. It got the name out there and all. And in the end it came out just before the album. It got on our nerves you know because all anyone knew was 'Cup O'Joe'; we had plenty of other songs but that was the one that everyone knew and wanted to hear. But it did help without question, and I've been friends with the guys from Blackout since we were in junior high. A lot of people didn't really know what to think of us at first because we didn't sound like a lot of the other bands out there. I've said it a hundred times and I'll say it again, we were like skinheads and were loving some of the Oi stuff that was coming out of the UK at that time, we loved it but we played faster music and took harder drugs, that was our addi-tion to the whole thing.

MM: Do you ever think that Sheer Terror was underappreciated, that you didn't get the recognition that you rightfully deserved?

PB: Yes and no. Yes because the only people who are to blame are us, or rather me. We did-n't play the game, and I didn't kiss anybody's ass. If I didn't like you I'd tell you to go fuck yourself or something. I didn't, and I still don't, like the nicey nicey bullshit that goes on and that held us back for a while no doubt. Some of the other band members held us back as well. People were asking us why we didn't tour, why we didn't do this or that, and it wasn't just me, it was other people as well sometimes it was jobs, or families or whatever. For me it was just a case of getting out of my parent's basement or whatever and picking it back up when we got back. I'm still like that today; of course I want to make sure I've got my rent taken care of first, but after that I'm ready to leave at the drop of a hat.

MM: What's changed for you personally or musically since the 80s and 90s into this new run of the band?

PB: I've changed most definitely in my attitude and ideas over the years. I think the bands are worse now, for me anyway. It's different. I know things are supposed to change but these bands now, like with metal when you've got some kid screaming about breaking it down or some shit I don't get it. Or then you get some old guy and it's all family friends, friends family what the hell shit do you have going on your lives? What's really getting to you? Are you really sitting at home sweating that we're not united yet? Or are you troubled because your kid's on dope and you can't pay the fucking rent. What's troubling you? That's what I always write about, that's what important to me, something that matters, whether it's personal, political or global, it doesn't matter unless it means something; make it something that matters not just ephemera, like cheerleader shit. But stuff like that – it's their roots, you know? It makes me sick when people go on and say kids now should respect their roots and everything but you know what punk rock ain't their roots, it's not how they grew up and if they don't like it they don't fucking have to. When I was young I didn't want some older guy telling me I was wrong.

MM: One of our writers always refers to you as the Charles Bukowski of Hardcore; do you think that's an   accurate description? There are lots of references in your lyrics, is it some-thing you looked to while writing?

PB: I was never a fan to tell you the truth; I always thought he was just a fucking drunk guy who got lucky. Some of his stuff's okay, I think I have a collection that someone bought me and I think I've leafed thought it a couple of times but I was never a big fan of his writing. William Kennedy is one of my favourite writers, he's from and writes about Albany and things that happen there, I don't know why. I had this collection that I bought when I was a kid from a bookstore or a junkstore or something and I really liked it. I'm also a fan of T.S. Eliott; I dated a girl who is now an English professor, back then she was going for her doctor-ate and she taught me a lot of stuff. She used to play me this tape of someone reading T.S Eliott and it used to annoy the fucking hell out of me! Bukowski – I can see where he's com-ing from and stuff like that but he doesn't do much for me. The way I write it's about what's going on for me right then; I'm working at a bar, I'm just sitting at home saying 'fuck you' to the world…. It's like that. Actually I listen to a lot of old soul music, and country music as much as anything else.

MM: So you've never thought of writing a book...?

PB: Yeah I definitely have. I started writing an autobiographical thing, then I noticed every-body else was starting to do things like that asking myself whether my story was really all that interesting. It's tucked away right now, not to say that it will never come out but not right now; I get bored when I'm writing it because I know this shit already. Besides I think I tell it better writing a lyric than writing about me ..

MM: You've also done a lot to publicise the Autism Speaks charity, but you seem to have moved away from it of late; was it too time consuming – clashing with the band's schedule?

PB: No, no I just didn't like the way the organisation was handling... With, my help (I didn't do everything, I just helped) and all the generous donations that people gave, we raised over $40,000 for them over 3 years or so, and it was cool but they keep talking about it as a disease and they use these scare tactics in their advertisements and stuff like that and I didn't like that. I think with autism there are different ends to the spectrum, degrees of autism, and I always saw it as more of a social spectrum – a different way of looking at things. I sometimes think that I have a touch of it and I think that a lot of people in the punk rock and hardcore community suffer from a touch of it to be honest; it's a communication thing, and not a bad thing. These people kept talking about a cure all the time, but I think they should have been more concerned about the care rather than a cure. That's why I stopped working with them. I'd like to find another autism organisation to work with. We'll raise money online, wear the shirts, if there is a walk we'll show up.. whatever we can do to help. My nephew has Asperger's and it got me interested in all this kind of thing, to find out more about it, and that's pretty much how I got involved. Anything to help a kid out.

MM: How did the *Kaos for Kristen* seven inch come about? Was it for Mark Magee?

PB: He's an old friend of mine from when he was in Condemned 84 and the Anti Heroes, and he's been living in the states now for over 20 years and he met this girl down in Atlanta, fell in love and married her and she was 32 and diagnosed with cancer, and that's so young, it was sad. It progressed really quickly, and mutual friends told me about the hell he was going through, it was his wife and he loved her. He was watching this beautiful young girl fall apart, and the medical fucking leaches were draining their bank accounts and we thought what we could do. So I talked to a mutual friend of ours called Ally and told her that this was what I wanted to do. I want to do these three Sham songs that I've always wanted to sing, and I spoke to Randale records in Germany to see if they wanted to put it out, and they were up for it; then I spoke to my merch guys at Dead City Records and they wanted to get involved too so we put it together raise as much money as we can. It's still selling, I'm hoping it will at least put a dent in the bills. I'm no saint, I've done a lot of fucked up shit in my life but I'd like to think that it's a debt paid. I've had a lot of fucked up shit happen to me as well, and if you talk about karma, well whatever happens, happens, but I can be a real fucking asshole; and to be a really great asshole you have to really cherish the role. There is a difference... there's a jerk off and he doesn't know he's a jerk off, he's clueless, he thinks he's cool; but an asshole? He knows he's an asshole.

MM: So how did you enjoy your short trip to the UK in 2012?

PB: We loved it, it was great. We really want to come back, maybe next winter, and for a little bit longer. We came over for two days years ago as part of a European tour, so I flew over and I was supposed to do a bunch of press for 'Love Songs...' a couple of interviews, supposed to be on European MTV, then the day I get there they fucking cancel the Headbangers Ball. That was going to be my European TV debut but they stole it from me! So I hung around with Mickey from The Business in a pub, and drove around with Steve, went to a bunch of parties, met some girls it was a lot fun. We're definitely looking forward to coming back.

MM: You've just finished recording a new album right?

PB: Yeah, we're hoping to have it out for June or July

MM: Who's doing it?

PB: Reaper's doing it in the States, and Randale Records is doing it in Europe

MM: Did you keep any of the song titles you'd mentioned before like *Love Me Like a Leper*?

PB: I think we've changed a couple of titles but *Love Me Like a Leper* is still on there, and there is one: *The Revenge of Mr Jinks* which is a good song, a heavy song; *Cigarettes and Farts* is the title of another, and that's just because I just always wanted to have a song called *Cigarettes and Farts*. If anyone is a fan of the American TV show *The Odd Couple*, you'll get this song. I'm very happy with this record, I'm happy with all of the songs and reasonably happy with my vocals; when I listen to me singing in places these days it almost sounds like I'm singing with an English accent and it wasn't anything I'd meant to do, but I listened to it and thought 'Who's that English guy?'

MM: With *No Really, Go Fuck Yourself*, did have you any plans for a follow up to that, or doing stand-up?

PB: I do a spoken word here and there; I don't plan it out or write anything down, I just go out there and talk for about an hour. Honestly I'd like to do more acting. I did two no-budget movies for friends, then I had one line in a movie but it was cut out, but you can see me in the precinct scenes of a movie called *The Son of No-One*. I was a detective in that one, I had one line, but they cut it out, but you can see my shaved head walking around in there.

MM: So is this something you're going to chase or pursue?

PB: I'm never gonna chase that shit, that movie was like three years ago and I'm sometimes lazy and forgetful. I got the role because of my buddy who was from the hardcore scene in New York; he's got a new movie coming out now called Boulevard, and he's an old friend of mine; he gave me the role. So I worked with Channing Tatum and Ray Liotta, that was cool. I really enjoyed the whole project. I got one of the biggest fucking compliments off Ray Liotta actually, when a friend of mine came to visit the set in Queens and met Ray Liotta, and asked him 'did you meet my friend Paulie?', Ray Liotta said "Yeah that guy's gonna get work". Which was a great compliment. I love British film though, I made my girlfriend watch this film last night – I first saw it a couple of years ago – called 44 Inch Chest, with Ray Winstone and John Hurt and Ian McShane; they're ugly mugs but great you know?

MM: Have you seen *Sexy Beast*?

PB: Of course yes. That's a great movie. I'm a real fan of English cinema, Japanese cinema too.

MM: Is Joe Coffee done?

PB: We never say it's done, we just say 'We'll see'. Everybody's doing their own thing right now with work and family, so if we want to play another show, we'll play another show, if we're all going to be in the same place at the same time. I'd like to do another record and I always tell these guys if they have something written to throw it at me and we'll put something together.

MM: So what's next for you Paul?

PB: I'm babysitting a few drunk people tonight at work…. We're waiting for the new record to come out, so I'm trying to book shows here and there. We really only do weekends because of the work commitments of two of the members so we can't really tour, but that's alright, I've come to terms with that now. Sometimes we can play out for a week or so, but usually its weekends only; that's ok I don't want to be out there all the time, people would get tired of seeing me. Then we're going to be writing, and I'll do some spoken word, and there are some songs that didn't make it onto the album because they didn't have lyrics yet or whatever, and they are going to be coming out on the black and blue label, hopefully within the year. I have this one thing I've been playing with, which is kind of a novel, but the characters haven't really introduced themselves to me yet, and it just comes out of nowhere, and I don't know where because I'm, not really a novel type. It's basically about a widower, his father and his daughter, it's sort of rough now, I can't force it. I can't force writing, I have to let it come to me.

MM: Anything you'd like to add Paul?

PB: Anybody out there who is into Hardcore or punk rock just keep plugging away at it, enjoy it and if you get a kick out of it, at the end of the day that's all that really matters. Stay true to your art and don't fucking give in because of what everybody else is doing; even if everyone around you is telling you your wrong, just tell them to go fuck themselves. If they tell you you can't do something you tell them: "Watch me" and just keep fucking doing it.

Originally published in Mass Movement Presents: Sheer Terror, May 2014

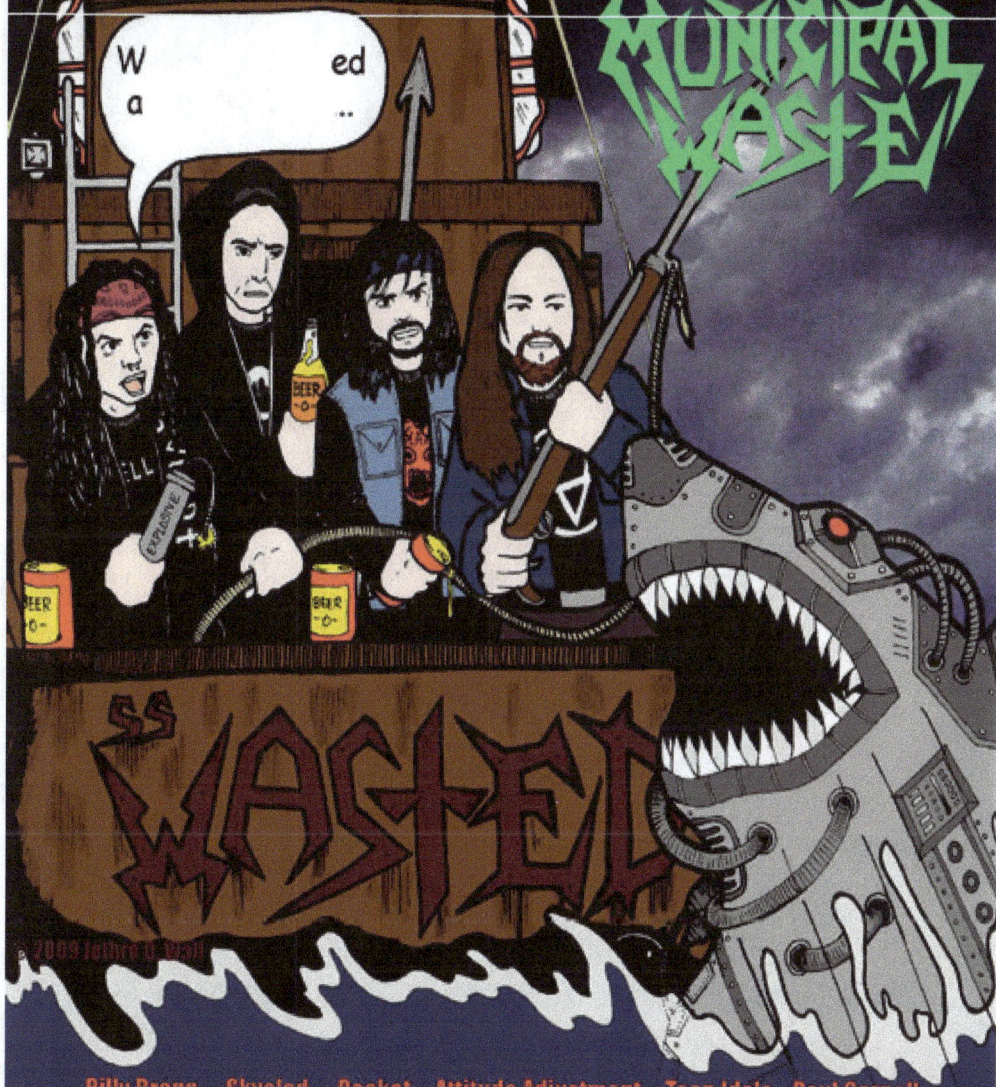

MASS MOVEMENT

24

MUNICIPAL WASTE

WASTED

© 2009 Jathro D. Wolf

Billy Bragg   Skyclad   Rocket   Attitude Adjustment   Teen Idols   Paul Cornell
Swashbuckle   Jasper Bark   Dead Lazlo's Place   Artillery   Charles Ryan   Unearth
Timothy Truman   No Friends   The Set Up   Snail   Gary Spencer Millidge   Testament
Darlings Of Chelsea   Unearth   Ancestors   Romeo Must Die   All Or Nothing   No Consequence

459

MASS MOVEMENT

26

CATHEDRAL

OVERKILL   PAT MILLS   ARMORED SAINT   FOZZY   JUGHEADS REVENGE   COM.X
NASTY   JAMES SWALLOW   BLACK BREATH   GOLDUST   KILLING TIME   MICKEY LEIGH
PRAIRIE COAST FILMS   MARTIAL ARTS IN HARCORE   THE DUNGEONS MASTER
STARBLAZER   RICHARD HERRING   JFA   AND MORE...

MASS MOVEMENT

27

UNDERDOG

GUY DAVIS

HOT WATER MUSIC

D.O.A.

BLACK CANDY STORE

TESCO VEE

SKULL CRUSHER

D.R.I.

STEVE JACKSON

AND

IAN LIVINGSTONE

YOUNG LIVERS

PETE STAHL

DUNGEONS AND DRAGONS RESEARCH AND DEVELOPMENT TEAM

PLUS LOADS MORE INTERVIEWS FEATURES COLUMNS AND REVIEWS...

462

MASS MOVEMENT 28

CRADLE OF FILTH

HELLOWEEN   STEVE IGNORANT   FORBIDDEN   CORROSION OF CONFORMITY

JOHN ARCUDI   wino   CHRIS JERICHO -FOZZY   JONATHAN MORRIS   Hail of Bullets

MASS MOVEMENT 23

DEW SCENTED

Thin Lizzy
MONSTER MAGNET
SYLOSIS
ALAN DAVIS
Onslaught
NO FRIENDS
FUNERAL FOR A FRIEND
brendonBurns
33
Nev Fountain

MASS MOVEMENT
30

DWARVES   DEFEATER      QUESTION THE MARK

Steve Jackson   THE DUNGEON'S MASTER

GWAR   THE DREADNOUGHTS   GALLIFREY   JASPER BARK

AMON AMARTH    Pentagram   SCREEN DAMAGE

ill niño   HammerFall

Richard HERRING   HIGHLANDER      MARK WATSON
EARTH

465

MASS MOVEMENT

ISSUE 31

AN INTERVIEW WITH **OFF!**

p.45

ALSO THIS ISSUE:

ANTHRAX

THE MELVINS

VENOM

PAT MILLS

KARMA TO BURN

EVAN DORKIN

MARK KERMODE

SEAWEED

BYFROST

JOHN HEFFERNAN

CHARRED WALLS OF THE DAMNED

THE SATELLITE YEAR

AND MUCH MORE...

MASS MOVEMENT PRESENTS...

SHEER TERROR

MASS MOVEMENT

With thanks

Mass Movement Magazine was brought you by Liam Ronan, George Tabb, Doug Crill, Tim 'Bunky' Davis, Tom Wilding, James McLaren, Brady Webb, Steve Scanner, Martijn Welzen, Jason Thomas, Marv Jolly, Ian Pickens, Tom Chapman, Pete Williams, Jethro Kamba-Wall, Leigh McAndrew, Jim Dodge, Ian Glasper, Mark Freebase, Kai Woolen-Lewis and Tim 'Mass Movement' Cundle

Dedicated to the memory of James McLaren, Dave Brockie, John Sicolo, Eric Brockman, Paul Spragg and Jason Sears. Until the next life. Slainte

Thank-you Andy Turner, Vique 'Simba' Martin, Chrissie Yiannou, Mosh Knockout, Johann at Reflections, Nanette & Wiebke (Fat Wreck Europe), Delphine Victory, Simon & Nita Keeler and Bill 'Doctor Strange' Plaster for believing in Mass Movement from the beginning - if it wasn't for you folks, we wouldn't be here today , Nathan Bean, Sophie Francois, Chris Andrews, Tom Chapman, Ian Pickens and Tony Fyler the current Mass Movement crew, Alan Wright, Rhodri 'Poggles' Dawe, Adam Caradog Thomas, Rachel Evans, Everyone at Earth Island Books, Engineer Records for sponsoring the Mass Movement podcast, Anna Hinds, Leanne Toy, Ross O'Brien, Jonathan Evans, Matthew Davies-Kreye, Neil Randle & Bang-On Brewery, Michael Davies, Welly Artcore, Gavin Gates, Darrel Sutton, The Legendary TJ's (the spiritual home of Mass Movement), Simon Phillips, Dean Beddis, Wayne 'Pig' Cole, Alexandros 'Alex' Anesiadis, Richard Torres, Marcus 'Mivvi' Davis, David 'Dog' O'Grady, Will Pywell, Dark Horse Comics, Titan Books & Comics, Turnaround Publishing Services, DC Comics, Epitaph Records, Bafflegab, Revelation Records, Big Finish, Fat Wreck Chords, Asmodee Games, Black Library, all the incredible bands, writers, artists, wrestlers, film makers that we've been fortunate enough to meet and interview during the last two and something decades, the labels, publishing and PR folk who rose above and beyond the call of duty when called on and last, and most importantly of all, my long suffering and (most of the time) understanding family (Emma, Siobhan and Ma) whose wisdom, guidance and help mean more to me than they will ever know - none of this would have been possible without you.

About Tim Cundle

Tim Cundle stumbled into the punk scene sometime in the mid-nineteen eighties and his life has never been the same since. Having worked as riflery instructor and drug counsellor and studied both English Literature and Behavioural Science at University, he decided his career lay down a different path and, having written for local newspapers since he was fifteen, did what most aspiring writers do. He became a journalist.

Currently the editor of Mass Movement Magazine, he has also contributed to, and written for, Doctor Who Magazine, Big Cheese, Fracture and many other publications. A lifelong geek and Disney, Star Wars and comic book fanatic, he spends far too much time obsessing over obscure Hardcore and Crossover bands, playing Dungeons & Dragons, reading genre literature, devoting himself to television shows and films that most people would consider to be puerile, recording and presenting the Mass Movement Presents podcast with his partner in audio crime Chris Andrews, drinking too much coffee, indulging his passion for craft beer and watching Professional Wrestling and Ice Hockey.

After "singing" for two Hardcore bands, Charlies Family Crisis and AxTxOxTx, he now considers that chapter of his life to be closed and the chances of him doing the band thing again are slim to non-existent. However, just like Sean Connery, Tim learned a long time ago to never say never again, so who knows? You may see him on stage again. But you probably won't.

The Best of Mass Movement: The Digital Years Volumes I & II are the result of a crazy five year period that saw Mass Movement reluctantly enter, and make its mark on the digital age. They are a testament to Tim's enduring love of the written word and the underground and capture the essence of a magazine and website that celebrated, and continues to champion, punk rock and geek culture.

Tim lives in a small, sleepy Welsh village with his wife Emma and daughter Siobhan and keeps himself busy by working on his upcoming books and Mass Movement, which takes up far too much of his time. He dreams about muscle cars, Disney World and disappearing to live in a small cabin in the wild woods of Tennessee